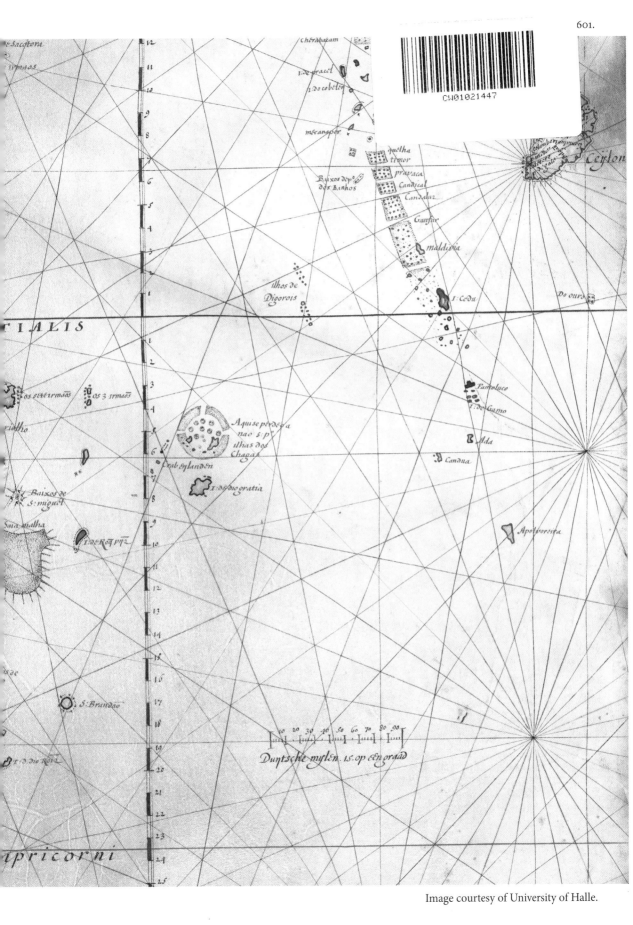

e Sacçtora

phnos

Cherbatam

I do pracil

I do cobelin

m cangaor

Buxos dep°
dos Banhos

RIALIS

os gtt trmaõs

os 3 irmaõs

riotho

Ilhos de
Digorois

Aquise perdeo a
nao s p°
ilhas dos
Chagas

Crab Eylanden

Baixos de
S: miguel

I do do gratia

saia malha

I de R oq v̄z

S: Brandao

B d.d. dio Roz

quelha
timor
pravaca
Candial
Candaluz

Ganfar

maldivia

I: Cedu

Do ours

Pamoluce

I: de Gamo

Ada

Candua

Apelltorvira

Ceylon

10 20 30 40 50 60 70 80 90

Duytsche mylen. 15. op EEn graad

pricorni

12
11
10
9
8
7
6
5
4
3
2
1
1
2
3
4
5
6
7
8
9
10
11
12
13
14
15
16
17
18
19
20
21
22
23
24
25

CHAGOS: A HISTORY

Exploration   Exploitation   Expulsion

NIGEL WENBAN-SMITH *and* MARINA CARTER

CHAGOS CONSERVATION TRUST, LONDON
www.chagos-trust.org

Published 2016 in Great Britain by
the Chagos Conservation Trust
23 The Avenue, Sandy
Bedfordshire SG19 1ER, UK

Dust jacket illustration:
Pointe du Bonnet Carré, Diego Garcia, 1819, by Maurits Ver Huell, courtesy Maritiem Museum, Rotterdam.

ISBN 978-0-9954596-0-1

Design and typesetting by Ray Perry; Jacket design by Jennifer Lassiter
Printed and bound by York Publishing Services Ltd., Hallfield Road, York, YO31 7ZQ, UK

Dedication

W
E would like to dedicate this book to all those who from the 1770s to the 1970s were fated to spend their lives on the islands of the Chagos Archipelago. It was their perseverance in the face of hardship and deprivation that allowed some profit to be wrested from the marginal natural resources of these remote islands. Documentary evidence of their lives provides the core of this story. We hope their descendants will find much of interest in these pages.

In particular, we would like to honour the memory of the brother and sister, Paul Caboche and Marcelle Lagesse, both of whose long lives ended before the book's completion. Marcelle Lagesse (1916–2011) we came to know more through her early writings than her converse; but those writings would have been undiscoverable had she not presented copies of them as a gesture to our enthusiasm. Had she lived to see what we drew from them, we are sure she would have found points to correct and many more to expand upon. Paul Caboche (1918–2012), her younger brother, we got to know much better, through long conversations and years of correspondence. As the children of a long-serving manager of the Salomon plantation, both were imbued with a deep regard for the old island life and both were glad to pass on documents, insights and direct recollections going back to the 1930s. Paul had moreover visited all the inhabited islands of the Archipelago by sailing ship and had (as a teenager) introduced radio communications to the Chagos, later operating the Royal Navy's radio station on Diego Garcia during the early years of the war.

Paul Caboche. Pensant aux problèmes de l'avenir afin de les resoudre

No less, this story owes a similar debt to Fernand Mandarin (b. 1943). As at least a fourth generation native of the Chagos Archipelago, Fernand brings a perspective quite different in time, place and circumstance, but like the other two, has been extraordinarily generous in allowing us to draw extensively on his recollections, distilled in an autobiography still in preparation. Indeed, his lively and detailed descriptions of growing up on Peros Banhos are so informative that they evolved into an entire chapter and contributed to several others. To him we offer our boundless thanks.

Contents

Preface

WE were drawn into exploring the history of the Chagos Archipelago from two very different starting points. One of us (MC) had encountered references to these islands and their inhabitants in the course of archival study of Mauritian history in the 18th and 19th centuries. Slave voyages, naval engagements, scandalous episodes involving brutality and murders were encountered repeatedly in records studied for other purposes. For the other (NW-S), whose several visits to Diego Garcia in the early 1980s as Commissioner of the British Indian Ocean Territory allowed him to fly low over the whole archipelago and to visit half a dozen of its islands by sea, there was left a residue of curiosity about the real character of the plantation life which the military installations on one island had replaced. What had gone on in those once-elegant villas, tumbled-down chapels, creeper-infested cottages, collapsed industrial structures with crazy rails leading to broken piers, still bearing the rusting frames of small wagons? In 2006, chance brought us to neighbouring desks in the Mauritius National Archive in Port Louis. We have been exchanging historical finds relating to these isolated atolls ever since.

Our separate researches have taken us over the past ten years not only to Mauritius and to the enormous resources of British libraries, museums and, especially, the National Archive at Kew, but also to Lisbon and Paris, Amsterdam and Rotterdam, Florence and Modena, Bedford MA and Rhode Island, not to speak of Mumbai and New Delhi. We have also corresponded with individuals having academic expertise or personal knowledge all over the world. We are however only too aware of gaps in our knowledge of, for example Russian, German and Spanish archives, and also conscious that our knowledge of United States official archives is largely second-hand. Broadly speaking, Parts 1 and 2 (Exploration and Exploitation) are the product of our joint efforts, while Part 3 (Expulsion) is the work of NWS alone.

The closure of the Chagos coconut plantations in the early 1970s and the consequences of the forced removal of the islands' civilian population have from the start been topics of great controversy, which continues to this day. This involuntary/imposed exile has spawned a host of media stories focussing on a 'Paradise Lost', without, however, providing a very clear understanding of what life was really like on those isolated coral atolls. Our purpose is to explore the little-known history of the discovery of the islands, their eventual settlement and the gradual development of a distinct community, all serving the single function of supplying coconuts and their derivative products to Mauritius. One of our chief objectives was to rescue from complete anonymity some at least of the individuals who made up this community of, at first, slaves and slave owners, who later emerged as the labourers, foremen and managers of Mauritian owned private companies. In this we have been less successful than we hoped: those most readily identifiable are those whose offences, alleged and real, brought them to the attention of magistrates. Their cases are valuable as indicators of social conditions, but too great an emphasis on misdeeds would give a wholly false impression of day-to-day life. We have attempted to redress the relative silence of the workers through our extensive use of testimony provided by Fernand Mandarin who has authored Chapter 20 and whose evocative memories of life on Peros Banhos and Diego Garcia have contributed to several sections of the book. Our researches have also revealed an interesting nexus of stakeholders in the exploitation of the Chagos, whose coinciding and competing interests determined their economic fate. Many, perhaps most, of those involved raised their families on Chagos and had a long and intimate relationship with the islands. Of these, the recollections of Paul Caboche and his sister Marcelle Lagesse have enriched our account in various ways.

We are not, of course, the first to look into the history of Mauritius' dependencies. Sir Robert Scott's *Limuria* (1961) remains a useful account of the discovery and exploration of these islands and the origins of the societies that emerged in them. Scott's focus differed, however, from ours. Concerned about the economic and social future of those Mascarene islands which depended on coconut products for their wellbeing – known collectively as the Oil Islands – he sought to record their distinct character and to look for ways of conserving it in the face of the rapid changes occurring in Mauritius and the world beyond. We write after those changes have engulfed the Chagos Archipelago. Moreover, by concentrating on this more limited area, which has now acquired a very specific identity, we can look in greater detail at each stage of its development. What we have found is the gradual emergence of a system of exploitation, initially conditioned by the islands' remoteness but later making cynical use of this distance from authority to retain unenlightened, under-capitalised, unproductive, unloved and, finally, unsustainable industries. What has also emerged is the extent to which the strategic pre-occupations of a succession of powerful states impinged on the Chagos in times of war and peace alike. Thirdly, of course, economic and political developments in Mauritius determined much of what happened in these distant Dependencies, but our chosen focus on the latter may have led us to reference inadequately some passing comments made on the former. Finally, we have been astonished at the extraordinary range of individuals, some well-known to history, whose lives were touched by these seemingly insignificant specks in the vastness of the Indian Ocean.

From Homer's *Odyssey* onwards, poets and dramatists have found that small islands in remote seas allow the mind to escape from mundane realities while providing focus for a concentrated mythic story. Shakespeare frequently employed this device, even making mention of the *Tigre*, the vessel later used for the second English voyage to the Chagos. In 1668, Henry Neville's *Isle of Pines* was placed in the same longitude as the Chagos but a dozen degrees further to the south, with a picaresque plot involving Dutch as well as English seafarers. More recently, *Smoke Island*, by Antony Trew (Collins, 1964) uses Eagle Island as a backdrop for the survivors of an air crash to explore South African racial issues. Cristina Pereira, a Portuguese historical novelist, has based her latest work (*Um Espião nas Descobertas,* volume III, 2011) on the real fate of a Portuguese ship, the *Conceição* on Peros Banhos in 1555. Coming closer to our own story, Mauritian novelist Marcelle Lagesse, who spent several years on Chagos as a young woman, wrote a charming story of the love of a daughter of the manager of Salomon Island for a visiting French sea captain in *Des Pas Sur Le Sable* (reprinted 2009, Editions du Printemps, Mauritius). Her *Notes d'un Carnet* (Editions Paul Mackay, 1967) gives a fictional account of the daily life of the Salomon islanders which must correspond closely to the reality she experienced from 1938–42. Finally, the life of the islanders exiled from the Chagos has also been presented in fictional form, for example, in Peter Benson's *A Lesser Dependency* (Macmillan, 1989) in French by Shenaz Patel's *Le Silence des Chagos*, (Editions l'Olivier, 2005) and *Out of the Cyclone* by Guy-Sylvio Bigaignon (ELP Publications, Mauritius, 2011). This is by no means an exhaustive list and the literature inspired by the exile of the Chagos islanders continues to grow.

The term 'Chagossian' is of much more recent date than 1973; in this book, therefore, we refer to the island inhabitants as 'Ilois', or 'workers' and 'labourers' according to the relevant French and English language records consulted. Those who have come to identify themselves as members of the Chagossian community, principally individuals employed as workers – and some as managers – in the islands (and their descendants) have enriched this work with their memories and photographs. We know of one individual who can trace his ancestry back to 1840, and one of our objectives has been to recall as many names as we can from the archival records. We hope that this unfinished work will be continued by others and that eventually many more Chagossians will be able to identify links going back beyond the recall of oral memory. Of course, we have been unable to include here all the names derived from passenger lists and civil status records that we have unearthed. A website with additional materials is being compiled; please visit www.chagos.info for further details. We hope to add further to this over time, as new research and records appear and are shared.

As far as this work is concerned, we hope it will help provide a base for future studies, by bringing to light the reality of conditions in these islands, before speedy transport and instant communication could help mitigate the effects of great distance and miniscule size. We hope that the story which unfolds in the following pages will provide all interested in the history of these atolls and particularly the Chagossians and their descendants with an understanding of the social and economic history of the archipelago over the last two centuries.

NW-S   MC

Acknowledgements

WE have received unstinting help from many quarters. There are people having professional or familial links with the Chagos, whether as former managers of the plantations (or, mostly, their descendants) served with military or civilian organisations either during the Second World War or since the establishment of BIOT. From individuals in these two groups, we have been fortunate to obtain many photographs, anecdotes and memoirs. These have supplemented, corrected and enlivened the dry contents of official records which are necessarily the primary foundation of this study. In this context, we should like in particular to mention Jocelyn Chaillet, Gerard Commins, Pierre Commins, Kirby Crawford, Richard Grainger, Paul Lemière, Francis Lionnet, Adrian McCloy, Margaret McCloy, Ted Morris, Charles Moulinié, Marcel Moulinié, Alix and Karl Mülnier, Alix de Robillard, Roland Schaeffer, Larry Sellers, Medgé Smith, Robert Talbot, the late Donald Taylor, Tim Taylor, Ingrid Todd, Daniel Urish, Carl Villanueva and Allen Vincatassin.

A number of those having academic or professional engagement with Chagossian issues have given freely of their expertise, advice and provision of documents. Others assisted hugely with their linguistic or technical skills, most particularly in translating Dutch, German, Kreol and Portuguese texts, but also in manipulating text and illustrations. To all these too we would like to express our gratitude. They include Atholl Anderson, Françoise Botte-Noyan, Larry Bowman, Pete Carr, Anthony Cheke, Jean-Marie Chelin, Bob Conrich, Andrew Cook, Chris Cuniah, Richard Dunn, Richard Dunne, Julien Durup, Edward Duyker, Manonmani Filliozat-Restif, Giulia Fiorenzoli, Steven Forsberg, Robert Furlong, Richard Gifford, Anne Green, Margaret Hall, Michael Hewitt, Chris Hillman, Laura Jeffery, Stephanie Jones, Lucy McCann, Pauline MacGregor-Currien, José and Cristina Manuel Malhão-Pereira, Yvan Martial, James de Montille, the late Amédée Nagapen, Götz Reinicke, Howard Resnikoff, Emmanuel Richon, Hans van Rijn, Peter Sand, Giovanni Scorcioni, Rachel Smith, Hervé Sylva, Malcolm Tompson, Raymond d'Unienville, Megan Vaughan, and Diederick Wildeman,

We are no less grateful to the staff of libraries, museums and other institutions visited or consulted in the course of our researches, such as the National Archives of Australia, Britain, India, Mauritius, and France, the Lisbon Geographical Society, the Galileo Museum in Florence, the Cambridge University Library, the Bodleian and Rhodes Memorial Libraries in Oxford, the British Library, the National Maritime Museum in Greenwich, the Mauritius National Library, the Scheepvaartmuseum in Amsterdam, the Maritiem Museum in Rotterdam, the New Bedford Whaling Museum and the Blue Penny Museum in Port Louis. Similarly, several commercial organisations gave freely of their knowledge and advice, in particular Paulus Swaen Old Maps, and Victorian Photos of Derby.

Old friends and chance acquaintances helped too, among them Antony Wood and Janine Huisman. So did those involved in the production of this book, not only leading lights of the Chagos Conservation Trust, such as Anne and Charles Sheppard and Simon Hughes, but also Edie Campbell, Susan Doubls and Alice Wenban-Smith. A special word of thanks is owed to Ray Perry, who gave his skills and untold hours of his time to the design and preparation of this work for publication.

Lastly, we owe thanks and praise beyond measure to our respective partners, Mark Hall – who provided technical support for video interviews and website development, and to Frances Barlow, for the years of forbearance of a husband whose mind was too often focused faraway from the warp and weft of our life together.

Selected Maps

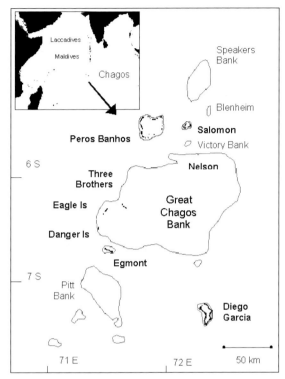

Chagos Archipelago. Image courtesy of Prof. Charles Sheppard.

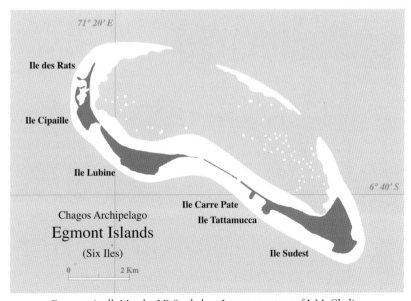

Egmont Atoll. Map by J.F. Sookaher. Image courtesy of J-M. Chelin.

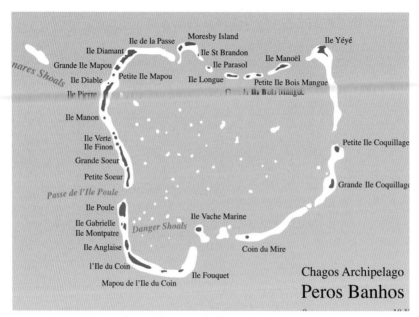

Peros Banhos Atoll. Map by J.F. Sookaher. Image courtesy of J-M. Chelin.

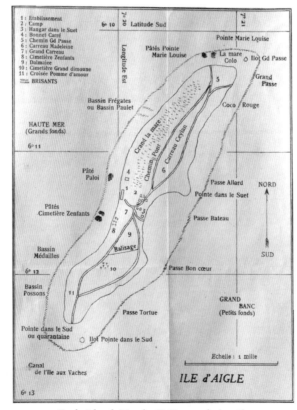

Eagle Island. Map by R. Dussercle (1936).

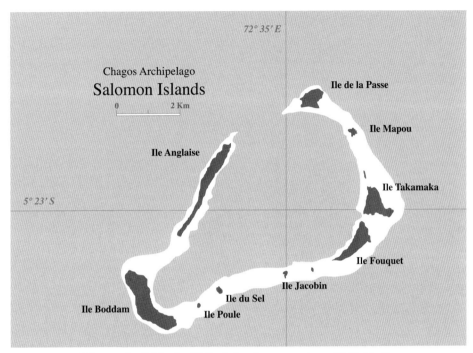

Salomon Atoll. Map by J.F. Sookaher. Image courtesy of J-M. Chelin.

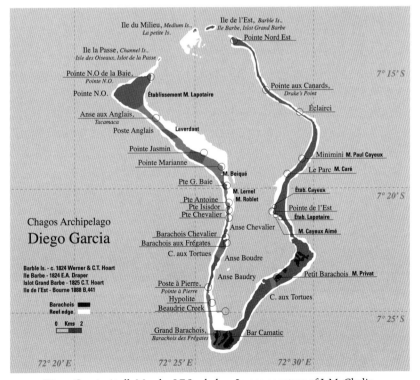

Diego Garcia Atoll. Map by J.F. Sookaher. Image courtesy of J-M. Chelin.

PART ONE

Exploration

1

Origins and Introductions

Peaks of Limuria

> The anomalies of the mammal fauna of Madagascar can best be explained by supposing that … a large continent occupied parts of the Atlantic and Indian Oceans … that this continent was broken up into islands, some of which have become amalgamated with … Africa, some … with what is now Asia; and that in Madagascar and the Mascarene Islands[1] we have existing relics of this great continent, for which … I should propose the name Lemuria.[2]

THIS proposition, based on earlier theories of a similar kind, was a gallant, but misguided attempt to explain the origin of the scattered islands of the western Indian Ocean; it also spawned a wide range of speculation, both semi-scientific and quasi-religious. Lemuria, often spelt Limuria, gradually came to be considered the eastern counterpart to Atlantis, its equivalent in classical mythology. It was thus an apt title for Sir Robert Scott's beautifully written book about Mauritius' remote Dependencies,[3] picked up again in Richard Edis' briefer history of one of them, Diego Garcia.[4] Here, the focus is intermediate, concentrating upon the Chagos Archipelago, a geologically distinct area of this Limurian space, and the authors' aim to dispel, not perpetuate mythology. So the term Limuria will be avoided in this volume wherever possible.

Bedrock

The area's history is, however, so profoundly determined by its geology that we must begin in far-off times. Deep below the earth's crust, a hot spot gives rise to volcanic activity, visible today in the island of Réunion, but leaving its traces in the Deccan flats of southern India and in the line of undersea ridges left behind as the tectonic plate bearing India headed – or, rather, heads – inexorably northwards. From south to north, visible island groups, such as the Mascarenes, Chagos, Maldives and Laccadives, rest upon successively more ancient volcanic remains. The huge volcanoes are heavy – so heavy that they sink slowly into the earth's crust. Corals, for their part, build reefs whenever they can find a hard substrate close enough to the surface of tropical waters. While at first this was on the flanks of the volcanoes, as the latter subsided corals grew on top of the old reefs. Today the coral rock may be one or two kilometres thick on top of the original volcano. Over the same millions of years, erosion, climatic changes and the consequent rising and falling of sea levels complicate analysis of individual atolls, but this basic explanation of their formation holds good everywhere. It was yet another of Darwin's insights; not only that, it was one first propounded on the basis of a short stay at the Cocos-Keeling islands and, after sailing on past the Chagos in the *Beagle*, on a lengthy correspondence with Commander Robert Moresby, whose beautiful charts of the latter islands grace this book. Indeed, Moresby, who in 1837 surveyed the Archipelago after completing similar surveys of the Laccadives and Maldives, reached similar conclusions independently. After describing one small islet, 'covered with luxuriant and beautiful vegetation from edge to edge, and surrounded by a white band of foam and spray' as being like 'an immense flower-pot rising out of the ocean', he gives a vivid description of the growth of corals and the eventual formation of islands above the cones of ancient volcanoes.[5] Darwin's own sketches explain themselves:

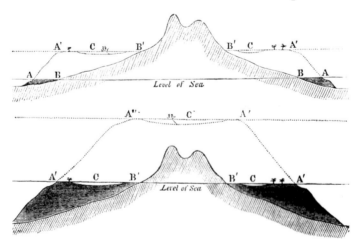

As a result of this formation, the Chagos atolls have probably existed for 50 million years, from the time when the volcanoes developed there. The corals that have continuously grown in the shallowest sunlit zone, on the tops of their forebears, still grow, forming the shallow reefs and islands seen today. The islands rise directly from the ocean floor, causing up-welling currents to bring to local waters the minerals and nutrients essential to marine life and, coincidentally, protect the low-lying islands from tsunamis. The latter, caused mostly by violent movements of the earth's crust at the intersection of its plates, require a gradually sloping shoreline to transform wave energy from speed to height, and thus to produce their well-known destructive effects. For the Chagos, this is just as well; mere distance from the source of a tsunami does not protect. In any case, it now seems that the sea bed close by is less stable than hitherto generally believed – though not by Moresby, who remarked upon 'the earth-quakes, that frequently disturb the foundations of the Archipelago, and will probably some day submerge all its lovely green circlets beneath the waves'. Indeed, tectonic plate boundaries apart, 'Chagos is possibly one of the most intense locations of oceanic seismicity today';[6] also, as for the past several thousand years, the islands' average elevation above sea level remains at no more than two metres.

Second only in importance to the islands' structure are the surrounding sea conditions, determined largely by latitude. As Earth spins on its axis, tilted in relation to its passage around the sun, it produces seasonal variations in weather patterns. Two major effects are relevant to this story. In the mid-southern latitudes of the Indian Ocean, strong south-easterly winds dominate from June to late September; for the remaining seven months of the year, the winds, interspersed with flat calms and violent storms, come generally from the north-west; and the direction of the surface currents follows the same alternation. South of these latitudes, strong westerly winds prevail throughout the year. To the north lies the Inter-Tropical Convergence Zone, a variable band of unpredictable calms and storms, affecting both sides of the equator. Just like the doldrums of the Atlantic, this zone brings delay and danger to sailing vessels, but on a scale vastly diminished by improvements over the centuries in design, rigging, navigational techniques and, not least, weather forecasting. As the illustration overleaf shows, the Chagos lies within range of the I-TCZ's southward oscillation. Of course, in contrast to the monsoon seasons of the northern Indian Ocean, all these features had still to be discovered when Portugal's *naus*[7] first ventured east of the Cape of Good Hope – and there too it mattered greatly at what season they sailed, whether outward or homeward bound.

The Islands

Fewer than half the atolls built upon the remains of volcanic peaks in this area of the Indian Ocean now reach its surface, but the platform from which they rise extends for some 200 miles from south to north and 120 miles east to west. At its centre lies the Great Chagos Bank, the world's largest atoll, with very little of its vast perimeter exposed. Just south-west of it, Egmont, a separate atoll, has six

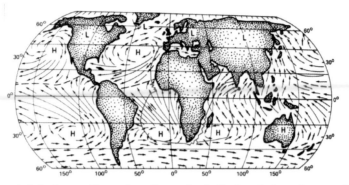

Average surface winds in August. Voyage from Portugal to India. In red, through Mozambique Channel (*por dentro*), in green outside (*por fora*).

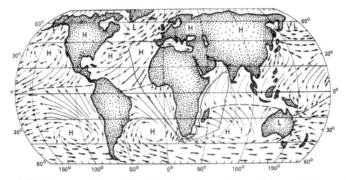

Average surface winds in January. Voyage from India to Portugal. In red, through Mozambique Channel (*por dentro*). In green, voyage outside all the islands and shoals of the Indian Ocean (*por fora*). In blue, voyage (*por fora de tudo*).

J. M. M. Pereira *O Cabo da Boa Esperança* (pages 35–36), by kind permission of the author.

linked islets (whose linking reefs are increasingly exposed), with a land area of some 300 hectares. On the Bank's western fringe are three small island groups, comprising six islands: Danger, Sea Cow, Eagle and the Three Brothers. These, together with a single island on its northern edge, Nelson, have a total land area of about 445 hectares. Some twenty miles to the north of the Bank are three more atolls: Peros Banhos, roughly circular, with twenty two islets (900 ha) scattered around its rim; Salomon, having eleven islets (311 ha) around an almost enclosed lagoon; Blenheim Reef, once boasting some sandy islets, but now consisting of rocks exposed only at low tide. Finally, far to the south, is Diego Garcia, an atoll forming the largest island of the group by far (2733 ha), with a lagoon which provides an extensive harbour. By including bits of land which are scarcely more than rocks, the archipelago as a whole can be said to comprise 55 islands, with a total land area of less than 6000 ha (60 km^2), the same as that of Barra, one of the smallest islands of the Outer Hebrides. A chart showing the whole archipelago is reproduced on the inside back cover of this book and includes the submerged atolls, which are vital to its ecology and marine resources.

The discovery of the archipelago, the establishment of the exact positions of its component parts and the emergence of an agreed set of names were processes taking nearly three hundred years. Those processes are of course part of this history, but readers need not relive all of the many hazards and navigational errors which prolonged and confused the efforts of the seafarers concerned. Better, perhaps, to begin by describing the distinctive features – often noted by the very first observers – which were to determine the development and eventual fate of each of the islands, once humans did arrive. Their common coraline structure and their geographical proximity resulted in their having virtually identical flora, fauna and weather conditions. Yet each atoll and each of the single islands had features which made it more or less difficult to exploit; none indeed could be exploited in exactly the same way as the others. The soil might be richer or poorer; ease of access and anchorage varied hugely; lagoons were shallower or deeper, some more, some less encumbered by coral heads; economic viability and social character would also be affected by geographical characteristics; and all this before taking account of the vagaries of chance in original ownership and subsequent management.

For the purpose of initial description and familiarisation, it is convenient both to use the names borne by the islands today and to 'travel' clockwise around the archipelago, starting with the island most likely to be encountered first by vessels making the voyage from the Cape of Good Hope towards India. Such encounters were however usually haphazard and fleeting. The 1602 map reproduced on the inside front cover of this book shows how little was known by the end of the 16th century. It was not until well into the 18th century that more organised observations of individual islands began to be made. The most consistent set of observations was that of Lieutenant Archibald Blair, employed by the British East India Company to investigate Diego Garcia and its 'adjacent islands' in 1786; except where otherwise indicated, the quotations below are drawn from his report.[8]

Egmont (always known to the French as **Six Iles**) was an atoll of some six miles in length and two in breadth; it had (and has) a very shallow lagoon offering a single entrance to vessels of modest size. The first recorded visit to it was made on 15 June 1605 by crew from the English ship *Tigre*, captained by Sir Edward Michelborne. The record of his voyage describes the islands of this atoll as being 'five in number, abounding with fowl, fish and cocoa nuts, whereof they brought great store aboard, and found to be excellent food. On searching both the south and west shore, they could find no anchoring; for in some places there was no good ground close under the shore, and such sharp rocks and shoals in other places, that they durst not anchor'.[9]

Danger Island was 'covered with thick wood and a few coconut trees near the centre'. It is very narrow and only about a mile long from south to north. Blair was not the last person to find it hard to approach and devoid of safe anchorage.[10] Half a century later, in 1837, Moresby gave up an attempt to land on it.

Sea Cow 'an Inconsiderable Spot covered with jungle' is separated from its close neighbour, **Eagle Island**, by a two-mile-wide channel with fast-flowing currents. The island was observed as 'two miles in extent, covered with coconut trees, and others common to these islands, no soundings except very close on the west side'; while the boat despatched to examine the shallow eastward side was prevented by the current from completing its task.

Three Brothers 'are small, two abounding with coconut trees and are connected by shoals and a small fourth island which cannot be seen unless very close in, having but small bushes on it'. The waters surrounding them are also extremely shallow, making landing hazardous and only possible in small boats. These islands had first been spotted by James Lancaster's expedition in 1602, and were noticed again, but not investigated, by the Dutch in 1744 and the French ships *Heure du Berger* and *Etoile du Matin* in 1771.

Peros Banhos, with well over twenty islets, encloses a lagoon stretching 15 miles from west to east and 12 miles north to south, an area of more than 100 square miles. This impressive expanse of quite deep water, dotted with innumerable coral heads, is often rough, particularly when the south-east trade winds blow, for there is no dry land on that edge of the atoll. Only the south-western corner of the lagoon provides good, safe anchorage; even there, corals prevent close access to the land. Only a few of the islets have soil fertile enough to support a varied flora and, even before habitation, there were few broad-leaved trees. Moreover, the atoll's topography ensured that any economic exploitation would entail the use of many small boats and expert seamanship. Blair confined himself to making a first class external survey. 'The first French chart of the islands of the Chagos Archipelago is certainly that of Lazare Picault in the *Elizabeth*, who reached Peros Banhos on 16 April 1744. He depicted on a summary chart the islets, surrounded by reefs, together with indicated tracks to show the route to take, soundings and the two places where he had anchored.'[11]

Salomon, in contrast to Peros Banhos, has a lagoon only five miles long and three miles at its widest, protected by eleven reef-linked islets and enticingly calm. At the same time, its single shallow entrance and maze of coral heads within make it inaccessible to vessels of deep draught. These characteristics were first described in 1757, by M. Rivière, the officer in charge of a dinghy sent in from a French ship, *Le Favori*. Rivière was however primarily interested – for good reason, as will be seen later – in issues of survival. When Blair, in his survey vessel *Viper*, entered the lagoon in 1786 and investigated two of the larger islets, he was enthusiastic: 'If a judgment may be formed from the soil and production, these may be supposed much older than any we have visited. The soil is tolerable and much deeper than Diego Garcia or Peros Banhos and consequently the trees take much deeper root, and grow to a larger size, one sort peculiar to these islands, which appears to be very good timber, grows the height of 130 feet, many very straight, some 4 feet diameter & 40 feet from the ground to the branches, the young timber is white, but the decayed trees are of a deep chocolate colour and the timber perfectly sound.' He might also have remarked that, with four of the islets accounting for most of the land area, management of this productive capacity would be greatly eased.

Blenheim Reef, 15 miles to the north-east of Salomon and slightly larger in size, is now no more than a circle of rocks, partly exposed at low tide. Blair, however, 'discovered from the masthead three sandy islands, where I expected to have seen breakers'. A globe based on what was known to British geographers in 1799 indeed shows a 'Sandy Island' in that very position.[12]

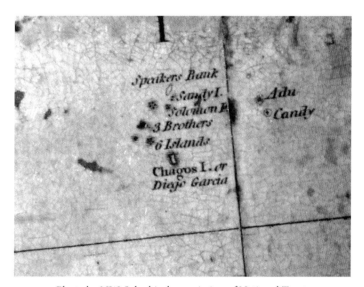

Photo by NW-S, by kind permission of National Trust.

A similar distance to the south-east of Salomon is **Nelson Island**, hardly more than a two-mile-long ridge on the northern extremity of the Great Chagos Bank. This islet, with vegetation consisting mainly of shrubs and bushes, is home to large colonies of seabirds. It was not discovered until 1820, by a schooner captain called Alexis Legour, after whom it was initially named.

The atoll of **Diego Garcia**, with a major and a minor pass at its northern end, contains a lagoon 13 miles long and 5 miles wide for about half its length, being bounded by a winding and mostly very narrow ribbon of land, almost 40 miles long. The first surviving description is that of John Davis, navigator of the *Tigre,* an English ship of 240 tons, on 19 June 1605.[13] Passing the island, he noted that it was ten or twelve leagues long and abounded with birds and fish, as well as being 'entirely covered with a wood of cocoa trees'. Davis also commented that 'this seemeth to be a very pleasant Island, and of good refreshing if there be any place to come to an anchor'. Alas, a 'bad wind' was forcing the ship toward the shore and it did not stay in the area very long. A somewhat closer look was taken in 1745, when, as we shall describe more fully (see page 24), Captain Lindsay of the English ship *Pelham* 'stood in with boat very near the land but could discover nothing inhabited'. It was not until about 1769 that we get a more detailed account, by the French cartographer, Abbé Rochon:

> That island, which we judged to be about twelve leagues in circumference, has a very pleasing aspect. Its form is like that of a horse-shoe. Its greatest breadth is not above a quarter of a league: yet the land is enough to inclose and shelter a vast basin, capable of containing the largest fleet. This basin is about four leagues in length, and its breadth is about one. It forms an excellent harbour, and has two entrances on the northern side. These passages are exceedingly beautiful.[14]

Before it was inhabited, the land was thickly forested with a mixture of coconut and broad-leafed trees, with a near-impenetrable undergrowth of creepers and ferns. On the widest part of the island, to the north-west, there were substantial marshy areas; there were also – and still are – watery inlets (*barachois*) at the southern tip, leaving only a very narrow band of land between lagoon and ocean. Although much of the lagoon was deep, with a sandy bottom providing excellent anchorage, it also contained many substantial coral heads. The main pass faced north-west, complicating entry by sailing ships during the season of south-east trade winds and making exit difficult at other times of year. Even in calms, close approach to the island could be extremely hazardous, given the sometimes strong westerly currents; indeed, a map published in 1786 marked 'many wrecks' on both the north-eastern and south-western coasts.[15] The island's infestation by rats, remarked on by the French as early as 1770, was a natural consequence of shipwreck.

Notes to Chapter 1

1 These islands, named after the Portuguese explorer Pedro Mascarenhas (see page 16), comprise the islands of Mauritius, Reunion and Rodrigues.

2 Sclater, Philip, zoologist and biogeographer, 'The Mammals of Madagascar', *Quarterly Journal of Science*, 1864.

3 Scott, Robert, *Limuria* Oxford University Press, 1961.

4 Richard Edis, *Peak of Limuria*, Bellew Publishing, London 1993.

5 Moresby, R. and Elwon, T., article printed by the order of the Court of Directors, East India Company London by Black & Co., 1841, and reprinted as 'Surveys of the Indian Navy' in *The Foreign Quarterly Review*, July 1845. This article, insofar as it deals with the Chagos, was based on a manuscript Memoir by Moresby, following his 1837 survey. The Memoir is mentioned by Darwin as having been lent to him by Moresby, but we have not been able to trace its text.

6 Sheppard, C., and Seaward, M. (editors), *The Ecology of the Chagos Archipelago*, Linnean Society, London, 1999. This work provides a much fuller introduction to the geological and many other natural features of the area than space allows here.

7 The *naus* were mainly three-masted vessels, with two rectangular sails on the fore and main masts, a lateen sail on the short mizzen mast and a small rectangular sail suspended from the bowsprit. They were heavy and difficult to steer or manoeuvre, with very poor ability to make progress into the wind. Their characteristics, routes and navigational instruments are explained with great clarity in José Manuel Malhão Pereira's (bilingual) study *O Cabo de Bõa Esperança e O Espólio Náutico Submerso* (2005).

8 Blair, Lieut. A., *Remarks and Observations on a Survey of the Chagos Archipelago*, London, 1788.

9 Astley, T., *Voyages and Travels* (Vol 1), London 1745. Michelborne, or rather his very experienced pilot, John Davis, considered that he had reached 'the Isle of Peros Banhos', a statement that has been taken at face value by many writers, despite his correct identification of the island's latitude as 6° 37′ South. The assertion made here is attested, not just by the latitude, and by the *Tigre*'s encounter with Diego Garcia a few days later, but also by the description given of Egmont by Lieutenant Blair in 1786: it then consisted of six islets (and, when the French first noticed it, called by them Six Iles), which 'are all very low, covered with wood, three only abound with coconut trees, they are connected by shoals which appear to be fordable, four extend to WNW the other two trend to NE with breakers connected with the two extreme islands, form an appearance of a small harbour, on the NE side of them. I examined it and found it difficult of access and dangerous from within from the number and closeness of the shoals … there is no safe anchorage near them…' Blair and his French contemporaries relied on their knowledge of Egmont's precise position, established by the visit there of the *Eagle* during an eclipse of the moon in 1763; and this caused Alexander Dalrymple, hydrographer of the East India Company, to refer, in a little-noticed aside, to Michelborne's 'going eastward from *Pedro Banhos* or Egmont Islands to *Diego Gratiosa* …' (*Memoir concerning the Chagos and Adjacent Islands,* 1786, p. 13). However, what appears to be the same island is shown on an anonymous Dutch chart (see inside front cover) thought to date from 1601, with the words *Crab Eylanden* added. It is a name that appears nowhere else and one that suggests it had already been visited.

10 In 1985, NW-S was among those washed ashore in a modern rigid inflatable boat, swamped by the surf.

11 Filliozat-Restif, M., unpublished doctoral thesis *L'Océan Oriental: connaissances hydrographiques françaises aux XVIIe et XVIIIe siècles*, Paris, Ecole pratique des Hautes-Etudes, 2002.

12 This globe, originally presented to Sir Joseph Banks, President of the Royal Society, is now conserved in Belton House, Grantham. Photo reproduced by kind permission of the National Trust.

13 Astley, T., *op. cit.*

14 Archives Nationales de France [AN] 3JJ 358 *Mémoire de M l'Abbé Rochon et répliques de M le Chevalie Grenier.*

15 Map of Diego Garcia attributed to Capt. Thomas Forrest, publ. by A. Dalrymple, 1786. This map has been reproduced in Edis, *Peak of Limuria*, Bellew 1993 (after p. 38).

Anonymous Portuguese chart, c. 1630 (detail)

2

Navigators and Cartographers

THESE islands had remained, it seems, virtually unnoticed (and unnamed) until early in the 16th century, scarcely investigated until well into the 18th century and not even partially settled until 1776. Apart from Diego Garcia's rats they were pure and pristine. Yet the Indian Ocean was no stranger to ocean-borne trade from at least the 9th century, while the Pacific Ocean, with much less trade, an even vaster area and microscopic islands scattered yet more sparsely, had been populated by seafaring settlers several thousand years earlier. How is this striking difference to be explained?

One obvious possibility is that there were early inhabitants, whose traces have been extinguished. An experienced multi-disciplinary team from the Australian National University examined Diego Garcia in 2010 and could find no archaeological evidence of pre-European contact. In addition, their sedimentary cores taken from swamps showed, generally, that natural fires caused by lightning strikes occurred seldom and were localised and short-lived. However, in one core there was evidence of sustained burning accompanied by an opening up in the forest and a rise in the growth of shrubs and ferns. This episode appears to have lasted for at least several decades and it was radiocarbon dated to the early second millennium AD. While increased burning during an unusually long dry spell cannot be ruled out the more plausible explanation is that it was the result of a period of human occupation. The core shows that forest had regrown completely in this area by the beginning of the 15th century and it was not opened up again until the early 18th century.[1]

Speculation that sailors from the Maldives, less than 200 miles to the north of the Chagos, were aware of their southern neighbours, and that Arab traders, or migrants from Indonesia en route to Madagascar, might have sailed close by remains just that, speculation. Or perhaps there was a shipwreck, whose survivors eked out a Robinson Crusoe existence until they died. Another proposition, that the great Chinese navigator, Admiral Zheng He (or 'Cheng Ho'), might have passed close by early in the 15th century, can now be laid firmly to rest: his fleet hugged the eastern coast of Africa.[2] All the same, it is certain that Arab or Persian navigators were aware of a few islands to the east of Madagascar, since these bore Arabic names when the first Portuguese explorers entered the Indian Ocean at the very end of the 15th century. Indeed, the Portuguese encountered Arabic-speaking merchants on Madagascar. The evidence that such knowledge extended as far to the east as the Chagos is however limited to a single, albeit important, map dated to 1502 (see inset). This shows, very indistinctly, a group of islands in the position in fact occupied by the Chagos.[3] It would appear therefore that the answer to the conundrum posed at the start of this chapter is that the dangers presented to primitive vessels by the intertropical convergence zone and the lucrative attractions of monsoon trading to the north combined to keep humans away.

Arissam, Tranom & Sapom in the Cantino Map, 1502

In the Cantino map, Armando Cortesão[4] estimates that 'the Maldives and Chagos are represented with extraordinary accuracy' for the time and considers that this 'amazing progress in geographical knowledge' suggests that 'some Arab or Malay maps were utilized'. The three larger islands, south of the Equator, corresponding to the Chagos Archipelago, in his view, bear the names 'Arissam', 'Tranom' and 'Sapom', in addition to which two groups of three smaller islands are depicted, one to the north and one to the south, each apparently representing low banks. In nearly all the later maps of the Cantino type this representation of the Maldives and Chagos is more or less to be found. However the reproduction of the names is not always very faithful; for instance, the island 'Sapom', spelt in the same manner in the Canerio becomes 'Saponin' in the Ruysch (1508), 'Saponi' in the Egerton MS-2803 (c.1510) 'Sapotu' in the Carta Marina Portugalensiumo (1513). In addition to these islands the Cantino map shows eastward a group of four islands, one just on the Equator, named 'armacora', and three more southward – 'lissam', 'sissam' and 'montizmoto'. These, in spite of being placed more westward, correspond better to the 'Ilhas Rado' of the British Museum map, and still better to the similar but nameless group of small islands in the Jorge Reinel world-map of 1519.

For what it may be worth, the important Atlas Miller, by the Portuguese cartographers Pedro and Jorge Reinel (1519), shows no sign of the Chagos, which make their first appearance in two anonymous maps held by the Lisbon Geographical Society and said to date from 1515 and 1540. Both show, south of the equator and a little west of due south of the Maldives, a group of many islands just to the north of a single island. On the earlier map, the single island is labelled 'Chagas', in the later, 'Diogo Gracia'; while the northerly group, indecipherable in the 1515 map, is called 'Islas das Chagas' in that of 1540. The 1540 nomenclature is retained in the great Atlas Universal (1558) by Diogo Homem. Diego Garcia (correctly placed and having its distinctive shape) is also named 'Diogo Gracia' in the 1540 mariners' chart illustrated on page 23. It must therefore not only have been sighted before that date, but also examined quite closely.

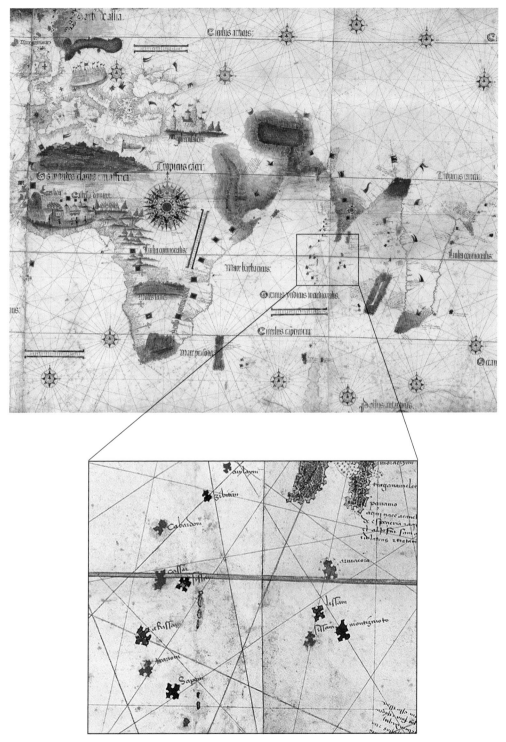

Cantino map, 1502. Image courtesy of Biblioteca Estense, University of Modena. (*Su concessione del Ministero dei Beni e delle Attività Culturali e del turismo.*)

The Portuguese

Initially, the many islands of the Indian Ocean could not readily be sorted into their distinct groupings. They – and their associated submerged reefs – represented little more than random hazards to navigation. The main trade routes tended to follow the northern coast of the ocean from India towards the Persian Gulf and Red Sea, and from those areas southwards down the East African coast. Knowledge of the SW and NE monsoons north of the equator gradually made possible safe passage between western Indian ports and equatorial East Africa. When the Portuguese first ventured into the Indian Ocean, they in turn followed the coast northwards until they linked up with the routes familiar to Arab traders. The Portuguese were however almost certainly the first to make a deliberate decision to cross directly to India from south of Madagascar.[5] Evidently, the fleet which left Lisbon under the command of Dom Garcia[6] de Noronha in the spring of 1511 had been ordered by King Manuel to seek such a route, because so many ships had already been lost in the Mozambique Channel. It took the fleet almost a year to reach Mozambique, whence one ship, the *Santa Euphemia*,

captained by Pedro Mascarenhas [pictured left] was sent ahead, because her crew was least debilitated by scurvy. After being driven south as far as Reunion, he succeeded in reaching Goa.[7] It is not clear whether any of the Chagos group were sighted on this voyage.[8] Many researchers have sought in vain for proof of a link between Mascarenhas' fleet and the Chagos and, given the certainty that reports of these early voyages would have been made to the King, it must be presumed that they were lost in 1755, with the burning down of the Royal Archives in the great fire which followed the earthquake that year. For the present authors, the facts that the earliest cartographers called the island 'Don Gracia' and that Noronha's name in the earliest manuscript is given as Dom Gracia provide great plausibility for this

Pedro Mascarenhas

theory. Be that as it may, the success of this voyage led naturally to the adoption of this route for many succeeding voyages.

While the names Chagas and Diogo Gracia (and variants of the latter) began to appear as names on charts commissioned by Portuguese and Spanish rulers, seafarers had the more immediate preoccupation of avoiding reefs and shoals. The pilots learnt their trade by experience and incorporated their wisdom in *roteiros* (or, to the English pilots, rutters) – sailing instructions, of which few examples survive concerning the Indian Ocean. They distrusted charts: 'From São Lourenço [Madagascar] to the equator you should steer night and day with a lot of care and vigil, recognising that the charts don't show the shallows, nor place islands in their correct latitudes; and there are many more islands and shallows than are shown on the charts....' Following compass courses, watching out for changes of wind direction and water colour, taking soundings, looking out for indicators such as birds or unusual fish – those were their stock-in-trade 'and don't trust yourselves, but in God and your good vigilance'.[9] In fact, the Portuguese pilots began by identifying two separate areas of danger, the '*Baixo das Chagas*' and the '*Pero dos Banhos*'. To date no written record has emerged of deliberate Portuguese attempts to explore or settle the Chagos.

Navigational problems and solutions

Apart from natural indicators, navigators were armed with magnetic compasses and with instruments to calculate latitude, notably astrolabes. Having only the most rudimentary means of keeping track of time and of the distance covered, let alone any detailed knowledge of mid-oceanic currents, accurate estimation of longitude was difficult indeed. The Portuguese however found a way around this difficulty. Discovering by experience that the extent of magnetic variation of their compasses from true North corresponded with the various places or sea conditions encountered along their way, they could guess with considerable accuracy how far they had progressed to the east or west. As we know, magnetic variation itself varies over time, but quite slowly. In effect, they now had a proxy measure for longitude. The *roteiros* are thus full of references to changes in magnetic variation and the changes of course to be made as a consequence. It was not until the middle of the 18th century that a chart was made of the readings to be expected at different positions in the oceans, even though this information was recorded in the daily logbooks kept by ships' captains.

The only fully documented Portuguese landing occurred in 1555, when a *não* called the *Conçeição* ran aground on the '*baixos de Pero dos Banhos*'.[10] Historians have traditionally interpreted this as being Peros Banhos, although the description given by the survivor who recorded the event makes it hard to accept this as likely.[11] There was indeed much uncertainty among cartographers, if not pilots, about the placing of these and other bits of land in relation to each other. One early chart, published in 1598 by the Dutch voyager, Huigen van Linschoten, shows '*Peros dos Banhos*' twice, close to present-day Peros Banhos and also to the north-west of the Maldives. The map which provides the frontispiece to the present work even shows a third shoal of this name! The confusion rife among

The fate of the *Conçeição*, 21 August 1555.[12]

cartographers was finally resolved in 1958 by Commander Humberto Leitão.[13] His detailed and persuasive study concludes that 'the group in the north of the archipelago formed by Peros Banhos, Blenheim Reef and Spenser [Speaker] Bank covers about 50 miles from north to south, and its central latitude is about 5° 00'. We believe that this is the group the Portuguese named '*Baixo das Chagas*', whereas 'the old '*Pero dos Banhos*' comprised the Great Chagos Bank, the Six Islands [Egmont], possibly Pitt Bank and perhaps Wight Bank'. In short, the names applied to the two groups had become transposed. Furthermore, what the accounts of particular ships' voyages and the *roteiros* show is that captains aimed to pass to the west of the Chagos on their outward voyages and to the east when homeward bound. If Leitão is right, as we believe,[14] the *Conçeição* must have run aground somewhere on the Great Chagos Bank. The two fundamental assertions of the survivor's story are that the wreck happened after many hours of sailing northwards over shallow waters and that the island concerned was small, virtually treeless and out of sight of other land. Nelson Island alone meets all these conditions.[15] Clearly, the *Conçeição* must have been well to the east of her intended course.

Wherever the grounding took place, the events which followed it were so terrible that they could only reinforce the desire to avoid this area. Only one day after the shipwreck, the captain and pilot, accompanied by various nobles and sailors – some forty people all told – returned in the ship's longboat, loaded it with supplies and treasure, then set sail for India. According to the contemporary Jesuit records,[16] the captain and about 20 men reached Cochin early in November. Ships were sent to rescue those left behind and soon encountered a second group of some 30 survivors, who had constructed a raft from the *Conçeição*'s timbers. Finally, a year later, on 27 November 1556, 12 other survivors reached Cochin, all that remained of a group of 27 who had constructed a second raft. These included Manoel Rangel, whose account of the wreck and his subsequent ordeal is recorded in the *Historia Tragica Maritima*.[17] Unfortunately, the Jesuit records shed no light whatsoever on where exactly the *Conçeição* went aground, how the survivors found their way to India or how many perished.

Calculations based on various figures mentioned by Rangel suggest that about 300 died at the site of the wreck, and more than 40 of those who managed to leave it.

Other Portuguese ships are said to have been lost on the shoals of 'Peros Banhos', in particular, the *São João* in 1577 and the *São Pedro* in 1578.[18] Only the second of these is mentioned in the British Library's manuscript (cf Note 4) – and in an intriguing manner: after remarking that the ship set out in 1577 and was wrecked on the shoals of 'Peros dos Banhos' without loss of life, it adds that, according to another account, she was lost on the '*Baixas das Chagas*', but that the crew used the ship's own boats to reach India. Clearly, there was still considerable uncertainty about the relative positions of both shoal areas. An anonymous Dutch chart of the Indian Ocean, considered to date from 1601, shows not only the '*Islas dos Chagas*', but mention of the *São Pedro*'s sinking (see map on inside front cover). It also represents another island close by, which some Dutch user of the chart has called Crab Islands, suggesting that he had been ashore.[19]

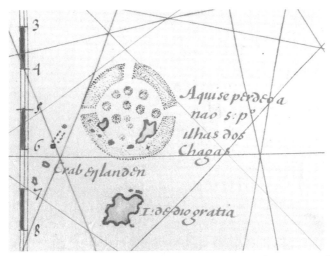

Anonymous Dutch chart of 1601 (detail). Image courtesy of University of Halle.

The Dutch

The Dutch were aware of the Chagos by the end of the 16th century. In 1583, a Dutchman, Jan Huigen van Linschoten, despatched to Lisbon to discover the secrets of Portuguese trade with the Indies, inveigled for himself a position in the entourage of the Portuguese archbishop being appointed to Goa. Returning in 1592, he published an account of his travels and discoveries, which provided his backers with just the encouragement they needed to plan an expedition to attack the Portuguese monopoly. His report quickly reached England, where an English translation was submitted to, among others, Robert, Earl of Essex.

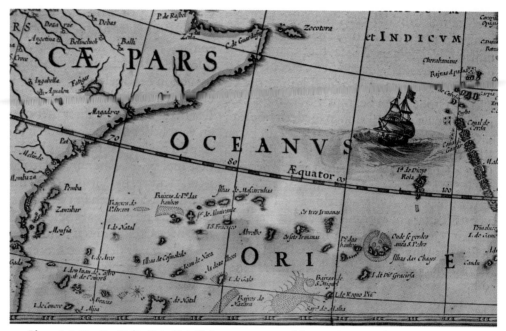

Blaeu Asia Noviter Delimitata (detail). Image courtesy of Stewart Museum (Montréal, Canada).

Taking a leaf from the Dutch book, he instructed a well-known mariner, John Davis of Sandridge, to seek employment as one of the pilots in the Dutch expedition which set out in 1595, returning in 1599.[20] Three days after reaching England, Davis sent Essex a meticulous journal of his adventures 'according to those directions which your Lordship gave me in charge at my departure; when it pleased You to employ me in this voyage for the Discovering of the Eastern Ports of the World, to the service of Her Majesty and the good of our Country'.[21] Another Dutch expedition set out in 1598 and one of its vessels, the *Vriesland*, passed close to Diego Garcia on 15 November that year, noting the sharp drop-off to deep water at its southern end.[22] Direct evidence of Dutch shipwrecks in the Chagos is lacking. However, in about 1998, a considerable quantity of broken pottery was found on the reef of Egmont Island.[23] Identified as being Ming trade ware of the late 16th or early 17th century, the most likely explanation is that it came from a ship, quite probably Dutch, wrecked on her return journey from south-east Asia.

The Dutch East India Company soon took a very close interest in establishing which routes to the east were best overall. As early as 1616, it issued instructions that all its ships should head due east from the Cape to use the prevailing westerly winds, only altering course northwards to catch the south-easterly trades at around 80° East. On the return route, ships from Batavia (today's Jakarta) were to head south-west after passing through the Sunda Strait; ships from Ceylon and Bengal were to use the north-east monsoon to steer southwards until reaching Lat. 10° South, then south-westerly until they reached between 30°–32° South. This made encounters with the Chagos very unlikely. In fact, the first land Dutch crews were expected to sight was the coast of Natal. However, several charts of the area, evidently used more than once, show that some ships bound from the East Indies for India did in fact steer due west from the Sunda Strait, then turn northwards immediately after passing the Chagos.[24] During the rest of the 17th century, when Dutch wealth and power were at their zenith, the country's map-makers also led the field, with the Blaeu family amongst the most prolific. Pictured opposite is part of a chart by Willem Janszen Blaeu, printed in 1635, but first published in 1617 under the title Asia Noviter Delimitata.

Later still, it was the captain of a Dutch ship, the *Kerkwyck*, who in 1744 reported the exact position of Diego Garcia, which he called 'Chagos Island'. In 1747, the same captain produced a number of sketches and partial charts of Chagos islands. One of those shows three islands, with another more distant, close to the west of a reef described as *'Baixos dos Peros Banhos'*. The latitude and longitude shown make it highly likely that the views are of the Three Brothers, with Eagle Island behind – a further indication of the correctness of Leitão's theory.[25]

The English

The English arrived in the Indian Ocean almost a century later than the Portuguese, spurred on by fear of losing trade to the Dutch and emboldened by the destruction of the Spanish Armada.[26] Having made peace with Spain in 1600, Queen Elizabeth gave her charter to London's Company of Merchants to promote England's trade with the East. A year later, the new company sent its first expedition on its way, a fleet of four well-armed ships under the overall command of the merchant James Lancaster aboard the 600-ton *Red Dragon*.[27] The expedition's chief pilot was John Davis, the protégé of the Earl of Essex already mentioned, and the latter's approval was sought for his appointment as 'Pylott Major' of the fleet.[28] The ships set off from Torbay on 22 April 1601 and, pausing only to relieve a Portuguese mer-

James Lancaster. Photo by kind permission of Tanners Guild, London.

chantman of her cargo near Madeira, rounded the Cape of Good Hope and headed east.[29] Lancaster and his fellow-merchants left a vivid account of this voyage, shortly after their return in 1603,[30] but another surviving record is, for the Chagos story, more revealing. This is a rutter or sailing guide to the Indian Ocean, published in 1618 on the basis of five completed voyages, of which this was the second. Its author describes in detail the navigational problems encountered. During the voyage, his estimates of longitude were calculated afresh from each stop and, like his Portuguese equivalents, he attached great importance to measurements of magnetic variation, often finding 'no means to help myself, but by the variation, which is very sure, if you be careful in observing'. After passing close to Agalega (then known as 'Roquepiz'), the fleet found itself suddenly crossing a ledge of rock into an area of shallows and deeper channels, a 'pound' as Lancaster described it. Careful manoeuvring was required, with the *Dragon*'s pinnace leading the way, for the four ships to extricate themselves.

> The shoals called '*Baixos das Chagas*', have [sic] in latitude six degrees and in longitude fifty three degrees thirty six minutes from the Cape of Good Hope. The variation is 19° 50' from North to west. These shoals are very dangerous. There are three or four islands and other dry sands: we were twenty-four hours upon and among these shoals. There is in some places coral, in others some sand; sometimes ten fathoms and, by and by, six fathoms: the best water the ships had [under the keel] was four fathoms: but God be thanked, we had no hurt to any one of the ships. We were clear by keeping the isles South South-West from us: for upon the North North-East it is that we found the way out. If they had been well laid in our charts, we had missed them.[31]

So much for cartographers! But the calculation by the document's author of the position of the western edge of the Great Chagos Bank, at the latitude described, is very accurate. At any rate the expedition proceeded on its highly profitable way. It is, however, tempting to speculate what might have become of the East India Company, had its very first expedition, to which the majority of its initial capital had been committed, been overtaken by a sudden storm in those treacherous shallows.

Two years later, in December 1604, Davis set forth again, this time at the service of an adventurer, Sir Edward Michelborne [pictured left]. He too had earlier enjoyed the patronage of the Earl of Essex.[32] Only two ships were involved, the *Tigre* (240 tons) and her pinnace, the *Tigre's Whelp*. Their arrival at Egmont Island and their passage close to Diego Garcia have already been described (pages 7 and 9 above), but Davis' confident supposition was that his first encounter had been with the island of 'Peros Banhos' and that its longitude was 109°. He would clearly have known that he was sailing to the south of his previous track, with the names of islands marked on his chart; we can infer therefore that, as Leitão proposes, 'Peros Banhos' was shown to the south of the '*Baixos das Chagas*' (but with Diego Garcia shown as 'Diego Graciosa'). As to the longitude, estimated from the Cape in 1602, during a voyage in which he had begun his calculations afresh at several points, including the Lizard (in Cornwall) at the start and Cape San Antonio (on the east coast of Brazil), it is obvious that on this occasion he had continued with his estimation based on the latter point, whose longitude is 37° 40′ West. Simple arithmetic demonstrates that Egmont, with a longitude of 72° 10′ East of Greenwich, is exactly 109° 50′ east of San Antonio. Any doubt remaining is dispelled by the fact that Lieut. Blair's description of Egmont in 1786 is, almost word for word, the same as that of the *Tigre*'s navigator. Below is shown part of a chart produced in 1540, similar to that available to the *Tigre*, showing very clearly the contemporary understanding of the islands' positions (although here, as in many Portuguese charts of the period, the baseline meridian is that of Ferro, an islet adjoining Madeira's sister island, Porto Santo). However, the main consequence of these encounters with the Chagos was to cause the English, like the Portuguese, to give them a wide berth for a century and a half.

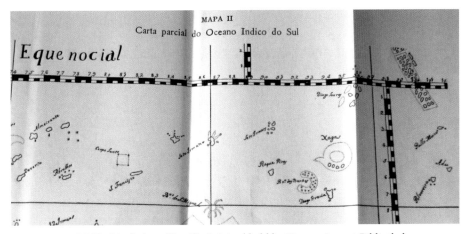

Wolfenbittel chart (detail). Original held by Herzog August Bibliothek.

Before continuing our narrative, it is necessary to mention an anomaly. The author of the rutter quoted above is stated to be John Davis of Limehouse, whose first known voyage to the Indian Ocean was in 1608. No mention is made in it of John Davis of Sandridge. The latter in fact never returned to England, suffering a violent death in December 1605 at the hands of Japanese pirates, from whom Michelborne himself was lucky to escape. How so much of the west-countryman's experience came to be disseminated by a Londoner of the same name is a mystery.

English ships, like those of other nations, must have continued to skirt the Chagos. These included the *Stringer* (1712) and *Grantham* (1728), whose exact courses are unknown. 'On the 12th January 1745' the *Pelham*, as her captain, Lindsay, reported in his log,

> very unexpectedly on our passage from the Cape of Good Hope to the Malabar Coast [of South West India], fell in with the basse de Chargoes [*sic*], bearing from SW to W3W, dis[tance] 5 leagues, Lat 7°11, dist from the Cape of Good Hope 53°11, we stood in with boat very near the land but could discover nothing inhabited we saw great number of birds and trees but during the time we were about this island could get no soundings. On the 14th standing towards this island our people saw ... a sandy beach the officer in the pinnace finding the ground very rocky stood towards the ship ... the island appears very fruitful some small hummocks on it there is no anchoring ground that we could discover.[33]

In 1748, Admiral Boscawen, with a fleet of 28 ships, sailed from Mauritius (which he considered attacking) to the Coromandel coast [of South East India], but did not apparently even sight the islands.[34] Unfortunately, his own flagship, the *Namur*, while anchored at Pondicherry and left unmanned, was lost in a hurricane that same year and, with her, all records of her fast (four week) crossing. In the year following, islands, probably Salomon, were seen from the *Griffin*.[35] Other ships, for example the *Cornish* (1762) and the *Admiral Pocock* (1763), are known to have passed through Chagos waters, while three more, the *Egmont* (1760), *Speaker* and *Pitt* (both 1763), made discoveries which are discussed in our next chapter.

The French

French explorers ventured twice into the Indian Ocean in the 16th century.[36] First, in 1526, Jean Ango, a protégé of King François I, received the latter's encouragement to accompany two Italian brothers, Giovanni and Girolamo Verrazano. Three years later, in 1529, two French brothers, Jean and Raoul Parmentier, set out in their two vessels, reaching and returning successfully from Sumatra. Then, in 1601, merchants of Saint Malo, operating without noble patronage, despatched two ships of their own, the *Corbin* and the *Croissant*. The records of these voyages and voyagers, though fascinating in many respects, make it clear that none encountered the Chagos.

It was not until much later that the French turned their minds to a more systematic examination of what lay between their Mascarene and Indian possessions. In 1744, for example, Captain Lazare Picault, in the *Elisabeth*, sent by the Governor-General, Mahé de La Bourdonnais, seems to have been the first person to encounter Peros Banhos atoll. This fact can be inferred from Picault's calculation of its latitude and statement that he found himself surrounded by 21 islets. He named the group after the Governor and made a sketch map.[37] Although the name 'Iles Labourdonnays' did not stick, the pass by which Picault entered the lagoon is called 'Passe Elisabeth' to this day. Picault depicted the islets, surrounded by reefs, together with indicated tracks to show the route to take, soundings and the two places where he had anchored, on a summary chart. In 1757, another vessel, *Le Favori*, on her way from Mauritius to Narsapour on the Coromandel coast, encountered Salomon atoll. Captain Moreau imagined that at his estimated position (5° 5′ S, 76° E of Paris) he would be close to the island of 'Adu', which was marked on some charts. It being calm weather, he sent an officer with a party of eight others to investigate, using a 16-foot dinghy with sails and oars, and instructed them to seek a way into the group. Their adventures – the first known human sojourn anywhere in the Chagos since the wrecking of the *Conçeição* – are worthy of a detailed retelling.[38]

On 26 March, M. Rivière, the officer in charge, together with the ship's gunner, M. Richer, and a passenger, M. Guillemette, together with a crew of seven Lascar seamen, set out with all the insouciance of a picnic party. For food they took two thirds of a turkey and half-a-dozen packets of ship's biscuits; for drink, a small barrel of water and a bottle each of syrup and brandy; in case of trouble, four guns, two pistols, two sabres, three axes and 35 cartridges of gunpowder. As they drew closer to land, the wind fell and they had to row, but could find no break in the surf. Night fell and, with the *Favori* no longer in sight, they found a passable anchorage. The next two days were equally frustrating and full of anxiety. On the third, they anchored closer to the surf, then plunged into it, disregarding the enormous sharks which surrounded their boat; one lascar, unable to swim, was left behind and retrieved next day by means of a makeshift stretcher. That night the wind rose and carried their boat through rocks and surf. To their amazement, it was soon found, waterlogged but intact, with only one object missing: their compass.

Three months of castaway life ensued. Coconuts there were aplenty, but the first small islet on which they found themselves soon ran out of birds to eat; moreover, they failed to discover potable water by digging.[39] After exploring the lagoon and others of the dozen islands with no better luck in finding water, they nevertheless transferred to the largest island, which offered more food and also a safe beach on which to leave the dinghy. A substantial shelter was built of poles and coconut leaves, with separate sections for the sailors and the three Frenchmen. Guillemette, who had suffered from seriously inflamed sunburn on his legs, recovered by having the fat of Boobies massaged regularly into his skin. A turtle once provided a welcome change of diet. Then it was time to move once more, along the shallows at low tide to the next island and fresh supplies of seabirds.

Here, Rivière turned his thoughts from survival to escape. This island was well supplied with virgin *mapou* timber. He knew that June brought the arrival of the south-easterly trade winds and with them the best hope of crossing the equator safely to pick up the south-westerlies of the northern hemisphere so as to reach the Maldives, India or Ceylon. All hands were set to work, cutting 5 logs, each as thick as a man's body and 25 feet long; spinning the coir of coconut husks to make cord and rope; boring apertures into the various wooden components so as to lace them together to form decking, cabin, steering oar, not to speak of masts and stays; making netting sufficient to store 500 coconuts on this new raft, with another 100 in the dinghy. The raft was completed with the fabrication of a mainsail of matted coconut fronds and a mizzen sewn from the dried skins of seals. With rain now falling more copiously, the water barrel was refilled and additional water storage created by the adaptation of bamboos washed up on the shore. On 22 June, at last, the two disparate craft set off, the dinghy in the lead and the raft trailing behind, attached by a painter. Five of the lascars travelled in the raft.

For two days, all went well, with moderate seas and steady following winds. Then, during the night, with high winds and heavy seas, a momentary lapse in the concentration of the raft's steersman caused it to veer at the moment when the dinghy's rope gave a sudden tug. In a trice, the raft capsized. Rivière was able to get everyone aboard the dinghy again, but was obliged then to cut the rope, thus abandoning most of their provisions. The men, Rivière later recorded, could only look to a Higher Power: the three French vowed, if they survived, to walk barefoot and in rags to make their oblations at the chapel of Saint Anne at Pondicherry; the Lascars vowed to Mahomet that they would buy and give to the needy three sheep and a sack of rice. The storm lasted another three days, before being succeeded by sunshine and, after about two further weeks, continuous rain. On 10 July, the last supplies of the dinghy's food ran out, with nothing to eat, apart from one small flying fish, until they were washed up on the western coast of India on 21 July.

They had been deposited on a patch of sand at Cananor, immediately beneath the walls of a Dutch fort. Their calls in the dark had roused the sentry, who fired a warning shot. Thanks to Guillemette's knowledge of Dutch, they were hauled up, but then dumped overnight in a hovel with a bowl of rice. Gracious amends were made by the Governor next day and, after time to recover from their five-month ordeal, the survivors were duly united with their ship at Pondicherry.

If this story and this chapter have happy endings, they illustrate also the extraordinary courage and endurance required to survive the dangers of negotiating the central Indian Ocean by sail. Those qualities were to be demanded of many others to face similar challenges in the years to come. Mostly, however, the Chagos Archipelago, now deliberately avoided rather than simply beyond human ken, was left to resume its slumber – but not for much longer.

Notes to Chapter 2

1 Anderson, A., Camens, A., Clark, G. & Haberle, S. (In press) Investigating pre-modern colonisation of the Indian Ocean: the remote islands enigma. In: *Connecting Continents: archaeology and history in the Indian Ocean* (ed. by K. Seetah & R. Allen). Ohio University Press, Athens (Ohio).

2 Pereira, José Manuel Malhão, and Jin Guo Ping, *Navegações Chinesas no Século XV: realidade e ficção*, Academia de Marinha, Lisbon, 2006; also Wade, Geoff, 'The Zheng He Voyages: a reassessment', *Journal of the Malaysian Branch of the Royal Asiatic Society*, vol 78, Part 1, No. 228, 2005.

3 The 'Cantino map', now preserved in Modena. Cantino was an emissary of the Duke of Ferrara to Lisbon and brought the map back with him in 1502. Close examination of a high resolution scan of this map, with the help of its curator, Dr Annalisa Bottini, demonstrates that the Portuguese at least had no direct knowledge of the Chagos at that time. Indeed, islands shown in position of the Seychelles carry the simple description 'Islands observed by Vasco da Gama during his second voyage'.

4 Cortesão, Armando, 'A hitherto Unrecognized Map by Pedro Reinel in the British Museum' *The Geographical Journal*, Vol. 87, No. 6, June 1936 (pp. 518–524); see also his *History of Portuguese Cartography*, Junta de Investigações do Ultramar, Lisbon, 1969.

5 The original inhabitants of Madagascar, who sailed from Indonesia in the 9th century may constitute an exception, but not the Chinese expedition of Admiral Zeng He in 1421, who (if he sailed round the Cape of Good Hope) would have followed the traditional Arab dhow route close to the African coast.

6 In the earliest manuscript record of the voyages to the East Indies, *Relação das Naos e Armadas da India* (BL, Códice Add. 20902), his name is spelled Gracia de Noronha. We discount the suggestion that Diego Garcia was discovered by an explorer of that name. A Portuguese, Diogo Garcia, working for Spain, explored southern Brazil during the 1520s. Any visit he may have made to the Indian Ocean would have happened later – by which time the island was already beginning to appear on maps.

7 de Visdelou-Guimbeau, Georges, *La Découverte des îles Mascareignes*, General Printing and Stationery, Port Louis, 1948.

8 Robert Scott (*op. cit* pp. 33-35) takes the view that the Chagos were very probably spotted. However, Alfred North-Coombes, in his admirable survey of the evidence, casts doubt on Scott, without coming to a conclusion of his own (*La Découverte des Mascareignes par les Arabes et les Portugais: retrospective et mise au point*, Service Bureau, Port Louis, 1979).

9 Pereira, G. (ed.), *Roteiros Portuguezes da Viagem de Lisboa á India*, Sociedade Geographia de Lisboa, 1898.

10 Wenban-Smith, N., 'The *Conception*: a 450-year-old mystery', in *Chagos News,* January 2007.

11 Rangel, Manoel, Relação do naufragio da não Conceyção, *História Trágico-Máritima*, I, 169-217.

12 From the *Livro de Lisuarte de Abreu*, an illustrated manuscript record of results of the fleets despatched annually from Portugal during the 16th century. Image courtesy of J.M.M. Pereira.

13 Leitão, Commandante Humberto, 'Identificão dos Baixos de Pero dos Banhos e das Chagas', in *Studia: Revista semestral do Centro de Estudos Ultramarinos*, 1 Lisbon, 1958, pp. 118-122.

14 Apart from evidence cited by Leitão, Michelborne's belief that he had landed on Peros Banhos in the latitude of 6°37′S suggests that he possessed a chart with this identification.

15 Admittedly, one near-contemporary chart shows 'Peros Banhos', i.e. Egmont, at the south-west corner of the Chagos group. Yet only 50 years later, it bore no resemblance to the one described by Rangel. In any case, the shallows to the south (Pitt Bank) would only have needed a few hours to cross.

16 *Documenta Indica*, Vol III, 1553-1557.

17 Gomes de Brito, Bernardo, Lisbon 1735–36.

18 Da Fonseca, Henrique Quirino, *Os Portugueses no Mar*, Ministerio de Marinha, Lisbon, 1926. This work lists a third name, the *Algarvia*, but makes clear that it was a nickname for the *Conceição*.

19 This chart, illustrated on p. 253 of the catalogue of charts published in *Dutch Asiatic Shipping* by J.R. Bruin and others, is also reproduced on the inside front cover of this book.

20 John Davis (or Davys, as he spelled his own name) was born close to Dartmouth and served under Raleigh at Cadiz, before embarking on a career of exploration, notably in making several attempts to discover a Northwest passage to China. He also invented new navigational instruments and wrote a

popular treatise on navigation, *Seaman's Secrets* (1594).

21 Dutch plans to break Portugal's stranglehold on oceanic trade with the Indies and the subsequent development of Dutch power in the area are fully described in George Masselman's study *The Cradle of Colonialism* (Yale University Press, 1963). John Davis' statement is quoted on p. 124 of that work.

22 'De Tweede Schipvaart der Nederlanders naar Oost-Indië onder Jacob Cornelisz van Neck en Wybrant Warwijck, 1598-1600', *Der Linschoten Vereenigen*, XLVIII, publ. Martinus Nijhoff, The Hague, 1944.

23 Samples given to NW-S were shown for identification to Miss Jessica Harrison-Hall, British Museum Curator of Chinese ceramics, on 20 May 2007.

24 An important source of Dutch cartographic and nautical information is *Dutch Asiatic Shipping in the 17th and 18th Centuries,* by J.R. Bruin and others, publ. Martinus Nijhoff, The Hague, 1987 (3 volumes).

25 The *Kerkwyck*'s voyage is described in the Dutch cartographer, Van Keulen's *De Nieuwe Lichtende Zee-Fakkel* (1753), pp. 17-18 and in 1786 led the distinguished British hydrographer, Arthur Dalrymple to name the islets now known as the Three Brothers as the 'Kerkwyck Islands'.

26 The complex commercial rivalries between Portuguese, Dutch and English merchants over the European markets for eastern luxuries, and England's response, are excellently described in K.N. Chaudhuri's *The English East India Company*, Frank Cass & Co., London, 1965.

27 Later to be knighted and become a Governor of the East India Company.

28 The other ships in Lancaster's fleet were the *Hector* (300 tons), *Ascension* (260 tons) and *Susan* (240 tons). Seventy per cent of the value of their cargo was in the form of bullion, to finance initial purchases, mainly of pepper. All four ships returned and the expedition made a profit of nearly 100%.

29 East India Company (EIC) Court Minutes, 30 September and 16 December 1600 in *The Dawn of British Trade*, Henry Stevens & Son, London, 1886. Essex, beheaded for treason on 25 February 1601, did not live to see the expedition set sail, just as Queen Elizabeth herself died on 24 March 1603, six months before Lancaster's triumphant return on 11 September that year.

30 *A True and Large Discourse of the Voyage…*, (William Aspley, London, 1603) reprinted in *East Indian Trade*, Gregg Press, London, 1968.

31 Davis, John, in Samuel Purchas *Purchas His Pilgrimes* (Part I, Fourth Book, p. 448), Wm Stansby, London, 1625. The 'small islands' must have been those that came to be known as the Three Brothers.

32 Michelborne, a soldier who had served under Essex in Ireland, and there been knighted by him, had been put forward by Lord Buckhurst, Lord High Treasurer, as one of the 'principal commanders' for the Lancaster voyage. The EIC Court rejected him, not wanting 'any gentleman', but only 'men of their own quality'; later the Court dismissed him from the Company altogether, on suspicion of involvement with Essex's rebellion against the Queen (EIC Court minutes, 3 October 1600 and 6 July 1601). With the accession of King James, he was able to obtain his very own Charter to trade in the East.

33 Most unusually, this fragment of Capt. Lindsay's log is to be found, not in any British archive, but in the French marine records, AN MAR 4 JJ 86.

34 Scott, *op. cit.* (p.63).

35 Dalrymple, *The Oriental Repertory.*

36 Here, as elsewhere in our account of French involvement in the Indian Ocean up to the end of the 18th century, a great deal is owed to the work of Mme. Manonmani Filliozat-Restif (see chapter 1 note 8). In consultation with her, an English translation of the passage in this thesis concerning the mapping of the Chagos was published in 2005 (*Chagos News*, No. 25).

37 French National Archive (AN MAR 4 JJ 86). Picault's original record is very hard to read and this text relies also on Mme. Filliozat-Restif's interpretation of the same documents (*op.cit*, p. 261).

38 *Ibid*. The full French account, of which a translated summary is given here, is entitled *Relation que fait le Sr Rivière officier du Bot le Favori de son voyage dans le canot de ce Bot aux Isles Adu et des événemens facheux dont il a été accompagné*, AN MAR 4 JJ 86.

39 Rivière's report allows us to establish that he and his companions landed first on what acquired the name 'Ile de la Passe' and then moved successively to what became known as 'Ile Anglaise', 'Ile Boddam' and, probably, 'Ile Takamaka'. Although Rivière does not say so, this was the best choice for his getaway, being directly up-wind from the lagoon entrance.

3

Anglo-French Competition and Co-operation

THE first encounters with Chagos described in the preceding chapter had been fortuitous and accidental; the results were marked down in log-books, principally designed to provide a source of information and a warning to fellow mariners. At this juncture, few passing sailors had the time or inclination to conduct detailed voyages of exploration around the archipelago and the presence of the various atolls and banks were seen rather in the guise of obstacles to be circumvented than as islands to be investigated. Moreover, as we have seen, both the Portuguese and Dutch regarded the Chagos as irrelevant to their interests and had settled on sailing routes to avoid the archipelago. That became less and less true for the French and the British. The French, having occupied Mauritius and Bourbon (Reunion), began to use these islands to project their influence in the Indian Ocean and to defend their Indian posses-sions.[1] The British left it largely to the East India Company to defend its own interests, not only in India but on the route to India. The perennial rivalry between the two nations was thus set to intensify in this arena; on the other hand, they had a shared interest in establishing safer and quicker passage for their mariners and merchants. A further complication was that, as they learned more about the mid-oceanic islands, the French took an increasing interest in their resources, whereas the British concerns were primarily strategic.

Thesis: the French

Within only a few decades of French settlement on the Isle of France (present day Mauritius) its natural resources began to be depleted. The *Intendant* (local representative of the French East Indies Company) was a certain Pierre Poivre, a man justly credited with promoting the scientific exploration of the North-East Archipelago, as the French then described the area which included the

Chagos.[2] Better known to us today for his botanical interests – the 'Peter Piper' who 'picked a peck of pickled pepper' in the English nursery rhyme – Poivre (pictured left) was, as the ditty suggests, a keen collector and disseminator of spices; he also had his eye on turtles and tortoises. Already by 1770 the *Intendant* had informed his superiors in France that 'Tortoises are starting to become rare on the island of Rodrigues. It would be as well to abandon it for a while to allow the population to recover. When we get more familiar with the archipelago that lies further to the north, we may hope to find islands as abundant in tortoises as Rodrigues used to be'.[3] Poivre remarked that earlier brief sightings of Diego Garcia had indicated an abundance of tortoises or turtles, and proposed that his best officers should be despatched to explore the archipelago in the *belle saison*. The north-east archipelago was therefore now of importance both as an area of dangerous shoals and banks which needed to be properly mapped and as the potential source of meat valued for its supposed power to combat leprosy.

In fact, help was already on its way. Jacques-Raymond, Vicomte de Grenier, born in Martinique in 1736, had embarked on a naval career at the age of 20 and had already been involved in several campaigns – his most recent against the Barbary corsairs – when he was selected for duty in the Indian Ocean.[4] In 1767 he was named commander of the corvette *L'Heure du Berger*, for service at the Isles of France and Bourbon. Judging this to offer only limited career prospects he requested the French naval minister's permission to 'undertake observations and even to make discoveries in these seas' and to embark with him two specialists: the Abbé Rochon '*pour faire les Observations astronomiques*', and a hydrographic draughtsman ('*dessinateur hydrographe*'). The Duc de Praslin acceded to all these demands in a letter dated 13 October 1767. After much discussion with fellow naval officers, Grenier became convinced that 'no-one had yet tried to investigate these waters, on account of their anticipated dangers' and he therefore set for himself the task of finding 'a shorter all-season route between the Isle of France and India'. Rochon, already recognised as one of France's foremost astronomers, was not able to accompany Grenier at once, but lost no time, once he had caught up with the ambitious mariner, in seeking to demonstrate the superiority of science over seamanship. His primary task, however, was to prepare for an important astronomical event, a transit of the planet Venus across the sun in June 1769, which would be visible from Rodrigues.

Shortly before the departure of the corvette, Jean-Baptiste d'Après de Mannevillette forwarded to Grenier a map of the Indian Ocean on which he had traced 'in yellow the places about which our knowledge remains very sketchy'.[5] On arriving at the Isle of France Grenier was requested by the Governor, Dumas, to undertake a voyage along the east coast of Madagascar. He carried out this task, but still burning to find a better route to India he finally obtained the agreement of Dumas and Poivre to set out on this mission, which they described as 'to traverse the seas which lie between here and the Maldive Islands and Ceylon, to

Abbé Rochon, shown here with ship's captain Bory.

reconnoitre their reefs and islands; to look for the most direct, and thus shortest, route to take between the Isle of France and the Coromandel coast at all times of year'. Rochon could not go with him, on account of his duties in Rodrigues – though, as Fate would have it, his ship was wrecked on the nearby Cargados shoals. The day before his departure, Grenier was given a copy of the map made by Picault in the 1740s and after consulting it, he decided to follow the 5th parallel (as Picault had done as far as Seychelles), a course that, if maintained, would take him across Speaker's Bank and on without obstacle to the Sunda Strait.

On 30 May 1769 he set sail northwards from the Isle of France, sighting Saint Brandon on 2 June, the bank of Saya de Malha on 4 June and arriving at the Seychelles on 14 June. His route to the Indies, Grenier reasoned correctly, should take him close to the 'Adu islands', which had been recorded in detail only by Moreau and Rivière from *Le Favori* in March 1757. Moreau's journal had described his approach to and the position of these islands as follows:

> From 25-27 March 1757. Observed white seabirds all afternoon; yesterday at 6 in the evening saw bottom, with no land in sight; took soundings, revealing rocks, and more soundings to establish the depth; had 19 fathoms, with the bottom consisting of coral and broken shells. At 6.45 large red coral; the same at 7.30, but hardly any rocks and the lead brought up a small red fish, still alive, plus some tiny shrimps and shellfish, with beautiful, pure white sand; at 8.45 bottom rocky, depth 15 fathoms; immediately sounded again and found same bottom, but 21 fathoms;

at 9.30, fine white sand at 47 fathoms. We were close-hauled on a port tack, wind NW. At 11.30, same bottom at 49 fathoms; at midnight, same bottom at 45 fathoms; at 6 a.m. today espied land to the NNW at an estimated distance of 6-7 leagues; at 7.30 spotted another island to the SSE; at 8 o'clock sounded again without finding bottom at 75 fathoms. At this point the westernmost island lay a little to the north of north-west and we had covered about 8 and a half leagues* upon it; allowing for the necessary corrections, it probably extended further northwards. At 8 a.m., as it was fine weather, with a very calm sea, we dispatched the ship's dinghy … At midday, the observed latitude was S. 5° 05', as against our expected lat of S 5° 11'. At midday the land visible lay as follows: the most southerly islet at a little westward of NW; the most northerly a little northwards of NE, the nearest land being one and a half leagues distant.[6]

* One French league was equal to three English nautical miles.

Grenier had consulted this record and concluded that the 'Adu islands' must be along his projected new route to the Indies. As we have already explained, however, in the last pages of Chapter 2, the islands encountered by Moreau were those of Salomon, centred on Lat 5° 20' S Long 69° 51' East of Paris. Moreau's meticulous soundings enable us to calculate that the bank over which *Le Favori* passed during the night was Victory bank, while the island visible to the SE must have been Nelson Island, not knowingly seen again until 1820.

Thus, when *L'Heure du Berger* passed Moreau's estimated position, there were many seabirds – the vessel was close to Speakers Bank, but no islands in view. Grenier concluded, again correctly, that Moreau had been somewhat further south than he believed. When Rochon and Grenier made the trip together later in the year, with the same result, Rochon was able to argue that Grenier had simply not made his case: there were still unknown dangers. On their return to France, their rival claims to be the best person to chart the new 'route to the Indies', either through or around Chagos, stirred up a controversy which necessitated the intervention of French ministers and notable academicians, dragged in Jean-Baptiste d'Après de Mannevillette (1707-1780)[7] and Alexandre Guy Pingré (1711-1796) astronomer and naval geographer, who were forced to judge their peers, and precipitated a storm of mémoires and counter-mémoires, which are breathtakingly vituperative but a useful source of material for the truly committed historian of Chagos cartography.

Both men were right; their arguments were not mutually exclusive. At first, the venerable academicians came down firmly on the side of Grenier, agreeing that the route proposed was shorter and attacking the '*sophismes*' of Rochon. For example, they countered Rochon's argument that this was already a well-travelled route, demonstrating that James Lancaster had followed a different trajectory:

That Admiral, who left Antongil Bay on 6 March 1602 and, after observing the

Island of Roquepiz on the 16th, headed south as far as the 6 degree line, between the isles and reefs of Pedros Banhos and those to the NW of Chagas Island, his route demonstrating that his successful transit of the archipelago had nothing in common with the route proposed by Monsieur Grenier.[8]

The arguments raged until July 1771. Then the 'great and good' reached a more nuanced view: the route was a new and shorter one, for which Grenier deserved credit, whilst admitting their ignorance about other possible 'dangers' and supporting the need for further exploration. Indeed both men later returned to Mauritius to pursue their researches. A full account of their quarrel need not detain the reader here.[9] Suffice it to say that Rochon, in his 1791 publication *Voyage à Madagascar, et aux Indes Orientales*, was to have the last word:

> Vessels leaving the Isle of France for India were forced, during both monsoon seasons, to take a long, indirect route so as to avoid the archipelago of islands and reefs to the north of the Isle. As long as the real positions of these dangers remained unknown, there remained risks for any squadron which might attempt to take a more direct route … If improved knowledge of the Archipelago allows a more direct route to be tried in both seasons, I dare to flatter myself that I have played a part in rendering this service to navigation, given that I have been the first to establish, through astronomical observations, the precise position of the main hazards.[10]

On a more general point, that the shortest route was not necessarily the fastest, Rochon could also have claimed victory. In the mid-1770s, the Governor of the Isle of France, the Chevalier de Ternay, offered his opinion on the 'new route to the Indies' of Grenier, which all had supported against Rochon. He commented, 'Every vessel leaving here in 1775 and following the route proposed by Mr Grenier has experienced storms, calms and contrary winds, which have occasioned prodigious delays, even, in one case, resulting in a voyage which took four months to reach the Malabar coast'.[11]

Having said that, the efforts of Rochon and Grenier had in reality accomplished less than either claimed. In particular, their supposition that they had observed Peros Banhos was mistaken; their visit to Diego Garcia established its exact latitude while still mistaking its longitude by two whole degrees; they did not recognise the islets now known as the Three Brothers, did not notice Danger, Egmont or Eagle Islands and they did not find the islands already visited by Moreau in 1757.

Diego Garcia: the Coiled Serpent

If the efforts of the French to establish the best route to India were inconclusive, the visit of Rochon and Grenier to Diego Garcia alerted the French authorities to that island's strategic potential. According to Mauritian historian Auguste Toussaint, Lorient-born sailor Claude Deschiens (later known as Deschiens de Kerulvay) was appointed Captain of the *Cheval Marin* [*Seahorse*] in 1774 with a mission to explore the Chagos islands. An undated *mémoire* by Kerulvay himself, mentions a voyage to Diego Garcia in 1776, when he realised it to be the same as the island called 'Chagas' at this time. He revisited Diego Garcia in May and October 1777, each time rectifying errors on the maps then in use. Deschiens returned to Chagos, in 1781, this time to draw a map of the archipelago for the benefit of those intending to follow the route to India indicated by the Chevalier Grenier. He visited what he terms the Speaker islands [as being near Speaker's bank] and which he asserts to be the same as the 'Adu islands' where *le Favori* abandoned its dinghy. He next described the islands of 'Pedro Branbos' which were easy to recognise he says, because they 'form a circle towards the west and are encircled by sandy reefs.'[12] By 1780, a new and more up to date description of the island of Diego Garcia was in the possession of the French naval ministry, based upon the visits of ships following Grenier's routes to the Indies and that of a M. Barreault in 1780, who also drew a plan of the island:

> The island of Diego Garcia lies 400 leagues to the north-east of the Isle of France and is a part of what is known as the North East Archipelago
>
> Diego Garcia's latitude is S 7° 20' S and its longitude 68° East of the Paris meridian.
>
> This island has the exact shape of a coiled snake, whose head and tail lie close to each other, enclosing a vast bay in which many vessels may anchor safely. The island is four leagues long from north to south and has a maximum width of two leagues. The entrance to the bay is no wider than 400 yards, and capable of being defended easily, while the continuous reef which surrounds the outer rim of the island prevents access to it from any other point. Even the largest vessels can anchor in the bay and be careened there. If the island were productive and had a greater land area, Diego Garcia would merit greater attention from the European nations that trade with India, on account of the size and security of its harbour. It lacks fresh water; or rather, water is obtained by digging wells in the earth, but the product is nothing but filtered seawater.
>
> The island's soil consists of sand on a base of corals and limestone, and covered by trees; the only kind of any utility as timber is a sort of beech, not very tall or thick, and suitable only for minor marine purposes. Otherwise, there are just vast numbers of coconut trees. The island abounds in turtles, fish and two sorts of lobster – marine and terrestrial.
>
> The flesh of the abundant coconuts could be used as fodder for goats, pigs and poultry.
>
> On the eastern side, there are some slightly higher sand dunes, up which, it appears, quantities of turtles climb to lay their eggs; and we observed some huge specimens of these on the reef, as well as many Hawksbills in the lagoon.

This island is all the less suited to occupation, given that there is hardly any fresh water and no species of land mammal other than rats, which are present in vast numbers; there are however big land crabs which are good eating and plenty of sharks and other fish.

The bed of the lagoon consists mainly of rocks and coral, but also some deeper parts where the bottom is of fine sand, which needs a large kedge anchor to hold well. Since there is nothing to fear but changes of wind direction, one can be very relaxed; and I have marked on the chart the places I consider best as anchorages.

The whole length of the inner shore of the lagoon is bounded by banks of coral, which extend more or less to the open water, in some cases up to five or six hundred yards wide, without intersecting inlets. Some of the coral is exposed at low spring tides and, in the area close to the harbour entrance (approaching from the north) there are chunks or blocks of coral, quite close to each other, at a depth of between a half and two fathoms, such that, when one enters by this pass and the sun shines from the south, there is a severe risk of running into these obstacles, obscured as they are by the sun's reflection on the water. That way, I once anchored on very unsuitable ground between these blocks, where I was afraid that my cable might be parted at any moment. I passed a whole night thus and found my cable badly damaged.

Coming into the lagoon by this pass and keeping to the middle of the channel, I found myself crossing a bar having a depth of between 4½ and 5 fathoms and extending (as I discovered by sounding) for about 3 cable lengths, at which point I started encountering the coral blocks mentioned above.

Between the first and second islet, the channel has plenty of depth, but is narrow and so not really practicable, what with the south-easterly winds and the fact that it is bounded on either side by coral heads.

The best passage for both entry and exit is the one between the second and third islet, to the west. In the middle of the channel there is between 7 and 7½ fathoms and even quite close to the third islet and over the bar of the reef there are 6 fathoms. Furthermore, with just a few exceptions, this pass, whether on entering or leaving, has only a few dangerous coral heads and even those are covered by 7, 8 or 9 fathoms of water; so, provided that you take continuous soundings and everyone keeps a look out, you can tack in this pass in every type of vessel.

When, having entered via the eastern passage, you have passed the dotted line marked E on the map, you will find, where the bay narrows, a few coral heads, which can be avoided, as they all are visible, except when the reflection of the sun on the water blocks them from view.[13]

Antithesis: the British

Although the Bombay authorities had refused to sanction any organised exploration of the Chagos area in the 1750s,[14] they were spurred into action in 1770, when they learned officially of the French annexation of Seychelles. During the preceding decade, however, several East India Company ships' captains had taken pains to look closely at a number of the islands in the Archipelago. In 1760, the *Egmont* visited both Eagle and Egmont islands, establishing the real position of the first by observing an eclipse of the moon and giving the vessel's name to the second, already known to the French as *Six Iles*. Scott reports that Captain Dewar in the *Speaker* had explored the seas round the Salomon Islands in 1763, and Captain Stevens in the *Pitt* had surveyed the south of the Great Chagos Bank in the same year.[15] It was not until 1771 that the *Eagle* and the *Drake*, with two marine engineers aboard, W. Robinson and D. Thomas, were despatched by the Governor of Bombay to explore the islands of the western Indian Ocean. They began by investigating the Seychelles, the Amirantes and other small archipelagos nearby, producing maps of, in particular, Eagle Island and Bird Island in the Amirantes. They then turned eastwards towards the Chagos, where they observed a group of islands, probably the Egmont group, but did not reconnoitre them. This first expedition was followed by a second in 1772, during which the *Terrible* and the *Eagle* had time to reconnoitre several islands before being subjected to a violent storm. The *Eagle* alone was able to continue the cruise and reconnoitre the Egmont islands, the Chagos Bank and Peros Banhos. However, a dispute between her captain and the hydrographer brought the undertaking to a halt and ended in tragedy with a duel in Bombay, in which the hydrographer was killed. This resulted also in the disappearance of the charts made during the voyage, although Alexander Dalrymple, the hydrographer of the East India Company, obtained two – mutually contradictory – maps constructed by William Skynner, captain of the *Terrible*, before the latter's return to India.

In 1772, the government in Bombay also instructed Captain Thomas Neale in the *Swift* to reconnoitre several islands in the Sunda Strait, but in addition to establish the positions of the island groups shown on the charts as the Three Brothers and Seven Brothers.[16] According to Neale's own account, he first encountered (at night) the shallows of the Chagos Bank and took steps to get clear of them, coming next day upon two groups of islands, and choosing to head for the one lying more to the east. He noted that 'the Coco-Nut grows upon almost all this Range of Islands. There are ten of them in Number, and are joined to each other by a Reef of Rocks, over which the Surff breaks with great violence... the Latitude is 5° 23′ South ...' Neale sent a boat ashore through the surf, which returned laden with Coco-Nuts and Boobies, then sailed around to find the entrance to the lagoon and dispatched the boat again to see whether the *Swift* herself could enter the 'very fine Bason'. While a good landing place was found, and a safe anchorage, the rocky bottom made the venture too risky. So Neale, having without doubt visited Salomon,[17] continued on his way, eventually reaching Praslin in the Seychelles, but not encountering any other land during his return voyage to India. According to some sources, in particular William Spray, Neale did visit Diego Garcia during 1772 and reported favourably on its potential, but no primary source for this assertion has yet been traceable.[18] On the other hand Dalrymple bemoaned the fact that he could not obtain the 'Journal of the *Swift*, in 1774';[19] perhaps it was early in that year that Neale investigated Diego Garcia.

Whether or not that was the case, it was in the same year that Adam Sheriff, captain of the *Drake*, was instructed to have the surveyor, a Lieutenant Dickinson, make a plan of Diego Garcia's lagoon. Although the idea of a settlement came to nothing as a result of the Indian wars, explorations by the English continued, with visits by the *Drake* in July 1774 and the *Success* in 1776, resulting in a map by Lieutenant Ringrose, which Dalrymple had published. Captain Sheriff also deposited a variety of domestic animals on the island, with a view to testing their capacity to survive unaided. As subsequent visitors were to discover, few did.

Blair's Survey

British investigation of Diego Garcia did not resume until 1786, when the East India Company decided to establish a settlement there and also to produce a map of the whole Archipelago. The first topic occupies our next chapter. As to the second, reference may be made to Lieutenant Archibald Blair's *Remarks and Observations in a Survey of the Chagos Archipelago* in 1786 and 1787.[20] Along with it was published a chart of the archipelago, two views of the island and harbour of Diego Garcia, as well as a plan of two other groups of islands. After describing at length the currents and depths around Diego Garcia, Blair set off to describe the location and characteristics of the rest of the Archipelago, starting with Six Islands (Egmont). He estimated them to be 68 miles from Diego Garcia and having 'no safe anchorage near them', describing them thus:

> All very low, covered with wood, three only abound with Coconut Trees, they are connected by Shoals, which appear fordable, four extend in a direction to WNW the other two tend to NE; reefs with breakers, connected with the two extreme Islands, form an appearance of a small harbour, on the NE side of them; I examined it, and found it difficult of access, and dangerous within, from the number and closeness of the shoals.

Blair next reconnoitred Danger Island as '16 miles distant from the Six Islands bearing NNW, it is covered with thick wood, and a few Coconut Trees near the Centre'. Eleven miles away were Eagle Islands 'the southernmost is an inconsiderable spot, covered with jungle; the other is two miles in extent, covered with coconut trees, and others common to these islands'. From the Eagles he next saw, at a distance of thirteen miles, the Three Brothers: 'They are small, two abounding with coconut trees, and are connected by shoals, and a fourth island, which cannot be seen unless very close in, having but small bushes on it'. These descriptions are reflected in the map illustrated on p. 134.

Continuing on her journey to the northward, Blair's ship 'sounded on a coral bank 5½ fathoms'. He made a detailed survey of the channels around the Peros Banhos chain but mentioned 'I looked out in vain for "Les Isles Bourdé" and "Solimin" where they are laid down in a French Chart'. He did however establish that the former were identical with those Picault had called the 'Iles Bourdonnaises' and de Mannevillette had renamed 'Pedros Banhos', while the latter were those Moreau had supposed to be 'Adu'. Spending several days there, wooding and watering, he remarked

> The well was dug 5 feet deep, about 30 fathoms from high water mark, and in a Copse of Coconut Trees, on SE Island; the water was perfectly clear, well tasted, and in abundance; we caught 20 turtle, 2 large seals and fish enough, both for present consumption, and salting; but they are not so plenty as at Diego Garcia; probably from the number of seals.

Blair's men hoisted the English flag and saluted it with three volleys of musquetry, naming the cluster 'Governor Boddam's Islands'. The surveyor noted that the soil was 'much deeper than at Diego Garcia or Peros Banhos, consequently the trees take much deeper root and grow to a greater size'. He noted that one particular tree, 'peculiar to these islands' grew to a height of 130 feet, and that while the young timber was white, the old decayed trees were of a 'deep chocolate colour'. Blair made some interesting notes about the fauna he saw on Boddam's Islands:

> I did not see one rat on any of the Islands; with which vermine those in the neighbourhood are much infested, nor do I recollect to have seen insects, or reptiles, of any kind. Besides the sea fowl common to the adjacent islands, there is one sort, which seems peculiar to this cluster. They burrow in the ground, and make a noise more disagreeable than a jackall; curlew and small plover are in great abundance, of the latter we shot a great number which were very good.

Useful products of these islands, he concluded, were the timber, coconuts and tortoise shell, although the latter could not be procured in any great quantity.

Blair then set out to prove whether 'Ady' and 'Candy' (also known as 'Adu' and 'Candu') did exist where they were laid down in the charts, and came across 'three Sandy Islands', but concluded, correctly, that those islands he had named after Boddam were what had been previously described as 'Ady'. Bad weather then prevented him from carrying out his intention of surveying further and he returned to Diego Garcia.

Synthesis: Dalrymple and de Mannevillette

The task of mapping the Chagos was no easier than the task of discovery, since the existing nomenclature was even more haphazard than in the Seychelles group of islands and the number of islands oversimplified. Examination of the journals of the navigators involved has shown that they made many errors; partly, they could not be completely sure where they were and partly they were unable to check, by proper surveys, the distinguishing characteristics of each place they came across. One part of the mapmakers' work was to sort out which islands were real and which imaginary and also to identify the islands which bore different names on French and English charts.[21]

De Mannevillette (1707-1780), pictured above (left), and Dalrymple (1737-1808) (right), exchanged information and plans – a good example of international scientific collaboration even in time of intermittent warfare. As the author of a doctoral thesis on the subject writes:

> the two hydrographers kept up an important correspondence from 1767 until 1780 (the year of de Mannevillette's death). Admittedly the correspondence slowed down somewhat during Dalrymple's sojourn in India between 1775 and 1777 and became more difficult when the war with America broke out in 1778. But despite everything, it continued via intermediaries. Furthermore, the two hydrographers each distributed in their own countries the works published on the other side of the Channel. Dalrymple obtained several subscribers in England for the second edition (1775) of *Neptune Oriental* (the French cartographer's seminal achievement), while d'Après de Mannevillette spread knowledge in France of a collection of plans of ports in the East Indies with introductory explanations, which his cor-

respondent published in the same year. The letters show Dalrymple, notwith-standing the respect in which he held the aging French hydrographer, to have been a demanding and persistent questioner, who did not give up until he had secured the information he wanted; but, in return, he provided extracts from the journals and plans made during the voyages of English ships passing islands to the north-east of Madagascar.[22]

The culmination of their work is to be found in Dalrymple's *Memoir Concerning the Chagos and Adjacent Islands*, published in 1786, to which he appended his translation of de Mannevillette's own memoir, unpublished during its author's lifetime, which accompanied the 1775 edition of his *Neptune Oriental*. These two documents, taken together with Blair's survey, which was published from the East India Company manuscript by Dalrymple in 1788, provide a decisive analysis of the gradual identification of the Archipelago's individual islands and their positions relative to each other. If one of the French cartographer's many achievements was to establish that Diego Garcia and 'Chagas' were one and the same island, it was Dalrymple's, with the assistance of Blair, to do the same with *Six Iles* and Egmont, and with Peros Banhos and the 'Iles Bourdé'. He also disposed at last of the non-existent islands of 'Adu' and 'Candu', which represented sightings of various of the Chagos islands by ships capable only of vague estimations of longitude.

If we now 'travel' around the Archipelago once more, the results are as follows:

Egmont (Six Islands), known to the French as *Six Iles*, served as the base point for the construction of de Mannevillette's chart, since its longitude had been established accurately by the British vessel *Egmont* in 1760. De Mannevillette deduced, from the description of them in the ship's Journal, that this group had first been observed from the *Duc d'Orleans* in 1757, but not by any other French vessel until 1771, when *L'Heure du Berger* and *L'Etoile du Matin* passed nearby. Dalrymple, for his part, noted in an obscure footnote that what Michelborne thought in 1605 was 'Pedro Banhos', must be identified with Egmont. This matter was settled definitively by Blair in 1786. The French and English names were thereafter used interchangeably, with Six Islands being used at least as much as Egmont in English documents.

Ships did not have to be very far to the north of Egmont to discern **Danger**, then **Sea Cow** and **Eagle Islands**. These three, originally, as we have seen, labelled 'Peros Banhos', were christened the *Trois Frères*, seemingly by de Mannevillette in deliberate contrast to the *Six Iles*, as he worked out what had been observed from the many ships passing that way, in particular the *Grantham* (1728), *Kerkwyck* (1747), *L'Heure du Berger* and *L'Etoile du Matin* (1771), *Eagle* (1772), *Calcutta* (1775) and *La Buffonne* (1777). Dalrymple, for his part, drawing on the records of the East India Company, distinguished between the five islands of Egmont, as counted by the *Eagle* in 1772, and the group of three well-separated islands, which he called 'Eagle Islands', after the largest of them. It is not certain when Danger and Sea Cow islands acquired their present names. Danger could as easily have been so christened by British as French observers, but Sea Cow was almost certainly named 'Vache Marine' to begin with. This term was used in the Isle of France to describe seals, not dugongs. There has been no indisputable sighting of a dugong in the Chagos Archipelago, even though its extensive areas of sea grass might have offered a viable habitat.[23]

We have seen how Lancaster must have seen the **Three Brothers** in 1601, while in 1747 the captain of the *Kerkwyck* had seen these as well as the previously mentioned groups, thinking them all to be part of 'Pedro Banhos'. Dalrymple, however, gave them the name 'Kerkwyck Islands'. These three tiny islets do not appear to have been distinguished separately by the ships whose courses were tracked by de Mannevillette and do not seem to have become known as the Three Brothers until named as such in one of Blair's charts.

After Picault's visit in 1744, islands of the **Peros Banhos** atoll were shown by de Mannevillette to have been observed by quite a number of vessels, both French and British. It was not however until 1776 that a French captain, passing close by in the *Salomon*, christened them the 'Bourdé Islands' after his own name, Bourdé de la Villehuet, while de Mannevillette, considering these to be close to, but separate from the islands reconnoitred by Picault, chose to attach the name Pedro Banhos to the latter. Dalrymple favoured calling them the 'Elisabeth Islands', after Picault's ship. Precisely how 'Pedro' reverted to 'Peros' is not clear.

Several ships had seen islands to the south-west of Speaker's Bank, in particular, the *Griffin* in 1749, but by the time Dalrymple was writing, **Salomon**, the name given in 1776 by Bourdé, after his own ship, was well-established. Although Dalrymple expressed disappointment that the atoll could not be called the Griffin Islands, he turned down the proposal of Blair in 1787 that they be renamed the 'Boddam Islands', after the British Governor of Bombay at the time. Thanks however to Dalrymple, Boddam's name remains attached to the atoll's largest islet. Rather sadly, neither *Le Favori* (1757) nor the *Swift* (1772) gained recognition of their more substantive encounters.

Quite surprisingly, no-one (unless we count the probable sighting by *Le Favori* in 1757) seems to have recorded seeing **Nelson**, a small, nearly treeless, island until 1820, when a schooner captain, Alexis Legour, who had spent many years plying these waters, noticed and laid claim to it. As we shall see, the Governor of Mauritius gazetted his claim and authorised that it be called Ile Legour, a name which appeared in official Mauritius documents for many years alongside that of Nelson Island. The latter name was that of a sailing ship, which passed the island in 1835 and reported the sighting direct to the Hydrographer of the Navy.

There had been prolonged disagreement among cartographers whether **Diego Garcia** was the same as or different from another island, called Chagas. This issue was settled finally by de Mannevillette and Dalrymple, who agreed that there was only one island to the south of the Great Chagos Bank. Dalrymple, perversely, chose to call it 'Chagos Island', as being the largest of the whole Chagos group, which were known to English navigators by that name. He acknowledged nevertheless that the earliest English navigators had used the name 'Diego Gratiosa', as had some Portuguese. In fact, as noted in Chapter 2 (p. 16), the Portuguese had by 1540 settled on the name 'Diego' (or 'Diogo') 'Gracia' (or 'Garcia'). Speculation about the individual whose name is thus commemorated remains unresolved, but, for what it may be worth, the present authors favour the notion that Dom Gracia (or Garcia) da Noronha deserves this accolade (see page 16). Since the island's distinctive shape was clearly known to Portuguese navigators by 1540, at least one of them must have entered the lagoon, whereas several later navigators, such as those of the English ship *Pelham* (1745), observed only its southern part. That problem was finally resolved in 1769 by Grenier, accompanied by Rochon, as a result of which Captains Lafontaine of the *Vert-galant* and Du Roslan of *L'Heure du Berger* were dispatched in 1770 and 1771 to make plans of the island, as described above. They were soon followed by British navigators dispatched from Bombay, Neale of the *Swift* in 1774 (perhaps) and Sheriff of the *Drake* later the same year. Only then did the French and English authorities become alive to the possible strategic significance of Diego Garcia. This moment has been summarised admirably by an American researcher, Steven Forsberg. 'The English and the French were both expanding their interests, and their rivalry, into the Indian Ocean. This rivalry led to a renewed interest in once neglected locations like the Chagos Archipelago. The "zero sum" reasoning of great power competition meant that even if a nation was not interested in owning and exploiting some island, its rival might.'[24]

Notes to Chapter 3

In the notes below several French texts are quoted *in extenso*. We have made no attempt to modernise the original 18th century orthography.

1 Sir Robert Scott, in his *Limuria: the Lesser Dependencies of Mauritius* (Oxford University Press, 1961), describes this policy more fully, pp. 57-60.

2 Rochon, Abbé, *Voyage à Madagascar, et aux Indes Orientales*, Paris, 1791.

3 'Les tortues commencent à devenir rares à l'Isle de Rodrigues. Il seroit à souhaiter qu'on eut abandonner pendant quelque tems cette Isle pour y laisser les tortues se multiplier. Lorsque l'archipel qui est au nord des Isles sera un peu mieux connu, on espere d'y trouver quelque isles aussi abondante en tortues que l'a été

celle de Rodrigues. AN C/4/27 Ile de France Correspondance M Poivre, Intendant Divers Memoires et Projets 1770.' Rodrigues was already a dependency of the Ile de France (Mauritius).

4 Caron, F. *Le vicomte de Grenier, héritier de Bigot de Morogues ou fils spirituel de Suffren?* Institut de Stratégie Comparée [www.stratisc.org].

5 Grenier, M. *Memoires de la Campagne de Découvertes dans les Mers des Indes*, Brest MDCCLXX, pp. 2-10.

6 It seems from this extract as if the vessel had been heading a little to the east of due north and crossed the whole of the Great Chagos Bank from south to north. Given that the islands on which the dinghy crew landed could only have been Salomon, the island seen to the SSE must have been Nelson. The original French text reads as follows:

> Du 25 au 26 mars 1757. Vu des Goulettes blanches tout l'après midi; hier à 6 heures du soir vu le fond sous nous sans voir la terre; tout de suite sondé, eu fond de roches, resondé pour avoir le brassiage, et eu 19 brasses fond de corail et de coquillage pourri. A 6 heures ¾ gros corail rouge; à 7 heures ½ même fond, point de pierres, il est venu contre le plomb un petit poisson rouge tout vivant avec de petites ecrevisses et du coquillage, pour le sable très-blanc et beau; à 8 heures ¾, 15 brasses fond de roches, resondé tout de suite 21 brasses même fond; à 9 heures ½ 47 brasses fond de sable blanc très-fin. Nous sommes venus au plus près bâbord au vent, les Vents au N.O. [Nord Ouest] à 11 heures ½ , 49 brasses même fond; à minuit ¼ 45 brasses même fond; à 6 heures ce matin vu la terre dans le NNO estimée à 6 ou 7 lieues; à 7 heures ½ vu une autre Isle dans le SSE à 8 heures sondé et filé 75 brasses sans avoir fond, ayant l'Isle la plus Ouest au N ¼ N O conséquemment nous avons fait sur ce Banc 8 lieues ½ qui tout corrigé peuvent aller dans le Nord; à 8 heures du matin le tems beau et la mer très belle, nous avons mis le Canot à la Mer, etc.
>
> A midi, la latitude observée Sud de 5°05′
> La latitude estimeeé idem 5°11′
> Longitude arrivée 76°15′
> A midi relevé la terre comme il suit.
> L'Ile la plus Sud au N O ¼ O celle la plus Nord au N ¼ N E 50 Est à 1 lieu ½ de la plus proche terre.

7 De Manevillette had, from the 1730s, captained a number of ships of the French Compagnie des Indes, both around India and in the NW corner of the Indian Ocean. From the start, he had been a keen collector and corrector of charts, presenting the results of his work to his supportive employers. In the early 1760s, he was put in charge of the Company's map depot at Lorient. His growing collections of charts were issued to new captains until supplies ran out. Meanwhile, his work was taken increasingly seriously by the French national institutions and authorities, apart from the Director of the national chart depot, who had much of de Mannevillette's work destroyed! Fortunately, for the country's navigators, he eventually emerged victorious from these quarrels. The full story is recounted in the admirable (but still unpublished) doctoral thesis of Filliozat-Restif (see chapter 1, note 8).

8 The original French text reads:

> Cet amiral qui partoit le 6 mars 1602 de la baye d'Antongil eut la vue de l'isle Roquepiz, la 16 et tomba ensuite vers le 6e degré sud entre les Isles et écueils de Pedros Banhos, et ceux qui sont au NO de l'isle Chagas cette route fait connoitre que cet amiral traversoit l'archipel et na aucun rapport a celle que propose M Grenier.

9 More details of the cut and thrust of the two men's arguments may be found on the website set up by the authors – www.chagos.info.

10 Rochon, Abbé, *Voyage à Madagascar, et aux Indes Orientales*, Paris, 1791, pp. xli-xlii. The original French text reads :

> Les vaisseaux qui partent de l'isle de France pour l'Inde, étoient forcés de prendre, dans les deux moussons, une route indirecte et longue, afin d'éviter l'archipel d'isles et d'écueils situés au nord de l'isle de France. Tandis qu'on a ignoré la vraie position de ces dangers, il y avoit peu de sûreté pour une escadre de tenter une route plus directe … Si la connoissance plus parfaite de l'archipel permet de tenter dans les deux saisons, une route plus directe j'ose me flatter d'avoir eu quelque part à ce service rendu à la navigation, puisque j'ai été le premier à déterminer, par des observations astronomiques, la position des principaux dangers.

11 French National Archives AN 3II/358. Extract of letter dated 21 August 1776 from Chevalier De Ternay, Resident (Governor) of the Isle of France. The French text is:

> Tous les batimens qui sont partis d'icy en 1775 et qui ont voulu suivre la route indiquée par M Grenier, ont tous éprouvés des orages, des calmes, et des vents contraires qui les ont prodigieusement retardé il y en a un surtout qui a été quatre mois a se rendre a la côte de Malabar.

12 Toussaint, Auguste. 'Le corsaire lorientais Claude Deschiens de Kerulvay' *Annales de Bretagne et des pays de l'Ouest*, Tome 82, numéro 3, 1975. pp. 317-336; ANOM C/4/146 Mémoire de M Deschiens Kerulvay, undated.

13 The French text is as follows:

> L'Ile de Diego Garcia est située à 400 lieues au nord-est de l'Isle de France, et fait partie de l'archipel connu sous le nom d'archipel du nord est de l'Isle de France … Diego-Garcia est par 7° 20' de latitude sud et 68° 20' de longitude à l'Orient du méridien de Paris…. Cette Ile a exactement la figure d'un serpent recourbé dont la tête et la queue se rapprochent et forment dans son intérieur une vaste baye dans laquelle un grand nombre de vaisseaux peuvent mouiller en sureté. La longueur de l'Ile est de quatre lieues du nord au sud et sa plus grande largeur est de deux lieues. L'entrée de la baye n'a pas plus de 200 toises de largeur et peut être aisément déffendue, un récif non interrompu qui borde l'Ile sur son contour extérieur en rend l'abord impraticable par tout autre endroit – que l'entrée de la baye. Les plus grands vaisseaux peuvent mouiller dans la baye et s'y carener. Si l'Ile était productive, si son terrein avait plus de surface Diego garcia mériterait la plus grande attention de la part des nations Européennes qui commercent dans l'Inde, pour la sureté et l'étendue de son port. Il y manque d'eau; on s'en procure en creusant des puits dans la terre, mais cette eau n'est autre que celle de la mer qui a filtré. Le sol de l'Ile est de sable entassé sur des coraux et pierres à chaux couvertes de bois [le seul propre à être travaillé est une espèce de hêtre blanc de médiocre élévation, de peu de grosseur, qui ne peut être employé que pour de petites ouvrages de la marine], surtout d'une quantité prodigieuse de cocotiers. Elle abonde en tortues de mer en ecrevisses de terre et de mer et en différens poissons.
>
> L'amande de cocos qui y abonde pourrait nourrir des cabrits, des cochons et de la volaille.
>
> Dans la partie de l'est, il y a des dunes de sables un peu elevées, où il paroit que les tortues de mer abordent en quantités pour y faire leur pontes, nous en avons vu de fort grosses sur le récif avec beaucoup de carèts dans la rade. Cette isle est d'autant moins susceptible d'etablissement, qu'il n'y a point d'eau douce, il n'y a non plus aucune espece d'aminaux terrestres, excepté des rats qui y sont en grand nombre; il y a de gros chancres de terre bons a manger, beaucoup de requins et autres poissons. La Rade en général est un fond de roches et corail, il y a cependant en quelques endrois fond de sable extremement fin, qui ne donne bonne tenue que quand on a une grande touée, et comme il n'i a à craindre que le trait du vent, on y est fort tranquille, jay marqué sur le plan les endroits que j'ai reconnu être les meilleurs pour le mouillage. Toute la côte en dedans de la rade est bordée d'un banc de corail, qui s'etend plus ou moins au large, et dans la plus grande étendue d'environ 250 à 300 toise sans former aucun barachois. Une partie de ces coraux découvre à basse mer dans les grandes marées, il y a aussi a l'entrée de la rade quand on vient par la passe du nord, beaucoup de morceaux ou pâtés de corail, assez près les uns des autres, et sur lesquels il n'i a qu'une brasse ¾ ou 2 brasses d'eau, c'est pourquoi lorsqu'on entre par cette pass et que le soleil est dans la partie du sud, on court risque de tomber sur quelques uns des ces pâtés, attendu que la reverbération du soleil empêche de les appercevoir. C'est ce qui a été cause que j'ai mouillé entr'eux sur un très mauvais fond, où je craignois à chaque instant que mon cable n'eut été coupé. J'i passai une nuit et mon cable y fut très endommagé. En entrant par cette passe et tenant le mi-canal, je trouvai de 4 B ½ à 5 B fond de roches et corail, je l'aisondé depuis et trouvé le même proffondeur; cette barre s'étend d'environ 3 encablures, en venant dans la baye, et c'est là où se trouvent les pâtés de corail dont j'ai parlé ci-dessus. Entre le premier et le second islot, il y a bonne proffondeur, mais le chenal étant étroit, il est peu practicable à cause des vents de SE et au dedans il est bordé ainsi que l'autre de pâtés de corail. La passe la plus sûre pour l'entrée et la sortie, c'est entre le second et le troisieme islot qui est vers l'ouest, au milieu du canal il y a de 7 a 7 ½ brasses et assez pres du 3eme islot ainsi que de la bature ou récif il y a 6 brasses; d'ailleurs soit en entrant, soit en sortant par cette passe on trouve tres peu de pâtés dangereux, à l'exception de quelques uns, j'ai trouvé sur les autres 7, 8 et 9 brasses, ils sont d'ailleurs en petit nombre, ainsi avec la

précaution d'avoir toujours la sonde en main, et du monde en vigie, on peut louvoyer dans cette passe avec toutes sortes de vaisseaux. Lorsqu'en entrant par la passe de l'est on a passé la ligne ponctué E l'on trouve encore en allant dans l'enfoncement de la baie quelques pâtés de corail, mais en petite quantité, et comme ils sont tous visibles on peut les éviter, à moins que la reverbération du soleil sur la mer n'empêche de les découvrir.

14 In 1756, two men purchased a vessel in Bombay to examine the islands between the Maldives and Madagascar, but the Bombay government refused to allow them to sail. See Dalrymple, A. *A collection of Plans of Ports in the East Indies*, London 1787, pp. 57-8.

15 Scott, *Limuria*, p. 74.

16 *Account of Captain Neale's passage from Bencoolen towards the Seychelles Islands etc.*, BL. Shelfmark 147.F.19 (4). Since both the Three Brothers and the Seven Brothers were reported to lie at positions which put them firmly in the Seychelles, it is not surprising that he did not encounter them in the Chagos.

17 Capt. Neale neither named nor claimed this atoll, which Dalrymple felt should be called Griffin Islands, after the British vessel which had probably spotted them in 1760 (see page 24), but might more logically have been named after *Le Favori* (see pages 25–26).

18 Spray, W., British Surveys in the Chagos Archipelago, *The Mariner's Mirror* Vol. 56, No. 1 (January 1970), especially pp. 62-63. However, Spray's doctoral thesis, on which this article was based, made no mention of a visit by Neale to Diego Garcia. In subsequent correspondence with NW-S in 2005 Professor Spray accepted that the assertion in his (ground-breaking) article might have been mistaken. The thesis is titled *Surveying and Charting the Indian Ocean: the British Contribution 1750-1838* (Doctoral thesis, London University, 1966).

19 Dalrymple, *Memoir* (introductory 'Advertisement').

20 Blair's report was published as part of Dalrymple's *Memoir of a chart of the Indian Ocean exhibiting the coast, Islands, Rocks and Shoals from Madagascar to India ...*, London, 1788.

21 Filliozat-Restif, *op cit.*

22 *Ibid.*

23 Rivière, whose sojourn on Salomon was described in Chapter 2, did indeed report shooting *lamertins* (as dugongs are called in French), but his tentative identification cannot have been correct: dugong skins could not possibly have been used to make sails! We must therefore conclude that that the animals which gave Sea Cow Island its name were seals, as must be the case for the islets in Salomon and Peros Banhos also called *Ile Vache Marine*. Dr Anthony Cheke, co-author of an important work on Mascarene ecology, *Lost Land of the Dodo* (2008), has confirmed to us that the term *vache marine* was used in Mauritius to describe seals, before these animals became extinct there towards the end of the 18th century.

24 Forsberg, S., *History of Diego Garcia* 2005, Master's thesis, on deposit at Sam Houston State University, Huntsville, Texas.

4

Early Settlements: 1776–1789

DESPITE being in possession of the nearby Mascarene islands for many years, and making occasional use of Diego Garcia for a supply of turtles and coconuts, it was not until the 1770s that the French governors of the islands formally claimed and settled any part of the Chagos archipelago. Governor Souillac asserted that the *Vert Galant* had been sent to Diego Garcia by Chevalier Desroches to claim the island for the French in 1770 and that in 1778 Dupuis de la Faye, commander of the *Europe*, raised the French flag in the 'northern bay' of Diego Garcia as per the orders of the French governor M. le Chevalier de la Brillanne.[1] This did not prevent at least two British East Indiamen visiting the Chagos in the following year – the *Luconia* and the *Resolution*. In 1781, claimed the Vicomte de Souillac, de la Faye was succeeded by M. Pastor who was given the task of maintaining the flagstaff, and raising the French colours whenever circumstances required. Pastor also made an arrangement with the Government of the Isle of France to supply the Mascarenes with the produce of Diego Garcia.

The corsair of Chagos

Deschiens de Kérulvay, as we have seen (p. 34), had made several visits to the Chagos archipelago in the 1770s both for purposes of exploration and cartography and to exploit the produce of the atolls for the benefit of his sailors and the French settlers on the Isle of France. In 1776, he records that he set up an establishment there to capture turtles and to harvest coconuts, of which he delivered a large quantity to the Isle of France. After hostilities were declared between Britain and France in 1778, during the American Revolutionary War, Deschiens captained a corsair ship, *la Bouffonne*, later renamed *Philippine* and financed by the Pitot brothers. In December 1779, with a cargo of slaves on board, he reportedly stopped at Diego Garcia to 'refresh' them. Among the slaves sent ashore, four men and a woman ran away. What became of them is unknown. The instructions for Kérulvay's next voyage, dated 17 April 1780, were to commence with a visit to the Chagos islands, to take on board a supply of turtles. The corsair returned to France at the end of the war, and settled in Saint Brieuc where he married, and raised a family. In 1786 he addressed a memoir to the French naval minister requesting a 20 year concession of Diego Garcia and the use of two ships in order to set up a slave trading depot. He proposed to collect slaves from Africa and to bring them to Chagos where they could be 'refreshed' and 'acclimatised' before being taken to the Caribbean. However, he was too late – Diego Garcia had already been claimed by a French settler on the Isle of France. The minister wrote to Kerulvay, refusing his request on 16 June 1786.[2]

Le Normand's Southern Bay establishment

In 1783, Pastor and the French governor accepted the proposition of Sieur Le Normand to take over the establishment and the job of maintaining the flag staff on Diego Garcia. Le Normand accordingly settled in the southern bay. The map opposite, only recently discovered in the French Colonial Archives at Aix-en Provence, is of uncertain date and authorship, but appears to correspond closely to the state of knowledge in 1793.[3] The products of Diego Garcia which he intended to exploit are described as follows: coconuts and wood, including tatamaka, '*bois blanc*', described as good for building boats, and wood for burning. The island was found to abound in fish, turtles, seabirds and wild hens, but was without a good source of water, which could only be obtained by digging down into the sand which produced a brackish but not unhealthy drink.[4]

In a letter detailing his grievances, addressed to the Colonial Assembly of the Isle of France some years later, Le Normand provides further information concerning his concessionary arrangement. Anxious to establish his status as the first lessee, Le Normand denied claims of a pre-existing French establishment on Diego Garcia. He wrote that at the time he had demanded his concession, the island was uninhabited and virtually unknown. Le Normand claimed that the agreement made on his behalf on 24 February 1783 had alone forced the British to discontinue their visits. Le Normand stressed that the then Governor, Souillac, was pleased with his request for the concession and authorised him to make the necessary expenses, informing him that if no-one else claimed the island he could have the concession (*jouissance*).[5]

Following his arrangement with Souillac, Le Normand went to Diego Garcia with materials and slaves but departed early in 1784 leaving a set of instructions for his manager François and the workers. The document, subsequently trans-

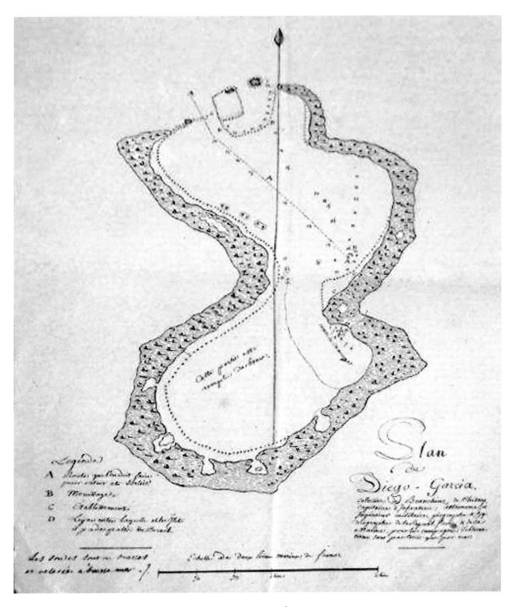

lated into English, but dated 1 May 1784 reads:

The property of the island of Diego Garcia having been granted to me ... I establish the herein named François to represent me during my absence and to work along with the negroes whom I have committed to his care at the several occupations respecting the trade of the partnership I have entered into with M. Lambert for the terrestrial and marine produce of the island. François de Moulereau shall assist him and shall be employed by the said François at whatever he may desire and shall represent him in case of death or sickness in every respect according to the following instructions.

Le Normand's instructions were that his black workers 'should seek receipts for employment on, and goods supplied to ships which touch at Diego Garcia'. The rate of labour for slaves so hired out to visiting vessels was set at 3 *livres* a day. The cost of providing a supply of coconuts and turtles for a ship was set at 80 *livres*. If a supply of coconuts was wanted as a cargo, he set the rate at 12 *livres* per 100 nuts.

He provided for the establishment of a fishing settlement near the entrance of the harbour, where a shed was to be constructed to secure utensils and provisions, and a scaffold measuring 2½ ft x 3 ft was to be erected to dry the daily catch of fish in the sun. When it was deemed too hot to fish the workers were to be employed collecting the feathers of sea birds, and on days of bad weather, their employment would be to pack the dry feathers into barrels. The workers were to be employed at fishing for two months, after which time they were to switch to gathering coconuts – 120,000 were to be collected and brought to the sea shore. When this number had been gathered and assembled, they were to continue fishing until Le Normand's ship returned. They could also be employed in catching turtles on the sea shore but 'they must only take those which come back from the northward'. Turtle shells gathered were to be packed in parcels.[6]

Le Normand's establishment, as described in 1786, consisted of a warehouse, huts for the manager and slaves, plus enclosures for pigs, chickens and turtles. On the opposite side of Diego Garcia a building to house lepers had been constructed, where six slaves – five men and a woman – were lodged.[7] The decision to house lepers on the island had been made some years earlier, based on the then current belief that the consumption of turtle and coconuts were effective antidotes to the disease; experience had shown this to be true, according to Le Normand. He described the cases of several slaves afflicted with leprosy who were 'cured' after a stay on Diego Garcia.[8] Souillac's careful documentation of the establishments on Diego Garcia was made in response to a serious challenge to French claims of ownership – from the British.

The British occupation of Diego Garcia, 1786

In the 1770s the Bombay Government was looking for a base for British shipping in a strategic location in the Indian Ocean, and in particular a suitable place from which to keep an eye on the French.[9] In 1771 the *Drake* and *Eagle* were sent out with two surveyors of the Bombay Marine, during which voyage they reportedly sighted the Egmont islands. The next year, the *Terrible* and *Eagle* went out, but their surveying voyages, for a variety of reasons discussed by Dalrymple and others, were curtailed before Diego Garcia was encountered. In 1774, the *Drake*, under Captain Sheriff, was sent to find and report upon Diego Garcia and to land sheep, goats and hogs on the island.[10]

A full decade then passed before, on 8 July 1785, the East India Company directors in London ordered the President in Council of Bombay to send 'with all possible dispatch' two small vessels 'to take possession of and settle the island Chagos or Diego Garcia lying 1,500 nautical miles to the south'. The plan was met with enthusiasm. Relying on the discretion of the local authorities as to who should be chosen to go on the expedition, it was directed that a survey of the harbour and island should be made, including the mapping of the 'numerous banks'. An account of the produce of the island was also asked for, together with the 'best means of settling it to make it a place of refreshment for ships.'[11]

On receipt of this document, the authorities in Bombay set about organising the expedition. On 16 January 1786 it was proposed that Mr Richard Thomas Benjamin Price should be sent in charge of the occupying party. Captain John Conrad Sartorius was selected to be engineer surveyor and commanding officer of the detachment, and Lieutenant Archibald Blair of the Marine was nominated as Assistant Surveyor. Mr Joseph James was selected to be the surgeon of the expedition, with a 'native Assistant and 2 dressers'. A subaltern from the Engineers would assist Capt. Sartorius and a Lieutenant of Artillery and a Lieutenant of a Sepoy corps would go in command of the respective detachments. It was recommended that the men sent on detachment should be chosen from among those who had been skilled artisans (carpenter, mason or smith) before entering the army. The Governor's plan was to despatch two vessels, the *Drake* and the *Viper*, with a country vessel, freighted as a store ship – to be sent out later, under the charge of Blair.[12]

A letter was accordingly drafted for Brigadier General Wilson, commander in chief of the forces, apprising him that Sartorius, Blair and an Ensign were to be employed 'on a secret service'. A detachment of artillery, and another of sepoys, along with ancillary staff such as washermen and labourers were also to be mobilised. Wilson was advised that those Europeans to be picked should be artificers and sober, steady men of sound constitution, 'for if they are diseased they will be burthensome, and if turbulent they will be the pest and plague of an infant settlement'. The sepoys should be volunteers 'and of such castes as will be the least troublesome and may be made the most useful at a new establishment'. In order to drum up volunteers it was proposed that arrears of pay and a 3 month advance of wages would be given out prior to their departure. Supplies of arrack and tobacco were to be laid on, spare clothing, one brass field piece and six pieces of iron ordnance and some carpenter, smith and entrenching tools, were also to be shipped.

In February 1786 it was reported that no lascars were willing to volunteer, and even the proposed leader of the expedition, Price, requested that he might relinquish his appointment in order to manage his private affairs in Bombay. This was rejected. Instead, on 7 March 1786, Price received a sixty paragraph letter outlining his instructions. He was given authority to 'preserve discipline, good order and harmony in the settlement', and an allowance of Rs 500 p.m. for table expenses. Sartorius was to command the troops, pioneers and artificers, Lieutenant Frederick the artillery, and Lieutenant Disney the sepoys. A ten month stock of provisions was to be loaded on the store ship, alongside those sent with the cruisers. On arriving at Diego Garcia, it was instructed that tents should be pitched at a commodious landing spot and a flagstaff set up. The British flag was to be hoisted, and possession taken in the name of King George III.[13]

A 'green conquest' plan

The first task of the occupation force was to survey the harbour and to look for a fresh water supply. If the harbour was considered unsafe and no water was found, the settlement was to be given up. Price was instructed to keep a diary of proceedings from the day of his arrival, and to send back anyone who became violent, or committed any felony. The surgeon was to keep a register of the sick and to mark any instances of disease arising from 'the air, water or vegetable productions'. This was evidently to be a 'green' conquest as both Price and James, the surgeon, were told to 'devote every spare hour to the search after and investigation of the several plants and samples' that could be found on the island. Price was particularly warned against committing what was considered a common error in this kind of enterprise – deforestation, 'under the pretence of clearing ground, without thought to cut down every tree that comes in the way, many of which would have been of the utmost consequence to the health and pleasantness of the settlement'. Instead, he was asked to send an account of all the different trees on the island, and indeed to seek to increase their number, 'as you are furnished with a variety of seeds as well for the field as the garden'. He was asked to pay special attention to 'the rearing of vegetables' and to send back regular reports.

During the earlier 1774 visit by the British to Diego Garcia a number of sheep, goats and hogs had been left on the island, and Price was asked to check whether these animals had multiplied, 'as there does not appear to have been on the island, any wild beasts to destroy them'. The expedition was to be supplied with cattle of various kinds and it was hoped that they could be maintained on the island to provide the settlers with fresh meat. It was expected that poultry could 'be raised with ease' on Diego Garcia. Information on the 'wild fowl' that frequented the island was also asked for, together with a 'list of common fish and whether they can be cured for the use of shipping'. The accounts of previous visitors had indicated that there were 'large turtle on the western side of the island'.

The East India Company made a point of noting that 'this important resource must be preserved', providing instructions to minimise disruption to the turtle population. Since they were likely to

> desert inhabited places on being much disturbed, we desire you will not admit of one single turtle to be turned or caught beyond what will be from time to time immediately wanted for your people, nor allow their common haunts to be unnecessarily molested.

Price was to carry grain with him, and was asked to 'mark out spots of ground to try experiments and to record which grains grow best'. A diurnal was to be kept of winds, weather and changes of temperature because it would be useful for instructions to shipping. Sartorius, for his part, was requested 'to form a judgement as to how [Diego Garcia] can be most easily made tenable against an attack'. However no fortifications were to be undertaken until a resolution had been made to maintain the settlement. Instead, temporary defence works could be constructed where wood and sand were plentiful, with the assistance of fascines and sandbags. Sartorius was to inform the Company as to the possibility of procuring building materials, including stone bricks and mortar.

Once these primary objects had been achieved, a survey of Diego Garcia was to be conducted – 'its coasts sounded, its form and dimensions ascertained and measured'. One of the expedition ships was also to be used 'to sound all parts of the coast without' to determine the dangers around Diego Garcia 'and the adjacent little islands of Red, Black and White Beaches'. The tides and currents, and other nautical observations were to be made by Blair 'to whom we have given the command of the new boat the *Experiment*'. No copies of surveys made were to be given away to anyone without permission.

Any 'straggling French'

In addition to the above, Price was issued with a set of 'Secret Instructions'. This informed the expedition leaders that should, against expectations, the French be in possession of Diego Garcia, they were merely to take on refreshments and return home. The secret instructions alleged that the British had a justified claim on the island, in view of the fact that they had 'discovered' Diego Garcia in 1712, and had since visited the island 'oftener than any other nation'. Consequently, Price was expressly told:

> You will not therefore deem any straggling French who may be accidentally there without authority as any settlement of that nation, or any post or pillar, or such like trifling marks of possession left there with an evil design to debar other nations (profiting from its situation) to be any impediment in the way of your establishing yourselves, and obeying our orders, which you will carry into

immediate effect. Being once settled … you will repel all hostile attempts, and to the utmost of your power defend the possessions of your Honourable Employers, yielding but to a superior force you find yourself unable to resist.[14]

Price was warned to treat any foreign vessels that might touch at Diego Garcia 'with civility and attention, and render them any assistance they may stand in need of … without permitting them to come into the harbour'.

Letters were also sent on the same date to Capt. Sartorius, ordering him to embark on board the *Drake* for a secret service mission, and to Captain William Robinson, advising him to 'proceed with the *Viper* cruiser, *Admiral Hughes* storeship and *Experiment* cutter to Anjengo where secret instructions await'.[15] These Robinson duly found awaiting him on his arrival there, informing him of his final destination – Diego Garcia – and offering him sailing directions according to the best knowledge of the time, especially with regard to the location of dangerous 'coral rocky banks'. On arrival he was to locate the same spot as that occupied in 1774 and to employ the *Experiment* and the boat 'to explore the bay or harbour, and finding good soundings, and a safe berth, move the vessels into it as soon as possible'. Similar sailing orders were given to Lt. Blair, and to the commanders of the *Admiral Hughes* storeship and the *Viper* snow. Blair was also asked to ascertain the 'true longitude' of the Chagos islands, for which purpose 'time pieces' were to be sent out from England.

The force left Bombay on 15 March 1786, and was expected to reach Diego Garcia by mid-April. The Governor General of India at Fort William (Calcutta), and the President of Fort St George (Madras) were apprised of the expedition at this time.[16] On the 22 March, Price wrote to the Bombay Government from Anjengo, informing them that rats on board the ship had already 'made great havoc among the rice and dholl [pigeon peas]', that one gunner – Edward Parks – found to have 'a stubborn venereal', was to be left behind, and that they would leave the next day to continue the voyage.[17]

Arrival, and an encounter with 'Caffrees'

On 27 April 1786 the British expedition arrived at Diego, and anchored in the lower bay on the east coast. A canoe approached them with five 'caffrees' on board who showed them three papers.[18] The first, dated 13 April 1776, stated that a Mr Normand and a Mr Lambert had set up an establishment on Diego Garcia, providing a list of persons associated with their business and utensils left on the island.[19] The second, dated 1 May 1784, detailed their concession of Diego Garcia with instructions for a fishery, and another list of persons associated with the enterprise. A third paper was simply a receipt for oil, and related to the arrival twelve days earlier of a M. Saintpi, who had left the Isle of France for the Seychelles, but, forced off his course, had stopped at Diego Garcia 'from stress of weather and leaky', and been supplied by the caffrees.[20]

After assessing the matter, Price decided that as the men then on Diego Garcia had not arrived before 1784, and because the concession paper was dated ten years after Capt. Sheriff had taken possession of the island for the British, the expedition should continue as planned. Le Normand, they were informed, had left in 1784 and had not returned. Price was helped to his conclusion that the French had no permanent settlement on Diego by the evidence of a ship hand of Captain Smith's who had earlier visited the island while aboard the *Concord* – taken by a French privateer – and who had at that time seen turtle there but no houses or people. Price concluded that the French resorted to the island for supplies of coconut oil and turtle, having noted that there was another turtle pen on the westerly side.[21]

One of the men on Diego, who identified himself as Jolicoeur, aka François, offered to pilot the British fleet to where he and the rest of the men were settled on a point of land on the inner bay, and where he stated that plentiful water was available. By 2 p.m. the fleet was anchored opposite what Price called the 'French village' and which he described as

> a dozen huts of the meanest appearance covered from top to bottom with dried branches of the cocoa[nut] tree ... a fine breed of hogs and fowls was perceived; the soil perfectly sandy and only so much of the ground cleared away as was sufficient for the erection of their huts ... on all sides were the cocoa[nut] tree, some of very extraordinary size ... and all below an impenetrable underwood. A passage had been cut thro' there, direct across to the sea shore, the breadth of the land appeared to be about 6 or 700 yards.

Diego Garcia was, at first glance, 'very low and woody'. A short excursion was made, the men returning by means of a passage made for a turtle cart. It was noted that the hogs and poultry 'feed on coconut and fresh herbs they pick up'.

Settling in

The difficulty of clearing a sufficiently large place for the tents of the expedition led Price to propose to Capt. Sartorius to take the boat next morning, on the 29 April, to a less woody spot at the upper end of the bay. They returned at 10 a.m. pronouncing it clear of impediments – Saintpi having resided there in March and early April – that a cart and road to the opposite shore for bringing turtle had been made and that a well of good water was located there. The cattle and some of the force were sent over, one Surat cow, however, breaking a leg in the transfer.

On Sunday 30 April, Sartorius and Robinson went to the western side of the upper bay but found it too narrow – only 150 yards – and 'jungly'. They then explored southward of the anchorage, where only young trees and underwood were found, and consequently began clearing the ground at that spot. On 1 May, the area was named 'Flagstaff Point' and arrangements were made for the formal ceremony, to be held on the 4th, which would mark the British possession of the island. On Tuesday and Wednesday some tents, tools, furniture and baggage were landed, but unsettled weather and heavy rain impeded progress. Marquee tents were handed out to the senior officers of the expedition, while smaller tents known as *rowtees* were distributed for various uses, including the storage of provisions, but these were soon soaked through. The pegs that came with them were too short to hold in the light sandy soil, so the carpenters were forced to make longer ones. As a result the tents were not finally pitched until the evening of the 9 May. The European artillery, lascars and sepoys meantime 'hutted themselves tolerably well'.

On Thursday 4 May at 10 a.m. the troops paraded near the flagstaff and the 'gentlemen' gathered at their commander's tent. The British colours were then hoisted and saluted by vessels and troops. Price's commission was read and saluted by 15 guns. An 'Instrument of Possession' – with company seal, was signed by Price and all the officers of the expedition. Over the next few days the bad weather continued, and the slaves on Diego Garcia, or 'French caffrees' as the British called them, explained that 'the surface of the ground was frequently covered with water from heavy rains [and] that the place swarmed with rats, worms and dangerous insects'. It was decided that a good foundation would be needed to protect the stores, and that the immediate priority would be to erect sheds for the cattle and stock, securing the straw and hay, 'no good grass being produced yet on the island', rather than to begin the survey of the harbour. Saturday 6 May was accordingly occupied in making passages through the woods, erecting houses for the cattle and their feed, and setting up cooking places. On Tuesday 9 May the weather improved and the provisions were brought on shore. The dholl, however, was found unfit to eat, the tank having overflowed onto the bags. An Englishman who had deserted from Saintpi's ship to remain on Diego Garcia was accused of having ill treated 'M. Normand's caffrees' and of having 'exposed the haunts of the turtle without permission' and it was decided that if he re-offended he would be kept a prisoner on board the *Drake* till the *Admiral Hughes* sailed back to Bombay with despatches, etc. Capt. Smith too was told 'not to turn so many turtle'.

On 11 and 12 May, the ground was cleared for planting, but very soon the first doubts began to be expressed about the viability of cultivating the soil and sustaining the settlement of Diego Garcia. The trees and plants were landed on the 13th and put into prepared ground, 'but we are under much doubt … there is depth of soil to bring them to any perfection, as the whole soil is a very light sand'. Various kinds of seeds were sown which 'have come up with surprising quickness, though 4 or 5 days after, the leaves have all become yellow'. The 'caffrees' reported 'that all they sow comes up a few inches and then dies' and that their sheep and goats had died in six weeks. Price wrote, 'should all our attempts to raise any kind of vegetable prove ineffectual we must be in a very distressed situation'. Meanwhile the sawyers had been occupied many days in sawing coconut trees for the storehouses, and the carpenters in making uprights, beams, etc. Price, however, complained that there were too few, and 'not one of them master of his business'. If the settlement was to be maintained, more and better workmen would have to be sent. Disagreements were also growing between the various groups of the expedition. Price complained again that the *Admiral Hughes* 'people' had 'turned many turtle' while cutting ballast for their ship, and also accused them of using up all the water in the well on the plain, which was now found to be dry.

On the positive side, many types of fish were found, 'tho few of any taste'. The best were 'cavallee', 'skait' and 'nair' fish. The skait was said to bury itself in the sand and strike with its tail – evidently an unpleasant discovery by Lt. Disney, who was stung on 16 May, and laid up for several days with a swollen foot. The habits and size of the local turtle population were also described:

> The turtle is to be caught in almost every part of the island … tho from 4 to 500 lbs weight it is nourishing and far from cloying … no care or attention shall be wanting on our part to prevent the disturbance of these animals, that seem to come upon the beach very near the year round, every 3 or 4 days – such numbers might be caught as to provision a few ships, were the island clearer and the communication more free, whereas at present we have but two places that roads are made to the outside.

Attempts to cultivate the soil, described as 'very poor, light and dry' continued. It was noted that the cattle refused to eat the local grass but that the hogs and fowls were thriving. The water supply seemed to be plentiful: 'wherever we have dug, water has flowed in with great briskness, apparently sweet and wholesome', but the ground, when watered, drained quickly, leaving the soil as dry as before. The French caffrees informed them that the wet season ran from December to April. Of the many types of vegetables planted, only potatoes and yams looked likely to succeed. Observing the coconut trees, Price was able to describe how they were propagated from the nuts but noted that they had 'no solidity or property for building'. His men had found no fruit trees on the island, 'or any eatable'. He speculated, however, that coconuts could be a good antiscorbutic vegetable for visiting ships.

On the 30 May, the *Atlas*, a snow under the command of Captain Wilson, coming from Bencoolen, was wrecked off Diego Garcia.[22] Help was given to recover the cargo. The supra cargo, a Mr Holst, reported that the lascars on board had committed 'all kinds of violence on the chests, bureaux etc in search, he imagined, of the treasure … that they likewise made free with the casks of liquor on board, and then left the vessel'. It was decided that the crew from the *Atlas* would leave on board the *Admiral Hughes* which was now ready to return to India, and which left on Sunday 4 June. This ship took back to Bombay the first letters of Price, and various documents, including the 'Instrument of Possession' and a number of reports by the various members of the expedition, including a meteorological journal and a harbour survey by Lt. Blair. Capt. Sartorius' report concluded that the best bay for shipping was 'along the inside shore of the Western point of the harbour' where Company ships could be brought to anchor in less than two hours. Three small islands at the mouth of the harbour could be equipped to defend it, and there was access to good water, coconuts, and fish. On the negative side, the water which appeared when the soil was dug would act as an obstacle to raising a foundation for any considerable building or fortification, while no tree fit for building had been found, nor any earth to make bricks or tiles and no stone fit for purpose. Sartorius suggested that if the island were to be kept – instead of erecting fortifications, the maintenance of a couple of ships of war at Diego Garcia would serve the purpose better.[23]

Disappointment and discord

As this information made its way back to Bombay, work continued in June with the building of a magazine, and the sowing of seeds at West Point, where the soil seemed better than at Flagstaff Point. Timber, planks and cordage was collected from the wreck of the *Atlas*. Early in July, however, it was found that the seedlings at West Point had also yellowed. Sheep, goats, poultry and pigeons died, while swarms of rats demolished any vegetables which managed to survive. The tents were rotting, and the store was full of rats 'which our utmost vigilance cannot prevent till we can build stone walls and better roofs'. Price criticised the magazine being built by Sartorius as 'too strong a structure and taking too long', and on the 22 July, Sartorius laid down plans to build a storehouse, a barrack for European artillery and a battery.

Not surprisingly, the workforce was beginning to lose heart. Absenteeism and thefts of poultry were deplored, and early in August, Price decided that 39 lashes from a cat-of-nine-tails was insufficient – the first court martial was declared on a persistent offender. Evidently, the caffrees were not faring much better. On 8 August the *Petit Cousin*, the vessel of Le Normand and Lambert, had arrived from Mauritius and anchored 'in a very dangerous place within West Island and West Point.' An officer went on board to explain that the British had taken possession of the island. That evening it was reported that Le Normand wished to take off his people and utensils, the attempt to develop the island commercially not being worth the expense and trouble of continuing. Le Normand had not been able to get the island to yield anything other than a bare subsistence for his slaves – 'they had had no rice, maize, biscuit or any of the commonest food produced in other countries for nearly 2 years before we arrived', stated Price. They lived on turtle meat, fish and coconut water. Price concluded, 'if such a people, whom we found infinitely more laborious than those we brought here, could effect nothing how much less may we expect to see it answer'.[24] The *Petit Cousin* wished to take on a load of coconuts and permission was given, on condition that they 'should take away the lepers on the western side of the island'. This proposal was resisted by Le Normand on the ground that it would be dangerous for the people of Mauritius; he also claimed that the French Governor was planning to make Peros Banhos the eventual destination for all lepers.

On Wednesday 9 August it was noted that the European placed in charge of the settlement by Le Normand had left for Mauritius to represent 'the barren state of the island and the distress of the people – having eaten all their rice, maize and bread'. On the 19th surgeon James cautioned against over consumption of turtle which he believed produced excess of red blood, leading to distended veins. He attempted to cure this by bloodletting. By the end of the month, the British felt able to offer further conclusions about the products of Diego Garcia. The only plants that thrived were represented to be coconuts and a species of wild mango. Potatoes and yams could be grown but were eaten by rats. The only wood fit for public use was *bois de palissade* and that only for 'trifling buildings'. Lime made from the coral was described as very fine and unless mixed with a coarser kind 'will not serve for water works or bear a plaister'. The hogs and fowls had survived, but did not produce many young, while most of the turkeys and ducks had died, those remaining being 'droopy and sickly'.[25]

Downsizing and departure

Back in Bombay, towards the end of July 1786, the Diego Garcia despatches were perused. The President in Council concluded that the island was only fit as a 'station for surveying and exploring the numerous islands and shoals about' and that French descriptions as to the extent of the island had proved deceptive. Evidently any settlement would be dependent on external supplies which would be expensive. The distance of Chagos from India was also a negative factor: 'placed where it is, its distant situation, the want of tides, the badness of the bottom and lowness of the land will render it of less value as a rendezvous for shipping, and more so still as they could here meet with no supplies beyond water, fish, turtle and coconuts'. Pending a final decision from the Court of Directors in London, to whom a report was made, a reduction of the establishment was proposed, which was unanimously agreed upon. It was decided to bring away Price, Sartorius, the European artillery and their field pieces and to leave the settlement in the charge of Capt. Smith, whose salary would be raised to Rs 1,200 a month, assisted by Mr Broughton, Lt. Disney in command of the Detachment and Ensign Emmitt in charge of surveying. Provisions for a further six months would be prepared and embarked on the *Scorpion* and the grab *Bombay*, the latter to return with Price and the rest.[26]

These decisions were communicated to Price on 31 July. Commendation was offered to Lt. Blair for his survey, performed 'with so much apparent accuracy in so short a period'. The Bombay Government's view of Le Normand's concession was dismissive. The papers, it was stated,

> appear to be framed for a private purpose and deserve neither credit nor notice for it is reasonable to suppose if any publick grant or authority had been given by the French Government to even a private adventurer, he would not have failed to have left an authentic copy of such grant to be occasionally produced by his settlers to any others who might thereafter arrive on the island and interfere with his views.

The government at Calcutta was less sanguine about the French threat. The Governor General of Fort William informed the Bombay Government, on 22 August, that in his opinion, 'no establishment can be formed upon the island for the advantage of the Company and that from its vicinity to Mauritius it will always be in the power of the French, in the event of war, to possess themselves of it'. The Calcutta authorities advised 'abandoning the island without delay'. In response, the Bombay Governor addressed the Governor General on 5 October, explaining the measures already taken to reduce the Diego Garcia establishment and confirming 'we shall take the necessary steps to withdraw our people from and evacuate Diego Garcia as soon as possible'.[27]

Before departing, Price had news of one botanical discovery from Diego Garcia. On 24 September he informed the Bombay government as follows:

> A stone cutter belonging to this settlement having been regularly bred a dyer, sometime since made a discovery of a shrub that grows in great abundance on this island and whose root gives a fine crimson purple and yellow colour to white cloths, and is the same that the Madras petticoats, chintz etc are stained with, but which he is of opinion is naturally much stronger and more flourishing than what grows in India, that the colours produced from it carry the appearance of more brightness and durability … but was not able to complete the experiments to his satisfaction owing to the water here not being proper for the purpose.

In November 1786, final arrangements were made to evacuate the island.[28] The settlement had been a failure but the survey of the islands, it has been said, 'redeemed the whole enterprise'.[29] However, this saga was not completely at an end. Wrangling over ownership of the island would continue with the French Governor of Mauritius until the outbreak of the Revolutionary wars would once again see the Chagos archipelago being used for the deadly cat-and-mouse games of privateers and naval cruisers.

The French reaction

Meanwhile on the Isle of France the Governor, Souillac, had learnt of the English intrusion from the return of the *Deux Cousins* [presumably the same ship as that named *Petit Cousin* in the Bombay Records]. He sent the corvette *Minerve* to Diego Garcia to regain possession, but on its arrival the English had already abandoned the island. The French captain therefore simply placed an engraved stone prepared for the purpose in a prominent position, which recorded that the island had been taken possession of in the name of France.[30]

Souillac penned a series of outraged despatches to France and a missive to the British Governor of Bombay between 19 and 31 October 1786 describing the attack on the French establishments there. He revealed that Sieur Figeac, a business associate of Le Normand, had been so intimidated that he had simply taken off his slaves without demanding the restitution of the animals and other property of himself and Le Normand. The captain of the *Deux Cousins* had been equally restrained – requesting only to take on a cargo of coconuts and turtles for the purposes of the voyage. He had, however, refused to take on board the leprous 'blacks'. The Governor also forwarded information gleaned from the *Madras Courier* which reported the shipwreck of the '*Atlas*' on Diego Garcia, where the crew were fortuitously aided by the arrival of the British force sent to occupy the island, adding 'Diego Gratia promises to become a place of great importance, its harbour when explored will be both safe and commodious – it will afford a shelter to our fleets during the monsoon, and the Turette fish and hogs the best of refreshments to give people – and as the hogs thrive well on the island should a proper method of preserving them be suggested, ships may be victualled with their flesh, which from the nature of the food the animals will feed upon, must be extremely delicate, and much more wholesome than that obtained in any other port of the country, or perhaps even in any Port of Europe. The cocoa nut tree will produce an article of commerce, and by no means an insignificant one; its oil is held in great esteem, and the materials it furnishes for making cables, ropes & c, are in great demand all over India'.[31]

Souillac was obliged to admit that at the time of the arrival of the English, no French were on the island, the only time since 1778 – he claimed – that this had been the case. Nevertheless there were present on Diego Garcia slaves belonging to the French with their commander. The Vicomte then decided to address a protest to the English Governor of Bombay, who had ordered the expedition, but no ship being available, a M. Dayot, having a commercial vessel about to depart for Malabar, was asked to forward a despatch addressed to M. d'Entrecasteaux (head of a French settlement in India).

Souillac reported that the British had with them around 450 persons, including sepoys, lascars and black and white workers, six 8-pounder cannons and four field pieces. The English fleet had unloaded wood to construct homes and warehouses and were beginning to build them when the *Deux Cousins* had left on 2 October. The English, he concluded, seemed to be planning to make Diego Garcia an entrepôt for their shipping. Attaching a plan of the island to his despatch, Souillac underscored the point that Diego Garcia was situated at a central point from which fleets could reach Ceylon or the Coromandel Coast of India or equally the Isle of France, and contended that its port was of great importance.

The British response was characteristic. Henry Dundas, the Viscount Melville, was in the midst of negotiations with the French over their rights in India and offered his passing views on the Diego Garcia question in April 1787 in a letter to Sir William Eden, Lord Auckland. After expressing an opinion that the French had no right in Diego Garcia, although the island was probably useless to the British, Dundas wrote 'When they [the French] talk any swaggering language upon that or any other subject, you are perfectly aware of the necessity of talking to them in a similar style, and I am more and more convinced every day that we shall soon feel ourselves in a situation in India that will cause all nations to think well before they disturb us'.[32]

Certainly the British had other options for their Indian Ocean bases. In September 1786 Captain James Scott had protested against the choice of Diego Garcia for a naval settlement, enumerating the superior advantages of Penang, and arguing:

> It is difficult to form an idea of the motives which has led to this measure.
>
> The island is situated in from 7 to 8 degrees of south latitude has the SE trade from April to October and the NW monsoon from October to April, it is a sand bank formed on an island of coral covered with coconuts and very little raised above the level of the sea – like all islands of this kind it has a lagoon in the middle with a dangerous and narrow opening, of difficult access at all times and no soundings without where ships may anchor to wait a favourable occasion. Its produce is confined to coconuts, and a precarious supply of turtle and fish.
>
> Such an island so situated can never be an object of commerce.
>
> As a port of retreat for refitting and refreshing our ships of war to me it seems equally unfit.
>
> 1st, because should our fleet have occasion to leave the coast any time from June to October they cannot return from Diego Garcia in less than 3 months allowing for the detention of repairs – even when they retire in October their

passage would be much retarded by calms, and they would reach their port about the setting in of the NW monsoon which in this parallel of latitude brings much such dirty weather as the NE monsoon brings on the coast of Coromandel.

2nd, the risque of running down in thick squally weather on a sand bank with no surrounding soundings is great. Yet it is necessary as getting to leeward would still be worse and when the fleet has made the island in unsettled squally weather the entrance of the lagoon is almost impracticable; even then in they must have chains to their cables as the ground is foul.

3rd. But let us suppose these difficulties overcome, the island made, the narrow passed and the fleet moored in safety in the bay by the 15th November; and that with extraordinary exertions they were enabled to sail again before the 25th December, the N and NE winds would so lengthen their passage that even good going ships could not reach Madras before the 20th January where they would arrive in want of everything and perhaps sickly.

If proposed as a port of rendezvous for our Europe fleets its contiguity to the French islands would occasion such an expence to render it secure as would over balance the attendant convenience …'[33]

In May 1787 Souillac received a verbal reply from the Governor of Bombay. This was relayed to him in a letter sent from M. de Saulnier, a naval lieutenant and commander of the corvette *Ecureuil*, which had gone to India to take the Governor's protest against the English intrusion on Diego Garcia. Saulnier reported that after some difficulty he had obtained from the Governor a verbal response, which as Souillac explained to the Minister in France, amounted to a qualified abandonment of Diego Garcia. While claiming that the British had been first to discover the island – in 1712 – the East India Company representative at Bombay now admitted that he was abandoning any claim to Diego Garcia and asserted that the British had all left.[34]

At the close of March 1787, news of the British occupation of Diego Garcia had, according to the British representative in Paris, 'occasioned some alarm here'.[35] The French Ambassador in London, the Count d'Adhemar, was instructed by the French court to make a formal remonstrance, denouncing the actions of Boddam, the Bombay governor who had seized the French establishment there in the absence of the concession holders. Lord Carmarthen replied smoothly that the intention had only been to take possession should no other power have already acquired that right, and that some time since, the Governor General had ordered the abandonment of the island.[36] In reality, of course, the British would continue to make use of the Chagos islands as it suited them, and more particularly, when hostilities were renewed with the French, as would shortly be the case.

Elias Hasket Derby Jr. and the mansion he built with the profits of Indian Ocean trade. *Source*: Peabody, R.E., Merchant Venturers of Old Salem, Riverside Press, Boston, 1912.

A storm off Diego and an American visitor

On 6 October 1788 an American ship arrived at the main harbour of the Isle of France. Its captain was a member of one of the most remarkable and wealthy familes of his day and he had an interesting story to tell.

The captain was Elias Hasket Derby Junior and his ship the *Sultana* had left the Isle of France on 14 April for a voyage to Bourbon. From there the ship had gone to Diego Garcia. Their stopover is probably the first recorded visit of Americans to the Chagos archipelago. After leaving Diego Garcia on 20 November 1788 Derby reported that his ship was caught in a hurricane which lasted six days. He also volunteered the information that a French corvette, which had left Diego Garcia at the same time as the *Sultana* and which he assumed had been sent for the 'perquisition of the brick of Sieur Dauget', was caught in the same storm and was probably lost.[37]

While the exact motive for Derby's stop over at Diego Garcia is unknown, the reason for an American ship being in the area is clear. In fact the Indian Ocean trade was key to the fortune of the first American millionaires (billionaires in today's money), the Derbys of Salem, Massachusetts. Elias Hasket Derby Senior founded his own Salem shipyards and his vessel the *Grand Turk* had, in 1784, been the first American ship to reach the Cape of Good Hope – gateway from the Atlantic to the Indian Ocean. In 1785 the *Grand Turk* became the first

American ship to be allowed to trade at the Isle of France. Derby trained his eldest son for the burgeoning Indian Ocean business by having him study English and French methods of trade *in situ*. He then sent him to India for three years where he built up trade interests for his father's firm.

In 1788 the proceeds of one cargo alone enabled Derby Jr. to buy a ship and a brigantine in the Isle of France which he sent to Bombay to load with cotton. Two other ships of his fleet, the *Astrea* and *Light Horse*, were loaded at Calcutta and Rangoon and ordered back to Salem. It was found, when the profits of these transactions were reckoned, that the little squadron had earned $100,000, the kind of sum an ordinary merchant family might spend a lifetime accruing. The Derby family made this fortune from one voyage alone.

Captain Moorsom's visit to Diego, 1789

On 21 August 1789, Captain Robert Moorsom and the *Ariel* arrived at Diego Garcia. He had been sent to follow up on Blair's survey work and to answer a specific set of questions. He reported that on his arrival he found a French brig at anchor in the upper part of the bay, loading coconuts and turtle for the Isle of France; 'they had been there seventeen days and sailed a few days after my arrival having some black slaves upon the island'.[38] He then proceeded to answer the questions he had been directed to investigate. To the question 'Whether in the harbour ships can lie sufficiently sheltered, notwithstanding the lowness of the coast from all winds', he replied:

> In some parts of the harbour ships may lie sheltered from all winds and that part which appears to me most convenient for anchorage near the sea they may lie safe except from winds at NNW to NEE, which winds I am informed seldom blow there with any violence – I do not think the lowness of the coast is any disadvantage to ships at anchor in any part of this harbour; during my stay there, though often blowing fresh gales, I never observed such gusts of wind as are experienced, when laying under high lands.

The second question suggests that the British were still contemplating a military role for Diego Garcia, as Moorsom was asked 'Whether at a small expence and a small force it might by log forts be rendered safe, or at least defensible against an enemy's squadron'. To this he responded:

> The first expence of building a fort at Diego Garcia will not be much if the timber of the island is made use of; there is plenty of it and the trees are large, some I measured from 15 to 20 feet round and very high. The timber is soft and juicy but it is used for the French turtle park and lasts from three to four years though there are many worms.

Moorsom considered that 'With a small force the West Island may be defended against one much superior' but added 'it will require … strong batteries at west entrance, middle and west island and also batteries on East Point and East Island'.

The next point of interest to the British was 'Whether water can be procured and of good quality'. Moorsom stated:

> Water may be procured in almost any part of the island – by making a well a few yards from the beach … I filled water for the ship from the wells at Flagstaff Point. That which was used by the people I had on shore was dug about twenty yards from the beach … the water was very good and at high water in plenty, but it dried on the ebb from not being deep enough.

To the question whether adequate refreshments could be procured there, he noted: 'water, fish, turtle and coconuts of these there is plenty. I had tents erected on shore and the men sent there were much refreshed by the food they received there'. Asked about 'the natural produce of the island' Moorsom commented that:

> The natural produce of the islands seems to be confined to three kinds of trees of high growth the coco nut tree and two others whose names I am not acquainted with, two of lesser growth and some weeds … of all these there is plenty so much as to render a passage through the woods impracticable without the labour of making a road by cutting down trees and clearing away the underwood – the vermin must prevent the growth of plants or shrubs if the soil produced them; rats and caterpillars are very numerous.

Evidently the British were contemplating whether Diego Garcia, from its geographical position, could function as a useful point from which intelligence might be sent from one settlement to another, and in particular from one side of the Indian peninsula to the other. Moorsom's opinion on this was a qualified one:

> Diego Garcia is advantageously situated with respect to India a place for intelligence when the commander of a squadron from Europe might be uncertain on which coast his force might be most necessary. The variation of the monsoon at the same time, on different sides of the equator, enables him from there to shape his course for either side of India and without loss of time for the coast of Coromandel or Bengal – during the SW monsoon there would be a loss of time if it was necessary to go to Bombay, the direct passage is to be preferred; but there would be none during the NE monsoon – it would also be a proper place for reinforcements from Europe for a squadron in India to proceed to for intelligence on which side the squadron was acting; and consequently a proper place for a small or any quantity of naval stores to be lodged at … The situation of Diego Garcia, I should think can only be made useful in this Respect, when there are

obstacles to interrupt the quicker modes of intelligence between the governments in India – it seems to be better situated as a centre of intelligence between the governments on the different sides of the peninsula and the settlements on Sumatra and eastern islands should any be made there.

The renewed interest in Diego Garcia was an indication that the British were seriously contemplating the possibility of a war with France. Come it did and, when it came, the Chagos islands would witness its destructive powers at first hand.

Notes to Chapter 4

1 Royal Society of Mauritius Archives [RSM], Papiers Doyen [PD] 22/36 Despatch of Vicomte de Souillac, 31 October 1786. The original quote reports that he 'fit un établissement dans la Baie du Nord et y éleva par les ordres de M le Chevalier de la Brillanne, Gouverneur Général, un mât de pavillon'.

2 Hébert, J.C. 'Les Français sur la Côte Ouest de Madagascar au Temps de Ravahiny [1780–1812]' *Omaly Si Anio*, 1983–4 p. 235, ANOM C/4/146 Mémoire de M Deschiens Kerulvay, undated.

3 The undated map, held by the Archives Nationales Outre Mer, Aix, is contained in a file of documents marked 'Diego Garcia, 1787–1809' and shows the location of two French '*établissements*' marked as 'C' on the map, along with a recommended route 'A' by which ships could reach the two anchorages 'B' located close by. The line of coral obstacles near the entrance is marked D. Comments in the bottom right-hand corner read: '*Plan de Diego Garcia [Collection de Branchinz de Chisny, capitaine d'infanterie, astronome et ingénieur militaire, géographe et hydrographe de la République Française et de sa Marine]*'.

4 MA TB 3/2.

5 MA TB 3/1. Souillac informed Le Normand that the matter had to be referred to France before a formal concession could be granted. This seems to have been rectified by 1791 when a written document established Le Normand as a supplier for coconuts, although he had no monopoly over turtles.

6 Maharashtra State Archives [MSA] Diary No. 34, Enclosure – Translation of Instructions left at Diego Garcia by Mr Le Normand for the French Negroes residing there, 1 May 1784.

7 RSM PD 22/36 Despatch of Vicomte de Souillac, 31 October 1786.

8 ANOM C/4/73 Le Normand to Souillac, 30 Oct 1786.

9 It is suggested that a further reason for British interest in Chagos at this time was concern over the recent French annexation of Seychelles – see Easton, G. & Boodhoo, R., 'Déjà en 1786 les Anglais convoitaient Diego Garcia' *La Gazette des Iles* 1986 p. 330.

10 Spray, *op. cit.*, p. 61. Spray's account, relied upon by later writers, is inaccurate in stating that Captain Neale in the *Swift* visited Diego Garcia in 1772 and admired its harbour. Neale's own record (published in William Herbert's *New Directory for the East Indies*, London, 1774) makes no mention of the island at all. There is thus no basis for Spray's assertion that it was Neale's report which led to Capt. Sheriff's being instructed to go there two years later. Interestingly Spray's doctoral thesis (London University, 1966), on which his article in the *Mariner's Mirror* is based, makes no mention of Neale's voyage.

11 MSA Secret & Political Diary No. 33A, East India Company to President in Council of Bombay, 8 July 1785. The interest of the East India Company in Diego Garcia had been aroused by a visit there in 1774 by the *Drake* ketch (it was common practice to identify vessels by both name and type – for the latter please see nautical glossary, p. 523).

12 Boddam, R H et al, *Bombay Castle to Court of Directors 18 March 1786*, pp. 99–100. Further details of the correspondence between the Bombay Government and the Directors of the East India Company can be found in Philips, C.H. & Misra B.B. Fort William-India House *Correspondence, vol XV Foreign*

and Secret 1782–1786, National Archives of India [NAI], Delhi, 1963.

13 MSA Secret & Political Diary No. 33A, Board's decision, 27 Feb 1786; Bombay Council to Price, 7 March 1786.

14 *Ibid.*, Secret Instructions to R.T.B. Price and John Richmond Smyth, 7 March 1786.

15 Anjengo is the name of a former Portuguese settlement between Quilon (Kollam) and Trivandrum in Kerala, India.

16 MSA Secret & Political Diary No. 33A, Bombay Government to Governor General and Council, Fort William, 18 March 1786, ditto to President and Council, Fort St George, 31 March 1786.

17 *Ibid.*, R. Price & R. Smyth, Anjengo to the Bombay Government, 22 March 1786.

18 'Caffree' or 'kaffir' was a term used to signify an African native, or a person who appeared to be such.

19 The *commandeur* François, nicknamed Jolicoeur, was a Malagasy. Four of his team – Hyacinthe, Jaso, Thomas and Domigne – were Mozambican, while three others – Casimir, Etienne and Henri – were Créoles de l'Ile de France. Another Malagasy – Sephir – belonged to Lambert. There were also two Mozambican women – Luni and Susanna – the latter having a daughter, Rose.

20 MSA Secret & Political Diary No. 34, Price & Smyth, Diego Garcia to Bombay Government, 3 June 1786.

21 MSA Reports of Factories and Residencies, Diego Garcia Diary No. 288, entry of Saturday 29 April.

22 Bencoolen is the colonial name for present day Bengkulu, Java, Sumatra. The wreck of the *Atlas* is also discussed in Fry, H.T. 'Early British Interest in the Chagos Archipelago and the Maldive Islands' *Mariners Mirror* Vol 53, No. 4, 1967, pp 343–356.

23 MSA Secret & Political Diary No. 34, Report of Sartorius, 3 June 1786.

24 *Ibid.*, letter of R. Price, Diego Garcia, 20 August 1786.

25 MSA Reports of Factories and Residencies, Diego Garcia Diary No. 288, entries of 2 and 9 August.

26 MSA Secret & Political Diary No. 34, President's Minute, 25 July 1786; Bombay Castle 26 July 1786; Bombay Government to Court of Directors, 31 July 1786.

27 *Ibid.*, Bombay Government to R. T. B. Price, 31 July; Bombay Governor to Governor General, 5 October 1786.

28 *Ibid.*, Bombay Government to John Richmond Smyth, 27 November 1786.

29 Fry, H.T. *op.cit.*, p. 347.

30 MA TB 3/2.

31 ANOM C/4/73 Letters of Souillac 19–30 October 1786, including transcription of Madras Courier; RSM PD 22/36 Despatch of Vicomte de Souillac, 31 October 1786.

32 Dundas to Eden, March 1787 quoted in Furber, H. *Henry Dundas, First Viscount Melville, 1742–1811,* OUP London 1931, p 67. For further details of ongoing disputes between Souillac and the British authorities in India and the Cathcart negotiations see Bolton, G.C. & Kennedy, B.E. 'William Eden and the Treaty of Mauritius, 1786–7' *The Historical Journal*, XV1, 4 (973), pp. 681–696.

33 India Office Records [IOR] G/34/2 Bengal Public (Separate) Proceedings, Letter of Captain James Scott, 25 Sept 1786.

34 RSM PD 22/36 Despatch of Souillac dated 2 May 1787.

35 IOR I/1/13 Duke of Dorset to the Marquis of Carmarthen, Paris, 29 March 1787. The Duke wrote, 'accounts have lately been received from the Isles of France and Bourbon which mention that two English ships, having on board 400 men had sailed from Bombay and taken possession of the island Diego Garcia … This intelligence, the particulars of which are variously represented seems to have occasioned some alarm here'.

36 *Ibid.*, Letter of Comte d'Adhemar, London 5 April 1787; Carmarthen to Comte d'Adhemar, from Whitehall, 17 April 1787.

37 MA OB 28 'Declaration d'arrivée du vaisseau ameriquain La Saltanna Capne Derby 6 oct 1788'.

38 TNA ADM 1/167 Letters from Commanders-in-Chief, East Indies, 1788–1794, Cornwallis to Philip Stephens, 11 Nov 1789, enclosures of Moorsom.

PART TWO

Exploitation

Battle on 7 October 1800 between the French corsair *Confiance* and the larger
East India Company ship *Kent*. *Source*: Wikimedia Commons.

5

Buffeted by Revolution, War and Aftershocks: 1793–1819

THE advantages and difficulties of establishing a viable settlement on Chagos were clear to both the French and the British. In the 1790s a summary of recent experiments provided a clear exposé of the disadvantages and benefits of Diego Garcia:

> occupied two years and an half by the French and English and evacuated by them successively, as affording no subsistence and as being flat, and exposed to attack. No timber could be found, nor lime manufactured. The island was capable of producing many kinds of culinary plants but no grain. Overrun by rats. No live stock throve there. The climate remarkably salubrious. The access to it difficult owing to the currents.[1]

Both nations had made claims over Diego Garcia and established temporary settlements there, but much of what was happening was non-formalised and opportunistic.

Sanatorium or commercial settlement?

In the late 18th century, M. Le Normand believed that he was the sole holder of a concession on Diego Garcia, but that did not stop the Isle of France government from permitting another colonist, M. Dauguet, to set up a fishing establishment there. Baron D'Unienville would later claim that neither man had a written contract from the government. Furthermore, he pointed out, the French administration had another destiny for Diego in mind – that of a lazaret or sanatorium for lepers.[2]

In December 1790 two inhabitants of the Isle of France requested special permission for one of their relatives, a 19-year-old man, who had reportedly been afflicted by leprosy following a trip to China, to be allowed to go to Diego Garcia for the benefit of his health. The young man, M. Liénard, had spent four months in hospital on the Isle of France, where Dr Laborde had recommended his discharge on the grounds that his treatment there had failed. His uncles, Messrs Suzor and Le Merle, hoped that the air and produce of Diego Garcia would help him recover his health, and requested that their nephew be ordered to the island to continue his treatment.[3]

Around the same time, and probably with an eye on preventing further British encroachment, the government at the Isle of France backed new schemes by its colonists to exploit the many coconut trees growing in the atolls. In 1793, Governor Malartic reportedly concluded an arrangement with M. Lapotaire whereby he would set up a coconut oil producing establishment at Diego Garcia. Scott asserts that the Lapotaire concession was a consequence of Governor Malartic's concerns about the rising price of oil, and his support for the establishment of an oil factory on Diego Garcia itself. Lapotaire consequently sent out two ships and soon had enough oil ready to supply both the government and local merchants.[4] Baron d'Unienville remarks that it was the South Indians, known as 'Malabars', settled on Mauritius who gave the French colonists the idea of making use of coconuts to manufacture oil.[5] Ships leaving for Diego Garcia to pick up oil were exempted from embargo measures.[6] However, the vulnerability of isolated settlements like those on Chagos was soon to be dramatically demonstrated with the outbreak of the Revolutionary Wars.

The 1793 British attacks on Diego

In late October 1793 the small settlement on Diego Garcia received a distinguished if unwelcome visitor. Rear-Admiral William Cornwallis, brother of the Governor of India, stopped there with two British vessels, the *Minerva* and *Bien Aimé*, on his way to Bombay, 'thinking it not unlikely that the French privateers might make that island a place of rendez-vous' as he later explained. The British narrowly missed a French corvette which had left the day before, he lamented, adding, 'I found only a brig loading with turtle, which I took away and having collected and embarked all the people that could be found upon the Island, I sailed from thence the 9th of November.'[7]

Fortunately William Richardson, a young Englishman pressed into service aboard the *Minerva*, has left a detailed account of the attack on Diego Garcia. He was in India when news arrived in June 1793 of war being declared between Great Britain and France; and mentions that 'the *Bien Aimé* a French Indiaman, with some other vessels of that nation lying here, were taken possession of, and their crews sent as prisoners to Fort William'. Shortly afterwards, losing most of his possessions in a shipwreck, Richardson had the additional misfortune of being pressed into naval service and sent on board HM frigate *Minerva*, commanded by Captain John Whitby. He describes the *Minerva* as 'a fine large frigate, with a poop lately erected on her for the convenience of the admiral and captain, and mounting 48 guns'. Richardson was stationed to 'do any duty in the maintop' and bemoans his predicament as follows:

> all my clothes were on my back, and with an old silver watch and one rupee, which constituted my all … a poor prospect I had before me. I had no bed, neither did I care for any, for my bones had got so hardened since I came to sea that I could sleep as comfortable on a chest lid or on the deck as on the best bed in the ship; and having only one shirt, I went without when I had to wash and dry it.

The *Bien Aimé* was brought into government service and officered from the *Minerva*, while the crews were completed by 'pressing out of the East Indiamen as they arrived from Europe, and a great many able seamen we got out of them'. Richardson was outfitted by the kindly first lieutenant Mr Robinson, who 'sent for me to his cabin; and then, taking a sheet from off his bed, gave it to me and told me to get some clothes made from it … I got a light jacket and two pairs of trousers made from the sheet, and was very thankful for his kindness to me, a stranger'. Later, Richardson was taught by his messmates to cut out and make a jacket, shirt and trousers from dungaree cloth handed out to the ship's company, 'by which means I soon got a good rig-out and a new straw hat, which I made by their instructions; as for shoes and stockings, they were not worn by sailors in this hot country'. It sounds very much as if the barefoot sailors in their simple clothes and straw hats might not have been dressed much better than the slaves on Diego Garcia whom they would soon encounter!

Expecting to meet with 'a French frigate and brig' that intelligence suggested were lying at Diego Garcia, the *Bien Aimé* and *Minerva* headed there, and en route 150 of the ships' crew were selected to be trained to the use of small arms. Richardson was one of the number:

> Nothing could be more diverting than to see the blunders we made at the first beginning: we were arranged in two lines along the quarterdeck, with the captain and fugleman in our front, and the booms full of people laughing and grinning at us; some put their muskets on the wrong shoulder, some let the butt fall on their next neighbour's toes, some could not stand with their backs straight up, and were threatened in having a cross-bar lashed to it, and some had their shoulders chalked by the captain that they might know the right from the left, which only bothered them the more; in short, there was nothing but blunders for a week or two, and then we began to mend.

This exercise was performed twice a day, and to the sound of drum and fife the men were marched round the quarterdeck gangway and forecastle, and rewarded in the evening with 'an extra pint of grog each'. Richardson notes, 'We improved so in the course of a few weeks that it was said we fired a better volley than the marines.' The men were thus prepared for a hostile reception at Diego Garcia. On arriving, the British ships hoisted French colours, and, 'though the wind was against us, worked the ship into the harbour and there came to anchor'. The French frigate had gone, but a brig was seen lying at the upper end of the harbour, and the ships sent out boats 'manned and armed to take possession of her, which they soon did, as the crew and few inhabitants, who are turtle catchers, fled into the woods for safety'. Richardson next describes the island and the encounter with some runaway lascars there, ending with a description of the use to which the turtles found were put:

> This is a noted place for catching turtle, and we found a pen with two hundred in it. The island is low and very woody, and the harbour a good-sized one; and, as we were in want of fresh water, we digged holes deep enough for each cask bung deep, and, putting them down in the evening, we found them full in the morning; but it was rather brackish, and only served for cooking. Our people caught several wild pigs here, which were good eating. In the course of their rambles several lascars who were hidden in the woods, hearing our people speak English, came and delivered themselves up to them: they said they had been wrecked here in an English ship belonging to Bombay several months ago, and, being afraid to deliver themselves up to the French for fear they would have sent them to the Mauritius and sold them for slaves, they had hid themselves in the woods and lived on coconuts and what else they could find there; so we took them all on board, and, when we arrived at Bombay, discharged them, to their great satisfaction. Having nothing more to do to draw our attention here, we loaded the brig with turtles, and got near fifty on board the *Minerva* and the *Bien Aimé*, being as many as we could conveniently stow on the main deck between the guns; then, setting fire to the poor Frenchmen's huts which happened to be on Guy Fawkes day, November 5th 1793, we got under way, and stood out to sea … and each day lived like aldermen on turtle soup; every evening for near six weeks, a turtle was hung up the skids by its two hind fins and the head cut off to let it bleed, and although each one was large enough to serve a day for our crew of three hundred men, scarcely half a pint of blood came from it. Next morning it was cut up and put into coppers, and when boiled, served out to all hands with two or three bucketsful of eggs into the bargain.[8]

Dauguet's report of destruction wreaked by the British on Diego Garcia in 1793 lies in the Reunion archives.[9] However, it seems that Cornwallis' squadron was the second group of British attackers to decimate his establishment, for the report mentions that the crew of a wrecked British ship had previously taken control of the Diego settlements. Indeed it was to re-establish control that the French frigate had been sent to Chagos. This frigate was reported to have left only the day before

Cornwallis arrived, and this would perhaps explain why the lascars had gone into hiding on Diego.[10] The Comité de Sûreté Publique in Paris offers an alternative perspective on these events in its denunciation of the royalist French admiral St Felix, accusing him of secretly favouring the English in his failure to defend French interests properly. The Comité claimed that on learning of a British ship wrecked at Diego Garcia, St Felix, after prevaricating for a fortnight, sent an unarmed corvette, the *Minerve*, rather than a frigate, and that this delay had given the shipwrecked mariners enough time to construct a boat, which the report described as a '*chaloupe pontée*' and in which they were reportedly able to carry off a considerable sum in gold and silver.[11] It would not be until 10 July 1794 that the Colonial Assembly on the Isle of France would record details of the hostile encounters, including the taking of the brig *Bonne Foi*, and its decision to compensate Dauguet for the total destruction of his establishment at Diego Garcia.[12]

Mauritian historian Raymond d'Unienville remarks that the fate of the civilian population transported to Bombay is unknown.[13] In such cases it was usual for the British navy to retain only those slaves who had maritime skills and to dispose of the others in British settlements around the Indian Ocean. Details of the exact size of the population on Diego Garcia at this time are scarce, but one source suggests that Le Normand's initial workforce sent out in 1784 numbered '79 Mozambican and Malagasy slaves as well as a few free coloureds who were skilled workers'.[14] Le Normand complained that his claims had not been dealt with correctly by the Isle of France authorities. In particular, he denounced M Maillard, the Intendant, who had refused to allow him to send his vessel to the island. As a result, he stated, his stack of firewood on the beach had been left to float out to sea while the government had refused to recompense him for the 'ruinous losses' he had suffered during the English occupation.

By the mid 1790s, the egalitarian principles and policies of the French revolution, as put into practice by the colonial assemblies of the Isles of France and Bourbon, were impacting upon the lives of traders and sea captains. The prohibition of the slave trade was progressively more closely enforced by the new legislators. In August 1796, owners of ships had to furnish financial guarantees that their vessels would not trade in slaves, and in 1797 the port authorities were given the right to search coasters for the same reason.[15] Around this time, a number of visits were made to Diego Garcia – the expedition of Lapotaire and a M. Bégué was recorded on 22 August 1796, and that of Messrs Desmarais and Le Corre in the *Elizabeth* in June 1797.[16] There is some speculation that these voyages were 'suspect' and that slave trading and the possible off-loading of slaves may have been involved.[17] It was certainly the case that the dependencies of Seychelles and the coral islands of Chagos were used by clandestine slavers in later years when the British measures abolishing the slave trade came into effect. One example was that of the *Chicken*, detailed on page 98–99.

HMS Victor *at Diego, 1801 and a naval battle*

It was unlikely that the French would have re-established themselves in any number on Diego Garcia at a time when the British navy was becoming accustomed to stop-overs at Chagos to take on turtle, water and other supplies, and no doubt was more than willing to avail itself of the 'fortune of war' to act even more forcefully in securing supplies than was usual. The myriad islands also gave the British an opportunity to flush out the odd French vessel, sheltering in a harbour, or itself taking on refreshments.

In August 1801 George Collier, captain of HM sloop *Victor*, put into Diego Garcia in order to refresh his sickly crew. After procuring what he described as 'a large supply of turtle and good water' he left his mooring at Diego on 27 August, and a few days later, approaching the Seychelles, he encountered the French national corvette *La Flèche*. In his report of the subsequent action, he wrote:

> I had the pleasure of bringing her to a close action at three quarters past five p.m. The disguised state of the *Victor* did not long deceive the enemy; the second broadside proved sufficient, the corvette hauling her wind and endeavouring to escape … the chace continued all night, frequently within gun-shot, and at sunset the following day, from the wind having favoured the enemy, she was four or five miles to windward; in the night of the 4th lost sight of the chace, when, probably by tacking, she escaped. In this affair I had one man wounded with two musket balls, and Mr. Middleton, master's mate, slightly; the damage sustained in the hull trifling, the foremast shot through, and I have to regret our sails and rigging much cut.

Collier pursued the French corvette towards the Seychelles and again attacked, 'in a few minutes her cable was cut, she cast round, and her bow grounded on a coral reef. Mr. McLean, the First Lieutenant, with a party of officers and men, were sent to board: though scarce had they put off, ere we discovered the enemy to be on fire'. *La Flèche*, commanded by Captain Bonamy, had left France four months earlier, with a complement of one hundred and forty-five men, some of whom had been left sick at Bourbon.[18]

A forced sojourner on Diego: the deportation of Thomas Privat

Despite the danger of British attack, the French continued to keep up a presence on Diego Garcia, and to send ships back and forth, as the naval and military reports in the Isle of France archives attest. It is recorded, for example, that a brick arrived from Diego on 21-22 Prairial, An 10 [30 May 1802].[19] However, the danger of spending time on such a vulnerable and isolated archipelago must have been apparent. Indeed as the strange case of Thomas Privat indicates, it seems evident that the prospect of being sent to Chagos could be conceived of as a stringent punishment.

Thomas Privat, a 30-year-old locksmith, came to the attention of the Colonial Assembly on the Isle of France in 1802, as a result of complaints made against him by the Municipality and by his own relatives. In the *procès-verbal* of the assembly it was reported that he cultivated a five *arpent* plot of land with the assistance of two slaves, but that the town council considered him a 'bad character', a drunken leper who bathed in the public canal of the district. He was also suspected of drinking with slaves. At this time, when the prospect of a slave uprising as in St Domingue was very real, fraternising with slaves was considered a serious offence, and a number of ordinary citizens suspected of *sans culotte* leanings were deported from the Mascarenes. Most went to other colonial settlements in the Indian Ocean – Batavia, Seychelles and India. The fact that Privat was a leper is therefore significant. The assembly noted that his own family had requested his expulsion. Speaking in his defence, Privat stated that he had only bathed in the canal once, and claimed that his relatives had requested his deportation merely because he had demanded his inheritance from them. He denied getting drunk with his slaves. The Assembly seemed inclined to accept that Privat might have had reason to be in dispute with his family but referred the matter to the municipality, who reiterated that due to his misbehaviour, and his disease, the wish of his relatives that he be sent to Diego should be respected. The assembly decided by majority vote to uphold his proposed deportation.[20] Perhaps Privat was among the six free men mentioned as being part of the leper community on Diego Garcia in 1809.[21]

The Chagos Archipelago in the Napoleonic era

After General Decaen, Napoleon's emissary, assumed control of the Mascarenes in 1803, further attempts were made to exploit Diego Garcia. No doubt the British blockade and its impact on the supply of goods into the Mascarenes was one factor, but a number of theories have been suggested for this belated and unlikely surge in activity in the far-flung atolls.[22] Evidently, at this time, there was some uncertainty in the British camp as to the status of Diego Garcia. The Commandant of the Seychelles, Jean Baptiste Queau de Quinssy, had secured for those islands a 'neutral status' which was to prove extremely useful to the French settled there during the period of the Napoleonic Wars. Not surprisingly, an attempt was then made to claim Diego Garcia as part of that group, in order to reap the same benefits. Jonathan Duncan, the Governor of Bombay, was sufficiently perplexed to consult Admiral Peter Rainier for his opinion on the question. Seeking evidence to prove that Diego Garcia was not considered part of the Seychelles, Rainier pointed to the report of the captain of HMS *Centurion* who, 'when he passed Diego Garcia at the latter part of the year 1797 in the ship he now commands, the French Republican Colours were then flying on this island'. The Admiral further expostulated, 'I know of no authority whereby the French have a right to claim the sovereignty of the island Diego Garcia not long after the Peace with France in 1783 it was held by a detachment from this presidency for the Hon'ble Company as your records will show'.[23]

In July 1808, Victor Duperrel[24] obtained a concession (*jouissance*) to exploit the Egmont atoll (Six Islands), while Lapotaire and a M. Cayeux were operating establishments on Diego Garcia itself. On 1st June 1809 Lapotaire addressed a long letter to Decaen, principally to reiterate the work carried out by himself and Cayeux on Diego Garcia and to complain about rival concessionaires Chessé and Blévec. In so doing he provided some intriguing details about the beginnings of the copra industry on Chagos. He explained that until 1791 the resources of Diego Garcia consisted principally in turtles and some coconuts, sold in their shells to the *'malabards'* – the Indian population of the Mascarenes. The difficulty of selling coconuts in large numbers had led Lapotaire, he claimed, to the idea of manufacturing oil on the spot, which he set up with another partner, following the method observed among the Indians for preparing copra. He transported 75 slaves to Diego Garcia, on two ships, as per authorisation of the then Governor, General Malartic. The establishment was set up at Pointe de l'Est, and this being adjacent to the property of Dauguet, eventually he joined forces with the owners of that establishment, including Cayeux and Chastan. He provided details of the oil mills and the slaves who worked them at each of the competing concessions. Governor Decaen, having granted an additional concession between East Point and North East Point, this was taken over by Chessé along with Lapotaire's former manager, Blévec. The latter subsequently petitioned Decaen for a larger concession, and for the right to manufacture oil on Diego itself, rather than transporting the copra which, they said, occasioned much loss. Having completed a slave trade at Bombetoka (in Madagascar) of whom 60 were retained at their establishment on Diego Garcia, they claimed that they would face financial ruin were their petition not acceded to.[25] On 2 May 1809 Decaen formally accorded three such concessions on Diego Garcia to Lapotaire, Cayeux and a M. Dédier, fixing the limits of their respective establishments (in order to prevent argument between them) and imposing on them the cost of maintaining the leper establishment there.[26] Among the more unusual products of the atolls that were then in vogue were sea cucumbers, exported to Batavia, and seabirds. The new concessionnaires (*propriétaires en jouissance*) were made responsible for running the leper establishments also – evidently the belief in the curative properties of Diego Garcia remained undiminished, since the leper colony now numbered six whites and six coloureds in addition to black slaves.[27] It is clear that with the proliferation of concessionaires the slave population of the islands increased, possibly to several hundred at its peak.[28] We shall discuss the terms of the *jouissances* and the numbers of those employed to work them in Chapter 6. Suffice it to remark here that the conditions set remained unchanged for many years after the islands fell under British jurisdiction. On the other hand, the population suffered wild variations as a result of the ongoing war.

In fact, the stepping-up of British blockade measures from 1808 onwards overlapped with the development of further projects for French establishments on Chagos, and while the two seem initially contradictory schemes, they were not unrelated. Food shortages were at times intense on the French islands, although the means of circumventing the blockading squadron were many and the captains of the small inter-island vessels were hugely resourceful. The French were of course taking a huge risk: in November 1808, for example, a lugger from the Isle of France was captured by the *Raisonable*, while returning from a visit to Diego Garcia. Lieutenant Walters reported that the lugger had 'people and materials on board her to colonise the island of Diego Garcia. Not being able to find it they were on their return to Port Louis'.[29] In late 1809 both the *Leopard* and the *Cornelia* reported making stop-overs at Diego Garcia. The log of the *Cornelia* is especially detailed, and records several visits ashore. One entry dated 24 November 1809 reads, 'Sent boats man'd & armed to examine the settlement where we found nothing but fish, a few slaves and a French man in charge of them, from whom we learnt that the brig which we chased on Sunday was the *Entreprenant* corvette.'

The following month, it was the turn of the French to register a naval success – the capture of HMS *Victor* in the Bay of Bengal. The explorer, Matthew Flinders, then a prisoner on the Isle of France, noted in his journal entry for Wednesday 3 January 1810 'Learned at noon, that the frigates *La Manche* and *La Bellone* had got into the port with a Portuguese frigate and our sloop of war the *Victor* (formerly *L'Iéna*)[30] and two of the three ships taken from the Company'. Frustratingly the blockading British squadron missed the chance to intercept the arrivals: 'In general our ships keep before

Matthew Flinders

the port, but at the time of the entry of the above two frigates and prizes, they were before the Black River, watching the *Venus*, and thus missed the finest occasion for rendering service', noted Flinders ruefully.[31] This event was to have momentous consequences for Diego Garcia. Admiral Drury ordered the *Sir Francis Drake* and the *Cornelia* back to the French Indian Ocean possessions to

Admiral Drury

search for the captured *Victor*. Accordingly, in February 1810 both ships were back at Diego Garcia. The *Cornelia* sent 'an officer and a party on shore to dig wells for watering' and another cutter with an officer 'to explore the upper part of the harbour.' David Patterson, senior lieutenant of the *Cornelia*, returned from shore with the information that the French Governor of the Mascarenes (Decaen) had established that settlement 'for the purpose of preparing coir and cocoa nut hemp for cordage, making cocoa nut oil and catching turtle and other fish for the use and service of the French squadron and of collecting stores for the French government and that vessels were sent periodically with the rations allowed them by the French government, and returned with the stores so prepared and collected'. Lt. Patterson was also informed that Diego Garcia 'was the resort of French cruizers as well as of American traders from India'.[32] Seeing a French ship rounding the Point, the *Drake* headed off in pursuit of her, while the *Cornelia* remained at anchor to complete the taking on of water. This was a job best performed at high water, which, on this occasion, required a petty officer and ten men to be left on shore to 'fill water all night'. The boats sent to examine the harbour returned the next day reporting that they had 'found five Frenchmen, a number of slaves, some turtle and dried fish'. On 17 February, fifteen turtle were received on board the *Cornelia*, and a day or two later the ships left.[33]

On their return to Madras, Adm. Drury was informed of the French establishment on Diego Garcia. Aware that the small dependencies like Chagos could be used to supply the Mascarene islands of Mauritius and Reunion, which were then being blockaded by British naval forces, he determined to destroy the settlement. Henry Edgell, commander of the *Cornelia*, was accordingly directed to proceed to Diego Garcia and given the following instructions by the Admiral:

> If you should discover any stores for the supply of the French islands in a state of close blockade you are to destroy them at the same time you are to be careful not to molest or injure the settlers the object being merely to prevent the islands under blockade from receiving supplies … As I am desirous other haunts of the enemies cruizers should be visited you are to … visit the Peros Banchos [*sic*] on Chagos Island and St Brandons Bay observing the same conduct.

In April 1810 the *Cornelia* and *Drake* returned once again to Diego Garcia, where the navy would remain for several weeks. Edgell's affidavit reports that while standing in for the anchorage at Diego Garcia, the British noticed a number of turtle floating out to sea, which they later found to have been 'sent adrift by the French men pursuant to an order from Gen. Decaen to prevent the English ships from obtaining supplies of that article. Going on shore, they determined that the establishment belonged to the French government, therefore it was 'broken up and destroyed' under the superintendance of Michael Matthews, senior lieutenant of the *Cornelia*.

The ships' logs however mention only that a party was sent on shore to 'dig wells' and boats were sent up the harbour to 'examine the French settlements' and to 'get turtle'. The captain of the *Cornelia* remarked 'Found the Frenchmen had hid several turtle, and a quantity of oil in the woods'. That day and the next a large number of slaves from the Diego Garcia concessions were embarked on board the British ships. The logs are almost casual in their description of these events. The *Cornelia* records, on 14 April 'Sent several of the slaves on board the *Drake* by their own request', and on the 15th, 'Several slaves volunteered and were taken on board the *Drake*'. The logs do not mention the information volunteered by Edgell much later, in 1827, when the prize status of the slaves in question was being settled. His affidavit asserts that in 1809 while in Ceylon with Adm. Drury and the island's Governor Sir Thomas Maitland, he was present at discussions which centred on 'the chance and probability of French Government slaves being found upon and attached to their establishments in their dependent islands'. Maitland, 'particularly and strongly urged their removal to Ceylon … for the purpose of their being received into His Majesty's Service and embodied in the African Regiments there'.

On 18 April, the *Cornelia* was off West Point East [*sic*] and recorded firing her guns at and boarding an Arab ship en route from Bengal to Muscat with rice.[34]

During May, the *Drake* continued her visits to the island, and on the 21st of that month, the log reports, 'wooding and watering parties on shore. Sent bark [boat] and wine on shore to the working parties. The turtle catchers returned with one turtle'. Meantime, the 'recruitment' of slaves continued. On 29 May the log recorded 'Received 11 slaves volunteered'. The next day's entry was rather more dramatic:

> 30th May. At 1 sent the boats on shore to bring the watering party & all the slaves off. At 2 squally. The yellow cutter swamped in coming off. At 2.30 made signal with a gun for all boats to assist her. At 3 the boats returned on board with the yellow cutter and found drowned Richard Hadden and 4 black men. Having received on board 103 black men 23 women 45 children … at 4.30 weighed and made sail … at 5.40 passed thro between Middle & West island.[35]

Surprisingly, the muster roll of the *Drake*, albeit including individual Malagasys and others embarked elsewhere, completely fails to record the sizeable contingent of Chagos slaves on board. Fortunately the 1827 Admiralty file gives a list of their names (see overleaf) and records that the slaves were disembarked at Ceylon, where, according to Maitland's wish, the men were incorporated into the 3rd Ceylon Regiment.

The affidavit of Lt. Matthews in the Admiralty file also provides an interesting insight into the role of Diego Garcia in the Napoleonic defence strategy in

List of Slaves removed from Diego Garcia in 1810 and taken to Ceylon

MEN

No.	Name	No.	Name	No.	Name
1	Chilevyn	36	Nandire	71	Molimant
2	Prosper	37	La Rame	72	Job
3	Arsilla	38	Savarang	73	Sas Mong
4	Lubyn	39	Compinio	74	Jirim
5	Charles	40	Masonga	75	Catandy
6	Elavi	41	Surmant	76	Jus
7	Dinear	42	Toomar	77	Zephir
8	Labram	43	Julien	78	Marca
9	Andrew	44	Figaro	79	Macaroni
10	Julicaire	45	Zemahall	80	Kedoheda
11	Artis	46	Francois	81	Nan Singolo
12	Epongeoa	47	Isantee	82	Siong Siongo
13	Emanuel	48	La Fleur	83	Caster
14	Jando	49	Nomparpara	84	Narson
15	Bien venu	50	Alexander	85	Singis
16	Over	51	Casper	86	Matomby
17	Francois[3]	52	Macadam	87	Mare Mema
18	Polit	53	Voltaire	88	Marni
19	Sans Souci	54	Emmanuel	89	Janquil
20	Preable	55	Establi	90	Scipion
21	Routina	56	Francois	91	Pistola
22	Sanson	57	Adonis	92	Se Rompa
23	Maher	58	Bourbon	93	Benoit Petit
24	Zenabo	59	Cesar	94	Tom
25	Blanfort	60	Armeda	95	Metame
26	Armandos	61	Armodeianda	96	Narcisse
27	Musamana	62	Balmire	97	Blanchi
28	Laventure	63	Capitos	98	Selapair
29	St Maria	64	Markir	99	Janti
30	Mistick	65	Jeannot	100	Sampir
31	Marcel	66	Bassar	101	Louis
32	Acasea	67	Massois	102	Maturyan
33	Benoit	68	La haur	103	Polisson
34	Sidon	69	Jarwar		
35	Carriat	70	Sesseong		

WOMEN

No.	Name
1	Mizia
2	Julia
3	Rosette
4	Rosella
5	Maria Anne [1]
6	Catherine [1]
7	Rosine
8	Parcelle
9	Maria Anne[2]
10	Clarissa
11	Mary
12	Nin
13	Catherine [2]
14	Harriet
15	Marina
16	Sophia
17	Louisa
18	Roselle
19	Mamise
20	Sacalla
21	Felicity
22	Lyark
23	Le Fukeva

8 children

Source: TNA HCA 32/1814

the Indian Ocean. While on shore Matthews mentioned that his party was

> visited by a Frenchman of the name of Le Loup who was able to converse tolerably well in the English language and who represented himself to be an officer acting under the French government of the Mauritius in charge of Post NW in the said island and further that there were two other posts designated Post SW and Post SE … Monsieur Le Loup appeared particularly desirous that his communication with them might not be made known to the Commandants of either of the other posts as, although he was the senior in the French Service, yet that a young Revolutionist Officer at Post SW was the General Superintendant of the island and was placed there as a spy over the rest by General DeCaen the Governor of the Mauritius.

This testimony is intriguing as it suggests that the settlements on Diego Garcia included French soldiers (at that time, soldiers were generally known by their nicknames, which doubtless explains the use of the name Le Loup – the wolf.) Tensions between monarchist and bonapartist settlers were rife in the Mascarenes, and appear, if Le Loup is to be believed, to have spread to Chagos also. Certainly the slaves on Diego Garcia had every reason to want to fraternise with the British. Le Loup remarked that the French ship which the British had chased was indeed their supply ship; its peremptory departure would be a 'very great and distressing inconvenience' as only a few more days' supplies remained on the island.

Matthews also provides further details of the momentous events that took place on Diego Garcia in mid-May 1810. He notes that the British remonstrated with the French officer regarding the turtle set adrift, and was informed that, having heard of the visit of English cruisers, Gen. Decaen had 'sent the most imperative command that on the appearance of any ship suspected of being English they were to do their utmost to prevent the possibility of their obtaining refreshments of any description and to withhold all communication with the said ships'. He added that

> the slaves upon the said island had been endeavored to be impressed with the strongest horror and aversion towards the English but notwithstanding the same and altho the most coercive and cruel measures had been resorted to prevent the said slaves from approaching the shore parties belonging to the British ships, yet notwithstanding the same the said slaves consisting of men women and children came down to the shore in collected numbers of from ten to twenty persons and waded so as to reach the said boats many of them bearing on their persons the marks of brutal treatment for having … merely attempted to look at or approach the said strange ships and boats.

The *Cornelia* and another ship, HMS *Diana* left Diego Garcia on 18 May after the slaves had been embarked on board the *Drake* and after all the stores that

HMS *Phaeton*. Image courtesy of NMM.

could be found either at the settlement or concealed in the woods had been destroyed. Some months later, while visiting Ceylon, Matthews noted that he 'saw several of the said slaves bearing arms and belonging to one of His Majesty's Regiments then doing duty at Point de Galle and ... was recognised by them as one of their deliverers from slavery'.

It may certainly have been the case that the Diego Garcia slaves would not have been reluctant to board the British ships, where the salted pork regularly served out to the seamen must have seemed a welcome change from their daily diet on shore, but their managers can hardly have been willing parties to these transactions. Their slaves were certainly not free to 'volunteer' aboard the naval vessels, nor is it clear that they were 'government slaves', as the affidavits of Edgell and others so confidently assert. Many must surely have belonged to the French concessionaires. A rather different version of these events, or of related incidents, occurs in French accounts, where it is stated that 'in May 1810 the English took Diego Garcia, destroyed the coconut oil station and took 147 workers as prisoners. The result was a shortage of oil in Ile de France'. At this time, according to Decaen, the coconut oil establishment was supplying all the wants of the French inhabitants on Mauritius and the price of oil consequently rose dramatically.[36]

A deserters' Paradise?

The British did not have everything their own way, insofar as Diego Garcia was concerned. For some of the soldiers and sailors on the naval vessels, the coral-fringed tropical atolls, with their seeming abundance of coconuts and fish, proved too much of a welcome contrast from the monotony and rigorous discipline of shipboard life to be resisted. On 21 May 1810, the *Drake*'s log, for example, had reported, 'Abraham Frith, one of the turtlers, saw William Wickham on the NE part of the island. On perceiving him, he made off to the jungle'.[37] Evidently Wickham was one of numerous crew men who regularly 'disappeared' when the ships stopped at Chagos. Scores of deserters, however, soon found that the archipelago was far from a welcoming environment and were quickly reduced to 'misery'. On 25 November 1810, thirteen men who were believed to have deserted from their ships when the *Hesper, Phaeton, Bucephalus* and *Russell* were at Diego Garcia, surely regretted it. It was reported that they 'lived chiefly upon coconuts and turtle' until they were secured and confined by the remaining 'Frenchmen and slaves' who resided on Diego – on the orders of Captain John Lloyd of HMS *Hesper*. Thomas O'Brien reported on the case in mid-1811:

> 13 unfortunate Europeans belonging to several of His British Majesty's ships who deserted on this island are laying in a most miserable situation these 3 months in a block, where they are confined as criminals, if you will take the trouble to come on the spot where they are detained, they are persuaded that their distressed situations will engage you to deliver them from their misery and carry them to Bombay where they will be able to meet with their own ships.
>
> They have conducted themselves in the most honest manner during the time they lived on the island, and the inhabitants of it can give you a testimony of their behaviour.
>
> To prove to you their sincerity of their wishing to return to their respective ships, they consent to be confined in the same manner on board of your cartel until your arrival in the port of your destination.

This proposal was accepted and they were landed in India on 5 July 1811, no doubt much chastened by their ordeal.[38]

As the foregoing accounts suggest, the movements of the sizeable force sent to conquer the French islands in late 1810 had occasioned an unaccustomed level of activity at the Chagos archipelago. Ships anchoring at Diego Garcia invariably reported one or more cases of desertion, but after a few weeks or months living on coconuts, turtle and fish, the runaways were usually happy to embark on the next visiting frigate – intriguing testimony to conditions both aboard and ashore.

A 'place of pain' – Diego Garcia in 1811

The British attacks on Diego Garcia led one French author, Roger Lepelley, to lament the position of the five white inhabitants in this '*lieu de douleur*,' noting that the crews of the enemy frigates had not simply destroyed their settlements and taken off their slaves, but had also killed the pig population of the island and had stolen even their own clothes. All that was left behind were the ailing Frenchmen and a few ill slaves – since only those in good health had been seized – left to eke out a subsistence which only their hunger could procure them.[39] Lepelley's book, which examines the fate of a trio of French ships sent – too late – to the Indian Ocean by Napoleon to protect his settlements, offers interesting details of the stop-over of the *Clorinde* at Chagos, taken from the log book of its commander, Jacques Saint-Cricq. The division had left Brest in February 1811, and arrived off Mauritius in May to discover the island already in British hands. Hence, unable to take on supplies there, the *Clorinde* decided to make for Diego Garcia. Here, it was planned to take on board turtles and some boat-loads of coconuts, to help stem the daily increasing cases of scurvy on board. Accordingly on 26 June 1811, the *Clorinde* arrived off the atoll, finding an anchorage between the second and third islet. The captain did not expect to find the island inhabited and was surprised when his boat brought on board two white men, creoles of Mauritius. The log states that the men claimed to be entrepreneurs, while their black slaves reported that they were in fact lepers. Saint-Cricq was surprised by the men's claims that French establishments had existed on Diego Garcia for some 40 years, writing in the log that the mariners had been unaware of this fact. He added that 'the unhappy beings exiled to this parcel of earth live very miserably; all they have for subsistence are coconuts, some chickens and turtles, it being impossible to glean anything from the sandy earth – all attempts at cultivation having been fruitless'.[40] The French sailors were at least able to obtain some water on digging in the sand, and two days later, after taking this on board, along with an ample supply of coconuts, they decided to weigh anchor, having failed to find turtles. They arranged however to purchase thirteen already caught and placed in the island's enclosure, which were paid for with the curtains of the captain's cabin and some cheese!

With this region of the Indian Ocean now safely in British hands, the Royal Navy were able to survey the atolls at leisure. In 1811, Lieutenant Owen, then in command of the *Barracouta*, spent some time examining the lagoon of Diego Garcia:

> I entered it by the western channel, and left it by the eastern, which, contrary to Mr Horsburgh's notice, I found quite clear and safe, with not less than three and a half fathoms in it. It is the place of banishment for lepers from the Mauritius and Isle Bourbon, where they make cocoa-nut oil, and catch turtle for exportation; and it is as famous in this way in these seas as Ascension in the Atlantic. Its lagoon forms one of the finest harbours in the world; but it is believed that

there are many others of a similar description, and equally good, in the other atollons.

Lt. (later Captain) Owen's biographer, E.H. Burrows, asserts that he discovered a coral bank nearby which is still charted as Owen Bank. R.M. Martin, Owen's crew mate aboard the *Barracouta* also mentioned the atoll in a later reference work, noting 'Diego Garcia is one of those numerous coral islands with which these seas abound. It contains plenty of turtle and has a few residents from the Mauritius'.[41]

During the course of the long 19th century, many more individuals, whether brought to Chagos involuntarily, as lepers, or, like the hapless mariners choosing to desert their ships, would find that these palm-fringed atolls, so beguiling at first sight, were not an easy place in which to thrive.

Pax Britannica

Britain's seizure of Mauritius was not ratified until signature of the Treaty of Paris in 1814. Only then was sovereignty over the island's many dependencies confirmed, but with Seychelles alone singled out for explicit mention. As far as the Chagos islands were concerned, the number and position of the individual islands had, as we have seen, been accepted by the authorities in the Isle of France. Nevertheless, it took the new British authorities in Port Louis more than a decade to examine their new domains, let alone establish real control over them; while in London there remained uncertainty about what these actually comprised. However, for the British government, it was immediately apparent that they had acquired a vast new area in which they could seek to stamp out the slave trade. This preoccupation was indeed to dominate policy towards Mauritius for the first 25 years of possession; it also conflicted with the decision to allow the French settlers to keep both their possessions and their local legislation. It certainly distracted attention from looking at such minor and distant dependencies as the Chagos as other than potential, indeed actual, slave entrepots. It is not part of our purpose to re-examine the wider issues of slavery or even, in any detail, the particular problems of suppressing the trade and, later, the institution of slavery in the Indian Ocean. Both elements did however loom large in the initial exploitation of the Archipelago's resources.

American and Dutch visitors

With the cessation of hostilities, French, British and other nations' merchant ships were once more able to operate freely in the Indian Ocean. For example, an American brig, the *Pickering*, was engaged in a three-year cruise. Having left part of her crew in the southern ocean to hunt seals, she sailed into Diego Garcia in March 1819 to load up with a full cargo of coconuts and fresh water, products that were respectively cheap and free (evidently the problem of finding potable water had now been solved). These were to keep alive the cattle she intended to embark in Madagascar for sale in Mauritius (where both commodities were dear). As she was about to leave harbour, her captain observed an 80-gun Dutch man o' war, the *Admiraal Evertsen*, struggling and failing to enter the lagoon. Setting sail at once, Captain Thomas B. Edes boarded the Dutch ship and was horrified to find water lapping at his feet; after eight days of pumping day and night, the crew and passengers were losing the battle to contain the inflow. Capt. Edes stayed aboard, as the *Admiraal Evertsen* drifted westward. By midnight, it became certain that she could not be saved and all 340 people aboard were transferred to the *Pickering*, a twelve-hour task. The drama was not quite over. As the brig sailed towards Diego Garcia, towing two of the *Admiraal Evertsen*'s longboats packed with sailors, a cannon boomed from the Dutch ship: one remaining crew member, the gunner, awoken from his drunken stupor, was signalling his presence. He was rescued, but burning powder set the ship alight. Many hours later, she went down in a pall of black smoke, destroyed in the end by fire, not water. The ship's commanding officer was Maurits Ver Huell, whose account of the shipwreck and his subsequent weeks on Diego Garcia has recently been published, together with a collection of the sketches and watercolour paintings he made while on the island.[42]

H.P.N. 't Hooft, *The Rescue of the Crew of the Ship of the Line Admiraal Evertsen*.
Maritiem Museum, Rotterdam.

Recounting his arrival at Diego Garcia, aboard the *Pickering*, he begins:

The sky was full of heavy rainclouds and when towards evening we were steering a middle course between the island of Millieu and the west point of Diego Garcia (as the wind was still against us), it rained very heavily and we suffered great discomfort. The night was dark. The rain poured down and the westerly wind soaked us with spray. We anchored in the wide, still bay. There was not enough room for everyone below decks and many found themselves a dry corner under the canvas. Cooked food was out of the question: hunger was assuaged with a piece of ship's biscuit and a slug of rum. Daylight was impatiently awaited; and with the welcome rays of the sun, which drove away the sombre clouds, we found new courage. The anchor was raised and the ship repositioned behind the Pointe de l'Est, where the main settlement is situated. The land looked very attractive and was thickly wooded: the jewelled crowns of the coconut palms stuck up above the other trees in countless numbers over the whole island. I went ashore immediately and was greeted warmly by the settler, a Monsieur Gebert from Mauritius. He showed me a row of spacious huts, where the negro slaves lived around the headquarters of the settlement, and, stretching out to the left and right in a semi-circle, more of the same. The first row of these was reserved forthwith for our stay; and then we began to unpack, with the happy prospect of an end to our many trials and tribulations.

His papers, brought to the brig by his servant, were lost in the ensuing mayhem. Fortunately, however, the offer of a reward resulted in the recovery of his sketch book. Another two weeks passed before the *Pickering*, having dumped her own cargo, could leave Diego Garcia for Mauritius with one half of the survivors, including the sick or injured and also some high ranking passengers; and a further month elapsed before she arrived back to pick up the remainder.[43] Ver Huell used this time to explore the island, to make some charming paintings, to examine its flora and fauna, as well as to note several aspects of daily life and the methods of production employed. We shall return to these matters. He also displayed the brisk, not to say brusque, characteristics of naval officers of the time.

I was sitting quietly in my little living room when a sailor came running up out of breath to say that he had seen a two-masted ship making for the bay … Thinking it might be the *Pickering*, I turned my gaze towards the beach and realised that it was a small schooner, probably looking to take on fresh water.

Giving strict orders for everyone to keep out of sight in case the skipper, seeing so many people, set out to sea again, he had his crew make ready the longboat with a full complement of oarsmen, and as soon as the schooner was behind Pointe Marianne, rowed out at full speed towards it.

The captain was dismayed when I boarded his vessel with my sailors and told him briefly the situation we found ourselves in. He replied that he was bound for the Seychelles and came from Ile de Bourbon [Reunion], with a cargo of linen.

Inspection soon revealed that under the bolts of cloth lay a hold full of rice. Ver Huell proposed that he buy enough rice for his people at market price in exchange for promissory notes from the government of the East Indies. An altercation ensued, with the schooner's skipper first accusing the Dutchman of theft, and then offering to sell the whole cargo. Taking no notice, Ver Huell had his men load their boat with rice, telling him to come and find them ashore. This the skipper did and, vastly outnumbered by Ver Huell's armed marines and officers, accepted the original deal.

Shipwreck at Salomon and piracy at Peros Banhos

The same year saw another case featuring both compassion and a total want of scruple. In August 1819 the Indian Government perused correspondence received from various interested parties concerning an incident that had taken place at the Salomon islands some months earlier. The documents were enclosed in a letter from the Acting Resident of the East India Company at Fort Marlborough, Bengkulu, on the coast of Sumatra, dated 1 April. This letter and its enclosures told a tale of skulduggery which seemed to have stepped out of the pages of a 17th-century pirate's memoir. The latterday pirate in question was Captain Lewis Jones of the *Iris*; his victims were the captain and crew of a French schooner, *La Vertu*. Their story, in their own words, was related to an official at Padang, western Sumatra on 10 March:

> We the undersigned, Captains, Officers and Mariners of the schooner *La Vertu*, certify and attest as follows, that being in the roads of the Salomon Islands the 8th February 1819 at 2 o'clock in the afternoon saw a ship to the southward, distance about two leagues standing apparently for the passage which she entered with all sails set at 4 pm. As she made no signals we imagined they were acquainted with the passage. At 5 she struck and sent a boat to the schooner for a pilot. We sent the boatswain. The ship lay the whole night in the passage. At 6 am he told us the bottom was stoved in and the ship made a great deal of water. We immediately proceeded to give them all the assistance in our power and assisted to save all that could be saved.
>
> The English captain asked us if we were to remain long at the Salomon islands. We answered about a month longer, and we offered to give them a passage to the Isle of France which in the first instance he accepted, but the next morning he told us he could not wait so long and offered 5,000 dollars to carry him to any port in Ceylon. We answered that we could not take upon ourselves such a voyage as our instructions were to proceed to Peros Banhos and that the schooner was insured and that the Resident of that Island was half owner of the vessel. He

asked to see him. We got under way on the 12th and came to an anchor on the 13th February at 10 pm at Peros Banhos. I Captain of the Schooner *La Vertu*, went on shore. The Resident was gone to another Island in the Vicinity. I gave orders to send for him, and returned immediately on board.

At day light we got under way to approach nearer the settlement. At 8 am the Resident came on board. The English captain asked him to freight him the schooner. The resident told him to let the vessel be made secure first and then we shall go on shore, and talk over the business with more composure. At 11 he came to and went on shore. The English captain took with him his carpenter, and I, Captain of the schooner, one of my sailors who could speak a little English to interpret. Being on shore the Resident asked him 6,000 piastres. The Captain and the Resident accepted to take the sum of 5,000 piastres which the Captain offered. An Agreement was immediately drawn out (of which the Captain has a copy), and all was settled and we were to sail the next day.

At 4 pm we returned on board, the moment we arrived on board the Captain ordered the arms to be seized by the sailors and the cable to be cut by his carpenter, to this cable was fastened 13 fathoms of chain. The Resident who was on board jumped immediately on the canoe with his sailors and the cabin boy and as soon as they shoved off the Captain ordered to fire at them, but we were ignorant if anybody was wounded. There now remained on board but two sailors, who turned against us the moment the vessel was seized. According to the Agreement made I was to have kept the command, but as soon as the vessel was seized the English Captain took the command himself and kept it to this port. We were kept continually on deck, not allowed to go down in the cabin in good or bad weather, constantly watched and not allowed to do anything of our own accord. We did consider ourselves on board after the behaviour of Captain Jones towards us, as prisoners, and … I look upon his conduct as that of a pirate until I can put my case in a court of justice.[44]

The captain of *La Vertu*, M. Alexis Legour, requested the Resident at Padang, a M. De Lamotte, to ensure that Capt. Jones be seized and be forbidden to take any property from the schooner. Jones retorted that he was willing to pay the master of the French schooner 'a reasonable freight for his vessel', adding, 'I am going to Calcutta with property saved from the late ship *Iris*. As there are regular courts of justice there if I have acted improperly the law will be open to him for redress'. De Lamotte accordingly advised Capt. Legour to seek redress at Calcutta. Legour was outraged, and pressed his claim in a letter to the Resident at Padang:

I beg leave to inform you that Captain Jones made a written agreement at Peros Banhos with Mr Lilliet part owner of the schooner, to carry him, passengers and treasure to Ceylon … The reason of our not being able to fetch India is that Captain Jones ordered the cable to be cut, seized the vessel by force of arms, and sailed from the island before water could be sent from shore.

He nevertheless expressed his willingness to retake charge of the schooner, provided that Jones agreed to indemnify him according to the agreement and with an additional charge for the anchor and cable.

In the event, Jones and Legour could not settle their argument and finding *La Vertu* still abandoned, Monsieur Ismail, a Frenchman residing at Padang took possession of her and brought her to a safer mooring. Legour, meantime, having asked for a passage to the Isle of France, 'where I am anxious to return, and inform my owners of the ill usage I have met with', eventually agreed to retake charge of his schooner.[45] Whether Capt. Jones was ever brought to book for his actions is unknown, but the incident served to underscore the potential for lawless behaviour in a corner of the British empire which was so isolated and so unpoliced. No matter how regulated in theory and principle the Chagos islands would be during the 19th century, in practice, as we shall see, an outlaw mentality would characterise the administration of the archipelago for decades to come, placing the powerless literally at the mercy of the strong.

For Legour, at least, the story had a happy ending. In 1820, still aboard *La Vertu*, he made a discovery that had eluded even Lt. Archibald Blair, of the low-lying islet which he was allowed to christen after himself, but which now bears the name Nelson. In December that year, he also obtained a *jouissance* to the island.

Between 1820 and 1827, *La Vertu*, not always under Legour's command, made at least eighteen round trips to the Chagos, most frequently to Peros Banhos, but also to all of the other Chagos islands with the exception of Egmont. The *Vertu*

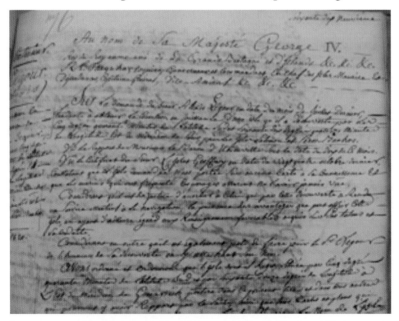

Grant of concession to Alexis Legour, with right to name island after himself. *Source*: MA LC24.

also supplied Eagle Island and Salomon, while Diego Garcia was most frequently supplied by a brig, the *Caroline*. Curiously, the brig *Brave*, which was used to supply Egmont, hardly features in the shipping returns. In a cruel twist of fate, however, another A. Legour, perhaps Alexis' son, was to lose his ship, the *Josephine*, in 1832 at the very spot where the *Iris* went down. Fortunately, captain and all but two of the crew were saved.

While the dramatic incidents described in this chapter illustrate how even the most adept navigators could face other dangers than natural hazards, the latter also resulted in a steady attrition. In general, however, the transport of goods and people, mainly slaves, to and from the Archipelago was undertaken by a small number of Mauritius-registered vessels, which carried on their business unimpeded. Similarly, as illustrated above, the process of granting concessions under the Crown, that is, *jouissances*, carried on unchanged following the transition from French to British sovereignty.

Notes to Chapter 5

1 IOR Home Miscellaneous H 606 'Notes relative to the Affairs of Native and foreign European States 1794-8'.

2 MA TB 3/2.

3 MA Z2B6 Police Report, Case of Sieur Liénard, 2 December 1790.

4 Scott, R. *op cit*. p. 96.

5 MA TB 3/2.

6 MA B 16/a and 18/a 18 orders of Thermidor an II and 5 Nivose an III.

7 TNA ADM 1/167 Cornwallis to Philip Stephens, Minerva, Spithead, 21 April 1794.

8 *A Mariner of England: An Account of William Richardson from Cabin Boy in the Merchant Service to Warrant Officer in the Royal Navy [1780-1819] as told by himself*, London, John Murray 1908, pp. 100-104.

9 See the report of Dauguet, head of a destroyed establishment in Archives Départmentales de la Réunion [ADR] L 312 letter to St Félix 22 October 1793, as quoted by Wanquet, C. 'Quelques remarques sur les relations des Mascareignes avec les Autres Pays de l'Océan Indien a l'Epoque de la Révolution Française', *Annuaire des Pays de l'Océan Indien* [APOI], vol VII, 1980, p. 211.

10 D'Unienville, R. *Malartic*, SHIM, Mauritius 2006, p. 139. 'L'établissement Dauguet, à Diego Garcia, étant occupé par des anglais provenant d'un bâtiment échoué, l'Assemblée voulut y envoyer un bâtiment de commerce armé afin de dégager l'île. Le vice-amiral [St Félix] s'y opposa et expédia la corvette La *Minerve* – qui s'en revenant, mission accomplie, quitta le mouillage de Diego 24 heures avant l'arrivée de la *Minerva* de Lord Cornwall.'

11 AN C/4/109 Correspondance générale M de Malartic M Du Puy, 1794-5.

12 MA B 16/11 22 messidor II [10 July 1794] quoted in D'Unienville, R. *Histoire Politique de l'Ile de France*, Mauritius Vol 2 1791-1794, Archives Publications No. 13, 14 and 15, 1975-1989, p. 39.

13 D'Unienville, R. *Malartic*, p. 240. Me. d'Unienville adds in a footnote 'Diego Garcia semble prédestinée à ce genre de traitement. L'histoire devait se répéter en 1968: avec cette nuance que les habitants de Diego étaient devenus britanniques et furent arrachés de leur île par des compatriotes.'

14 Peerthum, S., 'Origins & History of the Chagossians', *L'Express*, 11 November 2003.

15 D'Unienville, R. *Histoire Politique de l'Ile de France, 1795-1803*, p. 57.

16 These expeditions are recorded in MA B 24/54 and MA C 30.

17 See Lacroix, L., *Les Derniers Négriers*, Paris, 1977, especially chapter II 'Les expéditions suspectes', pp. 64-96.

18 Collier's letter recounting the attack was reproduced in the *London Gazette* and in *The Gentleman's Magazine, and Historical Chronicle*, Volume 72, Part 2 1802, pp. 662-3. The encounter is also discussed in Brenton, E.P. *The Naval History of Great Britain*, Vol 2, London, Henry Colburn, 1837, pp. 1-2, and in Phillips, M. *Ships of the Old Navy* www.ageofnelson.org

19 MA F 34 Rapports reçus de Général Desbrulys sur la service de terre, de mer et de l'hôpital.

20 MA D 10 C Assemblée Coloniale – Lettres reçues de divers.

21 MA TB 3/1. He was dead by 1829. See p. 120.

22 For further details, see Toussaint, A. *Histoire des Iles Mascareignes*, Paris, 1972, p. 129.

23 TNA ADM 1/173 Peter Rainier, Bombay harbour to Jonathan Duncan, Governor, Bombay 23 April 1803.

24 This concession is discussed in greater detail in Chapter 6 (see pp. 103–104).

25 Archives Nationales d'Outre Mer OIND 17 Letters of Diego Garcia concessionaires to Decaen, June 1809. This account supersedes that of Scott (*op. cit.*, p. 99).

26 MA TB 3/2 Notes compiled by Baron d'Unienville.

27 MA TB 3/1 Miscellaneous documents.

28 To date very little information about slave numbers in 18th-century Chagos has been published. See the discussions on this topic in Peerthum *op. cit.*, and Lassemillante, H. *L'esclavage aux Chagos Pendant les Dix-huitième et Dix-neuvième Siècles*, unpublished paper, 1998. Peerthum and Lassemillante enumerate Lapotaire's slave workforce at 100 strong.

29 Parkinson, C.N. *Samuel Walters, Lieutenant R.N.* Liverpool University Press, 1949, p. 67.

30 This vessel had previously belonged to the well-known privateer Surcouf, when she bore the name *Revenant*.

31 The capture was reported in *The Times* of Friday 20 April 1810 as follows: '*La Bellone* French frigate, arrived at the Isle of France on the 5th of January, with the *Victor* sloop of war, which she captured in the Bay of Bengal, after an action of four hours, and also a Portuguese frigate, called the *Minerva*.'

32 TNA HCA 32/1814 Affidavit of Henry Edgell, 1827. We are indebted to Mr Steve Forsberg for providing us with this reference.

33 TNA ADM 51/2518 Journal of the Proceedings of His Majesty's ship *Leopard* from 28 April 1808 to 20 July 1814; ADM 51/2045 Journal of the proceedings of His Majesty's Ship *Cornelia* from 6 October 1808 to 22 June 1813.

34 TNA ADM 53/363 Log of the *Cornelia*, 1808-1811.

35 TNA ADM 51/2826 Log of the *Sir Francis Drake*, 1808-1810.

36 This is quoted from Rigby, B. *Ever Glorious, the Story of the 22nd [Cheshire] Regiment*, vol 1, Evans & Sons, Chester, 1982, but the likely source is De Poyen whose account is based on Decaen's letter to the French Minsiter of 22 September 1810. He states 'Un petit évènement de guerre vint ajouter aux embarras financiers de la colonie. Les habitans de l'île de France avaient fait un établissement à Diego Garcia, l'île principale de l'archipel des Chagos pour y fabriquer de l'huile de coco et cet établissement fournissait à peu près toute la consommation de la colonie. Or, au mois de mai 1810, les Anglais firent une descente dans cette petite île, détruisirent presque complètement l'établissement et enlevèrent 147 noirs appartenant à des particuliers. Le résultat fut une pénurie d'huile à l'île de France et par suite une forte augmentation du prix de cette denrée dont on faisait un grand usage.' See 'La Guerre aux Iles de France et Bourbon 1809-1810' by De Poyen, *Nouvelle Revue Historique et Littéraire*, April 1898, No. 15, pp. 105-7.

37 TNA ADM 51/2826 Log of the *Sir Francis Drake*, 1808-1810.

38 MSA Bombay Political Dept Diaries Diary No. 376 Captain J. Prior, HMS *Arrogant* to F. Warden, 10 July 1811, and enclosure: Thomas O'Brien to Captain Pairandeau of the French cartel *La Camille*, at Diego Garcia, 3 June 1811.

39 Lepelley, R. *Croisières dans la Mer des Indes 1810-1811*, Keltia Graphic, France 1992, pp. 142-144.

40 *Ibid*; pp. 109-110, 142-144. The original French text is as follows: 'Ces messieurs nous apprirent que, depuis quarante ans, il s'était formé des établissements sur cette île, chose qu'il ait bien singulier que chacun de nous eut ignoré jusqu'alors. Ils vivent bien misérablement, les infortunés relégués sur ce coin

de terre. Tous leurs moyens se réduisent à des cocos, quelques poules et des tortues, mais il est impossible d'obtenir d'un sol de sable la moindre production recherchée par l'homme; tous les essays dans ce genre ont été infructueux.'

41 Owen, Captain W.F.W. RN *Journal of the Royal Geographical Society*, vol 2, paper dated April 9 1832 p. 88. Burrows, E.H. *Captain Owen of the African Survey*, A.A. Balkema, Rotterdam, 1979, p. 43; Martin, R.M. *History of the British Colonies*, London, James Cochrane, vol 4, 1835, p. 204. See also Fry, H.T. 'Early British Interest in the Chagos Archipelago and the Maldive Islands' *Mariners Mirror* pp. 343-351.

42 Fraassen, C.F. van and Klapwijk, P.J. (eds), *Herinnering aan een reis naar Oost-Indië*, Linschoten-Vereeniging, 2008. We are grateful to Rachel M.W. Smith for the translation of the passages quoted .

43 This account is taken from the memoirs of Hendrik Doeff, returning from nineteen years of near-captivity in Japan as the head of the Dutch trading post in Nagasaki. His heavily pregnant wife died four days into the voyage to Mauritius (*Recollections of Japan*, translated and annotated by Annick M. Doeff, publ. Trafford, Victoria, Canada, 2003).

44 NAI Delhi Home Public Consultations 6 August 1819, No. 15.

45 NAI Home Public Consultation 6 August 1819 No. 14 W.R. Jennings, Acting Resident, Fort Marlbro, 1 April 1819 to C. Lushington Esq, Sec'y Govt.

6

A Slave-based Plantation Society Emerges

I F there was little sign of the rule of law at sea, things were not much better on land, where utilisation of resources involved exploitation of enslaved people. Following the successive capitulations of the Mascarene islands of Rodrigues, Bourbon and Mauritius to British land and sea forces in 1809/10, their myriad small dependencies also came up for grabs. There ensued a somewhat unseemly scramble among British naval officers for the richer pickings of the Seychelles archipelago,[1] with the coterie around the new British Governor, Robert Townsend Farquhar, inevitably coming off best, while the less fancied Chagos atolls were left to the more adventurous of the French settlers to reclaim or request. Their efforts probably owed a good deal to the researches of the redoubtable Jean-Baptiste Lislet-Geoffroy (see vignette on p. 99), appointed at the turn of the century to the office of naval maps and plans in the Isle of France, where he had been gathering together documents to rectify the mapped locations and to chart new discoveries. In the case of the Chagos, he had 'followed, for the islands and shoals lying north of Diego Garcia, a chart given me by Lieutenant Blair',[2] as shown overleaf.

Most of the aspirant settlers obtained concessions under the Crown (*jouissances*), just as they had done before the British captured Mauritius, and all the concessions contained strict stipulations (on pain of forfeiture) concerning the conservation of the islands' natural resources, in particular coconut trees and turtles. However, sixteen years passed before any government official went to investigate how the concessions were being managed. Out of sight, out of mind, seemed to be the new Mauritius authorities' motto, though it is fair to concede that, with many pressing problems, that of examining scarcely known and scarcely inhabited islets 1,200 miles away could hardly have loomed large on their list of priorities. The consequences of neglect were however very slow to be grasped and the lessons learned were, as we shall see, repeatedly forgotten. What triggered the authorities' interest was the slave trade.

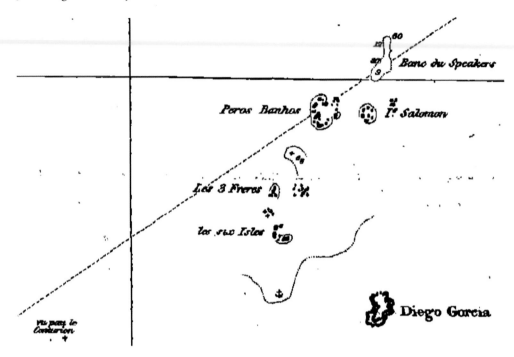

Chagos and the illegal slave trade

One of the biggest problems for the conquerors of Mauritius was to put into practice British regulations outlawing the slave trade. Governor Farquhar was a reluctant implementer of these laws, and such was his prevarication on the issue, and the consequent charges of illegal slave trading, that in the 1820s a Commission of Inquiry was set up to investigate the matter. The Commissioners found much evidence to suggest that the small dependencies of the Mascarenes and the smaller Seychelles islands offered many opportunities for traders to trans-ship slaves from Africa to Mauritius. They drew attention to the case of the *Chicken* commanded by a man named Piveteau, a creole of Mauritius 'who entered the harbour of Diego Garcia in 1825 with a cargo of Malay slaves'. The mate of the *Chicken*, named Tirant, was a creole of Seychelles.[3] The slave cargo comprised 40 seven- and eight-year-old boys acquired at Nias, an island off the east coast of Sumatra, well known for slave trading by Achinese and Chinese merchants. The French were believed to be regular purchasers.[4] Once the illegal slaves had been introduced to the dependencies, arrangements could be made to 'transfer' them to Mauritius on the grounds that they were the legitimate property of concession holders on the islands. Consequently memorials from proprietors requesting such transactions were frequent.[5]

Thus the first officials to visit the Chagos, in 1826, were Messrs Werner, Assistant Registrar of Slaves, and Hoart, the Sworn Surveyor. While they came

The Coloured Cartographer

When the British took over the administration of the Isle of France in December 1810, Governor Farquhar decided to adopt a policy of reconciliation. He retained many of the French settlers in their administrative posts.

Among the officials whose work straddled the French and British regimes was the extraordinary Jean-Baptiste Lislet-Geoffroy. As the mixed-race son of a white French officer and an African woman from Guinea named Niama, Geoffroy overcame all the disadvantages of his birth into a racially divided, hierarchical colonial society to become a revered cartographer and a legendary figure in Mascarene history.

Image © Christian Landry, La Réunion.

In 1819 he published – with a foreword by Farquhar – an interesting document entitled 'Memoir and notice explanatory of a chart of Madagascar and the North-Eastern Archipelago of Mauritius'. In this publication he explained that for the previous twenty years, since his appointment to the Office of Naval Maps and Plans in the Isle of France, he had been hoping to gather together documents to rectify the mapped locations and to chart new discoveries. He noted that a M. Quenot had assisted him in the revision of the small archipelago known as the Amirantes, and had discussed with him the correct position of Diego Garcia and the rocks seen by the *Centurion*, all of which he included in his new chart (opposite).

In his publication, Geoffroy offered the following conclusions as to the positions and the sources of information he had relied upon for the islands of the Chagos Archipelago:

'The isle of Diego Garcia is placed here at 70°50′ longitude and between 7°10′ and 7°30′ latitude South, according to what I, together with M. Quenot, ascertained. I owe besides to the latter the communication he made to me of a memorandum of the rocks seen by the Centurion, which lie 68°27′ longitude East and 7°30′ latitude South. I have followed, for the islands and shoals lying North of Diego Garcia, a chart given me by Lieutenant Blair. Our navigators, who frequent those parts, and amongst others Mr. David, who is provided with a good chronometer, affirm that it is very correct.

This group is composed chiefly of the Peros Banhos islands, the six islands, Salomon's islands, the Three Brothers, and many other small islands.'

back with details of the islands' positions, of concession holders and of the latter's commercial activities, their main purpose was to verify slave numbers. The prospect of eventual compensation, already held out, gave the owners a strong incentive to declare the identities of all their slaves. The resulting voluminous slave registration records, along with surviving ships' passenger lists, offer useful insights into how the concessionaires built up their Chagos workforce. Some of them also reveal not just the names, ages and ethnicity of many individual slave workers, but even their distinguishing marks and family relationships.

In contrast, we know little about how these early concession holders (*propriétaires en jouissance*) went about tasks similar to those facing Robinson Crusoe or the Swiss Family Robinson. Some of them were mariners already familiar with the area,[6] while others probably had estates or businesses involving import and export. All were clearly slave owners. What about the slaves they used to do the hard manual work? Were any sent merely as punishment? Were most newly acquired from dealers? If so, had they only recently been taken from their countries of origin? How many were picked to go to the Chagos because they had already acquired relevant skills, whether for harvesting coconuts, building houses or boats, or the nautical skills essential to work and survival in an environment of reefs and surf-encircled islets? Does that explain why some slaves were transferred from Seychelles, with its myriad coconut-treed islands? Those who visited the Chagos islands for operational reasons left few records, while other visitors were few and far between. We can only guess therefore at the answers to these questions and we can only wonder how many perished before the hard experience of the survivors had become translated into established Chagos practices, both in work and in social life.

Diego Garcia

This atoll had, as we have seen (p. 47) been settled after a fashion for nearly 30 years prior to the change of sovereignty. The concessions granted there served as a model for those made subsequently for the Archipelago's other islands, previously known only to navigators and cartographers.

Clearly, from the accounts of events on the island in 1810 and 1811, the concessionaires had done their best to continue production in spite of the surrounding turmoil. A recent study by Jean-Marie Chelin[7] includes valuable discoveries from Mauritian shipping records. These show that deliveries of oil, copra and coconuts continued unabated in the years following Mauritius' capture, with Diego Garcia as the main source.

An interesting vignette of life on the island is provided by the commander of the Dutch warship *Admiraal Evertsen*, Maurits Ver Huell, who was one of those obliged to spend over six weeks there in 1819 after his ship was wrecked in the circumstances described in the preceding chapter. Ver Huell tells us that

The whole island is divided into 5 settlements [*établissements*] – Mini Mini, le Parc, Pointe de l'Est, Anse David and Pointe Marianne, governed by individuals of mixed race [*Mestiezen*], most of whom were merchants based on Mauritius. The number of negro slaves, shared amongst the 5 settlements, amounted to around 300. Its products were: coconut oil, brandy distilled from the sap of this palm, soap, salt fish, and turtle shell. Pointe de l'Est brought in over 6,000 piasters a year.[8]

He added:

The climate, being in the tropics, is very healthy, albeit hot. I was assured that the horrific 'Lazarus Disease', which is prevalent amongst the slaves on Mauritius, improves relatively quickly here. Conceivably this can be ascribed to the curative properties of the turtle, which is the foremost source of nourishment for the islanders at certain times of year. I have often seen the negroes eagerly drinking the warm blood of these creatures, for they think that most of the power to free them from this dreadful disease is contained in the blood. There is no more hideous fate than this. The limbs of those that fall victim to it lose feeling, wither and drop off, whilst new skin forms over the joint. Many of these unfortunate people had missing fingers, toes and even hands and feet. The settlers thought that this illness was catching; which made our crew somewhat anxious but by God's grace none of us was affected by it …

Ver Huell *La Mare aux Lubines*. Image courtesy Maritiem Museum, Rotterdam.

The wealth of the island consists of the coconut palm; and almost nothing goes to waste from this precious commodity. Before the young tree develops a trunk, the crown provides very nutritious and tasty greens, eaten either cooked or as a salad, called *palmiet* or palm cabbage. Once it has become a proper tree, the branches are used to make twine for matting and bedding and roofing for houses. From the stalks of the flowers which grow in bunches, brooms are made. These are never cut without at the same time making the refreshing drink called *Caloo* here (but *toak* in the East Indies). To do this, a bottle or other receptacle is hung from the severed stalk and the sap collected in it. Although this fluid is itself a healthy drink, a sort of brandy is also distilled from it. Ten bottles of *Caloo* make one bottle of spirits. If the *Caloo* goes sour, it makes good vinegar; and you can also derive sugar from it.[9]

From the outermost skin of the nut, good strong rope is made. The nut itself is filled with sweet water; its flesh is the predominant food of the negro slaves and is at its most nutritious when it is beginning to germinate. From the coconut husks, charcoal is made. The fresh coconut oil is utilised in cooking and also, as it is throughout the Indies, for making soap. For lye, in place of caustic soda, they use certain shrubs which grow all around, called '*velouté*', which have wonderfully scented white flowers.

The collection and pressing of the coconut oil is done as follows:-

Early in the morning, after the slaves have been woken by the crack of a whip (which was never misused), they went out into the woods to pick the ripe coconuts and take off the outer husk by skilful use of the pointed end of a large shell. Towards midday, each brought his collection to the headquarters. Here the nuts were broken up and left for 4-5 days in the sunshine until the flesh became separated from the hard shell, and was thenceforth called copra, and left another 4-5 days. It was then ready for pressing and a special kind of mill is used, consisting of a hollow cylinder five or six feet high and about two feet in diameter, narrowing into a skittle shape at the bottom and provided with a hole through which the oil dripped. The cylinder was filled with copra, a round pole like a rolling pin put into it, squashing the contents against the sides of the cylinder, by means of a lever 10-12 feet long attached to the top end of the 'rolling pin' which was in turn chained to a horizontal beam turning in a groove at the bottom of the cylinder. At the end of this 'boom', on which a weight is placed to increase the pressure and to rub the 'rolling pin' with force against the side of the skittle-shaped inside of the cylinder, ran a negro, or sometimes a donkey, at a steady pace. The fibre left over from this process was fed to pigs and poultry. M. Gebert [manager of the East Point settlement] had some good-looking hounds, which also enjoyed eating the copra.

Ver Huell, who was a keen naturalist and collector, went on to discuss the many types of tree put to various uses, the most prized shrub being the *fouché* (a type of fig) from whose bark the workers made very strong fishing lines. He added that cotton had been planted, but gone wild, and seeded itself everywhere, but the settlers were short of labour to exploit it. In the settlers' gardens plants brought over from Mauritius were cultivated, for example tobacco, bananas, capsicums, melons and pumpkins. Of the *solanum* family, there were potatoes, aubergines and tomatoes. Honeybees, brought from Mauritius, lived in hollow tree trunks and provided quite good honey. The only four-footed wild animals, he remarks, 'inadvertently brought in on ships, and breeding well, are rats'. By then the Dutch had been on the island about six weeks. He wrote,

> Through God's goodness we all enjoyed good health, though for a while dysentery was rife amongst the slaves; yet with the skill and tireless care of our experienced Ship's Surgeon, Heer Efting, this infectious disease was brought under control. The treatment used the not very up to date medicines of the settlers. Very few of us were ill. Only one sailor who had a chronic illness died during our stay and was buried with full military honours.

The Dutch enjoyed a daily meal consisting of fish, cooked with coconut oil and palm nut vinegar; and from time to time a piglet was donated by a 'settler'. This was cut up into small pieces and cooked with some *palmiet* in cauldrons, producing a good soup. On their arrival, the Dutch had been distributed among the settlements and had recovered cauldrons once used for making soap from the abandoned settlement at Anse David. Efforts to catch fish for themselves proved rather unsuccessful and they also lost a lot of tackle on the coral reef. The 'settler' begged them to desist and to let his workers look after supplies, as there was a scarcity of iron on the island to make fish-hooks. Their pirogues returned each evening with the day's catch, which was divided into equal portions by the officer assigned to that duty for the day. Fires were lit and each man cooked his meal according to his own taste. With contributions from the other settlements, there were enough fish to go round. If they were lucky enough to catch a turtle, they had a splendid lunch (these weighed about 250 Dutch pounds, i.e. about 125 kilos). Ver Huell himself went fishing with Gebert and four workers. Their method was to strew a mixture of coral and fish fragments over the surface, lower the lines (which were suspended on a kind of horizontal frame) to the bottom and then pull them up to a foot or two above the seabed. The day's catch came to about 110 kilos of fish of all colours, the best-tasting of them being the surgeonfish. Sharks abounded and twice made off with their tackle. Once, they spotted a kind of ray known as a sea-devil.

Even where he tells how he and his fellow survivors spent their time, rather than giving descriptions of the island and its inhabitants, Ver Huell contrives to convey the prevailing atmosphere in a lively way, as the inset description of his trip to Middle Island shows. His romanticised paintings of his explorations of Diego Garcia bear equal witness to his fascination for the island. Indeed, it is hard to escape the conclusion that relief at his narrow escape from death and

Ver Huell *View of Middle Island*. Image courtesy Maritiem Museum, Rotterdam.

gratitude for the warmth of Gebert's hospitality coloured his view of conditions on the island. He relates a story of how, when Gebert's canoe had once capsized,

> His faithful negroes, only concerned to save their kindhearted and good master, heaved him out of the water to save him from the sharks. Fortunately none of these monsters was nearby and all got back safely into the boat.

All good things come to an end! The *Pickering* returned and a formal farewell party was held in the hut belonging to the 'good' Gebert. Ver Huell thanked the settlers, in particular those at Pointe de l'Est, on behalf of the whole ship's company, for the generous way in which each according to his ability had helped them in their hour of need and apologised for the burden they had imposed as a result of their plight. He was then congratulated in turn on the way in which his men had conducted themselves and the fact that no poultry or piglets went missing from those wandering around in the woods. Commenting on the experience, Ver Huell remarks that the 'gentlemen officers' behaved as if they were on a properly organised warship and this example had a good effect on the ship's company. He only once had to punish a man and that was for coming on duty in his underwear. The offender was shut in the punishment block for the slaves,

Excursion to Middle Island

Accompanied by one officer, with the 15-year-old son of Gebert (born on Diego Garcia and never having been elsewhere) as guide, and with four slaves to wait upon them and do the rowing, Ver Huell makes an overnight visit to Milieu Barbe island. They take only fishing tackle, coconut brandy, coconut oil and vinegar, a couple of cooking pots and drinking water. His aim is to look for baby boobies, and to augment his collection of conches and other shells.

He marvels at the crystal-clear water and the wonderful coral and sea life of every description. There are purple and gold giant clams. They see trumpet fish and the slaves pursue a stranded shark. They find a little hut and put 'our blacks' to work to clean it up and repair the roof in places, while 'we drink *caloo* spiked with a little brandy to refresh ourselves' before setting off in the canoe again to go booby-hunting on the neighbouring island of Grand Barbe. They collect about thirty boobies and slaughter plenty of seabirds which have difficulty getting airborne, with their short legs and long wings.

Back at the hut, they make a fire and the slaves deftly skin the boobies and spread them on sticks to dry. They are very hungry and prepare lunch, roasting the birds in coconut oil and baking their eggs in the ashes, with a few fish thrown in. *Palmiet* with vinegar and a bit of germinating coconut as relish complete the simple meal, which he rates more highly than fine wines, served on some broad leaves. 'We found the saying Hunger is the Best Chef to be very true.'

They spend the afternoon in a most successful hunt for conches and other shells. A shark, much too close for comfort, gives them a fright. They retreat to their cosy island with their canoe anchored in front of the hut. Their young friend goes to spear fish for their supper, eaten with more seabird eggs and *palmiet*. The idyllic evening wears on and the negroes make themselves shelter for the night in their own manner. Suddenly they are surrounded by hermit crabs in such large numbers that they can hear them scuffling about. Their sleeping platforms are luckily a few feet above ground and they fall asleep on the dried leaves spread out on them. They are woken in the morning by the slaves' voices and get them to make breakfast. They spend the day like the one before and then return to East Point, keeping close in to the east arm of Diego Garcia, seeing the settlement of Mini Mini on the way, and getting stuck – luckily not for long – on a coral head as it gets dark.

notwithstanding some people thinking this too harsh. In general, he had no complaints about the behaviour of his men; and the evidence of the 'settlers' corroborated this opinion.

While the rescued Dutchmen may have taken too rosy a view of the conditions, it is clear that Gebert must have provided continuity of management since the first days of the 19th century and that the East Point plantation at least was in good working order. It is impossible to tell from Ver Huell's account whether the availability of huts, the abandonment of Anse David and insufficiency of labour for cotton growing represented the continuing effects of the British

Ver Huell *L'Anse de l'Eclairci*.[10] Image courtesy Maritiem Museum, Rotterdam.

depredations of 1810. The two Dutch accounts varied widely in their estimates of population; Hoeff put it at about 150 workers in total, Ver Huell at double that. One contemporary record puts the figure (of slaves only) as low as 61. What we do know is that slave numbers were starting to increase. Seventy-four of them were transported to Diego Garcia under licence in the years 1818-1822[11] and, as the shipping records reveal,[12] all three concessionaires continued to send regular shipments of their slaves, the totals being as follows:-

Table 6.1

	Men	Women	Boys	Girls
Whites	5	1	–	–
Free Persons	1	4	6	3
Slaves	168	37	3	10
Leprous	30	5	–	2

<u>Source</u>: See note 12.

Quite early during this period, the concession holders began to delegate the task of running their establishments to subordinates, called *régisseurs*. Thus, Cayeux's *régisseur* at East Point (evidently the successor to Gebert) was a certain

M. Rival, and Lapotaire's at Pointe Marianne was Jean-Baptiste Le Camus (sometimes spelt Lecamus). Sometime in the early 1820s a separate *jouissance* had been granted for the southern portion of Cayeux's estate, known as Anse David, to Messrs Florigny and Pattée. Around the same time, reports began to reach Port Louis of bad relations between healthy slaves and the lepers and of maltreatment of the latter. Investigation from Port Louis of their problems proved ineffectual and in the end it took a visit by the sloop, HMS *Espoir* to secure redress, based on the detailed findings of the sloop's commander, Captain Greville, and his surgeon, T.T. Jones (pp. 108–112). We shall examine the specific problems of the lepers later in this chapter.

Meanwhile, back in Port Louis, both Lapotaire and Cayeux had already set up local oil mills to process copra from Diego Garcia, and seem to have been concentrating on the marketing of the oil produced by their plantations.[13] In 1819, we find Cayeux advertising his wares thus:-

> **A VENDRE**
> **Belle Huile de coco**
> **de Monsieur Cayeux**
> *livraison à volonté à*
> *12 livres par 10 veltes et à*
> *11 livres 10 shillings par 50 ou 100 veltes*
> *qu'on rendra chez l'acquéreur.*
>
> S'adresser a M.L. Floris, Rue de Paris.

In the same year, his behaviour locally, no less than in Diego Garcia, aroused the government's ire, as the following Notice in the Government Gazette shows:

> The attention of the Government having been drawn to the enormous extent to which the price of oils has risen lately – a matter of particular concern to the less well-off classes of the community, the Major General commanding gives notice that, should it be discovered that the present high price results from specu-lation or an illegal monopoly, the Government will find itself obliged to take at once whatever measures it judges most effective in order to relieve the citizens from the impact of such extortion.
>
> It has also pleased the Major General to instruct all those individuals who have obtained permission to establish themselves on any of the island Dependencies in the government's jurisdiction to present to the office of the Chief Secretary, within 8 days of this notification, the title deeds or authorisations by virtue of which their establishments have been set up. Similarly, the owners of the various installations for the production of coconut oil are invited to provide statements of the quantities of oil made or imported since the 1st. January this year and the quantities which their establishments are expected to produce by the end of the year.[14]

In fact the importance of oil produced in the dependencies and the political sensitivity of its price had been illustrated only three years earlier, when the main oil storage depot was burned down and the proprietor of Agalega gained kudos for deliberately lowering the price of his oil.[15]

We do not know how Cayeux fared in the matter of profiteering, but he was certainly taken to task for the behaviour of his minions on Diego Garcia; he excused himself by blaming his *régisseurs,* claiming to have sacked three of them since 1819 for treating slaves badly. Had Gebert, we might ask, completely pulled the wool over Commandant Ver Huell's eyes? Or had he been sacked for being too indulgent towards his charges? Cayeux also claimed credit for introducing maize to Diego Garcia and supplying it to his slaves. The latter were in addition, he said, given a pint of fermented liquor daily, a 'moderate' ration of spirituous liquor on Sundays, plus a weekly ounce of tobacco; twice yearly they were provided with an exchange of new clothes. Never was the comment *qui s'excuse s'accuse* more apt. By 1830 Cayeux's *jouissance* had passed to Le Camus, although another Cayeux, Joachim, perhaps the brother who is occasionally mentioned, obtained a concession in 1838.

The view from HMS Espoir

When Capt. Greville visited Diego Garcia in 1828, he found plenty to say about the condition of Diego Garcia's slaves and those in charge of them, visiting each of the island's establishments in turn. He detected 'no abuse of any kind' at Pointe Marianne. At Anse David, re-opened and now run by Florigny but owned by Laurent Barbé, where there were no asses to work the oil mills, Greville began by considering that the slaves engaged on this task were overworked, since only three of them were made to undertake a task normally accomplished by four. However, 'from all I could gather from the *régisseurs,* and the slaves themselves, the number was apparently sufficient ... however laborious and distressing the occupation may seem at a first view, the blacks do not appear to dread it more than other necessary labours of the establishment'. If this was a less than ringing endorsement, his comments on the East Point estate were unequivocal:

> [I am] obliged to state that the greatest discontent prevails, many of the slaves bear dreadful marks of very severe punishment (although I believe not recent). Mr Rival, the *Régisseur,* is a man without education and without method; he nevertheless appeared to have a strong desire to make the slaves and lepers comfortable.

Greville went on to explain the impossibility of reconciling this desire with the written instructions of the concessionaire (who had left the island for good in

1818) to limit the daily ration of rice to 8 ounces, rather the 14 ounces prescribed by law, this ration to be delivered in the form of soup. However, as an 'indulgence', the slaves were allowed to rear poultry, for which some *poonac* – the residue remaining after the crushing of copra – was supplied, giving the management in return a right to one chicken in three. 'Mr Cayeux,' commented Greville, [was someone] 'whose conduct when here and whose subsequent orders stamp him in my opinion as a man totally unfit to possess an estate so far removed from any satisfactory check upon his arbitrary disposition'.

Who were these hard-pressed humans at their slavemasters' mercy? The post-1810 legislation requiring slave owners to register their slaves and in particular the act of abolition of slavery on 1 February 1835 and the financial compensation offered to slave owners generated a good deal of paperwork which offers precious insights into the slave presence on Chagos. Ozille Majastre's claims (see inset overleaf) suggest that some members of the same slave family were distributed across the islands, for example the Fanchons. Similarly, when a claim was placed on behalf of a minor named Chery Edmond Marcel of Diego Garcia, we learn that the slave concerned, Jean Marie, was aged 50 in 1832, and his height was 5' 4½", classed as an 'inferior domestic' and valued at £40. This individual was from Mozambique and had been registered in 1826 by the leper Roblet in Diego Garcia.[16]

Not all of the slave owners in Diego Garcia had as large a workforce as Majastre. Some owned only a few domestic slaves, while others had domestic slaves additional to those they employed for plantation work. Thus Le Camus himself registered only three slaves – a couple with a child, who served as his domestics, whereas Jean-Baptiste Cayeux owned eighteen male and five female slaves (with five slave children, who were also listed as his property). A M. Treize (another free leper) of Diego Garcia possessed only two domestic servants, both from Mozambique and listed as 22-year-old Auguste Augustin, and 33-year-old Michel Hector.[17] Felix Dupuch registered only one slave at Diego Garcia – 27-year-old domestic servant Baptiste Victorine. There were also women slave owners at Diego Garcia – Adèle Garaud was the registered proprietor of 35-year-old Marie Jeune.

At the Anse David establishment on Diego Garcia, Lafauche and Florigny were listed as co-proprietors of a large workforce. The occupational status of their slaves reveals the diversity of tasks or skills in use at that time. A senior member of their workforce both in age and skill was 54-year-old Gracieux La Gaité, designated *chef huilier* (head mill operator). He was assisted by four other *huiliers*. Four carpenters were aged between 36 and 58, while another slave called Jean Marie was a *savonnier* or soap maker and 46-year-old Jean Baptiste Bongarçon did the job of *forgeron* (blacksmith). August Anna was employed at the mill, and 50-year-old François Cabot was a mason. Adonis Grave worked as

The Diego Garcia Slave Workforce of Mr Ozille Majastre, 1832

Name	Age	Height	Remarks	Place of Birth
Marie Louise Joseph	22	5'4		Creole of Mauritius
Marceline Joseph	16	5'2		ditto
Fanny Fanchon	31	5'0		Mozambique
Jean Baptiste Fanchon	12	4'2		Creole of Mauritius
Louise Fanchon	7	4'0		ditto
Louisa Fanchon	born 5 Dec 1829			ditto
Amedée Fanchon	born 28 March 1832			
Euphrasie Jacques	22	5'2		ditto
Pierre Louis Jacques	born July 1831			Creole of Diego Garcia
Ernestine Marie Jacques	born 25 Dec 1832			
David Paul	29	5'3		Creole of Mauritius
Henry L'Emoustille	22	5'4		Malgache
Frederic Jolicoeur	25	5'4		ditto
Philippe Le Roux	67		leper	Mozambique
Augustin Worhnitz	30		leper	Creole of Mauritius
Lindor Courtois	71	4'11		Indien
Gregoire Mathurin	51	5'3		Mozambique
Tranquille Capre	42	5'2		Malgache
Michel Mauvais Oeil	41	5'5		Mozambique
Azor Cupidon	55	5'7		ditto
Suffren Malnomm	50	5'2		ditto
Joseph Libertin	43	5'3		ditto
Pollux Prêt à Boire	40	5'5		ditto
Gerome Songor	28	4'11		ditto
Joseph Brigand	46	5'7		Creole of Mauritius
Avrie Bombay	59	5'7		Mozambique

a *tonnelier* (cooper). The *commandeur* (foreman/supervisor) was 52-year-old Foulon Docile. He was presumably in charge of the 32 slaves employed as *pioches* (fieldhands). Three of the slaves of Anse David – men aged between 40 and 59 – were listed as lepers. There were six children.

The other four atolls

Egmont/Six Iles

Readers will recall Lt. Blair's description of this atoll in 1786, with its six islands connected by apparently fordable shoals, but only three having coconut trees growing on them, and a small harbour, 'difficult and dangerous of access', on

Name	Age	Height	Remarks	Place of Birth
Pedre Sevenne	46	5'6		ditto
Cezar Duncan	40	5'2		ditto
Major Jacob	28	5'6		Malgache
Hipolite Hypolita	51	5'6		Indian
Fantaisie Michel	48	5'8		Malgache
Jolicoeur Albert	56		leper	ditto
Lindor André	36	5'4		ditto
La Jeunesse Guingan	52	5'5		ditto
John Joson	45	4'11		Creole of Mauritius
La Tulipe Adeur	40	5'2		Malgache
Lindor L'Aciota	38	5'4		ditto
Dimanche Congre	35	5'4		Mozambique
Pluton Jeudi	33	5'7		Malgache
Capitaine Barberousse	30	5'5		ditto
Thélémaque Marteau	29	5'4		Mozambique
Félicité Boule	51	5'3		ditto
Marguerite Sophie	40	4'10		Creole of Mauritius
Isabelle Ferrere	52	5'1		ditto
Suzette Lisette	41	4'11		ditto
Rosine Marie	41	5'0		Malgache
Felicia Rassare	40			ditto
Mie Joseph Trompeuse	28	5'1		Creole of Mauritius
Margueritte Jeanne	26	4'11		Malgache
Clarisse Lafolle	21	4'10		Creole of Mauritius

<u>Source</u>: MA IG 59 No. 5353 Mr Ozille Majastre claim for 52 slaves at Diego Garcia

the north-east side. Captain Robert Moresby's survey, just over 50 years later (illustrated on p. 135), shows that the only substantive change in the meantime had been the establishment of a settlement there.

A *jouissance* was granted in 1828 to an inhabitant of Mauritius, M. Victor Duperrel, but by then, according to an official report made in 1826, he had been in occupation of the island for nearly twenty years. Indeed, as Chelin reports and we can confirm, such a *jouissance* was granted on 26 April 1808.[18] The provenance and number of slaves initially brought to the atoll is unknown, but in 1823 22 slaves were brought from Seychelles, all bar one being the property of a M. E. Nageon. Unusually, all these slaves' names are known (see inset below). M. and Mme Nageon themselves took passage to the atoll in the brig *Espérance* in June 1826[19] and by 1829 Duperrel and Nageon, between them employing 37 slaves, were both listed as proprietors, although no actual *jouissance* was ever granted to Nageon (see inset below for details). Subsequently, Victor Duperrel (not long before his death) registered five slaves, all labourers, while his son Alphonse listed nine slaves, of whom 41-year-old Charlot Bontems was a leper.

In a survey of Mauritius' lesser dependencies in 1828, the soil of Six Islands is described as

> far superior to any of the others and, by the great industry of the proprietor, he has turned it to great account having an excellent and extensive garden, furnished with every kind of vegetable and several kinds of fruit. The maize is finer than in any of the other islands. Cotton also grows very luxuriantly and of very good quality. The Establishment is on the largest island.[20] On all the islands there is very good timber, one is quite covered in Tacamaka; the different sorts of wood are the Bois Blanc, Tacamaka, Chauve Souris, Badamier and Faujyac.[21] Very fine water is to be found here in wells. In the middle of Lubin island is a large marsh. The produce is a little coconut oil and the Bambara.[22]

Cotton was also exported; for example, in October 1823, the Mauritius Gazette reported that the lugger *Brave* visited Six Islands and returned with a cargo of cotton, this being only one of several references to this ship's voyages there. When HM Sloop *Espoir* visited the island in 1828, Capt. Greville found that 'the Blacks were healthy, well fed and not overworked' with only one case, quite dire enough, of oppression. Nyers Gertrude, who appeared unhappy and complained to the visitors of the treatment she had received, 'showed marks of severe, tho' not recent punishment'. Alphonse Duperrel, Victor's son, admitted to having caused her to receive 150 stripes with the stalk of a coconut frond, for making false allegations against him, with a view to having his own father remove him from the island. Scipio, another black person, confirmed Duperrel's account.

Slaves shipped to Six Islands on 30 January 1823 aboard Le Brave

Théophile Barbé	Louis Layette	César Jules
Fidèle Amant	Thilemaque Maque	Amis Amitié
Eole Vent	Alexis Alix	Philemon Magdelon
Jacques Maria	Marcia Maria*	Neptune Claude
Charlot Crabe	Fusil Cassé	François Bonti
Zamor Songois	Gertrude Suzette*	Paul Victime
Baptiste Victime	Jean Louis Victime	Lisette Louison*
Gustave Louison	Lamour Benet	

*females

All bar the first-named individual are listed as the property of M. E. Nageon. Théophile Barbé is listed as belonging to M. V. Duperrel

Trois Frères/Three Brothers

This heading requires clarification. As explained in Chapter 3 (p. 40), de Manne-villette used the term 'Trois Frères' to distinguish what are now known as Eagle, Danger and Sea Cow from Six Islands, known to the British as Egmont. The three tiny islets to the north of Eagle, now known as Three Brothers, were referred to as such in the 18th century by Lt. Blair but went unnamed in Lislet-Geoffroy's chart. Thus, when a M. Drieu and two Hulard brothers were granted a *jouissance* for this area on 13 May 1813, they were given *Permission de s'établir sur les Six Ilots dit les Trois Frères au nord de l'Ile de Diego Garcia.*[23] Throughout the time these islands were exploited, the enterprises concerned bore the name Trois Frères. From the start, however, Eagle Island was the base for exploitation of all of them; it was not only the largest, but the only one offering usable anchor-ages; one was on its west coast, only safe during the period of south-east winds; the other, on the eastern side, required negotiation of a narrow gap in the reef on the north-east point of the island, into a shallow lagoon. Concerning what we now know as the Three Brothers, identified separately as North, Middle and South Brother, two at least had at some stage been identified as 'Ile de la Terre' and 'Ile Diable'. They could only be approached in small boats in calm weather. Eagle Island alone was inhabited continuously.

How quickly the concessionaires acted to make use of these islands is uncer-tain. The earliest population counts state that there were 25 slaves there by 1818, a number which had grown to 34 by 1824. This followed transfer of the conces-sion in May 1823 to M. André Maure, who went regularly to the islands, perhaps for the first time in 1820.[24] Of those named above, it appears that Maure must have managed the islands as well as being holder of the *jouissance*, for full details of his workforce in 1826 are available (see inset overleaf for details).[25] Comparison of this entry with the slave register of 1830 reveals the birth of another member of the Legère family – Anastasia born on 15 June 1828 at Trois Frères, and of Juliette Aurore in 1827 and siblings Louise and Thomy Françoise in 1830 and 1834. The 1826 register itself provides a glimpse of family relationships, in par-ticular the absence of husbands. Clarissa Harlove, for example, a 35-year-old Malagasy woman, evidently had six children, of whom four were born in Mauritius and 1-year-old twins at Trois Frères. Pauline Legère also had a child born on the island. These children were also among the first recorded and named 'natives' of Chagos. By the time of the next registration the slave work-force had received a single addition in the person of Prosper Jean, a 25-year-old Malagasy leper.[26] Four more lepers must have arrived soon afterwards, for in 1828 the total population of 43 is listed as including 5 lepers, as well as 1 white, 2 free persons and 35 slaves. André Maure at Eagle Island and Laurent Barbé both managed large slave workforces.

Slaves of Mr André Maure, of Three Brothers island

Name	Age	Height	Remarks	Place of Birth
Clarisse Harlove	35	5'2		Malgache
Rosema Harlove	12	4'5		Creole of Mauritius
Frederic Harlove	10	4'5		ditto
Virginie Harlove	6	3'11		ditto
Noel Harlove	1			Creole of Trois Freres
Charlette Harlove	14	5'2		Creole of Mauritius
Belfort Harlove	1			Creole of Trois Freres
Pauline Legere	20	5'1		Creole of Mauritius
Belisaire Legère	2			Creole of Trois Freres
Jeanne Day	24	4'11		Creole of Mauritius
Larue Day	21	5'2		ditto
Lafleur Maria	24	5'1		Mozambique
Lafortune l'Endormi	41	5'7		ditto
Desire Figaro	29	5'4		ditto
Aaron Francois	30	5'3		ditto
Alcindor Coco	32	5'6		ditto
Jupiter Jupin	37	5'6		ditto
Isidore Isi	32	5'2		Malgache
François Arndua	40	4'11		Creole of Mauritius
Euphrasine Amota	32	5'1		ditto
Marie Louise Badoteuse	40	5'2		Creole of Bourbon
Adeline Françoise	18	5'1		Creole of Mauritius
Marie Louise Marroneuse	24	5'6		ditto
Marie Joseph Aurore	18		Leper	ditto

As regards production, Maure set up equipment for producing coconut oil, but seems also to have investigated other possibilities. Sea Cow island, which Blair had dismissed in 1786 as '…an Inconsiderable Spot covered with jungle' had been found to possess 'a small cove, where cocoa trees, fish and tortoise are in great plenty'. As to Danger Island, rarely mentioned except in relation to the risks it posed to navigators, it was many years before ways were found of landing safely and exploiting what Blair had described (see p. 37) as its 'thick wood and a few coconut trees near the centre …'.

Peros Banhos

As in the case of Trois Frères, a *jouissance* for the exploitation of Peros Banhos – for fishing and the harvesting of turtle and coconuts – was granted in 1813 (on 12 July), to Messrs Bigot and Allin. Nothing is known about how the concession-aires set about the task of gathering coconuts from the many islets at the edges

Ver Huell *East Point establishment on Diego Garcia* (detail). Image courtesy Maritiem Museum Rotterdam.

of the atoll's huge lagoon or even where they set up their first establishment. Indeed, nothing more was heard of either. When the first report on the number of slaves employed was made in 1816, the total was sixteen, but this number had built up rapidly to 113 by 1827. The shipping records show that a frequent traveller to the atoll was Ozille Majastre, usually accompanied by one or more new workers, and in 1823 he took over the *jouissance*.[27] Werner, the Assistant Registrar, described him as having established 'a rather attractive oil and fishing enterprise', although another observer considered it only 'tolerably good'. Majastre already had establishments both on Diego Garcia and on Coëtivy Island and a nearly contemporary report includes a sketch of the machine he used there for extracting oil.[28] Its frame was much lighter than that of later devices operated by donkeys rather than slaves. The one here illustrated was also designed to be worked by slaves, as described earlier in this chapter. It would be some years before this task was left to donkeys alone.

Majastre's claim for compensation for 96 slaves (see pp. 132–33) in his possession on the very day of abolition provides us with a snapshot of an entire slave workforce which also offers intriguing details of family ties and of Chagos-born offspring: Majastre's head man was valued at £160. Altogether 48 male and 28 female field labourers were worth £7,260, while a group of ten 'inferior' labourers (seven male and three female) were estimated to be worth £440 and nine children under six years of age were together valued at £270. The names of his workers are typical of those found across the slave registers of the Mascarene islands at this time. The obligation to register a surname at a time when slaves were usually known only by a first name led some owners to record nicknames or descriptive adjectives ranging from negative characteristics such as 'Dormeur', 'Le Gros', 'Moribonde' to the more positive sounding 'L'Utile', or the purely descriptive 'Petit' and 'Pêcheur'. A number of owners derived slave surnames from the first name of a parent; hence we find many examples in the workforce on Chagos such as Julie, François, Rosette, Fanny, etc. Some owners lazily created surnames out of the initial three letters of first names – hence Isidore Isi above.

Salomon

The first *jouissance* for Salomon's eleven islets was granted in 1813 to Jean Mallefille, but transferred in 1817 to Messrs Théodore and Pierre François Allain. Following the death of Pierre François, a British official, William Stone, obtained in 1822 the concession to the four 'Western' islets (Boddam, Diable, Anglaise and Passe), leaving Théodore's widow with seven 'Eastern' islets, only two (Takamaka and Fouquet) being of any consequence whatsoever. Interestingly, the concessionaires had differing objectives. Mallefille aimed to engage in coconut extraction and turtle exploitation, whereas the Allain brothers wanted to 'plant coconuts and to provide salted fish and seals'. Perhaps it was these contrasting objectives which made possible the shared exploitation, but, whatever the initial reasoning, this curious arrangement remained in place, though individual holders changed, until 1865.

When Lt. Blair visited Salomon in 1786, he was much impressed by the quality of its soil and timber, as well as by the absence of rats (see p. 38). Werner, in 1827, took a similarly favourable view, noting also that the lagoon 'presents an excellent anchorage to vessels of moderate burthen'. In that year, the population amounted to nine slaves, all of them the property of Stone or his single supervisor.[29] It is puzzling why an atoll so well endowed should be exploited so slowly. Part of the answer may lie in the curtailment of Legour's investigations (see page 90); he had been expecting to spend a further month there, perhaps reconnoitring where best to place a settlement, as well as harvesting timber, fish and turtles (with or without the concessionaires' permission is unclear). A second explanation could be that the atoll's tricky entrance and multiplicity of coral heads presented problems too difficult for the first concessionaires to solve.

The Chagos leper settlement

As we have seen, Diego Garcia had long been regarded as suitable for quarantining lepers and even curing them. That practice continued under British rule. However, by the early 1820s both the plantation proprietors and lepers on Diego Garcia had been complaining about their position. The *propriétaires* were consulted and, as might be expected, ascribed any such problems to the misbehaviour of the lepers. These representations resulted in a new Regulation promulgated in 1824, setting out rules applicable to all concerned.[30] The spokesman for the Diego Garcia proprietors in the framing of this Regulation was Lapotaire, proprietor of the Pointe Marianne plantation.

The main requirements were that lepers should keep to the areas reserved for them, and not allow their animals to stray; specifically they were forbidden to forage for firewood, coconuts or honey, or to cut growing timber; while encouraged to establish beehives and keep poultry, they were not to keep pigs (on the grounds that pork was bad for people in their condition); and penalties were laid down for transgressions: incarceration for a first offence, with up to fifteen lashes for any repetition. The plantation owners, for their part, were to allocate sufficient space for each leper to have at least 50 coconut trees; they were to provide each with 30 pounds of rice per month, against repayment for those able to make it; and, to the extent possible, each leper was to receive a pound of turtle meat each day (all turtles captured were to be regarded as the property of the plantation manager, with whom rested responsibility for distribution of its flesh and ensuring that all of the blood was reserved for lepers). Other provisions dealt with the reporting responsibilities of the owners, ship captains and police, who had to see to the transfer of lepers from Mauritius. The Government reserved to itself an additional sanction: the despatch to Middle Island of persistent offenders among the leper colony. In addition, the Governor, Sir George Lowry Cole, appointed Le Camus, Lapotaire's *régisseur*, to be the Government Agent (*Préposé*) on the island, with the primary duty of restoring peace between the lepers, the slaves and the proprietors.[31]

Cayeux (*aîné* i.e., the elder), owner of the East Point estate, had left the island in 1818, never to return. This gentleman had however left for the successive *régisseurs* who ran his plantation his own written instructions, of which only two full paragraphs survive, one requiring that those lepers who were free men be placed in a separate area at the northern end of the island, with a proper fence marking the boundary with Cayeux's younger brother's estate, the second that the *régisseur* ensure that the police enforced this provision, when allocating new arrivals to the various establishments – it was clear that the small numbers of free men among the lepers had been less than amenable to the demands of the plantation managers. A footnote required the *régisseurs* to provide maize grown on the island, rather than rice, for the lepers and, when maize was not available, to limit their rice ration to 8 ounces daily, reserving most of the rice for his slaves.

However, reports of maltreatment continued to be received, even after the visit by Werner and Hoart (Government Surveyor) in 1826, perhaps because that Commission did not concern itself particularly with these unfortunate beings. They merely noted *en passant* that Diego Garcia 'has for many years been the Depôt for Lepers and must formerly have been an eligible situation, as at one time great quantities of Turtle were taken, but latterly they have become extremely scarce'.

It is not clear whether the Werner Commission sent to examine the Dependencies in 1826 had included John Beachcroft Dixon, the Assistant Registrar of Slaves in Mauritius. However, this individual quit the colony that year and penned a 125-page tirade to the Colonial Secretary. The logic and legibility of this document leave much to be desired, but it includes a passage on the condition of the Diego Garcia lepers which appears to reflect first-hand observation: 'They stepped forth like troups of Spectres, so deeply had disease and famine entered into their very souls'. Dixon goes on to say that they had no food and no turtles, and quotes an Italian proverb *in terra di ciechi beato chi ha un occhio*, which is used to convey the idea that where conditions are bad even mediocrity can be considered satisfactory. Perhaps it was this passage that caused inquiries to be set in train. The Police Commissioner was to report on the numbers and distribution of lepers in the islands; the Chief Medical Officer was to advise on treatment, including the efficacy of turtle meat; and the Admiralty authorised the despatch of the sloop HMS *Espoir* to visit Diego Garcia, Seychelles and other named islands (none in the Chagos). In May 1829, the new Governor, Sir Charles Colville, reported the results and the action he had taken.[32]

By 1827, there were 85 lepers in the Chagos, 53 on Diego Garcia, of whom 39 were slaves; in Trois Frères, 17, 13 of them slaves; in Peros Banhos, 15, all slaves. When the *Espoir* made her visit in the following year, Capt. Greville was horrified by the condition of the lepers at Diego Garcia and found himself unable to discern much difference in the treatment of the lepers under the care of any of the three managers. All three were abominable. The lepers at Pointe Marianne were in 'very uncomfortable, wretched conditions'; though receiving the amount of rice stipulated by the Government, they were only rarely given small quantities of turtle, while the trees in the areas allocated to them rarely produced even the annual average of four coconuts found on Diego Garcia. Those on the elder Cayeux's estate were confined to an area where a single nut per year was all that could be expected. 'I must conclude by observing,' wrote Greville, that the lepers appear in want of every common necessary either for the amelioration of their dreadful disease or to make life even a tolerable burthen. There are 68 [slave] lepers on the island, 61 of them without clothing, without medicines or medical aid, and without the smallest rag to cover their sores; the remaining seven are government slaves and annually receive clothes from Mauritius.

The ship's Surgeon was even more graphic. Several of the lepers, he 'lamented to state', having lost part of their hands and feet, were confined to their huts which were totally unfit for their accommodation … while

those who are able to walk about are compelled to work and one of them, who was old, infirm and had lost nearly all his fingers and toes, bore marks of severe and recent punishment, which he incurred by having stolen some articles of clothing from one of his comrades; in short they all loudly complained of their treatment.

Dixon's infernal imagery had not been at all far-fetched.

Scientific interest

It was not mentioned in the report that the small group of leprous Africans and persons of mixed race resident on the 'oil islands'[33] of the Chagos archipelago were at this time the object of study and discussion by leading men of science of the day. Medical practitioners grappling with various ill-understood diseases found much of interest in the alleged cures employed on the remote atolls and the management of the afflicted.

As a result of the scientific interest in understanding and treating leprosy, observations made by visiting medical men to the Chagos islands were collected and stored by the Royal College of Physicians in London, where they can still be consulted. While most of these papers offer lengthy, and largely erroneous assumptions about the causes of the disease, they do provide further insights into life on Chagos at this time. For example, a letter preserved in the College's library, co-signed by T. T. Jones, surgeon to the *Espoir*, and R. McMath, dated 26 August 1828 at Diego Garcia, provides interesting assessments both relating to lepers and to slaves more generally. A few days after visiting the estate of Lapotaire, Jones and McMath noted approvingly, 'we did not detect a single case of venereal nor have we any reason to believe that more than two of the total number have ever been afflcited with that disease'; cases of hernia and rheumatism were however noted. They also observed that, during their stay on the island, the condition of the lepers had improved; 'the sores having healed'. They were adamant, however, that this was more likely to be due to the 'climate' rather than to use of 'turtle':

this change, in our opinion, is to be attributed solely to the influence of climate as they have had no medical treatment here and turtle, however salutary its effects may be in this disease, being scarce has been too seldom administered to have had any share in promoting their recovery.

More striking was their comment as to the evidence of corporal punishment of slaves, and the neglect of the welfare of slaves and lepers alike:

> Their diet consists chiefly in rice, one pound being allowed to each daily ... being also much in want of clothing and other necessaries they were dissatisfied with their present situation.
> On the 21st inst we visited the estate of Mr ... Several of the [slaves] were aged; and a very great proportion have the marks of severe punishments tho few seem to have been inflicted recently. They complained much of being overworked and not being well fed ... They are employed collecting coconuts and working at the oil mills ... We lament to state that we found the lepers here objects of commiseration, several of them having lost parts of their hands and feet, were confined to their huts (which were totally unfit for their accommodation) and appeared to be in want of every comfort not having dressings or bandages for their sores. On a third estate the lepers are in no better condition and we recommend that a medical person should look after them.[34]

Other documents in the Royal College's collections provide some statistical information as to the size and characteristics of the leper establishments on Diego Garcia. These indicate that at least seven white men (some of whom we have already encountered) had been part of the leper community on the island. A letter dated 21 January 1829 named those still living as Messieurs Gerardot, Treize, Ternel, and Achemain. Three others – Caret, Roblet and Lenpoen, were deceased. There were in addition a number of persons whose designation was that of 'free coloured', i.e., of mixed race. They were named as Albert, Rapp, Hypolite, Launai, Philogène, and Charles Fleury. Three of their number were also listed as deceased: Privat, Becquet and Narcisse. A third category of leper was given as that of 'convict', and the names: Sansat Chan, Sacordat, Conderda and Shankoo, suggest that at least two persons of Asian origin were among the number. Two men – Leveillé and Allison – were described as 'African Invalids' – this designation suggests that the men were among the number of 'liberated Africans' taken from slave ships by British government cruisers and 'freed' into long contracts of government service at the British-held islands of Mauritius and Seychelles.

A separate leper establishment at Eagle Island also included four persons of colour named as Pitois, Cadet, Alfred Dupont and Armand – the last-named died in November 1827. The total number of lepers domiciled on three separate establishments on the oil islands (not including a fourth at Providence Island,

Seychelles) had been given as follows:

Table 6.2   Lepers on Chagos, 1827

Dependency	Whites	Free Persons*	Convicts	Slaves	Total
Diego Garcia	4	5	5	39	53
Trois Frères		3		14	17
Peros Banhos				15	15

Source: RCP/OFFIP/4000/2 John Furness, Chief Constable of Police, Port Louis to G.A. Barry, Chief Secretary to Government.

*These would have been people of African descent freed from slaving vessels by the Royal Navy.

Making amends

Clearly, the dispatch of lepers to remote islands run by absentee concessionaires, where even the uncertain benefit of turtle meat was wanting, had been shown up as indefensible. No one could accuse a hard-bitten naval captain of uncalled-for solicitude. It was however noticed by the Surgeon's assistant that the health of some of the lepers did improve during their time spent on Diego Garcia, notwithstanding the absence of turtle meat; it seemed that the climate at least did have some beneficial effect. What then was the view of the Chief Medical Officer? Unfortunately, this official never got round to answering the Governor's question before retiring. Dr Shanks, his acting successor, took the view that the risk of contagion was not sufficiently serious to warrant the victims' exile and separation from their friends, family and medical care; better that the lepers should be accommodated together in one place, where they could be cared for and supervised in an adequate manner. Responding to this advice, the Mauritius Chief Secretary wrote to the Agent General in Seychelles to propose that Ile Curieuse be used for this purpose. This proposal was accepted and a contract to transport the sufferers put out to tender.

The owner of the *Hebe*, an English brig, won the contract with a bid of £400. She sailed from Mauritius on about 7 September 1829, reaching Diego Garcia a month later. Shortly after anchoring she was driven ashore in a gale and, with a plank stove in, immediately filled with water. After being made watertight once more with the assistance of the 'Blacks' on the island, she set sail on 30 October, carrying 37 lepers (3 others having absconded)[35] and picked up 3 from Eagle Island, 4 from Trois Frères and 15, plus 1 child, from Peros Banhos. En route, the *Hebe* passed Danger Island, where three lepers (the three absconders, perhaps) were reported to have been wrecked, but could not get close enough to pick them up. The vessel left for Mahé on 6 December, after a delay resulting from her crew's refusal to proceed until she had been made more seaworthy. She arrived there on 23 December. The 60 lepers were then duly transferred to Ile Curieuse, where proper preparations had been made for them to join the sufferers already installed. The Government Agent in Seychelles, Mr Harrison, had prepared a full list of all that would be required in terms of accommodation, clothing and utensils of every kind, to enable the victims to be so far as possible self-sufficient, with regular medical supervision. Subsequent inspections showed that these initial good intentions were properly fulfilled, providing an honourable end to a tragically misconceived and appallingly executed episode in the history of the Chagos.

Thus, to sum up, on the eve of the abolition of slavery in Mauritius and its dependencies, the total population of Chagos was approaching 500. The main activities were the gathering of fallen coconuts for de-husking and export or for processing into oil. Apart from the little that could be grown on the islands, all supplies had to be brought from Mauritius in ships chartered for the purpose, including the staple diet of rice. We have already described some of the hazards involved, but the capriciousness of the sea conditions between Mauritius and the Chagos was proving to be a constant source of anxiety. Experiments were being made into the islands' suitability for growing other cash crops, in particular cotton and maize, the latter also serving as food for the slaves, when supplies of rice ran short. Some of the abundant fish stocks were being caught and dried for sale in Mauritius. The provision of supplies of coconuts, wood and water for passing ships also earned money for the concessionaires. While poultry and pigs were shown to flourish on a diet of *poonac*, the once abundant green turtles were succumbing quickly to over-exploitation. Such information as exists suggests that the conditions in which the slaves lived were not only necessarily spartan, but often wantonly brutal. The concessionaires, once they had set up their settlements, tended to delegate local control to whatever individuals were prepared to undertake such work, well knowing that legal redress for criminal behaviour was all but unknown. It must be assumed that some profit was derived from the activities undertaken, including price manipulation in Port Louis. Certainly, Mauritius had need of coconut oil, which the Chagos islands, by virtue of being outside the hurricane zone, were well-placed to supply. However, the fairly frequent changes among concessionaires and the periodic abandonment of settlements suggest that profit was not easily achieved. These were conditions that, however distant, could not be tolerated indefinitely by any public authority having pretensions to civilised conduct.

Notes to Chapter 6

1 For example, two such, Philip Beaver and Charles Telfair, squabbled over the concession of St Anne and Cerf islands.

2 Lislet-Geffroy, J-B, *Memoir and notice explanatory of a chart of Madagascar and the North-Eastern archipelago of Mauritius*, 1819.

3 TNA CO 167/206, Printed Report of the commissioners of inquiry upon the slave trade at Mauritius, 1 June 1829, p. 33; further details are available in Appendix No. 62 of the report.

4 Allen, R.B., *A Traffic Repugnant to Humanity: Children and slave trading in the Southwestern Indian Ocean, 1770-1830* Conference on Slavery and Unfree Labour: Children and Slavery, Avignon, 19-21 May 2004.

5 TNA CO 167/108, 4 August (No. 58) report on dependencies.

6 Chelin, J-M., *Les Ziles La Haut* 2012 (privately printed). This careful examination of the contemporary records reveals, for example, that Pierre François Allain, who obtained the concession to Salomon in 1817, had captained a ship visiting Diego Garcia in 1812.

7 Chelin, *op. cit.*

8 Fraassen, C.F., and Klapwijk, P.J., *op. cit.* A piaster was worth about 2.2. guilders, roughly equivalent to USD 1.

9 As time passed, 'calou' (as it came to be spelt) became more sharply distinguished from the more fermented and alcoholic drink known as 'bacca'. A detailed description of the recipes for each is to be found on pp. 330-331.

10 This 'clearing' is, as some later maps showed, about one third south of the top of the island's eastern limb, just north of Cust Point (see map on page 503), where the island rim is still very narrow.

11 TNA CO 167/63.

12 TNA CO 167/63 and MA PP 1828 (205) Slaves in the Mauritius pp. 40–55 Enclosure 2 'Statement of the No of Slaves shipped from Mauritius since 20 May 1818 [the earliest date of any record extant in the custom house of Port Louis relative to the embarkation of slaves] down to the present period; distinguishing their sexes, the names of their owners, the names of the vessels on which embarked, and place of destination.'

13 Chelin, J-M *op. cit.*, p. 13, reports that Lapotaire employed 100 slaves on Diego Garcia to provide copra for his group's 12 oil mills at the Isle of France, where the Cayeux brothers set up 6 oil mills soon afterwards. Evidently, these must have been established before permission was granted to produce oil at Diego Garcia (for the reasons explained on page 78).

14 Government Gazette of 22 October 1819, quoted by Chelin *op. cit.* (p. 19). Major General Darling was administering the government in the temporary absence of Farquhar.

15 Dussercle, R. *Agalega: petite île*, General Printing & Stationery, Port Louis 1939, (p. 75). Agalega, 800 nautical miles NW of Mauritius, was second only to Diego Garcia as a producer of coconut oil. Its two closely adjacent islands suffered two inherent problems: very difficult access and, unlike the Chagos, periodic hurricanes.

16 MA PP 1826/7 [110] A Return of the Number of all the Islands which come under the denomination of Dependencies of Mauritius. Except where otherwise stated the statistics in this chapter are taken from this source.

17 MA IG 59 No. 5448 Greffe of Mr Treize, Habitant à Diego Garcia who has 2 slaves.

18 Chelin, J-M. *op. cit.* (p. 12).

19 *Mauritius Gazette* new series No. 64.

20 i.e. Ile Sudest, where Moresby's 1837 map shows it. The same statement regarding superior soil was also made of Salomon.

21 Presumably *Fauxgaiac*.

22 Werner Report, 1826. It has been stated that Bambara is a kind of groundnut, *Voandzeia* (or *Vigna*) *subterraneana*, the plant resembling that of peanut, but the nut being smaller and more like a bean, but elsewhere the word is translated as sea cucumber, almost certainly the correct interpretation here.

23 MA LC 23. Permission to settle on Six Islands north of Diego Garcia.

24 For source, see note 12 above. The examples cited here and in Note 27, in which 'owner' signifies ownership of the slave(s), not the vessel, show that the concessionaires not only visited their islands periodically, but were habitually accompanied by domestic slaves.

> *7 August 1820 Vertu owner Maure 5 men and 5 women to Isles Trois Frères*
> *13 March 1821 schooner La Vertu owner Dombreux 1 man Isles Trois Frères*
> *24 May Schooner Vertu owner M.A. Maure 1 male 1 female Isles Trois Frères*
> *26 April 1822 Schooner Vertu owner M.A. Maure 1 male Isles Trois Frères, owner Madame Chopart*
>   *1 female ditto; owner Mr Bomaniere 1 female ditto*
> *3 August Schooner Vertu owner Reybaud 1 female Isles Trois Freres returned 18 June 1823.*

25 The 1826 Werner Report gives the total population as 43.

26 MA IG 59 No. 5452.

27 For source, see note 12 above

> *1820 1 August Schooner La Vertu owner Cayeux 1 woman Peros Banhos returned 29 Dec 1820*
> *1822 8 August ditto owner Majastre 2 females Peros Banhos*
> *1824 14 June Schooner Vertu owner Majastre 1 male Peros Banhos*
> *1824 19 September schooner La Vertu owner Majastre 1 male 2 females Peros Banhos*
> *1824 22 September Schooner Vertue owner Majastre 3 to Peros Banhos (not identified)*
> *1825 7 February Schooner Vertu Mme Ve Michel 1 female Peros Banhos;*
> *3 May Schooner Vertu Mr Majastre 1 female Peros Banhos*
> *22 September Schooner Vertu owner Majastre 5 males Peros Banhos*
> *25 November Schooner Vertu owner Majastre 1 male 1 female Peros Banhos.*

28 AN 3JJ/358. The French description of the working of the machine is as follows:

> *Voici le croquis de la machine bien simple qui sert à broyer l'amande du coco pour en extraire l'huile, lorsqu'elle a été préalablement cassé et étendue au soleil pendant dix jours.*
>
> *A Coetivi, les mortiers et les pilons sont en bois dur, les leviers sont mus par des noirs. A Galéga, ce sont de vieilles mules qui tournent la manivelle et les mortiers sont au font.*
>
> Source: Copie d'un Rapport à M le Contre Amiral de Hell Gouverneur de Bourbon sur les iles Galéga et Coetivi ainsi que sur les dangers portés sur les cartes à l'ESE des Seychelles entre les méridiens de 57 à 60 degrés de longitude orientale, 1841.

29 MA PP 1826/7 [110]. d'Unienville [M.C.A.Marrier], *1827 An account of the islands and islets comprehended under the name of Dependencies of the Island of Mauritius, showing their geographical position, the extent of their territory, their population and their civil and military establishments, where there are any*. [printed report to British government, in French and English, no publisher, copy in Rhodes House Library, Oxford. A Return of the Number of all the Islands which come under the denomination of Dependencies of Mauritius.

30 TNA CO 167/107, Enclosure 3 to despatch dated 20 May 1829.

31 Royal College of Physicians [RCP] OFFIP/4000/1 26 August 1828.

32 Despatch 35, dated 20 May 1829, in reply to Colonial Office despatch 7, dated 25 July 1828.

33 This first reference to 'oil islands' is misleading. As emerges from later references (see Subject Index), it began as an informal term for all of those Mauritius' Lesser Dependencies where coconuts were exploited, including the Chagos islands and Agalega, but also Farquhar and Coëtivy. These last were however transferred to Seychelles in 1903. It is worth noting that the Mauritian Catholic diocesan records for the Chagos are mostly indexed under the heading 'Iles Huilières' [grave accent on first e of the second word]'

34 The discrepancy in numbers suggests that eleven had died in the preceding year, but some, including the obstreperous Roblet and perhaps other free lepers, may have been returned to Mauritius.

35 Robert Scott, R. *op. cit.* p. 128.

7

Chagos in the Time of Apprenticeship

WITH the passing of the Slave Abolition Order-in-Council in February 1835, it became necessary to consider what should be done in Mauritius' dependencies. Sir William Nicolay, the Governor, proposed the appointment of Special Justices, one for the Seychelles and one

> for the remaining smaller islands. The duties of the latter can only be performed by occasional circuits; and, at the present season of the year, the navigation among these islands is exceptionally hazardous. In this extraordinary situation, all that can be done is to carry into effect the provisions of the 'Abolition Act' as far the circumstances will possibly admit. The number of apprentices on each of the islands alluded to and which are scattered at great distances, is as follows: Agalega 213, Coetivi 36, Diego Garcia 142, Peros Banhos 93, Rodrigues 165, St. Brandon 6, Six Islands 114, Trois Frères 31.[1]

No such appointment was made until 1838. In the interim, however, it was decided that a more exact survey of the Chagos islands should be undertaken, led by the Indian Navy's best qualified officer, Captain Robert Moresby. His maps and charts, several of which illustrate this chapter, remain unsurpassed. In addition, Moresby compiled a 'memoir' on the Chagos, which he discussed with and lent to Charles Darwin in 1839. Sadly, archival searches have as yet failed to yield any copy of this document. Moresby was however co-author of an essay composed in 1841 and subsequently published in 1845 under the title *The Surveys of the Indian Navy*.[2] The latter appears to incorporate material from his 'memoir', offering a lively, but impressionistic account of the prevailing situation, as a few quotations demonstrate:

> The Chagos abound with cocoa-nut trees, and their produce in oil is about 120,000 gallons a year, worth about 120,000 rupees. They are capable of producing much more. The oil is made in the common mill, such as is used in India, and worked by the negroes, who, when the Archipelago was surveyed by Captain Moresby, were

still apprentices. Their labours are assisted by asses, which animals appear to thrive well on the island, and breed very fast. It appears that the proprietors of the several estates contribute nothing to the revenue for their produce; but are under a contract to supply government at the Mauritius with oil at a certain price, and, in fact, no oil is sold there but by these government contractors; for instance, on the arrival of a vessel at the Mauritius from India laden with this commodity, the contractors immediately lower the price and offer to buy what has been imported by others. As little or no profit is allowed, the importers must either sell it at a loss, or take it to some other port. Small vessels, such as brigs of 150 tons, are sent from the Mauritius by the proprietors of the Chagos Islands. They generally make two trips during the fair season, bringing with them rice and provisions for the settlement; and return full of oil and cocoa-nuts, as also the refuse of the cocoa-nuts after the oil is extracted, which sells well at the Mauritius for feeding cattle and poultry.

The vegetable productions of these islands are very similar to those of the Maldives, excepting the Salomon Islands, which produce the timber called *guyack* and *tuttamaca*, famous for building, being hard and durable … Indian corn [maize] grows most luxuriantly, but the negroes have neither the time nor the inclination to plant much. Tobacco, also, flourishes, and a small garden, occasionally looked after, produces all the year round. Cabbages, greens, sweet potatoes, onions, carrots, turnips, leeks, garlic, and all the common vegetables cultivated in India, with limes and citrons, thrive well, but few are planted. Pompions and plantains grow wild and are good flavor. Of the bread-fruit tree, when Captain Moresby first visited the islands, they had none: but he brought about thirty young plants from Ceylon, which succeeded well, as did the Malabar yam. The cotton plant grows on any part of the group, and, when carefully cultivated, produces the finest cotton of a long fibre. There are several grasses on which sheep and cows thrive well. Captain Moresby left a few to breed from on the island of Peros Banhos …

The treatment of the negroes, both male and female, is described by Captain Moresby as, upon the whole, praiseworthy. Occasionally they were hard worked and badly fed; but the contrary was the rule. All the provision supplied to them by the proprietors consisted of a pound and a quarter or a pound and a half of rice per day, with a small quantity of spirits from time to time; the rest, such as fowls, pigs, fresh vegetables and fruit, the negroes found for themselves. They worked from sunrise to sunset for six days in the week; the Sunday was their own; yet tasks were frequently completed on this day, which had remained unfinished on the Saturday. Turning the cocoa-mills in the heat of the burning sun appears to have been the hardest labour they had to perform. Two men were tasked to grind sufficient cocoa-nuts to make twenty-six or thirty gallons of oil, which they could accomplish between sunrise and noon. Four hours sometimes sufficed for the task, when the sun's rays, being very powerful, caused the oil to flow more freely from the nuts. The negro slaves might easily have been spared this labour, since asses, as we have seen, thrive well on the islands. When not working at the mills, the negroes and negresses were usually engaged in seeking cocoa-nuts in the woods as they fell from the trees; to collect 500 being cleaned from the husk being the daily task of each man and for a woman 300. Others were employed in breaking and exposing them to the sun.

There was but a small proportion of women to men. The laws of marriage were unknown, which may account for the scanty number of children; many of whom died young for want of care. According to one of the overseers, it was not an uncommon thing to suspect the women of causing their children's death by neglect, where they were not compelled to perform their maternal duties. There existed no means of instruction among these poor people, either religious or secular; they had scarcely an idea of a Supreme Being; and the overseers did not trouble themselves about them. Here, then, is a field, however small or obscure, for some missionary, who, without danger or difficulty, might confer very great benefit on humanity. He would, probably, have to begin with instructing the overseers themselves; Frenchmen, when removed from the public eye, having a strong tendency to degenerate into savages, as M. de Tocqueville frequently admits. Of course, the negroes on the Chagos group are now free – that is to say, nominally – though we entertain no doubt that, if their condition were inquired into, very little change would be found to have been effected in it.[3]

Moresby also had interesting remarks to make about the various animals, both wild and introduced, or which, in the case of cats, had become wild. Pigs and poultry, he noted, were 'the only stock to be obtained, but are not very cheap, because large quantities of them are annually sent to the Mauritius'. What is lacking from Moresby's account is any indication of the views and feelings of the workers themselves about the situation they were forced to endure; or of the character of the society of which they formed a critical part, as their labours transformed virgin forest into more or less productive plantations.

One reason for the ignorance of the British authorities in Mauritius was that, having no vessel of their own for asserting their power in the colony's Dependencies, they were reliant on such naval vessels as the Admiralty (or the responsible Admirals in the region) were ready to make available. For the Chagos, there was a further problem. Up to 1834, the Commander-in-Chief, East Indies Station, based at Colombo, included Mauritius in his area of operational responsibility; in that year, the Admiral in command of the Cape of Good Hope Station took over Mauritius, but not its many Dependencies. Nicolay had complained at once about the 'serious deficiency' resulting and, five years later, returned to the charge. 'The consequence [of these arrangements] is that there is no direct intercourse of vessels of war between this island and its dependencies, except upon the requisitions of the Governor for some special service, and these are of very rare occurrence.'[4] A month later, he reminded the Foreign Secretary that, while there had been an occasional ship's visit, no Admiral had visited Mauritius in the previous five years nor had any ship been stationed for the service of the Colony.

His plea for the latter solution, repeated by later Governors, fell upon deaf ears. Nevertheless, he had recently benefited from just such a 'special service'.

Apprenticeship at Chagos: the in-depth report of Magistrate Anderson

On 13 June 1838, one of the men sent out from Britain as Special Justices – to ensure that the rights of apprentice workers would not be neglected by colonial legislatures more used to upholding the will of slave-owners – was appointed to visit the island dependencies of Mauritius. His name was Charles Anderson. He was required to inquire into and report on the 'state and condition of the apprentices'. To enhance his role he was given a commission from the Governor 'giving you general jurisdiction upon each and all' of the islands visited.[5]

Nicolay was already becoming aware of the difficulty of overseeing islands which were only rarely visited by public officials and then for a very limited time period. He cautioned Anderson:

> it should be more the object of your mission to acquire information as to the actual condition and state of the apprentices and the treatment they receive generally from their masters and the overseers employed in the islands, with a view to ulterior improvement if required; than, by any temporary exercise of your authority upon the complaints that may be made to you either by overseers or apprentices, to hope to remedy the evils and grievances that may be represented to exist at the different islands.

It was therefore particularly important that the apprentices working at Chagos be helped to understand the terms and conditions of the Slavery Abolition Act. This law, which was designed to create a transitional period for both employers and ex-slaves, continued to bind the former slaves to their erstwhile masters, but now offered them rights which they had not enjoyed as slaves. Anderson was given the difficult task of explaining the reciprocal obligations of both parties. More joyfully, he was to inform the non praedial apprentices (those not employed in field labour, i.e., domestics) that on 1 February 1839 they would become fully free. Anderson was instructed to caution these newly freed men and women 'to avoid any neglect of duty, or unauthorized absence by which their liberation might be deferred for a much longer period'. Yet what would this mean in the context of Chagos where there was nowhere else to go?[6]

As well as acting to sort out any master-servant problems, and reporting on the food, clothing, hours of work and other details pertaining to the apprenticeship laws, Anderson was told, it will be desirable that you should acquire as much general information as possible with regard to the Islands themselves, the soil, climate, rains, wood etc, their capability of cultivation, facility of approach, nature of anchorage, and all other such facts connected with them, as may be useful to enable the government to come to an accurate conclusion as to their value and the future advantages that may be derived from them.

Anderson was to be accompanied by two police guards, and travelled aboard HMS *Leveret*. The visit of the magistrate helps to underscore how very isolated Chagos was from the huge socio-economic changes occurring in the British sugar colonies. In Mauritius the upheaval of slave abolition was accompanied, furthermore, by another revolution in the making – the wholesale importation of Indian labour which would dramatically affect the bargaining power of the ex-slave workforce. Nicolay apprised Anderson, through his Colonial Secretary, that this phenomenon did not yet apply to Chagos since he had 'refused to allow any Indians to be employed in the Dependencies on account of there being no means of ensuring due care and protection to them'.

Soon afterwards, the Colonial Secretary drafted a second letter to Anderson. He informed the magistrate that the Chief Commissary of Police had announced that:

he has reason to suspect that the vessels employed between Port Louis and the Minor Dependencies are in the practice of receiving on board and removing clandestinely from land, natives of India who have been brought from their country under engagements to serve for a fixed period in this island … the Governor request[s] that you will make inquiry into the fact in the several Islands which you are about to visit; and that you will warn the grantees of the several Islands or their overseers that by harbouring or receiving such deserters they subject themselves to the penalties of the law.[7]

Salomon

Anderson embarked on the *Leveret* on 18 June 1838. After visiting the Seychelles, the brig sailed for the Chagos archipelago from Curieuse Island on 25 July, arriving off Salomon on the evening of 9 August. He spent the next day exploring the atoll by boat, while the brig remained outside the lagoon's shallow entrance until he rejoined her in the evening. Six of the eleven islets he found to be 'mere specks with some brushwood upon them'. By contrast, the other five islands, which varied in size from ½ to 1½ a mile in length, were 'richly covered with trees of considerable dimensions, consisting of Fauxgaillac, Tatamaka, Bois de Feu and Bois Blanc'. Coconut trees were also found in abundance. Anderson thought it curious that despite the seemingly good soil the island group 'does not produce a single thing for the subsistence of man with the exception of the cocoa nut'. He also remarked that while the wood was of considerable value, it was 'fast decaying for want of cutting and thinning, and with only 10 free people on the establishment (3 of whom are women) the value of this group is lost'. The employees, he noted, were former government slaves from Port Louis. Their one year engagements specified a wage of $5 to $6 per month and rations.[8] They complained of 'having been left for many months without rations, and [of being] expected to work on Sunday'. Anderson noted that their contracts authorised Sunday working, but commented that the contracts were 'of a nature which in my opinion ought immediately to be discontinued as highly prejudicial to the encouragement of free labor'. When Capt. Moresby had surveyed the atoll the previous year, his only specific comment related to the export of timber. Apparently, the slow progress in exploiting this atoll's potential continued, for by 1851 the population had risen only to 34, although coconuts as well as timber were being produced. In fact, at the start of that year, the leaseholders asked to be allowed use of a plot of waste ground at the end of Hospital Street, Port Louis, for storage of their empty oil casks.[9] They claimed that the plot, located opposite the Indian immigration depot in the capital, was already being made use of by the holders of Agalega and Diego islands, and was large enough to accommodate their needs as well. Evidently, this development marked Salomon's adherence to the oil marketing cartel.

Source: British Library.

Peros Banhos

According to Capt. Moresby, as recorded in the 1841 (fifth) edition of Horsburgh's Directions for sailing to and from the East Indies, the principal establishment was then still on Ile Diamant,[10] with a smaller establishment on Ile du Coin. The latter provided a safer anchorage from the South East trade winds, while the former offered shelter from the North West. 'Plenty of poultry, fruit, vegetables, and pigs, at six Spanish dollars per cwt' were available for visiting ships; also water, which could be brought to the ships, using the establishment's flat-bottomed boats.

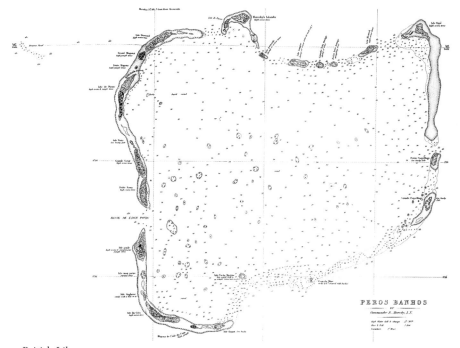

Source: British Library.

On 12 August 1838, Anderson visited these same islands. The brig reached an anchorage through the NW passage, about three miles from the establishment of 'Messrs Majastre' (presumably Ozille and a brother), which must therefore still have been on Isle Diamant. There Anderson enumerated 73 praedial apprentices, 12 free children, and 3 undeclared male apprentices, also gathering what he described as evidence of 'irregular transfers and improper classifications'. We can have some idea of who these people were by referencing Ozille Majastre's claim for compensation for 96 slaves in his possession on 1 February 1835. This document provides us with a snapshot of an entire slave workforce which also offers intriguing details of family ties and of Chagos-born offspring (see overleaf).

The Peros Banhos Slave Workforce of Mr Ozille Majastre, 1835

Name	Surname	Age in 1826	Height	Country
Euphrasine	Pona	31	5'2	Mozambique
Pauline	Pona	12	4'6	creole of Peros Banhos
Marie	Pona	10	4'4	ditto
Olivette	Pona	7	3'9	ditto
Joseph	Pona	born 11 Nov 1833		ditto
Virginie	Fanny	28	4'11	Mozambique
Isidor	Fanny	9	4'2	creole of Peros Banhos
Aurelie	Fanny	7	3'10	ditto
Auguste	Fanny	5	3'8	ditto
Antoine	Fanny	born 8 Sept 1834		ditto
Marie Anne	Fine	24	4'10	Mozambique
Milie	Fine	8	4'2	creole of Peros Banhos
Charles	Fine	3		ditto
Charlette	Fine	2		ditto
Marie	Françoise	34	5'3	Mozambique
Eugénie	Françoise	8	4'4	creole of Peros Banhos
Fifine	Françoise	7	3'10	ditto
Jeanne	Fanchon	24	5'2	Mozambique
Adèle	Fanchon	8	4'2	creole of Peros Banhos
Milie	Fanchon	7	4'4	ditto
Marie Rose	Fanchon	born 26 Oct 1833		ditto
Elisa	Fanchon	born 7 Sept 1834		ditto
Turlupine	La Cuisse	31	5'2	Mozambique
Eugène	La Cuisse	10	4'3	creole of Mauritius
Joseph	Philippe	35	5'4	Mozambique
Pierre	Lundi	23	5'6	ditto
Chaloume	Dimanche	32	5'6	ditto
Jupiter	Gai	27	5'4	ditto
Alexandre	Jean	25	5'6	ditto
Plantin	Bambou	21	5'6	ditto
Mathieu	Bezard	31	5'3	ditto
Crispin	Melomane	36	5'4	ditto
Jamier	Barbeau	34	5'2	ditto
Maconde	Bien Aimé	37	5'3	ditto
Panurge	l'Alerte	32	5'5	ditto
Alcindor	Dormeur	30	5'4	ditto
Myrtil	Bel Auteur	33	5'3	ditto
Jacques	Le Saint	38	5'2	ditto
Mardi	Trapu	25	5'6	ditto
Vesus	L'Ami	23	5'5	ditto
Sylvestre	Le Gros	24	5'6	ditto
Ambroise	Le Moine	25	5'4	ditto
Paul	L'Amant	35	5'7	ditto
Figaro	L'Utile	24	5'3	ditto
Bore	Le Vent	22	5'2	ditto
Achille	Charriot	28	5'8	ditto
Vaillant	Befort	23	5'3	ditto
Nicolas	Tuyau	26	5'4	ditto

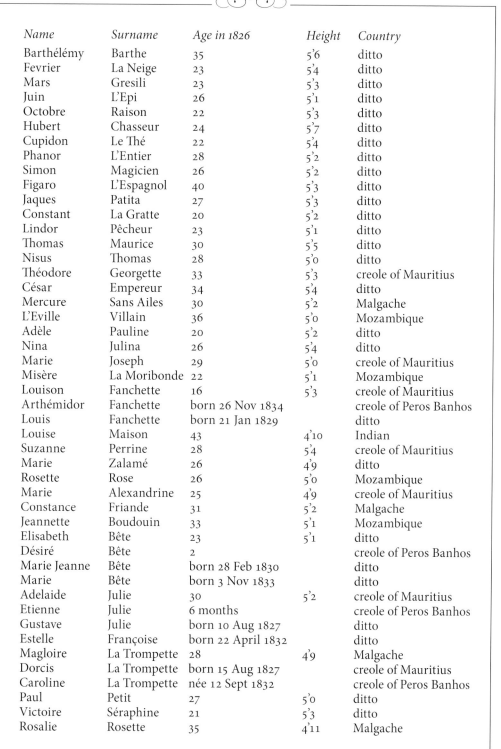

Name	Surname	Age in 1826	Height	Country
Barthélémy	Barthe	35	5'6	ditto
Fevrier	La Neige	23	5'4	ditto
Mars	Gresili	23	5'3	ditto
Juin	L'Epi	26	5'1	ditto
Octobre	Raison	22	5'3	ditto
Hubert	Chasseur	24	5'7	ditto
Cupidon	Le Thé	22	5'4	ditto
Phanor	L'Entier	28	5'2	ditto
Simon	Magicien	26	5'2	ditto
Figaro	L'Espagnol	40	5'3	ditto
Jaques	Patita	27	5'3	ditto
Constant	La Gratte	20	5'2	ditto
Lindor	Pêcheur	23	5'1	ditto
Thomas	Maurice	30	5'5	ditto
Nisus	Thomas	28	5'0	ditto
Théodore	Georgette	33	5'3	creole of Mauritius
César	Empereur	34	5'4	ditto
Mercure	Sans Ailes	30	5'2	Malgache
L'Eville	Villain	36	5'0	Mozambique
Adèle	Pauline	20	5'2	ditto
Nina	Julina	26	5'4	ditto
Marie	Joseph	29	5'0	creole of Mauritius
Misère	La Moribonde	22	5'1	Mozambique
Louison	Fanchette	16	5'3	creole of Mauritius
Arthémidor	Fanchette	born 26 Nov 1834		creole of Peros Banhos
Louis	Fanchette	born 21 Jan 1829		ditto
Louise	Maison	43	4'10	Indian
Suzanne	Perrine	28	5'4	creole of Mauritius
Marie	Zalamé	26	4'9	ditto
Rosette	Rose	26	5'0	Mozambique
Marie	Alexandrine	25	4'9	creole of Mauritius
Constance	Friande	31	5'2	Malgache
Jeannette	Boudouin	33	5'1	Mozambique
Elisabeth	Bête	23	5'1	ditto
Désiré	Bête	2		creole of Peros Banhos
Marie Jeanne	Bête	born 28 Feb 1830		ditto
Marie	Bête	born 3 Nov 1833		ditto
Adelaide	Julie	30	5'2	creole of Mauritius
Etienne	Julie	6 months		creole of Peros Banhos
Gustave	Julie	born 10 Aug 1827		ditto
Estelle	Françoise	born 22 April 1832		ditto
Magloire	La Trompette	28	4'9	Malgache
Dorcis	La Trompette	born 15 Aug 1827		creole of Mauritius
Caroline	La Trompette	née 12 Sept 1832		creole of Peros Banhos
Paul	Petit	27	5'0	ditto
Victoire	Séraphine	21	5'3	ditto
Rosalie	Rosette	35	4'11	Malgache

<u>*Source*</u>: MA IG 59 no 5355 Claim of Mr Ozille Majastre in the Island of Peros Banhos for compensation for 96 slaves in his possession as at 1 February 1835.

Anderson remarked that the apprentices grew some Indian corn, and spotted some banana and lemon trees. Otherwise the group produced only coconuts, generating 13,000 *veltes* (968,500 litres)[11] of oil annually, well below its potential. Anderson considered that the apprentices on the Majastre estate had light work and good rations of rice and tobacco, but that their living accommodation was poor, the amount of clothing supplied only half what the regulations stipulated, the hospital 'scarcely fit for a pig sty' and the management 'very indifferent'. He was particularly struck by the 'utter deficiency of medical attendance' and noted two urgent cases, one requiring surgical intervention.

Trois Frères/Eagle Island

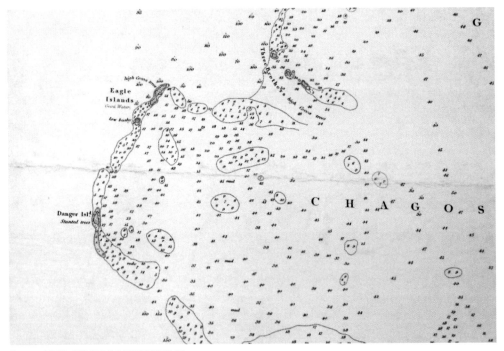

Source: TNA CO 700/MAURITIUS 18.

Adverse winds resulted in the *Leveret*'s taking four days to accomplish the 60-mile passage to Eagle Island, which Anderson reported to be known locally as the 'Île Des Marrons'.[12] Mr Maure's establishment was on its north-west side, safe only during the season of south-easterly winds, but with deep water so close to the shore that the brig could not anchor. En route, the magistrate had observed the 'Trois Frères' islets, covered in luxuriant coconut trees, but learned that Maure had, some time previously, abandoned, for want of labour, any harvesting of that part of his concession (it is clear from the phrasing of his report that

Anderson, like many others, was unsure how the separate geographical entities and the single concession of Trois Frères related to each other; and Capt. Moresby's chart, drawn, but not yet printed, solved the problem by labelling as Three Brothers the combined group of six islands. Coconuts and Indian corn were cultivated on the 2-mile-long Eagle Island, by 24 praedial apprentices. Seven children also lived on the island. Its annual produce, according to Anderson, was 3,000 *veltes* of coconut oil, 50,000 lbs of Indian corn with a few salt fish and some tortoise shell. He noted however, that with more labourers, oil production could be raised to 5,000 *veltes*. Relations between the manager and his workers were good and, in addition to their rations of rice and maize, they had space for gardens, on which poultry was reared in 'great quantities'. However, just as at Peros Banhos, the workers complained of the lack of clothing. Anderson found that the men had been given only a single shirt and pair of trousers, while women received a chemise and a petticoat annually: 'no coverings, hats or handkerchiefs'. So great was the desire for handkerchiefs, that the crew of the *Leveret*, whose offers of cash had been spurned, were able to obtain as much poultry as they wanted in exchange for them.

Six Islands (Egmont)

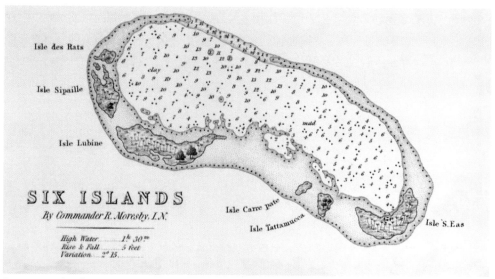

Source: British Library.

The next stop, equally brief, was at Six Islands. Here again, a short passage – 30 miles – took a long time – two days' sailing; and here too, access to the establishment, on Ile Sud-Est, was impossible; because of reefs, the *Leveret* could approach no closer than six miles. Duperrel's seventeen apprentices were 'treated with great liberality … They receive three suits of clothes annually. They are well fed and are allowed garden ground. Their huts are comfortable and well kept and their labor a very moderate task with which they are perfectly satisfied'. The establishment produced 2,400 *veltes* of coconut oil, 8,000 lbs of Indian corn, some tobacco and a few fruits. Pigs and poultry abounded. Anderson's impressions were in strong contrast to those of Capt. Moresby, who had surveyed this island only a year earlier and described it as being practically over-run by 600 pigs.[13]

> The utmost carelessness was exhibited towards these brutes. Nominally, they were said to be fed twice a day; that is, a small quantity of *punach* was thrown into troughs before some 200 or 300 half-famished animals, when a scramble took place, and the strongest of course got the lion's share … several large sows, with their litters, had taken up their quarters under the floors, which were raised about three feet above the ground, whence anything but sweet odours were emitted. The effluvia, combined with those issuing from a hundred other pigsties scattered in all directions, produced an intolerable atmosphere … The remains of a garden completely burrowed up by pigs seemed to confirm the impression of the extreme sloth and want of management prevailing.

With more in the same vein about the activities of innumerable bees, rats, cats and dogs, all engaged in Darwinian struggles for survival, Six Islands stood out from all the Chagos islands for incompetent management. It is unclear quite why an atoll so productive in 1828 (see pp. 111–112) should have declined so far into squalor. Perhaps it was because Nageon had left, taking his slaves with him: but Duperrel and his family were to remain its owners for a further half-century, keeping themselves to themselves. We shall encounter them regularly as this story continues …

Diego Garcia

The last island to be visited was Diego Garcia, described as 'much resorted to by whalers and vessels bound from England to India' on account of the abundance of water, firewood, pigs and poultry. Here Anderson spent two days examining the three establishments:

> Messrs Majastre's – containing 59 apprentices and 9 free children and producing annually 13,000 *veltes* of cocoa nut oil.
> Messrs Marcy & Enouf's formerly Florigny & Lafauche's, containing 48 apprentices and 9 free children and producing annually 16,000 *veltes* of cocoa nut oil.
> Mr Cayeux's containing 28 apprentices and 6 free children and producing annually 7,000 *veltes* of cocoa nut oil.

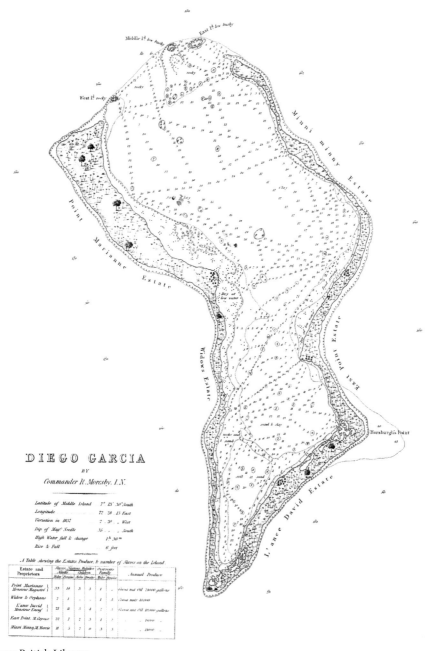

Anderson found the 'state and condition of the apprentices in all three establishments [to be] decidedly inferior to those of the labourers on the other islands.' The majority of the apprentices on the island were described as 'old, infirm and diseased people' and on each establishment Anderson found 'several deplorable cases of leprosy'. The magistrate stressed that most of the workers had come from Mauritius, where it had become customary to ship slaves off to Diego Garcia 'as a punishment'. Consequently, in Anderson's view, the apprentices were persons of 'indolent and idle habits'. This summary judgement of the workforce of the island is surprising given Anderson's otherwise diligent reporting. It also conflicts with the appraisal made by Capt. Lloyd in a private letter written at the close of the apprenticeship period who remarked that the 'most respectable' class of former slaves were those who had left Mauritius to establish themselves on 'Rodrigues, Diego Garcia, Agalega etc … This class are the most respectable because they export fish to Mauritius, and aid the proprietors of coconut oil establishments'.[14] Changes in the apprentice population resulted in some cases from transfers made by employers from their establishment on one island to another, or from one person to another. For example in October 1834 Marie Louise Bastia was transferred from P. Labauve Darifat to Le Camus and from Le Camus to O. Majastre. Zélie Cantal was also transferred to Majastre from Le Camus on 17 November 1834.[15] At the same time Anderson remarked that their allotted daily work was too severe, and ordered the task set to be reduced. He also criticised the want of medical aid, and the withholding of rice and clothing rations. He noted that nine former government slaves had recently arrived to work on Diego Garcia, for a wage of $8 per month with rations.

Anderson's overall conclusions

Anderson found no evidence of clandestinely introduced Indian labour and was cautiously positive about the prospects of the Chagos establishments weathering the coming challenge of the termination of apprenticeship. He believed it likely that – with the exception of Diego Garcia – the measures already in place to give workers an interest in continuing residence (allocation of space for gardening and permission to rear animals) would enable the management to obtain their labour as free men cheaply and easily. He considered that the work schedule of the small islands was much less onerous than the labour required on the sugar plantations of Mauritius, and concluded that the workers of the dependencies, including Chagos were

> a happier, a better conducted and, with some few exceptions, a more comfortable body of people, than any others of the same description which I have ever seen …
> I attribute it principally to so much of their own time being employed to their own advantage, to their very limited intercourse with strangers, and to being entirely deprived of … spirituous liquors, which have always been the bane of the apprentices of both sexes.

In concluding his report, Anderson adverted to the difficulty of navigation, the imperfections of existing charts, and the numerous shipwrecks which occurred in and around the reefs and shoals of the dependencies.[16]

If we put together the various figures for the population and economic activities of the Chagos islands, they can be tabulated thus:-

Table 7.1   Apprentices and Children at Chagos, 1838*

Names of Islands/Groups	Apprentices	Free Children	
Salomon's Group	10	??	
Peros Banhos Group	73	12	
Eagle Island/Trois Frères	24	7	
Six Islands	17	–	
Diego Garcia	135	24	
Total	>259	>43	>302

Source: TNA CO 167/204 Anderson Report, 1838.

*There are similar figures for 1835 in CO 167/182, folio 11 for apprentices, i.e., ex-slaves following emancipation: DG 142, PB 93, Six Iles 14, Trois Frères 31, but having no information about Salomon.

Table 7.2   Annual Production at Chagos, 1838

Names of Islands/Groups	Coconut Oil (veltes)	Indian Corn (lbs)	Salt Fish (lbs)	Turtle (lbs)	Tortoise Shell (lbs)	Shark Oil (veltes)	Fruits	Timber
Salomon	nuts abundant but neglected		?					plenty
Peros Banhos	13,000	small		?			scarce	
Eagle & 3 Frères	3,000	50,000	uncertain		uncertain			
Six Islands	2,400	8,000					scarce	
Diego Garcia	36,000						scarce	
Total	54,400							

Source: TNA CO 167/204 Anderson Report, 1838.

Reflections

Anderson's report provides little more than a snapshot of the situation prevailing in the Archipelago at this period. Rather oddly, he makes no mention of the reaction of either managers or workers to the news that the latter were no longer slaves. His visits to each island were, however, so brief that not much more could have been expected. What seems clear is that development of the islands' resources had made only limited progress; indeed, if his estimate of the amount of coconut oil produced was accurate, there had been a substantial reduction, from 120,000 gallons, as estimated by Capt. Moresby a year earlier, to approximately 90,000 gallons. Unfortunately, the records of Mauritius' trade with its Dependencies during this period make it impossible to obtain any clear picture of the amounts relating to the Chagos, let alone to its individual atolls. Anderson's remarks about shortages of labour suggest that the concessionaires may well have brought back some of their slaves to maintain numbers on their Mauritius estates. All the same, his comments about the problems of navigation and access to several of the lagoons were highly pertinent; and these were to prove permanent obstacles to profitable exploitation. Equally, his observation that the workers' relative contentment owed a great deal to the fact that much of their time was devoted to their private interests, with few temptations available, was perceptive as far as it went, but hardly indicative of long-term fulfilment. On the other hand, Anderson had no reason to suppose that the short-term contracts would be transformed by neglect into the emergence of an isolated island society or that the absence of medical care would be one of its continuing features. It would take another eighteen years for a clearer idea to begin to emerge of how the Chagos islands would be exploited and how its society would develop. It was not that nothing happened, merely that no official visitor would again venture there until 1856 and that there would then ensue a further gap of fifteen years before the next such visit.

Notes to Chapter 7

1 TNA CO 167/182. Despatch dated 16 February 1835.

2 Moresby, R. and Elwon, T., Commanders, Indian Navy, printed by order of the East India Company, Allen & Co, 1841; reprinted as 'Surveys of the Indian Navy', *The Foreign Quarterly Review*, July 1845. Much of this material reappeared in a work by Charles Pridham, published in 1849, *An Historical, Political and Statistical Account of Mauritius and its Dependencies*. The latter work is cited, for example, by Edis in *Peak of Limuria*, giving the impression that the account described the position as it was almost a decade later than was actually the case.

3 Moresby was not the only visitor to comment on the potential for growing food crops, other than the staple, rice. We speculate that there were two impediments: production on a scale to meet the needs of the whole population would have required additional labour with new skills and greater supervision; and great care would be needed to maintain the fertility of the generally thin soil.

4 TNA CO 167/213 Despatch No. 105 of 16 October 1839.

5 TNA CO 167/204 Colonial Secretary to Mr Special Justice Anderson, 13 June 1838.

6 TNA CO 167/210 Nicolay to Glenelg 17 May 1839 (61). Governor Nicolay expressed his regret, 'that the want of means of communicating with the minor dependencies of this govt, has hitherto prevented the promulgation in them of Her Majesty's Order in Council for terminating the praedial apprenticeship'.

7 TNA CO 167/204 Colonial Secretary to Mr Special Justice Anderson, 15 June 1838.

8 TNA CO 167/525 Enclosure to Mauritius Despatch No. 83 dated 5 April 1870. Many currencies were legal tender in Mauritius. In the early 1840s, the silver coins included Spanish, Mexican, South American, Sicilian, Austrian and United States dollars, as well as a Mauritian coin known as the Decaen dollar. Their value in sterling depended on the quantity of pure silver each contained. This varied from 4 shillings to 4 shillings and 4 pence.

9 MA RA 1135 A Louys, Bertin, Lemière & Plasson to Colonial Secretary 22 January 1851.

10 'Diamant' has nothing to do with diamonds, being the local Creole name for a species of small white tern, just as Yéyé, the name of another islet of Pros Banhos, is the Creole word for 'Sooty Tern'. We have

made no attempt to anglicise the names of these two islets..

11 *Veltes* were small casks, assumed to contain 7.45 litres of oil. The rather complex calculations of production and viability will be considered in a later chapter.

12 *Marrons* was the name given to slaves who had absconded and, if recaptured alive, were brutally punished. This nickname could indicate that Maure was an owner who offered banishment to the Chagos as an alternative.

13 Moresby did not himself name the island he was describing, but Scott, in his *Limuria*, made the identification. Scott and subsequent authors also ascribed these criticisms to Pridham (1846); the latter, however, was merely quoting Moresby without attribution, as can be seen from the work quoted more extensively in the final paragraphs of this chapter.

14 TNA CO 167/226 Captain Lloyd to Irving, 4 April 1840.

15 MA IG 59 No. 5353.

16 TNA CO 167/204 Apprentices in the Islands dependent on Mauritius: Instructions to and Report of Mr Special Justice Anderson to Colonial Secretary, dated 5 September 1838 and enclosed with Sir W. Nicolay's Despatch No. 105 of 23 October 1838.

8

Lives of Labour, Moments of Mayhem, 1840–1860

The Forties: out of sight and out of mind

IN MAURITIUS the joyful emotions of the day of final abolition – 1 February 1839 – were quickly followed by increasingly disquieting evidence that the slaves had simply been freed into what the coloured intellectual and journalist, Rémy Ollier called '*le plus affreux pauperisme*' (appalling poverty). Ollier used the pages of his mouthpiece *La Sentinelle* to decry the tactics used by the planter class – mass importation of Indian workers – to beat down the wages of creole labour. Unregulated before 1843, in that year the new government-sanctioned scheme of indentured labour brought thousands of Indians to Mauritius. By June 1844 Ollier was denouncing the policy of slave abolition in no uncertain terms:

> At the time of emancipation, most planters, on the basis of a generally accepted convention, offered their ex-slaves wages so pitifully low that the latter felt themselves under no obligation to accept. And what was the price of refusal? To be chased, on the very day they were given their freedom, from almost every one of the plantations.[1]

In the Chagos islands, it is likely that the upheavals of abolition and immigration caused fewer ripples initially, but the demographic revolution in train in the Mascarenes would inevitably be reflected in the smaller islands. An early report on the emancipated population was submitted by the Mauritius Surveyor-General, Captain Augustus Lloyd, R.E. Lloyd divided them into four groups or classes, one of which he described as 'sailing from Mauritius to Rodrigues, Diego Garcia, Agalega etc and living on the coastal strips reserved to the Crown (*pas géometriques*)[2] of these islands hunting and fishing etc. This class are the most respectable because they export fish to Mauritius and aid the proprietors of coconut oil establishments'. This description certainly underscores the continuing key role, utility and importance of ex-slaves to the upkeep of the oil establishments, but if this group were now to be classed as the most fortunate of the ex-slaves, it did not say much for the conditions and prospects of those who had remained on the main islands.[3]

Unfortunately for historians, very few observers other than the whaling captains visited the Chagos during the 1840s or even for most of the 1850s, a period during which the population gradually grew to more than 500. Admittedly, two surveys appeared, in 1848 and 1849, but both were largely recapitulations of material based on Capt. Moresby's information from a decade earlier.[4] The second of these (by an anonymous writer) does however deserve to be quoted briefly, since it conveys something of the atmosphere prevailing in the plantations.

> Incessant labour is more commonly the share of the negro, though intervals of partial rest occasionally intervene to break the monotony of weariness and toil. For the labour which renders these islands a mine of wealth to their proprietors, which causes the currents of industry to flow through the little archipelago, how is the negro rewarded? His daily pay varies from a quarter to half-a-pound of rice, with, from time to time, a wine-glass of spirits. It is necessary for him, therefore, to employ all his leisure hours in the struggle for existence; and fortunately the nature of the soil, its fertility, and the facility with which it springs into cultivation at the touch of the husbandman, render the task somewhat difficult [sic] of accomplishment … The negro apprentices, under the direction of their overseers, have erected commodious oil-stores and dwellings along the shores of the larger islands, whilst, in some localities, well-built and spacious boat-houses have been prepared for the convenience of the proprietors and their delegates in power, whilst the poor, laboring population must shift for itself and, out of the scanty leisure allowed, find food, habitation and every species of comforts which they can enjoy. We may expect, therefore, to find in such a community no trace of the progress of education … No attempt has yet been made to establish the foundation of better things, among these industrious but ignorant people, or, at least, what little has been only serves to exemplify how much more is needed to render them worthy of the country whose dependencies they are …

The Fifties: stirrings of official and commercial interest

It will be recalled that *jouissances* were held at the Crown's discretion. In 1849 Sir George Anderson, the newly-arrived Governor of Mauritius, was studying a number of applications to lease certain Seychelles island dependencies. He now sought permission to institute a system of longer leases, on the grounds that annual lease requirements, as envisaged in London, were impractical. Anderson explained, 'it is only by long leases – to persons of some capital and character, that any considerable improvement can be looked for either in the cultivation or condition of the Islands'. He noted the possibility that the islands could become valuable and yield a revenue, while in times of war they might 'become a refuge to hostile parties'. 'It is an object', he opined, 'to retain them – and an object to retain them at no cost to the parent state'.[5] Anderson was therefore instructed to take the following steps whenever an application was made for a lease in the Dependencies:

> … you will fix such a rent as you may consider to be fair and then give public notice in the Gazette of your intention to let it. If any other candidates beside the original applicant should appear you will put up the lease to public auction, but if there should be no competition you will grant it to the original applicant. In the first instance it would not be desirable to fix the lease at more than for ten years and a clause should be inserted authorising the resumption of the whole or any part of the land so let at any period if public service should require it, with compensation for improvements of any land thus leased.[6]

Since all the principal islands of the Chagos archipelago were occupied at this time, and seemed to be thriving, the Governor evidently saw no immediate occasion to apply the new policy. Indeed, later correspondence suggested that he believed the Colonial Office's instructions to be applicable only to the Seychelles.[7]

Not long afterwards, a larger, though related topic caught the Secretary of State's attention. It concerned the control of Crown lands around the perimeter of Mauritius, on which there had been steady encroachment. To study the issue, Anderson established a committee on which both officials and landowners were represented. One of its tasks was to 'investigate the nature and extent of existing *tenures en jouissance*', to achieve which the committee considered it would be 'necessary to ransack the public Archives, as well as those of the Land Court and the Surveyor General's Office … which would occupy much time …[and] would probably be difficult to execute with accuracy …'. The committee 'anticipated that His Grace [the Duke of Newcastle] would not require them to enter upon this difficult and almost hopeless task …'.[8] The result was that the question of *jouissances* in general dropped from view.

New sources of recruitment

The 1850s and early 1860s were a time of immense prosperity in the Mascarenes. With the global price of sugar rising, more and more land was brought under cane and the importation of Indian labour reached an all time high. Such was the demand for plantation workers that immigration schemes of many kinds were proposed. Plans to bring in Malagasy, Comorian and Chinese labour were mooted, and interest was shown in converting the slaves freed from Portuguese and French ships into 'liberated African apprentices'. Some of these new immigrants, with little local experience or contacts, would be among those contracted to work at the oil islands during these years. A concomitant development would have been increased demand in Mauritius for coconut oil, at the cheapest price possible, for the new arrivals.

In this period of heightened demand for labour in sugar-producing countries, the clandestine slave trade also resurfaced. The Royal Navy was active in intercepting Arab dhows and foreign – by this time chiefly Portuguese – ships carrying slaves. On numerous occasions in the second half of the 19th century, these 'liberated' slaves were brought to Mauritius and the Seychelles. The oil establishment manager-recruiters sought to supplement their workforce by securing some of the newly arrived 'liberated Africans' for the Chagos. In 1867, the Protector of Immigrants reported to the Colonial Secretary at Mauritius that 29 liberated Africans had been sent 'with their consent' to the Six Islands [Egmont] on a five-year contract.[9] African indentured immigrants were also recruited, but suffered by association with the slave trade, as when the French steamer *Mascareignes* arrived at Mauritius with 325 young boys from the east African coast. The *Mauritius Sentinel* reported the rumour, in its 1 February 1856 edition, that 'the 324 Africans introduced by M. Menon & Co., were bought by them, some for one or more lbs of gunpowder, and others for small sums of money'.[10] The presence on Chagos in 1859 of a small number of workers hailing from Johanna is an indication of the diverse immigration of these prosperous years. Johanna is the lesser of two main islands of the Comoros[11] and, at the time, was not only under British protection, but also had a coal depot much frequented by Royal Navy ships engaged in suppression of the slave trade. Similarly, some individuals were recruited directly from Madagascar to the Chagos, while the concern that Indians too might be taken there directly came to be realised in the 1850s, as we shall shortly describe. It is thus no accident that the population of the Chagos was steadily increasing, from its level of just on 300 in 1838 to nearly twice that number in 1861, with further growth to follow.

Table 8.1   The Population of Chagos Islands 1851-1871

	1851			1861			1871		
	M	F	Total	M	F	Total	M	F	Total
Diego Garcia	134	44	178	297	79	376	245	128	373
Peros Banhos	62	38	100	63	36	99	82	43	125
Salomon Island	31	3	34	36	16	52	66	33	99
Trois Frères	20	2	22	21	6	27	30	16	46
Six Islands	not enumerated			30	6	36	22	24	46
TOTAL	>247	>87	>334	447	143	590	445	244	689

Source: TNA CO 172/100 (1874 Blue Book, retabulated).

Alarm bells ring

While the numbers of workers in the Chagos might be on the increase, their conditions were self-evidently less well supervised than those at Mauritius, where magistrates and a 'Protector of Immigrants' were on hand to hear labourers' grievances. The workers, most of whom were illiterate, had to wait until their return and generally could hope to have their complaints heard only if they could afford to pay a petition writer. A group of ten workers at Peros Banhos managed to do just this when they sought redress for the failure to pay their wages. The following petition was drafted in September 1851 on their behalf:

> *Excellence*
>
> *Ont l'honneur de vous exposer très respectueusement les soussignés (au nombre de 10)*
>
> *Que s'étant embarqué comme labourers pour travailler sur l'Ile de M Duvergé Diégo dite Peros Banos qu'ayant rempli la mission depuis 2 et 3 années – Duvergé refuse de leur payer les 10 piastres….*

This rather makeshift French may be rendered roughly as 'Excellency, respectfully beg to submit on behalf of the undersigned (10 in number) that having been embarked as labourers to work on the island of Mr Duvergé known as Peros Banhos, and having fulfilled this work over a period of 2-3 years, Duvergé refused to pay the 10 piastres due'. Of the signatories (or those who marked the letter with a cross) nine were named as John Sanpath, Marie Orelie, Both Hyanth, Pascalle, Eloise Celina, Désiré, Désiré, Mozambique, and Estelle.[12]

The employees at Six Islands were to make the same accusation, to which the manager, Emile Régnaud's response was that they were paid in cash, but with deductions for purchases made in the company shop – a procedure wide open to abuses which remained unexposed for many years. Other forms of abuse were even worse.

Murder & mayhem in the Archipelago

As regards the illicit introduction of Indians into the Dependencies, Six Islands was, once again, involved. Between September 1854 and December 1855 no less than four deliveries arrived there from Cochin, involving in total 38 men, 4 women and 2 children. As none had experience of working with coconuts, the men were employed at wood cutting, clearing the coconut plantations and making roads, while the Indian women (who also received wages) were employed in clearing and burning the detritus along the plantation tracks.[13] The treatment of these people was to have very serious local consequences and to expose dramatically the results of a decade and a half of neglect by the authorities in Mauritius. We shall therefore tell their story in some detail.

Around the middle of 1856, an American whaling ship, cruising in the Indian Ocean, spotted a canoe floating in the sea. In it were six Indian men and a woman, all in a debilitated condition. They were landed at Salomon and eventually brought to Mauritius by a ship which happened to touch there. On arrival at Mauritius, the group explained that they had originally left Cochin, in a ship called the *Alexandre Auguste*, with the intention of coming to Mauritius as labourers. However the ship had taken them instead to Six Islands, where they had been compelled to land, and to work there, against their will, for about two years. During that time they were paid no wages for their labour and, they alleged, were subjected to such ill treatment that they had decided to escape in an open boat. When picked up, they had been at sea 21 days without any food. They stated that a number of their fellow countrymen, introduced under similar circumstances, remained at Six Islands where they were enduring very harsh treatment. Soon afterwards further disquieting news arrived from Chagos. It was said that the labourers on Six Islands 'had risen in revolt, had murdered the Manager, Paul Hugon, and had taken forcible possession of the *Alexandre Auguste*, which was lying there at the time'. The workers had compelled Captain Romain Rodrigues to take them back to India in his ship, and had appropriated a sum of about £900 in money, which they had found on board.

HMS *Frolic*. Image courtesy of NMM, Greenwich.

In November 1856 Governor Higginson duly reported these events to London, requesting that Commodore Trotter, naval commander at the Cape station, who was then at the island, be authorised to send HMS *Frolic* to the Six Islands to make further enquiries. The Governor asked Trotter to investigate the murder, but added that given the concerns about illegal importation of Indians from Cochin and the possibility that Indians might have been introduced illegally to the other islands, the *Frolic* should visit any of these (that is, Agalega, Diego Garcia, Coëtivy, Peros Banhos, Salomon Islands and St Brandon) 'more particularly as none of those Dependencies have been visited by a British ship of War for a number of years'. A separate letter was sent by the Colonial Secretary to the Protector of Immigrants asking him to investigate the report of the forced detention of Indians from Cochin.[14]

On 27 January 1857, before leaving Diego Garcia, Trotter prepared his report, based principally on information received from Mme Eve Albert Hugon, M. Pierre Dumazel (M. Paul Hugon's deputy) and the other creole residents of the Chagos. The summary of his findings was that the fifteen Indians concerned had been employed at the islet of Lubine cutting wood. They had a canoe with them which they used to return to the establishment periodically for provisions. In August 1856 Hugon visited them and found that very little progress had been made. On a second visit, finding no more work done, he struck the head-man with a piece of 1½ inch rope about 4 feet in length, which he generally carried with him. In response the Indians attacked him with axes and sticks. At first they could not overpower him, as he was a very strong man, but eventually he attempted to retreat, and was struck on the calf with an axe which brought him to the ground. Another Indian then struck him over the head causing death. They had then slit his throat, cut his feet and wrists off, ripped his stomach open, removed his entrails and placed them in his coat. The body had then been doubled up and buried head first in a hole about three feet deep. On the arrival of the *Alexandre Auguste* at Six Islands in September 1856, the Indians boarded and compelled the master to take them to the Malabar coast.[15]

Commander Lumley Peyton, the Acting Captain of HMS *Frolic*, also submitted a report from Diego Garcia on the same day. He stated that his ship reached Six Islands on 14 January where the labourers – seventeen men and one woman – were interviewed in the presence of Dumazel. Also in attendance was Thomas de Cruz, nephew of Capt. Rodrigues. The seventeen labourers were all creoles from Mauritius apart from three who were from Madagascar; some of whom had been on the island for years. Asked whether they had any complaints, the workers all replied yes, stating that they had not been paid since the previous July and were all anxious to leave for Mauritius. Their treatment at the hands of Hugon was also complained of, particularly his habit of stopping their provisions as a punishment. Peyton noted that during his four-day stay he frequently observed several of the labourers 'in a state of intoxication from drinking toddy'. Peyton nevertheless criticised the proprietor of the island for failing to send money by the *Sans Pareil* which had visited in December and suggested that Higginson should send a ship to take the labourers off the island.[16]

Meantime, in India, Capt. Rodrigues had finally come forward and made a deposition – on 23 December 1856. He stated that he sailed in his schooner from Mauritius on 20 September 1856 for Cochin, with instructions to call at the Six Islands en route. On his arrival he saw the oil mills working as usual and 'a gentleman dressed up to receive me' whom he guessed to be the overseer. However, on following that person into the house he was surrounded and cash taken from him. He was then compelled to navigate the schooner and landed between Allepey and Cochin on 30 September. Rodrigues claimed that he had failed to make a deposition earlier because he was in fear of his life. However he did write to Mauritius, and reported that Mr Ruffin, the agent at Cochin, had received a letter from there which had led him to persuade Rodrigues to make a deposition. Supporting statements were collected from crew members, and a number of the Indians who had been taken to Six Islands involuntarily also gave statements.[17]

By February 1857 the Colonial Office in London had received Higginson's despatches and had, after the event, approved of the sending of HMS *Frolic*. The officials there took the opportunity to request a full statement of the grounds for supposing that illegal introductions of Indian labourers had occurred and details of 'the means which exist for ascertaining from time to time what is going on in those dependencies'. It was pointed out (rather tardily, one might think), that 'no information seems to have been received at this Department, either in the form of Blue Book Reports, or other documents, concerning the state of those Islands or the means taken for the maintenance of law and order in them'.[18]

Dumazel and Mme Hugon had meanwhile returned to Mauritius where, in March 1857, they recorded statements in the office of the colony's chief legal officer, the Procureur Général. Dumazel explained that he went to Six Islands on 19 July 1855 as an overseer and remained there until January 1857. Five months after he arrived, Hugon replaced Régnaud as chief overseer. Eve Hugon confirmed that she had arrived with her husband at Six Islands in 1855, on 23 December. They resided at Chouette island [this seems to refer to what is more usually known as Ile Sud-Est] three miles from Lubine, which her husband had gone to visit at noon on 16 August. Dumazel explained that, after Hugon had failed to return from Lubine, he sent some creoles after him. He was then informed that the Indians from Lubine island had crossed over to the principal island by walking along the reef at low water and that they were in a very angry and excited state. He called together the creoles – seventeen in all – and asked them to protect the main house and Mme Hugon. The next day they were threatened by the Indians and, having no weapons, were obliged to accede to their demands. The Indians helped themselves to food and clothes and, when the schooner *Alexandre Auguste* arrived off Six Islands on 13 September, they shut up all the creoles in the camp and forced Dumazel to put on his best clothes and to walk about on the shore near the landing point. They also set two or three of the oil mills to work to give the appearance that all was in order. The crew of the schooner were nearly all Cochin men – the countrymen of the Indians at Six Islands.[19]

Statements were also taken from the Indians who had earlier escaped in the pirogue from Six Islands. Chaccoo, now working in Port Louis, had arrived on Mauritius with five men and one woman six months before. Describing their escape, he noted 'we took no food with us only 2 small casks of water. The casks leaked out before 24 hours were over'. The group had been twenty days at sea when they were picked up and taken to Salomon. He explained:

> we left Six Islands because we had been 2 years and 8 months there without receiving any wages and because we were beaten nearly every day by Mr Hugon the overseer. He used to beat us with a rope's end which he generally carried in his pocket. He made four men hold the arms and legs of those that were beaten. The arms and legs being extended spread eagle position … men were beaten till they fainted. Some of the men left at Six Islands bear scars … One day when Mr Hugon had beaten a creole named Gustave and Madame Hugon had remonstrated, Mr Hugon beat his wife for interfering … I heard the blows and saw Mrs Hugon a short time after sitting crying in a corner of the room.

An update on the case was sent by Higginson to Secretary of State Henry Labouchère in May 1857, and a number of letters were exchanged with the Government of India who forwarded information from the magistrate at Cochin, including the depositions of Capt. Rodrigues, of Alfred Perrier, an apprentice working on the schooner, and of Ochita, who explained how she and her son had been recruited and taken to the Six Islands, and how their requests to return home had gone unheeded. Ochita also explained that a black worker named Gregory had suffered an epileptic fit, had fallen into a fire and died. No other deaths had occurred while she had been working at the islands.[20] Finally, as far as the legal consequences were concerned, the dreadful story ended in June 1857 with the arrival in Mauritius of the newspapers from Madras. These reported the punishment at Cochin of Capt. Rodrigues for having kidnapped Indians from the Malabar coast and taken them to Diego; although initially considered too lenient, this was to levy a fine of Rs 1,200.[21] So much for Six Islands. However, the voyage of the *Frolic* also brought to light the state of affairs obtaining in the other islands of the Archipelago.

Conditions elsewhere in the Archipelago

On his way to Six Islands (which he reached on 14 January 1857), Cdr. Peyton called at Peros Banhos (6-10 January), Salomon (11 January) and Eagle Island (12 January). Leaving Six Islands on 18 January, he reached Diego Garcia the next day and, after completing his report, departed for Mauritius on 27 January.[22] For each of the islands, he supplied a detailed census. Valuable though this information is, we record here only the figures for the overall population of each establishment, leaving analysis, later in this chapter, to an altogether more exhaustive account compiled only two years later, by which time the total for the whole Archipelago had increased from 507 to 589.

(a) At Peros Banhos (population 60) Peyton reported that all of the labourers had been introduced in accordance with the rules. None had any complaint to make, but he also noted that the manager, a M. Ruaud, used to punish individuals by banishing them to Moresby islet.

(b) Peyton's next stop was at Salomon (population 89) where all was again described as in order. Most of the labourers at the Ile Fouquet establishment had been brought over legally by the existing manager. Peyton noted that the administrator for Isle Boddam, Gustave Hugon, was the half-brother of the murdered manager of Six Islands.

(c) At Eagle Island, Peyton visited the establishment, but also, being doubtless a victim of the habitual confusion over what was meant by 'Trois Frères', sent ashore Lieutenant Stephens at Three Brothers, where no-one was found. The population (35) were legitimately introduced creoles of Mauritius. The manager was a M. René Bernard.

(d) At Six Islands (population 24), the 18 labourers questioned all had complaints, as previously described (see page 147).

(e) The final stop was Diego Garcia (population 299), where the three establishments were inspected and found to be 'in a very flourishing condition'.[23] With the census data, Peyton forwarded a letter from a M. Dumat, owner and manager of Pointe Marianne estate, arguing the need for a magistrate and police force resident in the islands.

1859. Government takes a closer look

Consideration of Peyton's report in Port Louis and London led before long to a decision to appoint a Commission of Inquiry into the conditions obtaining in the remoter dependencies of Mauritius. The Commissioner, Lieutenant Henry Berkeley, RN, was supported by an interpreter, James Caldwell,[24] and they were accompanied by the Anglican Bishop of Mauritius, the Right Reverend Vincent Ryan. The last-named was taking advantage of the tour to revisit his flock in Seychelles and go for the first time to all of the inhabited islands of the Chagos. HMS *Lynx* (a steam sloop) was pressed into service; indeed Berkeley was her captain.

Lt. Berkeley set sail on 3 May 1859, armed with the instructions of Higginson's successor as Governor, Sir William Stevenson, to examine three potential areas of complaint: whether individuals had been brought to any islands against their will; whether any had been unlawfully detained there against their will, at the expiry of their contracts; and whether any had been treated cruelly or illegally imprisoned against their will. They were armed too with a Proclamation[25] issued by the governor in the name of Queen Victoria (see inset opposite). The *Lynx* visited the Chagos islands in the same order as had the *Frolic* thirty months

PROCLAMATION

In the Name of Her Majesty VICTORIA, of the UNITED Kingdom of Great Britain and Ireland QUEEN, &c. &c.

By His Excellency William Stevenson, CB, Governor of the Island of Mauritius and its Dependencies, &c. &c. &c.

WHEREAS it has hitherto been found difficult efficiently to administer Justice among the Residents in the smaller Islands Dependencies of this colony, on account of their distance from any Resident Magistracy;

AND WHEREAS it is very desirable that Law and Order should be preserved therein, and that the Inhabitants, like all other Subjects of Her Most Gracious Majesty, should be assured that they, their Rights and Liberties, will be protected and secured;

I DO hereby, in the Name of Her Most Gracious Majesty, Proclaim to all the Inhabitants of every Station and Degree, within the smaller Islands aforesaid, that they, their Persons and Properties and all their Rights and Liberties, are fully under the Protection of the Law, and will be protected and secured by Her Majesty's Government in this Colony of the Mauritius by every available means; and that Her Majesty's Government aforesaid will not only avail itself of every opportunity, but will from time to time appoint well-qualified Commissioners, to examine into their condition, to hear and as far as possible redress their grievances, and to promote their well-being.

AND WHEREAS it has come to the knowledge of Her Majesty's Government aforesaid that Labourers have been introduced into some of the said Islands unlawfully and against their will; and that some Masters therein have treated their Servants unjustly and cruelly, and have imprisoned them for real or supposed offences;

I DO therefore hereby Proclaim that every Labourer and Servant who shall satisfactorily show that he has been introduced into, or detained in, any of the said Dependencies unlawfully and against his will, shall be freed from such Compulsory Service, and his Master shall be compelled to make him reparation; and, moreover, that all cruelty or oppression and all illegal imprisonments, will be repressed and punished, upon complaints being properly made, when opportunity offers, to the Government of Mauritius, or to any visiting Commissioners; and, moreover, that upon satisfactory proof of such Complaints, the Engagements between the Complainants and their Masters will be broken.

I DO further Proclaim that, in order to carry out these objects, full power and authority has been given, and is hereby by me conferred upon Henry Berkeley, Esquire, a Lieutenant in Her Majesty's Royal Navy, Commanding Her Majesty's Steam Sloop *Lynx*, and James Caldwell, Esquire, of Port Louis, as joint and several Commissioners to investigate all complaints of the nature aforesaid, and to remove to Mauritius, or to one of the principal Islands of the Seychelles every labourer who shall shew that he has been unlawfully introduced into, or is unlawfully detained in, any of the said smaller Dependencies, or that he has been cruelly or oppressively treated, or illegally imprisoned by his Master, or those having his Master's authority.

At the same time, I DO caution all the Inhabitants of these Dependencies not to attempt to redress their own wrongs, but to complain to the commissioners above named, or those to be appointed from time to time as aforesaid, and to rely with confidence on the determination of Her Majesty's Government to protect them in all their just rights, and to advance their prosperity and happiness; and I DO hereby solemnly warn all labourers employed in any of these Dependencies that prompt and efficient justice will follow every criminal or violent act that they may commit, or attempt to commit, against those whom their own free contracts have placed over them:

And I admonish all such labourers and other servants who have engaged in any service whatever in any of these smaller Dependencies to be faithful and obedient to all lawful service and commands of their employers, and to use every endeavour to secure their good-will and confidence.

Moreover, I DO earnestly urge all the inhabitants of these Dependencies to cultivate mutual good faith, goodwill, and forbearance: because their just and kind treatment of each other will be far more effectual than any intervention of Government for promoting their prosperity and happiness.

Given at Government House, Mauritius, this Twelfth day of April 1859.

By Command: H. SANDWITH, Colonial Secretary.

earlier and Berkeley's general impressions were highly favourable towards the behaviour of the local managers. The very few complaints received concerned only the last of the categories of malpractice he had been instructed to examine. These are described in relation to the islands on which they occurred. Berkeley found no reason for believing, 'except in the case of a few old men, some of them remaining from the time of slavery,' that labourers had been introduced other than legally and from Mauritius; nor had he discovered any case where individuals had been retained against their will after their engagements had ended. The position was that

> no written engagements are ever made, nor are any engagements made as to time, the usual way being that the owners or their agents in Port Louis arrange with the labourers there to go and work in their islands and see if they like the work, offering them a return passage if they are not satisfied to remain. It is true, and frankly avowed by almost all the managers, that they try by every lawful means to induce the men to remain in the islands, but that they are not retained against their will …

In fact, several men were heard making such requests and, asked afterwards whether passages had been refused, answered in the negative.

Peros Banhos

After visiting Seychelles and Agalega, the *Lynx* reached Peros Banhos on 9 June. The atoll now belonged to Messrs. Levieux & Co. (Berkeley refers constantly to the *jouissance* holders as 'owners' and later correspondence revealed that there had been a steady transfer of the *jouissances*, in whole or in part, to relatives and friends of the original holders, only some of which had been authorised by the Land Court.) The newly arrived manager, a M. Houdet, being dangerously ill with dysentery, played little part in the proceedings, but his assistant, Jean Faure, was judged an able substitute. Annual oil production was around 20,000 *veltes*. Berkeley found 'a good store of excellent rice, the camp, the mills, all in good order and the oil store particularly well fitted up …' The supply of medicines was however inadequate. Giving details of pay and rations, Berkeley reported that neither element was reduced as a means of punishment. The mills were operated by about 100 asses.

Concerning cruel treatment, Cdr. Peyton had cited a case where a man had been punished by banishment to Moresby islet. Investigating, Berkeley discovered that three such cases had occurred under Houdet's predecessor, Ruaud, all of them duly recorded in the establishment's Journal,[26] and all involving unruly individuals awaiting return to Mauritius.[27] Another man, a Mozambican by the name of Carouga, had recently been sent there, for refusing to do the work assigned to him. Getting steam up, Berkeley took the *Lynx* to the islet to see matters for himself. He found Carouga near a hut where, with ten other men, a good meal of rice and fish was being cooked. Working parties were despatched there weekly, but Carouga, unlike the others, was not expected to work, though receiving normal rations. He nevertheless begged Berkeley to intercede with Houdet, and was transported back to Ile du Coin, where the manager was advised not to inflict such a punishment for offences of that kind.

Salomon

This atoll, where there were still two separate concessions, was reached on 11 June. As the *Lynx* could not enter the lagoon, she anchored to the south, off Ile Fouquet, while the Commission (and the bishop) were rowed ashore. This islet was reportedly 'owned' by a M. Sampsois [sic] of Port Louis – a name unknown to the records of the Land Court – and managed by Onézime Allard. Berkeley found 'everything here appeared very quiet though on a small scale. There was a good supply of provisions and no complaints from the men, the manager informing us that he had no trouble with them'. During the few hours the commission spent on Ile Fouquet no mention was made, nor questions asked, about the absconding of five people in a pirogue which reached Peros Banhos in August 1857, the very pirogue in which the six Indians had fled Six Islands earlier in that year (see note 25). As regards exports, the establishment produced only about 600 *veltes* of oil annually, but also considerable amounts of timber. At the time of Berkeley's visit, 800 pieces of *faux-gayac* (*Intsia bijuga*) were being prepared and the brigantine *Sans-Pareil* was in the lagoon waiting to load them. As rum and tobacco were only to be issued on completion of such tasks, it can be assumed that the workers would have been in a sunny mood!

The party was then rowed across the lagoon to visit in turn Boddam and Ile Anglaise, 'owned' by Messrs Auguste Louys, Hippolyte Lemière and Henri Plasson (who also acted as the group's Agent). This establishment was a good deal larger and exported annually about 7,000 *veltes* of oil, together with 12,000 cubic feet and 70,000 shingles of *faux-gayac*. Gustave Hugon, still its manager,[28] got off on the wrong foot with the Commissioners, by questioning the need for another inspection so soon after the last one. However, all appeared well with the establishment, except that Hugon admitted punishing men by fining them or sending them to one of the other islets. Berkeley then visited Ile Anglaise, where a number of men were working, and was disagreeably surprised to find among them a man banished there, for having killed a 'wild fowl'. Judging Hugon to have deceived him deliberately, but not having time to return to

Boddam to remonstrate, Berkeley recommended that the matter be taken up with Plasson in Port Louis.

Eagle Island

This island too was 'owned' by Messrs Louys, Lemière and Plasson, the manager being René Bernard. Arriving on 13 June and landing by boat through heavy surf, Berkeley and Caldwell found all the inhabitants assembled in the yard and were thus able to complete their business swiftly and 'get clear of a very uncertain anchorage'. With thirty donkeys to drive the mills, 8,000 *veltes* of oil were produced, from nuts collected on the Three Brothers and Danger, as well as Eagle Island itself. Supplies and management were judged approvingly, and it was noted that the only form of punishment was to force the miscreant's return to Mauritius. Berkeley also records that the workers' rewards include supplies of *poonac* to feed to their animals.

Six Islands

There being no anchorage, the *Lynx* stood offshore and, on the morning of 14 June, the Commission were rowed the five miles to the establishment. Six Islands remained in the hands of the Duperrel family, their agent in Port Louis being a M. Laporte and the current manager Théodore Raibaud [Ribault?] The island produced about 7,000 *veltes* of oil annually, using 45 donkeys to work the mills. Of the humans, only Raibaud and his workers emerged with credit from the Commission's examination. No vessel had visited since 1 January and in the store there remained only ten days' supply of rice, little salt and no rum (it had run out six weeks earlier). The rice 'we saw was little, if at all, superior to that generally sold in Port Louis as sweepings or damaged rice'. Berkeley also learned that, during the previous fourteen months, 'the labourers had been, on one occasion, *one month and a half* without any rice or other rations whatever'. As the vessel which usually serviced Six Islands was the *Sans-Pareil*, encountered at Salomon three days earlier, and was at the time waiting to load timber, it was less than likely that she would have had a cargo of provisions in her hold.

'It would be natural under such circumstances,' remarked Caldwell, 'to expect that we should have found a dissatisfied and turbulent body of men, refusing all labour and living in idleness. To the credit of both manager and men all the labourers were at work, and the best possible understanding existed between them and their masters'. Sixteen however wished to leave, either by the next vessel or the one following; and their wishes were formally recorded in the establishment's journal. Others declared that they would stay only as long as the present manager remained on the island. The latter must indeed have been a man of great perseverance, for he asked Berkeley to provide a passage for his wife and child, together with nephew dangerously ill with rheumatic fever, who in fact died a few days later. Summing up, Berkeley commented that Six Islands, capable of being as good as any other establishment he had visited, was in a state of dilapidation from want of necessary supplies of all kinds.

Diego Garcia

Arriving at Diego Garcia on the morning of 15 June, Berkeley visited in turn the establishments of Minni Minni, East Point and Pointe Marianne.

The proprietor of Minni Minni was Louis Mazéry (whose *jouissance* was not registered until 28 September 1865) and its manager Alexandre Mainguy. Production was 10,000 *veltes* annually and made use of 100 donkeys. After spending a day there, Berkeley pronounced it to be 'in excellent order with an abundant supply of food of first rate quality'. He reported that no punishments were inflicted and that, although not part of the terms of employment, workers were issued with rum and tobacco every evening.

Next morning Berkeley proceeded to East Point, belonging to the brothers Liénard of Port Louis (whose *jouissance* was issued on 8 May 1843). The estate now included the lands shown on Capt. Moresby's chart as Anse David and Widow's estate. It was managed by Régnaud (Hugon's predecessor on Six Islands) and produced 25,000 *veltes,* with 140 donkeys to operate the oil mills. Incentives to good work were gifts of rum and tobacco and 'punishments, cutting the grog'. Remarking upon the number of Indians working at the plantation, Berkeley reported that all had been legally recruited from Mauritius and had a perfect understanding of Creole; all in all, 'This is the largest estate we have visited and is in very fine order. Provisions and supplies of all kinds in abundance and a garden where we saw the tamarind, bois noir, bitter orange, lemon, sugar cane and vanilla growing'.

On the 16th, the Commission visited Pointe Marianne, 'owned' (like Peros Banhos) by Levieux & Co., of Port Louis, and managed by Emile Barry. Production of oil amounted to 16,000 *veltes*, with 103 donkeys. The same excellent conditions prevailed as at East Point. No complaint was made against the managers, but quite a number of workers complained of having come to blows with their fellows – and 'we dismissed those with a reprimand to both parties'.

Like Cdr. Peyton before him, Lt. Berkeley took a census of the inhabitants, but in much greater detail, as shown in Table 8.2 overleaf.[29] The most notable feature of this table is the increase it shows, compared to the size of population

Table 8.2   Population of Chagos Islands, 1859

| | PEROS BANHOS | | | | EAGLE ISLAND | | | | SALOMON ISLANDS | | | | | | | | | | | |
| | | | | | | | | | Ile Fouquet | | | | Boddam | | | | TOTAL | | | |
	M	W	B	G	M	W	B	G	M	W	B	G	M	W	B	G	M	W	B	G
Managers Families	2	1	–	–	1	1	1	2	1	2	–	1	1	1	1	1	2	3	1	2
Europeans	–	–	–	–	–	–	–	–	–	–	–	–	–	–	–	–	–	–	–	–
Indians	–	–	–	–	–	–	–	–	1	–	–	–	1	–	–	–	2	–	–	–
Mozambique	20	3	–	–	3	–	–	–	1	–	–	–	3	1	–	–	4	1	–	–
Malgache	19	1	–	–	4	1	–	–	3	–	–	–	24	1	–	–	27	1	–	–
Mauritians	15	6	–	–	7	–	2	1	11	1	–	–	9	3	2	4	20	4	2	4
Johanna	4	–	–	–	–	–	–	–	–	–	–	–	–	–	–	–	–	–	–	–
Seychelles	3	2	–	–	–	–	–	–	–	–	–	–	1	1	–	–	1	1	–	–
Diego Garcia	–	–	–	–	–	–	–	–	–	–	–	–	1	–	–	–	1	–	–	–
Agalega	–	1	–	–	2	–	–	–	–	–	–	–	–	–	–	–	–	–	–	–
Six Islands	–	–	–	–	1	–	–	–	–	–	–	–	–	–	–	–	–	–	–	–
Bourbon	–	–	–	–	–	–	–	–	–	–	–	–	1	–	–	–	1	–	–	–
Salomon Islands	–	–	–	–	–	–	–	–	–	–	–	–	–	–	–	–	–	–	–	–
Peros Banhos	4	7	8	8	–	–	–	–	–	–	–	–	–	–	–	–	–	–	–	–
	67	21	8	8	18	2	3	3	17	3	–	1	40	8	3	5	57	11	3	6
	104				26				21				56				77			

Peyton had observed little more than two years earlier: it had risen from 506 to 589. As Berkeley himself noted in figures appended to his table, another very striking feature was the huge disparity in all of the islands between the numbers of men and of women, the latter forming no more than 6% of the workforce in Six Islands, only 30% in Peros Banhos and a mere 15% in Diego Garcia, the largest and longest-settled island. As an inevitable consequence, a Chagos-born population could only emerge very slowly; at this stage it amounted to 75 individuals, less than 13% of the total. Another interesting feature was that by comparison with the observations made by Peyton, very few Mozambicans (25:117), remained on Diego Garcia, whose increased population was almost entirely

| | | | | DIEGO GARCIA | | | | | | | | | | | | | | | | |
| SIX ISLANDS | | | | Minni Minni | | | | East Point | | | | Pointe Marianne | | | | TOTAL | | | | |
M	W	B	G	M	W	B	G	M	W	B	G	M	W	B	G	M	W	B	G	
2	1	–	1	1	1	1	2	2	2	3	2	1	–	–	–	4	3	4	4	Managers Families
–	–	–	–	–	–	–	–	–	–	–	–	1	–	–	–	1	–	–	–	Europeans
–	–	–	–	1	–	–	–	35	2	–	–	10	–	–	–	46	2	–	–	Indians
5	1	–	–	7	2	–	–	11	1	–	–	4	–	–	–	22	3	–	–	Mozambique
14	2	–	–	6	–	–	–	10	–	–	–	13	1	–	–	29	1	–	–	Malgache
13	1	–	–	11	2	–	–	84	8	3	1	36	9	7	1	131	19	10	2	Mauritians
1	–	–	–	–	–	–	–	4	–	–	–	1	–	–	–	5	–	–	–	Johanna
1	–	–	–	3	–	–	–	3	2	–	–	1	–	–	–	7	2	–	–	Seychelles
–	–	1	1	5	2	8	7	5	2	1	–	2	3	2	3	12	7	11	10	Diego Garcia
–	–	–	–	–	–	–	–	–	–	–	–	–	–	–	–	–	–	–	–	Agalega
–	–	–	–	1	1	–	–	–	1	–	–	–	–	–	–	1	2	–	–	Six Islands
–	–	–	–	–	–	–	–	–	–	–	–	–	–	–	–	–	–	–	–	Bourbon
–	–	–	–	–	–	–	–	–	–	–	–	–	–	–	–	–	–	–	–	Salomon Islands
–	–	–	–	–	–	–	–	–	–	–	–	–	–	–	–	–	–	–	–	Peros Banhos
36	5	1	2	35	8	9	9	154	18	7	3	69	13	9	4	258	39	25	16	
44				61				182				95				338				

accounted for by additional Mauritian born workers, together with nearly 50 born in India. A few of Diego Garcia's Mozambicans could have been transferred to Peros Banhos, but nothing like enough to account for the Chagos-wide reduction in their numbers from 127 to 62. On the other hand, there had been a comparable increase (from 64 to 134) in the number of Malgaches (Madagascan-born) working in most parts of the Archipelago, especially Salomon. We hesitate to draw any significant conclusions from these changes. Perhaps the influx of Indians into Mauritius forced former slaves of African origin (many of them of course born in Mauritius) to take employment in the island Dependencies; there is also some anecdotal evidence to suggest that employers considered those hailing from Madagascar, Malagasys in English terminology, to be more adaptable and skilled than others; but we know of no explanation for the virtual disappearance of Mozambicans from Diego Garcia.

Conclusions of the Commission

Berkeley and Campbell's specific recommendations were as follows: that 'owners' and managers should do more to reduce the gender imbalance (a point on which the managers concurred); that in the future written agreements should be made in Mauritius with each new employee, and copies sent to the managers, so that all parties should have a clear point of reference in the event of disputes, and visitors a clear basis for handling any arguments relating to the due date of return or of voluntary extension of employment; also, at the managers' request, they had publicly insisted the workers should consume their issues of rum 'at the tub' (as in the Royal Navy), to prevent the clandestine accumulation of supplies. More generally, they believed that more frequent visits of inspection would provide the only effective means of fostering 'a kindly feeling between men already looking up to the Governor for justice and protection'. Most importantly, the Commissioners considered that conditions compared very favourably with those in Mauritius.

> The labour in these Islands is far less severe than the labour imposed upon similar persons in Mauritius, and the abundance of fish along all their coasts is such that they can, literally, walk into the water, and, in few minutes, get such supply as would be a banquet to many of a far superior class in Mauritius. As a general rule, as all the islands are healthy, and abound in all the necessities of life (except rice, with which they are amply supplied), the inhabitants have nothing to desire. Fowls and hogs come for the trouble of rearing them.

An ecclesiastical perspective

The archipelago of Chagos had been established as part of the Anglican diocese of Port Louis since 1847, but needless to say islands located some 1,300 miles away from Mauritius could not be easily or regularly ministered to.[30] In fact, Bishop Ryan may have been the first Christian priest to land in the Chagos since the *Conçeição* was wrecked in 1555. He wrote two accounts of his tour, a report to the Governor[31] and a public account of his episcopal experiences five years later.[32]

In the course of the *Lynx*'s visits, Ryan encountered quite a number of individuals already known to him, including several who had acquired some literacy and elements of Christian knowledge in Mauritius. One such, Amedée, whom he encountered at the first port of call, Peros Banhos, 'was formerly one of Thomas Jenkins' pupils in Port Louis, – a very intelligent man, *tonnelier* or cooper to the establishment, on good wages'. Accompanied by the ship's doctor, Ryan managed to make four visits to the 'camp' and meet a considerable number of the people there, including one with good reading skills. His observations also captured small incidents in the lives of the workers. For example,

> The most remarkable catch of fish I ever saw took place near the spot where I had bathed. Several men had a few gunny-bags tied together, with which they made a net. This was seized by a man at each end, taken about ten feet or so into the sea, put down and drawn to shore with the centre part full of fish. On walking up to them I observed what seemed to be a line of sea-weed, a few feet from the water-mark, but on looking nearer I found it was a bank of fish some forty yards in length by two yards or more in breadth. The explanation given of this is, that these fish make their way over the shallow reef just outside the island to avoid the pursuit of the larger fish in the deep water.

Bishop Vincent Ryan.

At Salomon too, Ryan met literate individuals already known to him. At the end of their inspection, as the visitors were rowed back to the *Lynx* in the establishment's whaler, they were treated to the 'rude singing of the men, preceded by the blowing of a shell with a deep trumpet-sound'. As Ryan recorded two years later, he also attracted new converts, whose subsequent lives and deaths illustrate both existing conditions and the ecclesiastical contribution to the slow spread of literacy. On Ile Anglaise, managed by the 'not very cordial' Hugon, a Malagasy known as Paul received a French language bible, constructed a chapel and organised daily prayers and instruction, against Hugon's strong opposition.[33] However, within two years he died of dysentery, the bible being buried with him by his friends. On Ile Fouquet, John, another convert, had also died, in a marine accident; but there the manager, a M. Allard, was eager to have more employees able, like John, to read and teach others. Indeed he made contact with Ryan in Mauritius for this very purpose.[34]

The bishop did not visit Eagle Island: 'The prospect of a useless wetting in the surf, and not feeling well after a wakeful night, and a tendency to shivering, kept me on board'. The same evening the *Lynx* reached Six Islands and in the morning the ship's boat took him through the pass. Ryan's account is quite revealing: 'Even when inside the circular reef, in the boat, there was need of great care to avoid the patches of coral, on which the sea often broke on both sides of us'. Once ashore, it is fascinating to note from Ryan's account that a rudimentary chapel was already in existence. He writes that the chapel was

> built by a Malegache convert, named Celestin Cyriacus, opposite to his own *caze* (hut), where he intended to gather as many as would come for united worship. Others had spoken to me of him as able to teach, but negligent. He and another Malegache came to me afterwards, expressing their need of books. A desire for knowledge of the right way is wonderfully spread among these poor people.

As regards Diego Garcia, the bishop's account adds welcome colour to Berkeley's laconic report. Once again, Ryan met people who were literate and known from their involvement with the church in Mauritius. These included an Indian from Bombay who had worked as a groom in Port Louis for thirteen years before signing up to work at the island. Another was a liberated African, who had been catechised by the Reverend Langrishe Banks and who was also one of the slaves brought to Mauritius aboard HMS *Lily*; and, like most of them, he had adopted the middle name Lily, thus helping ensure its survival as a surname up to the present day. At Minni Minni,

> Mr Mainguy, the manager, came out to meet us, and treated us with the most entire hospitality. He gave me a fine pig, which I sent to the ship's crew, and a basket of oranges and lemons … Mr. Barry, the manager of Point Maria Ann estate, and Mr. Régnaud, manager of South-East Point estate, came over also. There was much expression of courtesy and kindness from them all, and to each other. I went among the people and spoke a good deal with them. One of the slaves captured in the *Lily* was there and he remembered a good part of the Belief and the Lord's Prayer in English. Several causes tend to produce a bad state of morals among the labourers though, as far as physical comfort and supply went, they seemed to be remarkably well off.

Ryan went on to describe having walked from Minni Minni to East Point and having visited Pointe Marianne, making the 40-minute trip in the ship's whaler. He was particularly taken with East Point.

> Monsieur and Madame Régnaud, and their four children, occupied the spacious house, in front of which many mills were at work pressing out the oil. I never met with more cordial hospitality and kindness. Monsieur and Madame Bertin were in a pavilion close by. We were quite prepared by our walk for the excellent breakfast they gave us. Near the house is a nice garden, in front of which there were very large banyan and other trees, and in the garden were date-trees, orange trees, lemons, bananas, and vegetables of many kinds. There are more Malabars here than in any of the other islands. I spoke to several in Creole …

The bishop had nothing to say about the work of the official delegation he was accompanying, nor (except for his aside on the 'bad state of morals') about the general conditions prevailing. Only much later did Ryan comment that

> To my great regret I was only able to give a very inadequate reply to the demands made on me for help on those remote dependencies ... the appointment of a catechist in one island, the establishment of a school [*sic*] and the gift of books wherever I found any who could read was all that I could do.[35]

Evidently the plantations, especially on Diego Garcia, were working reasonably well. Régnaud was, incidentally, the same individual who had preceded Hugon as manager of Six Islands and come in for harsh criticism for ill-treatment of the workers there four years earlier. Perhaps he had learned his lesson – or perhaps the problems of operating that reef-girt island at a profit were insuperable.

Governor Stevenson forwarded to London the bishop's official report, commenting that future missionaries could expect useful co-operation from the island managers, but adding a strong warning:

> It is obvious, however, that any Missionaries who are sent for this duty should be liberal and tolerant in their views: otherwise, the good that they might accomplish might be, in some measure, counteracted by rash interferences or misplaced zeal, and against this they should be especially cautioned.

For whatever reason, this evidence of an unsatisfied desire for education, including religious education, fell on deaf ears in London. Nor did Stevenson consider it his business to include the dependencies in whatever educational arrangements were being introduced into Mauritius itself.

Why were things not worse?

Readers will have noticed that Six Islands had a much worse record than any other of the Chagos islands. In fact that group accounted for both of the major scandals resulting in and uncovered by the two Enquiries. Secondly, the Commissioners had narrow terms of reference: they were not asked to examine in depth the whole system of operations and employment conditions in the Archipelago, nor the social conditions of its inhabitants. Thus, the expression of satisfaction by Lt. Berkeley was based on rather limited evidence. Evidently, two conflicting trends were emerging. The first was the growing anxieties of the Colonial Office about the welfare of the islanders and the want of control over the entrepreneurs exploiting the islands. The second was the determination of the latter to increase their economic power and to maintain their freedom of action. We shall examine (in Chapter 10) how that came to be resolved. Here, it may suffice to answer the question posed by reference to the introduction, in general, of better-educated managers, a development related, perhaps, to the changes in effective ownership that had occurred from the time of slave emancipation.

It is not easy to piece together the process by which the original concession-aires passed on their holdings. A good number of the changes were authorised by the Land Court and are recorded in the Mauritius National Archives. Many more resulted from private agreements. In all cases, a named individual, known as the Agent, represented the 'owners' in their dealings with the authorities. Thus, taking Peros Banhos as a simple example, because there was never more than a single estate on this atoll, Ozille Majastre had the original *jouissance* of Messrs Bigot and Allain legally transferred to him on 18 May 1823,[36] with a series of further authorised changes in 1838, 1842, and 1844. By 1859, however, without further mention in the Land Court archive, Berkeley reported the owners as being Levieux & Co, while in 1862 the Surveyor General gave full details as fol-lows: Messrs Levieux, Dumat, Merandon, Duvergé and Mmes Majastre and Delafaye – 2/16 each; John Davy – 1/16; the (four) Liénard brothers – 1/16; and a group comprising Messrs Louys, Plasson, Mme Biron and the heirs to M. Pulve-nis – 2/16. In most cases, added this official (Captain Morrison, R.E.), 'a pre-mium, amounting to many thousands of dollars, was paid on the transfer of any share in an island, by the party obtaining possession'.[37]

These changes were typical of what was happening elsewhere in the Chagos and could only reflect a growing attractiveness of investment there. The out-standing exception was Six Islands, where in 1862 ownership remained entirely within the extended family of the deceased Victor Duperrel, with six individu-als having equal shares. Furthermore, there were increasing signs of individuals acquiring holdings, however small, in more than one of the islands. Notable among this group were Levieux and the Liénards (with interests in both Diego Garcia and Peros Banhos) and Messrs Plasson and Louys, who had begun with joint ownership of Coëtivy Island, but then extended steadily into the Chagos with holdings in Peros Banhos, Salomon, Eagle and, in a tiny way, Diego Garcia. After 1844, Plasson and Louys were joined by Hippolyte Lemière, an individual, as will be seen, of considerable standing and importance. From these facts it seems reasonable to conclude that the new investors were able to attract manag-ers of generally greater competence, better able to build a productive rapport with their workers. Certainly, the apparently irredeemable callousness and incompetence of the Duperrels and their minions must have owed something to their unwillingness or inability to attract fresh blood.

Unfortunately, many further years would pass before a coherent system of inspections of the islands would be instituted and much longer still before they became sufficiently frequent to constitute a reliable form of governance. Enough records do, however, survive to give a general impression of conditions in the interim as they were experienced by the two main constituents of Chagos society, the workers and the managerial groups. For example, castaways from merchant ships suffering disaster in the Indian Ocean occasionally fetched up in the Chagos, where the captains of the whaling ships also called for supplies and repairs. Their interactions with the islands' occupants are discussed next. After that, we shall revert once again to official contacts and preoccupations.

Notes to Chapter 8

1 *La Sentinelle* 4 June 1844.

2 The *pas géométrique* was, under French law, a ribbon of land along all coasts reserved to the Crown for whatever needs might arise. In Mauritius, landowners had to a great extent encroached on this land without penalty.

3 TNA CO 167/226 Captain Lloyd to Irving, 4 April 1840. For additional details about Lloyd, including his ownership of a pet elephant, see DMB, p. 143, 1942.

4 Pridham, C., *England's Colonial Empire: Mauritius and its Dependencies,* (Smith, Elder 1846), and an anonymous article in the *United Service Journal* (Henry Colbourne, London, 1849).

5 TNA CO 167/314 Anderson to Grey, 6 September 1849 (47). It should be noted that this correspondence had its origins in 1844, when the Colonial Office had first proposed that *jouissances* be replaced by single year rentals, which proved impractical. In 1849, as earlier, the specific islands concerned were all in the Seychelles.

6 *Ibid.* Colonial Secretary to Anderson, 26 December 1849.

7 TNA CO 167/449 Colonial Office Despatch No. 802, dated 23 October 1862 and Surveyor General's letter No. B/150 dated 1 June 1863.

8 TNA CO 167/356 (folio 49 and associated papers, February 1854).

9 TNA CO 167/497 Barkly to Carnarvon 2 April 1867 (68).

10 For further information on this case and the traffic in 'liberated Africans' see Carter, M. and others, *The Last Slaves: Liberated Africans in 19th Century Mauritius,* CRIOS, Mauritius, 2003.

11 Johanna was known to the French as Anjouan and is now called Anzouani by the Comorians.

12 MA RA 1135 Petition of ten labourers [although only nine signatories appear] at Peros Banhos, 18 September 1851.

13 Witness statement by Emile Régnaud, Manager of Six Islands 1854-1855, at the trial of Alexandre Gerard and Romain Rodrigues in June 1859. Régnaud testified that he had been Manager at Six Islands from 7 August 1854 to 31 December 1855, and that during his stay there 4 different bands of Cochin men arrived – on 2 September 1854, a band of 18 men; on 18 March 1855 15 including 4 women and 2 children; on 8 June 1855, 1 man; on 29 Sept 1855, 10 men. He could not speak Cochin, but had a creole with him named Gustave who could speak it. He states that the men were paid monthly in cash but that amounts were deducted for goods taken by them at the shop. He denies that the Indians complained or that they were flogged or burnt. With regard to employment at Six Islands he states 'Creoles used to strip 500 coconuts a day – the Indians none …'

14 TNA CO 167/379 Higginson to Labouchère, 22, 23 November 1856; Higginson to Trotter, 21 November 1856; MA PA 3 Colonial Secretary to PI, 2 October 1856.

15 TNA CO 167/386 Commodore Trotter of *Frolic,* at Diego Garcia, 27 January 1857.

16 MA RA 1386 Report of Peyton, 27 January 1857.

17 MA RA 1418 Chief Secretary Madras Government to Governor Mauritius 11 February 1857 and enclosures.

18 TNA CO 167/386 Colonial Office to Governor Mauritius 26 Feb 1857.

19 MA RA 1386 Statements of Pierre Tuldé Dumazel and Eve Albert, Veuve Paul Hugon.

20 TNA CO 167/386 Higginson to Labouchère May 1857; MA RA 1418 Foreign Letters, 1857.

21 *Commercial Gazette* 24, 30 June 1857; *Madras Spectator* 20 May 1857.

22 TNA CO 167/386 Higginson to Labouchère May 1857.

23 MA RA 1386 Report of Peyton, Acting Commander of HMS *Frolic*, 27 January 1857.

24 James Caldwell (xxxx–1887) had a long and varied career in the Mauritian civil service (see DMB, p. 448, 1944) and was the head interpreter for Creole and French in the Procureur Général's department.

25 TNA CO 167/386.

26 From scattered references to such documents, it is clear that each island manager was required by his employer to maintain a record of daily occurrences, ships' visits, production, punishments meted out, etc. Unfortunately, none of these documents has survived.

27 The first of these cases occurred in 1857 and involved five deserters from the Ile Fouquet establishment in Salomon atoll. Claiming, unconvincingly, that they had been excessively punished for destroying some young trees, they were put, with rations, onto Moresby islet, until taken away ten days later to Mauritius. Curious aspects of this incident were that the pirogue used was the very one which had been used by the Indians who had fled from Six Islands (see page **148**) and that one of the new absconders was also an Indian.

28 He was mentioned later as being master of the ship *Wizard* (*Mauritius Commercial Gazette*, 4 August 1864).

29 TNA CO 167/412 Report by Lt. Berkeley, enclosed with Mauritius Despatch No. 113 of 1859.

30 Nagapen, A. *L'Eglise à Diego Garcia*, typescript, 7p, n.d. p. 2.

31 TNA CO 167/412 Report, dated 14 July 1859 enclosed with Mauritius Despatch No. 113.

32 Ryan, V.W. *Journals of an Eight Years' Residence in the Diocese of Mauritius, and of a Visit to Madagascar.*

33 Quite possibly, of course, it was Protestantism rather than Christianity to which Hugo objected. At that time, hostility between Catholic and Protestant ministers in Mauritius was intense.

34 *Op. cit.* pp. 178–9, 192–3.

35 See TNA CO 167/540 for comments by Ryan on correspondence on ecclesiastical affairs in Mauritius in 1872.

36 MA LC 24/108.

37 TNA CO 167/449 Letter B/150 of Surveyor General, dated 1 June 1863.

9

Wrecks, Whalers and Castaways

MARITIME accidents occurred all too commonly in Chagos waters and early visitors to Diego Garcia spoke of its shores as having 'many wrecks'. The larger vessels plying the Indian Ocean in the mid-19th century were hardly less prone to disaster. In 1857 the American ship *Ocean Spray*, carrying a cargo of railway iron for Madras, sprang a leak and was wrecked on Ile Diamant of Peros Banhos. Part of the crew went to Mauritius in the *Two Cousins* and the remainder to Ceylon in the brig *Surprise*. They do not appear to have left any record of their experience.

In contrast, much more is known about the barque *Dalriada*. On 3 February 1859, this vessel left Bombay for her home port of Liverpool with a cargo of seed, cotton and oil and a crew of 36 men. The Captain, a Mr Ewing, was travelling with his wife and child. They had a pleasant voyage, as Ewing reported, until

> March 1, being in latitude 9.50 S and longitude 69 E, when at 5 pm an alarm of fire was raised … At 8 am the main and mizenmasts fell with a tremendous crash, and the ship was enveloped in one mass of flame. The crew, being divided into three boats, made sail, and stood to the north-eastward, hoping to meet with a ship, or to fetch some of the isles of the Chagos Archipelago. Next day, finding that the small boat could not sail so well as the others the people were taken out of her and she was set adrift, and they proceeded on their way, the captain, his wife and child and 21 men in the long boat, the chief mate with 13 men in the life boat. Providentially they encountered only fine weather, and for five weary days and nights they held anxiously on their course; and in the afternoon of the sixth day from leaving the burning wreck, all being well, they reached the island of Diego Garcia, where are three cocoanut oil manufactories, by the managers of which they were most kindly and hospitably received and cared for.

Capt. Ewing described their kindness – and especially that of their host M. Gassian, described as manager of the 'coconut oil works' – as beyond all expression. Here too, they were fortunate to find the *Futteh Salaam*, (Captain Croad), who was carrying a contingent of Indian labourers homeward bound from Mauritius and had put in for water during their voyage to Calcutta.[1] Reporting on this incident, the Mauritian newspaper, *Commercial Gazette* noted,

> at a time when the proceedings on some of the oil Islands have obtained an unenviable notoriety it is a pleasure to … shew that all those whose occupation leads them to spend their time on solitary islands do not degenerate into the inhuman monsters we have seen portrayed, but … in time of danger and desolation, a shield and a succour to the helpless and afflicted.[2]

One of the more unusual wrecks happened on 6 November 1865.[3] The *Shannon*, another almost new barque, had left Liverpool in May 1865, bound for Bombay with a general cargo of machinery, timber and spars. Severe gales in the southern Atlantic had delayed her progress and, more seriously, so damaged two iron tanks containing reserve supplies of fresh water as to cause most of it to be lost. The ship's chart showed Diego Garcia as a dot about ⅛ inch square, but with the aid of Horsburgh's sailing instructions Captain Frederick Dunbar found his way into the lagoon on 29 October. Just over a week later, as dawn began to break, he took the bearings necessary to set his course for the entrance and set sail. Let Capt. Dunbar tell the rest:

> I steered that course, but shortly after getting under weigh, a squall obscured all the marks and the tide set me to the eastward of my course without my being aware of it. I was so near the entrance of the harbour when the squall came on, that although I lost sight of the marks, I dared not round too, to anchor; there was nothing for it in my opinion but to run on, keeping the lead going; had I attempted to round the vessel too, either to port or starboard, she must have gone ashore; I suppose that after the squall struck her she was going at least 10 knots; whilst running at this rate she unfortunately struck on a coral reef and remained fast; from that time until the 6th of February, every effort was made by means of anchors, chains, hawsers &c., to get the vessel afloat; these efforts were continued till the 6th of February, during which time the ship made no water, neither did the hull show any sign of straining. During the time the vessel was frequently afloat, but I could not succeed in getting her clear of the coral ridges over which she had run while going so fast.

Three months!

> I had written to Mauritius and Cochin, and was constantly in expectation of assistance being sent from one or both of those ports; this made me unwilling to take the cargo out of the ship; besides which the only place that I could land it was 6 miles distant with no place for housing it. Having despatched my letters I waited two months for an answer. Two ships came to the port during that time, but one,

after communicating, left without attempting to do anything, and the offers of the other, a French Bark, the *Guipuzcoano* were so unreasonable that I could not accept them. She was a Bark of 333 tons, and her Commander asked £3,000 to carry a full cargo to Bombay. Our 'tween decks were very nearly full of large spars, planks and lumber; there was also about 300 tons of Coke on board. The other ship that called off the port was the *Genii*. She sent a boat in, but apparently not liking the place did not attempt to enter, but proceeded on her voyage to India … My vessel did not begin to leak till the 13th of February, although she was frequently on shore, and after striking hard, when suddenly without any previous warning, she began to fill rapidly, and in a few hours the water in the hold was level with the sea outside, although four pumps in excellent working order were at work. After this, we did the very utmost we could to save the stores and cargo, until the 13th day of March, when having first called a Board of Survey composed of the principal residents of the island, I abandoned my vessel, and shortly afterwards proceeded to Mauritius with my officers and crew. We had landed all the spars and planks, and some other cargo amounting in all, so far as I am able to form an opinion, to from 500 to 600 tons.

Unfortunately, virtually nothing is known of the interaction, during the four months elapsing between the stranding and sinking, except a single comment that 'the residents at Diego Garcia have borne flattering testimony to the exertions [of the Master, officers and crew]'.[4]

It was not only Diego Garcia and Peros Banhos that found themselves welcoming survivors. In 1862, another British sailing ship, the *Swithanley*, was wrecked on Blenheim Reef, to the north-east of Salomon.[5] By good fortune, the colonial schooner *Sphinx*, supplying that island group, had been close by and her skipper, a Captain Puren, managed with great skill to rescue all aboard and bring them to land. They had then been cared for by the island manager. As is explained in our next chapter, the island's proprietors made the most of what had happened to further their own interests.

A few years later, on 22 April 1869, a ship's boat suddenly appeared in the lagoon at Six Islands, bearing some exhausted and desperate seamen. They were the only survivors from an American ship, the *J.P. Whitney*. Built in Maine, USA, the *J.P. Whitney* had a varied career, carrying immigrants from Ireland to America in the 1850s, and later in the salt trade. The photograph overleaf of the ship is taken from a painting made at Malta in 1864, reproduced in John D. Whidden's *Ocean Life*. According to Whidden, a former captain of the *J.P. Whitney*, who was succeeded in her command by Captain George T. Avery in the 1860s, 'She was dismasted off the mouth of the Hoogly River to avoid being driven ashore, and afterwards refitted at Calcutta, sailed for Mauritius, and foundered with nearly all on board during a typhoon in the Indian Ocean'.

The shipwreck had occurred twelve days before the arrival of the survivors;

Ship *J. P. Whitney*, Capt. John D. Whidden at Port of Malta.
Copied from illustration in Capt. Whidden's *Ocean Life in Old Sailing Ship Days*.

her two other boats never reached land. The crew stayed at Six Islands until they were picked up two-and-a-half months later by the plantation's supply vessel, the brig *Ibis* (Captain J.L.R. Dolphin) and taken to Mauritius.[6]

Then, on 1 November 1876, the British barque *Teviotdale* caught fire 80 miles south-west of Diego Garcia, and was abandoned. Her crew of 26 succeeded in reaching the island after three days, and spent some weeks at Pointe Marianne.[7] The *Teviotdale* had been carrying a cargo of coal from Dundee to India. Some ten months later, on 17 September 1877, according to a report which subsequently appeared in the *Daily News*, the Peninsular and Oriental mail steamer *Hindostan*, approaching Aden from China, boarded an abandoned vessel which was completely gutted, with coal still smouldering in her hold. She was identified as the *Teviotdale*, of Glasgow, by the official number and registered tonnage marked on the main-hatch beam. An extraordinary last journey for this iron vessel!

Whalers: snippets from the log books

In the mid-19th century, as Special Magistrate Anderson had reported in 1838 (see page 136), the settlements on Chagos were well known to the men who regularly cruised the Indian Ocean whaling grounds. While not every whaler stopped in the Chagos for supplies, their presence was a familiar sight around the archipelago for several decades.[8] Some 200 American whalers, mostly from New England states, cruised the Indian Ocean between 1838 and 1875 and their log books survive in large enough numbers to provide a record of numerous whale hunting voyages, and occasional stop overs in this area.[9] The best time for whalers to visit the Chagos was between January and May, towards the end of the whaling season.[10] In general, the entries are frustratingly brief and tend to gloss over stays ashore to concentrate on recording data of whale chases and captures. The log of the *Montezuma* of New Bedford, Mass., is fairly typical in its brevity, merely recording in one day's entry for 1848 'at sunset we made the island Diego Garcia' and on the following day 'we were cruising off the island'.[11] Despite this, the dedicated researcher can find tantalising glimpses of the locations and activities of the whalers in and around the archipelago.

A preoccupation of those whale ships intending to call at Diego Garcia for supplies was to find a way through the shallow banks and sharp reefs and to take soundings in order to secure a firm anchorage. For example, the ship *Harbinger*, of Westport, Mass., mastered by Samuel Brownell, offers the following entry for Thursday 19 February 1846 'at 10 am saw the Island of Diego Grasha; at 11 am came to anchor at the said island in 10 fathoms of water'. On Monday 30 March 1846 the log again reports that 'Diego de Grachia in sight at sundown'. No other information about Chagos is given.[12] Peleg Sanford's log kept aboard the *Herald* of New Bedford recorded on Sunday 18 March 1834 'Diego Garcia in sight' and on Monday 19 March: 'Stood in for the harbour. Went in with the boat on survey returned on board and stood in to the harbour and come to anchor in 10 fathoms water hard bottom'.[13] The *Herald* spent several days at Diego Garcia between 20 and 29 March 1834 taking on supplies:

> *Tuesday 20th to Thursday 29th* The boats are going on shore and bringing off barrels of water, also wood and 80 fowls and 1 hog. The crew are also allowed on liberty ashore.
>
> *Friday March 30th 1834* At 10 got underway from anchorage and stood to sea at 4 pm last sight of the land.[14]

The *Tuscadora* also provided information of provisions procured at Chagos: the ship took on fish, bananas, fowls and eggs at Diego Garcia during a stop there in 1840.[15]

Some of the log books offer more specific details of place names and mention sighting or calling at other locations within the Chagos archipelago. The *Hector*'s approach to Diego Garcia in December 1846 was recorded as follows:

> Wednesday 9th December at 1 pm saw the island Diego Garcia bearing SW

dist 20 miles … at 7 am kept off SW for land at 10 am passed Middle Island at 12 am came to anchor at Mariana Establishment in 6 fathoms and furled the sails.[16]

Between 10 and 18 December the ship was 'employed getting wood, water & small refreshment', during which time the crew was given four days liberty, and a number of 'ships jobbs' were completed. On Sunday 20 December the *Hector* was ready for sea. A short while later at 6 pm on 31 December the crew 'saw island Diego Garcia bearing WSW dist 20 miles middle and later parts light airs so ends this day in Lat 7.22 S and Long 72.45 E'. Whales were evidently very close by as the log for the next day records:

> *January 1st 1847* … at 7 am saw a shoal of sperm whales at 8 lowered away the boats in chase at 10 starbord boat struck and parted line, larboard boat struck and killed waistboat likewise at 12 midday took one along side and kept ship off for the others so ends this day Lat 7 43 S.[17]

On 2 January the dead whale was taken alongside, cut and boiled, this work taking two days. The cruise then continued, and on the 6th, Diego Garcia was again sighted, along with 'a number of porpoises'. The entry for Saturday 16 January found the ship on Pitts bank and in view of Six Islands. The next day, writes the journal keeper, 'at 8 am saw bottom on Pitts bank sounded and found 8 fathoms water'. On each of the following three days sightings of porpoises were recorded and on Tuesday 19, the position of the ship was stated to be 'standing to NE Diego Garcia in sight bearing S dist 20 miles Lat 6.51 S Long 72.35'.

The travails of Samuel Braley

The most evocative journals of an American whaler in and around the Chagos islands, are surely those of Samuel Braley, who stopped at Diego Garcia several times in the *Arab* and the *Harrison*, in the late 1840s and 1850s. As Wray and Martin report, the popularity of the Chagos grounds developed around the same time as those of Ceylon, and

> vessels whaling western Indian Ocean grounds below the line could conveniently sail eastward to Chagos during the southwest monsoon. Braley favoured Chagos by 1850. That ground's remoteness was compensated for by abundant whales and the adjacent islands' provisions, many of which could be had for next to nothing, far from those developed ports which proved so alluring to deserters.[18]

Even at Diego Garcia, however, some seamen were lost. Between 30 March and 9 April 1847, Braley was there, 'filling up our water, getting a little wood and cleaning and painting ship'. Half of the ship's company were sent on shore each day alternately; one took the chance to hide:

Asa M Collier deserted the ship for the second time during the voyage … coming to the conclusion that the man is secreted by some white man that lives on the island and in such case I should not be able to get him at present I raised anchor and put to sea … There are but three white men upon the island and with one or the other of them he has made a league and he keeps him unknown to the blacks who are of the lowest grade of humanity and would sell a man's life for a bottle of rum and I have offered them money and have searched every place on the islands except the 3 houses belonging to the whites.

Braley returned to Diego Garcia later that month, still seeking news of the deserter. Initially he learnt only that 'he had been seen once by a black man who said that Collier wanted to get a passage to Mauritius and did not want to go on board of the *Arab* again because the Capt was a bad man'. However, sending his men on board another whaler which had stopped off at Diego Garcia, Braley was apprised that their crew had been secretly feeding Collier, and knew his hiding place. The captain found the deserter 'concealed among the bushes, which are very thick in some parts of the island. I caught him, tied his hands with my pocket handkerchief and led him to the house of the Regisseur of Miniminy Establishment and put him in the stocks which are of rather frail construction and were secured at the ends with nails'. The subsequent escape and fate of Collier is an interesting story, and reveals the sympathy of the residents on Chagos for the fate of the American sailors.

Some time in the night a black came and gave him an axe with which he managed to pry the stocks apart sufficiently to get out his leg, there being only one foot in and he took again to the bush … We looked all day and all the next and the next till noon when I received a note from the Regisseur at East Point establishment, that if I would come to his place he would give me some information concerning Collier; I lost no time in repairing to E Point where I found Mr Regnaud Regisseur at E Point, Capt Gerard of *Constance*, Capt Biney of the *Surveyor*, both Colonial Brigs belonging to Mauritius and two Gentleman passengers. Capt Gerard told me that my man had been to him and applied for a passage to Mauritius but he told that he could not give him one that the last thing he could do was to come to me and return to the *Arab*. Collier said he would go, but was afraid I would flog him as I had said that if I caught him that I would skin him from the neck to his heels. Gerard told him that he would send for me and if I would promise not to flog him that he must go with me and if I would not he might get away if he would … I told Gerard that I would not flog him if he came to me and gave himself up; he came and I told him that I would not flog him but to expect severe punishment in another way, accordingly that night I put him in irons for punishment and safe keeping till the ship came to take us on board … had him washed all over and clean cloths put on, and after walking the deck for an hour sent him below again … he refused to do any more duty on board the ship … on his refusing again I put him in the rigging and flogged him very lightly enough however to see that there was no signs of repentance in him and to be a warning to the ships company then took him down and sent him below without irons having made a place between decks for him that he may have no communication with the ships company.

Braley must indeed have been a hard master, or his voyages unsuccessful, for in August, an entire boat crew deserted.[19]

When the whales were not being captured, Chagos seems to have been a gloomy place for the mariners. A series of journal entries by Braley in May 1850 illustrate the point:

> *Friday 3rd* at daylight saw Dainger Island to SE. I am lonely and disconsolate with nothing to cheer my drooping spirits … I only eat just enough to keep my soul from taking its exit.
>
> *Monday 6th*
> Days of absence sad and dreary
> Clothed in sorrows dark array
> Days of absence I am weary
> Her I love is far away.
>
> The prospect frightens: men sick and no whales; if I find a chance I will send about six of my men home or somewhere else and ship others I have one thing to comfort me they can be no worse and possibly better.
>
> *Wednesday 8th* at 7 pm saw Eagle Island bearing SSE 20 miles … the ship is almost a hospital.
>
> *Monday May 13th* So goes the time and no whales I shan't stay in this place much longer if I don't see some soon, but go to the Seychelles and see the Girls and have some fun then to Ceylon for letters.
>
> *Thursday 16th* We have seen nothing today but the birds which we see every day in the morning flying off from the land and in the evening returning after having been in pursuit of fish all day and presume some of them return with their maws half stuffed to half starved young ones so it appears that they are under the curse as well as man.

Fortunately, the very next day, Braley's luck changed:

> *Friday 17th* at 7.30 am raised a large sperm whale lowered the boats and brought him to the ship at noon and began to cut.
>
> *Saturday 18th* We have finished the whale at least but it was hard work for everyone it is the largest whale that I have ever taken in the Indian Ocean.

In December and January 1851, Braley was back in the Chagos grounds, but once again, seems to have found the time there dragging, for in his journal entry of Friday 3 January 1851 he writes 'I am off out of this as fast as I can I shall try to find a place if there is one in the world where it does not rain every day in the week and pours on Sundays. I never see the like before. Good night'. In April that year, Braley had even more to complain about, having narrowly escaped a shipwreck close to Eagle island:

> Never in all my life was I in so bad a position as I was this morning at 4 o clock I was within ¼ of a mile of a reef where the sea was breaking with tremendous violence as could see and hear; the tide and swell both acting against us, and heaving us on towards it rapidly, not a breath of wind to fill a sail I could see nothing that would save the ship from destruction … as a last effort I was about sending the boats to try to tow her off but before I had given the order a breeze came, filled our sails and carried us clear of the danger … I consider that little breeze saved the ship from destruction, and never shall forget it, and hope that I never shall cease to be thankfull to God for it.

Between 5 and 17 May 1851, with bad weather making whaling success unlikely, Braley took the ship into Diego Garcia, anchoring off 'Miniminy' where his crew were employed in cutting wood, filling water and undertaking repairs. The next day he noted, 'I find that my old friends have left the island, but have found very worthy people in their places' and on Wednesday 7 May was entertained on shore:

> went on shore in the evening and passed an hour very agreeably with the lady of the establishment the worst of it is they cannot speak a word of English and therefore I have to speak French which is not of the purest dialect but I can make myself understood well; who can't when there is a pretty woman to listen? I … am haste to get away and I have much to do before I can go.

On 19 May, off Six Islands, an encounter with a pod of whales left two boats wrecked (see verbatim account overleaf), leading Braley to renewed despair.[20]

A third voyage of Braley to the Chagos grounds, undertaken in 1856–7, gives a further clue to the harsh conditions of life aboard the whalers, when his log reports that he intends to stop off at Diego Garcia 'for all on board are affected with scurvy or sick other ways and how it is I know not for it is not a month since we used the last of the vegetables yet so it is'. At Minni Minni, on 9 February 1856, he again found old friends, and others 'whose hearts are as warm and kind as those that have gone and I have spent a few days very pleasantly in their society'. Fourteen months later, on the evening of Saturday 18 April 1857, the whalers were back at Minni Minni 'all worn out with fatigue and 2 sick'. They were carrying with them the corpse of a 'native of the Cape Verde islands' named Julian De Borgue who had joined the ship at Mauritius. He was laid to rest 'in the burying place of the establishment'. On 10 May another crewman, John Canavan 'died at 10 pm after suffering the most severe pain for about 5 hours'. A coffin was quickly made up and he was interred by the side of his shipmate.[21]

Moby Dick, Chagos-style

Tuesday 19th [May 1851] steered to the northward in the morning till 10 and then kept away west to pass between the Six Islands and the bank to the south of them at 11 raised sperm whales going quick towards the land which was then about 10 miles off leeward from NW to NE at noon lowered the boats about 1 pm I got fast to a large whale which was apart from the shoal I called the 3rd mate to help me and let the other boats chase on for the shoal in about 10 minutes after just as I had the whale spouting thick blood I saw a wail set by a boat to leeward in distress; I dispatched the 3rd mate to their assistance. The larboard boat was stoven and the 2nd mate had picked out the crew etc It appears that he was stove in the following manner he was [g]owing on to a whale and when within a short distance of her she settled, and he layed his boat for another whale, but had gone but a little way, when he perceived the first whale coming under water for the boat, and too near and coming too quick to allow him a chance to avoid her: the whale took the boat amidships with her head and broke her nearly in two, and left her a compleat wreck. In the mean time I had taken the whale to the ship and made him fast, and the 2nd mate had brought the mate and crew to the ship and left the stoven boat I dispatched the 2nd mate to the assistance of the 3rd mate who was then close on to the whales; and sent the mate with the starboard boat to fetch the stoven one to the ship, and I kept the ship away for the whales and boats that were in chase and put out another boat. The stoven boat was brought on to her in and put up, the ship kept away again and the boats made ready for securing, the whales being not far from the ship and close to the boats that were already off and where I was on the point of going with the boats, the man at the masthead told me that he could [see] but one boat; I went down to her with my boat found the 2nd mate with the 3rd mate and boats crew in his boat and the bow boat in two or three pieces; a small piece of her stern head and a part of one side all the rest was mashed up fine. By this time the whales had started off and we gave them up … it is good for nothing but fire-wood. It appears that the third mate was going on to strike a whale, and when close to it another whale at a little distance ahead of the boat turned round, made for the boat on a clear rush, took her amidships with her head, and knocked everything flying and started off from here a little way but soon shied and came for her in the same way again and give her some more with her head which left her a complete wreck and again went up as before and again returned and as a third and last call mashed her with her tail then left the boat and went away to the shoal; then the men collected the three largest pieces of the boat tied them together with the lance warps and then remained until the 2nd mate come to their relief which was but a few minutes; how a boat could be smashed so and no-one hurt, I cannot see but thank God such is the case, there was no one hurt in the least by him, for which I am very thankfull for the same but with all that alone we had the good fortune to get one fine whale say 70 bbls [barrels] and I feel very thankfull for that and for there is a days work!! I never heard of the like nor do I believe that a paralell to it can be found in the annals of whaling, only to think! Two boats smashed, and neither of them darted, a pice of craft, and both by the same whale and she a very small cow! but so it is and be it so.

The Sea Fox *at Salomon*

In the late 1860s, the *Sea Fox* of Westport, Mass., made several whaling cruises in the Indian Ocean, during which time Eagle Island, Salomon Islands and Danger Island were reported as having been sighted.[22] The banks were popular fishing grounds for the whalers, with a number of logs in particular mentioning fishing on Pitts Bank, while the *Alto* also fished off Six Islands.[23] The log of the barque *John Dawson* of Fairhaven, Mass., on an 1868 cruise, offers some interesting information about a stop-over at Salomon. Sighting the 'Egmont or Six Islands off the lee bow', on 13 May, and the next few days 'cruising on Pitts Bank', the ship arrived off the north west of 'Saloman Island' on 25 May and anchored at 4 pm. A boat came to the ship, and the captain spent the night at a 'Frenchman's house'. The ship then anchored alongside the settlement, the log noting that the island was called Boddam by the French. Rafts were sent on shore and procured 100 barrels of water and 6 cords of wood 'given to us all out for nothing'. It was also recorded that the man in charge there, 'gives us all the coconuts that we want'. The log's entry for the next two days provides some interesting details about the activities of the crew on shore:

> *Wednesday May 27th 1868.* There never was a ship here before as long as they have been here [12 years]. M Decoiring and wife and child dine aboard this PM. All hands went ashore this afternoon some gunning after shells and coral got large quantity of the latter, brought some pigs aboard there is great many of them also fowl.
>
> *Thursday May 28th 1868.* Brought aboard this morning three boat loads of coconuts, plantains fowl and pigs, a present from Monsieur N Decoiring got underweigh at 8 am. We had to tow with [*sic*] all the way out about 8 miles crossed the shoal about low water with 3 fathoms of water. Mr Decoiring accompanied us out over the bar. The boys gave him three cheers when he left. Entrance to these Islands are at NW. Our course is W by N … Peros or Banhos Isle and Three Brothers on our weather beam this afternoon and evening.[24]

The Merlin: *Diego Garcia unveiled*

The most informative of the New England whaling accounts, insofar as the Chagos is concerned, is undoubtedly that of the *Merlin* of New Bedford, Mass. Time spent ashore was of course time lost from whaling and ships rarely entered harbour other than briefly for supplies or repairs. In the *Merlin*'s case, however, she had a disabled mast and the repairs required her to spend a whole fortnight there in February 1870. Fortunately for posterity, Captain David Allen's family accompanied him on this four-year voyage. His son Henry is mentioned only in passing, but his wife Harriet and daughter Helen both recorded their observations; to them we owe a most lively picture of the living conditions of the Diego Garcia managers. Helen (known as Nellie) was only seven when she journeyed to the Indian Ocean in the whaling barque, so that her account, which has been conserved in typescript in the New Bedford Whaling Museum, was obviously written many years later. After the account she gives of the storm in which the *Merlin* was damaged, there follows the section which concerns the family's stay at Diego Garcia:

> To repair our disabled mast we went to Diego Garcia, an island of coral formation encircling a lagoon. There were many cocoa-nut trees on the island, and the inhabitants were occupied in making cocoa-nut oil. There were three establishments, Minnie Minnie, Point East, and Point Marrianne, each run by a few white men with their families, and several hundred blacks.
>
> As soon as we had anchored, two French gentlemen came on board and gave us a very cordial invitation to go on shore at Point Marrianne. Father had been there before and knew what to expect, but we had no idea of seeing so many white people. Crowded together at the end of the pier, the ladies and children dressed in white, to my childish eyes it looked like a multitude awaiting us. Upon landing we were escorted to a large house and sat on the piazza for awhile looking at the sun set and the island, and trying to talk. They knew a little English, and we less French. One of the boys, Edouard Bonnier, son of the proprietor, seemed to be interested in me and tried to entertain me. By the aid of the sign language we got along famously, and later became great friends.
>
> After sitting on the piazza for some time we were shown the interior of the house, and soon dinner was served. After dinner there was music from a large hand organ which played forty tunes of various kinds, operatic, martial, dance, and which was operated by a huge colored man who kept audible time with his foot as he ground out the music. All the young people and some of the older ones danced, and we had a merry time. When it was bed time we were taken to a small house nearby which was at our disposal while we staid on shore. It seemed strange to me to go to a separate house to sleep.
>
> During our stay on shore, we were entertained at the other establishments, reaching them by going across the lagoon in boats. Our invitations were usually for breakfast, which was served about noon, and often out of doors. Of course we had a light breakfast earlier. I particularly remember our visit to Minnie Minnie where the Mangy [Mainguy] family lived. The morning was very pleasant and no one thought of rain, but just before we reached the landing place there was a down pour, and many of the party were drenched. Our boat had an awning which was a protection. Mother covered me with her long cape, so I escaped, but most of the party were very wet, and had to borrow dry clothing. In many cases the borrowed clothing did not fit and caused much amusement. Henry and Edouard wore long coats belonging to Jules Mangy, a young man of the family. However, the sun soon shone again, and by the time we were ready to leave the wet clothing

had been dried and pressed.

When the mast was repaired we made ready to leave the island, but before going we entertained all the white population at a breakfast on board the *Merlin*. Fortunately we had a steward who enjoyed having company, and was only too glad to carry out Mother's wishes in the matter. He provided a fine meal which was very much enjoyed. There was dancing on deck and a gay time generally. Henry and I had had such a fine time with the children we were very sorry to say goodbye. Later in the voyage we met the Bonnier family again at Mauritius and renewed our acquaintance.[25]

Mrs Harriet Allen's journal is longer than that of her daughter, but concentrates on details of clothing and furnishings of the homes of the European settlements, conversations, gossip, presents exchanged and much in the same vein which offers intriguing insights into the lives of those men who ran the establishments on Diego Garcia and that of their families, but very little else. Harriet's journal has been discussed *en passant* in secondary sources about whaling wives, but has never been published in full.[26] The segment of it which is of interest to us begins on Friday 4 February 1870 when she reports 'Six Islands and Danger island in sight. We will go in as far as we can to Diego Garcia.' On Monday 7 February she offers her initial impressions of the island:

Diego Garcia! This is a curious island of coral formation a mere rim of land encircling a large lagoon the entrance being at the north end. It is covered with trees chiefly coconuts. The inhabitants are wholly occupied in making coconut oil. At present there are three establishments at Minnie Minnie, Point East and at Point Marrianne at which place we are. D has been here before and knew what to expect. The children & I had no idea of seeing more than one white lady and perhaps a child or two. When we landed at the pier at about sunset, there seemed to be a multitude of ladies, gentleman and children to meet us – all in holiday attire. They welcomed us warmly and escorted us to a very picturesque house, where we were all seated upon the large verandah, from which the view is very fine. [27]

Harriet enumerates all the Europeans present to greet them, including 'Mr Bonnier, the chief of this establishment, about 50, his wife, much younger, their children Edouard nearly eleven, and little Cherie two and a half, and her nurse, an important personage with a red turban'. Also, 'a Madame Gosse aged 61 the first wife's mother and the first wife's two daughters Antoinette nearly 16 and Hercilia 13.' There were also three little girls, the children of the second in command, whose name Harriet could not spell. He had another three children who were not present. The chief (James Spurs, who will be described later) and second [M. Vital Hodoul] of Point East establishment, and 'Mr Mangy' (as Harriet spelt Mainguy), 'chief at Minnie Minnie' were also among the party. They,

Harriet stated, 'constitute the white population of the island. There are besides about five hundred blacks without counting children. The large number of servants and black people passing … in their holiday dress helped to give the impression of a crowd'.

In the 'salon' of the Bonnier house, 'a remarkable looking colored individual' provided the guests with musical accompaniment using a large hand organ. Mrs Allen described the room in detail, as oblong in shape, with a central table, six doors, two settees and decorated with portraits and engravings. The table was moved to one side to allow for dancing. During dinner a large fan or punkah was employed to cool the room. The dancing continued until a late hour. 'We were then conducted to our room by the ladies of the family and would have passed a very comfortable night but for the musquitoes.'

After breakfast the following morning Mainguy and his son Edouard arrived from Minni Minni. Mrs Allen learnt that Mainguy had 'lived seventeen years in Diego' while the other Europeans had been there 'two and a half years'. It was arranged that the young Edouard Mainguy would live on board ship while the *Merlin* was at anchor in order to learn English. On Tuesday, Mrs Allen reported, 'the children enjoy themselves exceedingly. Edouard & Henry are busy with boats and manage to understand each other. Nell makes friends with all'. On Wednesday 8 February a breakfast party was arranged at Minni Minni. Bonnier's schooner the *Antoinette* took the ladies, while the *Merlin*'s boat took some of the men. Harriet described the establishment at Minni Minni as follows:

> Mr Mangy has a good substantial house and quite a garden. Everything is very neat. His donkeys are not allowed to roam about like those at Point Marianne. Several lordly turkeys were strutting about. There were fowls of various kinds, turtles in large tubs, dogs etc. We visited the garden and grounds before breakfast after which the young folks played games.

Thursday was showery and the time passed with 'Music, dancing, singing, cards, dominoes'. A picnic excursion to Point North West was planned for the next day, but was cancelled due to bad weather. Mrs Allen remarked, 'We sit in the verandah in all kinds of weather. The children come and go, from house to house, as they like, rain or shine. No one thinks of their taking cold'. On Sunday prayers were said in the family chapel attached to Bonnier's house, after which the day was spent with 'more music, dancing, card playing and games for the children'. Monday 14 February was also a rainy day. Harriet learnt that Bonnier was

> a warm friend of the Emperor. Does not like Victor Hugo & the Radicals. Says he likes 'Prayers' and 'Education' but 'not a Republic for France'. He is a native of Britanny, North of France, is often 'melancholic for France'. Has not seen it for

twenty four years. Madame is a native of Bourbon, also Antoinette & Hersilie. They have lived a few years at Mauritius. It is wonderful how well we get on in conversation. We make comical work of it sometimes though. But by the aid of the dictionary, gesticulation and good guessing we manage to exchange our ideas. After sunset we all went to the beach and kindled a signal fire to announce our intention to go to 'Point East' tomorrow. We lingered until we saw the answering signal, then returned to the house to dinner.

On 15 February the schooner, the *Merlin*'s boat and that of the Point East establishment were put to use to ferry the visitors to and fro. The house there was described as 'very good' although 'not yet completed' and Harriet commented 'nowhere at Diego have I seen such nice beds in such spotless white, & every accommodation for the toilette so tastefully managed as here where there is no lady to superintend the household. Even the breakfast table had an air of refinement & taste not possible at Minnie Minnie or Point Marianne'. The garden, the soil of which came from Mauritius, was 'in excellent order,' and the same went for the 'the smaller gardens at Minnie Minnie & Point Marianne … since Diego furnishes nothing but coral'. A banyan tree and some other 'grand old trees under one of which is a swing' complete Harriet's description. As an afterthought she added, 'At Point East I first saw the cocoa nut mills in operation'. Returning to Pointe Marianne, the schooner was involved in an accident:

> Some time before we got to the anchorage we struck upon a rock & snagged some distance upon a reef. The shock was anything but pleasant. We felt our way a little further then left the schooner and came on in a boat sent to our assistance. Even then we had to be carried quite a distance in a chair. We found the whole family waiting for us in the moonlight.

The next day the schooner had to be hauled up to repair the damage. Harriet went on board the *Merlin* to make arrangements to entertain the 'Islanders'. On Thursday 17 February another excursion was made to Minni Minni. A shower of rain while the party were in the boats en route caused them to arrive drenched, and obliged them to borrow outfits from the Mainguy family, the comical effects of which are virtually the only comments on the day made by Harriet. On Saturday 19 February, a rather different outing was made to Point North West, when breakfast was eaten 'in a cocoa nut hut. Palm leaves & moss'. The sun was so hot that the party could not explore much, but Harriet noted that there were many fine trees and explained that there 'was formerly an establishment there, the same has been removed to Pointe Marianne'. Returning in Mainguy's boat, she comments, 'I enjoyed the singing of his African rowers'.

On Sunday 20 February, the Allens entertained the 'white inhabitants' of Diego Garcia on board the *Merlin*. Harriet was proud of the result: 'the ship was beautifully clean. There was an awning over the deck. The breakfast was excellent'. She was particularly pleased with the reactions of the 'nurses' who accompanied the children on board: 'the three nurses will not soon forget their dinner. They came to me & bowed almost to my feet thanking me. They had never sat at a table before'. On Monday 21 February, the date fixed for the departure of the ship, presents were received from the 'islanders'. Mainguy brought 'a turkey for Henry's birthday, fowls, eight small turtles, greens, bananas and a few shells from the young people'. Other gifts included 'honey in the comb, bananas, shells [chiefly armed oysters], roses, turtleshell and pigeons ... a pig, four ducks, eight hens, two bunches bananas, a turtle, a goat & kid and a dog for Nellie'. A pair of turtle shell bracelets, and two turtle shell napkin rings made by one of the manager's sons were also offered to the Allens. Among gifts given to the islanders in return by Harriet were clothing, slippers, an accordion, and a crochet needle. The families also exchanged photographs.

On Tuesday the ship departed, firing three guns, which were answered. Some time later it was discovered that Bonnier's blacksmith was on board, so that the *Merlin* was obliged to turn back. Further presents were exchanged with the Bonniers during the brief return to deposit the man, and Harriet's last words were, 'We shall remember this family particularly Antoinette. A delicate, gentle, lovely girl. I want to take her away from her surroundings. Now, we are off'. Harriet left Diego Garcia with 'four good sized boxes of shells & curiosities'; the officers of the *Merlin* had also amassed sizeable collections.

In the days following the departure from Diego two of the turtles given as gifts died, and the survivors were set free. The ship continued to cruise for whales in and around Chagos, sighting Diego again on 5 and 16 April. On 22 April Harriet reported 'Had wind. Got on the bank [Chagos]. Caught a few fish and porpoises'. She was now concerned with the need for a change of diet for her daughter who had become 'thin & pale'; at the same time she notes that she has become used to the 'roving life' and wishes that she and her husband could have their own ship to go where they please. Stays on shore were few and far between for the whalers, who could only earn their keep while out at sea and thus, while the ships might have the islands in sight many times during their voyages, only rarely would they seek to navigate their vessels close enough to gain supplies from the settlements on Chagos.

Which were the castaways?

The picture sketched by Harriet Allen was one of order and contentment, reflecting no doubt her delight at the contrast with incessant hunting for whales out of sight of land. The trouble taken by the island managers and their families must have been born out of an equal pleasure in the change from their own circumscribed lives. The unconfined joy of the children at making new friends – alluded to in the passages quoted – was also unsurprising, but indicative of a carefree way of life. There is no hint of fear of the plantation workers – nor much suggestion of mingling. The islanders, for their part, hardly feature apart from one initial mention of 'about five hundred blacks without counting children'. Harriet merely remarks that 'The large number of servants and black people passing in their holiday dress helped to give the impression of a crowd.' This vignette of social intercourse between two sets of middle-class people, far from their respective home bases, in which neither ranked high, but placed in circumstances where both were lifted above the 'lower orders', is charming but also misleading, only hinting at the habitual existence of either. The next chapter looks at other scant sources to attempt to unpack more details of labourers' lives on Chagos at this time.

As elsewhere in the world's oceans, intensive hunting decimated the whale populations. Fortunately, the discovery and exploitation of petroleum arrived just in time to save the whales from extinction, though not the whalers from bankruptcy. The effects of that intensive slaughter are felt in Chagos waters to this day. Petroleum, by replacing many end-uses of coconut oil, also began its slow undermining of the long-term profitability of the Chagos plantations – a topic of increasing concern in later decades.

Notes to Chapter 9

1 Wilmer and Smith's *European Times*, 7 June 1859.

2 *Commercial Gazette* 23 July 1859.

3 TNA CO 167/489 Report of Mauritius Marine Board hearing on 9 May 1866.

4 After the crew had departed, the *Shannon* must have been scavenged thoroughly; the deckhouse, for example, was re-erected in front of the Pointe Marianne manager's house, where, ten years later, it served as the establishment's dispensary.

5 TNA CO 167/445. Letter from Board of Trade to Colonial Office, dated 3 October 1862, enclosing report from Port Louis Shipping Master.

6 TNA CO 167/530. Letter dated 2 March 1870 from John Lothrop Motley, Head of the US Legation, London, to the Foreign Secretary (eventually forwarded to Port Louis from Board of Trade). The details of the ship and the photograph are from Whidden, J.D. *Ocean Life in the Old Sailing Ship Days: from forecastle to quarter-deck*, Little, Brown & Co, 1908, pp. 185–6.

7 TNA CO 167/573 J. Ackroyd, Report dated 26 January 1877. The *Teviotdale* was a barque launched in 1869 and closely resembled the well-known *Cutty Sark*, launched the same year. As this book goes to press, Stewart Jenkins, grandson of one of the vessel's crew, George Jenkins, is engaged in editing his forebear's diary of the accident and his sojourn in Diego Garcia.

8 Scott writes that 'during the 1860s and 1870s … and for a decade or so before and after, the seas around Diego Garcia were a favoured haunt of whalers, with some wrecked on its reefs'. Scott, R. *Limuria: the Lesser Dependencies of Mauritius*, OUP, 1961 [reprinted 1976 Greenwood, USA] p. 259.

9 Among the vessels whose logs are preserved in the New Bedford and Kendall Whaling Museums, the *Herald* (1834), *Tuskadora* (1840), *Harbinger* (1846), *Hector* (1846), *Montezuma* (1848) and *Merlin* (1870)

all visited Diego Garcia, while the *John Dawson* (1868) was given a warm reception at Salomon. Several other vessels reported sighting the various Chagos islands as they hunted the whales nearby – notably on Speakers, Pitt and Swift Banks.

10 Wray, P. & Martin, K. 'Historic Whaling Records from the Western Indian Ocean', *Report of the International Whaling Commission* 5, Cambridge, Mass. 1983, p. 223.

11 New Bedford Whaling Museum [NBWM] Old Dartmouth Historical [ODH] No. 44, Log of the *Montezuma* of New Bedford, Mass., mastered by William Allen, kept by mate Joseph Clark Smith, on voyage 10 October 1846–14 August 1849.

12 NBWM ODH No. 710, Log of the Harbinger 2 January 1845–1 October 1847. Brief mentions of Diego Garcia can also be found in Kendall Whaling Museum [KWM] No. 18 *Bevis* Bark of New Bedford Angles Snell master 4 June 1850–14 May 1853 and KWM No. 22 *A R Tucker* Bark of New Bedford Daniel Lake Ricketson master Annie Holmes Ricketson keeper 2 May 1871–17 October 1874, p. 239; KWM No. 148 *Montezuma* bark New Bedford William Allen master Prince Lawton keeper 15 September 1846–1849, pp. 103–6.

13 NBWM ODH Log 770, *Herald* of New Bedford, Mass., mastered by Frederick Ricketson, kept by Peleg Sanford, 1 July 1833–8 March 1834.

14 *Ibid.*

15 NBWM KWM No. 390 Log of the *Tuscadora*, Cold Spring Harbor, Edward Halsey, master 14 February 1840–13 May 1841, p. 74.

16 NBWM ODH No. 1052A, Log of the *Hector* (Bark) of Warren, Rhode Island, mastered by William Martin, on voyage from 8 July 1845–4 December 1847.

17 *Ibid.*

18 Wray, P. & Martin, K. *op. cit.*, p. 223.

19 NBWM KWM No. 259 Log of the *Arab* Samuel T. Braley Captain 1845–1849.

20 NBWM KWM No. 255 Log of the *Arab* at Fairhaven Samuel T. Braley master 22 March 1849–12 September 1852. During the cruise, the log recorded sighting Nelson Island, Peros Banhos, the Brothers Islands, and Eagle and Danger islands, as well as mentioning the names of Centurion Bank, Speakers Bank north of the archipelago, and Swift Bank.

21 NBWM KWM No. 261 Log of the *Harrison* Samuel T. Braley Capt 1854–7.

22 NBWM KWM No. 182 and No. 233 logs of the *Sea Fox* Joseph W. Lavers master 25 November 1869–14 February 1871, pp. 55–7, and July 1867–21 September 1869, pp. 49–51, 69–70.

23 NBWM KWM No. 14 Log of the *Alto* of New Bedford Angles Snell master 1 June 1854–7 April 1857, p. 70; KWM No. 255 Log of the *Arab*, p. 62. On a previous voyage the *Arab* apparently obtained turtle at Danger island: No. 259 Log of the *Arab* 22 November 1845–2 June 1849, p. 180; KWM No. 261 Log of the *Harrison*, 15 July 1854–15 September 1857, p. 102.

24 NBWM KWM No. 268 Log of the *John Dawson* Captain Wicks, Log keeper, Frederic Taber Fairhaven Mass. 1868.

25 NBWM KWM No. 402 *When I was Seven* account of the *Merlin* of New Bedford, kept by Helen [Nellie] C. Allen [daughter] 23 June 1868–12 April 1872, pp. 36–41.

26 Druett, J. & R. *Petticoat Whalers: whaling wives at sea, 1820–1920*, 2001, pp. 86–7 gives a brief mention to Harriet, noting that she played the 'bountiful hostess, inviting the local inhabitants on board for a meal'.

27 NBWM KWM No. 401 Journal of Harriet, wife of Captain David E. Allen of *Merlin* Bark, of New Bedford, Mass. All further citations to the journal of Harriet Allen are taken from this source.

The System Questioned: 1860–1874

Inspection problems persist

FOLLOWING the murder of Hugon in 1857, it had been agreed that, since the powers of the magistrates did not extend to the Lesser Dependencies, ships of the Royal Navy would periodically make cruises to these islands and their captains be appointed Commissioners having magisterial powers. The first such, as described in Chapter 8, was Lt. Berkeley, captain of HMS *Lynx*, who visited and reported on the state of the islands in 1859. However, this arrangement, being always subject to other demands on the Navy's resources, did not take long to break down. In 1860, the Governor requisitioned another vessel, HMS *Persian*, captained by Commander E. Hardinge, to undertake a similar voyage. He began by visiting Agalega and Des Roches, but, on reaching Victoria in the Seychelles, found a letter from his Admiral commanding him to return to Port Louis. There followed some testy correspondence between the Admiralty and Colonial Office about the powers of Colonial Governors to instruct ships' captains as distinct from seeking the assent of the relevant Admiral. In the first days of 1863, before the issue could be resolved, the ailing Governor of Mauritius, Sir William Stevenson, died a protracted and painful death, leaving the colony in the hands of the senior military officer, Major General Johnstone. The latter then aroused the indignation of the Admiralty afresh, by commandeering HMS *Rapid* to deal with an emergency in Madagascar.[1] Nearly four years had now passed since any representative of the colonial government had visited the Chagos and there was no telling when some new scandal might occur. In fact, just such a scandal was about to be revealed. Once again, the problem arose in Six Islands.

In 1861, some twenty Malagasys had been recruited from 'Ste. D'Amarée' [Cap Ste. Marie, now Tanjona Vohimena] in Madagascar. After a week in Mauritius, they were employed by a M. Gonard, self-styled proprietor and Agent of Six

Islands, on a three-year contract.[2] In May 1863, eleven of them fled from the island in a pirogue and, after spending 48 hours at sea without food or water, reached Eagle Island. There, the manager, a M. Gendron, received and treated them in a kindly manner, employing them as labourers for three months, until they could be sent on to Mauritius aboard the steamship *Sir John Burgoyne*. On arrival they reported, as instructed, to the new proprietor of Trois Frères, Henry Plasson, to ask for their wages. And then their sorry tale was investigated by the Procureur Général.[3]

When they first went to Six Islands, they had been well-treated by the manager, a M. Encelain [Asselin?[4]], who was in February 1862 replaced by Alfred Short. The latter had, according to the testimony of four individuals questioned in detail, behaved abominably from the start, cutting the rations provided, obliging them to make do with small quantities of Indian corn rather than rice, failing to pay wages, refusing to make available salt, rum or tobacco, and forcing them to work for the whole of every day of the week. The consequences of complaining were dire. As François Malagash, one of the witnesses, reported, his feet had been shackled at night and he had been beaten with a rattan cane almost daily for many months. Another, Milette, added that all the 20 Creoles and 21 Malagasys employed at Six Islands had been shackled at night and only the *sirdars* (i.e., *commandeurs*) left free; on one occasion Short came out with a loaded gun and shouted 'I am the Magistrate, the Police and the Master here. I will kill you and no-one will know'. Two others, Langar and Letchar, supported these claims, the first conceding that he had not been beaten hard enough to make him sick, the second adding that he had been forced on occasion to spend nights outside in the stocks.

Confronted with these accounts, Gonard confirmed that the schooner (*goëlette*) *Le Ramp*, on return from Six Islands in May, had reported the escape of eleven Malagasys. He had immediately despatched a letter of complaint to the Port Louis magistrate. He could not comment on the allegations now made without giving Short the chance to reply to them; however, he believed they were all lies; he himself had visited the island in August and spent eleven days there; everyone had been busy with loading and unloading; he had received not a single complaint during all that time. Interestingly, Gonard's indignation did not extend to any denial of the existence of stocks or an ample supply of leg irons. It was now September and Gen. Johnstone wrote to seek the urgent assistance of the newly appointed Commander-in-Chief of the Cape Naval Station, Rear-Admiral Sir Baldwin Walker. A month later, on 17 October, he forwarded a copy of that letter to the Secretary of State. 'Plainly', he commented, 'it is not possible to afford protection … by sending cruizers once perhaps every 2 or 3 years, and then only after the perpetration of some heinous crime'.

Johnstone then went on to suggest the outlines of a new system, under which the Navy would provide a ship once or twice a year, while law enforcement would be undertaken by a visiting magistrate based in Mauritius. He concluded by remarking, with manifest relief, that it would fall to the new Governor, Sir Henry Barkly, due to arrive on the next ship, to pursue this issue.[5]

Concessionaires seize their chance

These events might be thought to suggest that the colonial government had been careless in relying too heavily on the Navy to make up for the longstanding difficulty of exercising effective supervision in Mauritius' far-flung dependencies. That would be unfair. From at least 1862 the Governor and Surveyor General had been examining other ways of exerting pressure on the island proprietors, as well as obtaining some economic contribution from their enterprises. For their part, the proprietors were both tactically acute and well-placed to press their views. Hippolyte 'le Norman' Lemière was one such. His father, François, had emigrated from Normandy and married a Mauritian creole, Lolotte Pancique. Born in 1817, Hippolyte was a self-made entrepreneur, who gradually built up a portfolio of trading interests – exports to Europe of coconut oil from the Chagos islands, exports to Australia of Mauritius sugar and Madagascan beef, imports from Mauritius' outer islands of dried salted fish and guano to manure the sugar fields, as well as distillation of rum from a local sugar plantation, in which he also had holdings. He took an interest in the commercial and civic politics of Port Louis and in 1847, still only 30 years old, he was nominated to Mauritius' Legislative Council. Enjoying good relations with King Radama II of Madagascar, he helped promote British interests there and in 1862 this 'Merchant and Proprietor' was nominated by Radama as his Consul to Mauritius.[6] The Governor, commending him as 'in all respects a fitting representative', managed to secure London's agreement, contrary to precedent, for his *Exequatur*[7] to be issued without having the application sent afresh from the Madagascan monarch to the British Queen; he was similarly successful in obtaining permission for Lemière to wear a Madagascan decoration at official functions.

A month or two earlier in the same year, a British merchant ship, the *Swithanley*, had been wrecked on Blenheim Reef, to the south-east of Salomon (see page 169).[8] By good fortune, the colonial schooner *Sphinx*, supplying that island group, had been close by and her skipper, Captain Puren, had with great skill managed to rescue all aboard and bring them to land. They had then been cared for by the island manager. All this having been reported to the Board of Trade in London, a handsome gift was made to the captain and full reimbursement offered to the Salomon's proprietors, one of them being Lemière (the others were Plasson and Auguste Louys). The concessionaires refused to accept a cent. The fact was that, being aware of growing government interest in their affairs, they were themselves preparing to pre-empt any government initiative by putting forward one of their own.

Hippolyte Lemière. Image courtesy Paul Lemière.

They had reason for concern. The Surveyor General, Captain Morrison of the Royal Engineers, was undertaking, on his own initiative, a thorough study of the Oil Islands, covering not only their extent and ownership, but also their productivity and profitability. His main aim was to discover ways by which the Mauritius Treasury could benefit from their plantations. Finding it extremely difficult to establish the true facts from public sources, he privately consulted two of the *jouissance* holders, Plasson and one of the Liénard brothers. The results were twofold. His report to the Acting Governor,[9] made on 1 June 1863, was highly informative; his activity also stimulated the proprietors to submit, on 22 August, their own analysis together with proposals for a new dispensation. This took the form of a 'memorial' addressed directly to the Secretary of State for the Colonies, the Duke of Newcastle. Lemière's vigorous signature headed the list. The two parties' ideas were strikingly similar. Not surprisingly, the concessionaires' calculation of their profit was more modest than Capt. Morrison's; equally predictably, Morrison proposed exchanging the existing *jouissances* for 99-year leases, whereas the proprietors sought outright ownership of the islands. Gen. Johnstone, in forwarding the papers to London declared himself, on each point of difference, 'inclined to side with the memorialists'.[10]

At this stage, the Chagos islands were still producing well over half of Mauritius' requirement for coconut oil – 172,000 gallons out of 270,000 gallons. Of the difference, about 80,000 gallons were being imported from India, where new plantations were springing up, as they were also in Ceylon and the coastal areas of Malaya. The *jouissance* holders professed deep concern about this growing competition and claimed that the selling price in Mauritius was determined by production costs in India, where more modern processing methods were being introduced and would thus 'militate against healthy competition'; they held that *jouissances*, which could be terminated at any time by the Crown, provided an inadequate basis for committing sufficient capital to modernise the island plantations; they therefore sought outright ownership, for which they were prepared to pay 10% of the value of the current year's production, as well as a 6% tax on the declared value of the oil exported. In short, 'healthy competition' necessitated increased safeguards. The writers of the 'memorial' did however undertake

'at once [to] take steps to greatly increase the produce of these islets by the introduction of steam machinery and other adaptations, thus not only giving a considerable impulsion to commerce in these seas, but also increasing largely the
revenue accruing to government therefrom …' Capt. Morrison and Gen. Johnstone were convinced that stronger title would indeed lead to increased investment and also believed that the islands could produce anything up to double the
existing quantities of oil. In addition to the objective of securing, for the first
time, a return to the Mauritius treasury from the commercial activities being
carried on in the islands, they believed they could raise money to pay for better
oversight of the islands. As Johnstone put it,

> The increase of our income thus accruing to the Mauritius Treasury would
> entail responsibilities on the local government in relation to the moral condition
> and welfare of these outlying Dependencies, and might be appropriate[d] to the
> creation of hospitals, dispensaries and schools on the larger islands, as well as to
> the administration of justice by a travelling Commissioner, who might be
> appointed to make circuits at uncertain periods throughout all the outlying
> Dependencies of Mauritius, with instructions to enquire into the condition of the
> labourers, to exercise magisterial powers in cases of crime, and to make periodi-
> cal reports to the Mauritius Government upon all points relating to the material
> and moral welfare of the inhabitants.

In a follow-up despatch,[11] in which he reverted to the problems of securing the
Royal Navy's help more frequently than 'once perhaps every two or three years,
and then only after the perpetration of some heinous crime', Johnstone sought
the commitment of a cruiser once or twice a year. In that case 'it would be well
worth while to appoint a visiting magistrate whose Head Quarters might be at
Mauritius and [who] might avail himself of the visits of the cruizer'. This appears
to be the first mention of such a functionary.

Before considering the response of the Colonial Office, which first passed the
reports to the Land Board, it is worth pausing to describe what the two assessments revealed about the commercial health of the Chagos plantations. This is
not altogether simple, for it involves calculation amidst many statistical thick-
ets. First, the *jouissance* holders invariably used *veltes* as the unit of production
and sterling as the unit of value. *Veltes* were small casks, assumed to contain 7.45
litres of oil. The Surveyor General used these measures too, but also dollars and
gallons (by inference, Imperial gallons); occasionally, he provided comparisons,
but of a rough-and-ready kind, which assumed a sterling/dollar exchange rate of
£1:$5 and a *velte*/gallon equivalence of 1:1.5 (strictly, 1 *velte* = 7.45 litres = 1.64
gallons).[12] Second, the estimates of production by the *jouissance* holders were
invariably lower than those of Capt. Morrison; while the latter was seeking
objectivity, the former were concerned to reduce to the absolute limit of

plausibility the base figure for the calculation of the price they would pay for outright ownership of the islands. Thus Morrison reckoned that the production for 1862 had been 115,000 *veltes*, whereas the *jouissance* holders proposed a figure of 86,000. Thirdly, for a host of reasons, each island's production could vary markedly from year to year. A somewhat similar problem arose in the calculation of the cost of production and sale price. The latter was quite easily ascertainable, at around 7 shillings (7/-) per *velte*, but only the producers really knew what their costs were, proposing a figure of 5 shillings, as opposed to Morrison's estimate of 4 shillings. The latter was on this point ready to defer to the producers, remarking that a 40% profit could be considered adequate, even in Mauritius. However, when the papers were passed by the Colonial Office to the Land Board for expert assessment, the latter considered that the real figures should be 4/1 for production and 7/- for sale, a profit of 66%! Giving the *jouissance* holders the benefit of the doubt, it can be asserted that they were making a comfortable income, depending on how much was allocated to future investment. Assuming production of 100,000 *veltes* and a profit of 2/- on each, the total profit would amount to £10,000 per year. Some at least might have been allocated to new investment.

The plantations were not however the only source of income from coconut oil for most of the the *jouissance* holders. As the Surveyor General reported, the

> *Compagnie Générale des Huiles*, who are … the only extensive importers of foreign oil, are at the same time, I believe, the holders of almost all the Oil Islands, dependencies of Mauritius … the [company] enjoys a perfect monopoly of supply of oil that from their large capital, use of their own vessels &c they can afford to undersell, for the purpose of ruining, any other competitor – and their profits are enormous.[13]

While therefore, the *jouissance* holders had, as such, an interest in preferring oil from their own plantations, on which no duty was payable, to oil from India, on which the duty was 6% *ad valorem* on the invoice price, the payment was but a minor inconvenience. The *veltes* in which the oil arrived were leaking and dirty, nothing but a nuisance to Customs examiners, who charged a nominal 1/- per *velte* – a sum which was doubled, without a whisper of complaint, when the Chief of Customs was invited to comment on the Surveyor General's findings. If we now assume, in discussing the income actually received by individual holders of *jouissances*, that the whole sum of £10,000 mentioned above was available for distribution, readers may concede that their earnings have not been unduly exaggerated. Lemière was one of the lesser holders and probably obtained less than £300 per annum from this source. He must nevertheless have been, in the phrase of one of his living descendants, 'living in opulence at that time'. He must also, as we have described (see page 164), have been able to pay a good deal of money to buy his Chagos holdings.

Unfortunately for all concerned, the goose for whose golden eggs government and *jouissance* holders were contending was on the point of becoming a good deal less fertile. In May 1864, the Duke of Newcastle had received the Land Board's comments and had approved Capt. Morrison's proposals. He also gave the new Governor, Sir Henry Barkly, authority to settle as he saw fit the terms for the change of tenure; but he wished 'to be satisfied that adequate provision would be made for the protection of the labouring classes on [the islands]'.[14] Meanwhile, however, some of the *jouissance* holders living in Paris had dissociated themselves from the acceptance of any continuing tax on oil exported from the Chagos.[15] Disregarding the arguments adduced, regulations were published in August 1864 incorporating most of what had been proposed by Capt. Morrison and opening the way for individual applications to be made. None was forthcoming. Early the following year, the reasons became clear, when Barkly reported his conclusions drawn both from new representations by the concessionaires and from Morrison's own visit to the islands: the cost of production of 86-96 cents per *velte* and a sale price tumbling towards $1 per *velte* left no room for continuing profit. As Barkly explained, the decline

> may perhaps have been intensified by the anticipated introduction of Gas into Port Louis, but it has extended to all parts of the World, and it is clearly due to the recent great development of the American Petroleum Springs, and the improvement of the apparatus for burning Mineral Oils … the splendid Revenues once realised, which led the Holders to seek greater security of tenure, must be numbered with the past.[16]

The actual report of Capt. Morrison, drawn upon by the Governor, was however not forwarded to London. Indeed, this manuscript was only rediscovered in 2010, badly damaged by water, in the Mauritius National Archives in the course of our research for the present work. Interestingly, Morrison's conclusions scarcely support those conveyed to London by Sir Henry Barkly; in particular the Governor seriously exaggerated the production costs cited by his Surveyor General. While agreeing that pressure from gas and petroleum on the price of coconut oil was likely to continue, Morrison expressed himself robustly on the subject of the proprietors' own contribution to their difficulties:

> The establishments are of a very imperfect description: almost all the materials required in their construction or for their service, with the exception of iron for blacksmiths work may be obtained on the spot; the cost of the animals employed amounts to but very little; the salaries of the employés are not large; the freight is taken up in some instances by vessels belonging to the holders of the islands and the expense of whose maintenance cannot I believe be wholly charged to the establishments, inasmuch as at certain periods of the year such vessels are

employed in other services; the labor of planting involves but very small expense; and to a great extent the growth of the trees now in existence owes quite as much to nature as to the labor of man.

I believe that the outcry that has been made about the enormous expenses incurred by the holders of these islands involves a considerable amount of absurdity; and the hardship entailed by a presumed insufficient consideration thereof on the part of the Government is but one more sample of the supposititious injury to individuals which forms the *cheval de bataille* when the Government attempts to assert its just claims to defend its rights.

It is true that the value of these islands is liable to deterioration from the effects of hurricanes, but property of any description can scarcely be enjoyed without some attendant risks, and when a comparison is made between the annual profits, and these profits have been for many years past enjoyed by the holders and the amount of royalty upon payment of which freehold Isles are to be given by the government, I think that few, but the most interested parties, will be inclined to believe that the holders have met with aught but the most favorable terms from the government, terms which, had I been enabled to visit these islands a few months earlier, I should scarcely have felt inclined to have recommended the Government to accord.

The cost of the oil varies from 64 to 96 cents per *velte*, and such variation is apparently due to various causes – the number of laborers employed may be greater at one time of the year than another.

Before sending his despatch to the Colonial Office, Barkly convened a meeting with officials (including the Surveyor General) and four representatives of the holders, including Lemière and Plasson; agreement was reached that the down payment be based on production for 1864 and the idea of continuing royalties be held in abeyance against the possibility of change in market conditions. This proposal was accepted by the Secretary of State in September[17] and new certificates of ownership issued to all concerned, taking effect on 1 January 1866. The single payment to the Treasury in respect of the Chagos amounted to £12,000. In coveting this immediate gain – loss of an annual royalty was 'not unimportant … but as nothing compared with the importance of encouraging the chief production for which the soil and climate of these islands appears to be particularly fitted' – other public interests received less close scrutiny than they merited.

New dispensations, old impediments

No continuing arrangement was put in place immediately for ensuring the welfare of the island labourers (Morrison's suggestion, endorsed by the local managers, that a magistrate be appointed for the Oil Islands, with his headquarters at Diego Garcia, was lost to view). Perhaps this was because an inspection had just taken place. During November and December 1864 Adm. Walker had made available HMS *Rapid* to investigate the events alleged to have occurred more than a year earlier on Six Islands, with Morrison taking advantage of the tour for his own purposes. Charles Farquharson, the District and Stipendiary Magistrate for Seychelles, was entrusted with carrying out the undertakings given in the Secretary of State's Proclamation. He visited all the Chagos settlements and, with two exceptions, found conditions entirely satisfactory, with good management and contented workers, well supplied and burdened only lightly with labour. The exceptions were East Point on Diego Garcia and Eagle Island. Shortly after his arrival at the first,

> the whole of the Laborers came in a body, and in a clamorous and disorderly manner asked to be taken on board the *Rapid*, stating that the manager, Mr Houdet, used them very hardly, overworked them and did not feed them, &c., &c.. I soon found out the cause of these feelings towards the Manager: I ascertained that this gentleman had only taken over the management of the estate a short time previously and had succeeded to a person who had tolerated all kinds of abuses and license, which it had been his lot to reform. The measures which Mr Houdet had employed to reduce this unruly mob to a state of useful and wholesome discipline had raised the indignation of the most refractory, who vented their rage by exciting the quieter to raise the cry with which they met me.

Eventually, he questioned 14 out of the 180 workers and found 3 infractions which justified the imposition of a fine against the manager. 'What kind of cases?' was the marginal question of a Colonial Office official, pertinently perhaps in view of Farquharson's comments on Pointe Marianne and Minni Minni, two 'magnificent plantations', where 'the most perfect harmony and tranquillity reign[ed]' and a 'wholesome discipline appeared to pervade every department'. At this distance in time, no really objective comment can be made on the contrast between Lt. Berkeley's impression of the East Point establishment under Régnaud, Houdet's predecessor, and Farquharson's impression of Houdet (who had been encountered by Berkeley at Peros Banhos as its newly arrived manager). However, the testing of each other by workers and new managers was to become a recurring phenomenon.

Farquharson's next halt was at Six Islands, where all 41 labourers professed themselves 'perfectly contented and satisfied'. The only echo of previous problems was the discovery, a day later at Eagle Island, of a Malagasy, calling himself Cacanoul, who had previously been employed for eight years on Six Islands. He had only arrived at Eagle Island a few weeks previously, on 28 September, having come alone in one of the estate's canoes, and having spent six days at sea with only six coconuts to sustain him. He claimed to have left because Figaro, one of the sub-managers, had taken to beating him daily with the stick used to stir oil cake in the mill. The magistrate had great difficulty in extracting this explanation, and found Cacanoul 'silly'. On the other hand, he had considerable fault to find with the management of Eagle Island, where the books were very badly kept and, more seriously, a case of assault was proven against Gendron, the manager from whom the complainant was, in Farquharson's view, right to fear reprisals. There being no opportunity to revisit Six Islands, Cacanoul was removed and at his own request deposited at Salomon, the *Rapid*'s last port of call in the Chagos.

The comments on Farquharson's report, both in Port Louis and London, made clear the authorities' satisfaction both with his work and with conditions in the Chagos. Concerning Eagle Island, Barkly remarked in his covering despatch that 'the satisfaction of workers was shown by the fact that the men had all been long-term employees, all of whom had made several trips to Mauritius and then, at the first opportunity, returned to the islands'.[18] As for Gendron, Plasson had decided on his dismissal before Farquharson's return and a replacement, previously in government service, was already on his way. It is hard to resist the inference that relief was as important a sentiment as satisfaction in the official reactions, not least in the failure to pursue the anonymous Colonial Office official's pertinent question quoted above. Intriguingly, three years later, in the context of complaints from Seychelles about alleged growing French influence, the Governor remarked of Farquharson that, 'although his name did not betoken it, he was a Creole of British origin on the father's side only'. This curious comment evidently referred to Farquharson's Jacobite origins and possible want of objectivity in disputes between the French and British. Also known as Charles Farquharson Stuart, the magistrate was the last surviving male descendant of the Farquharsons of Auchriachan, who had settled in France in the 15th century and had for several generations used the name Stuart, maiden name of Charles's great-grandmother.[19]

Whatever might be the conditions of the islands' labourers, it was now clear that hopes of improved prosperity, in which Mauritius' public finances might share, depended on the unlikely disappearance of competing products and rival plantations. In consequence, the expectation of government and promise of the *jouissance* holders that secure tenure would be followed quickly by investment in modern machinery proved entirely chimerical. Indeed, the payment in cash for indefinite tenure took the whole of the profits for 1864, out of which any new machinery might have been purchased. Symptomatic of the changed commercial outlook was Lemière's own 'reverse of fortune', leading at the start of 1866 to his resignation from the Legislative Council after almost twenty years of, in Barkly's words, 'useful though unobtrusive service', having been the first person of Euro-African descent on whom that 'dignity had been conferred'.[20] The details remain scanty. Clearly, the unexpected financial outcome of the initiative, in which he had played such large part, to obtain full ownership of the Chagos, must have contributed. However, it appears that he must also have offended important interests when, as Mayor of Port Louis for the second time in 1863–64, he introduced gas lighting to the city. At the same time he became prominently embroiled in arguments between the Colony's rival Masonic lodges, La Triple Espérance (open only to white '*colons*') and 'La Paix' (open also to 'Englishmen' and '*population de couleur*'). Perhaps it was no coincidence that this development was followed immediately by the sudden decision of the Catholic Archbishop, citing the ruling of a 14th century Pope, to excommunicate all freemasons.[21] Lemière, who shared this fate, at least for some time, then spent the remaining years of his life in modest good works. He sold most of his Chagos share holdings to Plasson in 1866, but bequeathed the rest to one of his sons, Aristide, who had married the daughter of the proprietor of Minni Minni estate on Diego Garcia.[22]

Another decade of neglect

For the following eleven years the Chagos received no attention at all from the authorities. Admittedly, Mauritius itself was subjected to a succession of catastrophes: an outbreak of cholera in 1866 was quickly followed by the start of what proved to be three years of malarial fever, which carried off one tenth of the population and left many others permanently disabled; in the worst year, 1867, nearly 32,000 perished from this cause alone.[23] In 1868, an exceptional hurricane flattened many robust structures as well as the sugar plantations, whose apparent recovery was vitiated by an exceptionally low sugar content. Extreme financial stringency was the inevitable outcome; vacant posts were left unfilled, official salaries were reduced and all manner of plans held in abeyance. The Lesser Dependencies went unmentioned in the files. In 1869 however, Port Louis was reminded of their existence by reports of disturbances in the Saint Brandon fisheries.[24] Investigations duly revealed dire mistreatment of the labourers and steps were then taken to secure improvements. The police officer despatched for this purpose also commented in his report 'I am led to believe from hear-say that Galega and the Six Islands &c. are under much the same treatment with regard to the labourers, but as this is foreign to my report I simply mention it *en passant*'. In reporting these matters to London the Governor reverted to the desirability of instituting annual visits by a man-of-war, and remarked that none had been possible since no ship had been available since 1865 (nor, one might comment, had any visit been requested in that time).[25] Eighteen months later, discussions over the reduction in the Mauritius garrison provided another opportunity to raise this issue. The Acting Governor, Major General Smyth, duly did so, agreeing that the troops could go, but stating that it was 'much more important that a ship of war be placed permanently at this Station [for various purposes], but also to enable the Government to have the means of sending her occasionally to the various dependent Islands which otherwise can rarely be visited and which are in great want of supervision'.[26] It did not take long for the Admiralty to reject this proposal, while adding that their Lordships 'have taken a note of General Smyth's suggestion'.[27]

Taken as a whole, the years between 1860 and 1874 resulted, for all the effort expended, in no improvement in the governance of the Chagos islands. On the other hand, the owners (as they had now become), had obtained a huge gain in security of tenure at minimal risk or expense; they had even limited to two acres per plantation the amount of land which the government could claim back for public purposes, including the establishment of any Naval Station (for which two acres would be ludicrously inadequate). Furthermore, the assumption of the authorities that self-interest would cause the proprietors to fulfil their promises of increased investment proved entirely false. They had likewise left themselves without the means of applying pressure and without the tax income from which to fund more effective supervision. All that could be said was that, in the prevailing commercial circumstances, the proprietors had an interest in keeping sufficient peace in their establishments to ensure continuity of production and thus the continued flow of some income. The promises of Queen Victoria's Proclamation (see page 153) to the islanders remained hollow.

Not quite all was lost. Four years later, in 1874, an inspection of St Brandon and Agalega brought to light an improvement of conditions in the former, but very bad treatment in the latter. In a despatch, The acting Governor, Edward Newton commented that

> after all, nothing will be really efficient except the despatch from time to time of a competent officer to visit the islands. At the moment the overseers and managers are practically irresponsible – and that under such circumstances such men should be unfeeling or careless towards their labourers is only what might be expected ...[28]

Despairing of help from the Admiralty, Newton saw no alternative but to throw the expense of inspection on the revenue of Mauritius. He set his officials to work on a new Ordinance which would include:

 (i)   clear and positive regulations as to clothing, food, medicines, hospitals and lodging;
 (ii) control of the truck system so as to limit the maximum of profit to the shopkeepers;
 (iii) compulsory payment of wages in cash;

(iv)   restrictions on managers' powers of punishment;

(v)   abolition of verbal contracts and of transfers between islands, with all workers being obliged to sign contracts before a magistrate;

(vi)   the provision by all owners of bonds to secure proper treatment and the return passages of their workers;

(vii)   simple declarations by the man and woman concerned to be sufficient evidence of marriage and the cancellation of one partner's labour contract to entail the automatic cancellation of the other's;

(viii)   no renewal of a contract, except before a magistrate;

(ix)   rules regarding the treatment of women during pregnancy and after giving birth;

(x)   periodic reports to the Procureur Général on unusual occurrences, births and deaths, arrivals and departures, punishments, etc;

(xi)   annual or half-yearly visits to each island by a magistrate, at the owners' expense.

Before considering how these proposals were fulfilled, it is time to re-examine, from the scanty sources available, life on the islands themselves.

Mrs Allen's diary

Harriet Allen, the wife of an American whaleship captain whom we have already encountered (see pages 178–182), provides some insights into life on the individual establishments on Diego Garcia in 1870. East Point, by far the largest estate, was unusual in being managed by individuals coming from Seychelles rather than Mauritius. James Spurs was born on Mahé in Seychelles in 1838, a son of the chief mate (and acting captain) of the *Tiger*, a Liverpool sailing ship wrecked on Astove Island in 1836. He became manager of East Point in 1867. It would appear that he arrived shortly after his marriage (in Mauritius the previous year) to Alice Langlois. Their first child was born in September 1868 and Alice, herself not yet 21, died one week later. Harriet Allen's description of his house testifies both to Alice's taste and to Spurs' continuing grief. Intriguingly, Harriet, in conversation with Antoinette, the teenage daughter of the Pointe Marianne manager, elicited the comment about Spurs that 'he has no fault', an opinion shared by Harriet. The conversation then turned to Vital Hodoul, Spurs' younger assistant, whose hopes of marriage to Antoinette were dismissed by both the girl and her family on account of his lack of education. These objections were however overcome, for Hodoul did marry the girl, who returned with him to Seychelles for the birth of their daughter in 1873. The birth took place in the chateau at Les Mamelles, once the property of Hodoul's grandfather, the famous corsair Jean-François Hodoul. Spurs and Hodoul, who remained together at East Point until 1881, must have made an interesting, indeed formidable team. Both, if they lived up to their backgrounds, might be expected to emerge as rough diamonds.

In contrast, very little is known about the backgrounds of other managers of Chagos plantations. It may be reasonable, however, to speculate that at least Emile Régnaud, who had served in Six Islands and East Point a decade earlier, was (like Bonnier, who had entertained the Allens at Pointe Marianne), a man of some education, for he clearly had a connection with Dr Charles Régnaud. In 1860 the latter produced an interesting and learned paper on the nomenclature of Diego Garcia, involving reference to many obscure charts and atlases.[29] In it, he refers to the island as '*ma petite île*', one which he had surely visited, as evidenced by an article about coconut crabs in the English weekly magazine, *Household Words* in 1857.[30] In it the author mentions that 'Dr Reynaud [sic] has seen them [the 'sepoy crabs', a direct translation of the French *cipaille*] in great quantities upon the little islands at the entry of the bay of Diego Garcia'.

Coconut crab (*Birgus latro*). Image courtesy of Anne Sheppard.

The article adds the following intriguing information:

> The sepoy crabs are excellent eating. Gourmets of the Mauritius have them sent
> to them alive from the coco islands. They are sent in boxes which are strongly
> nailed down … there are a few holes made in the box to admit air, and a coco
> broken in two is placed within it; and then, without further precautions or other
> *nourriture*, the sepoy crab arrives in good condition after voyages of seven or
> eight days' duration.

Days of labour

Capt. Morrison's report on his visit in 1864 included descriptions of the daily
pattern of work, as did that of an official, E. Pakenham Brooks, appointed in
1875 as Special Magistrate 'to report on the condition of the labourers' employed
in the smaller dependencies.[31] We shall examine the circumstances of Brooks'
appointment and his findings in Chapter 11; but, since daily life, so far as it could
be inferred from his report, differed little from that observed by Morrison in
1864, we can fairly assume it remained pretty constant throughout the middle
part of the 19th century. For the moment, we may simply note that the proprietors had not taken any steps to modernise their methods of production, preferring to squeeze what profit they could by other means.

The estates existed in order to gather fallen nuts from the coconut trees, many
by this time being deliberately planted (rather than being thinned out remnants
of natural growth), de-husk them on the spot and transport them to the establishment, there to be broken open and have the flesh removed prior to crushing
in donkey-operated mills. The oil thus extracted was then stored for transport
to Mauritius. The numbers of workers engaged in these directly productive tasks
varied from nearly 100 at East Point on Diego Garcia, with up to 12 mills, down
to 25 at Six Islands, where there were only 3 mills. The mill operators and skilled
artisans were paid a little more than the standard monthly wage of $4 (see note
12), while women (whose main job was to remove the flesh from the opened
shells) rarely received more than $3. There was also a whole range of ancillary
tasks. All estates employed a few stablemen to look after the donkeys, while
some had regular grass cutters to obtain fodder. All but one had a 'pig attendant'. The managers of the larger estates had between four and eight domestic
staff, as well as a range of specialist artisans – carpenters, coopers, blacksmiths,
calou brewers – and odd job men – watchmen, gardeners, fishermen. Only East
Point employed full-time rat catchers, four of them, each required to catch 100
rats per week; only Peros Banhos needed full-time boatmen, nine in all; only
Salomon, with its fine timber, employed shingle makers. Every establishment

How they make Cocoa-nut Oil. — Page 29.

had one or more *commandeurs* – overseers – to make sure that the manager's instructions were carried out.

Each day began with a roll call at dawn and assignment of workers to specific tasks. The day's work was done when the task was finished. The norms varied only a little between one establishment and another. Thus, a man was expected to gather, de-husk and break 500 nuts, a woman to extract the flesh of between 1,000 and 1,500 nuts; and a mill operator to produce between 13½ and 22 *veltes* of oil, the disparities reflecting , it seems, the quality of the mills and nuts, not the arduousness of the task. Similarly, a man was required to gather 500 pounds of grass, a woman 300; or, where the job was to collect coconut leaves for hut construction, the amount set for a man was 10 bundles, each of 25 leaves, as compared to 12 bundles of 12 leaves for a woman. One other task deserves mention: making cinders, where, oddly the man's quota was only a half sack, a woman's three quarters; the cinders needed to be crushed finely for boiling down with coconut oil to make soap. For most workers on most days, tasks were completed by early afternoon at the latest, though individuals sent to remote parts of an estate might not get home so soon. On Sundays, on most estates, the only work required was *corvée*, cleaning the establishment and washing and feeding the animals. Of course, as is clear from Harriet Allen's account, this routine was disturbed from time to time when visitors arrived, notably by the need for crews to man the whalers, sailing boats and *pirogues*, which, for all the islands, were the main mode of transport. Likewise, every four months or so, when the owners' sailing ships came, everyone was involved in the unloading of supplies and loading of filled *veltes* of oil, not to speak of welcomes for new employees and farewells for those departing. In 1872, a children's book called *Palm Land: or, Dick Travers in the Chagos Islands*, probably based on accounts circulating among the whaling fraternity, introduced readers to several aspects of life in the Archipelago, including the technique for extracting coconut oil (as illustrated opposite).[32] This book is one of a series featuring the adventures of its youthful hero in various distant settings.

Food, drink, shelter and leisure activities

It is no longer possible to discern much about the social life of the islanders at this period. Cooking and eating must have taken up much of the remaining daylight hours after work, with a cheering *chopine* – half-litre mug – of *calou*; rations of rice (between 10½ and 12 pounds per adult, measured out in a metal *gamelle* – canister – were issued weekly, as was a tot of rum); the *commandeurs* and skilled artisans would, in addition, be given a bottle of oil each week. The rest had to make do with a half litre of oil each month, when all were also given a pound of salt. For the rest, the islanders had to rely on their chickens, on fish (where allowed) or on seabirds they caught; turtles were already a rarity and in any case were the company's property. A few islanders owned pigs, but most managers forbade this practice for fear that their employees would steal coconuts to feed them. *Poonac* – the residue from the oil mills – was the animals' usual fare. Vegetables and fruit (other than papayas) were hardly mentioned and, when Brooks visited in 1875, he recommended that the proprietors should provide *dholl* or lentils so as to achieve a better balanced diet. As regards accommodation, this consisted of individual huts, purchased directly from the estate for some $7, or constructed by the worker from materials freely provided, or bought from a departing worker. At the time of Brooks' visit, he found the huts to be well constructed and the 'camps' neatly laid out.

In *Palm Land*, we are also given the earliest account of a *séga* dance, in terms which suggest that it was not only a regular cultural event, but also one which

THE SERENADE. — Page 34.

was offered as entertainment for visitors. As with the donkey-powered oil mill, the illustration (above) of the dance suggests that the occasion had been witnessed by the artist.

At eight o'clock, the other members of the Frenchman's family and the captain came out on the veranda, and in a few moments after, a flame of fire was seen to shoot up from the pile of coconut shells, then others darted from it in every direction, until the whole mass was on fire, sending a brilliant light far into the grove of tropical trees, startling the birds that had gone to rest, and causing them to fly wildly about, while many darted into the flames and perished. Soon negro men and women began to come up in groups, until thirty or forty had assembled on the open space, or lawn, before the Frenchman's house. Then three negro men appeared, each with a large drum, eleven feet long, made of a hollow trunk of a tree, one end of which was open, the other covered with skin. Each of these drums, as they lay on their sides, were raised upon blocks ; and upon each a negro drummer seated himself astraddle, and began to drum with his fists, and at every beat to howl something in the Madagascar language; for they were all natives of Madagascar, and were formerly slaves in the isles of France, but were now liberated by the English government. All the men and women then formed into a large circle, and squat down, or sat on their heels, clapping their hands, and singing and shouting.

While they were singing, a large, fleshy negro woman, named Venus, whom Baptiste told Dick was the champion dancer, sprang into the circle; she was dressed in a red calico dress, and her head was ornamented with a huge red turban. Taking a gliding step to the time of the chorus, her movements at first were slow, and gradually became more rapid; and at apparently a challenge from her, a large black man jumped into the ring and joined her in the dance; and for fifteen minutes their chief object seemed to be to excel each other in rapidly moving their limbs. At last the man retired, amid shouts and hoots from his companions, thoroughly tired out; the perspiration rolling down his cheeks in great beads. But Venus, to Dick's amusement, continued the dance, without slackening her speed in the least, and was soon joined by another negro. Not till she had tired him, also, did she condescend to leave the ring, then apparently not in the least fatigued. Upon her exit, another took her place, and so the dance was kept up, accompanied by drumming, clapping of hands, and hooting or singing, until Dick's amusement began to change to weariness.

Eleven o'clock, and he began to doze in his chair; by half-past eleven the bonfire appeared to be nearer, and the negroes seemed to be horrible demons, yelling and dancing in the very midst of the flames. He was beginning to grow very uneasy, when the captain's voice, saying, 'It's over now,' brought him to his senses. Sitting up in his chair and rubbing his eyes, he saw the negroes moving slowly away, headed by those bearing the drums; and soon nothing remained of the serenade but a heap of live coals where the bonfire had blazed.

No further account of a *séga* in the Chagos appears until the 1930s, but it is clear that this form of entertainment continued to provide enjoyment, especially, one may assume, when not put on to amuse visitors. Now we must examine how the firmer regulation of the island plantations, as envisaged by Edward Newton, was brought into force, the impact there of the changes made and the reactions of the proprietors to the challenges they faced.

Notes to Chapter 10

1 TNA CO 167/455 Letters from the Admiralty to the Colonial Office, dated 2 September and 21 October 1863.

2 There is a mystery here. According to the report of the Surveyor General dated 1 June 1863, all the *jouissance* holders of Six Islands were members of the Duperrel family; according to the collective statement of the proprietors dated 11 August 1863, only Messrs Cloarec and Gérard were listed as owners of Six Islands, but with no indication of their shares. The name Gonard only appears as a widow with shares in Agalega – but some owners were resident in Paris. Perhaps the Gonard mentioned in this chapter was a son of widow Gonard.

3 Gendron's name is rendered as Sanderon in the victims' witness statements.

4 Both versions appear in the records, but clearly relate to the same individual. The name Encelain is otherwise unknown.

5 TNA CO 167/452 Mauritius Despatch No. 201, dated 17 October 1863.

6 TNA CO 167/443 Despatches No. 241, dated 1 November, and No. 273, dated 5 December 1862.

7 This is the document issued by the receiving state authorising a representative of another state to carry out consular functions.

8 TNA CO 167/445 Letter from Board of Trade to the Colonial Office, dated 3 October 1862, enclosing report from Port Louis Shipping Master.

9 TNA CO 167/449 Enclosure to Despatch dated 2 June 1863.

10 TNA CO 167/451 Despatch No. 199 dated 17 October 1863.

11 TNA CO 167/452 Despatch No. 201 of the same date.

12 TNA CO 167/508 Despatch dated 11 August 1868. Incidentally, 'dollars' did not apparently include the US dollar, but coins of Spain, Mexico and South America, that is Maria Theresa *thalers*, and the 'Decaen dollar', presumably a coin left over from the Napoleonic regime in Mauritius from 1803–1810. Readers may be readier to forgive the authors for a degree of confusion, when they learn of Governor Barkly's heartfelt comments on this topic 'There is probably no country in the world which would benefit more than Mauritius from the introduction of uniformity of weights, measures and coins. The accounts of the government are made up in British Sterling money, and duties are levied at the Custom House according to the Imperial standards of weight and size. The books of bankers and merchants are kept in dollars and cents and shopkeepers frequently price their goods in *livres* and *sous*, which, like the weights and measures invariably used in commercial transactions, are the same as those of France before the first Revolution! When it is added that a large proportion of the goods imported come from this latter country invoiced according to the decimal system which has been abolished there for 70 years, and charged for in modern French money, the complex calculations requisite for passing an entry at the Customs may be understood. The confusion and loss however caused to persons newly arrived in the country by having to make their purchases in *Gros* or *Aunes* or *Velts* and pay for them by exchanging real coins for nominal and imaginary ones, can hardly be conceived without a trial.' Students of numismatics may obtain further amusement and instruction from a legal memorandum on the French currency's validity in Mauritius and the Governor's covering Despatch a few months later (TNA CO 167/515 Despatch No. 23, dated 17 January 1869).

13 TNA CO 167/459 Report B/40, dated 25 January 1864, paragraphs 19 and 22.

14 TNA CO 167/47and CO 167/508, Colonial Office despatch No. 48, dated 4 June 1864. Letters of 26 March and 20 May 1864 from Land Board to Colonial Office.

15 TNA CO 167/474 Letter dated 9 March 1864 to Secretary of State, signed by three of the brothers Liénard and by Auguste Louys.

16 TNA CO 167/475 Despatch No. 42, dated 6 February 1865.

17 CO Despatch No. 488, dated 5 September 1865.

18 TNA CO 167/475 Despatch No. 21, dated 31 January 1865.

19 Dictionary of Mauritian Biography, p. 578.

20 TNA CO 167/486 Despatch No. 23, dated 30 January 1866.

21 TNA CO 167/358, 167/364, 167/371. The repercussions of this event shook the Mauritian establishment to its roots, and provoked unimaginably complex discussions about the limits of Church and State power. Lemière was a prominent member of the latter, having served as its 'Worshipful Master' in 1846; and he was the first signatory of a letter of protest to the Archbishop. For a more general discussion of Freemasonry in Mauritius, see Rivaltz Quenette's *La franc-maçonnerie de l'Ile de Maurice,1778–1878*, Port Louis, 2006.

22 TNA CO 167/467 and 167/502. In 1864, this gifted young man won one of the three scholarships awarded by the Royal College to complete his education in Britain and was called to the Bar at Middle Temple in 1867. He died childless.

23 TNA CO 167/523 Lieutenant Colonel Morrison, letter to Secretary of State dated 6 March 1869. One of the victims was the Surveyor General, who recovered but lost one of his three daughters, a second being left with the permanent affliction of St. Vitus' Dance, while the third, weakened by the disease, suffered an abscess requiring a foot to be amputated. Not surprisingly, when he had recovered in England, he resigned his post.

24 This islet, now known as Ile du Nord, lies at the northern end of the Cargados Carajos Bank, 300 miles NE of Mauritius.

25 TNA CO 167/515 Despatch No. 58, dated 6 March 1869.

26 TNA CO 167/529 Major General Smyth (Acting Governor, following departure of Sir Henry Barkly). Confidential Despatch dated 18 October 1870.

27 TNA CO 167/530 Admiralty letter to Colonial Office dated 19 December 1870.

28 TNA CO 167/561 Despatch No. 51A, dated 15 October 1874.

29 Régnaud, C. 'Quelques mots sur le veritable nom de l'île Diégo Garcia' *Transactions of the Royal Society of Arts and Sciences of Mauritius*, pp. 280-1. Later, in 1875, Dr Charles Régnaud is mentioned as chairman of a Commission set up to look into the state of fish stocks in Mauritian waters.

30 At the time, *Household Words* was edited by Charles Dickens. The article was published anonymously, but its author has been shown to be John Robertson, a Scotsman whom Dickens encountered in Paris, see Lohrli, A., *Household Words* Toronto University Press 1973.

31 MNA Appendix No. 5 to Minutes of Council No. 6 of 1876.

32 Samuels, Adelaide F., *Palm Land: or, Dick Travers in the Chagos Islands*, Lee and Shepard, New York 1872 and Boston 1892.

11

1875–1888: Magistrates Make their Mark

AS recounted (p. 196), the acting Governor, Edward Newton, had decided in 1874 that the government in Mauritius must itself take responsibility for improving the governance of its Dependencies. The proprietors, for their part, had good reasons of self-interest for improving their performance. The titular owners of individual shares in the different plantations formed, as it were, governing Boards, and each group placed day-to-day executive responsibility in the hands of an Agent, who organised shipping and recruitment, providing too the point of contact with official authorities. New investors, some of whom we have encountered, may also have contributed greater commercial acumen, as well as having more direct access to the Governor. The time was thus ripe for securing an enduring agreement on the governance of the Lesser Dependencies. The new Governor, Sir Arthur Phayre, who arrived at the end of November, was quick to endorse Newton's approach, soon securing his Council's agreement to the appointment of Brooks as Special Magistrate and to having the proprietors contribute £400 towards the costs of his inspection. While Brooks' account of daily life in the Chagos, already drawn upon, can reasonably be considered to describe the pre-existing situation of the mid-19th century, his critique of proprietors and managers more properly marks the beginning of a new era. The underlying story of this chapter is nevertheless the familiar struggle between government and proprietors, their respective aims being improved conditions for the workers and increased profits at minimal inconvenience.

1875. Brooks' tour

Brooks set out in July 1875 aboard the *Marghretta*,[1] a schooner chartered for a voyage which included Agalega and Coëtivy, as well as the Chagos islands. In the case of the Chagos, Brooks reached Six Islands on 30 September and finally departed from Diego Garcia in mid-November.[2] He counted the population, but went into much less detail than Berkeley had done a quarter of a century earlier (see pp. 158–159) or a later magistrate was to do in 1883 (see p. 227 below). Suffice it to say that the total population had increased modestly from 589 to 623.

Six Islands

This atoll's main owner, who also performed the function of Agent, was now Gustave Ritter.[3] Disembarking, Brooks' first discovery was that the road leading to the camp was obstructed by recently cut down tree branches. Charles Legrand, the local manager since about 1870, explained that he could not spare labour to clear them, since the workers were required to complete the building of his own house. That was the least of his problems. Brooks soon learnt that around one quarter of the workforce had been on strike for over a month. The seven men involved had refused to depart early to work one morning, in order to be present when their partners and other women (all with written engagements of employment) struck in protest at the excessive task expected of them: that of collecting 500 coconuts, the number required of male workers who, however, had additionally to de-husk them. As the results of an attempt to apply the law strictly would have been uncertain and, probably, perverse, Brooks arranged the cancellation of the contracts in respect of four couples, as well as ordering the grant of return passages to eight individuals, most of whose contracts had expired. Legrand told Brooks that he had been instructed to accept the departure of any who wanted to leave and that he expected sufficient replacements to arrive on the next supply vessel. A further major problem was that, yet again, deliveries of rice and other foodstuffs had been inadequate and irregular, the responsibility for this state of affairs lying mainly with the management in Mauritius. To quote Brooks:

> I must however in justice to the Manager state that during the greater part of the time when there was no rice on the islands, he was in the habit of giving the labourers in the morning a little *dholl* and maize or anything he had in store, and in the evening some '*bouillon*' and some bread, but as he confessed himself, the quantity of these articles was insignificant and not in any way equivalent to the stipulated rations. The labourers corroborated the Manager's statement and added that they were forced to go into the woods to collect *papayas*, which when eaten by their children occasioned a kind of black eruption all over their bodies.

Brooks ordered financial compensation to fifteen of the workers and, finding three women not guilty of stealing maize, expressed surprise that there was not more larceny. Nor need readers be surprised that, in the two months preceding Brooks' visit, there had been three births and four deaths of children under twelve. The figures are, all the same, shocking, given that there were only fifteen adult women and only twelve children at the time of his visit.[4] To complete this catalogue of misery, the manager admitted unblushingly that he received a 10% commission on sales in the plantation shop, where many goods were sold at double their cost price.[5]

Eagle Island

Brooks' next port of call was Eagle Island, which, with its neighbouring islets, was owned and directly controlled by Plasson. It presented in most respects a happier picture, reflected not least in higher production (8,000 *veltes*, as compared to 6,500 at Six Islands) from a smaller workforce (38, all Malagasy, compared with 51). As was often the case, the magistrate was brought from ship to shore in a pirogue through heavy surf; on this occasion the *Marghretta* was unable to anchor because the weather was calm (that is to say that the south-east trades, which would have held the vessel away from the reef had, as usual in October, died away). The new manager, Julian Paulet, seemed to enjoy an excellent relationship with his workers. Likewise, the physical conditions of the establishment at Eagle Island appeared good, with the huts neatly laid out and in very good condition. However, close questioning of the *chef commandeur*, Josselin, who had been on the island for 24 years, brought to light that rice had run out for a period of six weeks earlier in the year. As Brooks was to discover when he reached Salomon, which had suffered similarly, this had been the consequence of the loss at sea of the supply ship, *Adeline*. Altogether more culpably, Volcy Répécot, Paulet's predecessor, had committed many financial irregularities, hard to prove because he had taken away all the Eagle Island records. Apart from the normal over-pricing of goods in the company shop, Plasson's financial system, wide open to abuse, required the manager to make notes of the items taken by his customers and, at each month's end, to present the workers with vouchers, redeemable from Plasson in Mauritius, for the net sum due in wages, after deductions for the alleged total of their purchases. Two workers, Louis Malgache and his partner Adolphine, were able to present detailed accounts (falling short of conclusive evidence) of the way they had been defrauded, while others (also named) had similarly convincing complaints.

Salomon

Plasson had transferred Répécot to Salomon, now also in his primary ownership. On arriving there Brooks took these matters up, meeting with evasions of the questions he put to Répécot and an unpersuasive claim that the records relating to Eagle Island – such as they were – had been deposited in Mauritius; but the magistrate was at least able to collect back from Répécot some illegal fines (already repaid to the two workers concerned) that had been imposed arbitrarily for unproven thefts. Salomon no longer exported timber,[6] but produced around 18,000 *veltes* of coconut oil. The previous manager, a M. Bax, who had died a short while before, also used the 'Plasson system' of payments and shop purchases, but no previous records were available and Répécot had not had time to generate any of his own. He did however give an indication of his planned methods, asking Brooks to inform the workers that the manager was entitled to exact fines for petty larcenies and the like. Brooks declined, on the ground that there was no legal basis for such action, but gave Répécot his opinion that, as there was no continuous system of judicial supervision, he might do so, provided that a written record was kept and that the fine did not exceed a month's wages. Finally, on the last day of Brooks' visit, Répécot revealed his true colours. A fortnight previously, he had suddenly stopped providing *poonac* to feed the animals belonging to the two mill operators (Colas and Joseph Common), who complained to the magistrate. Questioned, the manager explained that the grant was done as a favour and he now needed all the available *poonac* for his own animals. Immediately afterwards, in revenge, Répécot stopped the two men's rations of *calou*. Brooks remonstrated, eliciting the response that *calou* was a 'gratification' which he could withhold as he wished; furthermore, he now feared that Common would create disorder after the magistrate's departure. The upshot was that, with the *Marghretta* short-handed and rations offered, Brooks agreed to embark the unfortunate man.

Peros Banhos

Before that, Brooks spent just over a week in Peros Banhos, owned by a M. Duvergé and others, including his brother Ajax, who acted as Agent. The atoll was managed by Julien Frédéric Cochaux. Production varied between 15,000 and 18,000 *veltes*. One feature, perhaps unique in the history of the Chagos, was the presence of an (unnamed) female *commandeur*. Here too there was scandal to be found in the establishment's shop. Many prices were not just double, but from three to five times the cost price, notably haricot beans and *dholl*, but also buttons and needles. The effect of the latter was to give the workers an incentive to use the trouser- and shirt-making service offered by the manager's wife, Mme Cochaux, the income being shared between her and the company (which paid a seamstress to do the actual work). As Brooks expressed it, 'no means here as elsewhere seem to be left untried to drain the unfortunate labourer of his wages'. Wages were paid every four months and most workers availed themselves of the credit the shop offered; many were in debt to the tune of six or more months' pay; and, over the most recent four-month period, shop sales had amounted to more than double the sum paid out in wages. On the other hand, health and accommodation were good and there was no sign of cruelty. The main

List of Prices at which Articles are supplied to Labourers on 'Peros Banhos Islands', together with the retail prices of the same in Mauritius

Articles	prices on Peros Banhos		prices in Mauritius		Articles	prices on Peros Banhos		prices in Mauritius	
	$	Cts	$	Cts		$	Cts	$	Cts
Dholl, per lb	0	25	0	05	Patna, per piece	1	25	0	75
Haricots, per lb	0	25	0	08	Conjon bleu, per piece	3	50	2	00
Sugar, per lb	0	16	0	09	Grey Calico, per piece	4	00	2	25
Coffee per lb	0	50	0	30	White Calico, per piece	2	25	1	50
Biscuits per lb	0	16	0	15	Indienne, per piece	2	00	1	00
Soap, per 3 lb bar	0	62½	0	30	Coutil, per *aune*	0	37½	0	18
Wine, per bottle	0	25	0	12½	Paliacats, each	0	50	0	15
Liqueurs, per bottle	0	75	0	25	Handkerchiefs (colour)	0	37½	0	12½
Dragées	1	00	0	50	Sewing cotton (ball)	0	02	0	01½
Spoons, each	0	06	0	03	Thread (bobbin)	0	06	0	04
Forks, each	0	06	0	03	Needles (packet)	0	25	0	06
Plates, each	0	25	0	06	Night lights (box)	0	06	0	04
Basins, large, each	0	50	0	15	Buttons (1 doz.)	0	12½	0	04
Basins, small, each	0	08	0	05	Padlocks, each	0	50	0	25
Tumblers, each	0	08	0	08	Eau de Cologne (bot)	0	50	0	25
Knives (Sailors) each	0	37½	0	12½	Belts, each	0	25	0	20
Marmites, each	0	50	0	25	Fil de Rennes (packet)	0	25	0	20
Do, (large), each	0	75	0	50	Looking glasses, each	0	25	0	12½
Pagne (Madagscar), each	0	25	0	12½	Straw hat (Seychelles)	1	50	0	50
Tobacco, per stick	0	12½	0	08	Do. (common)	0	25	0	15
Pipes, each	0	03	0	01½	Felt hats, each	2	00	1	00
Foot-baths, each	1	00	0	40	Pomatum (Jamaica)	0	25	0	12½
Frying pans, each	1	00	0	50	Razors, each	1	00	0	25
Tin pots, each	0	50	0	12½	Eau de Cologne (phial)	0	25	0	12½
Night pots, each	1	50	0	50					

Prices at which Articles of Clothing are made up in Manager's House

	$	Cts	
Making a pair of Trowsers	0	50	N.B. The Labourers
Making a Jacket	0	25	furnish their own
Making a Shirt	0	50	materials

<u>Source</u>: TNA CO 170/93 Appendix p. 1325 (1875 Report of E. Pakenham Brooks, App. No. 11)

complaints made by the workers related to the specific conditions of this atoll: most workers left camp on Mondays for the distant islets, lodged in huts there and returned towards the end of the week. One complaint was that too few pirogues were provided to complete the tasks efficiently; it emerged that boat-men were often careless about beaching the craft safely after use. Brooks negoti-ated a solution. A second complaint concerned the manager's refusal to permit the return of a gang sent to a given islet until all individuals had completed their allotted tasks. On examination, it became clear that this problem arose only when new workers were 'not fully broken in'. A third complaint concerned the manager's habit, which Brooks considered 'monstrous', of marking as absent for a whole week (and so docking a week's wages) any worker pleading sickness on a Monday morning. The manager agreed to desist, but one is tempted to wonder whether his penitence would survive future post-*séga* hangovers!

Diego Garcia

Pointe Marianne (production about 21,500 *veltes*) was also owned by Duvergé & Co. The manager was Edmond Desjardins, who had previously practised as an attorney in Mauritius. In general, although there had been a number of relatively minor incidents, living conditions were good and the workers well treated. However, shop prices and the four-monthly payment of workers reflected what happened in Peros Banhos. Indeed, the imbalance between total pay (less than $200) and nominal sales (more than $800) was even more striking, with workers' debts correspondingly greater. On the other hand, the manager received no commission and there was no clothes-sewing racket.

Minni Minni estate (production about 9,500 *veltes*) was owned by Louis Mazéry, whose Agent was his brother, Pierre. The local manager was Médéric d'Antoine, who had succeeded Mainguy earlier that year. Brooks was impressed by the manager's humanity and good treatment of the workers, including a few very old or disabled ones, who were paid token sums for token work, and women with infants, who were given extra rations of oil. Wages were paid monthly and in the shop (where the manager received an 8% commission on sales) prices were around 25% lower than elsewhere; d'Antoine admitted however that he rounded up prices on account of a shortage of small change. Brooks gave short shrift to this patently spurious excuse. Many chickens were reared by the workers, who were not allowed to keep pigs. D'Antoine explained that to do otherwise would be an inducement to the theft of coconuts; Brooks opined that the profit to be made from selling the meat of d'Antoine's many porkers was a more important consideration.

Next and last Brooks visited East Point, the archipelago's largest estate (production details not mentioned). It was owned by the Liénard brothers (who now lived in Paris, maintaining Eugène Mancel as their Agent in Mauritius) and managed by James Spurs, whom we have already introduced (see pages 179, 197–198). The tone of Brooks' report on this estate differs markedly from the rest, reflecting, but only in part, worker attitudes: the magistrate had to deal with an unusual number of unsubstantiated complaints, leading, for example, to absurd debates about the time when cocks crowed at the approach of dawn and the design of baskets in which coconuts were carried; and the atmosphere of the estate had clearly been disturbed by the arrival of a score of discontented new men, sixteen of whom requested and were granted passages back to Mauritius. Objectively, the estate was in many respects well run, with good accommodation, and well thought-out arrangements for new arrivals to choose the housing which best suited them; wages were paid monthly; and shop prices were less extortionate than most – but high enough for some workers to buy from the Minni Minni shop (Brooks was trenchant in his support for the canny customers, and unmoved by Spurs' loss of his 10% commission). On the other hand, recent life statistics were much less satisfactory than Brooks considered them to be, indeed, by far the worst for the whole archipelago: during 1875, with only twenty adult women on the estate, there had been twelve births and fourteen child deaths. Other incidents showed Spurs as inclined to react arbitrarily when displeased, for example in refusing use of the company pirogues for private fishing on account of the dirty state in which they had been left. Similarly, he had for excellent ecological reasons banned the killing of seabirds, but without doing anything to supply alternative nourishment.

Altogether more serious were three cases of vicious maltreatment and imprisonment. Louis Shane, who had complained one evening at the lateness of his return from work, was made to spend a week carrying stones between seashore and oil store and, after two days in hospital, to carry stones for two more days, then – legitimately, but vindictively – to carry coral from shore to kiln, followed by orders to return to stone carrying, which he refused. For this he was locked in an ill-ventilated structure of planks inside a storeroom, where he had spent a month by the time Brooks discovered him. The second case concerned Alfred Legris, who had previously been imprisoned for nine days on suspicion of dodging work in order to have an assignation with a woman called Amélia. Later he was shut in the *poonac* store and had been there 58 days when Brooks saw him. Spurs asserted that Legris had threatened violence against Amélia; and, while she denied this to Brooks, the latter found out that she had actually been struck on one occasion. Lastly, a worker called Kale had also been shut in the *poonac* store, for having left his load of coconuts behind at the end of a day's work. In fact, he had simply missed the boat and walked home. In full view, Brooks ordered Spurs to pay substantial fines, to restore the workers' wages for the days spent incarcerated and pay for the cost of transfer to Mauritius of Shane and Legris. He also explained in his report that more severe charges and harsher penalties were justified, but would have entailed removal of Spurs to Mauritius, with serious consequences for the plantation. Furthermore, he had been instructed to 'use every conciliatory means' to accomplish his task.

The foregoing paragraphs summarise a report which amounted to some 50 pages, not counting voluminous appendices, and we have tried to cite illustrative examples in preference to generalisations, however valid. In doing so, some similarities and also contrasts between the various establishments have been lost. As Brooks frequently remarked, marriage was an unknown condition among the islanders and, on account of the continuing gender imbalance, 'immorality' was widespread. On the other hand, though all islands had dispensaries with reasonable supplies of medicines, one noticeable contrast between the two larger and three smaller ones was the absence in the latter of either prisons or 'hospitals' – buildings that might be described more accurately as sick bays.

Ordinance No. 41 of 1875[7]

Brooks arrived back in Port Louis in late November 1875 and submitted his report on 16 December. During his absence work had continued on the drafting of an Ordinance that would consolidate and extend the legislation relating to the Lesser Dependencies. It was presented to the Council on 16 November and passed with minimal changes on 31 December. It authorised the appointment of an official having similar powers to those of existing district Magistrates, but with jurisdiction over all the minor dependencies. He would operate by making periodic visits, being entitled to free travel aboard the vessels used by the islands' proprietors, who would also be required to pay an annual subvention of £400 towards his costs.[8] Powers specific to the circumstances of the islands included the following: to annul contracts of engagement, to send employees back to Mauritius at their own or their employer's expense, and to sentence miscreants to terms of imprisonment in Mauritius. Further, all his judgments would be held as final, subject only to decision by the Governor that a point of law required consideration by a higher tribunal. A second section of the Ordinance made arrangements for the managers of each estate to be appointed Civil Status Officers, having a responsibility to keep records of births, deaths and marriages and power to certify the last mentioned on the basis of a single publication of the couple's intention to marry.[9] More generally, the magistrate was tasked with examining the 'conduct and state' of the Labourers and Servants and their treatment by their Masters in respect of payment, accommodation and provision of medicines. It would seem that existing regulations for the sugar estates in Mauritius provided recognised standards for, in particular, housing, sick bays and places of detention.

In March 1876, Governor Phayre himself addressed the Council on the subject of Brooks' report, summarising its findings thus:

> The following are the prominent grievances which demand redress: 1. Irregular settlement of wages at long intervals instead of by the month. 2. Excessive deductions from wages on account of absence from work. 3. Inferior quality of rice

furnished in some instances. 4. Exorbitant charges for necessary articles of food, the price being deducted from wages. 5. The absence of written Engagements and of a scale of rations. 6. The prohibition against fishing, or any occupation for acquiring an independent supply of food; apparently with the object of forcing the labourers to buy salt fish, salt, and other articles at the Store kept by the Manager. 7. Detaining labourers at the islands, long after they have expressed a wish to leave and go to Mauritius.[10]

1876–1881. *Enter Ackroyd*

The person appointed to use the new Ordinance to remedy these ills was John Henry Ackroyd, who held the post on an acting basis for three years, before being confirmed substantively on his return from leave in 1880. In 1879, the role was filled by another magistrate, Ivanoff Dupont, who went on to succeed Ackroyd in 1885. Dupont was in turn succeeded by Arthur Boucherat in 1887. It is through the prism of these three officials' reports and those of their successors that, bearing in mind the strong regulatory focus of their visits, we can glean most about what transpired in the Chagos over the remainder of the 19th century. Other visitors, having for example cultural interests, were few and far between. It was the first eight years of the new dispensation that set the pattern. During this time, Ackroyd visited Diego Garcia four times, Salomon, Eagle and Six Islands three times and Peros Banhos twice, while Dupont made one visit to Six Islands and two visits to each of the other atolls.[11]

The accounts by these and subsequent Visiting Magistrates provide a treasure house of factual information about the Chagos islands, but, of course, their primary objective was to establish how far the owners and managers were fulfilling their legal obligations; also to explain the basis for their judgments in specific cases of alleged wrongdoing by employees or employers. They had no remit to examine the sociology or sentiments of the island population for their own sake, nor to remark upon the commercial rationale of the local economy. To give but one simple example, the word *séga* is not mentioned in any of their 19th century reports.

The reports of both Ackroyd and Dupont followed a similar pattern. At each establishment, they began, for the first visit or two, by describing the geography and pattern of work, the numbers of workers and the attitudes of the managers, then seeking detailed information to discover which of the abuses they had been warned of were prevalent. As their reports built up in numbers, they targeted their enquiries more sharply and systematically. At the same time, the island populations, whether managers or labourers, became steadily more understanding of the magistrates' role, speaking frankly of their respective problems and in many cases resolving issues informally, rather than in official hearings. It also became clear that the expectation of magisterial visits at close to annual intervals helped to deter the serious abuses that Brooks had encountered.

We shall not deal with the issues as they were defined in Phayre's Minute (pp. 214–215 above), but rather as follows: basis of employment, working practices, pay and prices, food and drink, accommodation, discipline, health; also with four topics which the magistrates themselves found important: production levels, maritime risks, population changes and social stresses (which they addressed under the heading 'immorality').

Basis of employment

According to the Ordinance, all those hired to work in the islands were to have contracts sworn before a magistrate prior to departure, but, as successive reports by Ackroyd and Dupont showed, anything up to half the workers went on being employed on the basis of what were described as 'verbal contracts'. For example, at Six Islands in 1876,

> There are 16 of the (37) labourers under written contracts entered into in Mauritius; eight of these contracts are for a period of three years and eight for a period of one year. When the engagements have expired the labourers are sent to Mauritius, unless they themselves desire to stop. The other labourers are not now under written contracts. Those who are not engaged can go to Mauritius when they please and on giving notice the voyage previous.

This pattern continued well into the 1880s. Indeed, in 1882, when a revision of the Ordinance was under discussion – providing that no verbal contract should be of any effect – the owners protested vociferously, arguing that existing provisions made it difficult to recruit workers since 'the greater number of labourers who consent to go the Oil Islands are creoles, and that class of the population shows a great reluctance to appear before a magistrate in order to contract an engagement'.[12] This issue appeared to have remained unresolved, possibly because it was difficult to police, but mainly, we suspect, because it suited managers and labourers alike to keep things vague.

Working practices

As Spurs explained to Ackroyd, most of the work was unspecialised, with the ordinary labourers turning their hands to whatever was required on a given day. It may be taken for granted that those earning above the basic wage to undertake artisanal jobs were employed accordingly. It must also have been the case that men having the strength and aptitude for gathering and husking coconuts, just like the women who were the best at preparing the copra, were used to boost the establishment's productivity – and could increase their own earnings by exceeding the norms set. Again, although most of the men would have learnt from childhood to manage boats, the best sailors would become helmsmen and the best rowers man the Manager's whaler – an important and prestigious role on all the islands, but absolutely critical at Peros Banhos, Eagle and Six Islands.

Ackroyd's first visit to Peros Banhos revealed the system for overcoming the problems presented by the atoll's huge lagoon: a 12-ton 'coaster' conveyed workers close to the more distant islets, passing outside the atoll if conditions required it, also returning to collect the gathered coconuts; while a whaler or pirogue was used to transfer workers and cargo to and from the shore. As might be expected, the *chef commandeur* was also head boatman, with an Assistant and up to seventeen other boatmen to assist him. Even when conditions were not severe, this process involved risks and Ackroyd described an accident in which a man was drowned following a capsize.

From the very first, and with reason, official visitors to the Oil Islands had concerned themselves with the excessive demands put upon the islands' workers. We have already described in Chapter 10 the main elements of a working day, which changed little from year to year. By the time Ackroyd came on the scene, complaints about the amount of work demanded were rare and carried little conviction; magistrates regularly commented that the tasks were 'fair and reasonable'. Those words were also used in 1888 by Boucherat (the magistrate who succeeded Dupont) to sum up his observations on all the Oil Islands: 'Very often the men or women have performed a whole week's work in three, sometimes in four days. They are entitled then to holidays varying between two or three days a week. I have myself seen some of the women who had finished their day's task some at 8 some at 9 a.m.'.

Pay and prices

Most of Ackroyd's reports include lists of the numbers employed in various tasks and the wages paid for their completion. The pattern and pay rates did not vary greatly between one island and another, the example illustrated overleaf being typical.

To end the abuses observed by Brooks, the Ordinance required the workers to be paid monthly in cash. Before Ackroyd had set out from Mauritius on 12 July 1876, aboard the *Ada*, a vessel owned by Plasson, to visit Coëtivy, Salomon and Eagle islands, the two men had discussed what we have dubbed the 'Plasson system' relating to methods of payment for wages and shop purchases. Plasson

Work and Pay on Diego Garcia East Point Estate 1877

Nos.	Job description	Monthly wage	Nos.	Job description	Monthly wage
	Men/boys		2	Collecting manure/cinders	Rs 3‡
2	Overseers	Rs 12/Rs 11	20-30	Collecting and husking nuts	Rs 8
13	Millmen	Rs 9	7	Collecting grass/rods, making/covering huts	Rs 8
3	Carpenters/assistant	Rs 16/Rs 10/Rs 6	1	Cleaning up yard	Rs 4†
2	Blacksmiths	Rs 13/Rs 8		**Women/girls**	
4	Mason/assistants	Rs 10/Rs 8	1	Overlooker	Rs 10
4	Sawing/squaring wood	Rs 9	14	Taking nuts from the shells	Rs 6
4	Stableman/assistants	Rs 10/Rs 8	3	Cutting/collecting grass	Rs 6
1	Looking after fowls	Rs 8	2	Servants	Rs 8/Rs 6
1	Looking after pigs	Rs 8	1	Sewing	Rs 6
2	Gardeners	Rs 8	1	Making mats	Rs 6
1	Planting maize	Rs 8	1	Looking after fowls	Rs 6
1	Employed in oil store	Rs 11	2	Girls*	Rs 2
1	Miscellaneous work	Rs 8			
2	Servant/assistant	Rs 8/4†			
1	Cook	Rs 9			
1	Hospital attendant	Rs 6			
4	Rat catchers	Rs 8			

* doing half work, receiving half rations
† Boys
‡ Old men, who do but little work

Source: TNA CO 170/96 (Appendix, p. 1484).

wished to get rid of his shops altogether, arguing that, 'notwithstanding the high prices charged, very little profit was made owing to the quantity of goods spoiled and all those that remain unsold'. As regards the use of cash for wages and shop purchases, Plasson seems to have argued that this entailed locking up capital to no purpose; involved the risks of loss at sea and, in the absence of secure storage, of thefts between the workers; and, finally, made it impossible for the owner to know what amounts had actually been paid to the workers or what devices an unscrupulous manager might use to recoup cash from them. Ackroyd, for his part, considered the shops a necessity and was aware that most workers were destitute when they first arrived in the islands. He agreed nevertheless to consider the comparative strength of arguments advanced by Brooks and Plasson. Successive reports showed that the regulations were being implemented, but reluctantly; at Six Islands, Peros Banhos and occasionally elsewhere, the cash sent would be late or insufficient, with reversion to the use of credit vouchers. This may have reflected cashflow problems, for no theft of cash was ever reported; yet even in 1882 the owners were still arguing in favour of a return to the 'Plasson system' on the ground that supplying cash entailed too many risks, including 'danger for the manager'.

What happened to the cash was examined in detail by the magistrates. Roughly two-thirds of the money actually handed over would be spent in the establishment's shop, the remainder either being held by the individual or left with the manager for safe keeping. There were also arrangements for credit notes to be sent to Port Louis for the benefit of friends or relatives. There is no sign that this trust was ever abused. As to prices (which had to be displayed), the magistrates pressed steadily, with increasing success, to limit them to 25% above the amounts for which the goods had been purchased in Mauritius.

Food and drink

The basic rations, set by long tradition, were the weekly provision by the owners of 10½ lbs of rice, 3 lbs of fish (fresh or salted), and 4 ounces of salt. Under pressure from the magistrates, lentils were also usually provided. Coconut oil too was provided free, but in larger amounts to the better paid. Small quantities of wine and rum were similarly provided, but as 'gratifications' to be granted or withheld at the whim of the manager. On most islands, fresh *calou* was also provided on a daily basis. Expert advice on its preparation is to be found on page 330. The 1877 regulation required the owners to ensure that a minimum of six months' supply of the basic rations was available, the amount depending on average consumption by the resident population. Notwithstanding the periodic brushes with starvation, the owners managed in 1882 to find fault with proposals to increase the scale set for dry foods (on the ground that, for instance, flour and biscuits would not keep for six months).

Beyond these limited requirements, management was strongly encouraged to permit establishment boats to be used for fishing, while the islanders were generally free to forage, to keep poultry (and, with permission, pigs), as well as to grow their own vegetables. They could also buy foodstuffs in the establishment shop, including fresh pork and, ever more rarely, turtle meat. Wine and spirits were also stocked; indeed they were the best sellers. At East Point in 1880, Ackroyd calculated that in the preceding two years the adult population of about 150 had spent Rs 4,700, representing 9,400 bottles, i.e. just over 30 bottles a year each. At Minni Minni, Ackroyd noted, consumption per person was roughly double that amount. The East Point manager considered that some of this extra consumption of wine resulted from workers there selling it to his own employees (whom he rationed to a maximum of three pints per week, and not more than one per day, to be consumed at once on the premises). Excessive consumption, in Spurs' view, was the main cause of disorder; he could 'scarcely recollect any disturbance or offence, such as wounds and blows, that … had not arisen from liquor'. Of course, as readers will have noticed, the labourers had also from the beginning been given alcohol as reward or encouragement.

As to foraging, some islands were more favoured by nature than others. At Six

Islands in 1878, Ackroyd reported that

> … fish is very abundant and easily caught. Some of the men, however, mentioned to me that they did not often procure it. Why I cannot say … the canoes of the establishment are lent if they require it for fishing. The pumpkin plant grows plentifully, especially on Ile Cipaye, and although it very seldom bears pumpkins yet its leaves afford a good quantity of green '*brèdes*'. The papaye tree grows in considerable numbers and yields plenty of fruit. There are some banana trees growing on Ile Cipaye, but not many. I am also informed that crabs, crayfish and periwinkles or '*bigornos*' are easily procured. There is also on the Islands a large land crab called '*cypaye*' but it is not very readily caught. Seabirds are plentiful on Iles Cipaye and Aux Rats, and the labourers are not prevented from killing them. In certain seasons I am told great numbers of their eggs are found and are considered good eating.

Only at East Point did the consumption of sea birds (which was not forbidden by any law) arouse controversy. In 1875, Spurs, the manager, had crossed swords with Brooks, who refused to accept that the avian population could be in any danger, but the issue arose again in 1880. Three labourers complained that part of their wages had been stopped for killing sea birds. Ackroyd 'recommended' that Spurs repay the sums involved and this was done. Spurs, however, had a counter-claim. He had sent the three men to one of the islands at the lagoon entrance to keep watch over the birds, which were just beginning to frequent the island again; yet they had instead killed a good number. For this disobedience, not denied, Ackroyd inflicted fines close to a month's wages. He had in fact previously visited that part of the island with Spurs and become convinced of the harm done by indiscriminate slaughter. By late 1885, Spurs himself had left Diego Garcia for good, and a naturalist visiting Diego Garcia reported that 'Three species of terns breed in countless numbers on the undisturbed parts of the island, and were laying when I arrived on September 15th; the negroes soon made great havoc with their eggs. Frigate birds and boobies are abundant …'.[13]

Accommodation

It appears that the dimensions required (expressed in terms of cubic footage per person) for living quarters were those set for the Mauritius sugar plantations. By the late 1870s, it was rare for huts to be found which did not conform; but the managers clearly needed reminders to maintain these buildings in reasonable condition. They were also required to have prison and 'hospital' accommodation (with separate provision for men and women), of a size based on each establishment's population. Managers seemed to have little difficulty in meeting the prison requirements, but were frequently discovered to have failed to maintain (or even, in some cases, to build) sick bays. This was because most men and all women preferred to stay in their own huts when they were unwell – and were visited there by the managers. As the magistrates pointed out, one incentive for the men would be to treat as absentees any who claimed to be sick but refused to stay in the sick bay.

Discipline

Traditionally, managers had withheld 'gratifications' or rations, or simply put miscreants on the next boat to Mauritius. Later, they would fine or imprison workers for the various forms of misbehaviour – absenteeism, insubordination, larceny, violence. Except in their extreme forms, these punishments had been accepted as fair by the victims, even if they had no legal basis, as was often shown to be the case. Indeed, when Brooks, Ackroyd and Dupont came to hear complaints, they accepted that managers needed to have sanctions to maintain discipline, in the absence of any resident judicial authority. Quickly, however, they began to provide a body of case law, which managers and workers alike came to recognise and reflect in the complaints they made. The system was that, on arrival, the magistrate (occasionally accompanied by a police constable) would call for the workers to be assembled and ask if any had complaints. A time would then be set to hear them, with any witnesses to hand. Often, pre-liminary discussion would reveal that formal hearings would fail in their objec-tives, with mediation and admonitions securing much more constructive outcomes. The problem of giving the managers sufficient but not excessive power was never fully resolved; during the 1870s and 1880s several cases arose where an individual who had wounded another was removed prior to the death of the victim, effectively escaping justice. Also, since larceny, a very common occur-rence, could only be judged by a magistrate, the managers contrived to remon-strate in ways that provoked the insolence, insubordination, or disturbance that they were allowed to punish. Thus, for example, eleven out of fifteen offences at Eagle Island in 1882 fell into these categories.

   To illustrate the sort of problem that could occur, we may cite a most unusual incident at Peros Banhos in 1887. It began with the detention of a woman for 'insolence and insubordination'. A few hours later, after nightfall, her husband broke open the prison and set her free, at the same time creating much distur-bance. The manager, very ill at the time, ordered the husband's incarceration. Shortly afterwards a gang of the men, armed with knives, sticks and other weap-ons, again broke open the prison and released the man. 'There was a scene of great disorder. The sub-managers Button and Charles Lionnet,[14] who attempted to restore peace, narrowly escaped being beaten.' By the time the new magistrate,

Boucherat, heard about the event in May 1888, both man and wife had left the island.

Indiscipline was not confined to the workers. In contrast to the generally improving situation in the islands, in 1880 Ackroyd found himself confronted by a major case at East Point. Spurs' longstanding assistant manager, Hodoul, was accused of assaulting the manager of Pointe Marianne, Evelinor Nicolin; Ackroyd found him guilty of 'inflicting wounds and blows with premeditation' and sentenced him to ten days' imprisonment. Spurs also complained of having himself been libelled by Hodoul, but, as such a case would have required all involved to be heard in Mauritius, did not pursue the matter.[15]

Health

The visiting magistrates examined the health records kept by managers, including the birth and death statistics. The general pattern was that these island populations enjoyed good health and freedom from common infections, but probably had worse outcomes from disease and injury than people with access to proper medical care. However, perinatal mortality was very high. As Brooks had noticed in 1875, Six Islands seemed more prone than the others. In 1878 Ackroyd reported that, with an adult female population of about seventeen, there had over the preceding three years been twelve births and eight deaths, all in the first week or two of life and all with the same symptoms of 'cramp or a kind of tetanus'. Mme Lapeyre, the manager's wife, had done all she could to help, herself attending the births, but to no avail. Indeed, the primary purpose of that visit was to investigate the deaths of the Lapeyres' predecessors, Legrand and his wife, which had occurred in July the previous year. No foul play was involved, but the couple died very shortly after they lost their second new-born child in the same manner.[16]

Production levels

Most of the magistrates' reports mentioned the recent and anticipated amounts of coconut oil produced by each establishment, but not with sufficient consistency to tabulate the results. Their figures show that output was generally rising, but without any obvious correlation between increased labour and increased output, notably at Diego Garcia and Peros Banhos, which had the highest population growth. Some of the increased harvest can reasonably be ascribed to the fresh planting of the preceding decades, but other factors must also have been involved. One factor, hard to detect in specific examples, must have been the relationship between manager, *commandeurs* and labourers. In contrast to the frequent occurrence of misery at Six Islands, this atoll also provides a well-recorded instance of initiative by islanders. In 1877-78, Ackroyd reported, production had risen from 8,000 to 11,000 *veltes*, much of the increase achieved after the manager's death, through excellent management by the *chef commandeur*, Florimond Gaiqui; and the latter was aided by Verrapen, a man who had started as a common labourer and now kept the accounts with creditable accuracy.

Interestingly, the Board of Trade in London itself complained in 1883 about the paucity of trade statistics relating to transactions between Mauritius and its Dependencies; in response officials in Port Louis could only supply overall figures by value for the Minor Dependencies as a group and only for 1879-1882.[17] In later years, more detailed production and trade statistics became available, which will be drawn upon in our following chapters.

Maritime risks

Ackroyd's experiences of the voyages made in the course of his duties led him to give posterity an exceptionally vivid understanding of what these entailed for the islanders themselves (see inset overleaf). His dramatic escapades in 1881 were consequent upon a series of maritime accidents affecting the resupply of Six Islands. The Peruvian-registered barque *Maître Pierre* had been despatched there in December 1880. Her return being long overdue, in late March 1881 the *Eva Joshua* was instructed to call at the atoll with supplies on her way to Diego Garcia. The weather was too rough for this, but the dismasted *Maître Pierre* was seen inside the reef and close to the shore. On the *Eva Joshua*'s return, at the end of May, a small lugger, the *Arta* (26 tons), was despatched in haste. She too failed to reach her intended destination and finally put into Seychelles in distress. This information did not reach Port Louis until late July. The acting Governor then authorised the government's steam tug *Clavis* to make the voyage. Not surprisingly, that was her last long trip and, when Dupont made a tour of all five Chagos atolls in 1883, it was in the *Clavis*' replacement, the tug *Stella*, the round trip taking a mere six weeks. Next, towards the end of 1884, Dupont was authorised to use the government schooner *Harmonie*, to visit Diego Garcia and Peros Banhos. There were no mishaps, though only a few months later this vessel was to be declared unseaworthy.

Ackroyd's exertions did not only earn him the warm praise of the acting Governor; they also resulted in the immediate promulgation of new rules for the voyages to and from the Chagos.[18] These incorporated more rational standard sailing times, with seasonal variations. For example, the assumed voyage length

Witness to Neptune's Moods

The visiting magistrates did not just reveal conditions on land; their adventures at sea exposed, for the first time, what the islanders had long experienced in their passages to and from Mauritius. The seasonal variations in weather, described in Chapter 1, could be a matter of life and death. During the 1870s alone, one supply ship, the *Adeline*, was in 1874 simply lost at sea. In 1879, Dupont himself 'was wrecked at Agalega while aboard a French barque, the *Myosotis*. He did not get away until four months had elapsed'. Less than a year later, 'the French vessel *Africa* was wrecked on Eagle Island … She was taking labourers there & supplies, the anchorage at this place being for sailing vessels almost as bad as that of Agalega'.

More often the voyages entailed infinite varieties of endurance, as often through calm as storm. This was true even for short distances within the Archipelago. For example, in 1876, the schooner *Barso* took 11 days to sail the 70 miles separating Diego Garcia from Six Islands. In November the following year, this time aboard a much bigger vessel, 'the passage was a very trying one, as the *Virginie*, though a good vessel in some respects, was ill adapted for a tropical voyage' – and this time it took 47 days to reach Eagle Island. There, variable winds made things difficult enough, but on reaching Salomon (on 7 January 1878), there was too little wind for the *Virginie* to enter the lagoon; next day Ackroyd was rowed in over the reef in a boat sent out to collect urgently needed supplies. The brig followed on 10 January. After a failed attempt to depart on 17 January, she got clear of the lagoon a day later, but succeeded only in drifting into the Peros Banhos lagoon, which she was unable to leave until the 22nd.

Between June and September, high winds and heavy seas were the norm. For example, in July–August 1877, the barque *Eva Joshua* (285 tons) took 28 days to reach Diego Garcia, 'occasioned by strong head winds and heavy seas, which compelled the captain to keep his vessel under very reduced sail for 9 days, during which time we made little or no progress'. Conditions were much less predictable in the first and last months of the year. The *Virginie*'s long outward voyage in 1877 was followed, on her return, by violent storms. As Ackroyd recalled in a memorandum just over three years later, 'the discomfort, I might almost say misery of the [outward] voyage was so great that when I landed I was quite unfit for work; but it had to be done, & I accomplished it as well as I could. The return voyage was short but even more miserable and I felt the results of this trip for months afterwards'.[19]

Importantly, Ackroyd was interested in more than his own comfort. Depending on the design of the various vessels in which he sailed, the few cabins could be light and airy or cramped and stuffy; while labourers and artisans were lodged either on deck or in the hold. In the first case, they would be protected by awnings from the sun, and share the sailors' cramped accommodation when it rained; in the second, as in the *Virginie*, during the outward voyage, the labourers had travelled in the main hold with the hatch wide open, but those returning had a very different experience. 'Mr Nairac[20] called my attention to the fact that this hatch being closed almost, the only means of ventilation that existed was a small after hatch, and as this was on one occasion closed because it rained, the passengers must then have been nearly stifled.'

Two voyages in particular sum up the experiences available. In March/April 1878, the *Kroo Bay*, facing calms and light headwinds, took 30 days to reach Six Islands. 'The voyage was not only long, but very trying, for the cabins being below deck were very close, and the smell from the oil barrels, which were filled with salt-water as ballast, was most nauseous and at times insupportable.' As regards the labourers,

> They had to sleep on deck during the voyage to Six Islands and Diego Garcia, but as the temperature was very high and the weather fine they were none the worse for this, but coming to Mauritius we encountered a very severe gale which lasted nearly three days, during which torrents of rain fell and all the hatches, except the fore hatch, had to be carefully closed. The deck passengers were therefore compelled to share the small space reserved for the crew in the fore hold, and I was informed that they were very crowded and miserable.

Food and water were also wanting, there being only sufficient shipped (as required by the regulations) for 16 days, whereas the outward voyage alone took 30. The situation was saved, thanks to rain and the excess of rice provided by the managers at Diego Garcia.

The next decade began just as badly. Following the disastrous failures to resupply Six Isands in 1881, the acting Governor authorised the government's steam tug *Clavis* to make the voyage. Ackroyd immediately applied for a passage:

> The *Clavis* left Port Louis on the 1st of August 1881 and very soon had to encounter the full strength of the South-East trades and the heavy seas they raised. The decks of the *Clavis* were covered with water nearly all the voyage, and they leak in many places, one of which was my cabin. However, in that part of the cuddy not occupied by rice and other supplies, the deck was nearly watertight, and we were thus able to sleep and take our meals without getting wet.

The vessel finally arrived at Six Islands on 8 August, leaving again on 11 August. On the third day, it was realised that the tug had too little coal to reach Port Louis; the captain decided to seek refuge at St. Brandon (nearly 300 miles distant), making what use he could of auxiliary sail. By keeping steam pressure to the minimum and burning successive items of the vessel's wooden fittings, they reached the anchorage of the establishment at St. Raphael on 17 August. Two days were spent by members of the tug's crew in contacting members of the St. Brandon management and rowing with them in a vain search for a larger sailing vessel supposed to be near one or other of the widely scattered islets. Ackroyd (and others) then accompanied the tugboat's captain in the ship's gig, with an experienced local boatman as guide, to seek out the establishment's manager on another island. The party spent 23 hours in this open boat, bailing constantly and finding no land, but finally succeeded, through the captain's sure instinct, in returning to the *Clavis*. Next day, the party set forth once more, this time in a sailing boat, failed again and only a day later achieved their objective. This was to obtain the manager's permission to demolish one of his wooden huts as fuel for the tug. Enough to say that Ackroyd contrived to interview and report on the condition of the St. Brandon labourers and the *Clavis* did eventually reach port.

Source: MA Council Minutes No. 30 of 1881, p. 298.

for the return trip to Salomon was now 25 days from May to August and 37 days for September to April. Secondly, there was a new requirement to provide an adequate and balanced diet for ships' passengers – condensed milk for mothers with babies, lime juice for longer voyages, not to speak of port wine, with supplies of biscuit for issue when bad weather made cooking impossible. Of course, these regulations could not provide for every contingency. In 1887, there occurred a further set of maritime accidents, this time affecting Diego Garcia. The *Eva Joshua*, bound for the island with supplies and passengers, had to divert to Mahé on account of leaks. There, driven ashore and abandoned, she was eventually sold and sailed again, but never to the Chagos. Another barque, the *Ethell*, was freighted to take over the job, but also had an accident at Mahé, followed by a very protracted passage to the Chagos. Fortunately the *Cupido* happened to visit Diego Garcia only eight days after the last rice had been eaten. During that time, the population had to make do with coconuts and fish.

The magistrates also had to concern themselves with risks at a local level. At Eagle Island in 1882, one of the first matters Dupont had to attend to was the complaint by a worker, Booth Frantz, that the ketch *La Lucie* was unsafe. This was the vessel (doubtless built at Salomon) used to reach Danger Island and the Three Brothers, where coconuts were now being gathered and new trees planted. Together, the *Cupido*'s captain and the island manager, now Jean Louis (himself a master mariner), reached the same conclusion. Dupont ordered that she not be used again until properly repaired.

Lastly, no amount of regulation could remove the role of the Chagos as refuge of last resort for those wrecked in mid-ocean. In 1888, Diego Garcia once more received survivors, this time eight men from a very large Italian barque, the 1,200-ton *Fratellanza*, which had foundered 800 miles from the island. Only one of the two ship's boats reached it. Eight weeks later a visiting naval ship, H.M.S. *Griffon*, gave the victims passage to Zanzibar.

Population changes

As we have periodically recorded, the Chagos population grew quite steadily as the 19th century wore on. Virtually every official visitor made a count of the islands' inhabitants, but few made clear whether the management were included. Ackroyd and Dupont appear to have been meticulous, recording carefully not only totals, but the numbers and composition of those arriving and departing. Dupont, like Berkeley in 1859, also studied the ethno-linguistic affiliations of the islanders. Table 11.1 (opposite) brings together the counts made by Dupont during his tour of all the islands in 1883.

The most striking statistic in this Table is the sudden (and temporary)

Table 11.1   Chagos population 1883

	European				Creole				Malagasy				Mozambican				Indian				Total
	Adult		Child		Adult		Child		Adult		Child		Adult		Child		Adult		Child		
	M	F	M	F	M	F	M	F	M	F	M	F	M	F	M	F	M	F	M	F	
Diego Garcia																					
East Point	–	–	–	–	35	26	14	6	40	5	–	2	14	2	1	1	35	9	3	3	196
Pte. Marianne	–	–	–	–	30	14	11	12	46	4	–	1	4	3	–	–	1	–	–	–	126
Minni Minni	–	–	–	–	15	32	17	11	20	5	–	–	2	1	–	–	–	–	–	–	103
Peros Banhos	–	–	–	–	36	32	25	23	40	2	–	–	4	1	–	–	1	–	–	–	164
Salomon	–	–	–	–	19	12	3	5	21	3	2	1	2	1	–	–	2	–	–	–	71
Eagle Island					10	9	6	3	23	6	–	–	3	2	–	–	–	–	–	–	62
Six Islands	1	–	–	–	11	13	10	12	10	–	–	–	7	5	–	–	1	1	–	–	71
Total	1	–	–	–	156	138	86	72	200	25	2	4	36	15	1	1	40	10	3	3	793

In addition, on Diego Garcia, the Orient Line's coaling station at East Point employed 17 Europeans (assembling lighters) and 40 Somalis, engaged by the French Consul at Djibouti on 1-year contracts. One other European was the Agent for Lund & Co.

Source: TNA CO 170/118 (p. 578 *et sqq.*).

appearance of a substantial number of Indians at East Point (compared with the total of three counted by Ackroyd in 1880). The reason for this anomaly will be examined in Chapter 12. More interesting features are the great diminution in the numbers of Mozambicans and the preponderance of unaccompanied Malagasy men, for which we can offer only speculation. We may guess that the managers and Mozambicans underwent a mutual disenchantment. As to the Malagasys, many came to Mauritius as cattle drovers in the 1850s and found employment in the sugar plantations, later being replaced by Indian immigrants. Their own country being in the throes of civil war, they then very likely looked for alternatives to returning. Given that several of the share-holders in the Chagos were also engaged in commerce with Madagascar, they may very well have been pleased to recruit individuals having a reputation for competence and obedience. We may indeed suspect that it was Malagasys who were least often recruited in the presence of a magistrate.

Another aspect of population change is impossible to learn from these tables. How many left the islands and later returned? When Ackroyd visited Diego Garcia in 1877, he reported that 'the large majority of the labourers who came with me in the *Eva Joshua* had already worked on the island, and indeed of those who went to Pte Marianne only one was a new hand'. On the other hand, it is very rare to find records spanning a significant period of time. Ackroyd's report of his visit to Six Islands in 1881 is a valuable exception. Six vessels had arrived and departed between August 1878 and August 1881, in total bringing 64 people and taking away 72. Each of these figures included 20 children. Given that the population in 1881 was only 75, there was evidently a high degree of mobility, but it is impossible to know what proportion of those departing left for good. Similarly, when Dupont visited Diego Garcia in the same year, the *Eva Joshua* brought no less than 63 people to Pointe Marianne and removed only 18; even so, the resulting number of inhabitants was 163, which by 1883 had fallen to 126. In 1884 the number had fallen further to 92. From this small sample from the scores of voyages that took place, all we can say is that numbers fluctuated considerably and that significant numbers did return, for, as Ackroyd reported on an earlier voyage, workers could bring, free of charge, goods they had purchased in Mauritius for their friends in the islands.

Social stresses

This is a topic which the magistrates, concerned by the virtual absence of marriage and the heavy imbalance between men and women, addressed under the heading 'immorality'. Ackroyd consulted the owners about the problem of recruiting more women and reported their opinion that 'it is not easy to procure them, as women do not like to go to the Oil islands, although those who go there once generally return'. He also explained the inadequacy of the new Ordinance in respect of encouraging marriages. The main problems arose from the general absence of birth certificates and the impossibility of procuring affidavits in the absence of magistrates before whom they could be sworn; likewise with the problems of marrying minors in the absence of parents and guardians. Some of the cases which the magistrates had to consider supported the view that the main problem was one of supply and demand. One such concerned two workers at Salomon in 1879. Léonce had visited the hut of the blacksmith, Rampal, 'to call him to account for his behaviour towards his (Léonce's) concubine'. Following heated exchanges, Rampal fetched his *sagaye* [machete] and brandished it; Léonce had grabbed the blade, cutting his hand. Dupont found himself obliged to advise Léonce that his charge against Rampal would fail, as no intentional blow had been struck. Other cases, however, suggested the existence of more general tensions. At Six Islands in 1876, although the victims had not complained formally, two of the women had been knifed by the men they were living with (and one of the latter put in irons until he cooled down). Again, on Eagle Island in 1882 a violent death had occurred, in this case the perpetrator being a woman and the victim her lover; she, three male witnesses and the manager, together with his family, were brought back to Mauritius for the trial.

As in Mauritius itself, the authorities persevered in their efforts to encourage marriage and to achieve a more equal balance between men and women. In the same year, a revised Ordinance was being considered, of which Article 12 caused the owners to retort that

> Many of the labourers that go to the oil establishments are bachelors. Married men generally leave their wives and families here. Nevertheless, if the law was

carried out women should be sent not only in proportion to the number of bach-elors but also in proportion to the number of married men who may go to the islands without their wives. It is evident that the women who may be found and sent to the islands in order to comply with the exigencies of the law must be of the very lowest standard. They would surely be there a perpetual cause of trouble and debauch and this would interfere seriously with the working of the establish-ments and may possibly lead to crime. Labourers who go to the islands do not settle there except in a very few instances and they are satisfied to go alone. Why then should Government impose upon the oil establishments which for the last years have scarcely given any profit, the additional expense of sending thither women for their labourers?

The problem was never resolved fully, even though official efforts to encour-age civil marriages began to make some headway. In 1888, Boucherat, the new magistrate visiting Diego Garcia, found himself faced with two cases of alleged adultery. In the first, the husband succeeded in proving his claim against his wife and her lover and the guilty couple were condemned to fifteen days impris-onment. In the second, the case did not reach formal trial: the alleged paramour denied the husband's claim and the husband did not attempt to prove it; whereas the wife 'boldly admitted the charge, saying that she no longer cared for her husband and that no power on earth would prevent her going with [her lover]'.

Taken as a whole, the repeated visitations by magistrates with effective pow-ers resulted in improved living conditions for the ordinary labourers and the elimination of outrageous acts of both cruelty and financial abuse. On the other hand, the islanders remained cut off from any form of social development. Nei-ther the owners nor the government considered it necessary to provide improved medical care or any education at all. Moreover, we are left with the impression that the absence of major scandals convinced the authorities that they had solved the problems of governance. It is noticeable that, after 1884, the regularity of visits declined, as did the submission of the magistrates' reports to the Gov-ernor's Council. Had they been so submitted, their content would still be avail-able in the voluminous administrative appendixes to the Council Minutes. It is only from references in the single 1888 report to visits made in 1886 and 1887 that we know that any took place at all.

An idiosyncratic viewpoint

In September 1885, the naturalist, Gilbert Bourne arrived at Diego Garcia to spend several months examining its flora and fauna. He also found time to record his impressions of the life and work of the island's inhabitants.[21] Con-cerning the latter, he states that 'the labour on the estates is almost wholly

East Point plantation circa 1886. Photo by unknown passenger aboard
visiting P & O liner (NW-S collection).

supplied from Mauritius; very few of the labourers have been born on the island.
Those that have are known as '*enfants des îles*', and are a fine set of men, superior
both morally and physically to the imported labourers from Mauritius'.
Although his attitudes and opinions were decidedly blinkered, he provides
additional information on working practices and one important insight. On the
first point, he explains that the *commandeur* of a working party sent to gather
coconuts would allocate a particular area to each worker, whose nuts would be
counted before embarkation for return to the settlement, then re-counted after
being distributed in piles for the women to break up. He also describes how the
resulting heaps of copra were 'carefully protected from rain by a sort of pent-
house on wheels, which can be run over the heaps at a minute's notice'. The
contraptions shown in the contemporary photograph above are probably those
to which Bourne refers.[22] Indeed, such devices were still to be seen in use in the
1940s.

As to Bourne's insight, he recounts how Jules Leconte, a month after his first
arrival at Diego Garcia (to succeed Spurs as manager at East Point), found his
verandah 'besieged by a body of thirty men, armed with knives and bludgeons,
who declared that they would not leave the place until they had taken his life'.
Drawing his revolver, he parleyed with the group until the men calmed down.
Bourne then remarks that, on acquaintance, 'the ringleader of that very outbreak was one of the most civil-spoken and best workmen on the estate'. Our
interpretation of this incident is that, as had happened previously and would
happen again from time to time, the islanders were testing the mettle of their
new overlord – and that Leconte was not found wanting. Bourne, whose article

repeatedly makes clear his disparagement of Africans, duly saluted this example, as he saw it, of white courage overcoming black cowardice. He was, naturally, equally scathing about perceived African indolence:

> Nearly all the work done is task work, for the average negro, if set to work for a certain number of hours in the day, will manage to waste an inconceivable amount of time, and would do such a minimum of useful labour as would astonish even a 'knight of labour' in more civilised countries.

On the other hand, he also commented that

> in fact the employers were entirely in the hands of the negroes, who, in the case of a general and organised outbreak, could easily have made themselves masters of the island.

The reality, of course, was that workers and managers were mutually dependent and that if either pressed the other too hard, both would be losers. It was a reality generally well recognised and one where exceptions classically – and on occasion dramatically – proved the rule. Bourne was however right to hint at an issue which went to the heart of running such isolated enterprises: left to themselves, managers and workers could establish a tolerable *modus vivendi*; but progress and enduring profitability required serious incentives to mutually advantageous collaboration. That required commitment from the plantation owners in Mauritius more enlightened than the expedient of increasing or reducing the availability of alcohol.

Renewal and reform of ownership

Details about the ownership of the Chagos islands had never been easy to ascertain. The Surveyor General's report of 1863 (mentioned on p. 188) provided as complete an account as was then available, while the records of the Mauritius Land Court show some of what happened in the years immediately following the 1865 settlement. As we have mentioned, in 1866 Hippolyte Lemière passed on much of his holding to Henry Plasson, who remained actively involved for a decade. However, Plasson died a matter of days after propounding his views to Ackroyd on the eve of the latter's departure to visit the islands he owned.[23] A year later, Plasson's properties had been sold by judicial auction. The various islands in which he had held an interest had been bought by a group of eight individuals, led by James E. Deglos, who also took over as Agent.[24] Salomon was bought for Rs 65,010. Six Islands remained in separate ownership. In May 1880, another shake-up involved Peros Banhos and the Pointe Marianne establishment on Diego, following the deaths of Duvergé[25] and three out of the four Liénard brothers (who had also owned East Point). The 32 individuals having interests in the two establishments sold out to a 10-member consortium for the sum of Rs 500,000. These included the surviving François Liénard, Léopold Antelme, his wife Cécile Majastre and the widow of Ajax Duvergé, Marie Antelme – names providing an insight into the linkages between families long involved in exploiting the Chagos islands. Collectively known as the *Etablissement Huilier de Péros Banhos et Pointe Marianne*, this consortium also obtained 89% of the downtown oil store in Port Louis, the *Magasin Général des Huiles de Coco*.[26]

Next, early in 1883, a new law was passed to permit the creation of public companies having limited liability. The owners of all three Diego Garcia plantations, together with those of Peros Banhos, were among the first to take advantage of this legislation, with the Governor issuing a Proclamation on the formation of the *Société Huilière de Maurice*.[27] By August the same year, the company had renamed itself the *Société Huilière de Péros Banhos et Diégo Garcia*. Two hundred shares were issued with a nominal value of one rupee. According to the commercial press, the market value of the shares was Rs 75 each.[28] Its Agent/Secretary was Léopold Antelme *fils*, a well-connected entrepreneur with shipping interests; indeed, he probably owned the brig *Suzanne* (251 tons register), bought to replace the *Eva Joshua*.[29] By 1889 the company was reportedly worth Rs 1,080,000 while its individual shares were listed at Rs 100 each (there is no sign in the *Commercial Gazette* that any were traded). Meanwhile, on Diego Garcia, the three estates were first reduced to two by the amalgamation of East Point and Pointe Marianne; then Minni Minni was closed altogether and Pointe Marianne reopened as a subordinate establishment.

Thus, following the investigation by Brooks, major progress had been made in securing a degree of control and consistency of practice in the Chagos plantations. At the same time, the islands' proprietors had adopted more modern and integrated structures, offering the opportunity for improved management. There remained, however, no sign of investment in machinery or steamers, let alone social care for the inhabitants. Moreover, both the government and the proprietors found themselves having to deal with the wider issues to be discussed in our next chapter.

Notes to Chapter 11

1 The name of this vessel is differently spelled in the various sources, quite often as *Margretha* in press reports of shipping movements. We have used the spelling adopted by Dupont.

2 TNA CO 170/93, Appendix p. 1325.

3 Brooks himself does not give his name.

4 Moreover, Mme Legrand was herself to lose her two babies in their first weeks of life, leading, it appears, to the couple's joint suicide in 1877.

5 Attached to Brooks' report were appendices setting out, for all the plantations he visited, the articles for sale and the price of each in both the shop and in Mauritius.

6 Brooks had noticed and asked about 'some splendid *Fauxgayac* and *Tatamaka* trees, which had been cut down and left to wither away in the woods [on Boddam]'. He was told that they had been felled by a M. Hugon, a manager many years before, who believed that the timber trees impeded growth of the coconuts. Probably this was the Gustave Hugon we have already encountered, rather than Ferdinand Hugon, manager of Agalega at the time of Brooks' tour. Many years later, it was discovered that the fallen timber remained in excellent condition.

7 TNA CO 171/48 Mauritius Government Gazette No. 1 of 1876.

8 This official's annual salary was set at £500, plus travelling expenses up to £100. The penalty for failure by the proprietors to make their contribution by mid-January each year was to be a tax of a half-penny on every gallon of oil exported from the islands (equivalent, at the current rate of production, to slightly more than £400).

9 In return, each CSO was to receive Rs 20 per month.

10 TNA CO 170/93, Appendix p. 250.

11 We have been able to consult almost all of the Visiting Magistrates' reports, either in Mauritius or the British National Archives. In order to avoid a plethora of individual endnotes, we have sought in the text to provide enough detail (e.g., island(s) inspected, year of visit and magistrate involved) to ensure certain identification of the file references, which are as follows:-

TNA CO 170/93 Appendix p. 1325. 1876 July–September, Ackroyd by *Ada* to Eagle, Salomon.

TNA CO 170/95 Appendix 6 to Council Minutes No. 7. 1876 November–December, Ackroyd by *Barso*, Six Islands, Diego Garcia.

TNA CO 170/96 Appendix p. 1484. 1877 July–September, Ackroyd by *Eva Joshua* to Diego Garcia, Peros Banhos.

TNA CO 170/98 Appendix p. 397. 1877 November–1878 January, Ackroyd by *Virginie* to Eagle Island, Salomon.

TNA CO 170/98 Appendix p. 873. 1878 March–May, Ackroyd by *Kroo Bay* to Six Islands and Diego Garcia.

TNA CO 170/103 Appendix p. 1329. 1879 August, Dupont by *Marghretta* to Salomon, Eagle Island. Also 1880 April–May, Ackroyd by *Arsène* to Diego Garcia.

TNA CO 167/593 Enclosure 4 to Despatch 177 dated 18 April 1881. 1880 November–1881 January, Dupont by *Eva Joshua* to Peros Banhos and Diego Garcia.

MA Council Minutes No. 30 of 1881, p. 298, 1881 August, Ackroyd by *Clavis* to Six Islands.

TNA CO 170/114 Administration Reports p. 632. 1882 June–August, Dupont by *Cupido* to Salomon, Eagle.

TNA CO 170/118, Administrative Reports p. 578. 1883 April–May, Dupont by *Stella* to whole Archipelago.

TNA CO 170/123, Administrative Reports p. 44. 1883 November–1884 January, Dupont by *Eva Joshua* to Peros Banhos and Diego Garcia.

TNA CO 170/129, Administrative Reports p. 904. 1884 August–November, Dupont by *Harmonie* to whole Archipelago.

TNA CO 170/144, Administrative Reports p. 1134. 1888 April–June, Boucherat by *Suzanne* to Peros Banhos and Diego Garcia.

12 TNA CO 170/117 Appendix p. 492.

13 Bourne, G. 'On the Island of Diego Garcia of the Chagos Group', *Journal of the Royal Geographical Society* June 1886. Bourne stayed with Leconte. By this time the Minni Minni plantation had been abandoned, while the settlement at Pointe Marianne had also been run down, so that the amount of the island left 'undisturbed' would have increased. Bourne's pervasive disparagement of 'negroes', discussed on p. 231, does not, in our view, invalidate this specific observation.

14 Charles Lionnet is, surprisingly, not mentioned in the family's annals (*Mauritian Heritage*, edited by Dr Edward Duyker), but his name and elements of his career emerge from documents we have encountered; see Chapter 13, Note 7.

15 Evelinor Nicolin was an unlikely person to be assaulted, having for many years prior to his appointment as manager captained the *Eva Joshua*. By 1888, he had returned to seafaring, as captain of her replacement, the brig *Suzanne* (255 tons). As for Hodoul, he seems to have left the Chagos soon after this fracas, turning up a few years later at Farquhar Island in the Seychelles as manager for its new owner, James Spurs!

16 Ackroyd's report on the deaths is missing, but it can be inferred from the death of the Legrands' recently born child with cramps and convulsions a few days after her birth that they may well have committed suicide (it was learnt later that their first child had also died in the same way). Ackroyd was assisted by a police constable and a medical representative who examined the exhumed bodies.

17 MA SA 144 Minute by Acting Registrar General dated 16 February 1884.

18 TNA CO 167/593 Enclosure 5 to Mauritius Despatch 177 dated 18 April 1881, Proclamation No. 19 of 28/3/1881.

19 TNA CO 167/592 Enclosure 2 to Mauritius Despatch 119 dated 21 March 1881.

20 As mentioned in note 24 below, Nairac was one of the new owners and used this voyage to visit the two islands.

21 Bourne, *op. cit. On the Island of Diego Garcia of the Chagos Group, Journal of the Royal Geographical Society* June 1886.

22 This image on glass was advertised on the internet and brought to the authors' attention. Subsequent discussion with the seller, Aladdin's Cave of Derby (England), showed that the unknown photographer was aboard one of the Orient Company's ships en route from Liverpool to Adelaide, Australia in the early to mid 1880s. A second image is reproduced in our next chapter.

23 Ackroyd learned of the death on 23 July 1876, when the *Ada* called at Mahé in the Seychelles.

24 The other seven were Messrs Senneville, LeMaire, C. Nairac, St. Felix, Goupille, Clériceau and Larcher.

25 Ajax Duvergé had been involved with the Chagos as an Agent at least since 1864, when he was a passenger aboard the brig *Rio*, which arrived at Port Louis from Diego Garcia on 13 September (*Mauritius Commercial Gazette* for 15 September 1864).

26 Seychelles Archives [SA], Seychelles Volume 1 Notarial Deeds, No. 693 (408/80).

27 TNA CO 171/55, Proclamation No. 16, dated 5 March 1883. The detailed terms were set out in a deed drawn up by the Notary Public, but this text no longer survives.

28 *Mauritius Merchants and Planters Gazette* for 11 November 1883 (issue No. 222).

29 Advertisements in his name appeared in the *Mauritius Commercial Gazette* quoting Rs 5,000, later reduced to Rs 3,250, for a round voyage to the two islands in 1888 (on which Magistrate Boucherat was a passenger).

12

Proprietors take on the Empire

IN 1859, soon after Lt. Berkeley had presented his Commission of Inquiry's report, his interpreter, James Caldwell, submitted a report of his own.[1] It concerned not the Chagos plantations, but the Archipelago's strategic potential upon the eventual opening of a canal at Suez. The gestation of this scheme is a topic which goes well beyond the scope of this book. Enough to say that the British government opposed the project throughout the decade of its construction. Readers need not be surprised, therefore, that, when the Governor, Sir William Stevenson, forwarded Caldwell's analysis to the Colonial Office, which in turn forwarded it to the Admiralty, the latter should not go beyond admitting

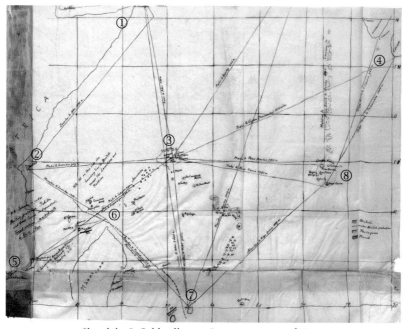

① Cape Gardafui
② Mombasa
③ Seychelles
④ Colombo
⑤ Mozambique
⑥ Comoros
⑦ Mauritius
⑧ Diego Garcia

Sketch by J. Caldwell, 1859. Image courtesy of TNA.

that Diego Garcia 'affords an admirable site for coal depots'.[2] Caldwell's memorandum was nevertheless a prescient document, the drift of which emerges clearly from the sketch map that its author appended (see above).

Steamships were encroaching steadily on the major Indian Ocean routes and the opening of the Suez Canal in 1869 gave a major fillip to this change. The routes between Europe and India, China and Australasia began to depend less on the seasonal patterns of wind and currents, more on differences of distance between major ports. As the range of coal-powered steamships increased, Mauritius' own importance as an entrepôt began to come under threat; indeed, the loss of lucrative victualling and ship repair businesses, combined with a major slump in sugar exports, produced an acute depression in Port Louis and thus led not only to many bankruptcies, but also to severe fiscal problems.[3] At the same time, Diego Garcia, all but intersecting the direct route between Aden and Australia and that between the Cape and India, offered entrepreneurs new potential. Four such approached the British government, imagining that its sovereignty gave it full power. They had not reckoned, however, with the new property rights in the Chagos and the determination of the proprietors.

In early 1879, a certain Fitzherbert Brooke asked the Colonial Office for permission to set up a coaling station on Diego Garcia and was invited to apply to the colonial government in Mauritius. He also proposed to the Admiralty that naval vessels should make use of this facility, once established; the Admiralty told him that they saw no necessity for it.[4] Brooke evidently then lost interest. In late 1880, the Orient Steam Navigation Company, deciding that Diego Garcia would be preferable to Aden as a refuelling stop for its regular services between England and Australia, wrote to the Secretary of State for the Colonies, Lord Kimberley, asking to buy a part of the island for the same purpose and, like Brooke, emphasised their interest in supplying the Navy.[5] Early in 1881, William Lund, a coal merchant with some shipping interests, embarked upon a similar enterprise. Unlike Brooke, he began by despatching a coal-laden ship to Diego Garcia before approaching the Colonial Office,[6] simultaneously securing introductions to Kimberley from two individuals of influence: one of them was a Member of Parliament, Reginald Brett,[7] who had been contacted, as he explained in his letter, by 'Chinese Gordon'; the other was Colonel Charles Gordon himself. Writing on 15 May from the Hotel Europe in Le Havre (where he was waiting for the ship that was to take him to Mauritius), Gordon excited Kimberley's interest by referring to the project as a 'very important subject to our maritime power'[8]. Disregarding official advice, Kimberley agreed to meet Lund, who thus achieved his first objective, ministerial encouragement to the Mauritius authorities to look favourably on his plans. The minister did however decline his request to be given a monopoly on the island. Two distinct ranges of activity then ensued: commercial competition in Mauritius and

General Gordon. Image: Butler, 1889.

examination of the naval and imperial interests in London, Ceylon and Diego Garcia itself.

By way of introduction to the latter, the role of Col. Gordon deserves mention. On 1 May 1881, he received a letter from an old friend who wished to avoid a posting to take charge of the Royal Engineer contingent in Mauritius, asking if he would take the job instead. Gordon accepted at once and the formalities were completed next day, to the delight of, among others, Queen Victoria.[9] He himself was thrown into gloom by his impulsive decision. He could not have considered in any depth Diego Garcia's strategic importance in the fortnight before he set off; the probability must be that Lund himself put the thought into his head, where it became firmly embedded. However, he had long taken the view that the Cape route to the East was strategically preferable to that of the Suez Canal and had corresponded with Brett on the topic. At some point, probably early in 1882, he wrote to Brett again, this time making specific reference to the Chagos:

> I spoke to you concerning Borneo and the necessity for coaling stations in the Eastern seas … I would select such places where no temptation would induce colonists to come, and I would use them as maritime fortresses. For instance, the only good place between Suez and Adelaide would be in the Chagos group, which contain a beautiful harbour at San Diego [*sic*]. My object is to secure this for the strengthening of our maritime power. These islands are of great strategical importance *vis à vis* with India, Suez and Singapore. Remember Aden has no harbour to speak of and has the need of a garrison, while Chagos could be kept by a company of soldiers …[10]

Gordon spent a year only in Mauritius, his main tasks there being to consider the defence requirements of that island and also those of Seychelles. He did not visit the Chagos (though he became a close friend of Ackroyd, then Visiting Magistrate to the islands), but his advocacy of Diego Garcia was to have long-lasting effects.

Following Lund's meeting with the Minister in 1881, events had moved with astonishing speed. Kimberley invited the Commission on Colonial Defence, already engaged in a wide-ranging survey of this subject, to examine the desirability of establishing a Naval Station, complete with local coal stores, on Diego Garcia. HMS *Eclipse* was despatched from Trincomalee on 26 May. Her commander, Captain Edmund Garforth, was accompanied by a Royal Engineer, Major Robert Barton. They concluded that a coaling station would best be sited at Eclipse Bay, as being close to the lagoon entrance and well protected from winds throughout the year; and a pier would need to be built to enable ships to refuel quickly. On the other hand, a naval refitting station – a much more dubious proposition – would be better sited at East Point.[11]

As to defences, the coaling station would require two batteries, each having two 6½ ton guns, with a further single gun to guard the rear; a naval station would need much more than this, probably a casemate battery, mounting about eight heavy guns. Maj. Barton remarked bluntly that, given Diego Garcia's isolation and the difficulty of finding troops to defend places of much greater importance, 'I am only wasting my time in considering the matter further, and I must give it as my opinion that the place is wholly unsuited to the requirements of a naval station'. As to the coaling station, the defences proposed would be inadequate for defence against any ships having armour plating and 'what may not be done thoroughly had better not be done at all'. In that case, it would be important to ensure that stocks required for civil use be removed when necessary:

> If ironclad ships can obtain coal at Diego Garcia, the fortifications of all our ports within a couple of thousand miles will be affected, take, for instance, Trincomalee … [where] all the batteries erected and proposed are designed on the assumption that ironclad ships cannot carry sufficient coal to operate with advantage in these seas.

Having considered this report, the Admiralty invited the Colonial Office to insist that contracts with those setting up coaling stations should include a clause providing for destruction or removal in time of emergency. In the event, the resulting instructions reached Port Louis just after contracts with both Orient and Lund had been signed. An attempt to reopen negotiations was abandoned in face of both companies' irate protests about compensation, with the Admiralty muttering that in extreme emergency it would take whatever action was required.

It was a question which continued to exercise the minds of naval officers in the area. In 1883, the C-in-C, Rear Admiral Sir Frederick Richards, was inclined to share the view of Capt. Garforth

> The Chagos Archipelago would also [in the event of war with France or Russia] require a force to protect the coal stored there for the use of the Orient Company and Diego Garcia would become a very important centre for a cruising Squadron. Although the increasing number of Coaling Stations is of the greatest importance and convenience to our merchant fleet, still in time of war they would no doubt be found a source of danger – offering in some cases an easy opportunity to an enemy's cruiser to fill up with coal etc, and it would probably be

advantageous to destroy any such stations immediately war broke out. One of the greatest safetys [*sic*] of the East Indies Station is the few neutral ports at which coal could be obtained by an enemy.[12]

Two years later, the captain of HMS *Euryalus* (which the Admiral considered 'the only really efficient and powerful vessel' under his command) reporting on the same issue, took a different view.

There are two opinions on the subject, one is that they should be destroyed on the outbreak of hostilities, and the other which I hold with is to retain them and give our adversaries the trouble of destroying them, for as we have more ships moving about in war time, so we could equally with other powers make use of them when opportunity arose, and to say nothing of the risk an enemy would run in attempting to take coal from such a position.[13]

In Port Louis meanwhile, tangled negotiations were under way between the competing coaling interests on the one hand and, on the other, between the colonial government and the proprietors of the East Point estate. Both Lund and Orient sought to strengthen their negotiating positions by sending coal-laden vessels to the island and anchoring them off East Point. Orient gained a slight local advantage by hiring Spurs, the longstanding manager of the East Point plantation, to manage their operation, but the plantation owners, perhaps out of pique, preferred to negotiate with Lund. Spurs, no doubt more conversant with

HMS *Euryalus*. Image courtesy NMM.

the terms of their tenure, was quicker in concluding a deal with Mauritius. Orient's 50-year lease of Middle and East Islands was finally signed by Blyth Brothers, their Agents in Port Louis, and a representative of the colonial government on 18 May 1882. Its provisions, back-dated to the start of the year, included the payment of an annual rent of Rs 250 and immediate return of the islands in the event that the Company's vessels ceased to use the station before expiry of the lease.[14] Lund, for his part, was negotiating a lease of West Island for himself, on the same terms as Orient's for the other two islets, and this entered into force in April 1883 (Lund must surely have been unaware just how insignificant and exposed this islet was). By the end of 1882, the stock of coal in his two hulks off East Point and on land totalled 4,000 tons, ready not only for his own ships, but also for those of the Royal Navy, one of which had already availed itself of this new facility. Early in 1883, the owners of East Point concluded a deal with Lund's representative, under which he would be given a monopoly to provide coal from the main island in exchange for their participation in the project. Spurs, who had brought two hulks of his own[15] and had continued to operate from East Point, employing labour from the plantation, was now given notice to remove himself to East Island, his hulks to what is now Rambler Bay, and his employees to Middle Island; the proprietors were insisting on their legal right under the 1865 concessions to control residence on the main island.

It did not take long for echoes of all this to reach London. 'A new state of things', the Governor reported on 19 April,

> of which little or nothing is known here, has sprung up in Diego Garcia since it became, some months ago, a coaling station of the Orient and Lund's lines of steamers … The proprietors of the island establishments have received complaints of disorder and difficulty arising from the arrival at this hitherto sequestered and primitive spot of large steamers crowded with passengers, and from the organisation of the two coal depots … It seems probable that some Police or other official authority will now have to be established at Diego Garcia …[16]

In fact, the government steamer, the *Stella*, had been despatched a day earlier, carrying Dupont, Acting Magistrate for the Lesser Dependencies, to investigate. He was on the lookout not only for legal and medical problems arising from the island's direct contacts with the outside world, but also for indications of unrest. He found nothing to concern him on any of these points: 'No disorder or debauchery have taken place and I am happy to be able to attribute it to the good order maintained by Mr Spurs.'[17] This was not altogether surprising, since, at the time of his visit in the first half of May 1883, both companies were still operating from East Point. Whatever problems were brewing, Spurs' relations with the new manager, Leconte, formerly his assistant in charge of Pointe Marianne, seem to have remained cordial.

The value of Dupont's report lies in his description, the only one surviving, of the early coaling operations. There were 7,000 tons of coal available; 3,000 belonged to Lund and were stored on land and in his two hulks (see illustration overleaf); of the remainder, belonging to Orient, 2,600 tons were stored in their two hulks and 1,400 tons on land. At that stage, only nineteen visits by steamers had taken place, the great majority being Orient's ships, each carrying some 300-400 passengers and taking up to 68 hours – much more than the 24 hours planned – to take coal on board. Spurs had hired 40 Somali workers from Port Said, but found them unproductive, expensive (at Rs 36 per month) and hard to manage; he was in the process of engaging some 50 Mauritians to replace them. He, like Lund, was hiring workers from the plantation, as and when required. Spurs had also brought in a team of European riveters and metal workers to assemble the twelve iron lighters he had imported in parts; these were to be used to bring coal from his hulks alongside the steamers. Spurs supplied coal only to Orient ships (and the Navy), whereas Lund sold his, at £2.5s per ton, to all comers. Altogether, Orient had imported 9,600 tons and Lund 5,500 tons since the start of their respective operations. Both foresaw major increases in their businesses, Spurs expecting the island's imports to rise to 50,000 tons per year and Lund's local agent, a Mr G. Worsell, claiming that 50 shipping lines trading between Europe and Australia had already signed contracts to take on coal at Diego Garcia. For their part, the local plantation managers stated that they had been paid £1,400 since the beginning of 1882 for the supply of labour to load and unload coal and for providing sand and coral for the colliers leaving in ballast. Spurs himself, using the steam tug he had imported, earned money by piloting all the vessels from and to the lagoon entrance for a fee of £6 (£8 for sailing ships) for each movement.

By the middle of 1883, the vicarious negotiations, via their respective agents in Port Louis, between Orient and the proprietors of all three estates on Diego Garcia had broken down. Each of the latter had presented differing, but completely unacceptable terms. They had also strengthened their hand by amalgamating their businesses into a single new company, the *Société Huilière de Maurice*. This company swiftly sought and obtained an injunction from Mauritius' Supreme Court against Orient while the new labourers, now 81 in number, were actually en route to Diego Garcia.[18] Warned by his agents in Port Louis, Spurs moved his operations to Middle Island just before their arrival at the end of August. Housing was immediately required, additional to that for the workers who had joined him from East Point. More than twenty of the latter were accompanied by their wives. By the end of the year, the process of replacing canvas shelters with decent huts was well under way. Dearth of acceptable drinking water, another severe problem, was on the way to being solved by the arrival of a 'distilling apparatus'. Dupont, who returned in mid-December for a normal

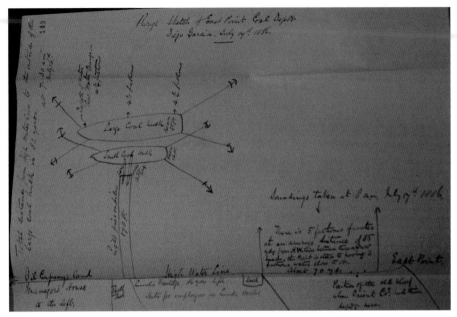

East Point coaling station, 1886. Image courtesy TNA.

inspection, examined Spurs' establishment early in January 1884. The population of his two islets was then 105, with further additions from East Point expected soon, doubtless encouraged by wages of up to Rs 16 per month. Dupont found fault with Spurs on a number of technical counts, but made no major criticisms and received no complaints from his employees.[19] Meanwhile, the operations of Lund and the enforced departure of Spurs from East Point had had an immediate impact on the island as a whole. The establishment at Minni Minni closed. Moreover, at East Point itself oil production for 1882-1883 had amounted to 25,500 *veltes* (190,000 litres), well below the 32,000 *veltes* (238,400 litres) anticipated. For want of labour similar reductions affected Pointe Marianne. It is clear that a considerable number of workers returned to Mauritius, apart from those who had defected with Spurs, and it seems highly unlikely that the terms of the deal between Lund and the island's proprietors outweighed this initial loss.[20] Lund too must have been disappointed by his financial results, for he approached the British government early in 1884 to propose, in return for an annual subsidy of £10,000, the introduction of a monthly steamship service between Mauritius and Ceylon, calling at Diego Garcia and timed to coincide with Orient's calls there. This proposal was duly put to Mauritius and rejected, the Governor's Council having only recently renewed its subsidy for the mail service via the Cape.[21]

Despite the obstacles put in their way, Orient persevered and Spurs maintained a preponderance of the trade. The commander of HMS *Dragon*, which visited the island in the first week of June 1885, reported approvingly on his arrangements: when an Orient steamer approached and needed coal, she would hoist the 'Rendezvous' flag, a signal for the colliers to set off for the lighters and hulk; the steamer would tie up alongside the latter, while Spurs' powerful tug would tow a lighter to the other side of the steamer. By this means 215 tons could be taken on in only five hours.[22] Yet the conditions of his workers were clearly unsuitable; apart from their crowding, they were not allowed even to visit their friends on the East Point estate and Spurs feared that there would be trouble, if this 'kind of imprisonment continued'. In London, Orient renewed their request to take a lease of land from the government; in Port Louis, the governor instructed senior officials to investigate what the *Société Huilière* might accept. The latter, through their Agent, M. Pelle, continued to 'object strongly'; the Acting Procureur Général reported back frustratedly that, as a result of the 1865 dispensation, 'this island, though a British possession, has entirely become a private estate in such a way that the owners may prevent any person from landing on any part of it'. Authorised to propose that the government should itself purchase 30-40 acres, he encountered the same determination to yield nothing beyond what their title deeds allowed it to take from the proprietors, a total of 6 acres for the whole island. Indeed, on that aspect, as we shall see, they showed themselves remarkably cooperative.

Not surprisingly, perhaps, in April 1885 another entrepreneur, Alfred Suart, who had been attracted by all this activity, despatched a certain R. A. McCallum to investigate. The latter reported that neither coaling station was doing well. Spurs, he claimed, was having difficulties because of troubles and sickness among his cramped and discontented workers, as well as through the loss of one of his hulks, driven ashore from its exposed anchorage; while Lund was having difficulties with the *Société Huilière*, who were trying to get rid of him, having been offered better terms from 'another quarter'. Suart then wrote to the Colonial Office to seek agreement to his leasing a site at Eclipse Bay, on the western side of the lagoon entrance.[23] His plan was to install a jetty and wagons, so that ships could be moored alongside and the coal be loaded and unloaded directly. Whether coincidentally or not, this was exactly what the Admiralty team had first envisaged in 1881. In his letter, Suart drew attention to the obstructionism of the *Société* and the threat this posed to England's imperial as well as its commercial interests. While nothing practical was to come of this approach, it triggered in Whitehall exactly the effect intended.

Sir Robert Herbert, the Permanent Secretary, penned a forceful minute to his Minister, averring that

> … the public interests concerned are too important to be disposed of there [Port Louis]. Diego Garcia has no natural connection with Mauritius, and it is only by an unfortunate accident that its destinies are in any way controlled by the

HMS *Bacchante*. Image NMM.

Colonial Government. The place is of the highest Imperial importance and I would suggest that we should discuss with the Admiralty the expediency of divorcing it from Mauritius and re-acquiring the Islands by compulsory purchase at a fair price based upon agricultural value; so as to be able to open them to the public on fair and safe terms.

Lord Derby agreed that the question of making Diego Garcia a separate Imperial Station should be considered by the Colonial Defence Committee. Officials then considered the possible options and difficulties, leading Herbert to offer the further thought that, if the Mauritius Council objected to providing land and paying off its proprietors, 'it may be best to pass an Order-in-Council supervising any person or company who may desire to establish a coal store and to purchase compulsorily the land required for that purpose'. Lord Derby agreed. 'What good', added a more junior official, 'is the possession of colonies like Mauritius if we cannot control their creoles in matters so much affecting our interests as this coaling at Diego Garcia?' The issues were duly submitted to the Colonial Defence Committee, which agreed.

Diego Garcia should be administered independently of Mauritius, with which it has no natural connection, and … whatever arrangements may be made for the civil government of the island steps should be taken to remove the impediments which now hinder the development of traffic. Every facility for the establishment of coal depots on the main island should be given, either by granting compulsory powers of purchase from the Oil Company, or by resuming on the part of the

Crown such land as may be required, in addition to 6 acres to which the Crown is entitled under the original agreement … and it would perhaps be desirable, failing any other equitable arrangement, that the Colonial Government should reacquire the whole of the main island at a price calculated on the agricultural value of the land.[24]

Moved by this political head of steam, officials in Mauritius considered more closely the legal devices by which the British government's objective might be achieved and accelerated their plans for the establishment of a small police contingent on the island. The Governor, Sir John Pope-Hennessy, reported his intention to visit Diego Garcia himself, if the Admiral on the East Indies Station could spare him the services of a man-of-war; soon after, in a separate despatch, he referred, most uncharacteristically, to 'the necessity of considering the urgent question of [Diego Garcia's] defence on Imperial grounds'.[25] The Colonial Office assured Orient that their wishes were being attended to. For their part, the Admiralty considered anew the desirability of establishing a naval station on the island. HMS *Rambler* was sent to undertake a fresh hydrographic survey of the lagoon and, a few months later, Rear-Adm. Richards in HMS *Bacchante* visited the island, noted the increasing number of ships using its coaling facilities, commented that the British Flag should be kept flying and reported that East Point was 'unquestionably the position most suitable for the proposed naval establishment'.[26] His enthusiasm was unabated when he visited Diego Garcia

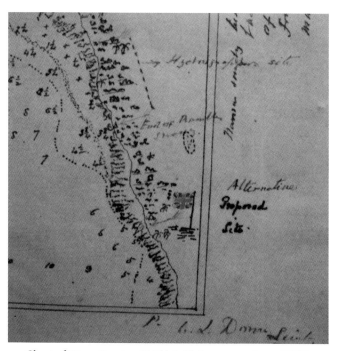

Chart of Diego Garcia, 1886 (detail). Image courtesy of TNA.

again a year later to choose a site (just to the south of the existing settlement), which he marked on the new chart with a neatly coloured Union Jack (see illustration).

For that visit, *Bacchante* was accompanied by three other vessels of his Squadron, HM Ships *Turquoise*, *Reindeer* and *Mariner*. A flurry of reports ensued. The Admiral recorded at once that he had 'carried out some submarine mining operations and other exercises and evolutions'.[27] We also know that these 'evolutions' included a theatrical performance aboard *Mariner*, attended by officers from the *Bacchante* and 'Europeans from the shore', as well as a performance ashore by the flagship's band. Earlier, 'the two Europeans came to the ship with their families to church services, just the 6 of them'.[28] The rare photograph below taken by a ship's passenger shows such a group, although the individuals cannot be identified for certain.[29] More importantly, Richards and all three of his captains put in enthusiastic reports on the importance of defended coaling stations in general and Diego Garcia in particular.[30] Their pleas, however, fell on deaf ears; the Admiralty declined to pay for fortifications, while the Colonial Office was satisfied by the Admiralty's Acknowledgement that it would defend Diego Garcia in time of war.[31]

Police

As has been noted, it was the concerns of Diego Garcia's proprietors that initially caused the government in Mauritius to consider installing a resident authority on the island. Once the government turned its attention to this

Diego Garcia managers and families, *c.*1886. Image NW-S collection.

objective, it received their cooperation and that of their friends in the Governor's Council. The Council quickly approved the Governor's proposal to send a police Inspector, with a corporal and five constables to assist him. In May 1885 an official surveyed the site offered, six acres of the former Minni Minni plantation. As well as being cannily placed between East Point and Orient's area of activity, it included the buildings of an abandoned oil factory. With considerable imagination these were transformed to provide a house for the Inspector, barracks for his force, a court-house and a six-cell prison. There was also a boat house, but no boat. Three wells, providing access to somewhat brackish water, were restored to working order and the police contingent duly arrived in October. It was led by Inspector Vere Butler, 'one of the finest looking men ever in the Mauritius police force, [whose] handsome appearance and fairly zealous attention to his duties were rewarded' by this appointment as Administrator of the island, which also gave him all the powers of a District Magistrate.[32] In addition, he was required to defray the cost of his contingent by levying charges from every vessel that called, at a rate of £5 or £10, according to size.

It was not a happy experiment. Lacking water transport of his own, Butler's effectiveness was severely limited. The legislation which gave him power to detain offenders for up to a fortnight had omitted to include cancellation of the managers' power to imprison employees for three days, causing constant conflicts with the latter.[33] The charge on shipping was equally resented by the coaling companies, especially Lund, who complained with reason that no service was provided in return; it was they who had buoyed the channel from the entrance to East Point, provided pilotage and rigged up simple lights. Even Adm. Richards was moved to argue in favour of reduced charges, mainly, as he later revealed, because he feared for the viability of the coaling stations and hence the availability of coal for the Navy.[34,35] In truth, just at the moment when the British government believed that its strategic objectives and administrative responsibilities were being fulfilled, both were beginning to unravel.

The first hint of trouble recognised by the Colonial Office came in a letter from Orient dated 25 February 1886. Capt. Waymouth announced that the company was considering closing its coaling station and, before offering it to others, wished to know if the British government might be interested. In a minute dated 27 February which shows signs of panic, E. Wingfield (the experienced desk officer) commented that the first thing was to find out if the company's attitude arose from the difficulties in getting the land they needed; if so, they should be assured that the government would press on with the unduly delayed ordinance for resuming possession of such land; it was 'absurd for the public to be perpetually boycotted by the French proprietors: Mr. Lund or Mr. Suart may presently take over from the Company'. Shortly afterwards, he made a note that Orient's departure would depend on whether their tender for a faster service to

Australia, precluding calls at Diego Garcia, were successful. Having consulted the Admiralty, which saw no reason, while supplies from Lund were available, to 'burden themselves with the cost and maintenance of a coal depot', he wrote declining Waymouth's offer.[36] In fact, there had been an earlier indication that Orient might be losing patience. In January 1885, Waymouth had reported that during Dupont's visit the latter had, with Spurs, 'marked off the proposed site for our coaling station at North East point'; in December, he wrote again to say that in May the Assistant Surveyor-General had visited Diego Garcia and measured off a plot of land at Minni Minni, some five miles south of the position Orient had proposed. The same letter reported that 'our late manager has recently returned to this country'.[37] Spurs, whether or not he had misunderstood the purpose for which the Minni Minni plot was required, had clearly despaired of gaining a proper base for his operations. He was never to revisit the island to which he had devoted so much energy and enterprise for almost twenty years. Instead, he bought the right to exploit the Seychelles island of Farquhar, where he lived until at least 1896, later going bankrupt and leaving his manager and old colleague, Hodoul, to face the fury of unpaid workers and angry authorities. Later, he held the contract to protect the wildlife of Aldabra. He died on Mahé in 1928.

Lund must now have decided that his hand was strengthened. In August 1886, he complained to the Colonial Office that the tonnage dues collected by the police since their arrival had provided no benefit whatever to shipping; all the buoys had (he claimed) been laid at his own company's expense and a member of his staff had piloted, without a single accident in five years, nearly every one of the 100 or so vessels which had visited the island (in late 1886, Dupont reported that 87 vessels had called during the preceding two-year period, the great majority of them to obtain or deliver coal).[38] Surely, Lund argued, these services and the provision of a light at the lagoon entrance should properly be provided out of the charges now being paid. The Colonial Office agreed and invited Port Louis to comply.[39]

Port Louis did not, however, consist merely of the Governor, but also of his Council and its powerful Finance Committee. The latter found in the new instruction from London a pretext to get rid of the interfering policemen and all the charges associated with their presence. In January 1887, the acting Governor relayed to London the arguments which had been adduced.[40] These were that, by September 1886, the cumulative deficit of the contingent had amounted to almost Rs 11,000, which would be increased greatly by the capital (Rs 60,000) and running costs (Rs 20,000) of installing harbour lights, with a steam launch and crew to service them. Still higher deficits would result from reducing the coaling charges, as proposed by the Colonial Office. Should the government seek to recoup these by increased taxation of the plantation companies, the latter, whose yearly income from oil produced on the island was about Rs 82,000, might be forced to give up altogether. Given the strength of feeling, the acting Governor doubted the possibility of obtaining agreement for an ordinance authorising compulsory purchase of part of Diego Garcia and sought fresh instructions. He was told to retain the police presence, but aim to finance it from a tax on the import of coal and on the export of produce from Diego Garcia. The Admiralty, whose views had also been sought, confined itself to stressing the importance of the island as a source of coal for HM ships.

While these issues were being considered, the Orient Line made a last attempt to obtain more land, writing to the Colonial Secretary in Mauritius and seeking support from the Colonial Office in London. Receiving no satisfaction, Capt. Waymouth informed the Colonial Office of the company's early intention to close the coaling station 'which has all along been a losing concern'; they had no further interest in acquiring land; and they expected to return their labourers to Mauritius and European staff to Britain early in 1888. In reply to a question from the Colonial Office, Waymouth asked for an extension of the three-month notice period for the cancellation of their leases and enquired whether the government wished to buy the ten navigation buoys they had laid down.[41] In January 1888 the same offer was turned down by the Admiralty, while in May the company informed the Colonial Office with manifest feeling that it was 'not their wish to continue in possession one day longer than necessary'.

Already, in April, a first-hand account had reached London, in the form of a report on the coaling stations' last days from the captain of HMS *Reindeer* to Adm. Richards.

> I beg to bring to your notice, that on my arrival at Diego Garcia I found the Orient Company had broken up their coaling station and the only coal they had left was in 2 lighters; this was taken by this ship and the *Kingfisher*, being just the quantity required. They have offered the whole of their plant, lighters etc., to Lund's Co., and the manager of the Orient Company was about to proceed to Colombo in the steam launch with a view to selling her there.
>
> I was informed by Mr. Butler (the Chief of Police & Magistrate) that the Orient Company had offered to sell the Buoys that mark the entrance (that I am told were laid down by the *Rambler*) to the Mauritius Gov't & that should the offer be refused the Company will then remove the Buoys. The answer to this offer is expected to arrive in the first week of March, but Mr. Butler went on to say that in the event of the Mauritius Gov't refusing to purchase these Buoys, they will be bought by a private individual with a view to selling them again. Should the Home Gov't wish to buy the Buoys Mr Paul Butler, Manager of Lund's coaling Station, Diego Garcia, could answer all enquiries & letters should be sent to him via Mauritius. The buoys are 8 feet buoys, 8 in number, moored by chain in 6 fathoms of water and laid down new 4 years since.

From enquiries I caused to be made I believe there is at Lund's Coaling Station about 1,800 tons of coal at the present time & this Company wish to obtain a contract for supplying HM Ships calling at the port.

Mr. Butler showed me an official confidential communication that he had received from the Gov't stating that it is the intention to establish Coaling Stations at Diego Garcia and Mahé; this communication he was directed to show to the Commander-in-Chief or Senior Naval Officer when visiting the port.

Sgd H. B. Lang, Commander[42]

To nip readers' curiosity in the bud, Paul Butler was indeed the Police Chief, Vere Butler's brother …

Let us now return to events in Mauritius. In August 1887, the acting Governor, Sir Francis Fleming, presented to his Council a proposal that the shipping tax be replaced by taxes on coal imported to Diego Garcia and goods exported from the Oil Islands. There was also a sweetener, worth Rs 4,000 annually, in the form of an offer to cancel the charge for the services of a visiting magistrate to the islands. All eleven official members of the Council supported the proposal; all twelve non-officials voted against it. The Governor would have had to cast both his own vote and the casting vote (available in case of a tie) in order to force the measure through. He decided not to press the matter, but to seek the Colonial Office's further views. The Office agreed only that he should ask for the original proposal to be reconsidered, but, if it were again rejected, he should withdraw the police contingent and place responsibility firmly on the Council for any disturbances or breaches of the peace which might occur. The Council next met in February 1888 and maintained its previous stance; one of their arguments was that the coaling station brought no benefit to Mauritius, but only to the Empire. The Governor suggested to the Colonial Office that he should put forward a more modest measure to pay the costs of a smaller contingent, mentioning *en passant* that there were rumours of the closure of Lund's enterprise at the end of that year, in which case the money levied on coal would be derisory. Did the Secretary of State wish him to press on?

It was now the Colonial Office's turn to prevaricate, by finding out whether the rumours regarding Lund were true. This took months. On 16 April, 1888 Lund wrote that he was 'contemplating' such a course and was 'thinking of ordering his manager home for personal enquiries on the subject'; on 1 June, he reported that a steamer, the ss *Murrumbidgee*, would call at Diego Garcia with a written request to the Manager, who 'might or might not be able to come'; and on 15 September that the Manager was in Britain and available. Wingfield met Paul Butler two days later and learned of his relationship to the police inspector. From their conversation, he gathered that Lund would probably continue his operation, if he could lease the islets and have a contract with the Admiralty. On 19 October Lund himself wrote to say that he 'had decided to discontinue selling coal at that place'; also that 'in case Mr Paul Butler should communicate for the purpose of establishing a similar business there on his own account, he had [Lund's] full permission to do so'. To the Colonial Office's request for clarification, Lund replied delphically that 'discontinue' did not mean 'abandon' and that he was still hoping to make the place commercially successful.[43] Exhausted, the Colonial Office instructed that the police contingent be withdrawn, a decision which the Governor 'deeply regretted, on Imperial grounds'.[44]

There must have been a good deal of celebration on the part of the Oil Island proprietors. All of them had put their names to petitions, arguing the injustice of the tax proposal which the Council considered in 1887. There were three petitions, reflecting respectively the interests of, first, Salomon and Trois Frères, second, Agalega and Six Islands and, third, Diego Garcia and Peros Banhos, by then the property of a single company, *Société Huilière de Diégo et Péros*. As can readily be imagined, each used arguments suiting their own case, citing highly selective statistics. Their main point was, nevertheless, a fair one: the police presence had only been rendered necessary (and only for one island) by the introduction of coaling stations. It was at the closing session of the Council in December 1888 that the Governor announced the decision to remove the police contingent;[45] the Orient Company's lease had been terminated with effect from 30 September. The *Société Huilière* wasted no time before applying, in February 1889, to take over the unexpired portion of the lease, a move agreed once a clause had been added to allow the government to withdraw it without compensation at any time the islets might be required for public purposes.[46] They had now achieved all they could have wished, save a profitable monopoly on the coaling business. Lund's last hope for making money – a contract with the Admiralty – also came to nothing: it had lost interest and declined the government's offer to transfer to them the Minni Minni establishment. That too was now leased back to the local proprietors, who purchased the buildings for the price set on them by the government's valuer.

Finally, there was an additional satisfaction for the proprietors. Inspector Butler and his policemen returned to Mauritius in the first days of 1889 straight into the arms of a Police Commission of Inquiry.[47] We owe to a very recent history by Jean-Marie Chelin an account of what transpired.[48] Various charges were laid against him by the East Point manager and others, of which Henri Leclézio, presiding, found him guilty of two, both involving his brother Paul. Vere had taken barrels of salted beef, pork and wine from official supplies, which he passed on to Paul to sell at a large profit in the boutique he ran at the East Point plantation; and he had perverted the course of justice by inflicting a mere month's imprisonment on a servant of his brother's who had committed murder, ignoring a key witness. Accusations of involvement in 'gross transactions of every sort' with visiting ships failed to stick. Quite apart from the accusations of the company, Butler had already come in for sharp criticism from the magistrate who visited Diego Garcia in 1888 and found himself having to try no less than six cases involving him, five of them as defendant.[49] Surprisingly, he obtained further appointments; unsurprisingly, they did not include the job he applied for, as Superintendent of Prisons.

The plantation owners had thus rid themselves of the naval and commercial interference of the *maudits anglais* into their private world. No-one will ever know, and it is useless to speculate, whether they had calculated, or even considered, the commercial benefits of a less narrow-minded approach. Likewise, we can only imagine how the economy of the islands and, later, their fate in times of war, might have been different, had the British government established a naval presence based on Diego Garcia in the late 19th century. It is time to revert to the development of the plantations and their governance during the years which followed the first decade of magisterial investigation.

Notes to Chapter 12

1   TNA CO 167/413 Enclosure to Mauritius confidential Despatch dated 7 September 1859. Caldwell's full-time post was that of Creole and French interpreter in the office of the chief legal official the Procureur Général.

2   TNA CO 167/415 Admiralty memorandum dated 2 December 1859.

3   Duyker, E. *Mauritian Heritage*, p. 60.

4   TNA CO 167/585 Admiralty correspondence, May 1879.

5   TNA CO 167/591 Letter dated 30 November 1880 from two Directors, Messrs Green and Anderson.

6   TNA CO 167/598 W. Lund letter to Wyndham Herbert dated 13 July 1881.

7   Brett, a rising political figure, at that time Parliamentary Private Secretary to the Secretary of State for India, was a close confidant and admirer of Gordon's judgment. Later ennobled as Lord Esher.

8   TNA CO 167/598 Col. C.G. Gordon letter to Lord Kimberley dated 15 May 1881.

9   The old friend was Col. Sir Howard Elphinstone, VC, enjoying an agreeable appointment in Aldershot, as Comptroller to the Queen's son, Prince Arthur, Duke of Connaught (Pollock, J. *Gordon: the man behind the legend*, Constable, London, 1993).

10   Gordon, H.W. *Events in the Life of Charles George Gordon,* p. 175, Kegan Paul, London, 1886.

11   TNA CO 167/598 Reports dated 28 June and 7 July 1881 and letters in 1882 between the various parties involved.

12   TNA ADM 127/14 Report on the Defences of Ports on the East Indies Station, sent from HMS *Euryalus* and dated 6 June 1883.

13   TNA ADM 1/6758 Report of Capt. A.P. Hastings, CB, dated 1 June 1885.

14   TNA CO 167/624 Text of lease enclosed with letter dated 21 April 1885 from A. Suart. This letter also supplies many of the details recorded in this and the following paragraphs.

15   These were both old sailing ships; the *Arran* (962 tons) and *Ronachan* (1,156 tons).

16   TNA CO 167/606 Despatch No. 153, dated 19 April 1883.

17   TNA CO 167/607 Ivanoff Dupont, Report dated 4 June 1883, enclosed with Despatch No. 57 dated 12 July 1883.

18   TNA CO 167/616 Letter from Blyth Brothers dated 11 August 1883, enclosed with letter from Captain Waymouth, Secretary of the Orient Line, to Lord Derby dated 16 February 1884.

19   MA Report dated 26 February 1884 (National Archive of Mauritius).

20 The Rs 6,357 accumulated workers' savings held by the manager had been reduced by two-thirds between August 1883 and January 1884.

21 TNA CO 167/613 Papers enclosed with Governor's Despatch No. 258, dated 6 July 1884.

22 TNA ADM 1/6758 Report by Commander Charles Anson dated 25 June 1885.

23 TNA CO 167/624 A. Suart, letter dated 21 April 1885.

24 TNA CO 537/39 Minutes of Colonial Defence Committee, 29 May 1885.

25 TNA CO 167/622 Confidential Despatch dated 26 October 1885.

26 TNA CO 167/623 Admiralty letter to Colonial Office dated 31 October 1885 (see also TNA ADM 1/6758 and 1/6807).

27 TNA ADM 6807/Sa 120 Letter to the Admiralty dated 20 July 1886.

28 Marsh, T. *A Naval History on the East Indies Station*, p. 19. Marsh was, at this point in his career, steward to the captain of HMS *Mariner*. He kept a diary, which he converted into a narrative during his retirement. It has since been published on the internet.

29 This slide was advertised on the internet and brought to the attention of NW-S. Subsequent discussion with the seller, Aladdin's Cave of Derby (England), showed that the unknown passenger was aboard one of Orient's ships en route from Liverpool to Adelaide, Australia. Initially, it seemed to show Spurs and Leconte together with their respective families, suggesting that it was taken before Spurs left East Point. A copy of the photo with its proposed identification was sent to the late Paul Caboche, from whose collection it was published by J-M. Chelin. But Spurs never married again after the death of his wife in 1868. It is more likely, we now think, that the images may be those of Leconte and his assistant, Lemasson. The latter had several daughters, for '3 Misses Lemasson' (and Mme Leconte) were among the passengers aboard the *Eva Joshua* on her voyage to Diego Garcia in August 1883 (Mauritius *Commercial Gazette*, September 1883, BL MC 1359).

30 Rear Admiral Richards to Admiralty, 3 August 1886.

31 Admiralty letter to Admiral Richards, dated 18 October 1886 and associated minuting.

32 Dictionary of Mauritian Biography.

33 TNA CO 167/631. This overlapping jurisdiction was not dealt with until May 1887.

34 TNA ADM 1/6807 Sa 141 Letter to Admiralty dated 31 August 1886.

35 TNA CO 167/635 Letter to Admiralty dated 21 December 1887.

36 TNA CO 167/628 Letter dated 2 April 1886 to Capt. Waymouth.

37 TNA CO 167/623 Letters dated 30 January and 3 December 1885. There is no reference in Dupont's reports to his having examined any such site.

38 TNA CO 167/630 Enclosure to Major General C.H. Hawley's Despatch No. 37 dated 17 January 1887.

39 TNA CO 167/629 Letter dated 20 Aug 1886 and associated minuting.

40 TNA CO 167/630 Despatch No. 37 (see Note 37 above).

41 TNA CO 167/636 Letters from Orient Line dated 3 February, 19 August, 1 September and 22 December 1887.

42 TNA CO 167/644 Letter from Admiralty dated 9 January and report dated 16 February 1888, forwarded on 13 April from Admiralty to Colonial Office.

43 Letters all in TNA CO 167/645.

44 TNA CO 167/646 Despatch No. 81 dated 10 February 1889.

45 TNA CO 167/642 Despatch No. 668 dated 21 December 1888.

46 TNA CO 167/647 Despatch No. 201 dated 11 May 1889.

47 Shipping records in the *Commercial Gazette* report the arrival of Inspector Butler and his family on 7 March 1889, while the issue for 10 May contains an extensive transcript of Butler's cross-examination of one of his accusers, ex-Constable Vandervoort, whom he had previously dismissed for forgery and false accounting. No other part of the Inquiry was reported.

48 Chelin, J-M. *Les Ziles Là Haut* Port Louis 2013, citing Paul, L-J. *Deux Siècles d'Histoire de la Police à l'Ile Maurice.*

49 TNA CO 170/144. Administrative Reports to Council, p. 1134, A. Boucherat on visit to Diego Garcia and Peros Banhos, July 1888.

13

1889–1914: Prosperity for Some

WITH the closure of the coaling stations on Diego Garcia (where the company immediately leased back the government's land), the proprietors could concentrate once more on their traditional activities. The authorities in Mauritius, for their part, acted for some time as if the problems of governing the islands in normal conditions had largely been resolved. While magistrates continued to make visits during the last years of the 19th century, their regularity and frequency were much reduced. Even the two biggest atolls were visited only three times between 1888 and 1901 – in 1890, 1894 and 1896; Salomon and Eagle Islands received visits in 1886, 1890, 1893 and 1899; whereas Six Islands was visited only in 1884, 1892 and 1897. The inevitable result of this period of neglect was deterioration in the workers' conditions.

Prelude: 1889–1892

On the surface, normality prevailed. The movement of people and goods continued their traditional rhythms. Between 1888 and 1891, the *Commercial Gazette*'s reports of shipping movements referred spasmodically to the names of cabin and numbers of deck passengers carried to and from the Chagos. The outward-bound figures for those four years totalled 148, 166, 88 and 65; the arrivals, evidently counted more zealously, came to 176, 107, 202 and 205. Implausibly, many sailings made no mention of deck passengers. These figures nevertheless provide some indication of the scale of movement between Mauritius and the islands. The press (see inset overleaf) likewise reported in considerable detail the cargoes being carried to the islands, providing evidence, if any were still needed, of their utter dependence on external supplies. As to production (discussed later in this chapter), improvements soon followed from the cessation of coaling activities, as Table 13.1 (p. 261) reveals. In December 1889, the

Chagos Supplies 1888/1889

1888 8th September Goods for Salomon Islands and Eagle Island
Venus, colonial schooner of 134 tons, F. Quineloc master; C. Nairac agent. Shippers: C. Nairac & Co

(*Salomon*) 2 pkges, and 1 c hardware, 2 c mercery, 2 c dress, 4 casks bread, 1 b flour, 1 b coffee, 4 casks wine, 5 b salt, 2 c haberdashery, 12 kegs paint, 2 bdles rattan, 12 blocks fuel, 4 pkges iron, 1 copper bar, 1 drum oil, 1 drum turpentine, 30 pkges cordage, 2 pkges copper sheets, 1 do nails, 1 do felt, 1 b beans, 1 b lentils, 1 b peas, 1 b dholl, 1 b tamarinds, 1 b onions, 1 bale tobacco, 25 planks, 12 empty tin buckets, 6 c brandy, 75 b rice, 235 emty casks, 4 bags sugar wg nett 299 kilos.

(*Eagle Island*) 8 pkges and 3 c hardware, 2 do mercery, 4 casks bread, 1 b flour, 1 b coffee, 3 casks wine, 5 b salt, 4 kegs paint, 5 pkges rope, 1 do rosin, 4 do iron, 1 iron sheet, 2 iron bars, 1 c dress, 1 b onions, 1 bale tobacco, 1 b turmeric, 1 b chillies, 25 planks, 24 empty tin pots, 5 c brandy, 50 b rice, 20 b cocoanuts, 500 empty bags

1888 Goods for Diego Garcia and Peros Banhos
24th July *Suzanne* colonial brig of 251 tons, E. Nicolin master, for Diego Garcia; Blyth Brothers & Co, agents. Shipper L. Antelme fils

1 bale rattan, 1 piece and 1 bale leather, 6 bundles iron, 20 bdles and 20 pkges hoop, 2 grindstones, 20 b salt, 2 c manufactured tobacco, 16 casks bread, 6 barrels wheat flour, 3 c leaf tobacco, 500 bags rice, 15 casks wine, 5 b coffee, 1 packet sugar, 5 pkges preserved provisions, 11 b sugar wg nett 796 kilos, 1 barrel pickles, 5 c composition candles, 2 c earthenware, 3 c mercery, 8 pkges earthenware, 50 kilos lentils, 30 kilos beans, 10 kilos peas, 50 kilos dried ginger, 75 kilos onions, 30 kilos garlic, 2 iron bars, 1 c iron mongery.

1889 2nd October Suzanne [same details], for Diego Garcia and Peros Banhos
(Diego Garcia) Shipper: L. Antelme

471 bgs rice, 1 parcel clothing, 208 empty casks, 21 cks wine, 25 bgs salt, 4 bgs bran, 2 c mercery, 1 piece stone, 4 c haberdashery, 5 c manufactured tobacco, 4 c drugs, 5 bales leaf tobacco, 1 c corks, 2 bgs wheat flour, 1 c olive oil, demi-john vinegar, 1 bg coffee, 4 c preserved provisions, 14 cks wheat flour, 18 cks biscuits, 2 bgs onions, 1 bale chillies, 1 bg curry powder, 2 bgs lentils, 1 bg peas, 1 bg dried ginger, 2 bgs dholl, 5 iron bars, 28 bdles iron, 2 drs linseed oil, 1 drum turpentine, 22 kegs paint, 6 iron sheets, 1 barrel pitch, 4 pkges coir rope, 3 c hardware, 1 iron anvil, 141 bgs sugar wg nett 1013 kilos.

(Peros Banhos) Shipper L. Antelme

300 empty casks, 10 cks wine, 300 bgs rice, 4 bgs salt, 1 c tin-plates, 2 pkgs coir rope, 2 drs linseed oil, 2 drs turpentine, 21 kegs paint, 16 pkges iron, 3 cks cement, 2 drs tar, 1 c tallow, 3 bdles rattan, 1 barrel coaltar, 4 copper bars, 5 pkges hardware, 12 cks biscuits, 1 bg coffee, 1 bg dates, 1 bg wheat flour, 3 c mercery, 2 c haberdashery, 1 c manufactured tobacco, 1 c drugs, 4 bales leaf tobacco, 108 iron pots, 25 planks, 51 pieces wood, 3 bgs sugar wg nett 211 kilos.

1889 Goods for Six Islands
14th September: *Venus*, Schooner of 131 tons, F. de Baize master; C. Nairac & Co, agents. Shippers L. Antelme

3 bgs sugar wg nett 217 kilos, 6 bales hay, 2 iron tanks, 2 bgs gram [*sic*], 2 bgs bran, 2 horses, 4 donkeys, 2 bgs oats, 4 cks biscuits, 1 c drugs, 10 kilos tallow, 12 pieces tinware, 2 cks wine, 2 c liqueurs, 3 bdles rattans, 1 c haberdashery, 1 ck rum, 100 bgs rice, 9 pieces wood, 1 c mercery, 250 empty casks, 3 pkges paint, 51 pkges hardware, 1 ck iron nails, 1 ck cement, 1 iron bar; A. de La Roche 1 ck wine.

Source: *Commercial Gazette* (mail edition) for 21 July 1888, 11 September 1888, 10 and 11 October 1889. Abbreviations as printed. We guess that c = case, b = bag, bdle = bundle, pkges = packages.

press also reported a sharp increase in the price of coconut oil (previously trading at around Rs 1.90 per *velte*) to Rs. 2.50 per *velte*, together with a rise in the cost of shares in the *Société Huilière* from Rs 1.00 to Rs 2.10.[1] A few months later, however, we find it reverting to Rs 1.00.[2]

The magistrate succeeding Arthur Boucherat was Hyacinthe Hewetson, who visited all the Chagos plantations during the three years of his appointment (for file references, see Note 17). In 1890, the situation confronting him on each of the islands resembled what had faced Ackroyd in 1876.

At both plantations on Diego Garcia (population 427), the manager, Jules Larcher, had been obliged to put the workforce onto half rations, with a three-day working week, owing to the insufficiency of rice delivered by the previous supply vessel. Moreover, the quantity brought in by the *Lady Harewood* was 100 bags short of the amount required to provide a six-month stock. Again, the manager had reverted to the custom, favoured by the workers, of issuing additional *calou*, rather than cash for extra work. The manager was also found technically to have transgressed the rules by fining and imprisoning offenders for acts which required prosecutions. On the other hand, there were no significant complaints, relatively few assaults, and a good medical situation. Shop prices met the rules and expenditure there took up no more than 70% of the wages paid. Annual production for the island as a whole amounted to about 60,000 *veltes*.

At Peros Banhos (population 167), managed by the recently promoted Charles Lionnet (see page 222), Hewetson's main criticism was that the women (as on Diego Garcia) were required to break coconuts as a Sunday *corvée* duty. However, he also remarked on the absence of vegetables in the workers' diet and the high proportion of infant deaths over the preceding eighteen months: eight of a total figure of fourteen deaths, there having been eighteen births. Like Ackroyd before him, Hewetson was highly critical of the conditions which the workers had to endure aboard ship. Inadequate drinking water was a constant source of complaint, to which the magistrate added:

> I would suggest that proper berths should be given to the labourers who are all huddled up together men women and children. They all sleep together on mattresses laid on the floor. These mattresses are never taken up and the floor is not swept – the labourers are not made to bathe. Such a state of things cannot be conducive to health or decency.

As to the three smaller islands, Hewetson visited Salomon (population 106) and Eagle Island (population 78) in September 1891. Neither had been visited for five years. The magistrate was highly critical of the state of affairs on both. At Salomon, managed by Alfred Delpit, dirt, disorganisation and squalor were evident everywhere. Many workers complained of callous treatment, some of which – for example, a diet of rice and salt only in the sick bay – conformed with regulations, while other elements, such as a charge of 25 cents for each person using the company fishing net, were odious given the absence of vegetables and paucity of fish, resulting in a diet 'worse than the one of prisons in Mauritius'. As elsewhere, the manager's use of imprisonment exceeded his authority, while the provision of *calou* as a substitute for extra pay was illegal. Not surprisingly, Hewetson found that, where imprisonment was justified, 'most of the cases were very serious and showed that the labourers freely used their knives'. Equally unsurprisingly, the vital statistics were dire: over the five years there had been 24 births and 29 deaths, most of them ascribed to dysentery or consumption. Production, however, was claimed to amount to some 21–22,000 *veltes* per year. At Eagle Island, it emerged that there had been frequent managerial changes prior to the arrival in 1890 of the current incumbent, a M. Giquel; the latter's assistant, a M. Boullé, had been temporarily in charge and had found the estate 'filthy beyond description'. As in years gone by, there was evidence of incompetent management from Mauritius. The rice available was of poor quality and full of grit; in 1890, none had been available for a full month; and the *gamelle* used to measure out rations contained 11¾, not the stipulated 12½ lbs. All except two of the uncomplaining workers were only under verbal contract and consequently ill-placed to assert legal rights. Hewetson ended his report with a strong recommendation that the owners be prosecuted. There were however signs of recent cleaning up and Giquel had begun to keep the requisite records. Again, the (sparse) vital statistics reflected the physical conditions: over the five years, there had been 17 births and 28 deaths. The stated production was 11,000 *veltes*.

It was not until a year later that Hewetson came to Six Islands, in September 1892, a full eight years after the previous magisterial visit. Here too management changes had resulted in the disappearance of some records, but there were no serious complaints to be made about callous behaviour or dirt. On the other hand, there were clear signs of casual attitudes on the part of the owners in Mauritius. The schooner *Emma Jane* (97 tons) usually visited only twice per year with six months' worth of supplies, thus, notwithstanding previous experiences, leaving no margin for error. On this occasion, what had run out was the entire stock of the plantation shop, which had been empty for three months; earlier still, the manager had run out of cash to pay the workers' wages, allowing the last items to be bought on credit. Fortunately both money and goods had just arrived. The other major issue, as so often in the past, was the continuation of high infant mortality. Over the preceding eight years, there had been 31 births and 18 deaths, 11 being of infants under a year old; but no register had been kept of the causes of death. Lastly, Hewetson records that the population on his arrival was 107, of whom 29 returned to Mauritius with his own departure. While production, at 16,000 *veltes*, was reasonable, it seems clear that the management must have decided to reduce its payroll.

During this period, a great deal more material becomes available concerning the Chagos economy and commerce, thanks to the fuller coverage given by the Mauritian press and more detailed trade statistics in Mauritius' annual Blue Books. From these and other sources, we can gain greater insights into the interaction between the main groups of interested parties: islanders, managers, owners, magistrates, government – as before – but also shippers and their suppliers. On the other hand, reporting by Visiting Magistrates became much more irregular. Levels of information about conditions obtaining in the Archipelago are therefore uneven. Against this background, it is most convenient to treat this whole period thematically. We shall begin with the Archipelago's economy and the development of the companies which operated it. Next, we revert to issues of governance, before considering once more the patterns of daily life in the plantations.

Better organised capitalism: 1893–1910

In 1892, economic conditions changed abruptly. On 29 April, a hurricane of great ferocity hit Mauritius. As Edward Duyker's *Mauritian Heritage* relates,[3] 'The sugar cane crop was completely devastated and the harbour of Port Louis was left a tangled mass of masts and wires', killing 1,100 people and leaving up to 50,000 homeless.[4] Like many other enterprises and individuals, the *Société Huilière* became bankrupt. From September that year, its shares ceased to be quoted. The following March, it was reported that its assets had been sold as a single lot at judicial auction for the sum of Rs 632,000. The purchaser was Henri Leclézio, said to be 'acting on behalf of a company'. The Leclézios were already powerful members of Mauritius society, providing leading representatives of the legal and commercial professions; Henri was later to use (and be known by) the anglicised spelling of his name, Henry. By August 1893, a new, this time private company, had indeed emerged: the *Nouvelle Société Huilière de Diégo et Péros*[5]. Its chairman was Leclézio, who had clearly made a profitable investment. Replacing Léopold Antelme[6] as its Agent and Secretary was Gabriel Théophile Lionnet.

In Duyker's words, Lionnet (1848–1911) was 'a sworn broker, with prosperous dealings in the island oil trade'. His first recorded connection with the Chagos was as the Agent for the *Star Queen*, a vessel sent to Diego Garcia in 1893 to bring back coal from East Point;[7] other Lionnets (identified only as 'Mr and Miss') had already appeared in the records as passengers to Six Islands in 1890, while Charles Lionnet, manager of Peros Banhos from 1890–1894 (see page 257 above), was Gabriel Théophile's cousin.[8] However, the Lionnet having the earliest known link with the Chagos was Gabriel Théophile's much younger half-brother Richard (1860–1934). As early as 1875, the previous company had employed him as a teenager to prevent pilferage of the supplies being taken through the docks for loading onto the Chagos-bound vessel; in those days, goods were taken by handcart, since donkeys did not flourish in Port Louis. The young lad was paid Rs 5 per month for his pains and given sleeping quarters. Exceptionally alert, he soon learned a great deal about the company's suppliers and it was not long before he was employed to help in choosing them. In 1881, the father of Gabriel Théophile and Richard, who had tried his luck on Australia's Victorian goldfields before returning to become a wealthy timber merchant during the development of the highland town of Curepipe, died, leaving bequests to both. In 1886, Richard, now 26, set up his own import enterprise there in partnership with an established wine merchant. Their stock-in-trade included many of the goods required in the Chagos. Within a few years, Richard was able to buy out his partner, leaving himself as sole proprietor of J.R. Lionnet & Co. Thus began a new stage in the concentration of power in the islands.

As regards the smaller island groups, some of the eight proprietors of Salomon and Eagle Islands (see page 234, Note 24) disappeared from view, while others, especially Jules Larcher and Charles Nairac, both mentioned as Agents, played increasingly prominent roles, as did E. D'Offay, owner and sometimes master of the schooner *Venus* (134 tons). The last-named appears to have been responsible for the abysmal state of affairs exposed by magistrate Hewetson in 1892. Six Islands was taken over by Antelme, after his removal from responsibility for Diego Garcia and Peros Banhos. Among the ships he used were the schooners *Gabriel* (78 tons), *Orénoque* (116 tons), *Little Annie* (227 tons), *Emma Jane* (97 tons) and *Cupido* (171 tons). It was not until around 1910 that the two groups joined forces in a company having the title *Société Huilière de Salomon, Trois Frères et Six Iles*, with Larcher as its Agent. This group was, of course, much less substantial. At the prevailing exchange rate of £1=Rs 13.50, its paid-up capital amounted to a little under £20,000, compared to nearly £50,000 for the larger concern.[9] As the inset on page 266 indicates, there was some cross holding of shares between members of one group and the other.

Trade between Chagos and Mauritius

All trade between the Chagos and Mauritius was accounted for by the inputs and outputs of the island plantations. The statistics for these exchanges are all contained in the Mauritius Customs records, describing what Mauritius imported from and exported to its individual island Dependencies. We have brought together the figures as they relate to the Archipelago as a whole. As Table 13.1 shows, the second half of the final decade of the 19th century was significantly more productive than the first. Coconut oil accounted for 95% of what the Chagos provided. De-husked nuts (*cocos barbes*) in vast numbers earned a further 2.2%, the remainder coming from such items as turtle shell, honey and beeswax, dried and salted fish, brooms and brushes. Occasionally, surplus pigs, donkeys and green turtles would be sent to Mauritius and, once, the enterprising manager of Six Islands extracted and exported the oil from a beached whale. The Table also shows that Mauritian exports to the Chagos, that is the goods required to operate the plantations, remained, despite the islands' growing population, virtually static. They certainly suggest that little or nothing can have been spent on modernising the machinery used or improving the islanders' standard of living (and, as has already been described, a high propor-tion of the cost of supplying the necessities of life was recouped from wages expended in the company shops). The available records do not identify shipping costs, nor include the cash to pay those employed. Also absent is any informa-tion concerning the profits or losses arising from the processing and onward sale of these imports.

Table 13.1   Mauritius imports from and exports to Chagos 1890-1900 by value (Rs '000)

	1890	1891	1892	1893	1894	1895	1896	1897	1898	1899	1900
Exports											
	98.3	107.2	103.4	101.5	100.0	101.8	98.9	105.6	116.3	99.4	127.3
Imports											
	93.7	138.1	165.6	152.4	157.7	211.6	205.7	203.3	188.1	207.0	215.9
Of which:											
Coconut oil											
DG	35.8	73.6	90.5	83.7	80.2	91.6	85.7	96.3	95.0	94.4	96.1
PB	17.3	17.6	28.8	22.7	29.3	36.3	31.5	38.8	36.3	34.1	39.2
Sal	14.4	19.6	17.8	25.7	21.7	29.7	34.5	25.7	20.2	28.8	24.0
Eag	6.9	7.9	8.8	9.1	11.4	14.8	18.0	8.9	5.0	21.4	9.4
6 I	15.5	13.2	16.1	8.6	9.9	29.4	24.2	17.8	15.4	21.4	27.7
Total	89.9	131.9	162	149.8	152.5	201.8	193.9	187.5	171.9	200.1	196.4

<u>Source</u>: Mauritius Blue Books (TNA CO 172 series).

In contrast to the 1890s, the first decade of the 20th century saw somewhat higher Mauritian exports to and distinctly lower imports from the Chagos (see Table 13.2 overleaf). The result was that the crude balance of trade between the two moved from a substantial surplus in favour of the proprietors to a rough balance. After 1910 the balance shifted substantially to an apparent deficit: the plantations were, it seems, costing more than they earned. There also seems to have been some attempt at diversification, for instance, in the reduction (from 95% to 85%) in the proportion of imports accounted for by coconut oil (only 1% of this difference could be accounted for by the increase, from 2% to 3%, in imports of unprocessed nuts).

Table 13.2   Mauritius exports to and imports from Chagos 1901–1915 by value (Rs '000)

	1901	1902	1903	1904	1905	1906	1907	1908	1909	1910	1911	1912	1913	1914	1915
Exports to Chagos															
	115.8	63.0	115.7	99.4	125.4	139.7	110.2	145.1	155.2	118.1	119.3	139.2	129.3	170.6	186.4
Total Imports															
	209.4	201.4	167.4	134.9	154.5	146.2	102.6	136.2	154.0	126.7	119.6	114.9	133.9	101.2	161.0
of which:															
Coconuts															
DG	1.2	2.0	1.7	1.7	1.8	1.3	1.4	1.2	2.2	1.9	2.1	3.0	1.7	3.1	2.0
PB	0.8	1.2	1.1	1.0	1.4	1.3	1.1	0.5	1.3	1.0	1.2	2.1	1.1	1.6	2.0
Sal	0.7	0.3	1.2	1.1	1.6	2.3	2.0	1.9	2.1	1.4	2.4	2.1	1.5	2.1	4.0
6 I	0.6	0.6	0.4	1.7	0.5	0.2	0.1	0.6	0.5	–	–	–	–	–	–
Eag	–	0.1	–	0.8	–	0.1	–	0.2	0.1	–	–	0.3	–	1.5	0.8
Total Chagos															
	3.3	4.2	4.4	6.3	5.3	5.2	4.6	4.4	6.2	4.3	5.7	7.5	4.3	8.3	8.8
Coco Oil															
DG	93.0	44.3	68.7	35.3	66.7	61.1	30.8	46.5	69.9	58.2	49.1	43.6	46.2	28.5	78.3
PB	41.9	17.2	29.2	58.4	32.9	33.7	20.1	45.8	34.5	30.2	25.1	26.8	25.8	7.0	31.7
Sal	32.9	10.8	27.3	19.1	19.5	18.1	19.2	14.3	10.2	16.6	17.9	15.5	19.9	15.1	13.5
6 I	20.5	8.5	18.5	15.9	14.6	11.3	13.7	10.3	10.2	6.9	8.6	9.0	5.5	–	–
Eag	9.6	2.9	8.8	10.5	6.1	5.7	5.4	8.1	6.3	4.9	5.6	5.2	10.9	1.5	11.4
Total Chagos															
	197.9	83.7	152.5	139.2	139.8	129.9	89.2	125	131.1	116.8	106.3	100.1	108.3	52.1	134.9
Copra/Poonac															
DG	–	–	–	–	–	0.6	0.4	0.2	0.1	<0.1	<0.1	0.3	0.7	10.1	2.3
PB	–	–	–	–	–	0.3	0.3	0.2	–	–	–	<0.1	0.1	5.8	5.2
Sal	<0.1	–	–	–	–	–	–	–	–	–	–	–	–	–	–
6 I	–	–	–	–	–	–	–	–	–	–	–	<0.1	–	–	–
Eag	<0.1	–	–	–	–	–	–	–	–	–	–	<0.1	–	–	–
Total Chagos															
	0.1	–	–	–	–	0.9	0.7	0.4	0.1	<0.1	<0.1	0.4	0.8	15.9	7.5
Other															
DG	3.2	6.3	5.8	7.2	5.0	6.2	3.0	3.7	4.5	4.3	3.2	4.0	11.7	11.0	6.2
PB	0.6	2.4	1.9	2.9	1.4	2.1	1.1	1.0	1.2	1.2	2.5	1.7	4.5	3.6	0.2
Sal	2.8	1.0	1.2	1.1	0.9	0.4	1.4	0.4	0.9	0.0	0.6	0.5	1.0	–	0.7
6 I	0.0	2.5	1.2	1.7	1.2	0.8	1.6	0.5	0.7	0.0	0.7	0.5	1.4	–	–
Eag	1.4	1.1	0.4	0.8	0.8	0.9	1.0	0.8	0.2	0.1	0.4	0.4	1.9	0.6	0.2
Total Chagos															
	8.0	13.3	10.5	13.7	9.3	10.4	8.1	6.4	7.5	5.6	7.4	7.1	20.5	15.2	7.3

<u>Source</u>: Mauritius Blue Books for years concerned. TNA CO 172 series.

What was going on? We may never know. The close connections between the shareholders in the various elements of the increasingly integrated Chagos business empire allowed huge scope for disguising the true costs of one part and another of the total operation. The economy and commercial performance of the Chagos plantations was described in general terms in *Mauritius Illustrated*.[10] The publication cited only 'average' figures for the amount of oil produced by

Diego Garcia (425,000 litres) and Peros Banhos (216,000 litres) over the previous ten years, in both cases a good deal higher than the latest official statistics suggested. The latter are however, extremely revealing, when compared with those for earlier periods. If production in 1862/3, as estimated by the Surveyor General prior to the transfer of ownership to the concessionaires, is compared with the Blue Book figures for 1889 (when the 1877 regulations had taken effect) and for 1912 (the last year prior to the shift to copra), it is apparent that the performance of the Chagos plantations, far from showing steady improvement, was highly uneven and nowhere near commensurate with the near doubling of the population over the 50-year period.

Table 13.3   Production of Coconut Oil in selected years

	Veltes*	1862 Litres	1889 Litres	1912 Litres
Diego Garcia	71,000	528,950	523,800	324,624
Peros Banhos	18,000	134,100	126,200	199,680
Salomon	10,000	74,500	160,495	108,680
Eagle Island	8,000	59,600	88,250	38,666
Six Islands	8,000	59,600	16,550	67,326
Total	115,000	856,750	915,295	738,976

*Note. In 1862, production was measured in *veltes*. For ease of comparison, we have calculated the litre equivalent, at 1 *v.* = 7.45 l.

These alarming statistics cannot explain all that was happening. Production naturally fluctuated from year to year, but, as Table 13.2 shows, there was a marked reduction in the level of earnings after 1909, which reflected a similar decline in production. To cite but four examples, the amount of oil exported to Mauritius in 1907 (1,191,204 litres) and 1908 (1,451,038 litres)[11] was in each case nearly twice that exported in the years 1911 (713,000 litres) and 1912 (738,976 litres). The companies were no doubt banking on the diversification from oil to copra to retrieve their position; but it is no wonder that the reporter for *Mauritius Illustrated* was fobbed off with averages, which disguised a situation likely to give shareholders just cause for concern.

Transport

Three other factors were also important to the overall financial health of the companies involved. The first was the cost of transport. We have seen only one specific indication of the cost of chartering a vessel to make the round voyage. In 1888, Antelme advertised the availability of his ship, the *Suzanne*, asking Rs 5,000. A few weeks later, this had come down to Rs 3,250.[12] The vessels used for conveyance to and from the Chagos were in general owned by the islands' proprietors, but were also used for trading with Madagascar, so spreading their costs. On the other hand, while their capital and running costs must have been relatively modest, the vessels used were slow, inefficient and all too frequently wrecked. The records do not allow us to establish with certainty when the plantation owners first purchased their own vessels, but by 1890 the owners of Salomon and Eagle Islands possessed the schooner *Venus* (134 tons) while the owner of Six Islands was making regular use of a smaller schooner, the 97-ton *Emma Jane*, which he went on using until at least 1900. Meanwhile, the *Venus* had been replaced until 1896 by the schooner *Earnest* (177 tons register). Although the owners of Diego Garcia and Peros Banhos had been making quite regular use of a 226-ton barque, the *Crocodile*, it was not until 1895 that the *Nouvelle Société* purchased their own barque, the 436-ton *William Turner*, which served them well until she was wrecked off Diego Garcia in about 1904.[13] In a rare exception to the general rule, the *William Turner*'s second and third voyages, in October 1895 and March 1896, took in Salomon and Eagle as well as the company's own two plantations, but evidently the attempt to economise by using the larger ship was not a success, probably because of the difficulty of gaining entry to Salomon and access to the jetty at Peros Banhos. After the loss of the *William Turner*, she was replaced by another barque, the *Ste. Marthe* (387 tons). In 1919, she too was wrecked, in tragic circumstances which we shall in due course describe.

Supplies

The second main commercial factor of importance concerned the control of supply costs. The company buyers were crucial in securing supplies of adequate quality at the lowest possible prices, usually achieved by competition between providers. Although this equation might seem simple, given that the company shops on each island enjoyed a monopoly and, with a permissible mark-up of 25% on the cost prices paid in Mauritius, were guaranteed to be profitable, there were limits to what the island workers would accept. Equally, there were limits to what, on their pitiful wages, they could afford; obviously, from the company's perspective, it would be self-defeating to supply goods which necessitated increased levels of pay. On the other hand, purchases from companies which were part of the same commercial grouping offered another route to enrichment for those involved. It is not possible to know how far this perception of the buyer's role was the product of Board policy, or whether the Managing Agent somehow believed this approach would best serve the Company's overall interest. We have, however, already seen how Gabriel Théophile Lionnet had employed his half-brother Richard as a buyer and how the latter had also established himself as a potential supplier. In 1911 Gabriel Théophile died suddenly and Richard was chosen to succeed him as Managing Agent. Richard (whom we must now call Richard *père*) in turn chose his eldest son, also called Richard (1892–1952), who was already employed by the *Nouvelle Société*, to take over his emporium in Curepipe. Only a few years later (by 1920 at the latest), Richard *père* passed the job of Managing Agent to his son, so that he himself could return to Curepipe. Thus there emerged from small beginnings a lucrative concentration of power. In fact, the early decades of the 20th century saw the fruition of this most convenient symbiosis, notably in the case of Diego Garcia and Peros Banhos. It was as Managing Agent that both Richard *père* and, later, Richard *fils* were to have many a tussle with Visiting Magistrates, who doubted whether the goods supplied to the islands were of adequate quality or reasonably priced.

Sales

The third factor, as already observed from the early days, was what would nowadays be called downstream integration. The proprietors had long been co-owners, with the Agalega Company, of the storage facility for the oil produced by all the Oil Islands. It should be kept in mind, however, that while the plantation companies effectively controlled the *Magasin Général des Huiles*, not everyone was a shareholder in both parts of the business.[14] The overall profit made by the companies would nevertheless be affected by the net profit gained from producing, storing, refining and then selling the oil produced. The quantities of and the prices at which oil from the Chagos was imported was recorded in the annual Mauritius Blue Books; so were the quantities and prices of the oil exported.[15] Thus the 713,000 litres imported in 1911 were valued at 15 cents per litre; in the same year, Mauritius exported just under 400,000 litres of oil at a price of 40 cents per litre. The remainder went to the local market, for domestic use or the manufacture of soap. The only other really profitable export from the islands was that of shells of Hawksbill turtles, known locally as *carets*.[16] The numbers of these turtles killed increased dramatically from 1903, adding little to Mauritian import costs, while the resulting highly fashionable 'tortoiseshell' made valuable profits for the Chagos companies when exported to Europe, until eventually supplanted by plastics. During the period from 1900 to 1918, 5411 kg of shell were shipped from the Chagos, representing over 140 animals per year, a rate which declining exports in later years proved as being unsustainable, but which helped the company to the tune of some Rs 5,700 annually, less Rs 420 for the Rs 3 per animal paid to the individual catchers. Or, to put matters another way, one Hawksbill was worth £3 to the Company – about as much as 1,000 coconuts.

Profits and the future

Whatever the underlying realities, it was not long before the *Nouvelle Société* began to pay out useful dividends. In its wide-ranging survey, *Mauritius Illustrated* (see Note 9) reported that the company's dividends averaged 12.1% over the years 1900–1911, but 17.8% over the last six of these years. Over the whole period this averaged at more than Rs 93,000 per annum (no comparable figures for the *Société Huilière de Salomon, Trois Frères et Six Iles* are known to us). Since the companies were private, share dealings were not reported by the stock market. Occasionally, however, they received mention in the Mauritius *Planters and Commercial Gazette* (see inset), which devoted a column to house sales, published wills and such like. Time consuming additional research might possibly reveal longer term trends in price and ownership.

Nouvelle Société Hullière de Diego et Péros (Capital 660,000 nominal 1 rupee shares in blocks of 500)

1910	29 Jan	Richard Lionnet holder of 500 shares [ambiguous]
	7 April	3 shares sold by Mrs Alexis Leclézio for Rs 2,850 (= Rs 950 each)
		5 shares sold by E.R. Lagane for Rs 4,750 (= Rs 950 each)
	19 April	1 share sold by E.R. Lagane for Rs 1090
	28 May	4 shares sold by L. Boullé for Rs 4,800 (= Rs 1,200 each)
	25 July	4 shares sold by Miss Hurquebie for Rs 4,800 (= Rs 1,200 each)
	29 August	4 shares sold by Miss C. Hurquebie for Rs 4,800 (= Rs 1,200 each)
	29 September	Mr T. Lionnet's shares valued at Rs 1,250
	1 October	2 shares sold by E.R, Lagane for Rs 2,300 (= Rs 1,150 each)
1911	28 February	2 shares sold by L. Rougier for Rs 2,200 (= Rs 1,100 each)
1912	28 February	2 shares sold between members of Lagane family for Rs 2,400
	14 March	1 share sold by Philippe de Caila for Rs 1,200

Société Huilière de Salomon, Trois Frères et Six Iles (Capital divided into 60 shares)

1911	29 April	2 shares sold by Richard Lionnet to Philippe de Caila for Rs 2,600
	28 October	1 share sold for Rs 1,140

<u>Source</u>: *Planters and Commercial Gazette* (available issues between Nos. 700-746 of Overland Mail Edition, held by BL)

Study of the Blue Books over the first half of the 20th century shows that the import price of coconut oil declined from over 20 cents per litre in 1900 to 14 cents by 1904, and remained close to that level for the next forty years. The Companies could not of course have known that that the reduction in price was to endure indefinitely, but the *Société Nouvelle*'s chairman, Henry (Henri) Leclézio, was as shrewd and well-placed as anyone in Mauritius to understand likely trends (see note 29) . There was indeed one harbinger of the major change that was to take place in later years: from 1905 onwards, the Diego Garcia plantations began to experiment with the export of small amounts of copra.[17] By 1914, Peros Banhos had followed suit; whereas in Salomon and Eagle, the product had been tried in 1901, but had soon been abandoned. Perhaps it was the necessary investment in sheds for drying and storing the new product that accounted for the sudden jump in exports to Chagos in 1914–1915. However, the key point to emerge is that the company must have taken a strategic decision to concentrate the processing of copra in Mauritius, rather than on the islands. It is easy to see why this might make commercial sense, but it entailed a fundamental downgrading of the role of the island communities. The long-forgotten promises of investment in improved facilities for producing coconut oil on the islands were now to be abandoned forever, leaving the islands undeveloped and their inhabitants bereft of advancement.

Governance

Magisterial problems

While the Chagos companies became generally more successful, at least after their resuscitation in 1893, the same could not be said of the Archipelago's governance. Momentum was lost after the re-assignment of Ackroyd and Dupont to other duties, and Boucherat's visit in 1888 to observe the end of the coaling stations was the only one made to Diego Garcia and Peros Banhos between 1885 and the last days of 1890. Salomon and Eagle islands were, apparently, visited in 1887, but the first report made after 1885 was that for 1891. Six Islands was not visited between 1885 and 1892. After that, the neglect became even more marked. Between 1889 and 1900, three visits were made to Diego Garcia and Peros Banhos, three to Salomon and Eagle Islands, but only two to Six Islands.[18] The lack of official interest in the affairs of the Oil Islands was evidenced by the fact that not a single magistrate's report was forwarded to the Colonial Office in the final decade of the 19th century. Only when a problem arose in Farquhar Island, causing the Administrator of Seychelles to address the Colonial Office, was fresh attention given. In a flurry of despatches, the new Governor of Mauritius,

Sir Charles Bruce, forwarded in 1901 all the reports made since 1890 and caused his Procureur Général to ask each of the magistrates concerned to account for his performance.[19]

Two main issues emerged. One arose from the longstanding problems of transport. For whatever reason, the government no longer made available vessels of its own, obliging the magistrates to use those of the proprietors and thus to make separate voyages to each of the three Chagos companies' plantations at timings convenient to the latter. Since the proprietors tended to take advantage of the same seasonal weather patterns, it was very hard for a magistrate to achieve more than one voyage in any given period. Furthermore, the companies were far from assiduous in giving the magistrate advance notice of their sailings. The other main issue reflected the difficulty in recruiting magistrates with the combination of qualities required. The corps of stipendiary magistrates in Mauritius was drawn from barristers qualified to practise at the English Bar, from which one (later two) were assigned to deal with the Dependencies. Quite frequently, in the absence of someone suitable for substantive appointment, an individual would be assigned to the islands on an acting basis, resulting in reports of uneven quality.

The Procureur Général began by analysing all the sailings made during the previous decade and then invited each of the four magistrates who had served during this time to account in writing for his performance. One (Hewetson) was able to point to his good record before he had been re-assigned to a Mauritius District; another (L.G. Rochery) sought to justify himself by explaining how much time he had needed to devote to the organisation of his marriage; Léon Leclézio cited concerns for his safety (and was able to point out that one of the ships on which he declined to set sail had been dismasted in a hurricane and driven onto the coast of Madagascar); the fourth, Yves Jollivet, aroused lengthy controversy about his suitability for substantive appointment. This controversy stemmed directly from the scandal occurring in Farquhar Island.[20] Jollivet had been sent to accompany the existing incumbent, Léon Leclézio, to look into the matter. Leclézio was a small, retiring man, for whom the tempestuous voyages to uncivilised islands were a living hell; Jollivet was a swashbuckling individual, who loved the experience and, apparently, the bottle. The tricky situation on Farquhar was resolved, but in a somewhat unorthodox manner, with some subsequent allegations that Jollivet had been 'intemperate'. While Jollivet continued to undertake the duties in an acting capacity, his applications for substantive appointment – citing his knowledge of Leclézio's impending retirement, his own sterling services and the sacrifice of his Bar practice – were until 1906 repeatedly turned down. The voluminous manuscript correspondence on this topic between senior officials (sometimes while on home leave!) brought to light the somewhat decrepit condition of the Mauritian magistracy, with the

Procureur Général despairing of its inexplicable judgments and the fact that one of its members (Boucherat) was about to be arraigned on bribery charges.[21]

Systemic difficulties

When Bruce's further despatch, explaining the action he was taking, reached London, it caused no discernible excitement.[22] Submitting it to his superiors, the desk officer commented thus:

> From the despatch and its voluminous enclosures, which scarcely repay perusal, I gather that all the magistrates are rather incompetent and that perhaps Mr Jollivet is the best of a very bad lot, but that even an efficient officer cannot do much until some new system is adopted …

His minute went on to outline three main options: to transfer the islands to the jurisdiction of Seychelles; to have a vessel dedicated to plying between the islands, which should also carry the magistrate; or to have the Admiralty provide a gunboat for the purpose, the costs of which would be reimbursed by the colony. All that he recommended, however, was to 'await further information'.

The three options were those already identified by Bruce. Discussion of the formation of a separate Colony based on Mahé was already advanced; but, as far as the Chagos islands were concerned, transfer of jurisdiction to Seychelles would merely have shifted the same frustrations to an equally distant, but much smaller Administration. In fact, as a result of company objections, all of the Oil Islands *except* Agalega and the Chagos were so transferred in 1903, with consequent simplification of the problems of Port Louis. There remained, however, at this stage, three ownership groups for the five atolls, each atoll having its own navigational constraints, rendering the notion of a single dedicated vessel 'plying between the islands' entirely chimerical, at least while sailing ships were the only available means of transport. Bruce himself simply stated, citing difficulties that had arisen in responding to an emergency on Coëtivy, that it was 'rarely possible' for the government to supplement the statutory means of communication by using the government tug or by chartering a vessel on its own account. The latter solution would certainly have been expensive, with no cargo to help defray the costs of a charter. Regarding the oft-contemplated use of a naval vessel, Bruce took advantage of a visit to Mauritius by HMS *Cossack* to discuss the matter directly with the C-in-C of the East Indies station. Admiral Day Bosanquet declined to give any general undertaking, agreeing only to assist Ackroyd, now re-appointed as acting Magistrate for the Lesser Dependencies, to visit the more northerly islands, that is, excluding the Chagos.[23]

Laws and Realities

The position of the Manager in the Oil Islands is very peculiar and in some cases he is compelled to act somewhat illegally. He is there alone, face to face, with a large number of labourers, has to rely entirely upon himself and one or two *employés* and is not in a position to obtain the protection of the Police nor of the law, except during the visits of the Magistrates, and even then their assistance is no more than moral, the powers of the Magistrate being very limited.

I often wondered as to the way in which I could enforce my judgments in the Islands, if the accused or convicted parties refused to obey my orders, the Magistrate having neither Usher nor Police Constables to execute his judgments.

If something is not done to assist the Manager, the labourers will certainly damage the crops to a large extent, for to drink one or two coconuts they cut a whole bunch which they leave in the fields. They are also very fond of germinated nuts and uproot growing coconut trees to eat the inside of the planted fruit.

In order to check this, it appears that the Managers have, for a very long time, instituted the fine system because, to have the labourers legally punished, accused and witnesses would have to be sent to Mauritius and remain here for at least three months. As the larcenies of fruits and plantations are of common occurrence, the whole staff of the Island should spend their time in Mauritius and this would be equivalent to utter ruin for the owners.

When the Magistrate is in the Islands, charges can be and are brought for such offences, but it often happens that the labourers return to Mauritius during the absence of the Magistrate and no remedy is given to the Manager against those men.

This difficulty was felt by the legislator and the right was given to the Manager to imprison for a period not exceeding three days labourers guilty of insubordination or insolence. As a pecuniary penalty is of a milder nature than imprisonment may be, the Managers thought they had the right to make themselves paid for the damage done.

Though none of the interested parties ever complained, I think it should be advisable that there should be some legislation to put an end to irregular proceedings, fixing for instance a maximum fine per coconut stolen or plucked, per tree destroyed and for each germinated coconut uprooted, also other cases in which pecuniary penalties might be decreed by the Manager, with the proviso that all such penalties shall not be final until they have been approved of by the Magistrate on his visits to the Islands. Part of such penalty to accrue to the owners as compensation for the damage suffered and part to the Crown.

I beg also to suggest that the Magistrate be given the right to appoint and swear in special constables to act as Police Constables on the Islands.

12 April 1901   Sgd. Yves Jollivet

<u>Source</u>: TNA CO 167/741.

Legislative solutions

The Governor then reverted to seeking a legislative solution to his problems, first seeking Ackroyd's views, which the latter offered soon after his return.[24] Ackroyd drew both on his own long experience and on ideas put forward by Jollivet in a memorandum; the full text no longer survives, but it included frank comments (see inset opposite) and recommendations made on the strength of a visit that same year. The papers were then passed to the Procureur Général, P.T. Piggott. Meanwhile, Léon Leclézio (now working in the judicial secretariat) had already been engaged in drafting a fresh Ordinance to replace that of 1875, a task which had featured spasmodically on the Legislative Council's agenda for almost twenty years. He had submitted it to the Procureur Général in February 1898.[25] Elements of this comprehensive document emerged in a fresh draft put forward by Piggott in June 1902.[26] It seems evident that Leclézio's draft must have been severely emasculated by the islands' owners. Notably, some very draconian paragraphs dealing with the protection of wildlife had disappeared entirely. Perhaps the most important Article in Piggott's version was one (Art. 6) which provided that 'all charges of administration are to be borne by the owners'. His justification for this provision was as follows:

> The provision of the draft seems to be justified by the circumstances of the case. The Islands are barren and only inhabited by the labourers sent there by the proprietors. They contribute practically nothing to the revenue of the Colony and the inhabitants can hardly be said to form part of the general community; so that the usual duty of the Government to provide for the administration of justice can hardly be said to arise. The principle has practically been admitted from the first, as the amount paid by the owners was intended to cover the salary of the Magistrate.

Other provisions defined more clearly the owners' contractual obligations regarding the employment, housing, feeding and health of their workers; as for the magistrates, two were to be appointed, each having jurisdiction throughout the Dependencies, so as to allow them to be diverted at short notice from one island to another; for the workers, there would be no distinction in the terms of employment between those born on the island in question or elsewhere, while penalties were introduced for any who signed on in Mauritius, took payment in advance, then failed to embark – apparently an all too frequent scam. The draft was then subjected to scrutiny in the Colonial Office and, more protractedly, in the Governor's Council, where those representing the companies' interests did their best to water down the new obligations. To this end, they submitted a detailed commentary to the Council, which the Governor forwarded together with his despatch recording the outcome of the Council's discussion.[27] For example, they weakened a proposal that each plantation should include a quali-fied medical dispenser on its staff. They also succeeded in eliminating a provi-sion that only individuals employed under written contracts should be allowed to work on the islands. As the owners explained,

> The obligation of having servants exclusively under written contracts in the Islands would be most injurious to the interests of the owners and would not, in the least, benefit those whom it is intended to protect. Many servants will not consent to enter into a written contract, and although they live happy on the islands they would have to be expelled therefrom. There are servants that have been there, who, either have never left the Islands, or who have come to Mauritius only on occasional trips. The islands are their home and they are the best of all servants. Artisans, such as masons, carpenters, coopers, blacksmiths etc., never consent to work under written contracts.

This argument is of twofold interest. As with the comments of the naturalist Gilbert Bourne in the mid-1880s (see pages 229–230), it provides evidence of the emergence of an island-born population having a distinctive character, but without offering any fresh indication of its size compared to those recruited elsewhere. One indicator of the relative numbers is to be found in the passenger lists of the vessels arriving at Port Louis.[28] Examination of the records of 21 voy-ages from the Chagos between 1900 and 1903, for most of which the passengers' places of birth are shown, make it clear that the vast majority of those travelling were born in Mauritius. It seems unlikely that this would have been the case had Mauritius-born workers not also constituted a substantial majority of the labour force at that time. Secondly, it turns on its head the Procureur Général's propo-sition that 'the Islands are barren and only inhabited by the labourers sent there by the proprietors'. The Governor was evidently impressed by the idea that – in his words – 'a certain number of labourers were in fact residents of the islands [who] … should be free to engage or not to engage as they liked'. Left unmen-tioned were the facts that the local managers asserted the owners' authority over all those on the islands, provided company rations to all and looked to magis-trates to enforce their authority. Ackroyd, for his part, devoted several para-graphs of his report to the issue without finding any disadvantage to the workers in having contracts; and it is hard to see how the insistence on written contracts should of itself reduce the inhabitants' happiness. Indeed, when Jollivet visited Diego Garcia in 1901, he had concluded no less than 52 individual contracts, 29 of three- and 23 of two-years' duration. It is plain that the benefits of leaving the status of locally-born people vague lay entirely with their employers.

 As regards artisans, the fact that individuals with transferable skills were those least amenable to signing contracts suggests rather that they were least ready to commit themselves at the rates of pay on offer. Their position was not even mentioned by Ackroyd.

At all events, following rather cursory examination by the Colonial Office, where officials noted that in almost every respect the text approved by the Council reflected the views expressed by the islands' owners, the new legislation was approved and finally came into force on 7 July 1904 as Ordinance No. 4 of that year.[29] Annexed was a standard text for individual workers' contracts. Possibly its most striking feature was that it entailed recognition of a category of island resident for whose general welfare neither the companies nor the government accepted responsibility. So long as the numbers involved were small, the implications might remain immaterial, but the higher the proportion of such individuals, the more the government would lay itself open to the charge of neglect. Yet, with occasional minor amendments, this Ordinance was what provided the framework for governance of the Dependencies up to 1973. This outcome was not surprising. The Council's members included both Henry Leclézio,[30] Chairman of the *Nouvelle Société*, and Léopold Antelme (*fils*), Chairman and principal shareholder of the *Société Huilière de Salomon, Trois Frères et Six Iles*, whose chief executives, Gabriel Théophile Lionnet and Jules Larcher, had signed the petition in question.

Coda: island life 1900–1914

For the first decade of the 20th century, magisterial visits remained only intermittent, but resumed in earnest from 1911 until 1915. Unfortunately, few of such reports as were made between 1901 and 1910 ever reached London and, of those few, none was retained when the files were bound.[31] While these reports, like the ones made in earlier years, provide the best single indicator of the state of the islands' inhabitants, an increasing range of other contemporary accounts is also available.

1900–1910

By 1900, all that remained of Diego Garcia's coaling station were a 60-ton heap of coal and a single buoy; all the rest, together with the hulks and lighters, had been removed or sunk (by 1903, even those traces were gone). Minni Minni estate was abandoned, its houses in ruins and covered by trees and bushes, making the remains invisible from the west. East Point had become the main settlement, with Pointe Marianne very much its poor relation. The *Valdivia*, a German ship (see illustration overleaf) engaged in surveying the world's oceans, spent a few days there and Dr Carl Chun, leader of the expedition, was as impressed by its inhabitants as by its natural beauties and the attractive layout of the settlements. The Manager, Philippe de Caila, came out to meet the vessel in his whaler,

Image courtesy of the family of Gerhard Schott, oceanographer to the *Valdivia* expedition.

crewed by smartly uniformed rowers,[32] representatives of a 'community … whose well-ordered activities proceed safe and free from trouble without the intervention of civil servants, judges and law enforcement officers'.[33] In a lively and accurate description of the pattern of work, Dr Chun noted that many of the workers,

> indeed as we were assured the most capable, are born on the island itself … All that is needed for the construction of buildings, of apparatus and for the necessary repairs is produced [sic] on the island. Blacksmiths, carpenters are constantly occupied; one is also surprised at their ability as well as their versatility and resourcefulness. Whoever has seen the fine rowing boats built on the island acquires a high opinion of the quality of the black workers.

Surprised too by the small number of white families – four – in a population of 527, he commented perceptively that 'all depends on the energy and tact of the Administrator'.

At the end of 1900, Jollivet inspected Diego Garcia, before visiting Peros Banhos in January 1901. His account of conditions at Diego Garcia was entirely consistent with that of Dr Chun, as was his view of de Caila: 'The labourers are very kindly treated and ought to be more thankful than they are for the kindness shown to them by the manager, the *employés* and their families'. On the day-to-day running of the island, Jollivet had no serious criticism to make. Production amounted to around 70,000 *veltes*, plus about 100,000 nuts and 'a few hundred pounds of beeswax'. The population, which he counted for the decennial census, totalled 509 (224 men, 142 women, 143 children). He also found himself having to try no less than 29 criminal cases, the great majority involving either violence between workers or 'plundering', and most, it must be assumed, of recent occurrence. No explanation of the contrasting elements of peace and discord was vouchsafed. Certainly, the quality of accommodation (126 huts at East Point and 70 at Pointe Marianne) was not an issue. On these Jollivet commented approvingly: 'they are built of timber and lined with coconut leaves, each house is surrounded by a small enclosure in which the labourers keep their fowls and ducks. Each house is at least 50 feet from the nearest hut. I found the camps well kept and very clean'. Remarks made in 1901 by Ackroyd (see Note 23) supported him. Housing, Ackroyd considered, was 'far better', going on to cite the following example:

> I saw at Cassis [a Port Louis suburb} the house of a man who had been thirty years at Diego Garcia or Peros Banhos and had saved enough money to build himself a very fair house for a man of his class; he told me however that he had a better house in the islands he had worked on and wished to return to Diego Garcia, notwithstanding his age. He assured me that the labourers on the Oil Islands were in a better position and more comfortable than in Mauritius.

Ackroyd also commented that stoppages of pay for indiscipline or idleness were on the same scale in the islands as in Mauritius itself, '[showing] that the Owners of these islands treat those they employ fairly'.

Other observers too noticed the coexistence of violence and contentment. Annie Commins, the daughter of the manager Walter Commins, has left some account of her happy childhood days:

> We often went fishing with our black nanny and afterwards walked round the island [Six Islands]. Like my father, we children loved the life on the islands; we did not have much in the way of material goods, but it was an easy and carefree time … When I was 10 years old we lived on Diego Garcia … My mother Valentine had plenty on her hands, although she had help in the house. The servants had to be taught things and supervised. All our clothes, including father's, were homemade. My mother also sewed extra goods like men's suits and beautiful pillowcases (which I helped to embroider) for sale to the Ilois. Her work was in great demand. She tended the sick, prayed at death-beds and was often consulted for advice and help by the Ilois. Father, as Administrator and in the absence of a priest, would baptize children, marry adults and pray at funerals.[34]

But Annie had also witnessed the perils of breakdown in the mutual dependence of management and workers:

> Once, during a fight in one of the compounds [on Salomon], Walter had to intervene to bring order; tempers were aroused, and he hit a man. Feelings ran high. It was an ugly time, with ill-feelings on all sides. The anxiety caused Valentine to give birth prematurely to twin babies … the infants did not survive.[35]

At Peros Banhos, Jollivet found nothing to alarm him. The atoll, managed by J.S. Leal, produced between 20,000 and 23,000 *veltes* of oil and its population amounted to 184 (94 men, 52 women, 38 children). Unusually, at the initial meeting, 'the men stated that they were all very happy. No complaints were brought either against or by the labourers'. As regards the two atolls' vital statistics, Jollivet provided only brief details relating to the five years preceding his visit. On Diego Garcia there had been a total of 86 births and 67 deaths; for Peros Banhos the totals were 25 and 24. As Note 30 reveals, no full text survives of the sixteen reports made between 1903 and 1910. This results in a severe dearth of evidence relating to one major source of concern in earlier years: health and, in particular, child mortality. A comparison of the death rates in the Chagos in 1900 with those of Mauritius, cited by Ackroyd (see Note 23), showed that infant mortality in the Chagos accounted for 70% of total deaths, as compared with a figure of 35% in Mauritius. On the other hand, the general rate of mortality came out in favour of the islands, at less than 2% per year, rather than the 3.5% for Mauritius. Indeed, those who survived the islands' sanitary and medical deficiencies often, thanks to the climate and style of employment, enjoyed extreme longevity. Two notable examples may be cited of people who would have been present at the time of Jollivet's visit. Mimi Auguste, born on Coëtivy Island in 1841 and taken to Peros Banhos at the age of three, died there in 1956 at the age of 115;[36] while in 1922 the visiting magistrate encountered in Diego Garcia a man reputed to be over 120 years old, a native of Madagascar, who 'would have been hale and hearty, were it not that he is totally blind. After one of his numerous love adventures as a young man of about 70, his injured neighbour robbed him of his sight by cruelly rubbing sand in his eyes'.[37]

A few months before Jollivet visited Diego Garcia, there began an extended series of deaths from beri-beri, which continued for just short of a year. One of the deaths occurred during his inspection, but escaped his attention (or was concealed by de Caila). In June 1900 a group of eight men and one woman had arrived from Anjouan in the Comoros, presumably as unofficially recruited labourers. Five were suffering from symptoms later identified as being beri-beri. Their condition did not markedly improve and two died in January 1901. Between March and June that year eight local inhabitants also died from the same condition. The surviving Comorians, along with 'their filthy belongings', were deported to Mauritius in mid June, after which the 'epidemic' ceased. These facts were reported by the Mauritius Sanitary Warden to the Colonial Office as evidence that beri-beri could be spread 'by a germ' (he noted in passing that *trismus neonatorum* and dysentery were the islands' main medical problems). The Medical Adviser to the Colonial Office accepted this baseless theory and published an account of the event to prove it.[38] All that Jollivet had to say on the subject of vegetables was that dholl was issued 'now and then', while the labourers 'obtain vegetables from the garden of the establishment whenever there are any available'. The real position must have been that the existing labourers and new arrivals alike were badly nourished. Then, late in November 1903, HMS *Pearl* visited the Archipelago and her commander, Captain Edward Ashe, reported that, according to the manager of Diego Garcia (still de Caila), 'quite 50% of children die shortly after childbirth, the principal cause being tetanus'.[39] This report, rightly alarming, went well beyond the facts of the situation, bad as those were: almost half the children were dying before their twelfth birthday.

There ensued correspondence between the Colonial Office and the Governor, whose medical advisers had discussed the topic in detail with de Caila.[40] The latter pointed to a variety of causes related to the ignorance and health of the parents, such as unhygienic management of the umbilical cord prescribed by traditional medicine, careless handling of infants, hereditary infections, and the prevalence of drunkenness. It was, he remarked, 'not uncommon to find a woman, who had within a couple of days given birth to her child, walk out with the almost naked babe in her arms into the cold rain and wind'. De Caila also distinguished between island-born workers and, as the Medical Director's report put it, the many members of the heterogeneous population of Malagasys, Africans, Creoles of Mauritius from Port Louis and a few Indians 'who are not permanent residents and, as a rule, are not recruited from the better class working people'. He was not however questioned about the employment conditions which deterred any absence from work. The conclusion of the officials consulted was that an experienced dispenser steward should be appointed to each island, backed up by regular visits of both doctors and ministers of religion. As mentioned above, the first element of this proposal, somewhat modified, did secure inclusion in the 1904 Ordinance. The issue of drunkenness must also have been discussed separately, for in 1906 a Regulation (No. 239) was passed providing that wine should be sold only on Saturdays and Sundays.[41]

The first reports made by the Visiting Magistrates after 1901 to be forwarded to London were those of Jollivet and L.J. Madelon in 1908, both being later weeded from the files. Jollivet's, however, aroused serious concerns in London, which caused the government in Port Louis to set in train investigations. The results of these, communicated by the Governor a full two years later, revealed a range of continuing inadequacies.[42] Further enquiries from London elicited, in July 1911, material relating to the conditions obtaining in the Archipelago five years earlier, in 1906.[43]

That year, it had fallen to Jollivet, at last appointed substantively to the office of Visiting Magistrate, to examine the plantations on Salomon, Eagle and Egmont. On the last-named, he found one case of beri-beri, which he ascribed to the consumption of Saigon rice, resulting in the issue of guidance on nutrition

Petit Jean's Story

It is rare indeed to come across the direct expression of individual islanders' attachment to particular islands. One striking example is that of Jean Adolphe Rodolphe, familiarly called Petit Jean.* This young man was born on Salomon in 1889, his mother, Marie Cécile Bakar, having gone there in about 1884. His father died in 1889, and, some time later, his mother moved in with the *Chef Commandeur*, Vital Joseph. In 1905, Petit Jean was implicated in a case of theft and was sentenced to be sent 'back' to Mauritius. After some weeks in which he scraped a living as a day labourer at a wage of 75 cents, he was employed on contract at St Brandon. When that contract ended after ten months, he was unable to find further work and contrived to attach himself to a band of labourers embarking for Salomon aboard the *Nonna Adèle*, which was also taking Magistrate Jollivet and Dr Keisler. Emerging from his hiding place between decks on arrival, the stowaway was examined by the doctor and judged fit for light duties. The manager therefore set him to work with the women, shelling coconuts at a monthly wage of Rs 5. Two months later he was allowed to work with the carpenters at a wage of Rs 6 and before long he graduated to the work of fit adult men, husking coconuts at a wage of Rs 8. He lived on his own, but was provided with meals and clothing by his mother, to whom he gave his wages every month. He was, nevertheless, diagnosed as suffering from tuberculosis. In 1907, his case was examined by the next magistrate to visit, Madelon. Petit Jean testified that he had never taken time off for sickness and concluded thus: 'I am very happy at Salomon, where I get work and earn my living. I was born at Salomon and all my relatives are on that island. I do not wish to leave a place where I am contented and happy, to go to Mauritius.' He stayed.

*TNA CO 167/784 Governor's Despatch 142, dated 11 May 1908.

to all the island managers.[44] He also found one man (George Alexis) suffering from leprosy and ordered his return to Mauritius (of 140 lepers in the main sanatorium in Mauritius in 1909, 5 originated in the Oil Islands). There were also a number of people suffering from conjunctivitis. The condition of the hospital bedding was deplorable. On all three islands, two substantial health hazards were the proximity of pigsties to human habitation, including the hospital on Eagle, and the use of the same wells for drinking water and laundry. On Salomon these risks were compounded by the presence of human excrement scattered among the workers' huts. Instructions were given to create cement slabs for laundering clothes, with purpose built reservoirs and drainage channels for the water, and all this a good distance from wells for drinking water. Likewise the managers were instructed to build latrines at a reasonable distance from the huts – pit latrines in the case of Eagle Island, bucket latrines elsewhere.

Health and hygiene were however far from being the only problems affecting the plantations. In August 1906, a murder took place on Eagle Island, prompting the despatch of Dr François Léon Keisler, the Assistant Sanitary Warden, to accompany Jollivet on his next visit.[45] At Salomon, Jollivet found six men who had arrived there from Eagle Island unintentionally: they had set out from Eagle for Danger Island on the morning of 28 June that year (1906) in an open boat without a compass; after being blown out to sea by squalls, they had drifted for about two weeks before reaching Salomon. This resulted in the drafting of regulations requiring that boats be properly equipped, supplied with emergency rations and put in the charge of a properly experienced coxswain.

Two years later, in 1908, Jollivet revisited Peros Banhos and Diego Garcia. He was accompanied by a police constable, who contributed to a series of criticisms of the manager of Peros Banhos, Leal, and his wife. The latter was accused of cornering supplies of flour, thread and cloth, then making a profit by using them to make clothes and bread rolls, for which she charged exorbitant prices. The manager himself was accused of using his power to favour selected workers by choosing only those to undertake extra tasks, which attracted extra rations as well as extra pay. At the same time he was said to manipulate the arrangements by which workers who missed a day's work (sometimes on account of bad weather) made it up by working double shifts; under the rules the second part of a double shift was to be paid at a higher rate, but he paid only the standard amount. What force there might be in these criticisms was never completely established, for Leal resigned a year later, shortly before the Company's comments – Théophile Lionnet's vigorous rebuttal of the criticisms – were finally received.

Another criticism concerned the arrangements governing the capture of Green turtles. Employees were free to catch the animals at sea, but were forbidden to do so without obtaining the manager's permission when they came ashore to lay their eggs (the taking of which was also forbidden). In either case, the catcher would be paid Rs 5, but the resulting meat was sold to purchasers for a total of Rs 12. This practice was defended by the company on the grounds that the animal was bought by the company, whereas the meat was sold at a fair market price. The ban on taking eggs or the animals laying them was also robustly defended as ensuring the conservation of a resource that could prove vital in an emergency. However, it appears that this admirable control had been imposed too late: the rarity of Green turtles, remarked upon by the captain of HMS *Pearl* in 1903, had then been ascribed to the practice of eating their eggs, without allowing any to hatch. In any case, as Jollivet himself observed at first hand, most of the turtles captured on land – all of these would of course be females – and then kept in seawater pens until required for food, proved on slaughter to contain large numbers of eggs; in other words, they were taken before having a chance to lay.[46]

By mid 1909, the issues raised by Jollivet concerning health and hygiene had been dealt with, except one. This concerned his finding that the rations which the companies were obliged to provide gratis under the 1904 Ordinance were in two respects inadequate. First, he considered the weekly allowance of 10½ lbs of rice should be increased to 12½ lbs. Second, he considered that the employers should be obliged to provide free 1 lb of lentils to each employee; his argument was that fish, turtle, pork and chicken did not supply the nitrogen essential to a balanced diet. His recommendations were supported by two doctors. Dr Keisler, who participated in his 1906 inspection (primarily to exhume the body of the murder victim mentioned above), found the inhabitants of Salomon to be 'generally speaking, weak, anaemic and sallow looking', the 'commonest complaints [being] anaemia and uterine disorders'. For these, he considered that 'the rations be altered and made to include some nitrogenous constituents'. Similarly, a Dr Powell, who accompanied Jollivet in 1908, found the women on Peros Banhos were 'all anaemic and most of them suffer from leucorrhea and partial descent of the womb'. There followed an animated debate between himself, a fellow magistrate called Le Conte, Dr Keisler and the companies, which was only settled after being considered in the Governor's Executive Council. In brief, Jollivet won on his second point, but (for the time being) lost on the first.

1911–1914

In contrast to the controversies which had loomed large during the preceding decade, the next few years were marked by tranquillity. There were nevertheless several unresolved issues still on the Council's agenda. These included the amount of rations to be in stock on the islands, (a reduced minimum of four months was fixed); the date from which wages were to be paid (on arrival, rather than date of embarkation); ownership of turtles caught (to 'be taken to be the property of the owners upon payment'); and clearer regulation of the arrangements for workers to repay time taken off by undertaking double shifts. All these decisions were to be incorporated in the standard employment contract. As readers will realise from the narrative in this chapter, the new regulation favoured the companies in virtually every respect.[47] The only problem left unresolved was that of providing evidence for the true prices paid for goods subsequently sold with a 25% mark-up on the islands.

With the revival of near-annual visits by magistrates, it is possible to construct a fresh impression of the conditions in the Archipelago, island by island (for file references, see Note 30). By a happy coincidence, the year 1911 also involved holding of the decennial census. The figures for the Chagos were as follows:-

Table 13.4

	Diego Garcia	Peros Banhos	Salomon	Six Islands	Eagle Island	Total
General population						
Male	288	156	80	82	55	661
Female	185	132	63	67	46	493
Indo-Mauritian population						
Male	6	9	1	5	–	21
Female	4	3	–	1	–	8
Total	483	300	144	155	101	1183

Source: MA 1911 Census Records, Table XVIII.

Diego Garcia and Peros Banhos

The managers of the two large plantations, visited by Jollivet in both 1911 and, for the last time, in 1912, were applauded for their 'flourishing state' and 'good order'.[48] In neither atoll were complaints raised by the workers, and there were few cases to be tried. This state of affairs enabled the magistrate to investigate other aspects of island life. For example, on Diego Garcia

> In accordance with the law, I visited the main camps on the islands; one camp at Pointe Est consisted of 108 huts; the camp at Pointe Marianne, 56 huts; that of 'Minni-Minni', one hut; at the Ile Grande Barbe, 2 huts; Camp 'Les Moulins', 3 huts; Camp of 'Roche Pointue' 3 huts; of 'Barachois Sylvain', 2 huts; of 'Baudry' 2 huts; of 'Anse David', one hut. There are besides 4 huts for domestic use.[49]

He found too that 12½ lbs of rice was normally distributed, meeting the concerns he had previously expressed and that, on Diego Garcia, 'to hard working labourers a certain quantity of dholl, extra rice, tobacco and oil is supplied as a reward and they are besides allowed boats, nets, lines and hooks to go out fishing and catch a sufficient quantity of fish. They also receive *poonac* to feed their poultry'. On Peros Banhos, only 'ill-doers and malingerers' were refused the use of boats and nets. We may guess too that the large amounts of Hawksbill turtle shell being exported during these years put noticeable amounts of cash into the labourers' pockets. The workers also knew where they stood regarding shop prices, rates of pay and definition of tasks, all of these being displayed prominently. On the last of these, Jollivet (uniquely) copied down and attached to his 1911 report on Peros Banhos what was required there (see inset overleaf).

In 1913 and 1914, a number of changes were noticed by the magistrates who had taken over from Jollivet, Messrs Louis Pilot and F.P. Genève. The most important development was the export of significant quantities of copra, with a

Standing Orders for Peros Banhos in 1911

Daily tasks for men earning Rs 8 per month

Gathering, de-husking and piling coconuts on beach ready for collection. 500 in respect of each of the northern islets from Ile Petite Soeur to Ile Moresby and Lapasse. Nuts from Ile Parasol to be taken to Ile Lapasse; those from Ile Bois Mangue to be taken to Ile Longue; those from Coquillage to be taken to Ile Yéyé or direct to the establishment; those from Vache Marine to be taken to the establishment. The quota for the following islands is 550: Monpath, Anglaise, Ile du Coin, Mapou and Fouquets. The quota for Ile Poule is 650 nuts.

Cutting down coconut trees: 20. Digging holes and planting seedlings: 15. *Cleaning palm frond stems of foliage [for use in making fences, furniture etc]: 144. **Stripping backs of palm fronds of material for bindings: 300

Straw cutting: 250 sheaves. Grass-gathering for animal feed: 400 lbs.

Transport per canoeist: 1,000 coconuts.

The coxswain shall occupy himself solely with keeping watch over the boat for which he is responsible.

Clearing and weeding. As judged sufficient in the circumstances by the staff member or *commandeur* in charge.

Mill operators

Processing 4 100-pound heaps of copra, which should produce 18 *veltes* and 4 bottles of oil.

Women, and men earning Rs 6 per month

Breaking and counting coconuts into 3 heaps of 1250 or extracting the flesh from 1250 nuts.

Making 6 brooms (or 18 brushes) by scraping and sewing.***

Making 18 mats. Collecting 300 lbs of grass.

Calcified ash: 1 basketful.

Corvée tasks on Sundays and Public Holidays

Men. Collecting 100 lbs of grass; cleaning and tidying the open area of the establishment, from 6 a.m. until 8 a.m. *Women.* As for men, but collecting 75 lbs of grass.

Legal Rations

10½ lbs rice per week and 1 lb salt per month

Discretionary Favours

Increase of rice ration to 12 lbs; ½ litre of oil per household; dry coconuts for grating without wastage; use of boats for fishing in fine weather; use of machine-made seine net for communal inshore fishing (twice yearly).

<u>Source</u>: TNA CO 167/799 Enclosure to Mauritius Despatch No. 328, dated 30 November 1911.

Note. We are indebted to a Seychellois researcher, Mr Julien Durup, for invaluable assistance in translating some of the expressions used, such as *'gaulettes de palmistes'* and **'amarrage à retirer'*. This involved wide consultations with people having experience of Creole island life, including Mr Fernand Mandarin. ***Durup himself in his youth used to make this type of broom from dry coconut fronds at La Digue; after the stems of the palm frond had been scraped clean, the leaves were sewn into bundles of 100 and three bundles stitched together to make one broom. Six brooms for a day's work was good going.

corresponding decrease in coconut oil, and an increase in the number of raw coconuts exported (see Table 13.2 on p. 260). It might seem curious that the consequential change in working patterns went unmentioned in the magistrates' reports, but as the inset overleaf reveals, the copra-making jobs had already been worked out, presumably to the workers' satisfaction. Also worth mentioning is that, at Peros Banhos, the 'hospital'- justifying this title for first time – now had a corrugated iron roof and comprised five rooms (male, female and lying-in wards, dispensary and waiting room). On the other hand, the rice supplied was found to be stale and the ratio of shop takings to total wages was creeping up, year by year, towards 100%, suggesting that the workers' wages were becoming insufficient to make the savings required for visits to Mauritius.

Salomon, Eagle and Six Islands

All three islands were visited by Genève in 1911 and 1913 and by Pilot in 1912 and 1914. In general, conditions were a great improvement on those encountered in the late 19th century. In particular, mortality levels were reduced, no doubt owing to the presence of competent and trusted Dispenser-Stewards. There were however, as in the past, occasional fatal accidents at sea. One unusual case of a different kind at Six Islands concerned the brief imprisonment of an individual charged with 'witchcraft'. The penalty was illegal, but could not be investigated, because the manager inflicting it had departed. However, the term witchcraft was habitually used to refer to death and burial rites associated with Madagascar – cultural manifestations which the Mauritian managers made every effort to stamp out.[50] There was also, in 1914, a serious problem resulting from the very poor quality of rice supplied by the owners. In addition, the magistrates devoted considerable attention to the proportion of shop sales accounted for by wine, on average around 25% of the total. They made no comment, however, on the reasons for or consequences of this state of affairs. Nor did they compare the figures they had collected for shop takings with total wages paid, the former in most cases being about 90% of the latter and in one case (Salomon in 1912) 110%. Thus, in the small as in the larger islands, little scope remained for the ordinary labourer to make savings.

Another development, which stemmed naturally from the establishment of a single company's ownership of all three islands, was that its vessel could, in a single voyage, visit all three of them. This was of course a boon to the magistracy, but the problems of access and anchorage continued to limit the size of the vessel chosen. This in turn limited the number of passengers that could be transported. In 1912, as Genève reported, the *Nonna Adèle* could accommodate only ten of the sixteen workers from Salomon, seeking passages to Mauritius at the end of their contracts, and only seven of the thirteen wishing to leave Eagle. This was a new issue, but one that would later recur in a more serious form.

A stocktaking

After all but 40 years of experiment and controversy, a settled structure for the exploitation of the Chagos islands had now emerged. The government had achieved an affordable legal framework for freeing the island workers from the constant threat of abuse. On the other hand, its demands had been reduced to a bare minimum of inconvenience to the proprietors; moreover, the system of annual magisterial visits depended upon the use of company vessels, making unheralded inspections impossible and ensuring their occurrence at moments when all the inhabitants were at their busiest. The proprietors, for their part, had been obliged to join forces, both in order to resist governmental pressures and to advance their own commercial interests. By involving the most powerful entrepreneurs in Mauritius society, they had achieved a decisive influence in the way their island businesses were conducted, as a monopoly in all but name. Furthermore, they had successfully disowned all obligation (apart from the employment of Dispenser-Stewards) to provide social improvements for their workers, even evading to large degree the adoption of enforceable contracts. By the end of this period, the meagre pay they offered was hardly attracting good quality workers; instead, they seemed to be set on reducing the work of the islands to that requiring no formal education, relying instead on the docility of those ignorant of anything other than island life.

Interposed between the island workers and their distant employers were the island managers and their staffs. These might enjoy greater creature comforts, but were as vulnerable to the many natural dangers as their workers and, while they needed to make sure that agreed output quotas were adhered to and also to nip in the bud any incipient troubles, wanted their workers to be contented. The labourers – at least those who survived the perils of infancy, though deprived of any form of schooling, benefited from an easy-going way of life, which could easily, if they kicked over the traces, end in return to Mauritius on a magistrate's orders. On the other hand, they had very few distractions and were as subject as any other small communities to quarrelsomeness and scandal. One cause of such problems was the imbalance between the sexes, with three males to two females the typical ratio in the 1901 census. In these circumstances, it suited the management to have quite strict rules concerning the amounts and frequency of wine consumption, but they were also tempted to offer additional wine as a reward. The workers for their part were equally tempted to find ways of increasing their alcohol intake by brewing their own coconut-based concoctions and buying up unwanted rations; but both workers and management suffered when over-indulgence ended in violence. There was in fact some debate about which type of alcohol was the more dangerous. Ackroyd held that 'sweet *calou*', the juice procured from the top of coconut palms, should be issued twice weekly in preference to wine, while Jollivet, having consulted the old and experienced former manager, Spurs, believed that the practice would lead to abuse, since *calou*, once fermented, formed 'a most intoxicating liquid'.[51]

This system, left undisturbed by external political or commercial forces, might have allowed the Chagos to subside gently, as a technically retarded backwater. However, as in the past, disturbance, distant but more violent than ever, would shortly ensue.

Notes to Chapter 13

1 Mauritius *Commercial Gazette* 11 November 1889 (issue No. 901).

2 *Ibid,* 11 July 1890 (issue No. 907).

3 Duyker, Dr E. (ed) *Mauritian Heritage,* Australian Mauritius Research Group, 1986. As this valuable work's subtitle explains, it is an 'anthology of the Lionnet, Commins and related families'. We owe almost all of the biographical information about these two families to this work and to Dr Duyker's introductions to descendants of those who played important roles in running the Chagos plantations from the late 19th century onwards.

4 *Mauritius Illustrated* (see Note 10 below).

5 Details of its shareholdings and organisation are scant, but a few years later the commercial press would from time to time report transfers of individuals' shareholdings. These transactions show that the company's capital was constituted as 660,000 shares, each having a nominal value of Rs 1 (Source: *Planters and Commercial Gazette* for 26 November 1901 and 25 February 1902 issue Nos. 331 and 333). However, a series of later reports in the same journal demonstrate that subscribers took up the shares in 1320 blocks of 500, each counting as a single share; a considerable proportion was taken up by Lewis Rogers, a leading Port Louis businessman, with other interests in shipping and sugar, founder of Rogers & Co., a conglomerate existing to this day.

6 TNA CO 167/769 Enclosure to Despatch dated 22 January 1904. Léopold Antelme, according to the report of the Captain of HMS *Pearl*, who visited Diego Garcia in 1904, was one of those forced by his losses in the 1892 hurricane to sell his interest in Diego Garcia.

7 Mauritius *The Merchants and Planters Gazette* 11 November 1893 (issue No. 233).

8 TNA CO 167/611 Enclosure to Mauritius Despatch No. 115, dated 30 March 1884. Charles Lionnet is not mentioned in *Mauritian Heritage*, but is referred to as 'my cousin' in a petition from Gabriel Théophile dated 29 February 1884, claiming compensation for both men from the French government. The claim related to losses suffered as a result of French bombardment of Vohémar (North East Madagascar), in which their trading store suffered a direct hit. Charles, according to the petition, was 'the only son of a destitute widow'.

9 TNA CO 167/879/4 Memorandum by Jules Leclézio [son of Henri], handed to the Colonial Office in October 1932 and attached to an official's minute dated 11 October.

10 Macmillan, A., ed., *Mauritius Illustrated*, W.H. & L. Collingridge, London 1914. This compilation, one of a series covering Britain's colonies, was first published in 1912. The prominence given to the *Nouvelle Société Huilière de Diégo et Péros* suggests that it was indeed at that time one of Mauritius' most

significant commercial institutions. In summary, it reported as follows: using 'very primitive' oil mills, Diego Garcia, with a total population of 517, was producing an average of 425,000 litres of raw coconut oil; Peros Banhos, with a population of 300 and eight working mills, was producing 216,000 litres and a considerable quantity of unprocessed nuts; Salomon, with a population of 160 and seven mills, produced coconut oil and turtle shell (quantities unstated) while Six Islands, with a population of 156 and seven mills, produced a 'small' quantity of oil, with much damage being caused by rats; Eagle Island, having 156 people and six mills, produced still less oil, but also brooms and salt fish.

11 TNA CO 170/233.

12 *Mauritius Commercial Gazette*, issues of 3 May and 27 July 1888.

13 TNA CO 167/793 Enclosure IV to Confidential Despatch dated 6 September 1910. Unfortunately, we have not been able to trace the details of this event, other than the allusion to it by Jollivet, who reported that the shipwrecked sailors had got into trouble with the local manager for spearing turtles in order to survive.

14 Macmillan, A., *op. cit*, lists Henri Leclézio as chairman of both companies and Richard Lionnet as a director of the Agalega company, but only as manager of the *Nouvelle Société Huilière*.

15 TNA CO 172 series.

16 Mortimer, Dr J., 'History of Turtle Exploitation in the Chagos' *Chagos News* issue No. 34 July 2009.

17 'Copperah', as it was described at first by the puzzled trade statisticians.

18 TNA CO 167/740 Enclosure to Secret Despatch dated 12 June 1901, October 1890–January 1891 Hewetson by *Lady Harewood* to Diego Garcia and Peros Banhos.

TNA CO/740 (as above), September–October 1891 Hewetson by *Venus* to Salomon and Eagle Islands.

TNA CO 167/740 (as above), August–September 1892 Hewetson by *Emma Jane* to Six Islands.

TNA CO 167/740 (as above), Hewetson by *Earnest* to Salomon and Eagle Islands.

TNA CO 167/740 (as above), November 1893–January 1894 Rochery by *Star Queen* to Peros Banhos and Diego Garcia.

TNA CO 167/740 (as above), July–September 1896 Leclézio by *William Turner* to Peros Banhos and Diego Garcia.

TNA 167/740 (as above), April 1897 Leclézio by *Emma Jane* to Six Islands.

TNA CO 167/740 (as above), June–July 1899 Leclézio by *Wild Rose* to Salomon and Eagle Islands.

19 TNA CO 167/739 Sir Charles Bruce, Secret Despatch dated 17 May 1901 and Annexes A to J.

20 The only connection this case had with our story is that it involved both James Spurs and Vital Hodoul, employed from 1885 to run the island, which Spurs had that year acquired. Spurs became bankrupt, leaving Hodoul to deal with the violent behaviour of his unpaid workforce.

21 TNA CO 167/769.

22 TNA CO 167/740 Sir Charles Bruce, Secret Despatch dated 12 June 1901.

23 TNA Co 167/740 Enclosures to Secret Despatch dated 27 June 1901.

24 TNA CO 167/741 J.H. Ackroyd, Report dated 12 October 1901, enclosed with Secret Despatch dated 15 November 1901.

25 TNA CO 167/740 Enclosure to Secret Despatch dated 17 May 1901.

26 TNA CO 167/750 Enclosure to Despatch No. 227, dated 23 June 1902, provides a précis of this document.

27 TNA CO 167/766 Despatch No. 142 dated 18 April 1904.

28 MA Z2D 159A – Z2D 171. Exceptionally, on one voyage from Salomon in 1901 and on one from Diego Garcia in 1902, one third of the passengers were locally born. These records have been posted on the website www.chagosinfo.org. Examination of a longer series of these records and of passenger lists of outward-bound voyages would be invaluable in showing how many undertook repeated contracts (in the sample cited, totalling 563 individuals, hardly any names recur). Researchers should be warned however that that the task is exceptionally time-consuming.

29 TNA CO 167/766 Telegram dated 30 June 1904.

30 As an indication of the influence of those involved in the Chagos, Leclézio had by now been honoured by the award of a CMG and would shortly be knighted; while Antelme, whatever financial

misfortune he may have suffered in 1892, was a leading socialite and devotee of hunting, chosen for this reason to entertain the Duke of York (the future King George V) during his 1901 visit to Mauritius. Both were members of the Legislative Council and in 1906 Leclézio was appointed to the Governor's inner Executive Council.

31 For clarity, references to reports, the texts of which have not survived, are here shown in *italics*.

TNA CO 167/739 December 1900–January 1901 Enclosure to Mauritius Despatch No. 126 dated 2 April 1901 Jollivet by *William Turner* to Diego Garcia and Peros Banhos.

TNA CO 170/209 Mauritius Despatch No. 409 dated 28 October 1903 *August 1903 Jollivet to Six Islands*.

TNA CO 170/213 Council Administrative Reports 1904 *Visits made to Diego Garcia, Peros Banhos and Salomon*.

TNA CO 170/217 Council Administrative Reports 1905 *Visits made to Salomon, Six Islands and Eagle Island*.

TNA CO 167/798 Enclosure to Confidential Despatch dated 14 November 1911 *Jollivet visited Six Islands and Eagle Island (murder inquiry)*.

TNA CO 167/793 Mauritius Despatch No. 142 dated 11 May 1908 *L. Madelon visited Salomon, Six Islands and Eagle Is in January 1908*. Also, Mauritius Despatch No. 157 dated 11 July 1908 *Jollivet visited Peros Banhos*.

TNA CO 167/799 Enclosure to Despatch No. 328 dated 30 November 1911 *Le Conte visited Diego Garcia and Peros Banhos in May 1909; also Peros Banhos in 1910*.

Ibid. Jollivet by *Ste.Marthe* to Diego Garcia and Peros Banhos (in August-September 1911).

TNA CO 167/801 Enclosure to Despatch No. 13 dated 20 January 1912 L. Madelon by *Nonna Adèle* to Salomon, Eagle Island and Six Islands.

TNA CO 167/806 Enclosure to Mauritius Despatch No. 41 dated 13 January 1913 Jollivet by *Ste. Marthe* to Diego Garcia and Peros Banhos. Also enclosure to Mauritius Despatch No. 93 dated 27 March 1913 L. Pilot by *Nonna Adèle* to Salomon, Eagle and Six Islands.

TNA CO 167/810 Enclosure to Mauritius Despatch No. 105 dated 23 February 1913 F.P. Genève by *Nonna Adèle* to Salomon, Eagle Island and Six Islands.

TNA CO 167/811 Enclosures to Despatch No. 244 dated 14 July 1914. L. Pilot by *Ste. Marthe* to Peros Banhos and Diego Garcia (in mid 1913). Also F.P. Genève to Diego Garcia and Peros Banhos (in March-May 1914).

TNA CO 167/813 Enclosure to Mauritius Despatch No. 70 dated 12 February 1915 L. Pilot by *Nonna Adèle* to Salomon, Eagle Island and Six Islands (in May-July 1914).

Note. We have not been able to obtain copies of any 20th century documents relating to the Chagos from the Mauritius National Archive; but it is possible that such material may exist in the vaults of Le Reduit, now the official residence of the President.

32 Following the visit by the *Valdivia*, the crew was issued with new uniforms, copied from those of the German naval ratings. They were made by Karl Mülnier, a German inhabitant of Mauritius who had lost all his property in the 1892 hurricane and found employment, initially as shop manager, on Diego Garcia; he later managed Peros Banhos and then Diego Garcia.

33 Chun, C., *Aus den Tiefen des Weltmeeres*, Gustav Fischer, Jena, 1903. Chapter XIX, describing the visit to Diego Garcia, was translated into English by Karl Mülnier (grandson of the individual mentioned in the preceding note) and published in *La Gazette des Iles* (No. 17, December 1987).

34 Duyker, E. *op. cit.* Walter Commins became Assistant Manager on Salomon in 1897, Manager of Six Iles from 1903 to 1914 and Manager of Diego Garcia from 1914 to 1915. Annie married Richard Lionnet, son of the founder of Lionnet & Co., in 1922. While old-fashioned in tone, her comments, written as a widow in Australia in the 1980s, reflect sadness not only at the loss of the islanders' way of life, but also at the demise of both the Diego Garcia Company and of Lionnet & Co., to which her husband had devoted his career.

35 *Ibid.*

36 Personal communication from Fernand Mandarin, whose mother, herself a centenarian, was Mimi Auguste's niece.

37   TNA CO 167/842 Report of W.J. Hanning on his visit to Diego Garcia.

38   Manson, P. 'A Discussion On Beri-Beri', *The British Medical Journal*, Vol. 2, No. 2177 (20 September 1902), pp. 830–839. In fact, beri-beri is specifically caused by thiamine (Vitamin B^1) deficiency resulting from a poor diet.

39   TNA CO 167/769 Report of Proceedings, forwarded to Mauritius under cover of Admiralty Despatch dated 22 January 1904.

40   TNA CO 167/767 First enclosure to Despatch No. 275 dated 30 July 1904.

41   TNA CO 170/219 Text approved by Executive Council on 13 July 1906.

42   TNA CO 167/793 Confidential Despatch dated 6 September 1910.

43   TNA CO 167/798 Enclosures to Confidential Despatch dated 14 August 1911.

44   TNA CO 167/784 Governor's Despatch No. 142 of 11 May 1908 and TNA CO 167/793 unnumbered Confidential Despatch of 6 September 1910. Jollivet's and other magistrates' reports have been destroyed, but material in the despatches allows the major problems he encountered to be reconstructed; the statistical material is of course beyond recall.

45   TNA CO 167/reference unavailable. This event was reported by Despatch No. 32 dated 11 January 1907, but the details, contained in the reports of Magistrate Jollivet and Dr Keisler, who conducted an autopsy, are no longer obtainable.

46   TNA CO 167/793 Enclosure IV to Despatch dated 8 September 1910 Magistrate Yves Jollivet, report dated 4 March 1910.

47   TNA CO 167/796 Confidential Despatch dated 26 April 1911; TNA CO 170/239 Minutes of Executive Council meeting of 4 August 1911.

48   Walter Commins and Karl Mülnier on Diego Garcia and Bussy de St. Romain on Peros Banhos.

49   Professor Vine (*Island of Shame* p. 29), evidently following the description in *Mauritius Illustrated*, refers to the existence of 'six villages on Diego Garcia alone'. The facts do not support his description. As regards Peros Banhos, Jollivet counted 97 huts at the Ile du Coin settlement, 4 on Ile Diamant and 1 on Vache Marine.

50   TNA CO 167/740 Enclosure to Mauritius Despatch dated 12 June 1901 Magistrate's 1890 report on Diego Garcia. For example, as Jollivet reported, in 1886 Louis Fidèle was given 21 hours in jail for 'sorcellerie dans le cimétière' [witchcraft in the cemetery].

51   TNA CO 167/741 Ackroyd, Confidential Report to Governor, dated 12 October 1901.

14

Wars Again Intrude

FROM the 1880s onwards, the interest of the Great Powers' navies in Diego Garcia, never totally absent, had shown signs of increasing, perhaps stimulated by the creation of the coaling station and consequent use by large steamers. In addition to the Royal Navy, visitors included ships from the navies of Germany (*Alexandrine,* 26 May 1889), Russia (*Dijghit,* 27 May 1890) and the Austro-Hungarian Empire (*Saida,* 2 November 1890).

In particular, Germany's colonial ambitions were extending from East Africa, possessed since 1884, into the Pacific and, by the turn of the century, were reflected in scientific expeditions and voyages to show the flag, for example those of the *Fürst Bismarck* and the *Marie* in 1899.[1] Through them Germany made sure that she had first-hand knowledge of the area. The voyage of the *Valdivia* has already been mentioned, but not Professor (as he now was) Chun's lyrically inviting description of Diego Garcia: 'No word can possibly render the magnificence of colour inside the lagoon … a superb and marvellously protected haven … highly developed plant canopy … an ancient specimen of *Calophyllum inophyllum* [*Takamaka*] which may have no equal in fineness on the earth'.[2] The Russian interest was less direct. In 1904, the British embassy in St. Petersburg picked up from the French Naval Attaché rumours of a plan by the Russian Baltic fleet to call in at Diego Garcia and take on board fresh supplies of coal from German colliers, en route to support other Russian forces engaged in its war with Japan. On instructions, the Ambassador warned his German colleague that the collier might encounter a British cruiser and the Russian government that its ships would not be allowed to take on coal there or use it as a base.[3] British naval intelligence then took a close interest in the fleet's progress eastwards and in the movements of an array of colliers standing by to supply it with coal. One French collier, the *Marie Thérèse*, did indeed receive orders in Djibouti to proceed to Diego Garcia, but naval intelligence picked up no evidence of the rendezvous having taken place.[4] This lacuna can now be filled. The

(British) Percy Sladen Trust mounted a scientific expedition to the Chagos in 1905. On its return, its leader remarked in an interview that 'a number of Russian colliers attached to Admiral Rozhdestvensky's fleet had been there a short time before our arrival, and had stopped several days'.[5] The fact remained that, for all its beauty and physical distance, this island was never far from the Great Powers' minds.

The Emden 'incident'

In 1913, the German light cruiser *Emden* was part of the East Asiatic Squadron, based at Tsingtao (now Qingdao), the German naval enclave in China. The newly promoted Admiral Graf von Spee, who commanded the Squadron, had carefully prepared plans for disrupting the supply lines of Germany's enemies in the event of European hostilities. Berlin, recognising that the Squadron would have largely to operate under its own initiative, had given the Admiral full discretion on the use of his force. The German Admiralty had also, for the same reason, made sure that the Squadron was composed only of its newest and fastest ships. As a result, it had a well-deserved reputation as the outstanding unit of the German navy in terms of efficiency. Unfortunately, the High Command's expectation that Japan would remain neutral in any Anglo-German conflict, notwithstanding her treaty of friendship with Britain, proved false: with other powers using the outbreak of hostilities in 1914 to snatch the small bits of territory comprising the German Empire in the East, Japan saw the opportunity to take Tsingtao and its mineral-rich hinterland. Von Spee therefore, foreseeing destruction by the combined British, French, Australian, Russian and Japanese forces ranged against him, decided to cross the Pacific and, by making use of South American neutral ports, to harry Britain's vital supply routes from the South Atlantic.[6]

At a mid-ocean Fleet conference to discuss this plan, Captain Karl von Müller, young, ambitious and extremely able, proposed that his ship, the *Emden*, should instead proceed on her own to see what damage she could do in the Indian Ocean; in a foray from Tsingtao she had already captured a Russian vessel. The Admiral assented: this would distract part of the enemy, relieve demand on his limited supplies of coal and, as *Emden* was his fastest vessel, could result in considerable disruption. So it proved. Within a month of the outbreak of war, Müller had captured or sunk ten ships, in every case ensuring the safety of their crews and passengers, and had set on fire the main oil storage tanks at Madras before deciding to seek fresh areas to raid in the Maldives. By this time, he badly needed to clean his hull of marine growths and make other repairs which could not be done at sea. He had also learned from intercepted radio messages that ships of the Royal Navy were now in pursuit. Diego Garcia, that 'miniature fairyland of coral banks covered in high palms and a sheltered bay which cannot be seen from the sea'[7] – had he read Chun's description? – offered the ideal haven. He reached the island at dawn on 9 October, accompanied by the *Buresk*, a British collier he had captured off Ceylon. There are many accounts of what then transpired, the best of them in the late Richard Edis' *Peak of Limuria*, from which the following is largely drawn.[8]

After the *Emden* and the *Buresk* had dropped anchor in the lagoon, a boat put out from shore bearing the assistant manager of the plantation, the francophone William Suzor. He was brought into the wardroom and (as recalled in the memoirs of one of Capt. Müller's officers, Lieutenant Franz Joseph, Prince of Hohenzollern, nephew of the Kaiser) 'made very good practice with the iced whisky and soda. For us the conversation became interesting from the moment we recognised – from his ignorance of the death of Pope Pius IX – that this manager and the inhabitants had no idea there was a war on in the world'.[9] Suzor also readily accepted the story that the German ship was involved in a major naval exercise involving other navies, including those of Britain and France. The party was then joined by Walter Commins, chief manager of the plantation and official British representative on the island, who took much more convincing.

> He looked suspiciously at the oil-stained deck, which had once been blue-white and examined the deep scratches and fraying with a jaundiced eye. He saw the thick matting hung about the guns as a protection against shell fragments, and he noticed all around the ship the shadow marks where something had once stood that was now gone. He looked into the wardroom and said something about the strangeness of having an officers' mess with a gun in the middle of the room. He said he had looked over the deck and he commented on the lack of paint and the repairs that were under way. Captain von Müller had a tale for him. The repairs were necessary because the ship had just come through a terrible storm, which had nearly caused her to capsize. The islanders nodded. They could understand storms like that.[10]

As a final proof of his good intentions, Capt. Müller responded enthusiastically to Commins' request for help in restoring his one motorboat to working order. All the accounts suggest that Commins was convinced by Müller, but this may not have been the case.[11]

Meanwhile the *Emden*'s crew manhandled on board 1,000 tons of coal from the *Buresk*. They also set to work to clean off the encrustations from the ship's bottom, flooding the port and starboard watertight compartments in turn so as to expose a fair part of the hull below the waterline. Before evening the plantation boat returned, laden with welcome gifts in the form of fresh fruit, fish and a live pig, together with an invitation to breakfast ashore next morning; an invitation declined in a gracious handwritten note referring to 'pressing matters of duty'. And, lest the Germans should be under any obligation to their albeit unaware enemies, the note was accompanied by gifts of wine, cognac and whisky, as well as boxes of cigars, rare commodities indeed in those parts. Next morning the two ships were gone. A plethora of published accounts, all of them inaccurate, describe the arrival within hours or days of two pursuing British ships, HMS *Hampshire* and the armed merchantman *Empress of Russia*. The facts, now easily established from reading the logbooks of the two vessels, are as follows.[12] The *Hampshire*, after keeping watch in the Maldives until 13 October, returned briefly to Colombo before heading to 'the Chagos Archipelago'. On 15 October, late in the afternoon, she sighted Peros Banhos, slowed down, halted (but did not lower any boats) and then, at 7 p.m. (no 24 hour time system then!), turned round and headed north back to Colombo. She did not visit Diego Garcia then or later. As for the *Empress*, she had been making her way westwards from Hong Kong, via Singapore, and did not encounter the *Hampshire* until 7 November, when she delivered provisions to the cruiser near Minicoy in the Maldives. The two ships then escorted a convoy eastwards and, on 15 November, encountered HMAS *Sydney* at approximately 4° N, 81° E, by then escorting a westbound convoy; the *Sydney* took over the eastbound convoy, leaving the *Hampshire* to protect the westbound ships all the way to Aden (and then head home to Britain). It was the *Empress* which, heading south from Colombo on 18 November at maximum speed, reached Diego Garcia late on 20 November, anchored overnight and left again for Colombo on 21 November.

In the intervening five weeks, the *Emden* had steamed north to the Maldives again where, from 15 October onwards,[13] she intercepted seven more merchantmen before vanishing into the eastern Indian Ocean, only to appear suddenly at the port of Penang in Malaya. Here a Russian cruiser and a French destroyer were sunk in short order by her torpedoes and guns. But the *Emden*'s luck finally ran out when she diverted to the British-ruled Cocos-Keeling Islands, sending a pinnace ashore to destroy its important wireless station. That mission was accomplished, but not before the station had despatched a signal, 'Strange ship off entrance'. This was picked up by HMAS *Sydney*, which was escorting a convoy of Australian troopships nearby and able to close in before *Emden* could make her getaway (but not before she had scuttled the *Buresk*, her eighteenth and last merchant victim). Outgunned, the German vessel was rapidly set ablaze and beached on 9 November, exactly one month after her visit to Diego Garcia. The surviving members of her crew were made prisoner but, by the order of Winston Churchill, Capt. Müller and his officers were allowed to keep their swords as a tribute to their daring, gallantry and respect for the rules of naval warfare. Finally, the *Hampshire* did play a small role in the drama, receiving the *Sydney*'s German prisoners at Suez and giving them passage as far as Malta.

Other naval manoeuvres

Knowledge of the *Emden*'s visit to the Chagos did not reach Mauritius until after her destruction a month later. But the islanders must surely have noticed an immediate disturbance in the pattern of their supply ships' arrivals. This seems the only possible explanation for the striking statistics of Table 13.2 (page 262), showing a steep decline of exports from the Chagos in 1914, followed by an exceptional resurgence in 1915. This was but a minor reflection of the disruption in trade between India and Mauritius brought about by the *Emden*'s daring exploits, with Indian merchants becoming reluctant to undertake such risky voyages and obliged to pay vastly inflated insurance for those that were undertaken. Although the Governor in Mauritius was under instructions to report any untoward events in the Chagos, naval watchers also took an interest. At the end of January 1915, HMAS *Pioneer* called at Diego Garcia on her way to Mombasa.[14] Just over a year later, on 16 April 1916, HMS *Minerva*, en route from Seychelles to Singapore, also made a brief stop there.[15] The Germans too drew lessons from what *Emden* had done.[16] Late in 1916, they despatched a raider *Wolf* with a submarine escort on a fourteen-month expedition to the Indian Ocean. She captured and sank eighteen merchantmen, while thirteen others were sunk by mines she had laid. The seas near Cape of Good Hope, Bombay and Colombo were among the areas attacked. Two of the victims, the *Jumna* and the *Wordsworth*, had disappeared without trace in the neighbourhood of the Chagos in mid-1917. As it happened, an Australian flotilla[17] of six destroyers was then on its way to assist in meeting the threat posed by German submarines in the Mediterranean. In mid July, the ships visited Diego Garcia, having spent some time searching the Archipelago for the missing vessels. It emerged later that the crews of both were brought back safely as prisoners to Kiel in February 1918.

The war's economic impact

Daily life on the islands proceeded as before. Magistrates visited though with diminishing regularity. Shipping records are not available for every year, but in 1916, the *Mauritius Almanac* lists the names of half-a-dozen vessels involved at times in the Chagos. These included two barques, *Ione* (510 tons) and *Ste. Marthe* (409 tons), owned respectively by Lewis Rogers and Richard Lionnet, and two schooners, *St. Géran* (290 tons) and *Nonna Adèle* (134 tons), owned by Messrs L. Couacaud and H.G. Ducray. The *Ste. Marthe* usually served both Diego Garcia and Peros Banhos; the schooners served the three small plantations. Two other vessels made cameo appearances: the 40 ton *Umvoti*, listed as a barque, and the government steamer, *Secunder* (993 tons). The latter's visit, since she was seldom used for this long voyage except in emergencies, could have been significant, but records are lacking. From 1915 onwards, the supply ships evidently functioned normally for, with the exception of Peros Banhos in 1918, no severe shortage was reported. Exports of oil and other coconut products fluctuated from year to year, but it was only in 1918 that the quantity diminished markedly. More noticeable, however, was a progressive increase in the cost of supplies from Mauritius, to the point where the islands had a significantly negative balance of trade, unsustainable had it continued longer.

Reports on conditions in Mauritius itself support these impressions. As early as February 1915, the Governor reported that 'on the outbreak of war freights rose considerably, in one case to three times the normal rate, and great difficulty was experienced in securing tonnage for the export of sugar'. The British Indian Steam Navigation Company's monthly service between Calcutta, Colombo and Port Louis suffered similar interruptions.[18] The complications did not only stem from enemy action or the fear of it. Early in the war, it was reported later,

> the sugar crop was purchased by the Imperial Government at a price considerably above the normal rates and the position of the sugar estates … was materially improved. The enormous increase which has since taken place in cost of all supplies and the rise in wages had not begun to be felt seriously in 1916 and the island, during that year, enjoyed a degree of prosperity which is unlikely to be repeated.

By 1917, the shipping direct to Britain of the bulk of the Mauritius sugar crop, added to the depredations of the *Wolf*, meant that trade with India became further disrupted, since the traditional pattern of transporting sugar exports and food imports by the same ships broke down. By mid-1917, the Governor had to appeal to London for urgent help and, in the absence of an immediate response, despatched a further telegram on 6 August:

> I am depending entirely on Rangoon for cheap rice which is main food of whole of labouring population. Present stock is exhausted. Only possess about 6 weeks supply best quality rice which is much too expensive for poorer classes. Ship from Rangoon not expected before end August bringing about 4 weeks supply rice. Have been informed no further tonnage available. Have endeavoured unsuccessfully to obtain rice Madagascar. Impossible wait for sailing [of] vessel starting from Rangoon even if available – essential foods such as dholl, lentils, rice, flour required from Karachi. It has been ascertained no tonnage available there. Flour from Australia too dear. *Secunder* [the government steamer] undergoing repairs Durban unlikely to be available for 3 months. Obliged to ask urgently for assistance. Colony produces only fraction of food of population. No reserves in stock. Situation may become dangerous if not relieved early … It is essential that not less than 9,000 tons of Rangoon rice should arrive before the end September and 7,000 before end of October.[19]

Ships were duly diverted from elsewhere and the situation retrieved.

The following year, however, a different combination of factors made for further difficulties. American entry into the war required a diversion of British merchant ships to assist in bringing troops and supplies from the United States. The British therefore delayed taking delivery of that year's Mauritius sugar crop, relying instead on supplies from Cuba; but they did not permit the Mauritians to dispose of their harvest elsewhere. The Mauritian producers thus found themselves with more sugar than could be stored, but not available to sell to India in return for rice and other supplies basic to Mauritian consumers, 70% of whom were of Indian origin and tastes. Their financial position was also seriously strained by a near-tripling of the import prices of the metals, chemicals and machinery essential to the sugar industry. As the war ended, the Indian government, under pressure to give priority to Indian and British rice requirements, sought to restrict exports to Mauritius, while at the same time putting obstacles in the way of the sale to Mauritius of (cheaper) Burmese rice. All this led to animated protests by the Chamber of Agriculture to the Governor,[20] a leading part being played by Sir Henry Leclézio, whose many roles still included that of chairmanship of the board of the *Nouvelle Société Huilière de Diégo et Péros*. It should however be added that the woes of the 'sugar barons', as they were colloquially called, were temporary. Once the war was over, the Governor, Sir Hesketh Bell, was required to disburse the staggering sum of £23 million paid by the British Sugar Corporation for the supplies received from Mauritius. As Bell later recalled, great fortunes were made, but disappeared over the next twenty years'.[21]

Mauritius government steamer, ss *Secunder*. <u>Source</u>: *Mauritius Illustrated* 1912.

While the Chagos plantations did not run out of supplies, they were not immune from events in Mauritius. The first workers to notice were those of Six Islands. When the Visiting Magistrates arrived there in early 1915, they complained that their rice ration, 'being dirty and mixed with chaff, lost about 25% of its weight after being pounded and fanned'. Magistrate Pilot took their complaint seriously and had samples tested of the new supplies carried in the vessel which was taking him to Eagle and Salomon as well as Six Islands. Those for Six Islands were found to have 30.5% 'dust and heads', those for Salomon 33.3% and those for Eagle an astonishing 75.8%. Taken to task, the new Agent in Mauritius of the company owning all three plantations was able to blame a departed predecessor and swear that nothing but the best rice would be offered in future.

The magistrate who inspected Six Islands and Eagle the following year made a point of examining the rice at both establishments and found it to be good quality Rangoon rice. On the other hand, examination of the rice at Peros Banhos the same year revealed that most of the sacks in store weighed 90-100 lbs, rather than the stated quantity of 150 lbs, mainly as a result of rat infestation. In 1917, only Diego Garcia and Peros Banhos were visited, but neither report was even sent to London.[22] In 1918 however the workers at Six Islands were again complaining about both the quantity and quality of the rice provided. The magistrate backed their complaints.[23] During the same voyage, a boat accosted the magistrate's vessel as it passed Peros Banhos to report that the atoll was running out of rice. Clearly, not all was well, but a thorough analysis would require more complete information than the few surviving reports can supply; in fact, even those that remain were less detailed than usual, while that for visits made in 1918 was not even signed until July 1919. The best that can be said is that, given the circumstances, things could have been worse, both for the owners and their island workers.

Notes to Chapter 14

1 van der Vat, D., *Gentlemen at War* William and Morrow, New York, 1981.

2 Chun, C., *op. cit.* See Chapter 13, note 32.

3 TNA CO 167/769 Lord Hardinge, letter dated 7 December 1904.

4 TNA ADM 231/42 Diary of the Russo-Japanese War.

5 J. Stanley Gardiner, interview with Reuters, reported in *The Scotsman* of 16 January 1906.

6 He was not to know that the equally careful plans of his British opponent to contain and destroy his squadron had been disrupted by the decision of the First Sea Lord, Winston Churchill, to override the discretion previously given; nor that the Japanese had given their priority to seizing Tsingtao; nor (subsequently) that the alarm caused by the *Emden* resulted in Australia's most powerful ship, HMAS *Australia*, being diverted from the Pacific to protect the country's troopships heading across the Indian Ocean.

7 Hohenzollern, Lt. Franz Joseph, Prince of *My Experiences in SMS Emden*, Herbert Jenkins, London, 1928.

8   Edis, R., *op. cit.* pp. 53–56.

9   *Ibid.*, p. 133.

10   Duyker, E., 'The *Emden* at Diego Garcia', in *Mauritian Heritage*, Australian Mauritian Research Group. Victoria, 1986.

11   M.A. Duvivier, postcard dated 12 March 1913, from items possessed by Commins' daughter Annie and held, pending conveyance to National Library of Australia, by Dr. Edward Duyker. In 2011, there came to light a postcard sent to Commins in Diego Garcia in early 1913, drawing attention to newspapers on their way to him and remarking (in French) 'You will be able to see how tense relations have become between the great powers, and that a European war is inevitable'. Perhaps as a result of his experience of the *Emden* visit, Commins retired in 1915, being replaced as manager by Suzor.

12   TNA ADM 53/69703 (*Hampshire*) and ADM 53/40817 (*Empress of Russia*).

13   The first ship seized, on 15 October, was the *Clan Grant*. It is tempting to think that news of her capture on that date reached the *Hampshire*, resulting in her immediate return northwards, but this is not possible: that ship was not taken until about 10.30 p.m.

14   The *Pioneer* spent just 24 hours at anchor in Rambler Bay from dusk on 24 January 1915, taking on 400 tons of coal from a collier (the crew worked throughout the night). There is no evidence of contact with the settlement (copy of ship's log kindly supplied by Australian War Memorial staff).

15   TNA ADM 53/40817. This visit was also reported to the visiting magistrate a month later (TNA CO 167/817), with the comment that the captain had asked whether any German vessel had visited in the preceding week or so.

16   See website 'Count Dohna and his Seagull' (www.smsoewe.com).

17   Royal Australian Navy records (www.navy.gov.au/spc/history/ships/huon1.html).

18   TNA CO 167/813 Confidential Despatch dated 2 February 1915.

19   TNA CO 167/820 (folio 197).

20   TNA CO 167/829 Records of the Chamber of Agriculture forwarded to the Colonial Office on 3 January 1919.

21   Bell, H., *Witches and Fishes* London, 1948 (pp. 87–88).

22   TNA CO 167/834 In early November 1920 officials listed the reports made on the Chagos from 1912 onwards, showing nothing later than 1916. However, the magistrates reporting in 1920 both refer to visits being made to the two principal atolls in 1917.

23   TNA CO 167/827 Report of Magistrate A. Legras dated 16 July 1919.

15

A Dreadful Decade: 1919–1929

Postwar problems: Visiting Magistrates' findings

IT WOULD be satisfying to learn that with peace came renewed interest in what was going on in the Lesser Dependencies. The reality was that no official visited the Chagos until 1920. The first to set forth was the magistrate Genève, who went to the three smaller establishments during the months of July and August, followed by Magistrate L.M. Berenger, whose visits to Peros Banhos and Diego Garcia took up the months of October and November. Both were confronted with a backlog of records to be updated and many workers who complained at having been unable to return to Mauritius at the expiry of their contracts. Both also had complaints to make about the arrangements for transport to and from the islands. Their patience would certainly have been tried by having to make the outward voyages while the Southeast trade winds were still blowing strongly. Genève was aboard the brigantine *Nonna Adèle* (135 tons), while Berenger was able to use the barque *Kassa* (287 tons); the smaller vessel taking 26 days to reach Eagle Island, while the barque took 25 for the slightly longer passage to Peros Banhos, both needing only 10 days for their return to Port Louis.[1]

Genève was highly critical of two other aspects of what he found. Noting that meat was scarce, he commented that the 'labourers receive low wages indeed and they can very seldom afford to buy the delicacies of the shops, which are sold at 25% above Mauritius prices'. He gives few details of pay, except to say that it varied between Rs 6–10 per month – a slight increase on pre-war levels, but clearly not enough to match wartime inflation. As to the meat, virtually no pigs were provided on Salomon or Eagle, as compared to Six Islands, where about a dozen were killed annually for the workers. The gap was made up by the capture of green turtles, 85 for Salomon, 15 for Eagle and 45 for Six Islands over the period January 1918–August 1920. More harshly, Genève stated that

Nonna Adèle at Six Islands. Image courtesy of Dr Edward Duyker.

The type of labourers who are now sent to the islands leaves much to be desired. It seems that they are engaged indiscriminately without regard to their antecedents and state of health. Ex-convicts, jail-birds, consumptive and syphilitic men and women find their way out there. They poison the minds of the old labourers and the discipline has relaxed. They do not respect their masters as they used to and have become aggressive and turbulent ... I have noticed a great change [his previous visit took place in 1913] in their behaviour towards those in authority.

In the case of Diego Garcia and Peros Banhos, there was a substantial and tragic complication. In June 1919, the company's vessel, the barque *Ste. Marthe*, which had served them well for a decade, was wrecked on Horsburgh Point as she approached the island at night (see inset). Fourteen of the seventeen people aboard were drowned. It would appear that some of those lost were people about to take up work. The fresh stock of rice she carried was also lost. As a consequence, various other vessels had to be engaged at short notice to convey goods and people to and from the two atolls – in particular the *Ione*, the *St. Géran* (twice) and the *Utopia*.[2] Of these, only the last was properly registered to carry passengers; she removed 50 people, while the others took 22 between them. The result was that on both Diego Garcia and Peros Banhos there were in 1920 large numbers of workers whose contracts had expired and who were impatient to be returned to Mauritius.

The Ste. Marthe's *last voyage*

The barque *Ste. Marthe* was bought by the *Nouvelle Société* in about 1910 to convey goods and people to and from their plantations on Diego Garcia and Peros Banhos. From at least 1916 she was usually captained by Louis Albert Nicolin, who knew the Chagos extremely well. As a child, he had on occasion accompanied his father, Evelinor, who had captained a previous supply ship, the *Eva Joshua*, and had also served as a manager on Diego Garcia. The *Ste. Marthe*'s last voyage was unusual in only one respect: after leaving Port Louis on 23 April 1919, Nicolin first visited Seychelles, probably to show those islands to his wife, Louise Keisler, whom he had married just three weeks earlier. She was a daughter of the Dr F.L. Keisler who had visited Chagos in 1906 (see page 278).

Albert and Louise on their wedding day. Image courtesy of Mr Jocelyn Chaillet.

By mid-June, the south-easterly trade winds would normally be established, but unseasonable storms, with violently shifting winds, were by no means rare. One such struck the *Ste. Marthe* on 14 June, evidently carrying her past Diego Garcia. Whether the wind reverted to south-easterly or died away is not clear, but there would have been a strong current setting to the north-west. At around 10 p.m. that night she struck the reef at Horsburgh Point, named after the hydrogapher who, as a midshipman, had been wrecked at that very spot in May 1786 (see page 57). More recently, in 1904, the Point had claimed the *William Turner,* happily without human loss. In accordance with naval custom, Nicolin, after giving the order to abandon ship, remained aboard. His wife, a strong swimmer, helped two other passengers to reach the shore through the surf. Realising that her husband was still aboard, she re-entered the sea, but never reached the ship. He left last and swam ashore, one of only three survivors.

Albert Nicolin had often stayed with the manager, William Suzor and his family, and did so again as he waited for the next ship to take him home. The Suzors' four year-old son, Lewis, was later to recall to his own son-in-law (our informant) his vivid memories of the bodies washed ashore and the captain, silent and sitting alone, as he absorbed the tragedy that had befallen him and those for whom he was responsible.

Berenger's reports on these two establishments, where the plantations were owned by the *Nouvelle Société Huilière de Diégo et Péros*, bore many similarities to those of his colleague Genève on the plantations owned by the *Société Huilière de Salomon, Trois Frères et Six Iles*. While he made no comment on the character of new arrivals, Genève noted that pay had been increased by between Rs 2–4 per month, while 'wonder[ing] how they could make both ends meet' at the previous levels of Rs 6–8. Like Genève, Berenger examined the prices charged in the company shop, but found that for many staple items there was little or no mark-up on Mauritius levels. It was evident that at some level of management, the habitual 25% mark-up had been recognised as no longer tolerable.[3] He was also struck by the large numbers of workers whose contracts were long expired, but not enabled to return, as they wished, to Mauritius; at Diego Garcia these totalled 161 out of a total working population of 356 and at Peros Banhos 80 out of 253. At Diego there were also complaints about the inadequacy of the rice ration, from which it emerged that the local managers had increased the amount provided to 12 lbs per week when only 'Rangoon rice' had been available, but reduced it once the better rice from Madras, Madagascar or Saigon came back on the market. The magistrate also publicly tested the long-used container (*gamelle*) which, to everyone's surprise, contained eight ounces less than the stipulated 10½ lbs. It quickly being established there was no foul play,[4] the manager at once accepted the magistrate's proposal that for six months the ration would be increased to 11 lbs. As to Genève's remarks about increased truculence, Berenger, new to his job, simply enumerated the particular complaints he had been asked to examine, concluding in all but one of them that they were without foundation. Certainly, compared to those of earlier years, they read as being entirely frivolous. In addition neither magistrate found cause for criticism in the food, housing, medical facilities for the workers or in the general behaviour of the managers. It does seem therefore that some new spirit of self-confidence had begun to animate the islanders, especially those who had undergone the war-time privations of Mauritius.

Postwar problems: reactions of others

It is also quite clear that the management in Mauritius were no longer able to find good quality labour for the pittance they had offered in the past. In the absence of recent reports on the islands, it is not possible to be more precise about the developing changes.[5] The Governor, in forwarding the two reports for 1920, explained that there had been exceptional demands for magistrates' services on Mauritius itself. Given the sharp inflation that had occurred during the war, as mentioned in our last chapter, it is not surprising that the salaries of the Visiting Magistrates were also beginning to look inadequate; at the end of 1920 they were increased sharply from Rs 6,000 to Rs 9,000 (but with removal of the daily travelling allowance of Rs 5 received by those formally appointed to the Visiting posts).[6] The cost of this measure was passed on to the companies, whose annual levy was increased pro rata, from Rs 12,000 to Rs 18,000.

The Governor also forwarded to London replies from the Managing Agents of the two companies commenting on the magistrates' criticisms. These were typical of the genre. In the case of the three smaller islands, the Managing Agent de Caila had visited the islands soon after Genève; he claimed that, 'without any pressure', all who had asked for repatriation had withdrawn their requests. Turning to other issues, he suggested that the shortage of meat might have arisen in part from refusing permission for the workers to keep their own pigs, but that refusal was the direct result of their theft of the company's *poonac* to feed the animals and their invariable practice of killing the company's pigs rather than their own. As to medical examinations, the Government could certainly employ a doctor for this purpose, but it would put a full stop to recruitment: the company's 'vast experience of islanders' enabled them to state that 'the Creole takes little care of his health, because he does not like being looked at by doctors'. Finally, while it might be true that one or two unsavoury individuals had recently slipped through the net, the Agent would do his best to prevent this happening again. Richard Lionnet (*fils*), the new Managing Agent for the *Nouvelle Société* (responsible for Diego Garcia and Peros Banhos), did not allude to the issue of unmet requests for repatriation, but defended his company's position on other matters. Noting that his company had, before Berenger's comments were conveyed to them, already taken a lease on the *St. Géran* with permission to carry passengers, and had already increased the Rs 6 and Rs 8 wage rates to Rs 12 and Rs 16 respectively, he went on to give a vigorous account of the several ways in which workers could obtain extra protein – by fishing, keeping poultry, etc. – or earn extra cash, for example by sending dried, salted fish to their relatives in Mauritius.

It is of some interest that Richard Lionnet (*père*) who had played such an important part in the fortunes of the *Nouvelle Société* from 1911 onwards, should have decided to hand over the role of chief executive to his son, just as the problems of running its plantations accumulated. Perhaps the loss of the *Ste. Marthe* had been the final blow to his self-confidence, but in any case he had always been more interested in his emporium, J.R. Lionnet & Co. Richard Lionnet (*fils*), born in 1892, was still a young man and it would take him several years to put his own stamp on the way the plantations were managed. However, the problems requiring attention were urgent and substantial; and since they began quickly to affect productivity, it is reasonable to assume that the Board of the

Nouvelle Société, in particular Sir Henry Leclézio, its chairman, would have been closely involved – how closely we can only guess.

When the first post-war reports eventually reached London in mid 1921, quite a terse correspondence ensued. Leo Amery, then Parliamentary Secretary for the Colonies, was led to interest himself in the Chagos by an informant who told him that the workers there were being scandalously treated and that recently appointed magistrates had unduly close connections with the plantations' owners and managers.[7] Officials then looked into the declining frequency of reports after 1916 and pressed for improved performance. Nevertheless a further year was to elapse before the authorities in Mauritius succeeded in re-establishing near-annual visits of inspection. From 1921–1922 the Colonial Office was in the hands of Winston Churchill, who took up the Chagos plantations issue where Amery left off. It was to Churchill therefore that Hesketh Bell's deputy (during Bell's absence on leave) reported in 1922. Churchill however lost his seat in the 1922 elections and was succeeded by the Duke of Devonshire, who received reports on the plantations inspected later the same year. With these rapid changes, London's interest in the Chagos appeared to wane once more.

A bizarre Scandinavian irruption

In 1921, there was a further shipwreck, this time involving no loss of life. The *Elmaren*, a bran-new Swedish bulk carrier of nearly 6,000 tons with powerful twin diesel engines, was returning to Gothenburg from Australia with a cargo of wheat, barley and wool.[8] At night, but in calm weather, she grounded at full speed on the reefs of Six Islands, her captain believing himself to be still well to the east of the Chagos. At dawn, the astonished inhabitants approached the ship as she lay upright on the reef flat, only to be faced with crew members brandishing revolvers on the assumption that the near-naked workers were 'cannibals'. It took several days for the manager to persuade the crew to come ashore, set up their radio to report their plight and be given lodging in the establishment. The crew also brought ashore not only their personal possessions, but also the ship's piano, surely the first and last such instrument to find its way to the Chagos plantations (it was later sent to Mauritius).[9] Before they could be taken on their way in a sister-ship, the *Tisnaren*, they found themselves counted among the island's inhabitants by a visiting team of census enumerators. All this would hardly be credited in the plot of a comic opera, but, as will be described later, the ship's components, spewed out as the vessel was gradually destroyed by the ocean rollers, included poisonous materials which contaminated the reef fish and, apparently, severely harmed some islanders who caught and ate them.

Numbers, occupations and origins

More detailed figures are available for 1921 than for any other census which we have been able to examine. In terms of overall numbers, there had been virtually no change as compared with 1911, but this disguised quite considerable variations in populations of the individual islands, as this summary comparison shows:

Table 15.1   Chagos Population Summary, 1911 and 1921.

	Diego Garcia	Peros Banhos	Salomon	Six Islands	Eagle Island	Total
1911	483	300	144	155	101	1183
1921	465	350	143	115*	131	1204

*Of the actual total of 165, 50 were the stranded Swedish sailors from the *Elmaren*.

One set of the census tables provides details of the occupations of men and women in each of the islands.[10] The two 'catch-all' categories were those of 'labourer' and 'no specific occupation'; of the 1206 people listed for the whole Archipelago, the first accounted for 580 people, the second for 356, mainly the children. Unfortunately, it becomes clear that respondents were inconsistent in the descriptions of their work; for example only Diego Garcia and Six Islands acknowledged boatmen as a separate category. It is also clear that extremely few women were employed otherwise than as general labourers, one notable exception being a female cooper on Six Islands. Those in managerial and supervisory roles amounted to about 50 all told. However, the range of artisanal work is quite striking, those listed including millmen, gardeners, storekeepers, blacksmiths, tinsmiths, harness makers, carpenters, caulkers, coopers, sawyers, sailmakers, masons, hospital attendants, cooks, laundrymen, grooms, shoemakers and even a cartwright. Rarely would there be more than one specialist per island and only Diego Garcia covered the whole range, also having a particularly large number of carpenters (22). The main conclusion must however be that, as in the past, most workers were expected to turn their hands to whatever tasks required to be accomplished on a given day. Finally, this set of tables reveals that the inhabitants of Indo-Mauritian (and, in a few cases, Indian) origin (145 in total) were mostly labourers, but did also provide the sole person requiring knowledge of the internal combustion engine – Diego Garcia's motorboat driver.

The census also revealed many a detail concerning the birthplaces of people on the islands and the types of work they were engaged in. As regards origins, we have compiled from the separate tables relating to each of the islands the composite Table shown overleaf. Several points emerge. First, 499 out of the total population had been born within the Archipelago, 556 in Mauritius and 123 elsewhere in the western Indian Ocean. Thus, the crude percentage of those born within the Archipelago (42%) was still less than the proportion born in

Table 15.2   Chagos Population by place of origin and racial category (Africa: General Population/Indo–Mauritian*)

	Diego Garcia		Peros Banhos		Salomon		Six Islands		Eagle Island		Total
	GP	I–M	GP	I–M	GP	I–M	GP	I–M	GP	I–M	
Agalega	3	–	15	–	5	–	6	–	5	–	34
Coëtivy	–	–	1	–	–	–	–	–	–	–	1
D.G.	157	14	20	7	7	–	1	–	–	2	208
Mauritius	189	28	124	31	53	7	58	9	47	10	556
Madagascar	8	–	5	–	3	–	–	–	3	–	19
Peros B	5	–	101	16	1	–	1	–	7	2	133
Reunion	11	–	1	2	–	–	–	–	1	–	15
Rodrigues	–	–	3	–	2	–	2	–	–	–	7
Salomon	7	–	2	3	57	3	5	–	10	2	89
Seychelles	2	–	5	–	1	–	2	–	1	–	11
Egmont	4	–	7	–	3	–	22	–	6	–	42
Eagle	1	–	1	–	–	–	4	–	21	–	27
Africa	2	–	4	–	1	–	2	9	6	–	24
Other	10	2	–	–	–	–	–	–	–	–	12
Total	399	44	289	59	133	10	103	18	107	16	1178*

Source: 1921 census tables.

*We are not able to explain discrepancies between the total figures for the population categorised by age, as in Table 15.1 (1204), by occupation, as described on p. 305 (1206), and by origin, as in this Table (1178). We do not exclude error on our part.

Mauritius (47%), but since both figures include management as well as workers and virtually all the former would have been born outside the Chagos, the proportion of the workers born locally is probably understated. Second, there were at least 147 Indo-Mauritians (12.5%) at this stage, compared to 29 in 1911. The small number (23) born in the Chagos suggests that this increase – well over fourfold – had been a recent occurrence, the reasons for which can only be guessed at. Third, there seems to have been little movement between the Chagos islands and Agalega; in each, the number born in the other group was in the low thirties. Lastly, there were important variations in the ratio of locally – to Mauritius-born islanders. On Salomon the percentage was 42%, on Diego Garcia 39%, on Peros Banhos 34%; on Six Islands 18% and on Eagle Island a mere 17%, figures which suggest the smallest islands found it most necessary to recruit fresh employees.

Increasingly regular inspections

In 1922, the magistrates spent much longer than usual at each island, allowing them to make a careful study of conditions. At Diego Garcia and Peros Banhos, Magistrate W. J. Hanning, newly appointed, went out of his way to express satisfaction at the relations between workers and management:

> The labourers appeared to me to be a very quiet, orderly lot, easily managed and satisfied with their lot on the islands. Their one desire is that they should be able to enjoy a little trip to Mauritius, for a good time there, after which they usually return to the islands, to which they have become accustomed.

As regards prices and pay levels, many of the workers were able to save appreciable amounts, despite the 25% mark-up in the plantation shops; at the same time Hanning considered that calico, used to make the workers' clothes, should be sold at cost price. His main adverse finding concerned the high rate of child mortality at Diego Garcia, which he ascribed primarily to the incompetence and neglect of an habitually drunk midwife.[11] The magistrate was also struck by the more robust appearance of people born on the islands, as compared with those hailing from Mauritius, noting too the considerable numbers of very old individuals.

The state of affairs in the three smaller establishments, examined by Berenger, was more complicated. Some problems arose from chance factors: the ship used, the schooner *Union de la Digue*, had been delayed in Mauritius for repairs, departing some six weeks later than planned and then, with a voyage lasting nearly four weeks to Eagle Island, arriving to find stocks of food exhausted or running low in all three islands. Likewise, there was disruption arising from the need for the managers of both Salomon and Six Islands to go to Mauritius to give evidence at murder hearings. As regards the mismatch between levels of pay and the prices of goods in the company shop, matters had improved: workers were paid Rs 12 or Rs 10, rather than the Rs 8 or Rs 6 stated on their contracts, with a bonus for regular attendance; and the 25% mark-up was only selectively applied (and, for many staples, only on the wholesale price). On Eagle Island, there were few complaints and the magistrate was impressed by the sense of order and calm prevailing, attributable in large measure to the good sense of the manager, a M. J. St. Louis Deshayes, an old sailor with long experience in the islands. By contrast, morale on Six Islands was low. As the magistrate remarked,

> In consequence of the scarcity and dearness of labour in Mauritius, men of very inferior quality have been sent to the islands; able-bodied, hardworking, honest men and women could be numbered on one's fingers at Six Islands. The men are addicted to drinking. I had to issue an order restricting the consumption of wine by drunkards and other troublesome persons.

This state of affairs had evidently arisen under the island's manager, a M. Julienne, still absent in Mauritius in connection with the trial of an individual suspected of murdering three people in 1921 (the suspect died in prison). Other recent miseries had included the disappearance at sea of one of the island's *commandeurs* and the suicide of an individual following what he believed to have been a successful attempt to murder an Indian woman with whom he had quarrelled.

Moving on to Salomon, Berenger met with complaints about the type of rice supplied (Saigon), which the workers considered made them weak and sickly, and indeed discovered that there had been four recent cases of beri-beri. Further investigation showed that little pork, fish or turtle meat was consumed, that the workers did little or no fishing on their own account and that, because thefts were so commonplace, they had all but abandoned rearing poultry or growing vegetables. Finally, Berenger needed to investigate a murder which had occurred on the preceding New Year's Eve. It emerged that to celebrate the occasion the manager, Jean-Baptiste Adam ('an experienced old hand'), had donated a bottle of wine to every worker, male and female, and had allowed all who wanted to buy nearly half a litre more. Half of the witnesses to the murder admitted to having been drunk at the time. When Berenger quit the island, he left strict instructions about adherence to the legal limits on alcohol consumption and took with him thirteen witnesses, the manager and the accused.[12] Fortunately, the return passage to Port Louis took only nine days, for space had to be found for a total of 40 deck passengers, the construction of extra shelter for them having contributed to the *Union de la Digue*'s late departure.

1923 was – if we except a higher than normal number of deaths in sailing accidents (see inset), four in Diego Garcia and two in Peros Banhos – an uneventful year (the other three plantations went uninspected). It is however worth referring to the very detailed attention given by magistrates to 'housekeeping' matters. The cleanliness of the 'camp', measurements of the workers' accommodation, the state of the hospitals[13] and their equipment, the keeping of attendance and payment records, the shop accounts, the adequacy of the prisons, the crime records – all these were meticulously checked, not infrequently bringing to light over-casual supervision of employees such as the shop managers. As in earlier times, one of the most frequent sources of controversy was the amount and quality of rice provided. The standard ration was measured out in a *gamelle* intended to hold 10½ lbs. However, different sorts of rice had differing weight/volume ratios, with the result that tests made at the time of magistrates' visits sometimes showed over and sometimes under-provision … Another problem, which we have already encountered, now emerged on a more serious scale. In 1920, one of the consequences of the loss of the *Ste. Marthe* had been that few of the ships chartered to bring supplies were authorised under the Passenger Acts to carry any substantial number of passengers. Consequently, on each visit, some of the workers whose contracts had expired had to wait for the next ship. Despite the magistrates' clear recommendations on the subject, no steps were being taken to get the ships certified. Given that all the islands were short of their full complement of labour, it is hard to escape the conclusion that the companies were using this as a technique to keep workers against their will without incurring the substantial fines that would otherwise apply. At the same time, the magistrates invariably reported that the daily tasks set for the workers were far from excessive and were most often completed well before midday.

All these matters came into sharper focus the following year. In fact, only seven months had elapsed between Berenger's visit in October 1923 aboard the non-certified schooner *St. Géran* (290 tons) and his return in May 1924 to the two larger atolls, this time aboard the barque *Ione* (520 tons), a vessel slightly better able to cope with that voyage's close encounter with the cyclone that had destroyed some 1,500 coconut palms on those islands. To the magistrate's astonishment, however, the *Ione* too was not registered under the Passenger Acts and could not take more than twelve deck and cabin passengers, with the result that only nine of the eighteen workers who requested return passages could be accommodated. As to on-island problems, having little to investigate in the way of crimes or disasters, Berenger turned his attention to other matters, such as an unpleasant

Small boats, big risks

If storms at sea brought dangers for ocean going ships (in 1923, eight of the workers bound for Salomon aboard *Union de la Digue* died en route), rough weather was no less a hazard for the small vessels serving the Chagos islands' daily needs. In 1921, Elie, one of the *commandeurs* on Egmont, 'disappeared at sea'. In 1922, four men drowned when their boat capsized in a squall in the lagoon of Diego Garcia. In 1923, Peros Banhos lost its best *commandeur*, Aurélien Julien, who was the helmsman, and a member of the management staff, Noël Ducray, when the latter held on to the mainsheet, instead of releasing it during a gybe; only the three passengers survived the capsize to tell the tale. In the same year, two men with bad reputations, accompanied by a woman and child, stole Diego Garcia's valuable 5-ton pinnace and decamped at night, never being heard of again – without ballast the vessel would have been extremely unstable in the open sea. In 1924, a party of eight men were returning from Sea Cow Island, just to the south of Eagle Island, when their boat was struck by two huge waves, the first filling it with water and the second sinking it in a spot 'where boats often capsized'. Six of the crew swam to the shore, but the boatswain, Joseph Bonhomme, a *commandeur* and strong swimmer, drowned as he tried to save the fourteen-year-old Emmanuel Bistoquet, grandson of his partner. In 1926, a man known as Langouti drowned while attempting to cross the Diego Garcia bay on a stormy day in a small pirogue. And so it went on, with a series of accidents in Peros Banhos. In 1926, one man drowned off Ile Longue; in 1927, two disappeared at sea near Ile Poule; and in 1928 one other suffered the same fate close to Ile du Coin. Lastly, a man called Toussaint Baznath died at sea near Eagle Island in 1928; the magistrate referred the case to the Procureur Général, suggesting that either foul play or management liability was involved.

Source: Miscellaneous magistrates' reports.

contagious disease affecting the islands' asses and the nutritional problems of the workers at Peros Banhos (where lack of vegetables and the absence of supplies of castor oil were blamed for severe constipation). While praising the managers for succeeding in maintaining production levels with labour as much as 25% below the established complement, and admitting to his lack of expertise, he commented severely on the islands' 'antiquated methods' and low productivity: with a simple motor, oil extraction could reach 90%, instead of 70%; the asses could be left to forage, gain in health and be sold; the women employed in cutting grass for fodder would no longer be required; and the cost – say Rs 20,000 – of the investment soon be recouped in higher profits.

Needless to say, Berenger's criticisms, when conveyed to the *Nouvelle Société*, provoked a lengthy and spirited riposte. Richard Lionnet (*fils*), the Managing Agent, explained that, in the company's view, the problems affecting the islands' donkeys were in the main the result of inbreeding, but that the importation of fresh breeding stock from Mauritius would result in the transfer of other diseases, not found in the islands; as regards human sicknesses and remedies, it was in the company's interest to have fit workers and they always responded to every request made by their nurse-dispensers.[14] Concerning the workers' diet, the latter, according to Lionnet, had only themselves to blame:

> The natural indolence of the island creoles is the sole cause of their lack of well-being. In spite of all the facilities afforded to them, they prefer to do nothing rather than tend to gardening; the plots around their houses remain unkempt and they have no intention of cultivating them to provide vegetables. Nor can the company spare the manpower to grow vegetables for sale (apart from providing vegetable gardens for the hospital and prison). And here is an example of their indolence: ever since their pay was increased substantially in 1918, they have not gathered the beeswax which the company used to buy from them, even though beehives abound on the islands.

Turning to company matters, Lionnet maintained that it did keep up with progress. He cited the introduction of equipment to produce copra from 1911 onwards and experiments with a de-husking machine (which had not produced the results expected of it). At the same time, he claimed that the efforts of the *Emden*'s engineers in 1914 to repair the island's motorboat had been ineffectual – thus, apparently, seeking to demonstrate that internal combustion engines, with their tendency to break down, had little to contribute to the work of the plantations. As to the extraction of a higher proportion of coconut oil, this had the disadvantage of reducing the nutritional value of the residue, used to feed pigs, the only source of fresh meat on the islands. Regarding the use of vessels not registered to carry passengers Lionnet played his ace: the company had just bought the barque *Janes*, lying at Hull in northern England, and this vessel would be registered to carry up to 49 deck passengers, additional to those having cabins.[15] Meanwhile, alterations had been made to the *St. Géran*, to allow her also to carry passengers.

sv *Diego* under full sail. Image by kind permission of Adrian McCloy.

Rechristened *Diego*, the company's new ship, under the captaincy of Henri Adam, brother of the Salomon manager, was soon in service and made her first voyage with a magistrate aboard in September 1925.[16] She proved a robust and speedy vessel, once achieving an average speed of 9 knots over a 24 hour period. On this occasion her outward passage to Diego Garcia took twelve days and her return from Peros Banhos only eight days. The acting Magistrate, R. Le Cudennec, evidently armed with a copy of Berenger's previous report, was able to see that his predecessor's criticisms and recommendations had been fully attended to on both atolls. It was clear that both plantations were functioning smoothly with no serious disturbances, crimes or accidents. There had however been a sad event early in the year: Marcel Dupavillon, assistant manager of the East Point estate, and his wife had been found dead in their bed one morning. The manager, Suzor, had returned to Mauritius shortly afterwards, together with some others able to give evidence. Le Cudennec's investigation was therefore postponed until his return to Port Louis. No trace of the papers relating to the case has yet been discovered, but, since no charges were laid, it would appear that no other party was involved.

What then had been happening on the three small plantations since Berenger visited them in 1922? They were not visited in either 1923 or 1925. In 1924 an acting magistrate, E.J. Colin, found that for all three islands, although the workers were paid at least Rs 12 per month, rather than the Rs 8 of their contracts, almost the whole of the wages paid out over the preceding two years was spent in the company's shops. The main concern he expressed related to the high child mortality in Salomon and Eagle Island. In 1926 Berenger returned to all three. Eagle Island he found dirty, a condition which the new (unnamed) manager, as ever, blamed on his predecessor. At Six Islands, drunkenness was still a problem, while Berenger also cancelled the contracts of several workers on grounds of their habitual idleness; another individual, who had assaulted the chief *commandeur*, was sent to prison in Mauritius. At Salomon, the magistrate was glad to notice a workforce that was much more cheerful and healthy than those of the other two islands and also in comparison with what he had seen four years earlier. One most unusual incident had occurred: a man had broken into the house of the dispenser, who had taken out his revolver; the gun went off after the intruder had snatched at its barrel, leaving the intruder with severe wounds in his hip. Careful nursing by the dispenser was bringing about a good recovery at the time of Berenger's visit and, as the victim did not want to press charges, the magistrate let matters rest. As for prices, on all three islands substantial errors in the calculation of the 25% mark-up resulted in over-charging. When this was pointed out to the company's Agent (who was visiting the islands at the time), de Caila explained that the calculations had been done in Mauritius, by the company's accountant, 'who was not good at figures'. They would, he said, be checked carefully in future.

Diego Garcia: the Edouard d'Argent affair

As Berenger was completing his inspections early in September 1926, Le Cudennec had just reached Diego Garcia. The state of affairs there was dire.[17] The company had decided to close the Pointe Marianne establishment for good and, while most of the workers had been transferred to East Point, many buildings had still to be demolished. The population of the island had fallen to 386, with a working population (including staff and their dependents) of 287. The comparable figures for 1925 had been 446 and 326. Not only were labourers in short supply and in turmoil, but the manager who had replaced the calm and experienced Suzor had dismissed four of the six managerial staff. Of the other two, one had committed suicide on 3 May of that year, while the other, only two weeks later, had been murdered. News of these events had reached Mauritius in early July before Le Cudennec set out and he was therefore accompanied by a

Edouard d'Argent. Image courtesy of Margaret McCloy.

doctor and a police sergeant. His general conclusion was that 'the labourers are being roughly handled and ill-treated by the new Manager, Mr Edouard d'Argent who has no experience of the work in the Oil Islands. The *employés* too had to complain of ill-treatment'. D'Argent was, it should be added, still on Diego Garcia when the magistrate's visit took place; he returned to Mauritius soon afterwards.

The full story of the two deaths and their investigation proved complex and macabre, beginning with the exhumation of both bodies. The first to die, Sydney Fidelia, was judged to have shot himself and, although no clear motive could be established, 'the ill-treatment of the Manager … was certainly not foreign to it'. As to the death of Marcel Henri Bigara,[18] the post-mortem demonstrated that he had been murdered, but Le Cudennec was not able to say who was the perpetrator. Evidence found included subcutaneous blotches on the corpse, indicating a violent struggle, a knife at the scene too blunt to cause a cut so clean and deep as the one detected, the cut also being on the right side of the neck – impossible for the victim himself, a right-hander, to inflict. The Mauritius Procureur-Général, presented with Le Cudennec's report, decided that the case should be re-examined by the next magistrate to visit the island.

That visit took place one year later. Magistrate Hanning's report, made immediately upon his return, did not go into detail, but concluded as follows:

> I wish to place on record the great assistance I received from Police Sergeant Le Meme … and it is due to his clever police work that the true facts of the awful crime have been revealed. When I left Mauritius the chain of evidence consisted entirely of missing links, if I may be allowed such an Irishism; and at the time of writing two persons (including the Manager) have been arrested on a charge of murder.

Hanning had brought back with him nineteen witnesses from Diego Garcia and two from Peros Banhos, while d'Argent had already returned of his own accord. There ensued two trials. At the first, held on 8 May 1928, Patrice Besage, one of the *commandeurs*, nick-named Catawon, confessed to the murder, giving a detailed account also of the pressure to which he was subjected by d'Argent; this included making him drink a great deal of whisky and, armed with a pistol, accompanying him to Bigara's house (the two dwellings were quite close and faced each other across a courtyard). Only when d'Argent threatened to use the gun did Catawon strike the fatal blow (another macabre element was that Catawon's duties include butchering pigs and he used the knife provided for that purpose). The jury duly found Catawon guilty, but entered a strong plea for leniency, which the judge and Governor's Executive Council had no hesitation in accepting. Under the rules of evidence, Catawon's own testimony could not be used against d'Argent. The case presented against him rested primarily on the evidence given by two other *commandeurs*, which strongly corroborated that of Catawon, and also on an (unsuccessful) attempt by the prosecution to show that Bigara was over-familiar with Mrs d'Argent, thus providing a motive for the crime. The jury acquitted d'Argent of murder and, by 7-2 majority, of complicity by giving instructions to Catawon for the murder, but failed to agree (the vote was 6–3) on another charge, of aiding and abetting. Consequently a fresh trial had to be held. It took place on 23 July under a different judge and with a different jury, which found him guilty of this charge. Like Catawon, his sentence was for life imprisonment. It began in late 1928, but d'Argent died only two years later.

All accounts of d'Argent concur in describing him as (like his father and sister) 'very authoritarian'. One of his descendants explains that he made himself extremely unpopular by seeking to instil greater discipline and, by that means, increase the plantation's output – the purpose for which he had been appointed.[19] This last phrase suggests that the d'Argents were known to important members of the Company's board. Indeed, a member of the d'Argent family had served (briefly and badly) as Manager of Eagle Island in 1890, while the manager of Peros Banhos at that time (Charles Lionnet) had been a fellow passenger with another d'Argent on a return voyage to Mauritius in 1891.[20] D'Argent was born in 1877, so would have been about 47 or 48 when he became manager at East Point. His parents had both been born in Seychelles, but he himself had moved to Mauritius by the time he married Marie Mauricia Guillot in 1917. He was said to have been on the staff of a sugar estate called Riche en Eau. There was no formal link between this estate[21] and the *Nouvelle Société* and only a distant one between the Lionnets and d'Argent, in that the latter's sister had married a distant cousin of Richard (*fils*), but it is questionable whether the risky decision to appoint him would have been taken by Richard alone.[22]

Changes in production

Whatever the precise reasons for picking d'Argent, the problems observed by magistrates must have played a part in the fortunes of the *Nouvelle Société*. Over the decade from 1920–1930, production moved away from coconut oil to concentrate on copra. There were also several bumper years (notably 1922, 1926 and 1930 on Diego Garcia) and several very poor years (1927 on Diego Garcia, 1924 and 1926 on Peros Banhos). Clearly the performance of Diego Garcia in the last couple of years of Suzor's tenure must have been a disappointment; equally d'Argent's results in 1926, though bought at a heavy price, were a big improvement, as shown in Table 15.3 opposite (exceptional year figures underlined). For convenience, we include the comparable figures relating to the islands owned by the *Société Huilière de Salomon, Six Iles et Trois Frères.*

Table 15.3   Chagos Exports of coconut oil ('000 litres) and copra ('000 kg), 1920–1930

		1920	1921	1922	1923	1924	1925	1926	1927	1928	1929	1930
Diego	Oil	273	189	<u>442</u>	***	141	174	157	<u>61</u>	42	30	13
	Copra	40	137	<u>595</u>	–	253	246	<u>579</u>	<u>253</u>	401	480	<u>925</u>
Peros	Oil	153	71	146	–	<u>88</u>	120	<u>67</u>	38	16	11	–
	Copra	308	303	289	–	<u>180</u>	277	<u>200</u>	440	429	404	<u>548</u>
Salomon	Oil	111	137	126	–	145	101	85	57	11	–	12
	Copra	–	–	–	–	30	52	34	123	216	147	301
Six Islands	Oil	27	59	65	–	70	55	50	3	<1	–	5
	Copra	–	–	–	–	10	20	6	71	205	94	169
Eagle	Oil	67	59	48	–	41	51	51	–	–	–	2
	Copra	–	–	–	–	–	–	1	66	120	42	105

<u>Source</u>: Mauritius 'Blue Books' (TNA CO 172 series).

*** No detailed export figures were compiled for 1923

As we have already seen (page 267), the decision to concentrate oil production in Mauritius was taken in about 1910, but we can only guess whether any detailed attention was given to its consequences for the operations of the island plantations. Clearly, there would be need for many fewer of the highly paid *moulineurs*, who operated the oil mills; and there would have been knock-on effects for those involved in animal husbandry: less *poonac*, fewer pigs, fewer donkeys, less requirement for provender, and so, perhaps, fewer workers. Much more importantly, the change removed whatever incentive might have existed to improve the skills and education of the Chagos workforce. Also, notwithstanding the low price received for coconut oil, that of copra was likely to be lower, thus reducing the direct income of the plantations. We were able to compare the prices obtained for copra only for one short period, from 1927–1932. Two conclusions emerged: prices showed a steady decline from 1927 onwards; and the prices obtained by the *Nouvelle Société* for the two big plantations were invariably higher, usually by some 10%, than those for the three small islands. We shall return to this problem in Chapter 17 (see page 345 *et sqq.*).

The later 1920s

When Hanning visited Diego Garcia in July 1927, d'Argent was in Mauritius awaiting the outcome of the judicial investigation. Hanning found the people of the island greatly relieved that their manager had not returned. He remarked nevertheless that 'the type of labourers has also changed for the worse, and the old labourer is not the same good worker as before'.[23] His inspection of Peros Banhos immediately afterwards was uneventful and the conditions there entirely orderly. Although the magistrate did not name the manager there, he was John Lewis Powell, who was shortly afterwards transferred to Diego Garcia as d'Argent's replacement.[24] When Berenger inspected Diego Garcia in September 1928, he found plenty to criticise, in particular the dirty condition of the camp, attributable to the lack of labour (actually, the working population, at 299, was slightly higher than it had been the previous year), remarking also that 'the best men are still reluctant to engage for Diego and quite a number' – actually eighteen men, ten women and sixteen children – returned with him to Mauritius. He also renewed his critique of excessive drinking (see inset). All the same he was able to comment that

> Although things are not working very smoothly just now, and the men are inferior in all respects to those working at Peros Banhos, yet there has been a marked improvement. I attribute the change to Mr J. Powell's short but effective administration.[25]

Powell had however already decided to leave the Chagos and his replacement, a M. De Chasteigner Dumée (who had previously managed Agalega), had arrived on the same ship as the magistrate. After his visit to Diego Garcia, Berenger proceeded to Peros Banhos. He found no cause for complaint and noted that in general the men's physique was fine and that they had a strong and healthy appearance. It was unclear whether Powell had yet been replaced or, if he had, by whom.

No reports survive of inspections made to the three smaller plantations in 1927 or 1928, although Magistrate Raoul Brouard's reports for 1929 make it clear

Wine consumption at Diego Garcia in 1928

Ten casks of wine were sent by the last boat. Six casks, with 14° alcohol in it, sold at 75 ct the litre and four casks, with 16° alcohol, sold at Rs. 1.95 the litre. On inquiry I was informed that wine, with 14° alcohol, keeps very well for many months, in spite of the excessive heat registered on the islands. Being convinced most of the mischief done is traceable to the highly alcoholised and intoxicating wine which most of the men drink, with empty stomach, by ½ litre at a time, I recommend that only wine with 14° should be sent to the islands. The men's passion for strong drink is so great that the majority of them and many women drink from 3 to 4 litres of wine every month at Rs. 1.95 the litre [so that] more than 50% of their pay is spent on wine alone without mentioning tobacco, another important item of expenditure.

Source: TNA CO 167/862/8.

that a visit did take place in the previous year.[26] The most striking difference between the state of affairs in 1926 and that obtaining in 1929 is that the monthly pay rates, stated as being Rs 8 and Rs 6, make no reference to extra sums being paid. The working populations of both Salomon and Eagle Islands had declined; so had the animal populations, particularly of horses and pigs. Furthermore, Brouard reported that the company had recently instructed managers to prevent payments being made for extra work; indeed, in comparison with 1926, such payments had been reduced by an average of 90%. These changes may in part have resulted from the big decline in oil production, but also suggest financial difficulties.

In addition, the magistrate expressed some concern about the general health of the workers and in particular the prevalence of ankylostomiasis (hookworm) on these three islands. One of the islands' dispensers was then instructed how to identify and treat the disease, leading the Mauritius medical department to comment severely on the matter: 'The two serious difficulties in combating the disease at Six Islands are firstly soil sanitation and secondly the indifference of the population towards both treatment and the most elementary hygienic measures.' The fact of the matter was that, while magisterial inspection had brought home to managers the importance of keeping wells protected from contamination, the results of animal and human defecation were simply left to nature. Readers will recall the vivid descriptions of the messiness of Six Islands in the 1830s. Nothing much changed over the next century and magistrates tiptoed around the issue in their reports. In fact it was not until the 1950s that frank descriptions of the squalor appeared. When Brouard's report was drawn to the Company Agent's attention, all that Henri Sauvage, who had succeeded de Caila, could say was that progress in dealing with hookworm was proceeding rather slowly despite the measures taken.[27]

Diego Garcia and Peros Banhos were visited in August 1929 by Hanning, travelling by steamer, the ss *Surcouf*, rather than the sv *Diego*. He found himself confronted, more dramatically than Brouard, by the two major issues just discussed.[28] Attending roll-call on his first morning, he heard the new manager, M. Lois Chateignier Dumée, announcing serious and sudden reductions in the labourers' wages. He had clearly misunderstood his instructions and Hanning was able to intervene to see that no change was implemented pending further orders from Port Louis. In fact, much smaller reductions were planned, affecting only the bonus element of total pay. But the cause was just as serious: a drop in the copra market and the precarious position of the whole industry. As regards ankylostomiasis (the prevailing element in sick-bay attendance), the former establishment at Pointe Marianne had been disinfected, but Hanning had to advise that huts at East Point be moved to a fresh site, given the pervasiveness of infestation at the existing camp. As for population, however, only

Peros Banhos showed a decrease (10%), while Diego Garcia had some 20% more labourers than in 1926.[29]

Verdict

As readers will have observed, this account of developments in the decade following the end of the 1914–18 war relies almost exclusively on the (incomplete) series of reports by the Visiting Magistrates. Nevertheless, it is hard to avoid the conclusion that the two sets of owners did little to advance their long-term business interests, let alone to improve the squalid physical conditions, primitive welfare provisions or derisory pay of their employees. There was for example no investment in more modern equipment and no education or training, such as would bring about increased productivity. Indeed, wherever they had choices between increasing profitability in the islands and improving their processing operations in Mauritius they chose the latter. Additionally, the pay structure and pricing of goods in the island boutiques went to reinforce company power – and required constant close inspection by magistrates. Their whole strategy, in fact, was to use their monopoly power to benefit themselves and a small body of shareholders at the direct expense of the island workforce. The tremors they felt in 1929, set in motion by that year's bank crash in the United States, were however but the foretaste of much harsher economic conditions ahead, which the Chagos plantation owners were ill-placed to overcome.

Notes to Chapter 15

1 TNA CO 167/837 Both reports were enclosed with the Governor's Despatch No. 185 dated 15 May 1921. Sir Hesketh Bell explained the absence of reports in 1919 as being 'owing to the magistrates having to be continually employed in Mauritius' and the delay in forwarding the reports compiled in 1920 as the result of the protracted correspondence with the companies concerned.

2 After the *Ste. Marthe* was wrecked it became necessary to charter vessels such as the barque *Kassa* (287 tons). There were also changes of ownership: Richard Lionnet had sold the *Nonna Adèle* to a group including H.G. Ducray, while France Lionnet, Richard's cousin, now owned the *Ione*. The latter did not have much life left in her and by 1924 was being used simply as a cargo storage hulk; her role in trading with the smaller islands was transferred to another schooner, *Union de la Digue*.

3 At Peros Banhos, however, the workers had been deprived of the benefit due to them by the plantation's shopkeeper, who charged the traditional mark-up and pocketed the difference until he was found out and dismissed.

4 It appears that, following the loss of the *Ste. Marthe*, the reduced size *gamelle* was made to help eke out supplies until further deliveries of rice were received.

5 The last complete round of visits had taken place in 1916; in 1917 visits had been made to Diego Garcia and Peros Banhos (but the reports were not forwarded to London); in 1918 Salomon alone had been visited.

6 TNA CO 167/837 E. Koenig, Explanatory Report on Ordinance No. 54 of 1920, enclosed with Despatch No. 19 dated 14 January 1921.

7 TNA CO 167/837 ref 'Colonial Office'. A Dr Laurent called on Mr Amery in early November 1920, telling him of 'unsatisfactory rumours of the state of things in the Lesser Dependencies, especially as regards prison conditions, food and the prevalence of the truck system'. Amery evidently wrote a demi-official letter to the Governor, which was not however referred to in the subsequent reporting.

8 These details were reported by the *Sydney Daily Commercial News and Shipping List* (12 and 17 May 1921).

9 Chelin, J-M., *op.cit* (pp. 41–42). It was Captain Nicolin who passed on an account of this event to one of the dedicatees of this book, Paul Caboche.

10 Peros Banhos, Table 21; Six Islands, Table 39; Eagle Island, Table 54; Salomon, Table 59; Diego Garcia, Table 66.

11 TNA CO 167/842 Enclosure to Despatch dated 6 August 1922. Of a total of 50 deaths in the preceding fourteen months, no less than twenty were of children under the age of eight.

12 When M. Julienne had left Six Islands, he was temporarily replaced by Adam's assistant, William McIntyre, who returned to Salomon with Berenger to take temporary charge of the island; the very experienced dispenser R. Gonthier (who had taken passage with Berenger from Mauritius) was left in charge of Six Islands.

13 TNA CO 167/850 Enclosure to Despatch No. 24 dated 12 January 1925. In paragraph 5 of his report on Salomon, Eagle and Six Islands, Magistrate Colin described the buildings thus: 'The Hospital in each of these islands is a large coral building with a thatched roof consisting of two large wards, one for men and the other for women, and of a smaller room which is used for a pharmacy …'

14 TNA CO 167/852 Richard Lionnet, letter dated 13 October 1924, enclosed with Mauritius Despatch No. 24, dated 12 January 1925.

15 Launched in 1868 at the Sunderland yard of Iliff & Mountsey, 145 feet long and with a capacity for 370 tons of cargo below deck, she was christened *Charlotte* and used in the Mediterranean, where she was sold in 1907 to an Italian shipowner, who renamed her *Tomaso Drago*. In 1912, she was sold again, this time to a Swedish shipowner, who gave her his company's name, *Janes*. This ship was the pride and joy of Richard (*fils*),who had a full colour painting made from the photo of the vessel under sail. That photo was taken by his cousin, France Lionnet, who sailed in her as a deck-hand.

16 The ship's records show that she was initially sold to J.R. Lionnet & Co, but ownership passed fairly soon to the *Nouvelle Société*. Thus, to start with, the Lionnets would have been able to charge the *Société* for use of the vessel; but, once the latter had sufficient cash to purchase the ship, it could save itself a regular cost. The profits and losses to the individuals involved would make a fascinating study in conflicts of interest!

17 TNA CO 167/859 and TNA CO 167/810/10 are the most important of several files in which these events are discussed, particularly in despatches Nos. 334 dated 1 August 1927 and 433 dated 25 October 1928.

18 Henri, sometimes referred to as Marcel Bigara, a single man aged 23, was the shopkeeper at East Point and also a close friend of Fidelia. The account of the case by Chelin (*op.cit*. pp. 43–46) gives some additional details culled from contemporary press accounts, demonstrating great public interest in the case and a good deal of support for d'Argent.

19 Patrice Lionnet, a great-nephew, explained the matter thus: 'Il s'est fait mal aimer, voire détester, pensant par de l'autorité amener une plus grande discipline, et par là, faire remonter la production et justifier ainsi ce pour quoi on l'avait propulsé là.' [He made himself disliked, even detested, believing that by demonstrating his authority he would bring about improved discipline, increase the level of production and thereby achieve the purpose of his appointment to the post.]

20 TNA CO 167/740 Enclosure to Despatch dated 27 June 1901 Report of H. Hewetson dated 19 November 1891. This includes mention of an otherwise unidentified d'Argent as having been manager of Eagle Island from September to December 1890, one of a series of short-term appointments during a long period devoid of magisterial inspection. Shipping records (BL Colindale *Mauritius Commercial Gazette* Nos. 909, 913 and 923) however mention an A.F. d'Argent as having travelled to Eagle in September and

returned by the same vessel, the schooner *Venus*, in January 1891. They also list E. d'Argent and J. Lionnet as passengers aboard the *Lady Howard*, which arrived at Port Louis from Peros Banhos on 10 October 1891. The initials given hinder rather than help identification. Those of Edouard d'Argent were R.H.E., while his father's were A.R.H. The Lionnet who managed Peros was known as Charles, but it is probable that he had a Church-approved first name, the commonest such being Joseph; and passenger lists generally used the first initial on a traveller's passport. Thus it is reasonably certain that Edouard's father did not visit the Chagos, but not completely impossible that Edouard went as a teenager. What is clear is that the two families were acquainted in a Chagos context from as early as 1890.

21 During the 1920s the estate was owned by the Beau Vallon company, formed by members of the de Rochecouste family, its previous owners.

22 In 1927–29, the *Nouvelle Société*'s Board, chaired by Sir H. Leclézio, comprised Philippe de Caila, H. Ducray, A Hourquebie, Ivanoff Desvaux de Marigny, Joseph Mallac, France Lionnet, Ernest Lagane and Edouard Desbleds. Another company chaired by Leclézio and involving members of the Lionnet family was the Compagnie de Frégate Ltd., in which France Lionnet was one of five Board members and Richard *fils* the managing Agent.

23 TNA CO 167/861/10 Second enclosure to Despatch No. 241 dated 14 June.

24 Powell had first been employed as steward-dispenser in Peros Banhos after funds for his training as a doctor ran out. He was a son of Dr Powell, who had investigated medical conditions in the Archipelago in 1908 (see page 280). He later married the sister of Raoul Caboche, who became manager of Salomon in 1931. Powell's son in turn worked as the accountant for the Mauritian company which processed the Oil Islands' output. His was a typical example of the familial connections which proliferated in the management of these islands.

25 TNA CO 167/862/8 Enclosure to Despatch No. 481 dated 19 December 1928.

26 TNA CO 167/865/4 Enclosures to Mauritius Despatch No. 419, dated 22 October 1929.

27 *Ibid.* H. Sauvage, undated letter enclosed with Mauritius Despatch of 5 November 1929.

28 TNA CO 167/867/13 W.J. Hanning, Report on visit to Diego Garcia and Peros Banhos dated 31 December 1929, enclosed with Mauritius Despatch No. 35 of 5 February 1930.

29 As for animals, Peros Banhos showed little change, while Diego Garcia had many fewer pigs and quite a lot more donkeys.

16

Customs and Characters:
a kaleidoscope of island life

Introduction

So far, from this narrative of events, there has gradually emerged the out-line of a way of life characteristic of the Archipelago, which naturally had many features in common with other islands of the western Indian Ocean and indeed Creole society in Mauritius. Hints of its culture, as distinct from the organisation, work and development of economic activity, appear from time to time. However, it was not until the 1930s that coherent descriptions of the spe-cifically cultural aspects of life were undertaken. There are two main sources for these: Fr. Roger Dussercle[1] and Mme Marcelle Lagesse. Dussercle was a French Catholic priest (1902–1975), who undertook military service in Morocco before being ordained in 1926 and spent most of his career (1927–1951) in Mauritius. He served a parish in Port Louis, but also devoted himself to the spiritual welfare of the islanders of the archipelago, which he visited at least six times between 1933 and 1942; although he was no anthropologist and his affection for these *pauvres bougres*' is shot through with exasperation at what he considered to be the bar-barity of certain rituals, his first-hand observations of local conditions are lively and detailed, while his own adventures and misadventures give a vivid insight into the risks of inter-island travel. Marcelle Lagesse (1916–2011) was the daugh-ter of Raoul Caboche, manager of Salomon between 1931 and 1952. After being widowed at a young age, she spent the early years of the war with her father, before returning to Mauritius to work in secret operations against the Vichy regime in Reunion. Her 'cover' was that of a journalist for the government propaganda journal *Savez-vous Que?*, which printed short articles based on her experiences in the Chagos. She then turned to fiction and became a well-known author, but some of her early work was semi-fictional, in which the events were real, but the names invented.[2] Her final visit to the Chagos was made as a Social Security official in 1961.

Since descriptions by these two authors (and others) of the ceremonies and activities embodying the culture are distinct from our narrative, it may help readers too to have the cultural elements discussed separately. Both Dussercle and Lagesse, while deeply interested in and sympathetic towards the islanders, were nevertheless outsiders looking in on the culture they described. For a born-and-bred islander's own perspective readers must await Chapter 20, in which M. Fernand Mandarin, born in 1943, recalls life on Peros as he experienced it until his enforced exile in 1967. Here we draw only on his detailed description of the recipes for *calou* and *bacca*, the locally made alcoholic drinks. The contrast provided by Mandarin's memoir has two further dimensions. Just too old to attend the newly-opened school, he found himself, as an ordinary worker, required to turn his hand to whatever jobs the managers, good and bad, might require of him. Also, living a generation later than those whose lives occupy this Chapter, his memories demonstrate both the continuity of life style and the changes wrought by the passage of time. We hope, however, that the following paragraphs will offer helpful background to understanding daily life in the Archipelago. For example, our narrative of island life has not so far involved looking inside the workers' cottages, as Dussercle did, providing far more than a merely physical insight into their lives:

> They are all the same: rooms separated by partitions made of matted palm leaves and furnished in much the same way as those of the poorest Creoles – at least those living in rural areas – back home in Mauritius: a straw pallet set up on 'piling', clothing in tumbled heaps or hung up by string. That's for the bed chamber, if you can give it so pompous a name. As for the saloon – to be someone, you must have a saloon – the walls are plastered with postcards of all sorts, New Year, April Fools' Day, Joyous Easter, but mostly with illustrations of lovers sighing their amorous sighs: it's the craze. On a cheap sideboard knick-knacks fight for space with purely ornamental containers and, occasionally, a common-or-garden wind-up gramophone. Drums, covered in tightly tensioned goatskin and so essential to setting a *séga* going, are usually tucked away under the rafters – especially when the Reverend Father is visiting and getting so worked up with his railing against this savage African dance …[3]

The following year, 1934, Dussercle reported with evident glee his visit to the prison in Diego Garcia, where two young men had been incarcerated for killing a donkey, claiming to have found it dead and seeking the manager's permission to '*prend so lapeau pour faire ène tambour*' ['skin it to make a drum'].[4] Music was indeed a fundamental element of the islanders' lives, resorted to for every possible purpose. Singing especially drew on everyday experiences for its vitality, while dancing was based more on ancestral rhythms and instrumentation; and the two became combined when dances celebrated particular events. All this music was termed *séga*, a word originating in Mozambique and first mentioned in Agalega, where Auguste Leduc was the manager from 1827–1839. The latter's brother, St. Elme Leduc, left some manuscript notes, based on researches by Auguste, from which Dussercle quotes as follows:

> The *Tschiéga* or *Chéga*, a dance originating in Mozambique, is the one generally practised. However, those of Madagascan origin sometimes practise their own country's dance. This one is more modest, less lascivious; the dancers retain their balance without contorting themselves, their arms and hands waving gracefully, and stamping their feet lightly in perfect time, the dance being accompanied by a chorus of melancholy, languorous song, sung in unison to bring out its melody. The men, spear in hand – or a rod simulating a spear – pretend to fight, with threatening gestures, retreats, advances and a thousand contortions, emitting occasional shouts, as if to frighten an adversary.
>
> As for the *Tschiéga*, it can be seen as providing the most monstrously obscene spectacle; while the beat of the tom-tom and the simultaneous medley of shouting voices produce the most deafening and hellish concert anyone could imagine.

Evidently aware that this quotation was somewhat confusing, Dussercle goes on to explain that, in the Indian Ocean islands, the Mozambique *séga* (spelt *Tschiéga* by Leduc) and the gentler Madagascan version (spelt *Chéga*) have become amalgamated to produce the form of dance observable at the time he was writing.[5]

Some songs (*çantés zavirons*) helped oarsmen to maintain the rhythm of their rowing, often over long distances in the extreme heat of flat calms and, just like

Salomon manager's whaler. Image courtesy of J-M. Chelin.

the sea shanties of other societies, helped lighten the burden of heavy or boring collective tasks. Listened to across the lagoon, as Marcelle Lagesse recalled, the *çantés zavirons*, in which the singers drew out the final note of each line, matching the rhythm of their oars, gave a cadence that accentuated the themes of their songs, often laments about partings, separation, lost love, death, or sometimes extempore comment on the voyage in progress.

Likewise, the women, spending much of their day sitting on the ground scooping coconuts and chopping the flesh, played a major role in composing new verses. Thus, the *séga* songs came to provide a means of remembering dramatic or humorous events, making sly, not to say scabrous, comments about individuals, or adding to the atmosphere of dances celebrating special occasions. One example, cited by Dussercle as having a particularly catchy tune, told of an island manager who had taken a 'concubine'. Dussercle, for all his moral indignation about uninhibited dancing, was an educated musician, who wrote down both the words of several songs and the notation of their melodies.[6] Invariably, however, he disguised the names of identifiable individuals.

Whether or not dancing was involved, a lead singer would provide verses, often freshly minted, with choruses for all to join in. *Séga* dances, the only form of collective entertainment until the 1930s, were held on most Saturday nights, on certain feast days (for example, that of the Assumption – *Séga la Vierge,* New Year – *Séga banannée*), to celebrate marriages, baptisms or the departure of the company ship – *Séga Navire,* or, as Dussercle put it, whenever a pretext could be found.[7] One unusual example he cites is of a *Séga Zenfants,* to be danced by children, where the words relate the unhappiness of a little girl having only a very tattered dress to wear on New Year's Day and being cruelly chided by the rest, who are kitted out in smart new clothing.[8] A most valuable description of the role played by *séga* in the socio-economic conditions obtaining in the Chagos has recently been provided by a social anthropologist specialising in studies of the Chagos, Dr Laura Jeffery. She also gives examples of songs involving individual managers, including Raoul Caboche.[9] Indeed, Jeffery's work, although concerned primarily with a later period, is one of several sources for a growing corpus of *séga* material, both in the original Kreol and in translation.[10] The special value of Dussercle's work is that it covers a time period for which few if any oral testimonies survive.

Dussercle's disgust at *séga* dancing was exceeded only by his views of contemporary French dances, which the islanders also from time to time essayed. And yet, and yet … curiosity prevailed. He was persuaded to observe one dance, having in turn persuaded the young men that on this occasion it would take place close to the Manager's house and would end practically before it had begun, at the unheard of time of 8.30 p.m.

Two braziers are lit and sparkle before the square silhouette of the manager's house, spitting smoke and sparks from the crackling palm leaves into the night sky. The coral sand gleams; and the shadows of the *laboureurs* make furrows over the bay from the square of light. The drums are put close to the flames, to increase their resonance, while, like some wheezing Breton bagpipe, an accordion tunes up till all is ready. We, that is the managers and their wives, the ship's captain and myself, are up on the balcony. The drums start beating – *pan, panpan—pan, pan-pan—pan, panpan* – slowly at first, in time to the songs which begin to be hummed or almost grunted; all this prepares the way for the dance itself. Then the rhythm picks up and the voices grow louder, until they are positively bawling out (and this sometimes leads to frenzy). It's time to dance.

One man comes forward (he had to be promised a litre of wine!), raises his hat and bows to a woman; she will be his partner. Each then stamps in the sand in time to the drumbeat, slower or faster, the partners always keeping four or five feet apart. Thus the *séga* is normally a dance for couples, but one in which the partners never touch one another. The woman, with both hands, lifts the hem of her skirt, rather in the manner of 18th century ladies of fashion curtseying, and sways, sometimes with disdain in her bearing and countenance alike, sometimes with an air of encouragement and pleasure in the advances of her partner who, arms akimbo or waving around, mimes his appeal with a rather idiotic air. And then there's a change of partners; a new man doffs his cap towards the woman dancing and the first retires. That, at any rate, is how they danced in our presence.

But, in a footnote, Dussercle offers no guarantees about what transpires outside his ken, going on to wonder what happens later in the night, when wine has gone to their heads and Satan takes charge of the ball.[11]

Seamanship and risks

A recurring theme in Dussercle's accounts of his visits to the Chagos is the role played by the crews of the small boats. On all the islands, these were used daily to take the workers from islet to islet, to transport the gathered coconuts, and of course for fishing. They were also needed to go beyond the reefs to take goods and passengers from the sailing ships unable to enter lagoons or anchor safely outside. Again and again, there are matter-of-fact descriptions of the hazardous passage through passes to the open sea, involving negotiation of the breaking rollers close to shore. Eagle and Six Islands were the most affected. By the time of Dussercle's visits, these two plantations were (as we shall describe) in the process of being closed down and were being managed together, with the result that there was much coming and going between them, as well as fortnightly movement of workers to gather nuts from Danger Island. The seamanship required – and the physical strength to row heavily-laden boats on windless days – was exceptional, but completely taken for granted by visitors from Mauritius. We can be sure that many more accidents occurred than have been mentioned in this book; but what needs emphasising is that there was more to daily life than the gathering, husking and treatment of coconuts, all tasks of banality and repetitiveness. The challenges of seagoing life required not only strength and skill, but courage and initiative. Sadly, it was only in the rarest circumstances that an islander's individual achievement was recorded. As will be seen in our next chapter, Dussercle himself helped fill this gap.

Boats and boat-building

Lagesse affords space to a number of other individuals, of whom the most interesting is Désiré, the chief boat-builder, with a large number of variously-sized vessels to his credit. While he had been taught a little reading and writing in childhood, he had no need to follow plans to repeat previous designs; he would simply make a note of key measurements and stick it up on a wall. All else was done by eye. Recognising his talent, the manager arranged for him to spend several months in Mauritius learning about modern techniques. This led to an apprenticeship in an important shipyard. Yet Désiré returned to Salomon, bringing not only his new skills, a splendid gramophone and a more modern outlook, but also a firm decision to settle down for good in the Chagos: he had suffered a bad attack of malaria in Mauritius and had seen fellow islanders die of a disease to which they had no resistance, a fate he was determined his own children should not suffer.

Here is a translation of Lagesse's tribute to him:

> Sheltered under the roof of the beachside boat shed to the left of the jetty, and buttressed by timber supports, there rose the sharp silhouette of the sloop's hull, with the boat-builders busying themselves around it. There they were: Désiré, Mylius, Onésime, relentlessly hammering the steel chisel they used to stuff the gaps between hull and keel with strips of aloe fibre or coconut wadding. Beyond, an apprentice was blowing on a fire of wood shavings, while, all around, the air was heavy with the smell of resin and tar.
>
> Five months of labour it had taken and, in a few days, the sloop would be launched. Désiré and his colleagues were filled with pride and joy as they gazed on their handiwork. All of the island's fleet of boats had passed through their hands: the *St. Raphaël*, the *St. Georges*, the *St. Antoine* – used for transporting coconuts and constantly criss-crossing the lagoon; also the *Loup-Garou*, a decked sloop frequently sent on missions to the neighbouring islands of Peros Banhos. The team had also built *Monique*, the slender whaler, so elegant and, with her

beautiful figurehead, almost a living creature. At the opposite end of the scale, the team had patiently shaped and scraped the trunk of a huge *gaiac* tree to make *Zazakel* the dugout canoe, always tethered to the mooring ring at the end of the jetty, and used to get back after anchoring lighters a few cable lengths from the shore.[12]

Only five more days and it would be time for Léonce to spread the roll of sail-cloth on the green grass of the lawn and cut out pieces for the jibs, mizzen and mainsail, then sew them carefully together. And then would come the business of rigging the vessel: fitting the cordage to attach the jib and staysail, as well as installing the tackle for hauling up the topping-lift. What, finally, should the new vessel be called? Désiré had been responsible for designing her and wanted a name at once resonant and decorous, something like *Frégate* or *Alizé* … but he, a mere shipwright, could hardly expect to make the choice.[13]

In later years, there were many comments made about the high quality of locally-made sailing boats in the Chagos. Let one suffice:

> Inter-island communication is by locally built small ships. These are sloop-rigged, with a curious, quite short, additional mast to which the boom is made fast. The boom itself, made from a local tree, is anything but straight, but this matters little as the mainsail is not continuously attached thereto. Two or three loops of cord, at either end and in the centre, hold the sail sufficiently to go over with the boom when the ship goes about. And if much wind is spilled, there is plenty more – at least there was on the day on which I sailed in one of these vessels. We carried a quarter of a ton or so of copra as ballast, and the half-gale which blew from the south-east kept our coaming just not awash. We sailed fast: 'Galopez un peu,' said the dusky, smiling helmsman. We certainly did.'[14]

Voyaging: the passenger experience

Here and there, we have mentioned the complaints of visiting magistrates about the conditions which they had to endure on their way to and from the Chagos, several of them noting that the conditions for the islanders, in the hold or on deck, were a good deal worse. Things were tough for the crew too (see inset overleaf). What Dussercle does is to give a sense of the atmosphere and camaraderie that suffused such voyages. The *Diégo* is due to leave Peros Banhos for Diego Garcia and the return to Mauritius. A good number of the labourers are due to leave for one or other destination and the loading of cargo, belongings, animals and passengers takes a full day.

> Aboard, it's like Noah's ark. The passengers have all stowed their kit between decks – most of the packages are in one corner, taking up a third of the available space; and each person, having gathered up his or her straw mattress and

*The Diego : a deck hand's life**

I signed on in front of Captain Henri Adam. He was as strong as an ox. He looked at me, just turned 17, all skin and bone, then said, pointing to the tall masts and yards 'Look at my ship, she may look like a Church just now, but once we get outside it will be a different story. Are you sure you want to sign on?' Of course I did and found my way to the 'glory hole' where a bunk was allocated to me. There were eight bunks, four on either side of the ship and in the forward part was the space allocated to the storage of mooring ropes. At the after end were the port and starboard chain locker, From the fore and after end came awful smells which hit me at first but afterwards I was able to live with them. Above was the hard windlass and capstan but on the port side was a pig sty containing two fat, voracious beasts. The smell that emanated from such a place was really awful, to which was added the constant grunting of the animals.

I had purchased a straw mattress (donkey's breakfast) from the local store and spread it on the bare wooden boards in the bunk. I noticed a large number of holes in the wood. One of the crew saw my curiosity and said they were a breeding ground for bed bugs. He added that in a day or two we'll burn them out. This was done by heating a hairpin with a kerosene flame and inserting the hot metal into the holes. The stench was horrible but it gave respite from bug bites until the next breeding cycle came round. There was a five gallon drum for freshwater lashed to the stanchion at the head of our quarters and that was for drinking and restricted washing only. I remember once reading in a sailing ship story a statement from an old sailor

'We never had a bath unless it rained and lived like pigs within a dirty sty'.

Well, I was right in the thick of it, with the exception of the pigs, which lived in the fresh air above us. In a word, our living conditions were more than primitive, seating was provided by every man's wooden trunk placed alongside the bunk and the only light was from a hurricane lamp hooked to the deck beam. Above every bunk a large enamel plate swung in a sling made with a roping twine and each man also had an enamel mug which was used for water, tea and restricted washing of one's essential parts. Tins of condensed milk were also swinging in homemade slings and old cigarette tins were used for storing sugar. Butter and jam were never on the rations but the men usually bought a couple of tins of jam if any cash was left after the last session at the ship chandler's pub. All these items were great attractions for all creepy crawlies in hot weather…

The men worked so hard that sleep generally came through sheer exhaustion and the usual discomfort of the bunk went unnoticed. A dark coloured blanket was spread over a rough pillow but the luxury of sheets and pillow slips was unknown. Though the whole place could be defined as discomfort plus, I was to find out that it was to become a most welcome haven after a hard night watch with long spells in the rigging and at the braces.

Another discomfort was that the windlass was on the main deck and cables led through the hawse pipe at the after end of the 'glory hole' to the chain locker. The mud in Port Louis harbour was a malodorous filth and some of it inevitably came down the chain locker, in spite of the hose which washed most of it away.

Living in the forecastle was a hardship in the best of weather as the man had to carry a plate full of hot food, balancing it with one hand while holding on to the rigging or gunwale while walking forward. We went individually to collect our food. The deck house was known as the 'palace' and far more comfortable. It had six bunks, a folding table and two lockers to hang clothes. Forward we had none of these luxuries. Clothes would often be wet for days during the rainy season, with the only option of wringing them. Very often after a watch below one had to get back into the wet garments to go back on watch. It is amazing that the salt water did not give more painful boils and rashes. Poor food was also something the men devoured, they were always so hungry. [The writer's daughter adds her father's comment that the food was so awful that, on occasion, the only way he could get it down was to take a bite of raw chilli pepper first]

The main remedies in the steward's medicine chest were Castor Oil, Black drought cough and clap mixture. Raw turpentine was a wonderful disinfectant for cuts and scratches and a good rub on the chest after a wet watch often saved from catching pneumonia.

Rats and cockroaches were other vermin living happily in the fore peak of the sailing ship. In spite of the poison laid out for them, too many seemed to survive and make nuisances of themselves. On one occasion a man who was not known for being a paragon of cleanliness had one of his toes gnawed at night while asleep.

*One of the grandsons of Gabriel Théophile was Joseph Edouard France Lionnet (1912–1985). Always known as France, he was to become a Master Mariner, serve in the RNVR during the second world war and later work as a pilot in the Suez Canal. He began his life at sea by signing on as a deckhand on the *Diego*. This passage, hitherto unpublished, is the start of his planned autobiography, of which only four pages were completed. We are deeply grateful to his children, Margaret McCloy and Francis Lionnet, for permission to publish it.

whatever else is judged necessary for comfort, sets up a little square on the main deck. It's a free and easy arrangement; and, above the chaos, it teems with children – the tiny ones all squawking as if in competition with the poultry housed in the large cages surrounding the main hatch and the galley. Behind the mesh, the struggle for life carries on unabated: constant squabbling for grains of rice and morsels of *poonac* thrown to them as food. To one side, on top of the planks which half-close the hatch (the other side being left open to provide a way down to the 'tweendecks), there is a collapsed heap – one might almost say, shapeless mass – of women and old folk suffering to a greater or lesser degree from seasickness. There too people are eating, winnowing rice, doing their sewing, chattering – and how! Meanwhile, the men and even the women keep a sharp lookout for cigarette butts to be thrown onto the deck. These they smoke down to the last trace of tobacco, taking it in turns to *hisse éne dame* (take a puff) – sharing their poverty. Now they can unwind; and listlessness and tropical sloth pervade the air. And beside a winch three immense turtles are laid on their backs, waving their flippers in vain or gasping hoarsely, jaws agape, to re-fill their ventricles for the dives they will never make again – nature extinguished under the burning caresses of the equatorial sun.[15]

As it happened, on the return passage from Diego Garcia to Port Louis, the *Diégo* encountered a very severe storm, during which most of the sails had to be hauled down and, as the vessel rolled and pitched, the main deck was swept repeatedly by knee-deep water, which drowned many of the caged poultry and left the contents of cabins in shambles. Curiously, Dussercle, while praising the tireless efforts of the crew, makes no mention of the fate of the Ilois passengers in the hold.

Alcoholic drinks

For an authoritative account of the preparation of the two types of alcoholic beverage brewed locally, it would be hard to improve on that provided by Fernand Mandarin, who uses modern Kreol spelling in preference to *bacca* and *calou*, as found in earlier documents.

Baka

The adults on Chagos drank *baka*; the origin of this drink is said to be from Madagascar. The recipe is fermented alcohol from dried beans (black lentils, red lentils, dholl, corn; all crushed and left in a container for a day, then sugar and warm water is added and the mixture is then transferred to a jar. After two days the liquid begins to foam up. After 2–3 days, more sugar is added, more foam will appear, it will create a gas inside the container or large bottle (process of fermentation). During 15 days one can add fruits to it (sugarcane, bananas, breadfruit).

Alternative recipes, in the absence of grain were made with white guava which is widespread on the islands, or coconut palm meat, and grated coconut, or pineapple or orange skins, or coconut flower. The colour of the drink depends on the fruits used; one can add caramel. This strong drink was not kept for purely festive occasions – it was also drunk during the working week!

Kalou

Refreshment! (detail). Image courtesy of the artist, Clément Siatous.

This drink is made using the extract from a coconut tree, a tree 4–5 metres high with all its energy, where a 'baba' has grown among its branches, full of buttons, not clustered but vertically positioned. Baba coco, a type of coconut, contains a coconut flower, measuring almost one metre. After 2–3 days, all the flowers open. Inside the flowers there are lots of small coconuts. Bunches of coconuts develop and grow. It hangs on the tree; then another cluster of coconuts will form and will hang. Once dry, the coconut falls and is harvested for copra.

For *kalou*, before the stem opens, it is tied in several places and cut where the head is. A rope at the end of the stem is pulled a little, every day, very slowly, so that the stem becomes horizontal. After 3–4 days, once horizontal, they cut a little more, bees and yellow wasps will come, a liquid begins to trickle and they put it in a small container.

They begin to cut/trim it by 1 cm per day. The colour is similar to rice water, very sweet, with a high percentage of alcohol; to increase the alcohol content (if too sweet) leave for 24 hours, it will become less sweet; with extraordinary fermentation!

Alternatively, the roots can be used. Dug out and measuring 2 to 3 centimetres in diameter the roots would be tied and cut and the liquid collected in a container. This practice was not authorised and the establishment would remove the *kalou* when yeast was needed for bread. Otherwise *kalou* was used as a kind of remuneration for small tasks carried out outside working hours; paid with 'kata de kalou' (kata is the empty shell of coconut). *Kalou* was kept in a barrel at the administrator's place. In order to maintain communication with Mauritius a dynamo had to be cranked to charge the battery. The people who turned the crank were paid in *kalou*.[16]

The commandeurs

The roles and duties of the *commandeurs* – perhaps best translated as supervisors – have been described in various contexts in the course of this work. To be effective, they needed to retain the trust of the island workers at all levels

Salomon—Raoul Caboche avec ses commandeurs:-de g a d Edouard Moëdine, Fernand Souciant,Baba Simon (qui s'est pendu)Leonce Rabouine ,-Emile Rodolphe,Nemours Flore---Tous dans leur Jeunesse…

Salomon Island manager and his *commandeurs* c. 1936. Photo by Paul Caboche.

and that of the managers. Clearly, force of character was vital; and we are fortunate to have both a photograph and Lagesse's pen portraits of Salomon's *commandeurs* in the mid 1930s (see inset overleaf) illustrating the importance of the part they played in community life.[17] She adds, nevertheless, some sly general comments:

> They had, to be sure, their failings. But is it a failing, for a true native of the isles, to have the need, which almost all of them feel, to slake their thirst once night has fallen? Besides, what was this litre of wine, provided to them each Wednesday and Saturday? Nothing, a mere trifle! Were it not for their position as *commandeurs*, which enabled them to acquire on the sly a few more litres, offered by elderly matrons, or by young women keen to augment the savings they lodged each month with the manager, they would have been reduced to making their own mixture of grain, sugar and water, which, when nicely fermented, set their veins on fire – a good *bacca* or, as everyone knows, if made with palm juice, a good *calou*! Too risky to take, though, except on *séga* nights, when one could be forgiven for thinking that the collective wine ration wouldn't suffice to stimulate the levels of enthusiasm required. And the same went for funerary vigils or the eight-day mourning ceremonies …[18]

The shark whisperer

The traces of ancestral culture mentioned in the inset were seldom recorded directly, although from time to time magistrates were asked to deal with managers' complaints about disturbances in the islands' cemeteries, which might very well have related to such ceremonies. One fascinating exception has been

The Salomon commandeurs: a valiant team

Léonce Rabouine was the 70 year-old *Chef Commandeur* on Salomon. He had not been to Mauritius for twenty years and was married to Augustine, fifteen years younger than himself; they were an exemplary couple, devoted to each other, and no-one worried about the extra-conjugal adventures of long ago or now remembered the active part she had played, one *séga* night many years earlier, in an assassination. That indeed was the year when the island's sloop, with a six-man crew, disappeared without trace on a trip to Nelson Island. Léonce's working day began by sounding the 6 a.m. bell. After that, his job was to take charge of the copra kiln, keeping an eye on the quality of the product, deciding when, in the event of rain showers, to cover the drying copra and – no easy task! – to supervise the women who shelled the coconuts and chopped up the flesh. Thanks to his conscientiousness, there was no need to employ an assistant manager from Mauritius.

Of the other *commandeurs*, *Fernand Ladouce* was unusual for two reasons, most unusually found in combination. He was literate and an habitual reader of the Mauritian papers. Secondly, he was the island's most knowledgeable exponent of the population's ancestral cults, most particularly the ceremonies associated with death, culminating in the *ani wawah* by which the dead person's soul was released. Likewise, he could provide protective charms to those who needed them against witchcraft.

Edouard Moëdine and *Emile Rodolphe*, both *commandeurs*, were also 'blood brothers'* with a very unhappy relationship. Edouard, undoubtedly the island's best helmsman, was a magnificent sight as he stood at the sloop's stern, his corsair's gold earring glinting in the sun, the tiller between his thighs, leaning one way then the other to steer the vessel, or even more imposing, when using an oar to control its passage through the foaming breakers to the open sea. His colleagues all expected him to succeed Léonce one day. He was also a meticulous respecter of ancient rites, refusing to go to sea on 15 August or on 2 November, when he was in charge of arranging for gifts of food and drink to be left out for the souls of the departed. But his love life had been chequered, with three decent girls left in the lurch prior to his current relationship with the sweet and wise woman who had born his three children. He was also at continual risk from the magic of Emile Rodolphe. For some reason, Emile's detestation of Edouard could be traced back to the date of the sudden unexplained death of the island's nurse … and, when on dark nights Emile's crouching form could be seen scampering about, there would be a sense of dread that The Thing had returned to smash Edouard beneath its feet. Still, Edouard continued to live a charmed life, successful and unscathed.

Alexis Victor was the youngest man ever to be made a *commandeur*. If amongst the sounds at dawn one heard drumming, first calling quietly in short or longer bursts, then with a heavier beat, suggesting the quivering of strange and mysterious life, everyone knew at once that the evening's *séga* would be held at Alexis' house. Drumming was not his only skill; he had built his own outrigger canoe, which he would take out alone onto the open sea to go fishing. Sculling his craft or hove-to and holding a fishing line, he made an hilarious spectacle and, if things became difficult, would burst into familiar songs or compose new ones. When his latest *séga* was performed, it was Alexis who first took the floor and held out his white handkerchief to the woman he hoped to have as his partner for the first dance – Edouard's wife. Soon, as the drums speeded up, the couple were lost in a whirl of spinning skirts and the darkness surrounding the halo of flames from the fire…

Only one of Lagesse's list of *commandeurs*, **Nemours Flore**, went without a character sketch.

Authors' note. Another *commandeur*, not mentioned by Lagesse but appearing in the group photo, was **Eudoxe 'Baba' Simon**. Shortly after being promoted he offended the manager and was demoted. Next morning, unable to face the shame of his situation, he was found hanged, leaving a widow and six children. Within three months the family were adopted by a new partner.[19] That, Fernand Mandarin later told us, is how life was.

---

*As Lagesse explains 'Fernand would carry out the ceremony for those who swore lifelong mutual loyalty. It involved making a small cut in the fore-arm of each man, each then dipping a small piece of ginger into the blood of the other's incision and eating it. But this ceremony was only effective if accompanied by secret phrases uttered by someone, like Fernand, originating in La Grande Terre – Africa.'

Source: Lagesse, M., summarised extracts from articles in *Savez-vous Que?*

recorded by both Lagesse and her brother Paul Caboche. It concerns Adrien, a Malagasy who had found his way (with a compatriot bearing the uninventable name Both Mice) to Salomon in the early years of the 20th century. These two specialised in making coconut frond roofs for the workers' huts; Adrien was also an excellent diver, who was regularly used to free anchors snagged on coral heads. He had another skill too, vouched for by several other witnesses and Fernand Mandarin:

> From time to time, Adrien was taken by an urgent need to talk to his friends, the fish. He would set off swimming, singing an incantation which none could understand, and was soon surrounded by large fish; taking them in his hands, he would talk to them, take them in his arms, caress them and after a moment, still singing, return them to the water, pointing them towards the open sea, and they would set off. Sometimes too, when a turtle had been killed, he would ask for ten feet of the intestines, wrap them around his neck and enter the water, chanting his song. He would be surrounded by sharks, who would feed on the 'tripe', while he climbed on their backs, caressed them, talked to them and swam back to shore. As soon as he could stand up, he would again embrace and caress them, before pointing them to the open sea, whither they would set off. Adrien would threaten thunderbolts and the vengeance of his ancestors on anyone who might dare to try spearing or catching any of these fish.[20]

Women's lives and families

Only rarely did the number of women exceed that of men. By the 20th century, they generally represented about one third of an island's adult population. All of them were employed. Their work might involve *l'abbatis* – clearing weeds from around the coconut trees – or assisting men in making roofs from coconut fronds, or twisting coconut fibres into string, or making brooms and brushes, these last two tasks being reserved for those who were pregnant.[21] The main task reserved to the strongest of them was the breaking of the de-husked nuts. To do this, they sat on the flat, concreted area on which copra was dried. They would start at 6 a.m. and could usually expect to finish their day's stint by midday. During this time they would be surrounded by their babies and young children, who, by the age of four or five, would be lending a hand with the work. As Lagesse explained,

> For the women, a single cutlass blow sufficed to split each coconut of the daily quota of 700. This would take about an hour, after which they would take a break while the sun's heat penetrated the flesh, before returning to extract it – another hour or two's labour. Many a time would one woman slide some of her allocation of nuts toward her neighbour's pile, resulting in screams of protest, fisticuffs or

the tearing of each other's hair. Usually, it was enough for Léonce to stand silently over them to restore calm.

Like their menfolk, the women would have been woken by a bell at 5 a.m. Sleepily, they would go to the copra kiln to fetch burning charcoal to relight their own cooking fires and collect water in buckets from the well. Breakfast consisted of *rane mafane*, a mixture of rice boiled then grilled, washed down with a mug of hot, sugared water. Around 10 a.m. it was time for the lunch break. This and the evening meal, prepared by the women, would consist of rice with vegetables (*sénage, brèdes*) and fish, chicken or a bit of turtle stewed in coconut milk.

As for dress, Lagesse reports that 'women wear a full, many-pleated skirt, and a blouse which goes down to their hips. Altogether, they are a pleasant people, having unconsciously maintained the traditional charm of their dress and hairstyles'.

Birth and marriage

Births, until a much later period, do not appear to have been attended by much ceremony, perhaps because of the high rates of infant mortality (perhaps this also explains the existence of separate children's cemeteries quite close to the main establishments). There was however a legal requirement for the managers to register all births and for birth certificates to include the names of both parents. It was considered good form for the father to own up to paternity, though Lagesse cites a case where the mother was not at all sure whose name to give.

Formal marriages were the exception rather than the rule; the island managers had powers to conduct civil marriages, while religious, that is to say, Catholic marriages could only take place when a priest visited. It was however rare for a marriage to take place ahead of months or years of informal partnership. When Dussercle questioned individuals, they would invariably reply that it was essential, before committing oneself to marriage, to get to know the character of a partner. All accounts suggest that many liaisons were only temporary. For example, Marcel Didier comments, young women (who generally embarked on cohabitation around the ages of fourteen or fifteen, very often following a post-*séga* assignation) changed partners quite frequently; and there was an unwritten rule that when a pair split up and did not resume their relationship within a fortnight, the woman would be free to establish a new relationship.[22] Dussercle cites the case of a *commandeur* on Egmont, father of nine children by his third partner, and father by two previous partners of at least a dozen other children, 'already grown up and able to earn their own livings, who were now dispersed to the four corners of the Archipelago'.[23] However, the custom was that new partnerships should be announced formally to the manager ('I declare that I am leaving Sounane and setting up house with Zélia'); and, according to Didier, it then became the manager's responsibility to ensure that suitable accommodation was found.

What about adult women not in any partnership? Lagesse explains that single women were known as *femmes bossoirs,* a phrase derived in her view from the nautical term for the lookout stationed on a ship's bow.[24] These women and childless women from a broken partnership were required to live on a separate islet (Ile Takamaka in the case of Salomon), but were invited back every time there was a *séga.* As Lagesse put it, there was little surprise to find *femmes bossoirs* with several children or children brought up together as a family but bearing different patronyms. Couples who had broken up were expected to sort out the consequences for themselves, but usually consulted the *commandeur* Fernand Ladouce about the offerings to be made to protect themselves against the vengeance of those they had offended. For example, Alexina, mother of the *commandeur* Alexis Victor had been abandoned by her husband, Chéri Victor, but the latter had obtained from Fernand a little *gardien* [voodoo doll] tightly wrapped in unbleached cloth. For her part, Alexina had taken all the magical steps prescribed to bring a curse on his life, but to no effect.

Death and burial

Both Dussercle and Lagesse go into some detail on this subject, the latter concentrating on the ceremony to free the soul of the departed from any physical bond to his place of domicile. This took place around midnight on the eighth day following the dead person's demise. On the preceding night a vigil was kept, well lubricated by *bacca* or wine, during which events of the distant past were mimed, particularly events involving important French personages and their abundant treasure. All this helped provide the Dutch courage necessary for the dangerous acrobatics required by the actual ceremony. The leader, usually Fernand Ladouce, was required to leap from corner to corner of the house in the dark, laying about him with a hefty club and shrieking as he went, at the same time gathering up all the accumulated detritus swept into a corner at the time of death, in which the deceased's soul might have taken refuge; all this he had to stuff into a box and, leading his cortège without trembling back to the far end of the camp, pronounce the sacred formulae he alone knew, to which his followers chorused the response '*Ani wawah oh, ani wawah ohé*'. Next, he threw the rubbish-filled box among the roots of the ancient *gaiac* tree, immediately turning his back on it and, with the whole company, running for dear life without looking back. Next morning, the relatives of the deceased would offer Fernand appropriate gifts – of coins, wine or a few chickens.[25]

Dussercle was utterly scandalised by these rituals, to the point where he could not bring himself to describe them, only burst into exclamatory condemnation. The ceremonies were

> savage, barbarous and often bestial, bringing together friends and relatives ostensibly to offer ritual prayers but in fact to give free rein to enormities which one would only believe possible in the heart of Africa; orgies, pernicious discourse, sessions of spells and sorcery, hellish calls to the underworld, demonic incantations, lascivious dancing in lewd disguises, wild tumblings from the canopy of coconut trees onto the roof of the dead person's house – and all this accompanied by the periodic performance of horrific acts upon the corpse of the deceased.[26]

In the last of his four books about the Chagos, *Les Zîles là Haut* (pp. 93–108), Dussercle returned to this topic more calmly, though still unable to resist a long and critical description of the ceremonies beginning with death and continuing until, with a final flourish, the soul was on the eighth day declared free of the body – and thus unable to haunt those left behind. At the same time, he described these ceremonies as dying out and being replaced by Christian rituals. He also made a point of stating that it would have been a mistake simply to stamp out old practices; rather to see that the eight days of mourning should be observed in a dignified way in the chapel. It would appear that his efforts were largely successful. Little is heard of such ceremonies in later years (apart from an isolated complaint from the manager of Salomon in the early 1950s) and they form little part in the recollections today of former inhabitants of the islands. It is worth noting, however, a remark made privately in about 2004 to Dr Jeffery in Mauritius by a former inhabitant of the Chagos in his fifties:

> Chagossians conceal information … for a true history you have to take the bad as well as the good … There was a lot of voodoo, which is a serious matter and is kept secret, and there were struggles for leadership amongst islanders, in which those who were weak had to stay quiet because they had no power, whereas those who were dominant could take the others' women.[27]

Later, Dussercle attempted, in a dozen pages of prose as orgiastic as the ceremonies themselves, to describe a 'standard' example:

> Someone dies; at once the deceased's room fills up with women mourners, who add their lamentations to those of the grieving family. One should add that this grief is on occasion factitious, when the one who has departed to another world is not only not a loss to the community, but one of whom the latter is well rid – and one must admit that this sentiment occurs as well in civilised countries, for example when the death of an uncle or aunt opens the way to a legacy. Be that as

it may, the sudden upset of death brings out the peculiar mannerisms adopted by the professional mourners of yore, with each of the ladies showing off in their own way, either with artificial gesticulations or exaggerated hypocritical sighs. Then it is time to wash the corpse and prepare the chapel of rest; while the men, more practically, set about collecting coins small and large. They do this among their fellows, who see the death of one of their own as a unique chance to amuse themselves. Certainly, they do not hesitate to show their impatience when some poor wretch appears to be hanging onto life too long: '*Ah ben! Li pas va mort ène fois, donc! Longtemps nous na pas fine amisés*' [Isn't he going to die, then! It's ages since we've had some fun.] Yes, this is how it goes. With the money collected – and the more of it there is, the better the party will go – purchases are made from the company boutique of tea, coffee, sugar, tobacco, all these being required for the night of vigil; after all, you can't observe a death without something to drink … and, if you don't drink, you can't have much fun … Luckily, though, wine isn't on sale for these occasions!

The corpse, in his best, that is, cleanest, clothes, is stretched out on the couch. Now it is time for the '*pousse nâme*', the soul's send-off. While some of his friends make things ready for the night, others noisily arm themselves with palm branches, brooms and sticks; and, as the women mumble prayers, the men perform a wild saraband around the hut … [there follow two pages of animated description of these activities and the beverages taken to fortify the participants] … That is what strengthens the heart. And, while the deceased seems to rest from the strenuous activities that followed his death, the excitement outside reaches a pitch of moral fervour that far exceeds the physical effects of the smoking greenery held aloft. And, since the sound effects provided by a drum would be quite inadequate, sticks, tin cans, basins, cooking pots are brought along, in fact anything that can be banged. Sleep is out of the question. These orgies continue all night, accompanied by card games, discussions, even disputes requiring knife fights to settle them, and by songs and stories which alone could – at least, according to fairy stories – counter the effects of the orgiastic frenzy to which the old witches would devote themselves of a Saturday night.

Finally, after several more pages of exuberant description, Dussercle suggests that these ceremonies had, thanks to the efforts of '*one or two* managers' – the emphasis is Dussercle's – largely died out.

All the same, the priest did not suppose that brief annual visits would do much to eradicate deeply-ingrained traditions and, as he noted, was well aware of the mutterings of the young lads that they would have their fun as soon as he had gone on his way. Nevertheless, his caring ministrations clearly gave considerable joy and opened new perspectives to people deprived of any real interest from others in their lives and problems. He also played a part in strengthening more modern forms of amusement, notably in the encouragement of New Year's Day festivities. In 1934, he found himself in Diego Garcia and, together with the

Richard Lionnet (left) and Bishop Leen (centre), prior to their voyage to the Chagos.

Bp. Leen and Fr. Dussercle celebrate Mass at Salomon, 1937.

Images courtesy of Dr Edward Duyker.

plantation staff and his fellow visitors, organised a 'jolly day out', involving races of all kinds – running, swimming, sack, donkey, long and high jumping, tugs o' war (boys versus girls, *artisans* versus *commandeurs*), and the equivalent of a toffee-apple race, with horribly unchewable rolls substituted for apples; while, for 'orchestral accompaniment' an accordionist was found to play 'pop' tunes currently in vogue in Mauritius.[28]

It is unclear how far Dussercle's activities were supported by the company management as a deliberate means to maintain the docility of their workforce. Relations between Richard Lionnet (*père*) and the priest were very close (Dussercle took his funeral service in 1934) and the relationship continued with Richard (*fils*); the latter's copy of Dussercle's book about the voyage they made together contains a warm manuscript inscription: *Au cher M. Richard Lionnet, qui a été si bon pour nous lors de ce voyage – et qui le sera toujours, je le sais.*[29] The collaboration went further: Dussercle composed a special catechism designed for use with the '*Créoles des îles*', which included instructions that the island managers should hold themselves responsible for continuing to propagate the faith between his visits. Since most of the managers were Catholic, they would have felt themselves bound by this religious duty, which included an absolute ban on wakes such as those just described.[30]

Dussercle was not the first Catholic priest to have visited the Chagos, but previous visitors had been rare. Apparently the first such was Abbé Roze, who made a tour of all the Oil Islands in 1875.[31] Dussercle makes passing references to a coral cross set up on Six Islands in 1904 by the Jesuit Père Malaval and to the fact that his own visit to Salomon in 1933 was the first for over ten years,[32] but the first continuing effort to evangelise the Oil Islands appears to have come from Archishop Leen in the early 1930s, with Dussercle as his instrument. One of the latter's projects was to organise the construction of solid chapel buildings on the islands which lacked them, in particular Salomon and Peros Banhos. In 1937, on Dussercle's fourth visit, he was accompanied by the Archbishop himself, who performed the consecration of the church on Salomon.

The progressively more co-operative relationship between the Catholic Church and the creole descendants of slaves in Mauritius has been summarised in an admirable study by Rosabelle Boswell.[33] However, we believe that the diocesan archives in Port Louis may well contain more material of interest in relation to the Chagos than we had time to examine.

A cultural epilogue

In this context, the account of Chagos culture by Françoise Botte in 1980 is of considerable interest.[34] As a Mauritian creole, who had studied anthropology and worked closely with the exiled islanders as a teacher and social worker, she was well placed to understand the differences between the practices of the Chagos and mainland. As well as describing briefly the customs that her informants – all now deceased – recalled concerning birth and marriage, she gives an interesting account of how the rituals associated with death had become modified by and to some extent amalgamated with the Church's practices. Collective baptisms would take place during the periodic visits by a priest, sometimes with so little ceremonial as to be dismissed by the parents as *baptème lérat* – baptism for rats! Years later, as the children neared adulthood, they would make their first communions, for which they had been prepared by the managers' wives. When it came to marriage, Botte's description has elements not hinted at by Dussercle or Lagesse, suggesting that they developed later:

> Marriage was not a common thing on the islands. There were many *raccommodages* (patched marriages) on the visits of the priest. More often the brides and grooms were dressed in any colourful dress because it was a *raccommodage*. For the rare case of marriage, the future bride made a command at the shop of the island and the white material for her dress was ordered from Mauritius. For a *bon mariaze* – true wedding, the party began on the eve with the civil marriage ceremony. On the very day of the wedding, there is a big *salle verte,* a big hall of leaves ordinarily built in front of a house. The parents of the bride and groom would on both side kill a pig and many hens for the big banquet. The guests would spend the whole night dancing, but the bride would leave by midnight. On the next day the mother of the bridegroom came to see if the girl was still a virgin. If ever that was not the case, the bride should already have explained to the mother-in-law with full details about the past accident. If the bride tried to hide that fact she is repudiated upon its discovery.

Similarly, after describing the main elements of the ancient rituals following a death, Botte goes on to explain that

> Before the exile of the Ilois community from the Chagos, some Administrators

had forbidden the practice of the spirit seeker and the story-tellers on the advice of the priest. On the 8th day of the death of the late person, there used to be a bigger party, operating on the same system. But some practices remain even in Mauritius. The weeping women will be present on the 8th day. There will be a *Chapelle Ardente* (a table where they will put all the pictures of the Christian saints, with flowers and candles). There will be prayers till midnight, then they will turn back the sacred pictures and put all the flowers outside. By putting the flowers outside, they will tell you that they are putting the spirit outside.

Another practice is that, on the very day of the person's death, when the house is swept, all the rubbish will be kept in a corner outside. Only on the 9th day after that the wife or any women in that home will collect all the rubbish in a *vanne* (a large rounded tray used to clean the rice) and throw it very far away from the place. It is done to put the spirit from the place. It appeared to be some kind of African habit. The woman who has to throw away the rubbish is usually accompanied by a big group of neighbouring women. On their way back home, no-one will look back, for if any look back, the sprit will haunt the one who looks back.

The dangers of generalisation

This chapter (and the next) draw heavily on the factual information derived from Dussercle's writings. Those writings, however, reflect not only his preoccupations as a missionary priest, but also (and inevitably) the social attitudes of his time and the circles he moved in. Hints of these emerge from some of the passages we have quoted. The same could be said, but in our view with much less force, about Lagesse, the Salomon manager's daughter, devoted to her father and to her Catholic faith, yet – as befitted an emerging writer – much more open to an intuitive sympathy with the workers' predicament. This sympathy is particularly evident in her accounts of shared experiences with individual islanders, notably Adrien, the 'shark whisperer', whose son was left in her care and whom she visited as he lay stricken by elephantiasis in later years. In her memoir of her years on Salomon, she sums up her feelings thus:

> In Mauritius, I occasionally encounter a native of Salomon. After the usual exclamations and exchange of courtesies, they always confide what they feel most deeply: 'Madame, the fish – here we have to <u>buy</u> fish!' There is a look in their eyes that takes them way beyond Mauritius towards a horizon I know too. What they don't know is that I can never bring to mind that lost period of my life without recalling their kindness, their devotion, their sometimes clumsily expressed affection and their little universe of gossip, banter and limitations. Beyond the reefs encircling the lagoon, there was just the ocean and what the ocean deigned to bring us.[35]

When Dussercle yielded to the temptation to describe the general character of the islanders, innate paternalism overcame him:

> From the material point of view they could, if they wished, be the happiest people on earth. Their workload is not excessive and they can earn more pay by 'doing extras'. Their daily rice ration is provided and fish is ready to hand, or at least, to hook. They have no rent to pay for their huts, admittedly built of coconut fronds, which they can improve by adding small gardens and chicken runs. Sixty per cent of the labourers are '*enfants des îles*', descended from Madagascan forebears. These 'Ilois' are in general good, grown children, usually straightforward, obliging, industrious; but, regrettably, the remaining forty per cent, who come from Mauritius, don't always conform to the habits of calm and good order which, despite everything, normally supervene in the Islands.[36]

At the start of this chapter, we anticipated the emergence of contrasts between the perceptions of Dussercle and Lagesse and those of Mandarin, yet to be described (in Chapter 20). In general, informants about life on Chagos in the 1930s articulated views which, while less extreme than those of Bourne 50 years earlier, few would share today. Coming as they do from persons more closely associated with the managers than with the workers it is not surprising that the judgments concerning the general character of the Chagos population are more focussed on morals and bacchanalian rituals than with the economic exploitation and disregard of elementary rights which suffused the operation of the Chagos plantations.

Notes to Chapter 16

1   The books are: *Archipel de Chagos: en mission 10 Novembre 1933–11 Janvier 1934*; *Archipel de Chagos: en mission Diégo–Six Iles–Péros, Septembre – Novembre 1934*; *Naufrage de la Barque Diégo à l'Ile d'Aigle aux Chagos; Dans les 'Ziles là-Haut*. All were printed by the General Printing Company, Port Louis; a second edition of the third was published in 2006 by Editions du Hecquet, Port Louis. In 1949, Dussercle published a further book, *Agalega – petite île*, on the history and customs of Agalega. This includes references to and comparisons with the Chagos.

2   Lagesse, M., *D'un Carnet* (Editions Paul Mackay, Mauritius 1967) is largely factual, while her *Des Pas sur le Sable* (Les Editions du Printemps, Mauritius 1975, re-published 2009), though set in Salomon, is purely fictional. The author was kind enough to present NW-S with copies of both these works, while resolutely declining to reveal more about the boundary between fact and fiction in the first of these works.

3   Dussercle, R., *Archipel de Chagos: en mission Novembre 1933–Janvier 1934*, pp. 142–3.

4   Dussercle, R., *En Mission Septembre–Novembre 1934*, p. 56.

5   Dussercle, R., *Dans les Ziles là-Haut* p. 150.

6   At the time of writing, work is being undertaken to reconstruct the music from the material we have collected from Dussercle's writings. These include a whole chapter (pp. 137–174) of *Dans les Ziles là-Haut*, entitled 'Danses et Chansons aux Iles'. To the best of our knowledge, only one recording has been made live from a *séga* in progress prior to the islands' evacuation (see Note 31 on p. 497).

7 Marcelle Lagesse adds *séga la paie* (pay day?) and *séga d'avance* (loan day??).

8 An interesting contrast between the songs composed in the Chagos and those later in Mauritus has been noted by the anthropologist, Dr Jeffery: 'Whilst the lyrics of songs composed on the Chagos Archipelago concern the everyday sorrows and joys of life there, the lyrics of Chagossian songs composed in exile romanticise life on Chagos'. Jeffery, L., *Chagos Islanders in Mauritius and the UK* (p. 7), Manchester University Press 2011.

9 Jeffery, L., *op. cit.* (pp. 60–64).

10 For examples of sound archives, three Chagossian songs can be listened to here: http://www.cezame.co.uk/liste_titres_album.php?id_album=580. Also, a live recording (speech and song) of a *séga* in progress at Diego Garcia in 1969 can be found at http://www.chagos.info/The 1969Recordings . Similarly, a downloadable PDF featuring transcriptions of extracts from segas; information relating to creole sayings, folk culture etc of Chagos is available at: http://culture.gov.mu/English/DOCUMENTS/NIICH%20-%20CHAGOS.PDF

11 Dussercle, R., *En Mission Septembre–Novembre 1934*, pp. 69–72.

12 The dugout's name is derived from *zazakely*, the Malagasy word for 'baby'. Thus, in English, the canoe might have been called *Babe* or *Titch*.

13 Lagesse, M., 'La Nouvelle Lune s'élève à l'Ouest' (Part VI), one of a collection of nine articles (one is missing), which appeared in *Savez-vous Que?*, a monthly government broadsheet published between 1942 and 1950 (copies presented to NW-S by her brother, Paul Caboche).

14 Blood, Sir H., 'The Peaks of Lemuria' in the *Geographical Magazine* Vol XXIX No. 10, February 1957.

15 Dussercle, R., *Archipel de Chagos, en mission Novembre 1933–Janvier 1934* (pp. 136–138).

16 Extract from interview notes made by Robert Furlong (trans. MC) between 2010–2015.

17 Lagesse, M., *op. cit.* The photograph by her brother, Paul Caboche, identifies most of the individuals mentioned, as does Dussercle in reproducing the text of a document hidden in the island's chapel foundations at the time of the laying of its foundation stone in 1935.

18 Lagesse, M., *op. cit.*

19 This event made its way into official records for 1934 (TNA CO 167/885/12).

20 Paul Caboche, note dated 28 September 2005, citing as other witnesses a magistrate, Raoul Brouard and the captain of the sv *Diégo*, Captain Henri Mazoué. Caboche's sister, Marcelle Lagesse also wrote an account of this phenomenon, published in her book *D'un Carnet*. The brother and sister remained in contact with Adrien himself and his son and grandson for many years. Fernand Mandarin, in an interview with MC in 2010, was asked 'Have you heard a story about an individual who would swim among sharks?' His reply: 'Yes, and it's a true story, because his son is still alive! He lives in Mauritius, he is about 80 years old and is called Onésime. Now I will tell you how it happened. On Salomon and other islands, they always said be careful of sharks. He always said, sharks are my friends. There is a boat called Diego, his wife was taken to Mauritius to cure her. Onésime did not want to go, and threw himself into the sea. The Captain was worried and made a report when he arrived at Mauritius. But when the boat came back two months later, Onésime was there.'

21 This list is provided by Marcel Didier *Pages Africaines de l'Ile Maurice*, Centre Culturel Africain, Mauritius, 1987. Didier operated the Diego Garcia radio in the late 1940s and early 1950s.

22 Didier, M., *op.cit.*

23 Dussercle, R., *En Mission Septembre–Novembre 1934*, p. 105.

24 As Dussercle was to explain later (in *Agalega: petite île* pp. 166–7) a more complex explanation of this phrase arose from a practice long-established in Agalega. There, from the early 19th century, a formalised system of polyandry provided that, when a woman's official partner was absent, she would take an unofficial one, referred to as a *noir bonsoir*; and this word became corrupted to bossoir. Dussercle was however adamant that this practice was not found in the Chagos.

25 This description is taken directly from the seventh of Lagesse's articles in *Savez-vous Que?*

26 Dussercle, R., *op. cit.* p. 131.

27 Laura Jeffery *op. cit.* p. 67.

28 Dussercle, R., *op. cit.* pp. 159–162.

29 *Archipel de Chagos* (1934). The copy in question is now in the possession of NW-S. The sense of Dussercle's inscription may be conveyed as follows: To dear Richard Lionnet, who was so helpful to us during this voyage – and, I know, always will be so.

30 Dussercle, R., 'Petit catéchisme en créole, spécialement destiné à l'instruction des Créoles des Iles' (1936), re-published in volume 1 of *La Production Créolophone* (eds R. Furlong and V. Ramharai 2007).

31 Mgr. Amadée Nagapen, typescript note composed around 1971.

32 Dussercle, R., *En Mission 10 November 1933 – 11 January 1934*, pp. 54 and 114.

33 Boswell, R., *Le Malaise Créole* Berhahn Books 2006.

34 Botte, F., *The 'Ilois' community and the 'Ilois' women* (research project, 1980). Botte's work, like that of Jeffery, is primarily focused on the period after 1973, but both authors' remarks on cultural practices relate to a continuum unconstrained by time limits, such as those we have imposed on this story.

35 Lagesse, M., *D'un Carnet* (p. 52) Editions Paul Mackay 1967.

36 Dussercle, *Archipel de Chagos: en mission Novembre 1933–Janvier 1934*, pp. 9–10. It should be noted that 'les îles' include all Mauritius' island dependencies, not just the Chagos islands.

17

Stuck in a Deeper Rut: the 1930s

FROM the world of personal lives and emotions we must revert to the narration of material events. Triggered by the collapse of the United States banking system, a worldwide economic depression swiftly followed. Even so remote an area as the Chagos was not immune, given its dependence on the price of a single commodity, whether in the form of coconuts, copra, *poonac* or raw coconut oil. Ironically, the companies' efforts to increase copra production were at last beginning to bear fruit and 1930 was a bumper year, with production exceeding 2,000 tonnes. Soon, however, as Table 17.1 shows, international trade prices tumbled well below the reduced prices being paid to the plantations.

Table 17.1 Comparison of copra trade in triennia preceding and following the 'crash'.

Mauritius imports (cif) of copra from Chagos.

	Total		Average	
	Tonnes	Value (Rs)	Rs/t	£/t
1927–1929	3,491.9	808,450	231.5	16.18.0d
1930–1932	4,688.8	915,693	195.3	14.3.0d

Mauritius exports (fob) of copra worldwide

| 1927–1929 | 4,043.6 | 1,015,848 | 251.2 | 18.6.0d |
| 1930–1932 | 5,969.7 | 949,437 | 159.0 | 11.10.0d |

Source: Mauritius 'Blue Books' for relevant years (TNA CO 172/154–159).

It is not known what happened to the shareholders' dividends, but the company managements had little alternative to cost-cutting. The snag was that their longstanding parsimony had left the island communities ill-placed to cope with enhanced deprivation. Except for 1932, Visiting Magistrates visited all the plantations each year from 1930 to 1939.[1] Their reports revealed the interacting consequences of continuing with inadequate investment and outmoded production methods in the face of harsher conditions and the same range of maritime accidents and breakdowns in law and order as had occurred in the past. And, as before, funding and tariff protection were sought, largely in vain, from the authorities in Port Louis and London.

It would be possible to tell this part of the story *seriatim*, proceeding year by year in the magistrates' footsteps, but only at the cost of losing from sight the dynamics of the struggles engaged in by all concerned. We have therefore adopted an alternative approach: to begin with a summary of the Archipelago's problems in 1930–1931 and the reactions of government and higher management thereto; to recount in detail the circumstances leading to the complete abandonment of Eagle and Six Islands; to describe the loss of the *Diégo* and change from sail to steam; and to consider the economics of the three remaining plantations, before examining their contrasting characteristics. The chapter ends with a description of the local events foreshadowing the outbreak of another war.

The Archipelago in 1930–1931

In June 1930, W.J. Hanning visited Diego Garcia and Peros Banhos. As well as making the usual factual reports about both islands, he noted that Diego Garcia's East Point settlement (the only one remaining) was being completely rebuilt, with its huts, of more than ample dimensions, in straight lines rather than scattered haphazardly over a wide area. He used his initial meeting with the assembled workers to give 'a lecture to the men and women, the latter in particular, on the "genesis" and "exodus" of ankylostomiasis (Anglice = hookworm), its deleterious effect on the health of those suffering from its attacks and safeguards to take for its cure and prevention'. This sanitary discourse was followed by a visit to the hospital; it was in good condition, with only one case of hookworm identified in the preceding year. Altogether more revealing were two general observations, the first reading as follows:

> Before closing this report on Diego Garcia, I should like to add a few remarks as to the island itself, based on observations made by me during a period of 8½ years of my connection with the Lesser Dependencies. It has struck me forcibly that Diego Garcia, which has an area of about 30 square miles [comment: actually, under 11] under coconut cultivation is an estate of tremendous possibilities, and that the development of its resources to the fullest extent should be the aim of its owners. Unfortunately, quite the contrary is the case, the labour employed is insufficient, the drying machinery is old-fashioned and inadequate, and every building and apparatus breathes of stagnation. It is my opinion that this important island could produce six times of its actual export. A fibre [coir] industry could easily be worked; the fibre from the coconuts is now a waste product, and modern methods of hydraulic presses could be used instead of the antiquated one

of donkey power and crushing mills. The harbour itself is magnificent; about 40 square miles of deep water almost everywhere for the anchorage of the largest ships in the world, and there are two sites at least where deep-water quay accommodation exists. I have always asked myself why the owners do not sell their copra f.a.g.[*sic*]² Diego Garcia to any port in the world, thus saving loading and unloading charges and freight to Mauritius, and reloading on steamers there for export. A small auxiliary motor vessel to work between Peros Banhos and Diego Garcia would be all that would be necessary for the former group. Diego Garcia is on the steamer route between South Africa, Mauritius and Colombo. It should not be very costly to charter the British India steamers to call there with labour and stores, and bring the time-expired labourers to Mauritius on the return trip from Colombo. I believe in making these observations that on the progress and prosperity of these islands must depend the welfare of their inhabitants.

Some of the magistrate's remarks were inaccurate, and his imaginative proposals for alternative systems of resupply and export look to be based on some wishful thinking. Nor did he take account of the navigational and anchorage problems of the other four atolls. His central criticisms, that failure to invest condemned the island to continued torpor and undermined the welfare of its inhabitants were, however, very much to the point. Their welfare was indeed the subject of his second general comment – a plea for the introduction of radio transmitters and receivers, such as were already installed in the small outlying islands of the Seychelles. Noting the Archipelago's 'complete isolation from the rest of the world for months on end', he added, 'It is this feeling of isolation, and absence of news from relatives, which has in the past led to bitter feelings among the staff, and a consequent reaction on those of the labour population'.

The magistrate who visited the three small plantations in November 1930 was Pierre Rousset. No significant issues arose in Salomon or Eagle Island. The condition of Six Islands was altogether different. Francis Gendron, the recently arrived manager, had had little opportunity to make changes, but many huts were in disrepair and the sick bay was badly in need of a new roof; the physical condition of the workers was weak, largely on account of a lack of green vegetables; no less than 76 cases – the total population was only 56 – had required treatment during the previous fourteen months, not one resulting from violent behaviour; and there had been a rapid turnover of dispensers during the preceding three years. This time, the magistrate brought with him the dispenser from Eagle Island, a man who had already made several visits to make up for gaps between appointments. One fundamental problem was that the well water was polluted, though there was some uncertainty as to the cause of this. In addition, the previous manager's procedure for measuring out the wine ration had been highly insalubrious, with excess wine being left for days in a galvanised bucket before being returned to the barrel and with no washing of any of the utensils.

The island's animals were in an even worse state. Astonishingly, the Director of the Medical and Health Department in Port Louis described the report as disclosing 'a generally satisfactory state of affairs'.[3] It is not known what this gentleman might have thought a year later, when Hanning was the visiting magistrate and found that matters were, if anything, worse.[4] A 'strange disease' had been prevalent causing a sharp increase in the number of deaths, which, it seemed, might be ascribed to eating poisoned fish;[5] and so, for want of labour, the rebuilt sick bay remained roofless; nevertheless the number of cases treated had declined to 58. In case the well water were also contaminated from the sea, the magistrate counselled the population to stick to water from other islets of the atoll or to rain water, but commented in his report that the rainwater tanks were empty as there had been no rain for two months or more … As if this were not enough, the nursing assistant had died of strychnine poisoning. Perhaps it was not surprising that the *Saint Géran* on this visit brought only 8 individuals to Six Islands to replace the 22 who were leaving.

Six Islands was not the only establishment to have problems at this time. In June 1931, the manager at Diego Garcia complained that some of his 'labourers were in the habit of carrying knives and razors which they had a tendency to using in quarrels however insignificant', leading the magistrate to issue a strongly worded warning at the following morning's roll-call.[6] At his next stopping point, Peros Banhos, there was one serious case of wounding to try. Less than two months later, however, this atoll's latent tensions boiled over into a full-scale rebellion, in which the manager, Jean-Baptiste Adam, had lost control, his assistant had made matters worse by issuing extra wine to the ringleaders of the rebellion, the shop-keeper had drawn his revolver on workers who were on the point of looting his premises and a woman counselling restraint had been beaten up.

This was the situation when the *Diégo* (captained by the manager's brother) arrived on her next visit. Such was the attitude of the rebel elements that the ship had to sail away without unloading badly-needed supplies of rice (the manager was later able to send a boat, crewed by workers who had remained loyal, to borrow some from Salomon). The *Diégo* was fortunate in being able to make a fast voyage in both directions, arriving back at Peros Banhos within a month, this time bearing not only Magistrate Hanning, who now had ten years experience of the islands, but also a Police Inspector in command of a twelve-strong armed guard. It did not take long for the Inspector to piece together the events and to charge those responsible: 25 men were given sentences of between three and twelve months, to be served in Mauritius and to run consecutively in cases where they were found guilty on more than one count; this enabled the magistrate to maximise the impact of the punishments available without the expense of assize trials in Port Louis.[7] Ten women were given short sentences, to be served on Peros Banhos. Three of the *commandeurs* judged to have been insufficiently supportive of the manager were summarily dismissed. What seemed to lie at the root of these disturbances was manoeuvring by Adam's assistant, himself unpopular for his licentiousness, and the scope this offered to unruly elements, some having criminal records. One irony was that Hanning had himself been in Salomon at the time the disturbances began, but, in the absence of radio communication, entirely unaware of them; it was, of course, considered too expensive to the company to make good this deficiency.

Another issue to which Hanning drew attention in forceful terms was that of recruitment. The magistrate who had visited Diego Garcia and Peros Banhos in June 1931 (see note 5) had remarked that no labourers were engaged, unless they were in possession of a police certificate, but was clearly dubious about the diligence with which this rule was applied. When Hanning visited Agalega in July, he delivered himself of a general observation, applicable to all the Oil Islands:

> A point to which I attach great importance for the welfare of these islands is the unsatisfactory way in which labourers are recruited. I have noticed that several habitual criminals of the worst character are being sent; although the names of the men to be engaged are sent to the Police for enquiry as to their character before the signature of the contract, men of bad reputation and sometimes women of very loose morals (more or less infected with VD) are allowed to sign on. I am aware that some of these creatures give a false name, so that they would not be identified by the Police. In these circumstances, I am circularising the different agents informing them that in the future, any new labourer must produce his birth certificate …[8]

Although this report provided no specific evidence for his assertions, that on the Peros Banhos disturbances, written a few months later, gives the names of two such individuals among those returned to Mauritius; one had a single and the other six previous convictions, while each had two aliases.

Hanning's visit to Salomon, Eagle and Six Islands had been his first to that group. His view was that the 'far from flourishing' state of Six Islands (and Eagle) resulted from the 'abnormal drop in the price of copra', compounded by low productivity resulting from the difficulty of access to these islands. Low copra prices had already been causing difficulties in Agalega. Indeed, Hanning described the situation in the Lesser Dependencies as being one of acute depression:[9] as the market price of Rs 107 per ton was well below the production cost of Rs 145,[10] practically no sales had been made in the preceding seven months; indeed, the companies were even considering closing down their operations until prices picked up. Perhaps they wished this impression to reach the Governor, so touchingly did Hanning describe the implications of such a step for Mauritius. Be that as it might, early in 1932, Sir Wilfrid Jackson received joint representations by the companies concerned. He declined to consider their request for a protective duty against imported vegetable oils, which might make it worth establishing a refinery in Mauritius, without seeing detailed costings and plans for raising the capital required; and he rejected out of hand the notion that the Government might underwrite such an investment. Nor did he miss the opportunity to criticise the wastefulness of maintaining two independent vessels for the island trade.[11] The companies undertook to produce more detailed proposals.

Reactions in Port Louis and London

These developments led the Governor to reflect more widely on both the governance and the viability of the islands' economies; they were, he thought, being developed 'in a very haphazard and rudimentary fashion', though he was unable to make available an agricultural expert to examine their prospects on the ground.[12] Pointing out that Agalega was closer to Seychelles than to Mauritius and that the Chagos was more than halfway to Colombo, Jackson reverted to the problem of communications. As small steamers were already trading successfully on the Mauritius-Madagascar and Mauritius-Rodrigues routes, he believed that it was mainly capital constraints and the vested interests of the owners of the *Diégo* and *St. Géran* that stood in the way of a similar service to the Oil Islands. He noted too that some at least of the proprietors were willing to consider such a plan, for which the Government could hold out at least one financial inducement: the reduction from two to one in the number of magistrates assigned to the Dependencies, with the consequent halving of the Rs 18,000 per year paid by the companies for their services. Alternatively, as Magistrate Hanning had suggested (see page 347 above), the companies could together arrange for all Chagos produce to be brought to Diego Garcia, whence it could be collected and shipped direct to Colombo. However, after mulling over these options, Jackson concluded that the lack of enterprise and initiative of the closely related concessionaires represented an even greater obstacle and that, even if a larger enterprise could be persuaded to take an interest, it would have to overcome prolonged haggling from the existing owners, who could not simply be dispossessed. There remained the problem of governmental oversight, which events in Diego Garcia, Peros Banhos and Six Islands had exposed as inadequate; with a more frequent steamer service, magistrates could do more to mitigate the effects of poor management. Finally, Jackson noted the desirability of having more frequent calls made by Royal Navy ships. Lying behind this suggestion was an idea, put into his head by Vice-Admiral Fullerton, who had called at Diego Garcia aboard HMS *Effingham* in 1931, that the Governor should

HMS *Effingham*. Image courtesy of NMM.

use the occasion of a home leave to return via Colombo and then take passage
with him to visit the Dependencies on his way back to Port Louis.[13]

In November 1931, Jackson had raised this possibility with London, remarking that he would feel happier 'in the exercise of the responsibilities which vest
in me for the administration of these islands if I were able at some time to make
a personal inspection of at least some of them. The conditions as to communications however make this very difficult and uncertain, as with only sailing ships
available such a visit involves a prolonged and indefinite absence.'[14] The reaction
of the Colonial Office – to float the idea of hiving off the Chagos (and Agalega)
to become part of Seychelles Colony – was welcomed by the latter, but criticised by Jackson, who pointed out that the companies' problems in running the
islands would be made more complicated. It was left that the British government
would not help the companies obtain greater protection unless and until they
were prepared to improve efficiency by greater collaboration.

By the end of 1932 discussions amongst the oil companies had resulted in the
presentation of an agreed memorandum.[15] Its starting point was that production
of copra for export was no longer profitable, but that there would be an overall
benefit to the Mauritian economy in turning the copra into oil in Mauritius;
and it included a douceur in the form of an undertaking to introduce transport
by steamship. The case was neatly argued as providing continued employment
in the Dependencies (whose workers would otherwise worsen unemployment
in Mauritius), diversification for the Mauritius economy, near self-sufficiency
in vegetable oil products for the Colony, and price stability at existing levels;

but, to prevent dumping by the foreign producers threatened with displacement, there would need to be an adequate tariff and, to buy the machinery (mainly British and costing £30,000), a loan of £20,000 from the Colonial Development fund would have to be sought. This was exactly what Jackson had anticipated. Nevertheless, further discussion in London, involving company representatives and the Governor, resulted in approval for the project, which eventually proved valuable both to the private investors and to Mauritius: the former were able to make substantial profits from the new coconut processing company, Innova Ltd., for which the losses of the plantations were irrelevant; the latter gained in a major way when war broke out and supplies of vegetable oils from India and Ceylon were cut off. On the other hand, the expectation of British officials that they would obtain greater leverage over the plantation companies to improve conditions in the islands was not realised. The Chagos settlements were condemned to continued stagnation.

Closures, consolidation and the use of steamships

Nowhere was this truer than in those two sad islands, Eagle and Six Islands (maps on pages xiv and xiii). In both, poor management and company parsimony, combined with purely local difficulties, had made them more unprofitable than elsewhere in the Chagos. In 1932, the Company decided that its best course would be to close one establishment and have that plantation's coconuts gathered from the other. Eagle Island was the one to be shut down. The workers were moved to the establishment on Six Islands. From there a boat was sent at the start and middle of each month, taking a team of six *éplucheurs* to gather and husk the nuts and return with them after their fortnight's stint, to be replaced by a relief team. However, fresh problems arose. The *St. Géran*, which could enter the lagoons of both Eagle and Six Islands, lost her certificate of seaworthiness and was replaced in 1933 by the first steamer, ss *Wajao*. Sadly, this vessel had made only a couple of voyages to the Chagos before a freak wave lifted her bodily onto the reef at Agalega in November of the same year. This event finally precipitated the takeover of the *Société Salomon-Six Iles-Trois Frères* by its bigger associate. The terms of the takeover are no longer traceable, but the trade statistics do contain a single mention of the movement of bullion between the Chagos and Mauritius; that was the import of Rs 7,800 in 1935, presumably representing a tidying up of cash balances, little of it from the coffers of the smaller company.[16]

The Managing Agent of the *Société Huilière Diégo-Péros*, Richard Lionnet, lost no time in visiting his new acquisitions aboard the barque *Diégo*, which was henceforth to serve all the Chagos plantations. This enabled him to observe at first hand the problems of maintaining the two small islands and, rather dramatically, to experience the navigational difficulties they presented: the *Diégo*, with her 16-foot draft, could not always cross the bar into Eagle Island's lagoon, while the ocean anchorage on its western side was dangerously exposed; nor could she enter the lagoon at Six Islands at all. On this occasion, the *Diégo* anchored off Eagle's western shore, while Lionnet and his party inspected the forlorn, empty settlement and abandoned donkeys sheltering in its buildings. The others in his party were the Salomon manager, Raoul Caboche, his teenage son Paul and Fr. Dussercle, making the first of his many visits to the Archipelago. Rejoining the ship, they had to wait overnight for the first breath of wind and indeed it took the whole of the next day to reach Six Islands. Their approach was spotted and the plantation manager's whaler, the *Swan*, dispatched to meet them and bring them ashore. Unfortunately, the oarsmen lost sight of the bonfire lit to provide a marker in the fading light, the boat missed the narrow gap in the reef and they were unceremoniously dumped onto its shoulder-deep crest. By now it was nearly midnight. While four members of the crew concentrated on saving the boat, the Caboches hauled the others onto the dry land of the Ile des Rats and marched them to the next proper islet, Ile Cipaye. There the priest celebrated a midnight mass. Hours later, with the approach of dawn, the whaler arrived to transport this waterlogged band to the settlement. Meanwhile, the *Diégo* cruised beyond the reef. The following morning, they set off to rejoin her, this time by the sailing boat *Express* in a freshening breeze. By the time they reached the *Diégo* it was much too rough to come alongside and it was decided

View of the barque *Diego* from an approaching whaler. Photo courtesy of J-M. Chelin.

that they should follow their ship for the 30 mile journey back to calmer water at Eagle Island. It proved a wild ride and they only reached their destination after losing their foremast and improvising a jury rig. In case these adventures were not enough, the *Diégo* encountered, on her final departure from Diego Garcia to Mauritius, a storm of such violence that a steamer, itself in difficulties, altered course to see if the barque required help.[17]

This harsh encounter with the realities of Chagos seafaring resulted in a decision to reopen the Eagle Island establishment, reduce the numbers living on Six Islands and transport its produce to Eagle for transhipment. By the time Six Islands was next visited by a magistrate, in May 1934, the manager Gendron had already left to accompany his sick wife to Mauritius, his assistant, Lucien Quevauvilliers, was in charge and the coconuts and copra were being delivered to Eagle by small sailing boats. This arrangement was still in force when Dussercle next visited these islands in October of the same year. As should already have been apparent, this system was not efficient or even safe. Moreover, as Dussercle reported, loading the *Diégo* by lighter was a tricky operation requiring the barque to approach dangerously close to the reef; in fact, she would have been blown onto it, but for exceptional efforts of the lighter's oarsmen to tow her off.[18] Next, in February 1935, the *Express* was wrecked: towing the 28-foot open lighter *Vertige*, loaded with coconuts, she was blown past Eagle Island to the Three Brothers. After being marooned there for eighteen days, the crew managed to attach a jib to the lighter and take advantage of light winds and favourable currents to reach their intended destination.[19] The Company at last concluded that both the Eagle and Six Islands plantations must be abandoned for good. That was not quite the end of exploitation of the two small islands, for the energetic Raoul Caboche (manager of Salomon) persuaded the company that workers from Salomon could go and collect nuts from the islands involved, if a small vessel were put at his disposal. Accordingly, a 70-ton schooner, the *Germain*, was bought and a young Seychellois, Albert Lemarchand, taken on as her captain.[20] Monthly visits were made to Six Islands and some coconuts were gathered, but, as will be seen later, the experiment was fraught with difficulties.

It is only thanks to the writings of Dussercle that we have the names of the small boats so essential to the operation of the plantations, as well as examples of the skills and courage, but rarely the names, of the sailors who manned them. There is one striking exception. In June 1935, the *Diégo* was despatched to transfer the workers from the two islands to be abandoned. She began by taking 32 people from Six Islands to Salomon, while the remaining 27 sailed to Eagle Island in two of the small boats, *Sauveur* and *Swan*.[21] The *Diégo* then sailed to Eagle to transfer the new arrivals and a final cargo of coconuts and oil to Diego Garcia; and she returned once more to Eagle Island in order to remove the eleven people remaining there to Peros Banhos and Mauritius. Dussercle was again one of the passengers. On 20 June, shortly after her arrival and despite extraordinary efforts by Captain Henri Mazoué, a sudden unseasonal storm swept her onto the reef. Her predicament was observed from shore and, in the darkness, after many vain attempts, a *commandeur*, Arthur Tallat, managed to paddle a pirogue through the surf and take ashore a line, to which a thicker rope could be attached, enabling all the 35 people aboard to be taken in twos and threes to safety.

Survival of the wreck was only the start of a long ordeal.[22] There was little enough food on the island even for those already waiting to be taken off; there was no means of communicating news of the disaster; it was some time before small amounts of cargo could be salvaged; and, perhaps not surprisingly, the islanders were unhelpful, leaving it to the ship's crew to use their initiative in gathering edible vegetation, fishing and catching crayfish by torchlight. Both the *Sauveur* and the *Swan* had been swept away in the storm. The only seaworthy boat left there was the lighter, *Vertige*, which we have already encountered. Having rigged her up with decking, mast and sail, the *Diégo's* First Mate, R. Bérenger, set out with a crew of three for Peros Banhos. At the first attempt, he was driven back by strong winds; at the second, he succeeded. But Peros, itself waiting for the supplies which had gone down in the *Diégo*, could not provide all that was required, so the *Vertige* sailed and, as the wind dropped, was rowed on to Salomon, loaded up and rowed back. For the onward journey back to Eagle, Tallat took charge of the *Vertige*, while Bérenger captained one of the Peros Banhos fleet, the *Saint Louis*.[23] The two vessels arrived laden down with two huge green turtles, bunches of bananas, oranges, pumpkins and two or three kegs of salt pork, not to speak of 30 bags of rice, a crate of spare clothing, a litre of rum and a dozen packets of cigarettes (Dussercle was one chain smoker among many). We do not have to imagine the feelings of those stranded on Eagle Island. Capt. Mazoué immediately wrote to thank Caboche from the bottom of his heart for 'all his bounty, all his treats. When Bérenger got back, we were down to our last two bags of rice and nothing else … I do hope your son will be able to send a signal soon; I can't wait to get off – I just can't get the loss of the *Diégo* out of my mind. Before, the only place that always used to frighten me was the channel into Salomon'.[24]

The drama was not, of course, over. Bérenger had to return the *Saint Louis* to Peros Banhos promptly and this time he took Dussercle ('to provide him with a little distraction', as Mazoué delicately phrased it in his letter). Dussercle found plenty to interest him both on Peros Banhos and Salomon, but did not manage to return to Eagle, as he had hoped. After the vessel had been loaded in Salomon with fresh supplies of all kinds, including both a live and a salted hog, they had gone no further than Peros Banhos when another storm arose. They managed to return there for shelter, but Bérenger judged it prudent to leave Dussercle before setting out again. Meanwhile, with the *Diégo* long overdue, Port Louis arranged for the steamship *Clan MacPhee*, bound for Mauritius from India, to be diverted to the Chagos; it was only after calling in at Salomon and sounding her siren at several other islands that she found the survivors at Eagle Island on 2 September, bringing them (and the faithful *Vertige*) to Peros Banhos, but leaving the equally faithful *Saint Louis* riding peacefully at anchor. Then, after a few more weeks of waiting, the ss *Hatipara* anchored close to the Peros Banhos settlement, ready to take Bérenger, Mazoué, Dussercle and seventeen others back to Port Louis and a heroes' welcome. News of Tallat's contribution also reached the wider world. Following a report of the *Diégo's* fate in the London *Times*, small sums were raised for the survivors and for Tallat himself. The latter was also awarded the Silver Medal of the Royal Humane Society and brought to Port Louis to be presented with the medal. He was to spend the rest of his days on Peros Banhos, where he became quite a celebrity; he was presented, wearing his medal, to captains and crews of visiting ships and submarines, who showered him with gifts – he ended up with a fine collection of nautical headgear.

ss *Zambezia* at Diego Garcia. Images courtesy of Edward Duyker.

With the loss of the *Diégo*, pressure to replace her with a steamship finally became irresistible. Critical, of course, was the need to obtain a vessel with a shallow draft, so as to be able to enter the Salomon lagoon and anchor close to the jetty at Peros Banhos. The (coal-fired) *Zambezia* had been built in 1914 to work on the river from which she took her name and had even begun her life armed with a small cannon, in case of encounters with German invaders from Tanganyika. Now, in 1935, she had been abandoned on one of the Zambezi's many mudbanks and was, it must be supposed, going cheap. Her first voyage from Beira [Mozambique] to Mauritius revealed her propensity to roll, a propensity enhanced by a permanent list resulting from the original misalignment of her single screw; even when the Port Louis shipyard had added bilge keels on either side, she continued to '*roule, roule, roule*', as one *séga* refrain put it. For all that, she served the Chagos well for almost twenty years before being sold on once more to work on Indian rivers. It was in November, with Lionnet among her passengers, that she first visited the northern atolls, passing Eagle Island on the way. Sadly, the *Saint Louis* had disappeared without trace.

One company, three plantations

Notwithstanding the major changes of circumstance, the underlying pattern of life, with minor fluctuations, remained extraordinarily stable during the nineteen thirties. The population increased, but only by eleven:-

Table 17.2   Chagos population, 1931 and 1939.

	1931				1939			
	M	*W*	*C*	*Total*	*M*	*W*	*C*	*Total*
Diego Garcia	249	206	*	455	157	177	156	490
Peros Banhos	194	179	*	373	103	92	154	349
Salomon	65	40	*	105	80	66	93	239
Six Islands	37	21	*	58	–	–	–	–
Eagle Island	41	35	*	76	–	–	–	–
Chagos total				1067				1078

*not listed separately.

<u>Source</u>: 1931 Census (RHL ref. 912.s.18); 1939 Magistrate's reports (TNA CO 167/912/10).

The same was broadly true of the pattern of trade. Moreover, since the plantations *were* the Chagos from the point of view of trade – all exports had to go to Mauritius and all imports came from there – the trade figures reflect accurately what was going on in the plantation economy. It remained on an almost Lilliputian scale: over the decade Mauritius' annual imports (cif) from the Chagos were worth on average around Rs 225,000 (£16,700) and its exports (fob) around Rs 100,000 (£7,400). It would be surprising if even half of the difference represented company profit – offsetting items included the *Diégo*'s running costs, staff salaries and that (tiny) part of the employees' wages which did not come back directly in the form of purchases at the plantation boutique. Given the wider background of world economic conditions, it is hardly surprising that, however short-sighted this might seem in the abstract, resistance to any new expenditure was the guiding principle.

The islands, as ever, relied on imports for a very high proportion of their simple requirements, as can be seen from a quick glance at the annual Blue Book statistics: staple foodstuffs, such as rice, dholl, lentils, flour, sugar, salt, biscuit, tea, coffee and wine; tobacco and cigarettes; soap and toiletries; pottery, glassware, matches, candles, even joss sticks; cloth, plain or coloured, and haberdashery; supplies and equipment needed for the basic island activities, such as cement, ropes and cordage, paint, linseed oil, tar, galvanised iron and

innumerable gunny bags; occasionally, a horse, bull or cow. Machinery, petroleum and electrical goods were usually notable by their absence. On the export
side, the vast majority was accounted for by coconuts, copra (and *poonac*) and
coconut oil; the remaining 3% came from dried or salted fish, tortoiseshell, beeswax, pigs, and the occasional donkey, though mention should also be made of
the thousands of brooms and brushes, made by the women and sold in Mauritius at twenty to the rupee. This pattern applied to all the three remaining
plantations. Nevertheless, if we look at them in a little more detail, each had its
own ups and downs and its own character. Statistics, culled from Mauritius'
annual Blue Books and successive visiting magistrates' reports, tell part of the
story, as follows:-

Table 17.3   Production.

		Copra		Coconuts		Oil		Other	
		kg '000	%*	'000	%	l. '000	%	Rs '000	%
D.G.	1931–3	1494	80.8	555	6.3	197	9.9	8.8	3
	1934–6	1757	83.9	538	5.3	186	8.2	8.3	2.6
	1937–9	2126	86.7	364	4.2	38	2.7	10.8	3.5
P.B.	1931–3	1126	90.1	<0.1	0	74	7.2	5.9	2.6
	1934–6	1054	89.4	56	<1	122	7.7	4.8	2
	1937–9	1345	94.3	31	1	18	1.4	6.7	3.3
Sal.	1931–3	491	71.6	306	10.6	124	14.6	4	3.2
	1934–6	632	83.4	134	4.2	84	9.5	3.5	2.9
	1937–9	926	85.9	222	6.2	16	2.4	7.8	6

*The percentage figures represent the value of each product as a percentage of each island's total exports
for the triennium in question. Curiously, Peros Banhos exported no coconuts at all in 1931, 1932, 1936 or
1937.

Source: Mauritius annual 'Blue books' (TNA CO 172 series).

In 1939, apparently for the first time ever, the Chagos islands were visited by
a small team from the Mauritius Department of Agriculture. It was led by Dr
Octave Wiehe, a plant pathologist. His examination of the coconut plantations
focussed on both the initial planting and subsequent operation of the groves.
Except at Peros Banhos, which had an excellent nursery and carefully prepared
holes for planting the seedling palms, no selection was made of the seeds chosen for planting and little effort applied to preparation of the ground. The trees
were much too closely spaced, at 20 rather than 30 feet apart, resulting in excessive shade and low yields. The plantations all had large numbers of sterile trees,
easily recognisable by their more erect crowns. Nuts were gathered at roughly
monthly intervals, while weeding parties worked in rotation, clearing each area
about three times per year; as a result, many nuts were lost in the undergrowth
and had to be cleared as saplings. No fertiliser was applied. Rats ruined about
one third of the potential crop.[25]

Table 17.4 Labour Productivity* exports per employee.

		Population	Exports (Rs, annual average)	Rs per employee
D.G.	1931–33	328	94,000	287
	1934–36	273	111,000	407
	1937–39	331	103,000	311
P.B.	1931–33	227	75,000	330
	1934–36	178	78,000	438
	1937–39	187	67,000	358
Sal.	1931–33	87	42,000	483
	1934–36	115	39,800	346
	1937–39	128	43,300	338

*The population figures fluctuated from year to year and magistrates did not always distinguish between workers and staff (or even include the latter). All adults of both sexes have been assumed to work and children have been excluded. The 120 workers from the abandoned plantations on Eagle and Six Islands were mostly reassigned to the other three plantations in 1935. The production figures, which also fluctuated, have been averaged from the totals for each triennium. Perhaps owing to weather problems, production from all three plantations fell in 1937 to little more than half that for 1936, but rebounded in 1938.

Sources: Mauritius 'Blue Books' and annual magistrates' reports (TNA CO 172 and 167 series).

Table 17.5 Land Productivity yield per acre.*

	Approximate area (acres)	No. of coconuts picked yearly	Yield Nuts/Acre
Diego Garcia	6,000	5,300,000	885
Peros Banhos	2,835	3,536,395	1,225
Salomon	2,000	2,235,345	1,117

Comparative yields elsewhere: French Guiana (1893) 3–4,000; Zanzibar (1898) 4–8,000; Fiji (1914) 3–4,000; Ceylon (1935) 3–4,000.

*No allowance was made for marshy or other unusable areas, resulting in some understatement of productivity.

Source: Tables I and IV, Wiehe Report (1939).

As far as this last problem was concerned, the system at Diego Garcia was to organise mass drives, using dogs, which accounted for over 30,000 rats per year; while at Peros Banhos, where the problem was less severe, small tins of *poonac* laced with arsenic were placed in the tree crowns, apparently with some success. By way of remedy for the other faults, Wiehe explained how the best parent trees could be recognised, available guano applied as fertiliser, suitable creeping grasses and leguminous plants introduced, with clearing and replanting to reform the groves. While Wiehe made no comments on the time, expense or additional manpower necessary to achieve these improvements, it is clear that a sustained programme of change would be required. We do not know what attention may have been given to the report; but the outbreak of war a matter of weeks after its submission probably condemned it to oblivion.

Nevertheless, from the figures in the foregoing Tables, a few general conclusions can be drawn. In all the plantations, there was increasing concentration on copra, compared to the other uses of coconuts, but with nothing to show for it by way of increased output. Salomon's effort at diversification did not, however, raise its productivity. In each triennium Diego Garcia was less productive than the other two islands. Moreover, the increased output of copra appears to have occurred regardless of the decrease in the workforce in the first half of the decade and its greater rise in the later years. The decline in numbers employed may have resulted mainly from a decision to suspend recruitment as the economic situation worsened, but the increases after 1935 were largely the result of the reallocation to the three islands of those displaced by the closure of Eagle and Six Islands. Whatever the motivation for this decision, it is clear that greater production from the remaining plantations would have required increased investment as well as profitable markets for increased output. Neither condition was fulfilled. There was, all the same, more to the story than poor strategy.

Salomon

Let us begin with Salomon (map on page xv), not only the smallest and simplest case, but the one best documented, thanks to the availability of personal information from the family of Raoul Caboche, who managed the plantation almost continuously from 1931 until 1952. Salomon's lagoon was (and is) not only compact, but infested with coral heads, and its entrance both exceptionally shallow and host to an awkwardly placed rock (which had settled the fate of more than one ship – see page 93). Capt. Mazoué was right to fear it. With the establishment at the south-western corner, which as elsewhere was best protected from wind and wave, the loading and unloading of sea-going vessels was throughout its commercial history an unresolved problem. Given its small land area (a mere 311 hectares, only slightly more than Eagle or Six Islands), the idea of blasting entrance and lagoon in order to deepen both could never have been economic and, not surprisingly, had never been contemplated. But the atoll had three valuable advantages: the deepest and most fertile soil in the Chagos, with the most placid of all the lagoons, and also exceptionally fine native timber. These features made its artisanal, small-scale plantation easy to manage and, with a working population that rarely exceeded 100, the opportunity to establish a peaceful seigneurial system of control was self-evident. Equally obviously, there was no scope for economies of scale.

In terms of output, the performance of this plantation showed similar trends to the other two. Where it differed was in the manager's efforts to exploit the possibilities both for improving living conditions for the workers and for diversifying the range of products exported. Fallen timber, for example, was collected and used to make roofing shingles, both for export and to replace the traditional palm thatching. One result was to produce a steady and, cumulatively, very substantial improvement in the standard of workers' accommodation; by the end of the decade all the workers' palm-thatched huts had been replaced by neat cottages on cement bases, shingle-roofed[26] and each with its own water tank and latrine. Along with these innovations went efforts to vary the workers' diet and a constant concern for their welfare. Similarly, *poonac* was imported from other Chagos islands to feed pigs, which could then be exported or used to increase the supply of pork for local consumption. Salt, too, began to be made locally, as well as soap (750 lbs of which were exported to Mauritius in 1932). By 1933, the visiting magistrate went out of his way to remark that Caboche was 'the right man for the post he occupies. He has the knack of making himself popular with the men, and it is certain that his manner is [*sic*] for much in the zeal displayed by the personnel at their work'.[27]

Caboche's interest in modernisation was unflagging and one of his major contributions, in 1936, was to introduce radio communication to the Chagos for the first time, with his own teenage son as operator. Understandably, Caboche did not neglect his own comfort and the magistrate who visited in November that same year remarked

I wish to say here how I appreciated the management of Salomon Island. Mr. Caboche, who has a long experience of sugar estates in Mauritius, is making

Salomon's new workers' huts, c. 1935. Image courtesy of J-M. Chelin.

efforts to give the inhabitants of his island comfort and happiness. There – and only there – can one dine by the light of electric bulbs and enjoy, after dinner, in comfortable arm-chairs, concerts from Ceylon.[28] The moment is not very far, perhaps, when the Magistrate or visitor, when back at his home will, with deep melancholy, think of Salomon as some lost paradise."[29]

By chance, perhaps, the magistrate did not mention Raoul Caboche's refrigerator, which enabled another visitor to enjoy an ice-cold gin and tonic before dinner!

Only a year later, in 1937, the radio came into its own in an emergency. Caboche had become irritated by the tendency of *séga* evenings to degenerate into lasciviousness and fighting. He therefore imposed a ban on these events, which he intended should be temporary. As it happened, Magistrate Henri P. Dalais arrived only a few days later for the annual inspection and, inevitably, the ban on dancing was the topic of vociferous complaint by the workers. Leaving the jetty on his departure to rejoin the *Zambezia*, he called out that the workers need not worry; the *séga* would be restored. His audience, leaping to the conclusion that he had over-ruled the manager, set a dance going a few evenings later, despite Caboche's refusal of permission pending instructions from Port Louis. The manager immediately went to put a stop to the proceedings, confiscating the drums and instructing the *commandeur* to escort the drummers to the prison. On the way, the party was surrounded by an increasingly threatening crowd, whose ringleaders were starting to incite their followers to stone-throwing and violence – '*Dire li sourti la parcequi talere li pour trouve so drap mortuaire!*' ('Tell him to get out as very soon we will get his winding sheet!'). Deciding that discretion was the better part of valour, Caboche retreated to his house and, after his son Paul had radioed for assistance, put a guard on the transmitter, which the workers had threatened to destroy – '*Anous alle casse motere.*' For the next four days, the islanders were quiet, but sullen. On the fifth day the four individuals who had been ordered to go to the gaol entered it of their own accord and, one day later, the magistrate returned and held court, finding seven individuals guilty on various charges, of whom five were to serve their sentences in Mauritius and taken away on the *Zambezia*.[30]

Thus, for all Caboche's efforts, his plantation was not immune from the potential for sudden upsets, nor from commercial realities. It would appear that it may have been the initially exceptional productivity of Salomon which caused the Port Louis management to increase his workforce by 50%, but with very little increase in output to show for it. However, whether they knew it or not, the company allowed him to improve the comforts of Salomon for all its inhabitants at the expense of their 'bottom line'.

Peros Banhos

It was not until three years after the disturbances of 1931 (page 348 above) that a new and younger manager, Walter Thatcher, was appointed to this atoll (map on page xiv). To judge from successive magistrates' reports, he was both efficient and well liked. With a population diminished by the expulsions following the disturbances, his plantation scored the highest productivity per worker ever achieved in the Archipelago. Within a short time of his arrival, comments were being made about the comparatively better health of the population there and the good quality of the company *boutique*. By 1939, the docility and discipline of the workforce was being remarked on in similar vein. Dr Wiehe's comments (page 358 above) on his standards of cultivation speak for themselves. Given the character of the atoll, having a very large and potentially dangerous lagoon, with a multiplicity of small islets to be harvested and hence a large number of small boats sent off daily, with small numbers of workers spending nights, even weeks, on the more distant islets, good organisation was at a premium and good morale essential to production. Quite why the export of unprocessed coconuts was virtually abandoned is not known. Possibly, they needed to be exported when freshly gathered, a need more difficult to satisfy from a multiplicity of small islets, especially as there was little advance warning of the ship's arrival. When the *Diégo* or, later, the *Zambezia* suddenly hove into view, it would have entailed extraordinary efforts for the workers to return from the atoll's farthest corners to discharge the cargo and reload the vessel in the limited time available,

HMS *Hawkins*. Image courtesy of NMM.

if they also had to gather fresh supplies of fallen nuts.

All the plantations relied upon sailboats, ranging from simple *pirogues* made of hollowed-out logs and finely-trimmed whalers to substantial two-masted *côtiers* ('coastal' vessels capable of inter-island voyages) 30 feet or more in length. However, it was the Monday morning departure of the fleet from Ile de Coin at Peros that was the most spectacular. As Dussercle vividly described, the whole fleet was set in motion, with men, women and children stuffing the holds of their boats full of their belongings and setting off, whether to Grand Baie, Ile Pierre, Diamant, Moresby, Yéyé or Coquillage. He himself was taken in the *Hawkins*, pride of the fleet, fast as an arrow and, in the strong breeze, with her lee rail under water, despite the counterweight of the crew sitting to weather – a veritable *calèce difé* in the Creole expression.[31] Named after the Royal Navy cruiser which had visited Peros Banhos in 1933,[32] *Hawkins* was about 30 feet long, cutting a fine slender figure, with two large lateen sails and twin jibs, and looked every inch a yacht. The Peros Banhos whaler was the *Sir Henry*, used to convey the manager around the lagoon by a hand picked crew of smartly uniformed oarsmen.

Diego Garcia

As a plantation island, Diego Garcia (maps on pp. xv and 137) had never really fulfilled its promise, nor did it do so in the 1930s. We have already seen how the *Société Huilière de Diégo et Péros* responded to the impact of the economic crisis; indeed, in Diego Garcia its first action had been to cut the workers' wages. The same negativity was reflected in its response to the challenges thrown up by

Manager's pony cart, Diego Garcia, c. 1940. Image courtesy Paul Caboche.

its earlier acquisition of the Minni Minni and Pointe Marianne estates; these were simply left to wither, while labour and such investment as took place were concentrated on East Point. The Minni Minni establishment had been closed in 1884 and used to lodge the short-lived police contingent. By the time Dussercle arrived at Diego Garcia in 1934 and visited the site in the manager's pony cart, its roofless ruins were hard to distinguish amid the rampant vegetation. Only a couple of huts, providing temporary shelter for visiting *éplucheurs* (see p. 352), remained. In 1935 the company got round to informing government of its intention to abandon the lease, but, as examination by the magistrate showed that nuts were still being collected, it was forced to continue paying rent.[33] At Pointe Marianne, the settlement was formally closed in 1930, but still occupied by a score of workers under supervision, while its church, much larger than the one at East Point, continued to be used from time to time for special ceremonies.

Similarly, in replacing the murderous Edouard d'Argent by Lois de Chasteigner Dumée, the company opted for a kindly but ineffectual manager, rather than the dynamic moderniser that was required. Dumée certainly had his good qualities; the magistrate who visited in 1933 thought him the man exactly suited to his post, showing firmness and a deep sense of justice and tact, whose workers seemed happy and contented.[34] His main defect, the proximate source of many of the plantation's problems, was his complete lack of interest in the technical and scientific aspects of his job. For example, he took no interest in the idea of improving communications by installing radio telegraphy, which he thought would undermine his independence; he allowed the plantation machinery to fall steadily into disrepair; and he did virtually nothing to tackle the scourges of Diego Garcia, mentioned by virtually every visitor – the rats, flies and

Côtier at Diego Garcia 1937. Image courtesy J-M. Chelin.

mosquitoes. It is hard to resist the conclusion that, as the years went by, Dumée was overcome by the effort of achieving anything worthwhile in the face of local indifference and the company's neglect. In 1938, the visiting magistrate noted that there had been no flour available on the island for at least a month prior to his arrival and that the quantity of sugar left was so small that its distribution had to be carefully controlled. 'The manager declined all responsibility, stating that in spite of his numerous requests for larger quantities, he met with a curt refusal from the Mauritius agents.' Dumée was finally pensioned off in 1939, after being caught out in a profiteering scandal, and replaced on a temporary basis by Caboche.

Objectively, the problems of managing Diego Garcia resembled those of Peros Banhos, in that the lagoon was large and required a fleet of sturdy sailing boats to collect and transport the substantial quantities of coconuts from the subsidiary plantations. Theoretically, of course, the island's topography made possible the construction of a motorable perimeter road and the introduction of lorry transport, but this would have entailed fresh thinking and additional investment from Port Louis; Dumée was left to make do with an aging fleet bearing romantic names such as *Hermione, Queen Mary*[35] and *La Marne,* as well as a single motor boat, *Maréchal Foch.* Where the island differed was in its much larger land area and the existence of the basis for three significant dependent establishments, properly supervised. In fact, only at Pointe Marianne was there still a local manager (Gendron from Six Islands) and a small shop. Depending

Staff house at Pointe Marianne 1937, with Dussercle (left). Image courtesy of J-M. Chelin.

on the wind, it took Dumée a whole day to visit Pointe Marianne and even longer if he took his horse-drawn trap around the perimeter track. A local wireless network would of course have facilitated his management task …

The problems arising from the absence of radio communication have already been mentioned, for example in connection with the disturbances at Peros Banhos in 1931. In 1934, well before its introduction at Salomon on local initiative had proved its value, Magistrate L.J. Lincoln remarked perceptively that

> I do not think it out of place here to mention the advantages that could be derived from the creation of small wireless stations on these islands. I was particularly struck by the potentialities of Diego Garcia as a possible auxiliary naval station in time of war, and a proper wireless station there would not be out of place. For the time being, however, encouragement should be given to the different managers to build small receiving and transmitting sets, and perhaps the creation of a better station at Diego Garcia as economically as possible … with facilities for training young employees [in Mauritius].[36]

Like so many other attempts to spur the Chagos company into life, these comments sank without trace.

Approach of war

The approach of war can scarcely have been perceptible in the Chagos. The *Zambezia*, on her four-monthly visits, would surely have brought newspapers as well as letters and gossip from Mauritius. British cruisers of the East Indies Station had of course dropped in to Diego Garcia every few years to show the flag there as elsewhere in the Indian Ocean. There is, however, no trace of contingency planning for the Archipelago on the part of the Mauritius government; its highly-detailed Defence Plan, compiled in 1937, made no mention of any of its Dependencies other than Rodrigues. At one level, this was hardly surprising. The Chagos Archipelago was the remotest backwater of Mauritius' jurisdiction; similarly, at a more strategic level, the Chagos rated little attention – and, relatively speaking, deserved little in the grand scheme of things. The *Société Huilière de Diégo et Péros Banhos* was a congenitally reactive organisation and there is no evidence of any thought being given to the possibility that supplies to the islands might become more spasmodic or be cut off altogether. It is however possible that an interlocking series of managerial changes in 1939 reflected plans to have fresh management teams installed before war broke out. The successful partnership of Thatcher and his assistant, René Charoux from Peros Banhos was sent to Diego Garcia, with Charoux arriving ahead of Thatcher, while the latter took leave and before Dumée was pensioned off; a new man, Louis Monnier, was brought in to succeed Thatcher, but sent to the smaller plantation of Salomon to learn the ropes while Caboche held the fort temporarily in Diego Garcia until Thatcher's arrival. It is even possible that the striking superiority, noticed by Dr Wiehe, of the management of cultivation at Peros Banhos influenced these plans. Sadly, apart from the return of Caboche to Salomon, they were soon to go awry, but they were at least made.

There was one major exception to the general drift. Captain P.G. Taylor, an Australian aviator and close colleague of the better-known pioneer, Charles Kingsford Smith, was a visionary who foresaw the coming importance of aviation in both commercial and military terms.[37] Anticipating (in 1937) the difficulties Australia would face in the event of Japanese control of the Western Pacific Ocean, he set out to prove the feasibility of a trans-Indian Ocean air route between Western Australia and East Africa. Diego Garcia would be one of the intermediate stopping points. His proposals were at first rejected by the British government, despite the urging of the Australian Prime Minister. Finally, Taylor's persistence paid off and, with provision of the only suitable aircraft in existence (property of Richard Archbold, a wealthy and generous American aviator and naturalist), the flight took place in June 1939.[38] The British had now agreed to contribute up to £3,500 and, more importantly, to make available HMS *Manchester*, which was dispatched to Diego Garcia to lay a mooring buoy, provide stocks of fuel and lubricant and stand by to give any assistance Taylor might require. The aircraft, nick-named the *Guba*, a Consolidated PBY-2, was a forerunner of the PBY-5 Catalinas. She arrived there on 14 June, thus becoming the first aircraft to fly to the Chagos. One hundred copies of Taylor's formal report on the flight, with careful recommendations for developing the route for military and civilian purposes, were sent to the British authorities, who shelved them.

When Taylor made his brief visit, his impressions of the island were based largely on a conversation with Dumée, and concerned mainly the possibilities for establishing a staging post for flying boat passengers and crews. What he called the 'fairly cool and consistent climate' would be 'ideal for passengers', as would the lagoon, with its clear waters fringed by white sandy beaches. One blot on this idyllic scene was the 'plague of flies', which were 'very unpleasant and would need to be exterminated'. Taylor remarked too on the absence of any wireless or telegraph, which meant that the *Zambezia*'s four-monthly visits were the only means of contact with the outside world. Even the manager's radio set was broken. Other signs of disorganisation were to be noticed in the state of the island's one small motor boat, which lacked vital parts of its engine, and in the broken-down bandsaw, essential for construction work. But Taylor saw the substantial sailing boats capable of transporting timber or other freight within the lagoon and considered the standard of workmanship was such that satisfactory pontoons, lighters or similar craft could be built locally. Lastly, Taylor took comfort in the availability of food, in the form of poultry, pigs, fish and land crabs, and in the good health of the people, who – he must have been told – did not suffer from malaria or other tropical diseases. Dumée's optimistic account clearly suited Taylor's purpose. Intriguingly, his impending visit had also attracted the company's interest in Port Louis. Sensing perhaps a new source of income rather than undergoing a sudden conversion to modernity, they proposed to Paul Caboche that he should go to Diego Garcia aboard a steamer diverted for the purpose, in order to repair Dumée's set and act as radio operator during the visit, but offered a fee far too small to tempt him.[39]

Summing up the Depression years

On this banal note ended another decade of missed opportunities. The 1930s did however – more by accident than design – force upon the companies the much-needed consolidation essential to any long-term profitability. The decade also saw some modest improvements in the standard of care given to the islands' workers. Beyond this, Fr. Dussercle's ministrations encouraged progressive acceptance of Christian religious answers to the conundrums of existence and behaviour. The range of Catholic liturgies included processions to the cemetery and an annual procession for the blessing of the whole population and their vessels at the water's edge. The priest's visit to Diego Garcia in 1939 coincided with that of the *Manchester*, whose captain supplied a 30-strong detachment of smartly uniformed sailors to add colour to the occasion. Another, but completely unconscious, process was also under way: the consolidation of the inhabitants of the Chagos into a grouping distinct from the workers in the other minor dependencies of Mauritius. Even Dussercle, who did so much to chronicle these islanders' way of life in this period, seemed unaware that his writings might also contribute to the definition of a distinct society. We have attempted to describe elements of this society, presenting also a small selection of the photographs taken mainly by management staff of the period. Most of these were snapshots taken with simple cameras, defying high-quality digital reproduction. For an evocative array of such images, we commend to readers' attention Jean-Marie Chelin's recently published *Les Ziles La Haut*.[40]

While a distinctive society was emerging in the Chagos, the pattern of shorter term movements between Mauritius and these islands evidently continued unabated. On this topic, one poignant passage by Dussercle is indeed worth quoting at some length. Discussing (in the context of the imminent closure of the Six Islands plantation) the comparative advantages of life in the islands and in Mauritius, Dussercle comments as follows:

It isn't necessary to be rich to be happy; money has never created happiness. And I know about those who bite their nails at the prospect – so falsely embraced – of moving to Mauritius; to a Mauritius where, finding themselves outside the meanest of the local classes, they have nothing to eat: famine for themselves and fever for their children, children who are so well, so chubby in the islands, but wilt and die in the unfamiliar climate. It's as well to tell them the facts. A waste of breath! The experience of others counts for nothing. It's received with a smile or shrug of the shoulders, signifying the ignorance or malevolence of the offerer of such advice. Then, having undertaken the wretched experience of voyaging to the supposed Land of Cockayne, they come by the dozen to your door, hand outstretched

> *Mon Père, çarite moi dé trois cass, mo faim, trois zours sans manzer*

It's all too true. And when you ask if they've been able to find work, of course they reply in the negative – after all, how many poor Mauritians there are too, who have nothing with which to feed their children. Poor, poor grown-up children of the islands who are unwilling to understand their happy condition: there they are at least guaranteed their ration of rice. No wonder their one desire is to go back; how happy they consider themselves if they secure re-employment. And then they accept the truth of my observations.

> *Nous ti croire ous cause menti. Vrai même ça qui ous ti dire nous*

Yes, but all too often it's too late.[41]

Dussercle's comments are in their vocabulary redolent of their time, but his deep, if paternalist, affection for the islanders is beyond dispute. A recurring theme of this narrative has been the limited opportunities afforded by work in the islands, offset by the certainty of nourishment, adequacy of housing and an undemanding style of life. As visiting magistrates occasionally remarked, labourers in the Chagos were, at least in the early 1930s, 'economically many times better off than the Mauritian labourer'.[42] Despite these positive elements, the employers found it hard to attract workers even when unemployment in Mauritius was high. Low pay was one obvious disincentive, but it is hard to escape the conclusion that conditions on the islands were felt to be deeply unsatisfying to many who experienced them. In the absence of contemporary social analysis, we can only speculate about this problem; we do not even know whether it was primarily recently arrived individuals or those of island descent who sought escape. One explanation is the widespread bullying by the strong; women were particularly vulnerable and opportunities for the children to advance through education non-existent. If the 1920s showed the limitations of the pattern of exploitation of the Chagos developed over the preceding century, the 1930s put many difficulties in the way of profitable modernisation. Dussercle's view of the harsh realities of those desperate times was probably correct, but it is little wonder that some of the islanders were ready to chance their luck by going to Mauritius.

Notes to Chapter 17

1 TNA CO 167/867/13 W.J. Hanning to Diego Garcia and Peros Banhos, July–August 1930.

TNA CO 167/ 875/12 P. Rousset to Salomon, Eagle and Six Islands, November 1930; R. Espitalier Noël to Diego Garcia and Peros Banhos, May–June 1931.

TNA CO 167/ 879/3 W.J. Hanning to Salomon, Eagle and Six Islands, August–September 1931.

TNA CO 167/883/1 P. Rousset to Salomon and Six Islands, February–March 1933.

TNA CO 167/885/12 R. Espitalier Noël to Diego Garcia, Six Islands, Eagle Island, Salomon and Peros Banhos, September 1933; A.J. Lincoln to Six Islands, Eagle Island, Salomon, Peros Banhos and Diego Garcia, May–June 1934.

TNA CO 167/ 893/4 H.P. Dalais to Diego Garcia, Peros Banhos and Salomon, October 1935.

TNA CO 167/ 893/19 P. Rousset to Diego Garcia, Peros Banhos and Salomon, July 1936.

TNA CO 167/896/16 H.P. Dalais to Diego Garcia, Peros Banhos and Salomon, July 1937.

TNA CO 167/ 905/11 M. Lavoipierre to Diego Garcia, Peros Banhos and Salomon, October 1938.

TNA CO 167/912/10 P. Rousset to Diego Garcia, Peros Banhos and Salomon, May–June 1939.

2 We have been unable to discover the meaning of this expression – free against guarantee??

3 TNA CO 167/874/3 Enclosure to Despatch dated 31 May 1931.

4 TNA CO 167/879/3 Enclosure to Despatch dated 23 March 1932.

5 *Ibid.* The magistrate thought the cause might be the escape of heavy metal residues from the ruptured hull of the mv *El Maren* (see page 304), but analysis of the samples he took disproved this theory; the periodic toxicity of certain fish species was a naturally occurring event. Later (CO 167/905/11) it was thought that Dengue fever, which had broken out briefly in Australia, had been brought to Six Iles by the *El Maren* and had subsequently been carried via Eagle Island to Diego Garcia, all three having had outbreaks of *guimbé-guimbé*, as it was known locally.

6 TNA CO 167/875/12 Enclosure 2 of Despatch No. 437 dated 16 November 1931. Report of Magistrate R. Espitalier Noël.

7 TNA CO 167/879/4 Subsequently, the Procureur-Général in Port Louis decided that some sentences were *ultra vires*, but that their salutary effect should be maintained by quiet releases of all but the most serious offenders after twelve months in prison.

8 TNA CO 167/875/12 Enclosure 1 to Despatch dated 16 November 1931.

9 TNA CO 167/875/12 Report dated 17 August 1931.

10 It is not clear how these figures are to be reconciled with those derived from the Blue Books, but they show the same picture.

11 TNA CO 167/879/3 Sir Wilfrid Jackson, Despatch No. 106 dated 23 March 1932.

12 *Ibid.* Sir W. Jackson, Despatch dated 30 March 1932.

13 TNA CO 167/875/12.

14 *Ibid.* Despatch No. 437, dated 16 November 1931.

15 TNA CO 167/879/4.

16 Rs 3,600 from Diego Garcia, Rs 2,300 from Peros Banhos, Rs 1,800 from Salomon and a mere Rs 100 from Eagle Island.

17 This incident is related vividly in the first of Dussercle's books, *L'Archipel de Chagos – en mission Novembre 1933–Janvier 1934* (pp. 96–126).

18 Dussercle, R., *Archipel de Chagos: en mission Septembre–Novembre 1934* General Printing. Port Louis, 1935.

19 This drama became the subject for a *séga*, part of which has been recorded for posterity in Dussercle's *Dans les Ziles là-Haut* (pp. 154–55).

20 According to Paul Caboche (personal communication), the *Germain*, already on the shipping register in 1853, had been used to transport sugar from the Ferney estate (in SE Mauritius) to Port Louis, before road transport became more economic.

21 According to Dussercle (*En mission Septembre–Novembre 1934*, pp. 134–5), the population of Eagle in October 1934 had been not more than 30 all told, while that of Six Islands (*op. cit.* p. 97) had been just over 80; 32 men, 20 women and about 30 children. There must therefore have been some later reductions prior to the two islands' final closure in June 1935.

22 Dussercle, *Naufrage de la Barque Diégo à l'Ile d'Aigle aux Chagos,* General Printing, Port Louis, 1936.

23 As the *Saint Louis* was leaving Peros in the dusk, a small boat collided with her, smashing one of Bérenger's fingers, the top joint of which had to be amputated, but no one was ready to make the return voyage in the absence of his guidance …

24 Letter dated 17 July 1935 (copy provided to author by Paul Caboche). We are indebted to Mr Julien Durup for translations of some of the terms used in the original French, in particular, *tierçons de petits salé*, which we have rendered as kegs of salt pork. *Petits salé* appears in Breton recipes involving salted pork belly as an ingredient, while *tierçons* were a type of wooden box or barrel still found in Seychelles shops in the 1940s.

25 Library of Royal Botanic Gardens, Kew. Dr P.O. Wiehe *Report on a Visit to the Chagos Archipelago, 1939* (mimeographed).

26 According to the manager's son, Paul Caboche (personal communication), the very durable shingles were used for the roofs of the workers' huts only when Raoul Caboche learned that the shingles exported to Mauritius were not being sold, but purloined by the Directors to improve their own houses.

27 TNA CO 167/885/12 Report by R. Espitalier Noël. Raoul Caboche had been appointed manager in 1931, after the sugar plantation he managed had gone bankrupt following its destruction in that year's devastating cyclone.

28 By an extraordinary chance, the young Caboche had been given the *Diégo*'s radio receiver to repair just before her fatal trip to Eagle Island. He had no difficulty in getting it to work perfectly, as the magistrate discovered, but was still awaiting the components to make his own transmitter, which he introduced in 1936.

29 TNA CO 167/893/4 Report by Henri P. Dalais.

30 TNA CO 167/896/16 The magistrate's report includes further details, for example that the manager's son stood guard with his rifle all night to protect his father and the radio, a statement that Paul Caboche rejects categorically (personal communication dated 15 July 2005); it was clear that there was no love lost between Dalais and the Caboches. Marcel Didier, a later commentator, drew attention (*La Gazette des Iles*, issue 878 February 1988) to the coincidental timing of the fracas on Salomon with violent strikes in Mauritius, but offered no evidence of a causal link.

31 Dussercle, R., *Naufrage de la Barque Diégo*, p. 217. The literal meaning of this expression, in French *calèche du feu*, is 'a fiery coach'.

32 TNA ADM 53/78639 HMS *Hawkins* called at Peros Banhos on 5 May 1933 and spent two full days at Diego Garcia a few days later. Her Captain was T.S.V. Phillips, who, as Admiral Sir Tom Phillips, perished in HMS *Prince of Wales* at Singapore in 1941. Unfortunately, his Report of Proceedings for the Peros Banhos visit does not survive and the only account is to be found in a light-hearted book, *Nil Desperandum*, by the ship's chaplain, W.E. Rea, printed privately 'to enliven memories of all who served in HMS *Hawkins* between 1932 and 1935'; this remarks that the inhabitants 'with the humble means at their disposal – and here I speak for all those tiny isolated islands – do their best to make the Navy welcome. In Diego they sent on board dozens of crabs, most attractively mounted on neatly polished wood'.

33 TNA CO 167/893/4.

34 TNA CO 167/885/12.

35 Perhaps named after a 60-ton vessel in Mauritius, having both sails and a petrol engine, rather than the British liner, which did not make her maiden voyage until 1936.

36 TNA CO 167/885/12.

37 Sir Gordon Taylor GC *The Sky Beyond* Cassell Australia 1963.

38 TNA AVIA 2/2826.

39 Paul Caboche, personal communication.

40 J-M. Chelin *Les Ziles La Haut* 2012, printed by J & S Printing, Mauritius.

41 Dussercle, R., *En mission Septembre–Novembre 1934* (pp. 101–2). The two remarks in Kreol may be roughly translated as 'Father, out of your pity, give me three cents – I'm hungry. I haven't eaten for three days.' And 'We thought you were telling us lies. But what you said was the plain truth'.

42 TNA CO 167/879/4 For instance, W.J. Hanning, reporting on Peros Banhos in 1931.

18

At the Mercy of Events

I NEVITABLY, the Second World War was to have a much greater impact on the Chagos than did the First. The Indian Ocean's importance had grown in line with the world's increasing use of oil, much of it coming from the Persian Gulf and, once Italy had joined Germany as an enemy in June 1940, this importance became accentuated for Britain, with more and more of her troops and materials requiring to be transported to the Middle East via the Cape of Good Hope. Japan's involvement, with its implications for Australasian forces and supplies, though her actual attacks came eighteen months later, could only intensify the trend. The vast area of this ocean multiplied the difficulties of defending it, until long-range aircraft could be deployed to assist naval units in reconnaissance and communications. All these factors added to the potential of Diego Garcia as a mid-oceanic link, in the event that use of existing bases round the periphery were denied. As matters turned out, not all of the island's potential needed to be used: its radio communications proved themselves from the start; its harbour could and did allow ships up to the size of cruisers and light aircraft carriers to refuel; equally, its use as one of a chain of island flying boat bases increased vastly the utility of these aircraft; and, fortunately, the adequacy of the forces posted to defend it never had to be tested or even, in regard to extreme dangers, developed.

As will be seen, the usage of Diego Garcia in these varied roles reflected events far beyond its shores, but these swells from far-off storms had a major impact on all of the Archipelago's plantations and people. It was not simply a matter of accommodating a military component, but of bearing the losses and disruption resulting from enemy sinkings of merchant shipping. Moreover, the effect on the islands' civilians was cumulative, whereas, for the military personnel, life improved steadily, once the frantic preparations against direst emergency yielded to security and regular routines, as the Allies came to gain the upper hand from mid-1942 onwards. When war ended, the troops could go home, taking much of their impedimenta with them; but the islands and islanders were left with the negative consequences of investments foregone, links with families and friends in Mauritius loosened, and infrastructure neglected. With the exception of Dussercle, scarcely any civilian visitors came their way (after 1939, the next magistrates' visits took place in 1944 and 1945, but both reports have been weeded from the British National Archive). Thus we focus more on the war's impact upon the Chagos than on the Chagos' impact – or, more exactly, Diego Garcia's – upon the war. One effect of this approach has been to limit the appreciation given to the efforts of the units and individual members of the armed forces posted there. We are not oblivious to the debt owed to those concerned, but it must be repaid separately.

Initial naval activity and its impact on the Chagos

When war broke out, it was natural and sensible to guard quickly against repetition of the tactics employed to such devastating effect by the *Emden* in 1914. Not only did German strategy dictate that British naval forces should be diverted from direct defence of Britain, but intelligence reports indicated that as many as three German surface raiders were being sent to the Indian Ocean.[1] In fact, during August 1939 two pocket battleships had already been dispatched to the mid-Atlantic, each with her own supply ship and, in November, one of these, the *Graf Spee*, was to make a brief foray into the Indian Ocean, where she made one successful attack before resuming her South Atlantic predations and meeting her end a month later in the River Plate. On 3 September, immediately upon receiving news of the declaration of war against Germany, the Commander-in-Chief, East Indies (in Colombo) sent ships at his disposal to search for the raiders.[2] HMS *Cornwall* was dispatched to the Andaman Islands, HMS *Delight* to the Nicobars, HMS *Gloucester* to Mombasa and HMS *Birmingham* and *Eagle* first to the area west of Sumatra and thence to the Maldives, with *Eagle* carrying on southwards to the Chagos.

HMS *Eagle*. Image courtesy of NMM.

HMS *Odin*. Image courtesy of NMM.

A few weeks later, the Admiralty formed no less than eight powerful Hunting Groups. One of them, Force I (HM Ships *Cornwall*, *Eagle*, *Kent*, *Dorsetshire*, and later *Gloucester*, replacing *Eagle*), was dispatched to scour an area of the Indian Ocean bounded by the coordinates 10°N to 10°S and 70°E to 80°E. No raider was found and the conclusion was soon drawn that it was almost certainly the Germans themselves who had put about rumours designed to disperse the Royal Navy's resources over as wide an area as possible. It was therefore decided to use such vessels to protect the most important of the many convoys now moving troops and supplies from Australasia towards the Red Sea and from Europe round the Cape of Good Hope. To replace them, four submarines were detached from the China Station to form a new (Eighth) Flotilla of the East Indies Fleet. Three of these – HM Submarines *Otus*, *Odin* and *Orpheus* – were assigned to the area previously patrolled by the ships of Force I and, fortunately, three patrol reports, one for each submarine, survive.[3] Their interest lies mainly in the comments made on contacts with the island communities.

The first to examine the Chagos area, during the last three weeks of November 1939, was HMS *Otus*, which made several circuits of the Archipelago, initially to establish which islands were capable of providing anchorages suitable for raiders or their supply ships. Only Peros Banhos and Diego Garcia were found adequate and *Otus* visited both, as well as Salomon, meeting all the managers and the captain of the *Zambezia*, which happened to be delivering supplies to the islands. The commander of *Otus*, Lieutenant-Commander Nicolay, a great-nephew of a Governor of Mauritius, established very good relations with his interlocutors.[4] He also made a start on improving their radio communications – Diego Garcia's radio was completely useless: key components were being repaired in Mauritius, and the generator, repaired by the *Otus*, was broken again immediately by the unskilled operator. Commenting on Nicolay's report on his patrol, the Flotilla Commander noted that 'the most suitable and economic way to search the Great Chagos Bank would be to employ aircraft, preferably flying boats' which, if based at Peros Banhos or Diego Garcia, could reach all the anchorages in a few hours.[5] He also commented that in Diego Garcia there was already one flying boat mooring laid and stores of aviation spirit and engine oil – these were of course relics of the still recent *Guba* visit (see p. 368).

Otus was relieved by *Odin* (whose report of this patrol is missing), which was in turn relieved by *Orpheus*, arriving at a Peros Banhos rendezvous on 20 December. Nothing of operational significance occurred during the 24 days she spent in Chagos waters. The submarine did however provide the islanders with a Christmas Day present: she encountered the schooner *Germain*, which had left Six Islands a week earlier and was bound for Salomon, taking 25 workers home. They had run short of fresh water and were given 100 gallons. What then happened to the *Germain* remains a mystery, for when *Orpheus* next visited Salomon on New Year's Day 1940, there was great concern at the schooner's non-arrival. After a vain search, the submarine continued her patrol, but then on 12 January encountered the schooner once more, close to the entrance to Diego Garcia, and apparently en route *from* Six Islands.

The schooner *Germain*. Image courtesy of J-M. Chelin.

There is then a gap in the reporting sequence, with the next patrol report being that of HMS *Odin*, which arrived off Salomon on 8 February. Again, the submarine's visit to the Chagos was operationally uneventful, but of considerable importance to the inhabitants. In the first place, *Odin* helped solve the *Germain*'s problems, taking her broken chronometer to Diego Garcia for repair and helping Captain Lemarchand by inviting him aboard the submarine to copy out the relevant bits of the Nautical Tables – and remarking drily in his report 'lacking these two aids to navigation, it is perhaps hardly surprising that this schooner so often loses herself'. Second, *Odin* went to a great deal of trouble to solve the three islands' communications problems. At Salomon, the island's efficient and enthusiastic radio operator came aboard for instruction on how to use the Playfair Code, but, listening in afterwards, the submariners could hear both Salomon and Ceylon transmitting without contacting each other. As for Peros Banhos, the plantation remained without wireless telegraphy – in fact *Odin* gave the manager a lift to Salomon and back to put the two plantations in touch! It was during this trip that the manager explained an even more important concern: a severe shortage of rice. The shortage appears at first sight inexplicable. When the *Zambezia* had visited at the end of May 1939, the visiting magistrate reported the amount of existing stocks and of the supplies then delivered. He also reported the managers' estimates of monthly consumption, from which it is easy to work out how long the stocks could be expected to last; six months in the case of Salomon, eight months for Peros Banhos and over eleven months for Diego Garcia.[6] After consultation with Colombo, the *Odin* was instructed to fetch 100 bags of rice from Diego Garcia;[7] returning from this mission via Salomon, she once more encountered the *Germain*, this time arriving with a cargo of rice for that island. These events, together with the coincidence of the arrivals at Salomon of the *Otus* and *Zambezia* in November 1939, strongly suggest that the outbreak of war must have caused the latter's sailing from Port Louis to be delayed. Moreover, the shortage at Peros Banhos only a few months later and the need to dispatch the *Germain* to replenish Salomon's stocks from Diego Garcia, make clear that the company had skimped on the supplies dispatched in November.

The last submarine patrol of the Chagos, once again by HMS *Odin*, (though her captain's report has not survived) took place in late March; and in April the submarines of the Eighth Flotilla were ordered to the Mediterranean. In May, however, rumours of German raiders gave way to reality. Two powerfully-armed vessels, disguised as merchantmen, rounded the Cape. One, the *Atlantis*, operating over a wide area between (roughly) Mauritius and Sumatra, was to sink twelve ships between June and November, with the other, the *Pinguin*, causing similar devastation further south. Thus it was that, in the same month, HMS *Kent* was dispatched to visit the three main atolls. The ship's crew used an afternoon in the Peros Banhos lagoon to conduct crossing-the-line ceremonies, while the ship's pinnace investigated Salomon – a visit documented by Marcelle Lagesse and also by HRH the Duke of Edinburgh; the latter's Midshipman's journal providing corroboration of his light-hearted exchanges with the island's managers and the *Germain*'s captain and his wife (see inset overleaf). After anchoring overnight at Diego Garcia, the *Kent* returned to Colombo. No sign of a German presence was detected.

HMS *Kent*. Image courtesy of NMM.

The war's impact intensifies

Meanwhile, the situations in the Mediterranean and Red Seas had become ever more difficult in the run-up to Italy's formal declaration of war on 11 June 1940 and the fall of France a week later. Among the casualties, *Odin* was sunk on 13 June and *Otus* on 19 June. Much traffic between Britain and the East had in consequence to be diverted round the Cape of Good Hope. The concentration of

The Prince of Salomon*

The cruiser HMS *Kent* is at Aden on 12 May 1940. In the ship's log we find this entry:

1720 Joined Midshipman HRH Prince Philip of Greece.

Next day, the Kent sailed for Colombo and, after a short stay, sailed again southwards, visiting the Maldives; and then, on 27 May

1035 Lowered pinnace to obtain intelligence from inhabitants of Salomon Is.

The following extracts from HRH's Midshipman's Journal for 2 June 1940 describe his participation in this proceeding:

'We were back on our original job, which has since come to be known as Island hunting. We passed the Maldive Islands and soon after we sighted the first of the Chagos group which was our destination. We passed several close to, keeping good lookout for any masts showing above the coconut palms … We left the ship about 1030 having filled the boat up with our lunch and tea, rifles, ammunition, revolvers, wireless sets and telegraphists. After a rather haphazard navigation of the rocks in the lagoon, we eventually came alongside a small jetty. We were very cordially met by the French manager, his wireless operator and the skipper of a copra schooner which was lying in the lagoon … A long and complicated bilingual cross-examination ensued while the schooner captain seemed to take a great delight in airing the least printable words in the English language on people who

HRH Prince Philip of Greece

could fully appreciate them. Eventually all the necessary information was wheedled out of the reluctant and somewhat suspicious manager. He then told us rather resignedly that every time a British warship came through he had to answer exactly the same questions.

We then decided it was time for some food and having offered the manager's daughter some fresh meat and bread as a peace offering, we returned to the boat, assured the crew that the natives were friendly and the sharks tame, and collected our lunch. We returned to the house and broke our bread while the hosts drank coffee. The skipper's wife joined us there. She was small and pretty in a French way and spoke no English, in fact she hardly spoke at all. After lunch we were shown the island. Before we left the ship, the Captain had expressed a (universal) desire for fresh fish, so having made enquiries at the island, we left with a guide the Navy's efforts on protection of the most important convoys meant that traffic of lower priority, including ships bound to and from Mauritius, were particularly vulnerable to attack by the German raiders. A third development of consequence to the Indian Ocean was the accession to power of the French Vichy regime under Maréchal Pétain, hero of Verdun: the consequent bitter division between the Pétainists and the Free French under de Gaulle was to be felt not only in Madagascar and Reunion, which both opted for Vichy, but also

and proceeded to blow them up with small charges. We let go about four charges and collected about fifty or sixty fish. This was probably the most amusing episode of the day. Four of us got into bathing suits and as the fish came to the surface we dived in and threw them into the boat. Eventually, after a most interesting day we returned aboard at 1800.

The ship in the meanwhile had gone to another island to pay a similar call. The same thing happened next day when we visited the largest and most southerly of the Chagos group, Diego Garcia, of Blue Lagoon fame. We left the same afternoon and returned to Colombo without further adventure. Having spent Thursday, Friday and Saturday in Colombo we left again for Bombay and after that another secret job as yet not announced.'

Marcelle Lagesse published her own account of this visit in 1947, on the occasion of Prince Philip's engagement to the then Princess Elisabeth.

P. Caboche, M. Lagesse (l) and Sylvie Lemarchand (r). Image courtesy Paul Caboche.

'Lieutenant Commander Blundell announced briskly that the Midshipman Philip Mountbatten was related to Admiral Mountbatten and was a descendant of Queen Victoria ... Nothing astonished us any more. Not even that this tall, fair-haired young man, with a sailor's tan, cheerful smile and generous heart, who looked you in the eye, should have thought of bringing us poor savages a thousand comforts AND fresh meat, an unheard of delicacy on our island. What could be more natural than that this young man should be of royal descent and conduct himself as a normal mortal? Or that he should appreciate our simple boiled breadfruit with butter? Or that, when I complimented him on his impeccable French, he should remark 'I lived for nine years in France and I'm very fond of that country'?

After tea, our visitors asked to take a stroll. Philip Mountbatten filmed our departure, our passage along the verandah, decorated with its anchors and lifebuoy, our halt at the garden fence, some scenes of daily life, the silhouettes of some women, including the sailing captain's wife [Sylvie Lemarchand], who spent 18 months with us – all souvenirs to remember when he got home, when the world was at peace again.

My own souvenirs were our visitors' visiting cards and a sailor's hat that someone gave me and which I still wear when I go sailing.'

Abridged from an article published in Chagos News No. 27 (Spring 2006)

*TNA ADM 53/112525; Mauritius *Journal Officiel* 1947 *Savez-vous Que?*

in Mauritius[8] and faraway Chagos.

From 1940 onwards, ships of the Royal and Australian navies began using the lagoon of Diego Garcia for refuelling operations.[9] It was important that these vessels, and others transiting the area, should be able to report that they were safe, without giving away their positions by using radio while on passage. There was also a need for daily weather reports. There was thus an immediate requirement to improve radio communications with Diego Garcia by the recruitment of a properly trained Wireless Telegraphist. The choice made was an inspired one: Raoul Caboche's son Paul was one of a small band of Mauritian self-taught radio enthusiasts, capable, as we have seen, of designing and building sets as well as operating them; in addition to these technical accomplishments, he was, by virtue of his teenage voyages in sv *Diégo*, familiar with the Chagos Archipelago as a whole. Indeed, he had even been acting as the *Zambezia's* radio operator at the moment when HMS *Otus* had first appeared off Salomon. His duties now were to transmit to Mauritius daily weather reports; to transmit coded signals from the naval and merchant ships which called in to record their safe passages; in addition, he was to provide the plantation's own communications. This last was to cause friction with Walter Thatcher, the newly appointed manager, who considered himself to have first call on Caboche's services and to be entitled to be privy to the content of coded messages (Caboche arranged for a sharp reprimand).[10] Thatcher also chose to make do without the services of Charoux, his erstwhile colleague from Peros Banhos.[11] Charoux was replaced by Louis Talbot, an outspoken individual, who made no secret of his Pétainist views. Thus began the unravelling of the Company's plans for better management of the island.

Salomon, in contrast, benefited from continuity of management, but also from the determined efforts by Raoul Caboche and his daughter to maintain morale, by organising events such as V-for-Victory sign writing campaigns. The islanders were also encouraged to keep a lookout for strange ships approaching: for example, radio reports were made from Salomon in July 1940 about the close passage of what proved to be HMAS *Westralia*. Similarly, when news came of the loss of the *Otus*, flags were flown at half-mast for three days in honour of her crew. There was never any doubt where the Caboche family's loyalties lay. At Peros Banhos, Louis Monnier was a new manager, who had been assistant manager at Agalega, but had had only the shortest of local apprenticeships in Salomon. At first he had to administer the widely dispersed plantation on his own, but the eventual arrival of an assistant was to prove disastrous. Early in 1941, a ship arrived at Diego Garcia to remove Talbot from his Pointe Marianne house at an hour's notice and take him to Mauritius, his family being left behind with no word of explanation. No doubt he was paying the price for expressing his views. After Talbot had spent a month in detention, the company's chairman,

Jules Leclézio,[12] interceded with the Governor on Talbot's behalf and secured his release for posting to Peros Banhos to help Monnier. Then, late in 1941, it emerged that Monnier, on arriving at Peros Banhos (before the fall of France), had christened the establishment's new whaler *Admiral Darlan*.[13] This was apparently considered provocative by the military authorities now installed on Diego Garcia. The armed merchant cruiser, HMS *Ranchi*, was diverted via Peros Banhos on her way to Mauritius and Paul Caboche, who was leaving the Chagos for other duties, found himself instructed to watch over Monnier and Talbot for their journey back. Who then was to manage Peros Banhos? Gaston Vielle, a widowed mine manager from Madagascar, who had recently come to Diego Garcia to manage the shop, found himself thrust into unexpected authority.[14] Politics aside, these managerial upheavals can only have set back what Thatcher had achieved on the atoll, while leaving him to manage the Diego Garcia plantations largely on his own.

Fr. Dussercle (right) and Walter Thatcher set off for Gaston Vielle's wedding (see note 14). Image courtesy of Fernand Mandarin.

Collapse of the Nouvelle Société

If the early naval visits were but the harbinger of maritime warfare, the problems in supplying the plantations also signalled more serious difficulties affecting *La Nouvelle Société*. It is not certain how many visits were made by the *Zambezia* in 1940, since the Chagos shipping figures were aggregated with those for Agalega, but the low total tonnage makes it certain that there were fewer than three voyages.[15] One reason for this could have been interruption to Mauritian imports of supplies from India. Whatever the precipitant, there must have been a collapse in the company's financial situation, for on 13 January 1941 an Extraordinary General Meeting was called, at which the company went into liquidation. A month later, it was sold at judicial auction for Rs 655,000.[16] The purchaser was Jules Leclézio, son of Henry Leclézio who had taken similar action in 1893 (see page 259). Jules had also, like his father, emerged as a key figure in Mauritius society and close confidant of the Governor. It is even possible that his purchase was made at the governor's request (with the release of Talbot as a return favour), given the implications of abandonment for the Chagos population. Having renamed the company Diego Ltd.,[17] Leclézio was to retain its chairmanship until shortly before his death in 1951. Richard Lionnet remained as Managing Agent. Whether the local managers, let alone the employees, had any inkling of the potential sudden ending of their whole way of life remains a mystery to this day.

Increasing use of Diego Garcia

The concentration of the Eastern Fleet's resources on convoy protection work, entirely sensible as it was, brought into focus the lack of surveillance capacity in the Indian Ocean, leading the C-in-C, East Indies, to express 'grave concern' at the fact of having only one Catalina flying boat at his disposal.[18] One consequence was that patrolling of the Chagos became an ad hoc process, achieved by the occasional diversion of ships not required for convoy protection. It was not until April 1941 that two Catalinas from the Singapore-based Squadron 205 could be spared to begin surveillance operations in the western Indian Ocean.[19] Plans were also then made to establish simple base facilities on Mauritius, Seychelles, the Maldives and the Chagos; so the RAF Auxiliary *Ann* was dispatched to these places, to install moorings, stores of fuel and ammunition, and also sufficient accommodation and rations to last one Catalina crew for a month. In the case of Diego Garcia, the *Ann* and another auxiliary, the RAFA *Shengking*, had by early June provided 275 tons of fuel and lubricants, together with sixty 250-pound bombs. In July, naval planners, considering the options for Indian Ocean defence in the event of Japanese attacks making Singapore unusable, decided that Diego Garcia's initial role should be as a refuelling base for cruisers and smaller ships.[20] Thus, for the first time in its history, the island became a base for military operations.

The first Catalina actually to visit Diego Garcia arrived there from Ceylon on 16 May 1941. This was not simply a proving flight but an operational mission to look for the supply ship of a German raider sunk a week earlier. The pilot chosen to undertake this task was a Canadian, Alex Jardine.[21] A few weeks later, two Catalinas moored overnight in Diego Garcia. By July, a policy for using this new capacity (individual aircraft being relieved by others from Singapore) had been agreed. The planes would be used only to make definite searches when there was positive indication of a raider's presence, to search unfrequented areas where a raider's supply ship might lurk or to examine areas through which important ships or convoys were to be routed; they would not undertake routine patrols. There were also losses. One 'Cat', bound for Diego Garcia, crashed shortly after taking off from Seychelles. In September, Catalinas flew from Diego Garcia in support of Operation SNIP, and one of these was lost in the sea after failing to find her way back to the island.[22] The four ships involved in this operation, to intercept a Vichy French convoy reported to be heading westward to Madagascar, also assembled at Diego Garcia to refuel, but, owing to faulty intelligence and lacking air support, searched an area too far north of the convoy's actual route. This operational experience (and the paucity of available aircraft) exposed the difficulty of prioritising the competing demands of long range activity and the protective surveillance of Ceylon's coastal waters, which remained unresolved until November. Then, at a meeting of C-in-Cs in Colombo, the C-in-C Eastern Fleet pressed the need for the Catalinas to operate on regular reconnaissance between Seychelles and Diego Garcia, but the overall Commander, General Wavell – wisely, as it proved – decided that they should not be diverted from Ceylon without further reference to the Chiefs of Staff Committee.[23]

Mauritius had always been garrisoned, but the Seychelles, Chagos and Maldives (all three already being used as cruiser refuelling points, as well as for Catalina operations) were completely undefended. It was therefore decided in mid-1941 to garrison and install coastal batteries in all three territories, and to develop Addu Atoll in the Maldives much more substantially – for this atoll had a harbour big and deep enough to constitute, in the event of Ceylon's becoming unusable, a major reserve base for the East Indies Fleet. For Diego Garcia, an advance party of a single officer and ten other ranks was dispatched from Mauritius in September, while steps were being taken to raise the additional forces required. In December, HMIS *Clive* arrived to survey the harbour and install an indicator net at its entrance. In January 1942, there followed the *Clan Forbes*, a requisitioned merchant ship bringing a Royal Marine unit to install what came to be called the Kerry battery. With the assistance of Indian Army engineers, these tasks were completed by mid-March. The battery – still in place – consisted of two naval six-inch guns salvaged from an old ship and mounted at Kerry Point, although, owing to a string of accidents, no range-finding equipment ever reached the Point, so that, in the event of attack, the guns would have had by good luck to hit their target at the first attempt, or else be annihilated.

There were three distinct tasks for army personnel: to man the battery, to protect both it and the RAF installations at East Point, and to construct the buildings and infrastructure for all these forces. This last element was provided from the start by the Indian Army, with an 83-strong Section of an Artisan Works Company arriving in December 1941. After initial disagreements about who should provide troops to man the battery and defend the island, hastily assembled units of the Mauritian territorial reserves (215 all ranks, including some British officers of the Royal Artillery) were dispatched to Diego Garcia in February 1942, arriving ahead of the stores and tents being supplied from Ceylon. The initial confusion was gradually put to rights, but the ill-prepared Mauritians never really adjusted to the primitive conditions which faced them.

These preparations proved, at least in principle, to be timely, since they coincided with the events that transformed the strategic situation in the Indian Ocean – Japan's entry into the war in December 1941, with destruction of the American fleet at Pearl Harbour and the sinking a few days later of HMS *Prince of Wales* and HMS *Repulse*,[24] followed in early 1942 by her occupation of Malaya and the fall of Singapore. The United States having joined Britain as a belligerent immediately after Pearl Harbour, both countries needed to react quickly and in close collaboration. So far as Diego Garcia was concerned, the US was the first to act, dispatching the *Capetown Clipper*, a requisitioned luxury flying boat, in early March 1942, to investigate the possibility of constructing an airfield there.[25] This visit – the first hint of any American military interest in the island – came with only 48 hours warning.

Britain's major concern in this theatre was that the Japanese would exploit at once the opportunity they now possessed to overwhelm British power in the

The *Capetown Clipper*. Internet image.

area, with all that would imply for oil supplies from Persia, convoys from Australasia and the passage of reinforcements of troops and materials round the Cape bound for the Middle East. Diego Garcia, if Addu Atoll were over-run, could be required as much more than a secondary naval refuelling and air surveillance base. The decision was quickly taken to send a reconnaissance team to Diego Garcia to plan the ambitious project of defending the island against major attack by the Japanese fleet.[26] The team arrived in April and submitted their final report in the first days of June. Their proposals entailed the establishment of 4,000 personnel on the island and included plans for an airstrip, basing these on the very rough proposals made by the American team, who had visited the island ten days earlier. Before returning to Britain, they met Leclézio and Lionnet in Port Louis to agree on the basis for compensating the Company for any diminution of coconut production.[27]

Scarcely had the reconnaissance team left Diego Garcia than the Japanese fleet mounted its major raids on Colombo and Trincomalee, involving further losses to the Royal Navy's Eastern Fleet. What is now a mere 'might-have-been' had become a real and present danger. However, after several weeks of uncertainty, it became clear that the Japanese were altogether more interested in the Pacific theatre, where, fortunately for the Allies, they overplayed their hand and brought upon themselves the strategic reversal begun at the battle of Midway in June. Thus it was that, on 12 June, only a week after its submission, the team's recommendations were shelved for good. There was one exception; this was that the Mauritius infantry company ('inadequately trained and of poor physique') should as soon as possible be replaced by a much more substantial garrison of Indian troops.[28] The change was duly implemented during August and September, with the result that the total garrison amounted to about 500, made up of units from 12 Indian Coastal Battery, 25/4 Bombay Grenadiers and some Indian Engineers. A small number of officers and specialist NCOs were British. The base was also removed from Mauritian control and put under the GOC, Ceylon.

From a military point of view, the key assets of the island were the Kerry Battery, close to Eclipse Point, and the RAF installations at East Point, with the total force being split in a ratio of about 1:2 between the former and the latter. Apart from organising themselves for the island's defence, the new Indian troops undertook a good deal of building work, including a pier at Eclipse Point, rest rooms for the soldiers, barracks for both Army and RAF, and the construction of a more solid W/T station to be operated by the RAF, as well as completion of the island's primitive roads so as to make it possible for a lorry to pass all the way around the island's perimeter from Eclipse to Barton Points. As this work neared completion at the end of 1942, the risk of attack had greatly diminished. Unsurprisingly, Sir Henry Pownall, the newly appointed GOC, Ceylon, concluded that the garrison could be reduced by half and, when he visited Diego

Garcia in December as part of an inspection of the Indian Ocean bases, a Captain Boyagis presented him with a forthright assessment: 'In the event of an enemy attack, we can expect no assistance … The garrison will maintain their defensive position to the last round and the last man.'[29] On a more cheerful note, there arrived on 23 December the Dutch transport, *Zuider-Kruis*, escorted by HMAS *Maryborough*, bringing Christmas fare.

Ironically, the strategic shift in the Allies' favour was what made things worse in the western Indian Ocean: in 1943 the Eastern Fleet could begin to focus more on plans for recovering control east of Ceylon, but at the same time was required to send no less than 48 of its ships to take part in the invasion of Sicily. Well might Admiral Somerville, the C-in-C, write to the First Sea Lord that 'As a boy, I always had a hankering after coral atolls; anyone can have the things now, as far as I am concerned.'[30] Nevertheless, Diego Garcia was entering its most active phase in the whole war, being used to refuel many ships and to support ever-growing numbers of Catalina and, as they became available, Sunderland flying boats.

Short 'Sunderland' flying boat. Internet image.

Both types of aircraft were being used to help provide surveillance ahead of convoys and to mount search and rescue operations for survivors from the merchant ships that had been sunk. Although it was not until 1944 that its operations (30 sorties were made in July alone) were judged to require the establishment of its own Advanced Flying Boat Base (AFB 29), what had been demonstrated was the value, in such a vast area of sea, of having a network of island bases, of which Diego Garcia was the central and indispensable link. As Captain Roskill noted

> One interesting side of the sea-air operations carried out in the Indian Ocean in 1944 was the number of occasions on which the flying boats and land-based aircraft of Nos. 222 and 225 Groups sighted and reported lifeboats containing survivors from sunken merchantmen, so enabling warships to be sent to rescue

them. To give only one example of this work, when the P. and O. liner *Nellore*, with 341 persons aboard, and the American ship *Jean Nicolet* were sunk by Japanese submarines on the 29th of June and 2nd of July respectively to the south of the Maldive Islands, Catalinas and Liberators from Diego Garcia and other bases flew prolonged and widespread searches with the triple object of finding the enemy, escorting other ships through the danger zone and locating survivors. It was entirely thanks to aircraft spotting the lifeboats that we were able to save 234 of the *Nellore*'s complement and 23 of the ill-fated crew of the *Jean Nicolet*.[31]

Those rescued were brought to Diego Garcia. A temporary rest camp was organised by the base, where '100 were fed and flown away within 18 hours. Over 100 suffering from extreme exposure were fed, clothed and cared for during 8 days; several cases of malaria occurred amongst these survivors'.[32]

Civilian life under military occupation

For the civilian inhabitants of the Chagos, the war had two continuing effects. The first was the gradual reduction in supplies from Mauritius; thus, in 1941, the *Zambezia* came only twice, in March and August. The second, confined to Diego Garcia, was the growing disruption brought about by military activities.

No independent account exists of how Vielle coped with life on Peros Banhos, but Lagesse has described a particularly fraught period for both the northern atolls between 5 September 1941, when the *Zambezia* departed from Salomon, and June 1942. As stocks of food diminished, boats were dispatched to Nelson Island to bring back turtles and rice reduced to half, then to one third, of the normal ration. She continues:

> The war was on. We had not been re-supplied for 10 months. Let us pass over in silence the misery of those days.
>
> One evening, when we'd given up hope, a radio message from Mauritius brought the news that a cargo vessel was sailing for Peros Banhos and would deposit there the supplies destined for Salomon. My father, the next thing to God on the island, decided to dispatch the *Germain* … It took us a mere nine hours to cover the thirty miles separating the two atolls. And then the waiting began, ten days of waiting … The rations allotted to us from Salomon were meagre – a little of that panacea, tea, and a few kilos of flour. But, on the makeshift table, these looked impressive, once we'd added a rich turtle stew or a breadfruit, baked in its skin in the ashes beneath the oven.
>
> Time dragged on as we waited. The desire to live well overcame the abnormal circumstances of our situation. The plantation manager had already slaughtered the hog for our dinner of welcome and uncorked his last bottle of wine …
>
> On Salomon, we were well organized and knew how to distract ourselves: there

was the daily tour of the island to be made, to hear the kids recite the alphabet and their catechism; and we had the radio. On the Ile du Coin [at Peros Banhos], things were altogether different. We found ourselves disconcerted – even disoriented – by the curious atmosphere prevailing among the inhabitants. We were used to making spontaneous exchanges of bread or salt; they mumbled 'What are we going to do today?'

But, at last …

As the first luminous glow of a new day appeared, there arose a happy murmuring which filled the whole island. With a few bounds, we were on the beach, shouting like the rest and, like the rest, overwhelmed by the indescribable emotion which takes hold of and shakes every inhabitant of these isles, as they watch that plume of smoke smudging the horizon.[33]

The *Germain* had a capacity of 70 tonnes and returned laden down with rice, flour and barrel-loads of supplies, including, perhaps, the 'cheese, olive oil and bottles of Lea & Perrins [sauce]' that had loomed large in their hungry imaginations.[34]

As regards Diego Garcia, matters were more complex. During 1941 and 1942, the establishment and usage of the flying boat base and the increasingly frequent ship visits would have very little direct impact on the work of the plantations. Indeed, a few new items were imported, such as the first lorry, together with some fuel and oil. The idea was to make use of the perimeter road being constructed by the military. However, neither the Company nor Thatcher understood how to use it to improve productivity; the vehicle was old and its tyres worn, with no spares or extra inner tubes supplied, and its driver soon returned to Mauritius where he could earn a better wage. Meanwhile, the manager's house at East Point had been offered by Monnier to the Royal Air Force as its operational headquarters, so that he (and subsequently Thatcher) used the assistant's house.

Subsequently, to provide liaison between the military and the islanders, Thatcher was obliged to move to tented accommodation close to the army encampment on the north-west of the island, far from the main settlement and coconut groves. This must seriously have disrupted his managerial functions and indeed led him to resign and depart.[35] The military however made few demands on the plantation employees, whose utility they roundly disparaged – 'They obtain an easy living from the work required of them by the Diego Garcia Company and will be of no use whatsoever as labourers'.[36] The only skill which the military thought might be of use was that of the women in matting palm fronds, for which an order was placed for 500 per week. There is also some evidence that the islanders took to selling local fish and chickens (with the price for the latter rising sharply) – pursuits which they found more agreeable than coconut gathering. It also seems likely that, whenever they got the chance, the visiting forces bought or (in one case at least) stole fresh fruit and vegetables, to the disadvantage of the local population – these items were barely adequate at the best of times and their absence was a constant source of complaint from the garrison commanders; it was not until 1943 that a cold store was constructed. By the end of that year, however, the newly arrived Major Mackay in charge of the Eclipse Point garrison could report positively on the state of his troops and optimistically on the improvements in their diet. Part of this resulted from the establishment of a vegetable garden and the provision of geese and goats; admittedly the former provided no eggs, while the latter, all being male animals, failed to breed.[37]

Progressive economic effects of war

The anecdotes cited above show that the war had an early and significant effect on the provision of supplies to the Chagos; but they reveal nothing about the inevitable consequences for the Archipelago's earnings from exports. Trade statistics were not compiled for 1941, while for 1943 figures for exports from the Chagos were amalgamated with those relating to Agalega. Nevertheless, Table 18.1 (below) shows that, with some ups and downs, the war involved an average diminution of almost 30% in the value of products exported annually from the Chagos, with a similar increase in value of goods supplied. While the latter fig-

Table 18.1 Trade trends 1939-1945.

Mauritius Imports from Chagos (Rs '000)							Total* 1940– 1945	Averages* 1940– 1945	1937– 1939
	1939	*1940*	*1942*	*1943*	*1944*	*1945*			
D.G.	108	75	74.4	n/a	86.4	64.3	300.1	75	103
P.B.	61.9	30	50.3	n/a	54.2	36.3	170.8	42.5	67
Sal.	46.6	19	37.5	n/a	41.8	30.2	128.5	32.3	43
Total	216.5	124	162.2	n/a	182.4	130.8	599.4	149.8	213

Mauritius Exports to Chagos (Rs '000)									
Total	107.1	113	69.6	(170.3)	209.7	142.9	536.2	133.9	95.2
of which									
D.G.	54.9	48	32	(83.3)	97.6	80.2	257.8	64.5	49
P.B.	29.4	39	19.6	(55.7)	74	44.5	177.1	44.3	28.6
Sal.	22.8	26	18	(31.3)	38.1	18.2	100.3	25.1	17.6

*The import statistics for 1943 combine the figures for all the Oil Islands, making it impossible to provide separate figures for the Chagos. In order therefore to compare the wartime and pre-war averages, the 1943 exports have not been added into the totals.

Source: Mauritius Blue Books (TNA CO 172 series).

ure must have included some supplies for the military, they are not apparent from the detailed trade figures. It would seem therefore that the company, both before and after its collapse and reconstitution, must have been in still greater difficulties.

We have tried to investigate what lay behind these figures. It is clear that the disruptions to management, combined with those to shipping, must have reduced the output of copra. For example, in 1943 the *Zambezia* only visited once, as did one other ship, probably one of the Norwegian cargo vessels, operated independently by crews having no desire to return to occupied Oslo. That year too, the price of coconut oil in Mauritius rose for the first time since 1904, and rose fivefold, though the quantities still being imported from the islands were too small to improve the profitability of Chagos Ltd., as distinct from that of Innova Ltd. (see page 352), which had several of the same shareholders. The Chagos plantations did, however, increase slightly their tiny exports of fish, pigs and preserved fruit, as well as supplying some guano for the first time.

But by far the biggest change was one which affected the islanders rather than the company's finances. This was the reduction and eventual disappearance of rice. As Table 18.2 reveals, the disruption of the early years was dwarfed by what happened from 1943 to 1945. The shock of having to turn to wheat and then maize as a staple must have been immense; and, in 1943 and 1944, the amounts available were hardly enough to go round. It was not as if there had been any appreciable reduction in the size of the population. A census, delayed from 1941, was held in 1944, showing a total of 1048,[38] only 30 less than in 1939, made up as follows: Diego Garcia 501 (246 male/255 female); Peros Banhos 332 (160 male/172 female); Salomon 215 (115 male/100 female). Following the loss of Burma to the Japanese, rice had been in short supply throughout the Indian Ocean; but what the Chagos islanders were experiencing was the additional impact of German and Japanese submarine activities: few ships bound for Mauritius could be given the protection of sailing in convoy and Mauritius – including its Dependencies – paid the price.[39] What little we know of the reactions of the islanders themselves comes from comments made by Fernand Mandarin in 2010, recalling a time when, as a little boy 'I ate coconuts and drank coconut water. There was no

Table 18.2 Supplies of staple foodstuffs to Chagos (kgs '000), 1937–1945.

	1937	1938	1939	1940	1942	1943	1944	1945
Rice	205.5	194.0	204.2	212.2	93.7	3.8	0.4	4.2
Wheat flour	12.7	4.0	5.2	11.6	33.9	124.2	123.3	20.1
Maize/ 'rice-maize'	–	–	–	–	–	6.0	12.0	68.6

Note: In addition, the normal amount of pulses (dholl and lentils) supplied was about 5-6 tonnes of each; in 1944 and 1945, none of either commodity was sent.

Source: Mauritius Blue Books (TNA CO 172 series).

milk, no sugar. We ate turtles and grilled fish. That lasted for nine months'.[40]

The impact of the war upon Mauritius itself goes beyond the scope of this study, except in relation to its effects upon Diego Ltd. and its suppliers. One indicator of the severity of the situation was the outbreak of rioting in 1943 in response to food shortages and inflation; workers' wages had risen by 10–20%, whereas the cost of foodstuffs had risen by 100% and that of clothing by 300%.[41] The difficulties of Diego Ltd. emerge clearly from the descriptions of Lionnet's own misfortunes by one of his nieces, Maryse, and by his daughter Christiane:

> The war years brought a steady decline in business profits [for J.R. Lionnet & Co.] … To make matters worse, the family's other investments also suffered severely during the war years. The Chagos Islands investments brought no returns at all during the war and their capital value decreased rapidly.[42]
>
> Although his salary was supplemented by dividends from the family business, Richard found it hard to make a comfortable living for his family. There was trouble at work as well; war rationing was enforced and the anger of those who felt they were not getting their share of the precious oil was quickly aroused. One day there was a dispute in front of the Company's building and an angry man threw a brick which hit Richard on the head. He suffered concussion and had to take to bed for a week.[43]

These auguries of the future could hardly be worse, whether for the family enterprise or the plantation company itself.

Islanders and the military: attitudes and accidents

The physical conditions of Diego Garcia exposed interesting contrasts between the experiences and attitudes of its temporary military inhabitants and the long-established islanders. For example, the planning team which visited the island in 1942 found it difficult to work hard or even to think hard – but did not see any link with the islanders' more languid approach to life. As regards health, the islanders were not as free of ailments as the captain of the *Guba* had been led to suppose. Nevertheless, they evidently had greater resistance to the local diseases than did the soldiers, among whom an epidemic of dengue fever broke out at one point; while on another occasion several airmen suffered from fish poisoning and orders were issued prohibiting the eating of fish caught in Ramblers Bay. Some too suffered severely from the tropical heat and humidity, most notably (and volubly) the Scottish Marine Captain in charge of installing the Kerry battery, who was a martyr to prickly heat.[44] Early in 1942, the support ship for this task, the *Clan Forbes*, was stationed in the north-west corner of the lagoon, where she also provided hospital support for serious cases. There were several such, most arising from accidents in landing and moving heavy pieces of equipment. At East Point, a Sikh doctor, who was one of two medical staff attached to the Indian contingent, held a daily sick parade, his patients standing smartly to attention; in the absence of medical supplies, he would pick stems of grass, and, with a short homily, hand one in turn to each soldier, who would salute smartly and make off. 'It works well in their villages', he explained. Meanwhile, the military took such opportunities as arose to help the local inhabitants out of difficulties. For instance, in 1942, the RAF had to evacuate to Ceylon one islander suffering a severe case of beri-beri. Other examples included the rescue of fishermen, whose boats had capsized in the lagoon and who had spent many hours in the water, and the importation of a surgeon from the hospital at Addu Atoll to perform a successful eye operation on a small boy who was going blind as a result of an accident.

At a more general level, relations between the islanders and the military, especially at East Point, never became warm. On the whole the two parties kept themselves to themselves; in any case, the rule laid down from the military side, if not always followed, was 'No fraternisation'. The relationship between the Company and the military likewise had its good and bad moments. The military considered that the Company could and should provide their protectors with more assistance, for instance labour 'to help carry out such urgently needed tasks as the removal of the store of old petrol cans, removal of the piggery and donkey stables, and the reconstruction of the pier'. More dramatically, in October 1944,

> trouble broke out among a section of the native population, who broke open the jail and began behaving in an unruly and riotous manner. The Company's [acting] Manager appealed to the CO for assistance, and a party of 8 volunteers under his command restored order after a display of force which succeeded in cowing the rowdy element. No damage or casualties occurred and the Manager was most grateful for the assistance rendered.[45]

Official relations underwent a more marked improvement a month later, following the arrival, as Thatcher's substantive replacement, of Louis Monnier, who was no doubt greatly relieved to find himself restored to grace. The military authorities found him 'very anxious to co-operate with the RAF to the full', including provision of the labour which had previously been refused. Gifts of fruit and meat from the management followed, and individuals were also offered 'gifts of native Rum and Vin Rouge, with results which might have proved unpleasant'. It was promised that similar gifts would not be made in future. Even so, not all was sweetness and light. In early February 1945, as food supplies for the Indian troops neared exhaustion, Monnier reported that a large number of his poultry had been stolen overnight. He had seen the thieves on his premises, but was unable to give any information as to their identity. On the other hand, a few weeks later, guards had to be set, following thefts from the military's own chicken runs; there were also break-ins to the military storage sheds to steal petrol and kerosene; and even Monnier declined to make available labour to do the Army's washing.[46]

Debris and departure

In May 1945, the garrison and the air base began to be run down, with most of the military paraphernalia being removed by the departing units. However, it was not until the beginning of 1946 that the last Sunderland flying boat left the island. Paul Caboche has informed us that the plantation managers also succeeded in removing a considerable number of items of commercial value to Mauritius. The only physical reminders of war were the two naval guns and the carcass of a Catalina blown ashore in a storm in September 1944. Increasingly derelict, there they still remain. The plantations too must have been neglected, and the islanders bereft of opportunities to increase their earnings by undertaking extra work. Clearly, it would be an uphill task for Diego Ltd. to restore prewar levels of production, let alone achieve levels of output and prosperity that had previously eluded the Chagos.

Notes to Chapter 18

1   Roskill, W.S. HMSO, 1954 (*The War at Sea*, p. 111) describes the utility of raiders well.

2   TNA ADM 199/382 C-in-C (East Indies Station) War Diary.

3   TNA, ADM 199/1839.

4   TNA ADM 199/1831. He even arranged for a Walrus spotter plane from HMS *Eagle* to drop a message giving notice of the position at which *Otus* would take on board mail from the island for onward transmission.

5   TNA ADM 199/1831.

6   TNA CO 167/912/10.

7   Another example of Diego Garcia's sleepiness, compared to Salomon. At the latter, *Otus* had been spotted approaching the island; this time – admittedly in heavy rain, *Odin* had entered and anchored off Minni Minni, where she spent two hours trying unsuccessfully to attract attention and having then to move to East Point. Marcelle Lagesse's account has it that the *Zambezia* had not visited the northern islands for ten months; so it would appear that the company had been relying on the *Germain* to forward stocks delivered to Diego Garcia.

8   TNA CO 875/7/3 The secret operations to put a stop to pro-Vichy activities in Mauritius and later to subvert the Vichy regimes in Madagascar and Reunion go far beyond the scope of this work. A succinct account of the contrasting strands of public opinion in Mauritius, and reactions to wartime developments is contained in a note on the local government's propaganda work forwarded to the Colonial Office in 1943. It will also come as no surprise to readers to learn that Paul Caboche was recalled to Mauritius to operate secret radio communications and to be trained as a saboteur, ready for action in the event of invasion by the Japanese. His sister Marcelle Lagesse, back from Salomon, was involved sepa-

rately, in conjunction with Captain Lemarchand, by then skippering a tugboat, in clandestine transfers of men and materiel between Mauritius and Reunion. In addition, she contributed to the government's propaganda organ, *Savez-Vous Que?*

9 TNA ADM 53/114643 For example, the oiler *British Genius* refuelled the ships involved in Operation SNIP in Diego Garcia's lagoon on 18-19 September.

10 Caboche, J.P., 'Diego Garcia pendant la Guerre', 1999. This unpublished typescript (21 pages) is an invaluable adjunct to the sparse official reports and, together with subsequent conversations and correspondence, helped establish much of what we know about the personalities involved in the Chagos during this period.

11 Charoux, brother-in-law of Raoul Caboche, had visited Salomon and picked up some ideas, which he implemented on Peros Banhos after Thatcher's departure in 1939, achieving a sudden increase in output. Talbot had had difficulty in explaining matters to his masters in Port Louis and, immediately on arriving at Diego Garcia, forced Charoux to resign (personal communication from Paul Caboche).

12 Jules Leclézio (1877-1951) was the third son of Sir Henry Leclézio and, as a major sugar producer with many other interests, secured election to the Legislative Council and was picked by the governor as a member of his Executive Council, achieving the same degree of influence as his father. He became a CBE in 1934 and was knighted in 1942. His business interests included directorships of the *Nouvelle Société Huilière* and the *Compagnie Générale de Quicaillarie*, one of the *Société*'s major suppliers.

13 Admiral Darlan was C-in-C of the French Fleet, an important part of which was, in July 1940, destroyed by the British while at anchor at Mers-el-Kebir, for fear that Germany might make use of such an important asset. The action, which killed 2,000 French sailors, provoked great bitterness in France and among French communities abroad.

14 Vielle did not go alone to Peros Banhos. While at Diego Garcia he married Germaine Tournier, the sister-in-law of Lucien Quevauvilliers, manager of the company shop (and previously a manager of Six Islands – see p. 354). In this close-knit community, it was inevitably Paul Caboche who escorted the bride by ox-cart to the ceremony, Raoul Caboche who conducted it and Fr. Dussercle who later blessed the couple. They were to spend thirteen years managing the atoll, where most of their five children were born. Two of their daughters were later to compose a lively and prize-winning vignette of island life, *Bor'Endan Bor'Déhors* (Marie Descroizilles and Alix Mülnier, Editions de L'Océan Indien, Mauritius 1999).

15 The *Zambezia* may only have made a single visit, for at least one supply visit was made that year by the *Norwegian III* (source: Caboche's unpublished typescript (p. 17), already mentioned in Note 10 above).

16 TNA WO 32/21294. Thus, the assets of the company possessing the whole archipelago were only worth Rs 23,000 more than was paid for Diego Garcia and Peros Banhos alone in 1893.

17 TNA WO 32/21294 Mauritius Mortgage Register of Transcriptions Vol. 461, No. 90, dated 2 June 1941.

18 Roskill, *op. cit.*, Vol II, pp. 80-81. Indicative of the scale of the continuing disparity between need and provision was an Admiralty assessment made in March 1942. The total requirement for aircraft to operate over the Indian Ocean at that time was, including 90 flying boats, 570; total availability was 42, including 6 flying boats.

19 TNA AIR 23/4792.

20 TNA ADM 53/112525.

21 Jardine was an experienced long-range flier, but the skill he showed in finding his remote island destinations, despite primitive instrumentation and the absence of local radio beacons, led to his being awarded the AFC for these exploits. He was subsequently captured by the Japanese, but survived his ordeal to enjoy a distinguished post-war career in the RCAF. A full account of his career is to be found in his biography, *Lucky Alex* (Colin Castle, 1961, in co-operation with Trafford Publishing, Victoria, Canada).

22 Paul Caboche listened to the pilot's last message, as he was forced to land in the sea during a violent storm. Paul's sister, Marcelle Lagesse, later wrote, perhaps fictitiously, of finding the wing of a 'Cat' washed up on the beach in Salomon. The ships involved included HMS *Hermes* and HMS *Mauritius*.

23 TNA ADM 199/383, /391, /398, /408, /425 and /426 War Diaries of the C-in-C, East Indies Station,

Colombo, and the Royal Indian Navy provide many details of the naval and RAF visits to the Chagos in 1941-1942.

24 Paul Caboche, *op. cit.*, included these two ships in his list of those that had called at the lagoon entrance to report their positions. Unfortunately, despite assiduous searches, we have been unable to discover any evidence to support this assertion. Study of *Repulse*'s movements eliminates the possibility of such a call, while, in the case of the *Prince of Wales*, only the ship's logbook, lost when she was sunk, could have established Caboche's claim.

25 TNA WO 1063/3719 and ADM 1/26876. An account of the visit is to be found in Edis, R.S., *Peak of Limuria* (p. 63, 2004 edition), based on detailed information provided by Paul Caboche and Ian Smith (Commanding Officer of the small Mauritian garrison, interview November 2003).

26 TNA WO 106/3781.

27 TNA WO 106/3719 and ADM 1/1308. In the event, no formal agreement was signed.

28 TNA ADM 199/426.

29 TNA WO 172/1502.

30 Quoted in Roskill, *op. cit.*, Vol II, Pt. I, p. 425.

31 *Ibid.*, Vol. III, Pt II, p. 326.

32 TNA AIR 29/34 Royal Air Force Operations Record Book, No. 29 Advanced Flying Boat Base.

33 Lagesse, M., *D'un Carnet*.

34 There is a mystery about the actual requirements. Trade figures showed that the average monthly export (1935-1940) was around 17 tonnes, equivalent to a daily ration of roughly half a kilo per person, with managers then and later consistently reporting their monthly consumption, collectively, as about 200 bags. This suggests that each bag must have weighed 85 kilos, unless the managers were understating their needs – which could be one cause of their reserves running out.

35 The only source for this account of Thatcher's peregrinations is Caboche, an interested party, whose description (see notes 10 and 11 above) is somewhat vague, but plausible. He also lets fall that the Assistant Manager's house was known as the Devil's cottage (*case de diable*) – it was where Bigara had been murdered in 1926 (see p. 313).

36 TNA WO 106/3719 Elsewhere, the reconnaissance team remark that 'people less likely to be able to do work of any kind can scarcely be imagined'.

37 TNA WO 203/1211 Report dated 1 January 1944.

38 RHL 912.s.18. Also TNA CO 1032/132 Enclosure 1 Despatch No. 293 of 31 October 1951, which provides additional information culled from the records of the island managers, which we can tabulate thus:-

	1941	1942	1943	1944*	1944	1945
Diego Garcia	n/a	n/a	n/a	502	n/a	n/a
Peros Banhos	330	364	387	332	360	372
Salomon	235	n/a	211	215	222	221
Total				1049		

*Quoting census report. Comment: It is clear that the record-keeping at Diego Garcia had been neglected (and no explanation can be found for the discrepancy between the total quoted here (502) and that in our main text (501). Nevertheless, figures for births and deaths (including infant deaths) were maintained. On Diego Garcia, the annual death rate in the years 1941-43 averaged 26, compared with about 16 in later years, the difference probably being accounted for by deaths among military personnel. There was also a sudden spike in infant deaths, ten occurring in both 1942 and 1943, compared with less than three normally (and still lower figures on the other two atolls). The author of the report speculated that the high level of infant mortality could have resulted from the mothers' attention being diverted from their babies to the visiting military. We think it more likely that there was a prolonged delay between the departure of the resident midwife and her replacement.

39 Roskill, *op. cit.,* Vol. III, Part II, Appendix ZZ, Table II. In the Indian Ocean alone, 205 Allied merchant ships (724,485 tons) were sunk in 1942; 82 (486,324 tons) in 1943; 50 (322,802 tons) in 1944.

From 1939-41 the total number of sinkings had been only 45.

40   Interview with MC March 2010.

41   Jackson, A., *War and Empire in Mauritius and the Indian Ocean* (p. 154), Palgrave, Basingstoke 2001.

42   Duyker, E., (ed.) *Mauritian Heritage*. Contribution by Maryse Duyker (née Commins) (p.186) Australian Mauritian Research Group, Victoria 1986.

43   *Ibid*. Contribution by Christiane Belde (née Lionnet) (p. 152).

44   Thompson, J.A., *Only the Sun Remembers*, Andrew Dakers 1950. This impressionistic memoir includes highly-coloured descriptions of the islanders' character and of a *séga* he was taken to observe.

45   *Ibid*.

46   TNA AIR 29/34 (Operations Record Book of the No. 29 Advanced Flying Boat Base) is the source for almost all the information summarised in the foregoing paragraph.

19

1945–1955: Company Mismanagement and Intervention by Governors

State of the islands in the late 1940s

> The inference to be drawn from the numerous reports of Magistrates who have visited [the Chagos and Agalega] is that the recommendations they have made with a view to bettering the life of both overseers and labourers have in most cases been overlooked by the management … Many suggestions put forward in the past have been opposed on the ground that the expenditure involved was too heavy. If exploitation of islands cannot be a paying concern there is no compulsion in running them at all. Their small population can easily be transferred elsewhere. If on the other hand there is to be a settlement, it is indispensable that from manager to labourer everyone should enjoy a minimum of comfort, which is most certainly not the case at present.[1]

W ITH this introduction to their report dated 26 June 1946, three senior officials of three key social departments of the colonial government, dispatched by the Governor within months of the final victory, went on to set out a string of recommendations for 'drastic changes' in all aspects of the running of the plantations. The note struck was wholly different from the tentative and spasmodic proposals made by magistrates (whose principal remit was of course to satisfy themselves that existing rules were being followed). The authors began by drawing attention to the importance of a good understanding between the Mauritius management and the island one – which was lacking – and of competence among the latter, which was also frequently absent. Without improved management, they saw little chance of success in the specific changes they went on to propose, concerning health, nutrition, housing, education, religious instruction, amenities, communications, policing, alcohol consumption and wages. Of all these, pay and education were considered fundamental; staff had been paid between Rs 60–90 per month in 1940; and labourers had been signing contracts, even in 1946, at rates of Rs 8 per month. The first was usually insufficient to attract 'the better sort of employee' – 'how often has the fate of the islanders been in the hands of persons incapable of looking properly even after their own selves'. The second rates 'were obviously fictitious'; the point of them was to give managers the opportunity to prevent workers who displeased them from earning anything beyond this minimum. As to education, its total absence was simply 'the greatest deficiency of these islands'.

This fresh interest on the part of the colonial administration in Mauritius was timely, for it coincided with the start of considerable changes of managers and shipping for the islands. Also in 1946, Richard Lionnet suffered a slight stroke, retiring from Diego Ltd. soon afterwards. In December of the same, year, Richard's brother Felix, who had been managing Lionnet & Co. at Curepipe, emigrated to Australia, setting off a general exodus of the Lionnet and closely-related Commins families, completed with Richard's departure in 1951. The family firm's assets – except for its name – were sold to defray the costs. Thus some 60 years of engagement with the provisioning and management of the Chagos sputtered to its end.[2] That same year, Sir Jules Leclézio died, breaking another key link with the islands, but his name lived on with entry into service of the ship named after him.[3] The 711 ton mv *Sir Jules*, replacing the coal-powered *Zambezia*, was, however, no faster and just as prone to rolling.

mv *Sir Jules*. Image courtesy of Fernand Mandarin.

Quite soon the new ship attracted her own charming *séga*,[4] which includes the following lines:

Ena ène joli bateau	*There is a beautiful ship*
comment dire ene ti chateau	*which is like a castle*
Temps en temps li allé dans île	*Very often it comes to the island*
nous appelle li p'tit Sir Jules	*we call it little 'Sir Jules'*
Rouler, rouler, rouler mon p'tit Sir Jules	*Roll, roll, roll on my little 'Sir Jules'*
Courant li trop fort	*The water current is too strong*
ramène moi dans port	*take me back to port*
Captaine ecque ingénieur	*The Captain and the Engineer*
pénan pli grand Bonheur	*know no greater happiness*
qui chante ène ti séga	*than to sing a little Sega song*
pou blié zotte tracas	*to forget their troubles*

Intriguingly, her captain and the engineer also had links to the past, the former being Edouard d'Argent, a piratical-looking man known for the '*impitoy-able* [merciless] *truculence de son langage*' and the latter his brother Philippe. They were the nephews of the murderous manager of Diego Garcia, already encountered in these pages. Thus there was an element of familial continuity as well as changes in equipment and management. The question naturally arising from the latter, for example the death of Raoul Caboche in 1952 and the retirement of Gaston Vielle in 1955, is whether they would lead to any fundamental improvement in the way the company operated and its workers were treated. To answer this question it is necessary, at the risk of repetitiveness, to review the observations made by a fresh generation of official visitors.

The report of the magistrate who visited the Chagos in 1947 no longer survives, but a later despatch from Mauritius, in December 1948, refers to modest progress being made in dealing with some of its recommendations, for example the replacement of an incompetent midwife and improved training of medical dispensers appointed to the islands.[5] Discussions were also continuing about the type of education most suitable for the islanders and the division between government and company of financial responsibilities for providing it. By the time this despatch was on its way, a further report had already been presented. For this visit, in October 1948, the magistrate had been accompanied by the Catholic bishop and one of his priests, as well as by Joseph Lamusse, Lionnet's successor as Secretary (Agent) of the Diego Company. The magistrate found that there had been a major improvement in health care; housing too had mostly been improved; while education, curiously, was not mentioned. By this time too, wages had been increased. The rate for male workers was now Rs 14.30 per month and for females Rs 10.40, with each entitled also to receive gratis 10½ lbs of rice and 2 ounces of salt per week. In practice, varying amounts of coconut oil, pork, turtle meat, lentils or beans were also distributed free of charge. All other needs had to be met by purchases from the company shop, for example coffee, sugar, tea, condensed milk, wine, cigarettes and soap, as well as extra fish, meat and eggs, when available. The magistrate commented that, while the shop made little if any profit, expenditure on necessities took up virtually all of the workers' basic pay; there were however plenty of opportunities to earn extra income to purchase clothing or make modest savings. All the same, his report's main conclusion was that the basic wage should be increased by 20%, a conclusion which Lamusse was invited to bring to his Board's attention.

Three months later, on 28 March 1949, this report in turn was sent on to London, with the Acting Governor noting the Company's refusal to make any change in rates of pay and his Labour Commissioner's view that more detailed information about living conditions on the islands would need to be collected before the government could take any action.[6] This was, it seems, the same Commissioner who had been unable to spare an officer to accompany the magistrate, notwithstanding the previous Governor's recommendation that this should happen. Officialdom was stirring, but not yet with undue haste.

In the plantations themselves, life went on much as it had done before the war. In one respect, an interesting element of flexible working had been introduced. Extra pay for extra tasks was earned as before (at a rate of 1/30 of the monthly cash wage per task); but in addition a worker could build up a credit, entitling him to take a day off without prior notice and without forfeiting a day's rations. The result was that, when the weather and tides were right for fishing, few males turned up for work. The *séga*, of course, remained as popular as ever, to the distress of visiting magistrates called upon to try the resulting cases: 'The people living on these islands are generally of good behaviour,' remarked M. J. Desplaces in 1948, 'except occasionally when they have been drinking and take to their favourite dance, the *séga*, when they get very excited, are then quarrelsome and get easily to their knives. I have given them a very severe warning …'

While the isolation of the islands had been reduced, thanks to the availability of long-wave radio, including the overseas broadcasts from Mauritius, the more popular domestic service of the Mauritius Broadcasting Corporation was still out of reach. At the same time, the *Zambezia*'s visits had become less frequent, with two sailings now the annual norm. No doubt the Company regarded this as a straightforward economy, whose feasibility had been proved by its necessity during the war years. For the islanders, however, there was an emotional price; on one occasion, as the vessel's siren blew to signal departure, the manager and employees, with tears in their eyes, signalled the captain to stop. There was another price too: the phenomenon known as 'Zambezia Epidemic' became, even if short-lived, more severe; diseases such as whooping cough, measles and influenza, brought from Mauritius, took a firmer, sometimes fatal, grip on the islanders' unprepared immune systems.

In general, however, the islanders' health was quite good; in fact, as observers remarked afresh, it compared favourably with that of ordinary workers in Mauritius. While their diet could be improved by consuming more vegetables and fruit, this required increased enthusiasm for cultivation on their part as much, if not more than, the managerial encouragement already provided in the form of prizes for the best and second-best garden on each of the plantations. Meanwhile, the open-air life and, especially for the men, vigorous physical exercise of seafaring and plantation work served them well. The most serious, widespread and continuing form of debilitation was filariasis, whose visible signs were grossly swollen limbs and/or testicles. The local mosquitoes, immune to DDT and almost as overwhelmingly numerous as the flies, were the main vectors of this disease, but its elimination, no less than the elimination of flies, required huge improvements in human hygiene and plantation management.

It was not only official visitors who commented on matters of health and hygiene. Marcel Didier, who operated Diego Garcia's radio transmitter during the late 1940s and early 1950s, provided a vivid account of his recollections in 1985.[7] The most important element concerned the part played by the islands' radio operators themselves. When a patient's malady was beyond the competence of the dispenser or midwife to diagnose or treat, they would send a radio message to the operator in Mauritius (still Volcy de Robillard[8]), who would consult a Dr Duvivier and radio back instructions. In less serious cases, the three atolls' operators would act as intermediaries between the local dispensers. As to what happened when a dispenser fell sick or died, Didier quotes a case where the radio operator took over the medical duties, with the midwife attending to female patients. Three themes predominate in Didier's account, all of which attest to the wretched living conditions on the island. First, the paucity of latrines and their location close to the wells from which drinking water was obtained. Second, the malign consequences of poisoning from fish, crustacea or, most frequently, alcohol. As regards the last, the desperate longing for this 'poisonous solace' led some to insist on a daily dose of cough mixture, for the traces of alcohol it contained. Finally, there was the sad lot of the women, rendered anaemic by the frequency of their pregnancies and unable to provide adequate nutrition to their infants. Their prayer should be, suggests Didier, 'Deliver us, Lord, from the male of the species!'

For his part, Caboche had a low opinion of his company's performance and his exasperation eventually boiled over in a twelve-page manuscript account of its failings.[9] Two main themes emerge from his catalogue of criticisms ranging widely in time and topic: the company's persistence in endless false economies and its failure to adopt the modern techniques essential to survival. The first category included: reductions in the pay and privileges of the local managers as well as in the number of such posts, resulting in inadequate supervision of the workers; the introduction of a lorry to Diego Garcia – but not a new vehicle with a proper supply of spare parts, rather a third-hand machine with worn tyres, no extra inner tubes and, when the first tyre became unusable, only one spare sent out, such that the lorry was repeatedly put out of use for long periods; the failure to pay drivers and mechanics sufficiently to retain their services; and pay scales at all levels which failed to recognise the need to cover triennial holidays in Mauritius, where nothing was provided in kind. Regarding the failure to make use of new technology, Caboche drew particular attention to the primitive copra-drying arrangements used in the Chagos, a 'bastard system' requiring partial sun-drying and completion of the process by a husk-fed boiler; this resulted in great wastage and produced a blackened and smoky product incapable of competing with that emerging from the electric kilns employed elsewhere in the Indian Ocean; likewise, when machines were supplied, for example the bandsaw on Salomon (driven by an electric motor powered by a dynamo, which in turn was driven by a motor fuelled by gas from charcoal), the breakdown of one component was liable to be followed by the ruination of others by salt or sand – and thus, as he did not fail to point out, by the collapse of a nice little trade in roof shingles for Mauritius. And all this was compounded by a tendency to recruit managers having little or no interest in modernisation. Caboche's indignation is best captured in the original French: '*Je me souviens qu'en passant par Diego d'avoir eu l'occasion de parler de 'progrès' à l'Administrateur de l'île à cette époque. Eh bien !! Croyez-vous, il était, comme dit l'Anglais, DEAD AGAINST tout à fait. Il alla jusqu'à me dire que si par exemple le bureau de Port Louis lui envoyait un Moteur pour être monté, il n'en ferait rien et le laisserait tout bonnement dans sa caisse.*'[10]

The swish of new brooms

In May 1949 there took place the long-proposed visit by an official of the Labour Department, a Mr G. Mayer.[11] As he himself admitted, his resulting report did not provide the detailed analysis needed for well-founded recommendations. His arrival on the *Zambezia* surprised management as much as the workers:

> Owing to the general emotional upset of the arrival of the ship I had to act with caution. I proceeded to explain my presence to each of the managers of Diego, Peros and Salomon, emphasising the value of the services I could render in obtaining a satisfied labour force. The labourers I found regarded me with undisguised cynicism as a piece of administrative window dressing.

Fearing that close questioning of the workers on their expenditure on clothing, drinking, etc., might be 'too much for order and discipline', he asked the managers to gather this information later. Nevertheless, his examination of the books demonstrated that the workers on Salomon, where the island's resources were already being exploited to the maximum, were managing to save even less of their earnings than those of Diego Garcia and Peros Banhos. He therefore recommended that the mark-up of prices in the company shop, which the Company had recently halved to 12½% for all three plantations, should on Salomon be reduced further. Rather characteristically, this recommendation was not passed to Lamusse until November and by May 1950 – a full year after the actual visit – when the papers 'mislaid in the Secretariat' were submitted for the first time to the new Governor, no response had been received.

The new Governor, Sir Hilary Blood, quite soon discovered that criticism of the plantation companies extended beyond officials dealing directly with the various islands to the increasingly vociferous members of his Legislative Council. The latter, he explained, regarded the companies as 'capitalist concerns which exploit the islands for the benefit of their own pockets and to the detriment of persons employed therein'.[12] His own view of the islands – whose beauty later enthralled him[13] – was that they provided produce much needed by Mauritius and that the existing system for exploiting their resources was probably the only one practicable; but that greater supervision, including visits by the Governor, should result in improved development. He was as good as his word, making visits to the Dependencies in each of the next three years, and ensuring detailed follow-up by experts.

After his first visit, in September 1951, Blood summed up his aims as follows:

> It is of the greatest importance to this Government that the maximum use should be made of these islands as producers of copra so that we may be, as far as possible, self-supporting in vegetable oils. Secondly, we have to see that the conditions of life of the people of these islands are safeguarded and that the company does not regard them merely as dividend producing robots … One very obvious defect … is the class of persons employed by the Company as local managers. These people are badly paid, they have no experience of coconut growing outside the oil islands of Mauritius, and they appear to be almost entirely ignorant of some of the most elementary facts relating to tropical hygiene and public health.[14]

Among those accompanying the governor was the (acting) Director of Medical Services, Dr Maurice Lavoipierre, whose own very detailed report was enclosed with that of the Governor. Some of his observations provided new insights, for example:

On pay, Lavoipierre calculated that, including rations worth Rs 18 per month and the value of free housing, basic wages were the equivalent of Rs 38, 34 and 28 for men, women and young persons, enough only for childless couples where both partners were working.

On the composition of the work force, 'a large proportion of the labourers are born, live and die on the islands and can perhaps visit Mauritius on one or two occasions during their lifetime. The remainder of the labour force is recruited from Mauritius, and it is noted that there was a new departure last year [1950], when about 100 men and women came over from Seychelles to work at Diego Garcia'.

On health and hygiene, only on Salomon were efforts made in these regards, with Diego Garcia the most depressing; anaemia and parasitic conditions of every kind abounded; infants in particular were 'frankly debilitated'. Dr Lavoipierre took most of the blood tests himself and found that even the healthiest looking individuals had parasitic conditions.

On nutrition, pulses had recently been cut from the rations provided; pork was available from time to time, but only rarely on Diego Garcia, given the size of its population (600); turtle meat was very rare, except at Peros Banhos, where six to ten animals were captured every month;[15] the local hens were small and poor layers; also 'as in Mauritius, petty thieving seems to be of common occurrence and moreover dogs – some owners having five or six – are specially trained to catch the neighbours' chickens'; as to vegetables, the situation was 'disastrous', mainly on account of the freely ranging pigs and donkeys; and, although citrus and other trees, including the valuable banana, grew well, there were far too few of them.

Finally, concerning the disposal of refuse of all kinds, Lavoipierre could hardly contain his disgust: '… household refuse and junk is lying all over the settlements, particularly in Diego Garcia. There are no privies … and intestinal diseases are spread by the residents who use the beaches and the settlement perimeter for the purposes of nature'.

On two of his three visits, Blood took directors of the Company with him. The result was a series of well-informed and detailed reports, starting with that of Lavoipierre, leading to the measurement of results and firm pressure on it. This last was reinforced by the establishment of a small committee of the Governor's Executive Council to undertake 'discussions' of the islands' needs with the Company's representatives. Quite soon, these discussions brought into the open some rather tricky problems. World prices for copra and other coconut products had risen substantially above the controlled prices set for Mauritius' domestic market; yet all island produce had to be sold in Mauritius at these lower prices, which helped sugar producers to contain union demands for higher wages.[16] This issue aroused understandable concern in the Colonial Office and was eventually – but only temporarily – resolved by an *ex gratia* grant of Rs 2 million to the Company. Another issue was the absence of any government contribution to the social welfare of the islanders, notwithstanding that both the

Company and its staff contributed to the tax revenues. At the same time, the plantation companies were under-capitalised and hard put to raise the funds needed to install new equipment and attract better managers.

These dilemmas did not however distract Blood from the task in hand. In three years he had seen to: the establishment of a school on Diego Garcia and the introduction of teaching in the other islands by the lay Catholic Sisters of Charity; hugely improved sanitary arrangements; elimination of the plagues of flies and mosquitoes – and hence filariasis; better diet – Lavoipierre supplied Australorp cockerels from his own pens to improve the chicken population; the provision of simple social amenities; various measures to prevent the provision of alcohol from remaining an integral part of the pay structure; and he had helped the Company, for example, by securing the agreement of the Mauritius Cooperative Society to accept all the salted and dried fish the Chagos produced, to find new sources of income for the islands. There are two criteria against which to judge this energetic Governor's achievements: how far did they improve the lives of the islands' inhabitants? And how far did they ensure the permanence of the Chagos Archipelago's contribution to the Colony of Mauritius' economy?

On the first of these issues, Blood's achievement was remarkable. He shone a bright light into some very murky corners of his realm and then, by sending out officials for sufficient lengths of time, saw to it that the changes they made would take hold. At the technical level, these were quite straightforward. A sanitary inspector oversaw the building of latrines and drains, clearance of the puddles and rat-chewed coconuts in which mosquitoes bred, and containment in modern sties of the ubiquitous semi-wild pigs; he likewise organised teams for the daily disposal of waste and ordure and, in a neat example of biological control, introduced four white egrets (whose numbers soon increased[17]) to consume the maggots of the flies overjoyed by the new dung heaps. The personal commitment of the inspector appointed, Philippe Houeix, also went a long way to securing the support of the islanders themselves – it was he who cleared a patch of ground for a football pitch (Stade Houeix as it became known), while two visiting officials shared the cost of a Cup for competition between the islanders and the steamer crew. Similarly, in the fields of education and medicine, Blood took an interest in the suitability of candidates appointed to teaching and nursing jobs. The brightest of the 'torches' he shone was however Miss Mary Darlow OBE, his Public Assistance Commissioner and Social Welfare Adviser. Although she spent only nine days all told on Diego Garcia, four on Peros Banhos and two on Salomon, her 70-page report on the Chagos remains perhaps the most revealing ever penned.[18] Even Blood was taken aback by it, commenting tartly that it 'covers a large number of subjects which can hardly be considered as falling within the province of [her job]'. All the same, he secured his Executive

Council's agreement to the recommendation requiring their approval, that they should foot the bill for a modified form of old-age pensions.

While Mary Darlow provides a wealth of detailed information about the contemporary working activities and social structures of the islands, most striking are her insights relating to the degrading conditions of the workers, especially the women, and to the importance of the leadership (or lack of it) by the Company's managers. Since all the population fell into one or other of these categories, the two elements were inextricably connected. And, for those born in the Chagos, the problems began at birth. By the 1950s, women nearing childbirth were well cared for, with less work required of them and supervision by the midwives. There was very little mortality in childbirth and there was no requirement to resume work until 40 days afterwards. However, as there was no maternity benefit (other than a present of three chickens) and no pay or rations during this period, the enforced idleness was unpopular. Babies were generally breast fed for a year and thrived during this time, but did less well thereafter, especially before they were old enough to consume the same food as adults (one undersized three-year-old was spotted in her house, sharing some rice with a chicken). Crèches were provided, at least on Diego Garcia, offering 'merely a shelter' for (50–60) babies and young children whose mothers were at work. Toys were all but unknown – 'boundless joy is given by a single rubber band'! An application to the Directors for a small supply of footballs was turned down on the grounds of cost. At the age of about six or seven, the boys and girls started light work (often having helped their mothers from an even younger age), with the boys moving on to husking jobs in their late teens. Even in Diego Garcia, the newly established school's curriculum was devoid of practical instruction and the teacher took no interest outside the classroom; in short, 'the children everywhere have arrears of affection and interest due to them, though they respond easily and happily'.

As regards the school, the Governor had secured the Catholic bishop's agreement to fund the building of schools on all three atolls and to recruit teachers through the Roman Catholic Education Authority; their salaries would be met by government, while their passages to and from the islands would be provided free of charge by the Company. Diego Garcia's school was opened in September 1951, with an initial intake of 92 pupils; Peros Banhos had to wait until 1955 and Salomon until 1956. However, as Darlow's remarks indicate, these institutions were not well-adapted to the society they were intended to serve and, notwithstanding the Company's support, struggled to survive.[19] By 1953, the school register at Diego Garcia had declined to 75, with a far lower number attending regularly.

Distribution of labour recapitulated

Between 1946 and 1952 the population of the Chagos rose gradually towards a total not seen since the 1920s. But, as the table below shows, it is evident that the population of Salomon was very stable, at a level close to that obtaining during the war years (see chapter 18, note 38 on page 397). In contrast, the population of Diego Garcia expanded markedly, while that of Peros declined to a similar degree, after an increase in comparison to the pre-war years. Whether any significant transfers were made from one to the other is unknown, but it would appear that few people can have left Peros Banhos before the war ended. It is of course possible that improving survival rates for infants were leading to larger proportions of children, but the necessary statistics are lacking.

Table 19.1   Chagos population 1946–52

	1946	1947	1948	1949	1950	1951	1952*
Diego Garcia	n/a	447	536	568	604	637	615
Peros Banhos	372	313	323	328	314	306	325
Salomon	219	220	224	228	223	220	211
Total		980	1083	1124	1141	1163	1151

*Mauritius census 1952. Figures for other years were obtained from island managers.

<u>Source</u>: TNA CO 1032/132 Enclosure 1, Despatch No. 293 of 31/10/1951.

For those of working age, there continued to be a settled hierarchy. At the pinnacle was the manager (*Administrateur*), supported by a small managerial staff. On Salomon and Peros Banhos, there was rarely more than one assistant to the manager; but by the early 1950s, Diego Garcia had no less than seven. All were Franco-Mauritians or Franco-Seychellois. Below these were the workers, who fell into three classes: *Commandeurs* (supervisors), *Artisans* and *Laboreurs* (including, with rare exceptions, all the women). As an indication of the relative numbers in each class, the 393 workers on Diego Garcia at this period included 20 *commandeurs* and 33 *artisans*. The numbers on Peros Banhos (and Salomon) were 182–11–17 (and 130–n/a–n/a). The *artisans* included blacksmiths, sawmill workers, boat-builders, sail-makers, masons, gardeners, mechanics, fishermen and pig-keepers. As we have already seen, the key labouring tasks were the gathering and de-husking of coconuts (by men) and their reduction to copra (by women); but these jobs were allocated only to quite small numbers of the best workers, in the case of Peros Banhos sixteen and ten respectively. The rest were occupied on the multifarious tasks involved in maintaining the plantations – transporting the nuts, weighing and bagging copra, operating the oil mills and furnaces, charcoal burning, clearance and new plantings, farm and timber operations, guano collection, not to mention the hunting of rats or, for the women, the manufacture from palm leaves of twine, cordage, matting and brooms. The workers, as in the past, were virtually all Creoles of French-African or French-Malagasy origin, with scarcely half-a-dozen of Indian parentage. Only on Diego Garcia was there an imbalance between the sexes, largely accounted for by the high proportion of men (79) to women (32) among the one-fifth of the workers who had been recruited recently from Seychelles.

This recitation of plantation activities suggests the potential at least for a harmonious and productive, if poorly educated and culturally impoverished society. However, as in earlier times, the isolation of the islands put a premium on good local management, properly supported and directed from headquarters and, just as in earlier times, these conditions were, to a greater or lesser extent, still unfulfilled. There were indeed significant contrasts between each of the three plantations and these, as Mary Darlow recognised, stemmed more from managerial problems, rather than intrinsic differences resulting from geography, which we have examined earlier (see pages 357–366).

Management and social life

Diego Garcia

Diego Garcia provided an object lesson in the importance of good management. From 1948 the island was managed by Henri D'Unienville. During his tenure the island fell into complete chaos. He himself was habitually drunk, failing to supervise his subordinate staff or to take any interest in the workers. As a consequence, weed clearance was abandoned and parts of the plantation soon became impenetrable; the grounds and buildings of the establishment were abandoned to dirt and decay; the pigsties and stables became filthy; the yard where the women worked resembled a hen run; and the furnace for treating the copra no longer operated. As Darlow commented,

> the workers naturally idled if the bosses did not work. They had been allowed liberties, particularly as the *Administrateur* and his immediate subordinates had relations with many of the women of the island, some of whom were actually established in their houses. The blacksmith, for example, who is probably the principal artisan, was insubordinate because his daughter lived in the *grand' maison*.

Inevitably, there were wider social consequences, evidenced by a very high proportion of wounds, blows and contusions in the hospital's outpatient records. Mismanagement was, however, not the only reason for these. Because of the difficulty – hardly surprising – of recruiting labour for this island, nearly 80 male

Seychellois workers had been hired, together with 32 women, upsetting both the homogeneity and the gender balance of the population, with inevitable consequences in such unruly conditions. It is perhaps surprising that only one murder was committed, and that between two men who on that very morning had sworn themselves to blood-brotherhood. Finally, the whole island went on strike.

Blood's first visit to Diego Garcia in 1951 had allowed him to see at firsthand what was going on and, fortunately, he was accompanied by one of Diego Limited's Directors, a Dr Lanier. The latter was a particularly well-qualified observer, having had direct experience of coconut cultivation in the Seychelles, where he had also been Director of Medical Services. Within nine months, D'Unienville had been dismissed and a Captain Lanier, presumably related to the Director, installed, together with several new assistants. When Blood made his second brief visit in October 1952, he found great improvements under way and was able to perform the official opening of the new school.[21] By the time of Darlow's visit in mid-1953, the situation had been transformed. Violence (and accidents to the establishment's three lorries) had sharply declined; the house and kitchen gardens had been cleared and freshly planted; the copra preparation area had been provided with a cement floor and protective roof; four rolling roofs installed to protect the drying copra from showers; various old buildings restored and both the new school and new pigsties built; the workshops were working, with one new boat constructed and others repaired; and clearance of the creepers and *cocos Bon Dié* ('saving His presence, badly spaced and often not upright') was well under way. Furthermore, work was better organised and supervised; for a start, the *appel* [call to assemble] was sounded at 6.10, with work from 6.45 until 10.45, rather than two hours work from 7.30 until 9.30, following *appel* at 7 a.m.

Three voyagers have left accounts of Capt. Lanier. In 1948, F. D. Ommaney, whose *Shoals of Capricorn* remains a classic description of the western Indian Ocean, sailed in the three-masted schooner *Diolinda*, when Lanier was her captain. 'He was an old French sea dog, tough and wiry, with a russet face seamed with a million tiny wrinkles worn by the sun and wind of many years. The blood of the corsairs ran in his veins … he swore loudly and volubly in English and French and creole and chased his crew aloft with oaths in the traditional manner.'[22] Shortly after Lanier's arrival in Diego Garcia, the French single-handed yachtsman, Bernard Moitessier, was wrecked there and was taken to the manager's house by some of the islanders. They called out and 'roars came from within and there appeared the awesome figure of Captain Lanier, grasping a cudgel in his fist and ready to subdue the rebellion … a bluff character, blunt and straightforward, with a heart of gold'.[23] Three years later, he had become 'a small agile, twinkling man, a sailor turned farmer. He had been in sail all his days at sea and the most immediately remarkable legacy of his early years is his voice, which, having retained the pitch to make it audible above the screech of the trades in the rigging, is at first a little disconcerting in an enclosed space'.[24] No wonder Lanier, with the help of his fourth wife, made things shipshape in Diego Garcia.

Operation Concubine

On 1 November 1952, a few months after Captain Lanier had embarked on his Herculean task, there arrived the first Sunderland flying boat to visit Diego Garcia since the closure of the wartime base. It brought an Air Force team, whose mission (Operation Concubine) was to assess various islands' suitability as sites for a staging post.[20] As in the war, the result of this operation was to give priority to developing Gan in the Addu Atoll. Also, like their American predecessors in 1942, this British team concentrated their attentions on the north-west corner of the island, which they found to be covered in heavy jungle, at the end of a dirt track barely passable by the Landrover in which they travelled. The team's report on conditions on the island was highly critical: 'Living and sanitary conditions are extremely bad. Flies and mosquitoes abound, faeces and refuse are deposited on the ground around dwellings, and wells are open to every kind of contamination.' The echoes of Marcel Didier's account are unmistakeable. Their photographs included one of a 'typical hut'.

The team noted, however, that improvements were under way, with better latrines and also a new piggery to 'replace the appallingly filthy enclosure [adjacent to Lanier's house] which at present houses the numerous pigs and provides the bulk of the fly breeding in the vicinity'. They were told that the working population was about 400, of which 200 were indigenous and the rest imported from Mauritius or Seychelles on three-year contracts. These figures are consistent with those reported in the census earlier that year (Table 19.1).

Peros Banhos

In Peros Banhos, the fundamental problems for managers stemmed from the atoll's geography – its vast, rough lagoon, the plethora of small islets, and the fact that the jetty could only be approached at high tide, thus severely disrupting loading and unloading of the *Sir Jules*. By 1952, Vielle, now 61 and with twelve years' service there as manager, was suffering from deteriorating health, as well as the loss of his experienced assistant, Philippe Talbot. As visiting magistrates noticed, a lot of trouble had evidently been taken to display attractively the goods available in the company boutique; but this attractiveness appeared to have encouraged excessive wine consumption. Other visitors, as we shall see, were to comment how charmingly the Ile de Coin as a whole had been developed. What went by the board was regular inspection of the atoll's remoter islands, where undergrowth, debris and rats took an increasing toll on productivity. Other problems were not of Vielle's making. He fell seriously ill and had to allow a junior assistant, a certain M. Arnal, take charge. This individual sought to increase production by setting impossible daily targets and, when they went unmet, withholding the weekly rations. He also took to brandishing a home-made whip of plaited coconut leaves. His come-uppance came swiftly. The *Sir Jules* arrived and was unloaded. Then the workers, brandishing their knives, barricaded Arnal into his house and refused to load the export crop until he agreed to board the vessel himself, ready to return to Mauritius. Vielle restored calm, though he had no choice but to accept Arnal's departure. Soon afterwards, Philippe Talbot was transferred and replaced by Robert Talbot, apparently not related to the former but a son of Louis Talbot, who had been removed from the Chagos in 1942 (see pages 382–383).

Salomon

In Salomon, Raoul Caboche, the manager since 1933, had died at his post in 1952, leaving his plantation, Darlow considered, 'in good fettle'. Philippe Talbot, who had succeeded him, was judged an able administrator, keen, popular, just and firm. Not surprisingly, the coconuts were looked after better than in either Diego Garcia or Peros Banhos; while the subsidiary export of pigs, developed by Caboche, enabled the new manager to purchase various comforts of benefit both to manager and employees, e.g., a refrigerator and, by 1953, a Friesian bull, two cows and a calf for the supply of fresh milk. Another relic of Caboche's tenure, apart from the shingle-roofed huts for the workers, was the policy of gathering all the sound trunks of fallen hardwood trees to make shingles for export to Mauritius. Although the island had no motorboat or lorry, there was a fully-functioning diesel engine used to replace manual labour in the saw mill. Even making allowance for the smaller quantities involved, the arrangements for loading the ship were more efficient than elsewhere. As for the islanders themselves, they were better-regarded by Darlow than those of the other islands, as being less prone to violence – wine consumption was better regulated – and displaying greater initiative (for example, some had built their own boats). In sum, 'this group of islands is definitely the best of the three groups in every respect'. Philippe Talbot was, however, like Dussercle before the war, disenchanted by their 'primitive customs', for example, the abandonment of personal cleanliness for the week following a death.

Management weaknesses and sub-optimal production

By the early 1950s, problems in the Archipelago could no longer be blamed on the effects of war. As we have seen, visitors had been inclined to consider pay rates as the main barrier to better performance. When the situation was studied in closer detail in 1953 by Darlow and the visiting magistrate, this time Etienne Bouloux, an experienced official of the Industrial Court, they found a different explanation for the curious paradox of shortage of labour coexisting with the excessive leisure of those employed. The basic wage was based on the production expected of the slowest workers, who could complete their daily tasks within three hours; and the main incentive offered for doing more was an increased allocation of wine. Taken together with, on the one hand, the free provision of most necessities of life and, on the other, of a paucity of interesting goods for purchase, it was hardly surprising that, as Bouloux caustically remarked, 'the summum of bliss is the minimum of exertion'.

Sale of alcohol in the islands was, in theory, still regulated by the law of 1906 (see page 277). It provided that no spirituous liquor should be sold in the archipelago; that no wine should be sold to a person under sixteen; and that the amount sold to an adult should not exceed half a litre on one day, with a weekly maximum of two and a half litres. As far as spirits were concerned, rum had begun to arrive in increasing quantities during the war, but there was also substantial consumption of locally distilled *bacca*, which infamously helped *ségas* to go with a swing. Regarding wine, the actual arrangements varied over time and in the different islands, but in general wine went on sale twice each week and there was a requirement that it be consumed on the premises. What regularly happened in practice was that the head of a family would take delivery of its whole ration, say two litres, consume it on the spot and collapse drunk outside the store (in 1951, Lavoipierre counted seven or eight men in this condition on a single afternoon). Similarly, a woman – women often did not like the wine – might collect her half-litre, then sell it to someone else at three or four times the purchase price. The wine had an alcohol content of 14%, this being the minimum that enabled it to keep in the local climate. Generally speaking it had been produced in Mauritius and dispatched in barrels. The only detailed description of its manufacture dates from 1954, when Sir Robert Scott, then Governor, participated in an unannounced Customs raid on several factories, but there is no reason to suppose that better procedures were used in earlier years. Writing to his mother, he commented that the vinegar factory,

> was quite indescribable … Two of the wine factories (where the basic liquor was made by fermenting imported raisins in water and sugar) were pretty grim also, but nothing like so bad, although if I'd ever had any idea of sampling the local wines I no longer would. The stuff in the fermenting rooms looked exactly like pigswill and there was nothing to prevent the sparrows or mice etc from popping in for a swim; [even the best] was more like a burlesque than a business.[25]

Trade statistics show that the fob cost of the wine supplied to the Chagos was for many years 1 Rupee per 2 litres.[26] It seems unlikely to have been the best quality available.

This then was the spur to greater zeal. In Diego Garcia, for example, 'men husking 5,000 coconuts in a week receive an additional free issue of one litre and women are entitled to a free issue of one fifth of a litre for every additional task … and I have no doubt that part of the labour force is suffering from the effects of chronic alcoholism'.[27] Related to this was the absence of other incentives; and even if money were used for this purpose, there was little available locally to spend it on. To quote Lavoipierre again, 'A special mention must be made of the islands' shops. They are dirty and uninviting. The buildings are in need of repairs, goods are piled up higgley-piggledy and dust is to be found everywhere. As they represent the settlements' larders, I recommend that immediate attention be given … to render them sanitary …'[28] By 1953, Capt. Lanier on Diego Garcia had got a grip on the situation, against strong resistance from his workers, while on Salomon the issue of wine was already well-regulated and only on Peros Banhos were there still signs of excessive indulgence. These local improvements were also beginning to be reflected in better attendance and increased earnings.

Wider economic constraints

Yet local change could really only have a local impact. Certain disadvantages of the Chagos islands were hardly capable of remedy – for instance, the distance from markets and sources of supply, the absence of a social infrastructure affordable only in larger societies, the fragmentation of production (above all on

Peros Banhos), and the absence of scope for economies of scale. Others were more acute than they needed to be – for example, the *Sir Jules* was notoriously under-powered and therefore slow; the lagoons and entrances thereto prevented efficient loading and unloading; communications between the plantations, whether by boat or telegraph, were antiquated and inadequate; and a pall of lethargy hung over the whole system. There was also a largely unacknowledged difficulty: only in the Oil Islands and Seychelles was coconut production a traditional activity; even though Mauritius suffered from unemployment among its largely Indian population, it could not supply labour having the required skills or interest in the Creole lifestyle and even though these skills were available in Seychelles (where the Company maintained a recruiting agent), the Creoles there did not mix easily with the Ilois. As Blood had recognised, the essential ingredients for greater commercial success included more intensive and diversified production (involving additional workers), the introduction of better equipment, regular consultation between the three plantation managers, firmer and more interested involvement of the Company's Directors and, not least, increased capital investment. Soon after his visit in 1953, Blood retired.

Sir Robert Scott

There appears to have been a certain loss of momentum, while Scott, Blood's successor, settled in and it was not until December 1954 that he responded to the Colonial Secretary's comments, made in February, on the detailed reports submitted the previous year.[29] In the interim, however, there had been a somewhat unusual exchange of demi-official letters between the new Governor and Sir John Martin, a senior official in the Colonial Office.[30] Scott reported that he had

> seen two departmental reports, which are discursive and detailed; one seems to be reasonably objective while the other is very much the reverse. The first [he appears to have in mind that of Lavoipierre] consists, however, of the kind of notes which a not very experienced Assistant District Officer would keep for his District Commissioner's benefit. The second [evidently that by Darlow] is a mélange of sundowner gossip, 'bazaar' chat and unco-ordinated observations on this and that …

Noting that he was turning over in his mind the problem of the Lesser Dependencies, he did not think it a good idea that such reports be forwarded undigested to the Colonial Office. The reply was brisk and unequivocal: existing procedures worked well and all three of the reports resulting from the visits made in 1953 had been of considerable interest. Clearly, London did not want any loosening of the grip achieved by Blood.

In his December despatch, Scott reported what had been done to implement some of the recommendations made, as well as the difficulties preventing fulfilment of others, and concluded that the Company seemed to be taking a reasonably enlightened view of its responsibilities in regard to welfare, but that the primary need was for regular and experienced administrative (rather than legal) supervision. At the same time, he commented (forwarding only the statistical appendix!) on the report of the magistrate who had visited the Archipelago in July.[31] It appears that conditions, especially on Diego Garcia, had continued to improve, but that discipline on Peros Banhos was increasingly lax, with the likelihood of trouble ensuing for whoever was chosen to succeed the ailing Vielle. Much more dramatically, however, there had been severe problems of insubordination in Salomon towards the end of June 1954. These had been reported by radio, enabling a very experienced magistrate, accompanied by three police officers, to be substituted for the inexperienced individual who had been on the point of leaving for the islands. In brief, the manager's efforts to restore calm after an alcohol-induced brawl resulted in his being threatened by a knife and having in turn to draw his revolver. The ringleaders were three Seychellois, one of whom proved to have had a criminal record before being recruited; all were sentenced to short terms of imprisonment and removal from the island. The magistrate's view was that the underlying cause of the event was resentment at Philippe Talbot's efforts to tighten discipline, which had been allowed to decline under his predecessor. Be that as it might, two full and peaceful years had passed between Caboche's death and this first fracas, time enough, one might think, to seek blame elsewhere than in a predecessor's tomb.

In 1955, Governor Scott, aboard the frigate HMS *Loch Killisport*, was able to visit the Archipelago himself.[32] As well as providing material for an official report, this visit supplied brilliant local colour for his highly-praised history of the Lesser Dependencies, *Limuria*, published after his retirement.[33] Even more vivid was the description he penned to his mother, immediately upon his return to Port Louis.[34] This is worth quoting in some detail, both as an antidote to the unfortunate events recounted above and because it best explains how the Chagos might, however briefly and superficially, be confused with Paradise. More seriously, the islanders, many of whom had undergone two decades of poor management and penury, followed by wartime deprivations and then even worse management by d'Unienville, must have been enthused by the interest shown and changes wrought under Blood's stewardship. It was not so much that there had been any fundamental improvements in their standard of living or opportunities for self-advancement. Rather, but only slightly less importantly, it was a matter of relative transformation in the atmosphere in which their daily lives were lived.

East Point is like a portion of a French fishing village transported to a clearing in a forest. As I found to be the case in most of the main villages in the islands, it has an extensive green as its centre, with a cross at the seaward end. There is a 'big house', in this case a red roofed, small château with a horseshoe staircase on the outside, in a walled garden with an arch over the gate. Behind it was a little plantation with some fruit trees (mainly citrus and breadfruit) and a lot of timber trees. The factories and workshops are on two sides of the square and, grouped round at a little distance, are the shop, hospital, school, church and crèche. In the case of East Point, the bungalows of the principal members of the staff are beyond these central groups at one end and the main village is at the other end. Everything has to be fenced or walled because of the donkeys: there are about a hundred ranging free on the island. There are also herds of horses, but nothing like so many as on Agalega. The school at East Point was the best in the islands although (perhaps, because) the mistress was a bit of a dragon and raspberries flowed freely during my visit. The children had been at the pier head to meet me, the girls in white or bright cotton frocks and the boys in coloured shirts and white shorts. They sang the Queen very nicely and the head boy (11 yrs) presented me with a large bouquet of pink roses; there were plenty of them in East Point, also apricot cannas and cosmos and lots of hibiscus. The village was built irregularly over a large area – cottages of palm fibre and thatch on timber frames. There were mild attempts at gardening, but what seemed to interest the islanders more were poultry and ducks (I noted three different varieties and many crosses) which were all over the place. The flies in the whole of Diego were an absolute menace but nobody had to be as unpolished as [Lavoipierre] suggested and keep a hand over their beer glass, for little wooden lids, neatly turned from a dark local timber, were supplied. There is a very good range of local timbers and the Met Officer had made some interesting and elegant experiments in cabinet making. The store was very well stocked, their pride being that they had a jewellery department (artificial pearl necklaces, rolled gold wedding rings and brooches etc.) and a sanitary department (arty tin-tins).

After a day at East Point, Scott took a jeep trip northwards along the bumpy, forested road, enlivened by bright cardinal birds and acrobatic rats in the canopy, past three little villages and the ruins of the Minni Minni establishment to Barton Point. There a rain storm soaked everyone to the skin and, on the way back, the jeep broke down, leaving them stranded for an hour before a search party arrived. Moving on to Salomon, Scott found time to sail to Ile Anglaise (with its small village) and Ile de la Passe, enjoying successful fishing along the way. Lastly, he spent two days at Peros Banhos. For a contrasting insight into the Company's efforts to make a good impression on the Governor (see inset), we can draw on the recently compiled recollections of one islander, Fernand Mandarin, to whom readers have already been introduced. From the Governor's perspective, the visit's highlights included an all-day fishing trip to the Benares

Bank in a local schooner, with a total of 600 lbs of fish being caught, with Scott proudly landing the single biggest, weighing 24 lbs. That evening, he attended a *séga*.

> There were very catchy, half-sad tunes sung to an accompaniment of outsize tambourines and drums. The star performers among the girls were three white-starched petticoats under bright dresses whose skirts opened down the front. In the whirling movements the petticoats went out like ballet skirts. We left to loud singing of 'Au revoir le Gouverneur'.

Scott was clearly delighted.

> The fruit and vegetable garden was the best of all the islands, having among other attractions many orange trees in full bearing. The people, who are the merriest, except perhaps for the Agalegans, have a good reputation for honesty – hence the success of the garden. The island itself was very trim, the coconut groves being maintained like a park ...

Scott's despatch is more prosaic and also more penetrating.[35] Apart from its factual survey of the system of operations in the Archipelago, he focused on three main topics: the impact of the reforms set in hand by his predecessor; the composition of the population; and his concern about the islands' economic outlook. On the first of these, he came close to waxing lyrical. There was potential for abuse of the population, but no sign of it; spasmodic disturbances had arisen 'mainly from the misdeeds of imported bad-hats and faults, not assigna-

Governor Scott's visit to Peros Banhos

The Governor was going to visit us, in Peros Banhos, and the administrator requested that we be taught how to sing in English in preparation for the arrival of Governor Scott. At the time I was 7 years old; we were in a group of children from the age of 6 up to 14 years. We were learning the song 'God Save The Queen'. So as soon as the Governor would step on the quay, we would start singing and we would be holding and waving a little Union Jack in our hand. The Governor came down with his feathered hat, he applauded, he was pleased to hear us singing that song. He then asked the administrator, 'Are they the school children here on the island?', to which the administrator replied 'There is no school here'. He was shocked, he could not believe that there was no school on Peros. He said we should have a school here for these children; it was then 1955. A man called Michel Domaingue was in the delegation. During his stay on the island, he showed us a Charlie Chaplin movie. It was a great discovery for all the inhabitants of Peros Banhos. We all came to watch this projection in the go-down. There was also a projection of Johnny Weissmuller in the role of Tarzan!

Source: Mandarin, F., extract from unpublished memoirs recorded by M. Robert Furlong (trans. MC).

ble to any one quarter, in the system of operation'; schooling and vegetable-growing were encouraged, though with some continuing resistance from adults; and in general the people were healthy and happy. Most striking were the sharp increases in earnings, savings and imports of consumer goods, for which the management (now virtually free of misfits) deserved credit.

As to the character of the people, Scott was 'surprised to find that a relatively high proportion of the residents regard the islands as their permanent home and they have their characteristic way of life, unlike that of those Creoles of Mauritius who most resemble them physically'. These 'natives' were supplemented by constantly changing infusions of Seychellois, imported on contract, who usually kept themselves very much to themselves, but (for the reasons previously described) did not make for harmony. Scott goes on:

> The overseer class consists either of 'natives', who were described as being generally too easy-going or slow thinking, or Mauritians and Seychellois on contract, whose quality varied considerably. Artisans and mechanics (also Creoles) are usually brought from Mauritius and, although a number are skilful and hard-working, I was told that they found great difficulty in settling down to the life of the islands and some have definitely been quite unsuitable and have had to be repatriated. The managerial staffs, school teachers, book-keepers and dressers, Mauritian and Seychellois, are in the main members of the 'coloured' community with a few individuals of European blood in the highest posts. With very few exceptions, they have no vocations for careers in out-stations: their natural surroundings would be the pavements, shop-windows and cinemas of a small town in Mauritius.

Finally, Scott observed, 'It is the economic future of the Oil Islands which gives me some misgiving'. The companies were meeting increasingly keen competition in Mauritius from vegetable oils imported from elsewhere. Anyway, only in Diego Garcia did Scott see scope for increasing production, but only if the capital costs involved in clearing and replanting abandoned areas were to be economic; on the other atolls, coconut and timber used all the land available. There was some scope for exporting guano deposits, but other activities, for example fishing and the conversion of copra into pork, seemed 'most unlikely', because of transport difficulties, to be capable of development for more than local requirements. In conclusion, 'it appears to me to be abundantly clear that the future well-being and development of the Oil Islands are primarily and almost exclusively bound up with the coconut and that industry will require constant attention'. In short, for all the change of atmosphere, fundamental problems affecting the islands' future remained. As he penned his comments, Scott was waiting to learn the views of the Company's chairman, who had visited the islands at the end of 1955.

Notes to Chapter 19

1 TNA CO 167/912/10 Joint report of Maurice Lavoipierre and Harold Glover, heads of the Medical and Education Departments, and Pierre Rousset, Magistrate, Port Louis, 26 June 1946.

2 Duyker, E., *Mauritian Heritage: an anthology of the Lionnet, Commins and related families* (p. 152), Australian Mauritius Research Group, Melbourne 1986.

3 This small ship, with a single 450 horsepower diesel engine, was built in Holland in 1949. She had an average speed of less than 8 knots, with 40,000 cubic feet of cargo and sheltered deck space, plus accommodation for 42 passengers, 18 of them in steerage.

4 These lyrics were collected by Jacques Cantin, together with those of many other old *ségas*, and this translation into English is largely the work of L.C. Cuniah. Its full text is to be found at http://www.chagos.info/. We have seen a slightly different version in a collection found online, where the *Sir Jules* is compared to a *cateau* (a type of fish) and the poem begins, in its English translation: 'I am the negro with seven skins [a Mauritian proverb]. Look how robust I am. Not even a blow with a knife can cut through my skin'.

5 TNA CO 859/194/8 Despatch No. 324 dated 14 December 1948.

6 *Ibid*. Despatch No. 74, dated 28 March 1949.

7 *L'Express* 3 June 1985, summarised by Yvan Martial in the same weekly in June 2010, in his regular column *Il y a 25 ans*. The full text of Didier's recollections can be found at http://www.chagos.info/.

8 De Robillard had been a youthful radio enthusiast, wartime operator and close companion of Paul Caboche, who married his sister.

9 This document was discovered in his attic by Caboche's son Paul in October 2008. From internal evidence it must have been composed early in 1949, but whether it (or, more likely, a considered text based on it) was ever submitted to higher management is not known.

10 I recall making a visit to Diego Garcia and having occasion to mention the word 'progress' to the island's manager at the time. Well, would you believe it! He was, as the English say, totally DEAD AGAINST it. Indeed, he went so far as to say that, if, for instance, the company's Port Louis office sent him some Machine to install, he'd do nothing of the kind, just leave it well and truly in its crate.

11 Report by Mayer (undated), submitted to C.O. under cover of telegram 302 Saving of 12 May 1950.

12 TNA CO 859/194/8 Despatch No. 269, dated 15 December 1950.

13 Blood, 'The Peaks of Limuria', article in the *Geographical Magazine* Vol. XXIX, No. 10, February 1957. 'Most of [the dependent islands] are uninhabited, unexplored and undeveloped, visions of tropical beauty, pocket-handkerchief paradises, protected in their unspoiled loveliness by the sweep of the ocean, known to bird and fish but not to man, inviolate save by sun and storm, existing for the glory of God, who cannot but look with pleasure on these gems of his creation.'

14 TNA CO 1023/132 Despatch No. 293 dated 31 October 1951.

15 The survival of turtles in Peros Banhos helps to explain why its inhabitants retained memories of the traditional recipe, known as *carangaie*. As Fernand Mandarin, who was born and brought up on that atoll, explained (interview in January 2010), the custom was to cook the turtle's meat, tripes, etc., over an open fire in the shell, then mix in the rice. When the *carangaie* had been consumed, the children would climb in and scrape the shell clean. Then the shells would be exported to Mauritius to be boiled down into glue.

16 A compendium of the local press (*Weekly Report*) for 20 February 1952 included an item about the Oil Islands. The writer stated that in the financial year ending in September 1951, the companies concerned had posted a loss of Rs 300,000. This arose from the fact that they were not allowed to sell their copra at a price exceeding Rs 580 per tonne, whereas the world market price was Rs 967.25.

17 These birds, cattle egrets (*Bulbulcus ibis*), are now so well established that periodic culling is required to limit the risk they pose to aircraft.

18 TNA CO 1023/132.

19 Mgr. Amédée Nagapen, undated report 'Archipel Chagos: L'Eglise à Diego Garcia' (post 1972).

20 TNA AIR 20/10220 and AIR 23/8712 Report by Squadron Leader P.F. Eames, November 1952.

21 TNA CO 1023/132 Despatch dated 8 November 1952.

22 Ommaney himself visited Diego Garcia in 1948, but not in the *Diolinda*. He made little comment on the island, except to remark on the traces of wartime activities, including 'what used to be the Operations Room with a large operational map still in place on the wall, RAF emblems and pin-up girls ogling at nothing in the dusty heat'.

23 Moitessier, B., *Sailing to the Reefs*, adapted from his *Un Vagabond des Mers du Sud* (Flammarion, 1960).

24 Sir Robert Scott, who visited the Chagos in 1955, in his evocative *Limuria* (p. 243) 1961, Oxford University Press.

25 RHL MSS Brit Emp s. 417.7.

26 We have not tabulated the usual statistics recorded in Mauritius 'Blue Books', which during this decade showed unusual fluctuations and changes in price levels, as well as changed categorisations, the latter probably reflecting application of the rules of the General Agreement on Tariffs and Trade (GATT) after 1952. Serious analysis would, we believe, require specialist expertise.

27 TNA CO 1023/132 Report dated 17 October 1951.

28 *Ibid.*

29 TNA CO 1036/138 Despatch No. 971, dated 10 December 1954.

30 *Ibid.* Lettter dated 9 July 1954.

31 No trace in TNA.

32 TNA CO 1036/138 Despatch No. 3 dated 16 January 1956, reporting a visit which took place during September and October, 1955.

33 Scott, R., *op. cit.*

34 RHL MSS Brit Emp s. 417(7), letter dated 7 October 1955.

35 TNA CO 1036/138 Despatch dated 16 January 1956.

20

Living Memories: a worker's view of the 1950s

By FERNAND MANDARIN[1], with illustrations by CLEMENT SIATOUS[2]

I WAS not brought up by my biological parents but by my adoptive parents. My grandmother's sister and her husband, Leonel Casimir, did not have any children; they wanted to adopt me, as they had other members of our extended family. It was an adoption carried out on verbal trust, with no official document involved; this type of adoption was commonplace throughout the archipelago, for boys and for girls, and it was done very quickly. The child who goes through this adoption process knows his biological parents, and visits them often; and also carries out some filial duties, while at the same time becoming emotionally attached to the adoptive parents, and to the adoptive siblings just the same as blood siblings. I grew up in this adoptive family, composed of a mother, father and ten children.

During that time my biological mother was sick and they needed to come to Mauritius because there was no doctor on the island, just a nurse. I wanted to come to Mauritius, but my biological parents said no, you do not live with us. One day when your adoptive mother goes there, to Mauritius, then you can go; I wept, for I wanted to go. I wanted to go because I was tempted by the lovely things I see people come back with. Every time someone comes back from Mauritius, they have a lovely pair of shoes, clothes, etc. My other brothers and sisters followed my biological parents and came to Mauritius and spent roughly about a year here. I was the only one that was left behind. Today when I look back I realise that I have known Chagos better than them, because I have been there, I did not leave, and I have witnessed everything that went on there during their absence.

Leonel Casimir was a cooper by trade and also worked in copra. He taught me these two trades when I was very young; I was seven years of age, when I would keep him company at work. His duty was to ensure the copra was being put in the mill and he was also the overseer, in charge of groups of workers who pick coconuts and sort them out, making sure the work was being carried out properly on the islands.

My father, Louis Raoul Mandarin, was the seventh child in the family; he worked with several administrators and has lived on three of the five inhabited islands: Salomon, Egmont and Ile du Coin where he passed away. The births of his children took place on many of the islands. That is why my blood is found on all the inhabited islands of Chagos!

My father spent a lot of his time in the blacksmith shop. All industrial activities linked with the exploitation of copra needed wrought iron in one way or another: horseshoes and accoutrements for horses used to pull carts, nails of all dimensions for various usages; plates placed under boats to protect them from the reef; the rudder, anchors, metalwork for masts, along with tools used in coconut cultivation and other implements used on the islands. My father also made soap for the factory.[3] The soap was sold in the local shop – one could buy a bar, or if money was tight, a piece of a bar, sold by weight.

Ile du Coin

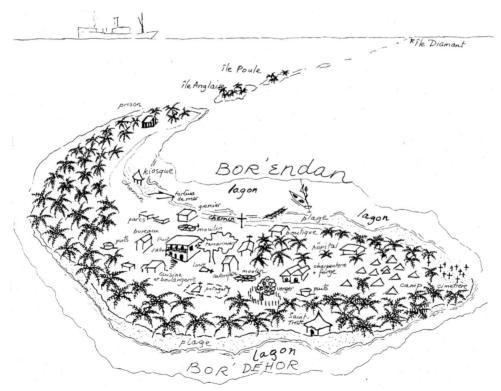

Image reproduced by kind permission of Mme. Alix Mülnier.[4]

The village on Ile du Coin [Peros Banhos atoll] was fairly well-equipped; it comprised a shop, together with a 'go-down' where food products were kept. There were houses for all staff of the *état-major*: the administrator and other personnel (nurse, assistants, mechanic, carpenter, joiner, etc.). There were a number of hangars: one used for boats; one as a marine carpenter's workshop; one for wood-cutting and another for a joiner's workshop. There was a stable for horses; blacksmith's and cooper's workshops. There was a prison, a chapel (with a small and a large bell, which communicated time, etc., to the islanders), and the mission. There were factories, with a go-down for coconut kernels (with a furnace and oven inside). There was a mill for crushing the coconut kernels (copra) to extract oil. There was a power house, for electricity; for radio and communication. There were offices: one for daily workers' attendance, and one to carry out administrative work. There were cow and sea turtle pens, and a slaughterhouse. There was a pier, to facilitate the transportation of goods to and from ships. There was also a flagpole for the Union Jack. Each house in the village had a tank, to store rain water.

On the outer coast (known as Bor' Déhor) of the lagoon, between the village and the workers' camp, which consisted of 72 houses (after 1954), there was a football ground, facing the hospital. There was also a school and a crèche. The workers' camp was about 100 m from the village; the houses in the camp were all identical. A family dwelling was made of four wooden walls, a thatched roof (coconut fronds), with a floor of lime. The measurements were 1000 sq. ft., with a verandah in front; 18 m long x 6 m wide. The occupier customised the interior as he pleased; some made a space for an interior kitchen with sandy floor; for cooking there was straw, wood and charcoal; the cooking was done on a three-legged metal wood-burner; some people used a *réchaud* (a kind of basic stove); there was a small wooden table, a cooking-pot (*marmite*); water was obtained from a communal well and, also, each house had its own well, deep enough to keep water (2 m 50 or 2.5 m), each inhabitant looked after and maintained his own well; the water was a bit salty – brackish water, but it was drinkable. There were outside bathrooms, people used water from the well; and toilets, all with no roofs – communal latrines for four to five houses. Before that people would go in the woods; the emptying of the sewage in the sea – in the bay, was organised by the administrator.

The road was 10 to 15 m wide with houses on each side. There was a space of roughly 10 m between houses, and each inhabitant organised his own little vegetable garden in front of his house. There was a farmyard, for chickens, and different types of ducks, such as kanar patuyar [mallard] and kanar mile [mallard/Muscovy cross]; different types of birds were fattened for the table: hens, ducks and cockerels. Workers were not allowed to keep pigs; this was a privilege afforded only to those in the plantation house. Those animals were for domestic

The village square, painted by Clément Siatous. Image courtesy of the artist.

use only, not a commercial enterprise; only, every now and then, eggs or live chickens were sold to those who did not have a farmyard.

Later, there were two long hangars built for ten to fifteen workers, who came from the Seychelles – they came to work on Ile du Coin as there was a shortage of labour.

Childhood

Parents were generally very strict and demanded respect and good manners. They ensured proper values were inculcated: the children were, for example, not allowed to drink or smoke. Friendship and family were very important. The core value was the sense of sharing, and also understanding others. We were sometimes reprimanded for our actions or behaviour and the *rotin-bazar* (rattan cane) had the last word!

At a very young age our parents taught us their trades, skills; and usually the son of a cooper or shipwright/carpenter became a skilled cooper or shipwright. In my case, from the age of seven I was taught some skills in cooperage, together with my adoptive brothers. But our leisure times were spent playing games such as *gard-maron* [hide and seek in the woods]; *boul-kaskot* [break-rib bowls] – played with a ball the size of a tennis ball, thrown in the air, the one who caught it would hit any other player with it, and so on, or *kanet* [marbles]; or making little boats with paper and sticks, then floating them on water. Football was not a popular game or that common because we did not have a ball. With the sea all around us, we practised swimming; and also we learnt various ways of catching fish: fishing with a *gaulette* [wooden rod]; with a line spun by hand; using a net called the *épervier* [sparrowhawk]; everything caught was for our own use and not for sale.

Girls would be taught how to carry out the daily chores at home, how to cook, wash, iron, etc. by a female member of the family. Their leisure activities would include skipping, walking in circles (sometimes with boys), while singing rhymes such as:

La pli la pompe la rivière du rhone	The rain, the pump, the Rhone river,
Premier m'a couté m'a couté cinq louis	The first one cost me, it cost me five louis
Perdi mon ti kok deras	I've lost my prize cockerel
C'est là haut dan filao	Up in the filao tree

Some girls also worked at the administrator's place or with the families of the staff at the *état-major*; most, however, stayed at home, kept busy with their domestic chores.

Education

In Mauritius, parents always had high expectations regarding their children. Schooling was gradually opened to all children; and for many families, education brought hope for social progress. In the Chagos there was no school for a long time except for the upper echelons of the administration for whom a tutor came from Mauritius and taught them the basics. The ambitions were there anyway: to improve our situation, becoming a *commandeur* or boat manager depending on one's skills and competence. The ambition was that one day the native Chagossians would form part of the administration.

Before the arrival of primary education on the island, Chagossians' parents wanted their children to learn a profession, to get some skills, to become a carpenter, a cooper like me, construction worker, blacksmith, shipwright, sailboat worker, *nougat* [*sic*], sawyer, lumberjack, etc. It was the kind of business that allows children to make a living while serving the copra industry. They were not interested in reading and writing because they were not aware of the importance of these skills. It was Governor Scott's visit (see page 419) that brought change. And the first school opened in 1956!

The arrival of the school was a dream come true. Nearly 30 to 35 children, under 10 years, including my little brother, were admitted to receive primary education; to learn reading, writing and arithmetic. As for me, I was unfortu-

School on Chagos. Image courtesy of Paul Caboche.

nately too old and had to wait for some time before I was able to learn to read and write, like many other Chagossian adults of my generation.

The school was like a large hall, with no partitions. There were only two teachers: the male teacher was called Manyepa and the female teacher was called Miss Celine. They were employed by the establishment. Whoever came from Mauritius, whether a nurse, a teacher, etc. they were all employed by the establishment; it was a private enterprise. *Ardoise*, a rectangular piece of slate was sold in the shop for 10 cents. We did not have satchels at the time; my little brother would carry a piece of khaki material, sewn into a little bag, in which he would keep his slate and crayon. Every year the children would move to a higher class, up to 5th grade.

Working life

I was working already at 12/13 years of age, in 1955–6, in the boiler room of the factory. I had a two-part salary, one given in money: Rs 7 monthly and the other given weekly as a ration: 1 lb of rice for each working day, given on a Saturday, some dholl, lentils, peas and butterbeans, ½ lb of salt, 1 lb of flour, ½ bottle of coconut oil. This would be my labourer's salary until the age of 16.

When I was 15 years old, in 1958, I became a construction apprentice with a group of seven qualified workers. The group I joined was run by Walter Rab-ouine, whose father was also in construction. Our project was the construction of a pier on concrete plinths. It measured more than 100 m in length – from the village to the coral reef. This was to facilitate the movements of merchandise to and from boats arriving and departing from the harbour. The job lasted six to seven months. The pier is still there, although it is a bit battered by the weather and the passage of time.

Afterwards, I started working on putting concrete floors in the workers' houses and for the staff of the *état-major*.

The material used in construction on Peros was mostly lime made from burning coral. For macadam and gravel, stones of all dimensions are gathered on the beach at low season. Larger stones of various sizes could be found on all the islands, whenever there were big waves or tsunamis in the region; not at high tide *marée kinox*. The stones were picked up by carts and stored where construction workers could access them. The coral used in lime on the road and on walls was *tête de mort* [boulder (porites)]; it is very soft, easy to remove and break into different sizes for use.

Another type of stone used is called *roche de carrière* [quarry stone], it is white in colour and found underground although easy to access. The stone known as *roche galet* [loose boulders] was used when building the pier. Another type of stone found in large quantity on Peros is *pierre ponse* [pumice]; it is white, like

Peros Banhos pier in 1984. Photo by NW-S.

a hard dry sponge; used when doing ironing; to polish or sharpen metal; to remove rust, etc.

At the end of that period of work in construction, when I was 16 years of age, I became an apprentice fisherman for nine months (1959–60). It involved fishing in a small boat and using a line under the order of the chief fisherman. This work was for the benefit of the establishment. In my case, the chief fisherman was Eugène Safir, and if he was ill, he was replaced by Joassin Bésage, a Malagasy born in Chagos but who still spoke a Malagasy language. We would leave very early in the morning so as to be back by late afternoon. Each day, we brought heavy catches of fish, of which a few varieties are known in Mauritius: many types of reef fish, such as grouper, snapper, wrasse, parrotfish and jobfish, as well pelagic species such as tunas and barracudas.[5] The lagoon was full of fish. Nylon string either did not exist at the time or we simply did not have it. Our fishing line was made out of fine threads of ordinary cotton. The fishermen had to bring all the fish caught to the administrator's yard, and lay it out on a concrete table; sharing the fish with all staff, the fishermen had the right to at least one fish each. Once a week, a big fishing trip was organised on the further islands. We also hunted birds and sea turtles.

A *séga zavirons* [rowing song]

Blanc, blanc, blanc,	White, white, white,
Mo dire toi Bernard ki'allé	There goes Bernard,
Blanc, blanc, blanc	White, white, white,
Mo dire toi Bernard ki'allé	There goes Bernard,
[Other rowers sing in unison at this point]	[Other rowers sing in unison at this point]
Blanc, blanc, blanc,	White, white, white,
Mo dire toi Bernard ki'allé calçon blanc	There goes Bernard with his white trousers
Mo dire toi Bernard ki'allé …	There goes Bernard …

These *ségas zavirons* would be sung to the rhythm of the sound made by the oars hitting against the rowlocks, known as a *dam*.

After 16 years of age, the work became the work of an adult, which changed the amount of money I was earning: Rs 18 per month, together with the following rations: 1 kilo of rice, 1 bottle of oil, dholl, butter-beans, lentils and flour; the salary was paid at the end of the month, but the rations were given on a weekly basis.

Each adult worker had the right to a thatched house, constructed by the administration, in a place that they saw fit. There were times when one was given a vacant house, left by someone else; sometimes people would get half a house, sharing with another adult. We had to agree to the working conditions imposed on us; we did not know who negotiated those conditions for us.

As a labourer, my first job was to de-husk coconuts. For six months in 1960, every week I had to de-husk 3,000 coconuts; 12,000 coconuts per month and 72,000 for this period. It was hard work, for after de-husking all the coconuts, I had to take them to the beach to be transported by boat. I had to walk 100–150 m with a basket full of coconuts, roughly about 150 coconuts minimum on my head. From there I started working on the boats, transporting coconuts, and this job lasted for ten months. This kind of work depends a lot on the weather and the tides. As boatmen we were responsible for the upload of coconuts that the workers had de-husked, taking and unloading them at the village. Each boat could carry up to 36,000 coconuts depending on the tides; fewer coconuts at low tide. We worked in a group of six.[6] We loaded the coconuts without the husks, carrying them in baskets made on site, using *rotin* (rattan, imported from Mauritius).To keep track of how much we loaded, we had a traditional system of counting using coconut leaves, which we cut; each boatman had his own symbol, e.g. *levañtay* [a fan shape].

In 1961 I went back to de-husking coconuts, for ten months. I had to carry a sharp machete and a basket on my head. I used the machete to spear the coconuts and place them in the basket. The basket was very heavy. Not everyone could do this work. The first time I did it my hands were raw. After a few days one got used to it. Some people could not do it and went back to Mauritius. I

De-husking. Image courtesy of K. Mülnier.

Clearing groves and gathering coconuts, by Clément Siatous. Image courtesy of the artist.

then again returned to work as a boatman; it all depended on where I was required to work. At the end of 1962, I returned to construction, building houses;
I learned to cut wood for scaffolding, standing to a height of 9–10 m. I did different types of work, for example in the *calorifère*[7] and, whenever a large ship came
with merchandise, I would join others to unload the ship of its cargo. Some
of the work on the island was quite arduous. It amounted to a form of slavery.
For example, while working on the boats, if the wind dropped the boat would
remain at sea for days – there was a kitchen on the boat but it was hard to cook
and eat. At such times, life was very hard.

Working women

The wives of labourers also had to work, to help their husbands, if only to be
entitled to a salary (Rs 11) and a ration (the same as their husbands – no extra
was given to very young children). They were allocated a number of supporting
tasks:

   *helping with *l'abbatis* [cutting down, i.e. clearing undergrowth];

The Different Types of Coconuts on Chagos

The whole archipelago was covered with coconut trees. Most of them measured 15 to 20 metres in height, with bunches of coconuts. One tree can hold bunches of up to 50 coconuts. The coconut water was chosen according to its maturity; there are several types:

The 'tender coconut' is rarely consumed, for it has no cream and is not sweet.

The *'coco-madaf'* is very good to drink, it has a good taste, it is transparent, with a tender coconut cream, which is very nice to eat. How is one to know that the coconut has reached the required maturity? Workers became very good at this – they look at the colour of its skin.

The *'coco mir'* [ripe coconut] is not very refreshing; it has not got much water, as it has been reduced through fermentation. *'Li pena bon gout, mais ou la tête viré quand ou boire sa dilo la!'* [It doesn't taste nice, but your head can spin with that sort of water!]

The *'coco sek'* (dry coconut) is good for copra; it will fall by itself from the trees. After approximately two months on the ground, it will start to germinate. The shoot was very important to the workers, especially at times of food scarcity; it grows up to 5 cm in diameter. It was eaten regularly, the islanders loved it.

The *'coco la reine'* (queen coconut), was not found in the woods or in the wild, it was planted in people's yards. It does not grow too big, it is of medium size. It was not used for copra. Its water did not taste very good but renders the drinker tipsy very quickly. This type of coconut was also used for decoration; it was known for its aesthetic quality. It was handcrafted and used as gifts.

The *'coco selan'* or Ceylon coconut was an experimental coconut. It produced big fruit, it was enormous and full of water. It was found all over the archipelago; it was big inside, and was used as a bowl (*kata*); but the trunk was like the other trees.

The *'coco betel'* comes in bunches; it produces, right after flowering, small coconuts, which gradually grow to the size of a grapefruit. It has water, but not sweet, and has no cream. It was used for copra.

Images taken from paintings by Clement Siatous.

*cleaning the factory floors;

*making coconut matting to cover the coconuts placed in a pyramid shape in the drying area;

*making *bastin* (coconut rope/string) from the fibrous coconut husk – this was beaten, sun-dried and rolled by hand on the thigh; each task assigned required a worker to make about a 100 m of cord – used to secure the wall panels used in houses. Panels for homes were also made of dry fallen leaves.

*searching for coral in the lagoons to make lime (as required once every two to three years).

*removing the shells of coconuts.

The women also travelled in groups to remote islands, to help with various tasks. Pregnant women were given different tasks – such as turning/weaving the ropes; doing light work. After giving birth in the maternity unit, they were paid for a few days while recovering at home.

Making copra under cover, by Clément Siatous. Image courtesy of the artist.

The administrators and the commandeurs

The quality of life depended very much where one was working and living, or more importantly with which administrator; some were good while others were bad. There were many differences. The islands were private property, and there were no laws, no journalists, no union members, and no civil status officer. There was only a chief administrator, and a second administrator, a nurse and a mechanic. One administrator called Mr Adam[8] was very bad. When a boat came from Mauritius with supplies, the workers would not unload it – there was a strike. All the supplies remained on the boat on its way back to Mauritius. The boat came back two weeks later and took 60 of the strikers and put them in prison in Mauritius. During the second strike, I was there. Another administrator, Mr Vielle, he was not bad, his second administrator, Paul Arnal, was very bad. He had no children, just his wife, she was very good.[9] There was another administrator in my time, called Robert Talbot. He loved to hit people, and he liked young girls. And if the girl did not like him, she was obliged to go with him. It was inhuman. If the girl's father did not agree, he was sent to Mauritius. My uncle who came from Mauritius was put in prison by Talbot until the boat came to prevent him from making trouble.

There was no police force on the islands to resolve disputes, fights or any crimes; the inhabitants would call on the *commandeurs*. The latter had no uniform; they would dress like any other islanders. The *commandeurs* were chosen by the administrator from amongst the inhabitants. They lived together with the islanders, and were respected for the position they occupied. Whenever there were arguments or fights, they would resolve the matter. If necessary people would be put in prison. Prison was hard, those incarcerated had to live on a few dry grains of rice with some salt for six days, or it could be for twelve days depending on the crime. There would be an inquiry, and the administrator would decide.

Food sources

Fish was generally cooked in coconut milk, smoked or grilled over charcoal. According to the method employed called *obernwar*, the fish was grilled with its skin and scales were removed only afterwards, so the fish preserved all its nutritional qualities. The best fish for eating were the *vieille*, *sacrechien* and *croissant*. Reef sharks were not eaten; they were often found in the lagoon and were very aggressive; the shark '*demoiselle*' however could be eaten, it had good tasty flesh. Shark fishing was carried out using a metal wire and a large hook, in a motor boat; sharks of between 4 and 10 feet were taken; the shark's liver would be removed and melted for oil; put in barrels it was exported to Mauritius as a variant on cod liver oil.

Catch of the day, by Clément Siatous. Image courtesy of the artist.

Turtles were found on all the islands; they slept on the reef, we used harpoons to get them. During the war, if there had been no turtles I would not be alive now. There were only two types of turtle, *tortue verte* [Green Turtle] with a round head and *tortue caret* [Hawksbill] which has a pointy head with a beak, and a square pattern on its carapace. The latter is toxic and should not be consumed. The green turtle provided good meat. The islanders had their own techniques on how to hunt the turtles. They would also look for the turtle's eggs under the sand, one metre deep; a turtle can lay at least 200 eggs in one sitting. The turtle will leave a trail behind when it drags itself back to the sea. The people who are hunting for the sea turtles, will wait for the turtles to come back after fifteen days; they will pick the ones they want by turning them upside down; sometimes they will find the turtles stranded in isolated ponds; or, they will catch them while they are mating, as it takes them quite a long time – almost 24 hours. They hunt them with a harpoon [a nail of 4 cm in length on a coconut stick]; when it is dark, the fishermen will use fire torches in a boat, they will go behind the coral reef; the sea turtles sleep there amongst the corals. The fishermen do not use the sail, only oars; once they have found the turtle, they harpoon the creature, the nail goes through the carapace, then they pull it on board and take it to shore. Each turtle killed had to be declared. The administrator would then buy the turtle, then it would be cut in pieces, each weighing 1 kilo and sold to all those willing to buy.

The turtle's eggs were eaten boiled, but also used to make various types of cakes. Sea turtles are full of vitamins; we used the turtles to prepare rich soups, especially for children. The turtle meat with its fat was also chopped and mixed with the turtle eggs to make a paste, the whole then put into the oven. When cooked, a kind of marzipan was obtained which we called *mapinba*. Turtle meat was delicious when served with the fish Red Snapper, Spotted Unicorn Fish and Bluelip Mullet. Turtle meat was cooked as one cooks chicken, with its fat, looking grey and green, mixed with all the interior parts: the liver, tripes, intestines, etc., then adding a little bit of salt, and cooking for a while (no ginger, garlic or onions, etc.). A dish of choice; the flippers were cooked with coconut milk. Finally, we would make a barbecue and eat the rest of the meat, using the carapace as a container.

Turtles were not only a source of food; the carapace of the Green Turtle was boiled until soft, the bones removed and left to dry. It would be sent to Mauritius and utilised to make very strong glue, which the joiners used to glue wooden furniture. As for the *tortues carets*, which were available from February to October, they had to be sold to the administrator for Rs 3 each; he then had them cleaned and kept underground for up to a week; the scale/shell would come apart and the scales were used to make jewellery. Turtle shells fetched a lot of money. A lot of work was involved in getting the turtle shell looking beautiful for export.

Crab and lobster could easily be found and caught. Dolphin (which we called *marsouin*) was at one time found at the market in Port Louis, they used it as meat. I know how to call them and used to play with the dolphins; there is a type of plant called *liane lafous* which they like.

Seabirds were another important source of nourishment. The most common were the terns or noddies, which frequented many islets of Peros Banhos and elsewhere in the Chagos. I also had a technique for calling the terns. Their nesting seasons were from December to February and then July to September. The islanders were careful not to destroy the nest or habitat. The birds always came back in larger numbers. The islanders used a whip to kill the birds. They plucked the feathers, cleaned the dead birds then preserved them using coarse salt; they cooked the flesh as they would cook chicken, in *masala*, coconut milk, stew, etc. The meat was tasty and lean. The diet must have been healthy because every year when the doctor came to visit, very few people were ill; there were times when they had to close the hospital because there are very few ill people.

The terns laid their eggs on the ground and it was easy to pick them up. The islanders kept the eggs in a wooden box; sometimes they made *kapas* with coconut leaves, in the shape of a basket. The islanders used the eggs to make omelettes, or as an ingredient for cakes; and, when the eggs were plentiful, they would make biscuits, often sending them as gifts for relatives in Mauritius. By the way, the bird's egg is just like the egg of a chicken; however, when it is broken, the yolk is pink coloured.

There were other birds that were also good to eat such as the larger species of Booby, which tasted like duck; other Booby species, Shearwaters (which lay their eggs in burrows) and Noddies were also taken for food.[10] There were also sedentary birds: *Marianne* and *mandarin*. Some birds were not eaten. These included several species of tern, tropic birds, herons, plovers, fodies and miscellaneous migrant shorebirds.[11]

I would like you to know that the Chagossians were respectful of nature, coral, fish, bird, plants; our motto is: 'use but not abuse'. Respect for nature has been passed down by the old generation. They would release the small fish, and would only take the big fish; the same with turtles, to capture only large ones.

During the holiday seasons, at the end of the year, the ration was improved; the islanders were allowed 1 lb of pork meat. Pig farming was restricted only to the administration. For vegetables, meat or fish, everyone had to fend for himself – to go fishing. Every month, the administration would ask for some animals (pork, beef) to be killed and the meat would be sold.

Leisure activities & religious practices

Sega music[12]

Various types of *séga* were popular on Chagos, including the Seychellois and Rodriguan versions. On certain religious holidays such as Easter, *séga* was played all night. Traditional instruments used included: *amakalapo*, *bobre*, harmonica, and the *tambour* which was made not only from goat's skin, but also from sea animals. There was an instrument called *gès* and another known as *bom*.

Crafts

Details from Clément Siatous' paintings. Images courtesy of the artist.

Amongst the islanders, coconuts had many uses; the shells were made into cooking utensils and big coconuts were used as bottles to carry fresh water from one place to another and also to store the same for later use. The shell could be cut in half and skilfully crafted into jewellery boxes, and cigarette holders, either

Coconut Recipes

Coconut Cake

To make coconut cake, grate a coconut, then soak in water; afterwards wring to remove the milk; the milk is poured in rice-flour, then sugar is added. Place the paste in banana leaves, or in small coconuts, then fold banana leaves and/or tied-up small coconuts. Boil water in a pan, and then put the ingredient into the pan, leave to boil for 45 minutes. Get rid of water, then leave to cool down: the cake is cooked, like a *poutou* [rice cake]. Cake can be kept for up to 15 days at least, hung in a basket, in open air; it will dry up but will still retain its flavour/taste.

Motouftwa Cake[13]

Break the coconuts in the same way, grate, wring to remove milk; add the grated flesh to flour, mix into a dough; place in a coconut shoot leaf (from a one metre high tree), close the leaf, tie it up; give it the shape of a carrot; make a hole in the sand, stick it in; light a fire over it; when the wood fire has been reduced to smouldering charcoals, cover it for about 30 minutes, then remove it – it is cooked. The leaf should be in good condition, not burnt; the cake golden on top like bread; it can be kept for a whole month; it is not sweet, but savoury – add salt. It will sate your hunger.

Merveille cake or kol kote

Dry coconut, do not remove the milk; grate finely; add sugar and water; put in a pan and cook until water is reduced; leave to cool down; add flour. Take more grated coconut, which has been wrung of its milk; take the milk and mix it with flour and make a dough; cut into circles by pressing a glass over the dough; put coconut on top, close it and then fry in hot oil (similar to the way one cooks sweet potato cake). The cake will last up to one week.

Maize cake gato mai or maize pudding pudding mai

Grate coconut, wring to remove milk; add to flour; make the dough a bit runny; add grated coconut; sugar; place in a baking tray, then place in an oven; leave to cook for 30 minutes. Once it is cooked, cut into pieces, just like maize pudding; soft cake, it will last only a few days.

Dulpiti

Sweet cake cooked with milk, flour and water, similar to making roti; roll the dough in hands until both ends are tapered; like macaroni, 3 cms in length; drop them in boiling water; do not let them stick together; pour the water out, then add milk and sugar and leave to boil.

Rice cake or douri coco

Cook the rice, pour the water out, and then add coconut milk and sugar.

Sweet potato cake or sweet potato and coconut milk/ yam and coconut milk/ breadfruit and coconut milk/ green banana/ plain potato.

Cut the sweet potato or yam, then steam-cook [*bain-marie*] do not boil too much, because it will be cooked again in the coconut milk. Pour out water, replace it with coconut milk, add sugar, do not leave it to dry (for banana: cut into round slices).

Fish curry with coconut milk

Different types of fish can be used; clean well, then season with salt. Put the fish in a pot on the stove, cover; pour in 10–15 cl of water to prevent the fish from burning or sticking to the pot; leave to cook on medium fire. Grate coconut, wring/press milk out of it; sieve it; pour into pot to replace water, leave to cook. Add chilli according to taste; leave to boil but not to dry; add any other spices.

Coconut milk: this is used in a variety of ways: in tea or coffee, when there is a shortage of ordinary milk on the market, but it is not good for use in a baby bottle as it is too rich.

for the islanders' own use or to be exported. The coconut husks were used for *kayam* – to make musical instruments. Fishermen would handcraft trapping boxes with coconut branches and leaves to trap fish, crabs, lobsters, etc., instead of using bamboo. The women made baskets of various sizes, hats, mats, bags, etc., for their own use; they aso used coconut leaves to make brooms, to make a type of string known as *corde coco* or would cut the coconut in half to make brushes called *brosses cocos*. The women used the coconut leaves to make large-bowls and trays. Coconut husks were also used in religious ceremonies. Indeed, on the islands, nothing was lost of the coconut; just as with the sugar cane in Mauritius.

Catechism and Communion.

It usually fell to the wife of the administrator or a female member of staff, such as a nurse, to teach the catechism and prayers such as Our Father, Hail Mary, Act of Contrition, Act of Faith. At seven years of age the children received the First Communion; the Church was open as early as 5 a.m. Ceremonial clothing – white canvas pants, long white khaki cuffs – would be worn. Confessions were carried out by the priest. Mass was held on Sunday, always in the afternoon, between 4 p.m. or 5 p.m. and the big bell was used to call people to prayer. The little bell was used for special announcements. Both bells were used on occasions such as Christmas Mass.

Lent and Easter

The administrator would announce the beginning of Lent and the chapel would be left open so that people could go in to pray. Fasting – abstaining from milk, butter and cheese – would be observed. On Friday evenings leading up to Holy Week a 'Stations of the Cross' procession would be held led by the wife of the administrator or his representative. The stations were designated by photographs. During Holy Week workers tried to abstain from using hammer and nails out of respect for Jesus Christ who had been nailed on the cross. Holy Friday commemorating the death on the cross was a half-day's work up to 1 p.m. The ceremony of the death of Jesus was then held. An altar would be constructed upon which a cross with the effigy of Christ was placed. Personal adoration of the cross begins; people will come, following in a long queue; individually, each one will kiss the cross. The chapel closed at 6 p.m. On Saturday the chapel was kept open for the whole night. Preparation for the Easter Resurrection ceremony was underway inside. Midnight Mass would last for one hour. Everyone attended, even those who had been camping on the islands. After Mass, fasting was over and the Easter Holiday began. Pigs were killed and sold by the establishment. The traditional *séga* was played. Everyone took part. All the houses were cleaned and beautifully decorated; sometimes with a new set of curtains, as at Christmas or the New Year.

Rites of passage

Baptism

As soon as the wife gave birth, if there was no priest on the island at the time, it was the administrator, who took a book and filled in the details of the newborn. In the administrator's office, the father, mother, the child and godparents would be present. There were two registers, one for the church and one for the civil status office. The priest or administrator asked if the couple are married, if they have chosen a name; and who will declare the child, for sometimes there are arguments about it. This was the case with my grandfather who was separated from his wife, but who carried on declaring the children she was having with someone else. Once the civil status procedure is over, and they have signed in the register, the priest or administrator opens the church register and writes inside. From that day forward the child is a catholic. If it is a boy, the child will be known as Louis; if a girl, she'll be known as Marie. Thereafter there will be a party; drink, food, dancing, christening cake, vermouth and *dragées* [sugared almonds] from the shop are shared with the islanders.

Marriage

Priests came rarely to the islands, so most wedding ceremonies were presided over by the administrator. Before the celebration, the administrator went through the civil registration procedures. Thereafter he gave his blessing to the newly-weds. There were lots of preparations; the couple would get engaged first, close relatives and acquaintances would be invited. According to the tradition in the Chagos, a house would be prepared for the couple on the plantation, a rustic house; and also a wedding *trousseau* (linen and clothes, bed sheets, pillow cases, cooking pots, etc.); gifts would be received from the islanders.

When the ceremony started in the chapel, there was chanting, and the bells (big and small) ringing in the background like music. When the two bells rang at the same time – it meant a special event was taking place. A 'green room' was prepared in front of the bride's house, using a tarpaulin lent by the administrator, with coconut leaves for decorations, and benches and chairs borrowed from the hospital and chapel. It would be used for two whole days of eating and drinking, chicken and duck prepared by the two families would be served. The bride's uncle would make a speech; a gramophone would be brought to the venue, powered by batteries. Little bottles of vermouth and brandy would be used to decorate the bride's table. For the afternoon celebration, a procession on foot would be made to the chapel; the wedding party then returned to the green room, to party until early in the morning; they used petrol and gas lamps provided by the administrator. An accordion might be played but the *séga* was not allowed. The people would wear some special clothing: boys would wear white khaki suits or clothes from Mauritius. The girls also dressed in a white material, with fine stitches, often made in Mauritius. There was a maid of honour and a best man for bride and groom respectively. At the time, no one had a camera, so wedding photographs are very rare. A toast would be made to good health; speeches of good wishes, congratulations and romantic stories in Kreol would be told by the old people.

The newly-wed couple would then go to their house. The old aunties would visit the room afterwards to check if the girl was a virgin. The outcome can cause trouble and argument, at that time or at a later stage. Virginity was considered very important. There was no frolicking. A minor could get married if the families on both sides agreed; the wedding is celebrated; if they become parents while still minors, the mother or father of the boy will declare the child. Young people were taught discipline and strictness; moral education; girls were made aware that they could not go out whenever they wanted or with whoever they wanted. Girls always wore dresses or a skirt and blouse/jacket, never a pair of trousers. There were cases of rape which was known as being '*trompé par un homme*' [deceived], such cases remained secret. There was a sense of responsibility; the boy and girl would meet each other in secret; if they were seen together, the person in question talked to the parents, who would discipline them. Engagement letters were sent in a little basket; the party concerned would request the nurse or someone else to write up the letter. In the case of two young lovers, if the family of one or the other was not happy they might decide to elope together; they would go to the parents who did not oppose the match; this would be viewed as scandalous behaviour and could cause such couples problem with their rations, until the woman involved declared herself to be the wife of the labourer.

Funerals

Formerly, there were many old practices observed during the wake for a deceased person. Traditional stories would be told (Tizan,[14] Red Riding Hood and ghost tales from Chagos or Mauritius); old songs and dances would be performed. When there was a death, the whole community would participate in the mourning. Lemon and orange tea would be served, visitors would play cards or dominoes. A service would be held in the chapel; labourers from the camp contributed 50 cents or one rupee, from their pay through the deputy administrator to cover the cost of such rites. A coffin would be made by the shipwrights using white wood; it would be covered with black fabric for an adult death, or a white cloth if a child had died. People from the camp would bring the body to the chapel. The administrator said a prayer for the dead and blessed the person, with the close family at the front. A grave would be dug by the labourers. Islanders who had visited Mauritius would buy items from there to decorate the grave site. There were no local tomb makers on Chagos, so any tomb stone or artefact or wreath had to be purchased by labourers. After burial, every night, for 8 days, candles would be lit and prayers said by people from the camp. After 8 days a festive day, with songs, but no sega or gramophone music, would be held. The few items left by the deceased would be distributed; spouses could remarry after a decent interval, say 1 or 2 years. The cemetery was very well maintained. When a priest visited the islands a procession of Corpus Christi was held and the priest would bless all those who passed away during the interval since his last visit. There was no sacristan so the chapel would usually be prepared for such ceremonies by the wife of a staff member, who would be tasked to put up the necessary decorations as required.

Notes to Chapter 20

1 Writing the history of the Chagos archipelago is dependent largely on archival and written sources. These are concerned chiefly, as is evident from this book, with governance, commerce and strategy. A few visitors and residents like Mary Darlow, Roger Dussercle and Marcelle Lagesse, sought to assess and interpret the lives of the islanders; their insights are valuable but the perspective is unavoidably that of outsiders looking in. This chapter attempts to redress the imbalance by offering the first-hand testimony of Fernand Mandarin who grew up on the atoll of Peros Banhos. The material in this chapter is based on the authors' interviews with Fernand Mandarin which were videotaped, transcribed and translated from Kreol with the assistance of Mr Chris Cuniah; on the French/Kreol typescript compiled from further interviews conducted by Robert Furlong; and interview data collected by James De Montille and transcribed in English. In transcribing Creole words and names, we have received great assistance from Robert Furlong and Anthony Cheke, especially in introducing modern standard orthography where possible.

2 For further details re Clément Siatous see Jeffery, L., and Johannessen, S., (2011) 'Reflections on the Life and Art of the Chagossian Painter Clément Siatous', *Wasafiri*, 26:2, 72-77.

3 See the local methods of soap manufacture described on pp. 200–201.

4 This drawing appears in *Bord' Endan, Bord' Déhors*, an award-winning account of island life by Alix Mülnier and Marie Descroizilles, daughters of Gaston Vielle, the island manager. They consulted two islanders, whom they had known well as children: one was Fernand Mandarin, the other Clément Siatous.

5 The fish mentioned by Mandarin are, using standardised Kreol spelling: *vyel ruz = Epinephalus fasciatus* [Blacktip Grouper], *vyel roz = ? Cephalopolis leopardus* [Leopard Hind], or *Epinephelus longispinis* [Longspine Grouper], *vyel makonde = Epinephalus chlorostigma* [Brown-spotted Grouper], *vyel labu = Epinephalus morrhua* [Comet Grouper], *varavara = Lutjanus bohar* [Twinspot or Red Snapper], *babon = Epinephalus tauvina* [Greasy Grouper], or *Plectropomus punctatus* [Marbled Coral-grouper], *vakwa = Aprion virescens* [Green Jobfish], *kaya = Lethrinus reticulatus* [Red-snout Emperor], *simiz = Lutjanus*

russellii [John's Snapper], *tiruz* = *Ostorhinchus fleurieu* [Ring-tailed Cardinal-fish], *tazar* = *various species of Sphyraena* [barracuda], *toñ* = *tuna* [several species in different genera], *toñ blañ* = *Gymnosarda unicolor* [Dogtooth tuna], *madras* = *Lutjanus kasmira* [Blue-lined or Blue-stripe Snapper], *grostet* = *kapiten grostet* = *Monotaxis grandoculis* [Bigeye Emperor], *maldak* = *species of Bodianus* [wrasse], *kato blañ* = *Scarus dubius*, probably *S.globiceps* [Violet-lined Parrotfish], *kato ruz* = *Scarus rubroviolaceus* [Redlip Parrotfish], *sakresyeñ blañ* = *Pristipomoides filamentosus* [Crimson Jobfish], *sakresyeñ ruz* = *Etelis carbunculus* [Deep-water Red Snapper or Ruby Snapper], *sakresyeñ dor* = *?* [not identified], *grañ lake* = *sakresyeñ grañ lake* = *Etelis oculatus* [not certainly identified]. We are greatly indebted to Dr Anthony Cheke for his work in identifying the species involved, drawing on a variety of specialist sources. The most important of these is Baker & Hookoomsing's *Dictionary of Mauritian Creole*, used here (except for ñ, represented by them as a n with a dot above)

6 If conditions allowed, the boats would be overloaded to reduce the number of trips required and gain extra free time (although Fernand makes no mention of accidents having occurred for this reason, he cites half a dozen examples where deaths resulted from nautical mishaps).

7 Hangar where the copra was artificially dried.

8 See also account of this affair on pages 348–349.

9 For further details of the strike as a result of which the workers forced Arnal's departure (see page 413).

10 Mandarin mentions the following species: *fu pat ble* (identical to *fu zenero*, also referred to as *fu albatros*) = *Sula dactylatra* [Masked Booby], *fu pat roz* = *S. sula* [Red-footed Booby], *fu labek zon/fu kapisiñ* = *S. leucogaster* [Brown Booby], *fuke* = probably *Puffinus bailloni* [Tropical Shearwaters], *tayvoñ* = *P. pacificus* [Wedge-tailed Shearwaters]; also two more sedentary species, *mayrian/mañdrin* (used interchangeably) = *Anous tenuirostris* and *A. stolidus* [both Brown and Lesser Noddies].

11 Mandarin refers specifically to: *golet blañ* = *Gygis alba* [Fairy Tern], *gliñ* = *Sterna bergii* [Crested Tern], *fañsiñ* = (probably) *Sterna fuscata* [Sooty Tern], *payañke* = *Phaethon lepturus* [White-tailed Tropic Bird], *gro mizo* = perhaps *Dromas ardeola* [probably Crab Plover], *makak* = *Butorides striatus* [Striated Heron], *kanar sarsel* = *Anas querquedula* [Garganey], *seriñ* = *Foudia madagascariensis* [Madagascar Fody] and *zwalet* = miscellaneous [(migrant) shorebirds].

12 See also Note 6 to Chapter 16 (p. 341).

13 The Kreol phrase '*mo tuf twa*' literally means 'I will choke you'!

14 Tizan is a character common to most French-based creole islands from Reunion to Guadeloupe and Martinique. He is the mythic little boy able to solve any problem, to get things right for everybody and for his family, to get out of terrible situations … the little intelligent hero.

21

Decline and Fall

S IR Robert Scott's visit to the Chagos islands had, as we have seen, left him
nervous about their economic prospects and worried too about the outlook for the island populations, with their distinctive way of life. The next
few years were to demonstrate how well-founded were his concerns and, ahead
of Scott's retirement in 1959, to reveal two major additional threats to the status
quo: revived Seychelles interest in acquiring the islands and, for the first time,
an American strategic interest in this area.

Diagnosis

Dubruel de Broglio was the Acting Chairman of both Agalega Ltd. and Diego
Ltd., which were technically separate, but inextricably entwined; indeed they
were at that moment contemplating amalgamation. By profession an independent financial expert, he had been brought in to see if the plantations' long-term
outlook could be restored. In a five-week trip, de Broglio not only visited the
three operational plantations but also landed briefly at both Eagle and Egmont
islands. His impressions[1] added to and contrasted with those of Scott.

The two abandoned plantations had been taken over by dense jungle. Having
cut a path into the interior of Eagle Island, and observing the paucity of coconuts, de Broglio concluded at once that it would not be worth attempting to
revive the plantation. Egmont he found much more productive and its Ile Cipaye,
which was less overgrown and had palms laden with nuts, the most attractive
sight in the whole archipelago. However, exploitation would entail the acquisition of a seagoing motorboat, a search for additional labour, and the diversion of
heavy expenditure from tasks of much higher priority.

Salomon impressed de Broglio. The palms were well looked after and in full
bearing. For the current year a crop of 225 tonnes, worth Rs 157,500, was in

prospect. Likewise, the atoll's buildings and equipment were all in good order. In general, all of the area available was being utilised, with not more than an additional 50 tonnes of copra potentially available. Its quality was not, however, yet up to Seychelles standards (a prerequisite for international export). De Broglio also noted that the atoll's motorboat was equipped only with an old car engine, which would soon need to be replaced by a reliable marine version. Other points to strike him were the atoll's self-sufficiency in building timber, thanks to a carefully-tended 50–60 acre forest of takamaka trees on the islet of that name; the presence of 120 pigs, 100 of them running free; and the poor quality of the wine supplied (in leaking barrels). The working population of 125 (of a total of 197) could usefully be increased by 15, but this was not essential.

Peros Banhos, with its 32 islands, made a wholly different impression. De Broglio was particularly 'shocked' by the state of the production facilities on Ile du Coin. Many of the buildings were in a very bad condition, including the main warehouse, and the mobile covers to protect copra from passing showers had ceased to function, so that the resulting product was *vilain* (lousy). The newly-appointed manager, Robert Talbot, had made a start on clearing the undergrowth from the more neglected plantation areas, but a huge task lay ahead, with fewer workers than were needed both to make good deficiencies and to replace old trees with new. Only 10% of the cultivated area was made up of orderly groves; the rest consisted of '*cocos bon Dié*'. Accommodation, for staff and labourers alike, was ill-maintained – the shopkeeper, for example, whose wife was paid by the Government to run the school, was on the point of resigning on this account. The only bright spot was the establishment's powerful motorboat *Capitaine Picot*, with a supporting fleet of nine boats to ferry the workers, plus two sailboats and a barge to transport the nuts from the 21 islets on which palms were harvested. Most of these were in a good state, but suffered high wear and tear as a result of being beached on the rocky islets at low tide. Another problem was that loading for export could only take place when the tide was in, that is, for only 8 hours in every 24, involving night work at higher rates of pay.

On a lighter note, de Broglio commented favourably on the productiveness of the atoll's banana, guava and breadfruit trees and the excellent state of the management's vegetable garden, noting that most workers also grew vegetables. He also remarked on the animal populations – 70 pigs (25 only in the piggery); 60 donkeys, damaging palm saplings on Ile du Coin and shortly to be exiled to Ile Diamant; and the management's chicken pens, installed rather appropriately on Ile Poule. The population was 315, of whom 24 were Seychellois and the rest Ilois.[2] Of the total, 187 were in employment, all but 2 of the residue being children. Talbot considered that an extra 30 men and women should be recruited and hoped that these could be found among the former Ilois inhabitants of Peros Banhos who had settled in Mauritius; failing that, it would be necessary to seek labour from Seychelles.

Diego Garcia's cultivable area was about 6,000 acres, more than the combined totals of Peros (3,000) and Salomon (2,000). Potentially the jewel in the Company's crown, the island's plantations were on the verge of exhaustion, very little replacement of old trees having been undertaken for many years and many parts allowed to be overtaken by the luxuriant growth of weeds and saplings profiting from the island's high humidity. 'Unless measures are taken immediately', concluded de Broglio, 'to revive the existing plantations and establish new ones, Diego, our finest island, is destined to suffer a slow death.' The achievements of the manager, Captain Lanier, over the preceding three years were very good, but a vast amount still needed to be done. De Broglio detailed a whole series of steps that should be taken with a view to increasing production and bringing its quality up to Seychelles standards. In addition, he instructed that the island's substantial deposits of guano (some 30,000 tonnes, he thought) should be exploited as a matter of urgency, with the aim of exporting 1,000 tonnes annually. The existing population, excluding management, was then 551, of whom 437 were in employment (of the difference between these two figures, all but four were children). Lanier considered that the minimum number of adults needed was 550 and de Broglio undertook to seek 50–75 additional workers from Seychelles. Thus, the total population of the Chagos, almost certainly excluding management staff and their families, amounted to 1063.

As elsewhere, de Broglio had interesting observations to make on the cultivation of animals, fruits and vegetables. Here, all 80 pigs were kept in a government-designed sty, whose expensive tin roof made the animals much too hot; free pork was distributed four times per year to the workers, to mark Christmas, New Year, Assumption and the anniversary of the Queen's coronation. There were ducks and chickens aplenty. Donkeys were not mentioned, but the extreme rarity of Green turtles was noted. Bananas did well and there was enough for everyone, but more breadfruit and lemons needed to be planted. Finally, in Diego too, much wine was lost to leakage.

However, of all the facts revealed in de Broglio's very detailed report, the most astonishing are that this was the first year in which an annual budget had been set and that no previous attempt had been made to calculate depreciation of the Company's fixed assets. Consequently, there had been no means of coherent financial management, combined with persistent overpayments of tax. De Broglio calculated that for 1955/56, taking account of urgent expenditure to make good the poor state of the buildings at Peros Banhos and to set in motion the improvements envisaged for Diego Garcia, the overall balance, island by island, would be:-

Table 21.1 Estimated company income and expenditure 1955/56

	Diego Garcia	*Peros Banhos*	*Salomon*
Income (Rs)	590,000	330.000	172,500
Outgoings (Rs)	625,000	288,500	213,500

<u>Source</u>: TNA CO 1036/421 De Broglio's visit report.

His detailed recommendations included a series of ideas for improving quality and reducing waste, for making better use of *Sir Jules* when not required for
visits to the islands, and for doing everything possible to ensure that Mauritius'
requirements for coconut oil and *poonac* were reserved to Diego Ltd. Rebates
were already being sought from the tax commissioners. On the other hand, he
also attached great importance to improving the salaries, housing and general
living conditions for all the Company's staff in order to secure better employees
and greater commitment – all proposals entailing increased costs. What de Broglio's report did not address was the question of how the overall shortfall of Rs
34,500 was to be funded or the existing bank overdraft cleared.

De Broglio's conclusions were duly endorsed by the companies' Boards. The
latter also concluded that oil produced from the islands' copra could not com-
pete in the Mauritius market with imported oils, unless the manufacturing
company (Innova Ltd., a jointly-owned subsidiary) installed new machinery;
and they took an immediate decision to do this. By the time de Broglio reported
all this to Scott,[3] he could also report that 1,500 acres of new coconut plantations
were to be established in Diego Garcia, to which an additional 80 Seychellois
workers had already been sent. As regards copra, the quality was not competi-
tive on world markets, but he had arranged for a trial shipment of 200 tons
(prepared with special care) to be sent to Britain; at the same time, he was investigating ways of improving the production methods employed in the islands.
The economics of converting copra into pork for export had also been examined, but the conclusion had been that this enterprise would not succeed; on the
other hand, it had been decided to experiment with free-ranging pigs on certain
islands which had perennial water supplies and abundant natural foodstuffs,
but which were not used for coconut production. The companies had also resur-
veyed the guano deposits on Diego Garcia and concluded that exports could be
increased to 1,300 tons per year, without detriment to the expansion of their
plantations.[4] Other measures were being taken to improve supervision from
Mauritius, increase emoluments, plant more citrus and breadfruit trees and to
see if the *Sir Jules* could be fitted with new engines, in order that it might contribute to rather than be a burden on their profitability. De Broglio commented
that, if the companies had not abandoned their policy of admitting no changes
that would entail additional expenditure, they would be brought close to the
rocks. Scott was too experienced to miss the implications of this exposition:

while the companies' analysis was a promising first step towards restoring the viability of the islands' economies, it was far from certain that they would succeed in raising the Rs 750,000 necessary to the fulfilment of their plans. He had no doubt that there would in due course be an approach to Government.

A way out?

Sometime late in 1956, there were signs of interest from Seychelles in purchasing the Oil Islands. The first surviving evidence of this is to be found in a letter[5] from de Broglio in January 1957, supplying basic details of the Diego Company's operations in both Agalega and the Chagos.[6] Although de Broglio was evidently still involved, he explained that he was no longer Chairman, this position now being held by Maurice Doger de Spéville. In June 1957, the latter, accompanied by a M. Richard de Chazal, representing Agalega, called on the Governor.[7] They explained that they were in preliminary discussions about the sale of their plantations to 'a Seychellois', who would be interested in a deal, but only if jurisdiction over the islands were also to be transferred to Seychelles. Meanwhile, the companies were not able to raise the capital necessary to turn the islands into a profitable investment, a process that would in any case take a decade. Their view was therefore that their shareholders' interests would best be served by recovering their capital forthwith.

Scott replied by indicating the considerations he would have to bear in mind if he were ever to seek to satisfy the Secretary of State that a transfer of the Oil Islands would be justified. In summary, these were the economic implications for Mauritius; the well-being of the islanders; and the domestic political reactions. On the first point Scott noted that the oil processing subsidiary, Innova Ltd., made a contribution both to employment and to the colony's balance of payments. On the second, Scott said that a 'very considerable proportion in all the islands were truly native, i.e. deriving from families settled there for some generations and often without other roots'. His impression, when visiting the islands, was that the inhabitants did not much like the Seychellois and he foresaw an accentuation of the tendency to employ the latter 'at the expense of the islanders rather than the Mauritians, who were relatively few and mainly artisans etc.'. Thirdly, Scott anticipated a 'pretty sharp' political reaction. Finally, Scott offered his personal opinion that the companies had not really got to grips with the problem of making the Oil Islands pay.

Wider considerations

While the companies digested his reactions, Scott turned at once to wider policy issues. In a second letter of the same date[8] he raised the possibility of a government buy-out of the companies, despite the likelihood that this would lead, sooner or later, to their greater Indianisation; and he also suggested that London, which had recently considered the strategic value of the islands, particularly Diego Garcia, should look further at the strategic implications of their retention by Mauritius. The reply he received from a senior official, T.C.D. Jerrom, was uncompromisingly dismissive.

> We have not thought it necessary to ask the chiefs of Staff for a full scale appreciation of the strategic importance of the islands … We know that the Joint Planning Staff do not attach any great importance to the Chagos Archipelago or the other islands … Her Majesty's Government is making arrangements as far as possible to safeguard the defence facilities it requires at Gan.[9]

As far as Indianisation was concerned, the Colonial Office would prefer to avoid it, but did not think strategy should be altered to secure such an objective. Jerrom was no less dismissive about the supposed interest of 'Seychelles speculators … men of straw', with long odds against their producing any firm commercial proposition.

Birth of American interest

In fact (unbeknownst to the British), this was just the moment when American interest in Diego Garcia was germinating and, according to the testimony of one insider, a very senior American admiral was making an unannounced visit to Diego Garcia.[10] A brief account of the gestation of this interest appeared in the 2004 edition of *Peak of Limuria*, to be succeeded by an altogether more detailed exposition in David Vine's *Island of Shame*, published in 2009. In 1956, a civilian researcher employed in the US Navy's Long Range Objectives Group, Stuart Barber, developed what he termed the Strategic Island Concept. Observing the trend towards colonial independence from western European countries and the latter's declining strategic power, not least that of Britain in the Indian Ocean (where the United States had no footholds of its own), he scoured atlases for potential island bases. Vine's researches of the primary sources describe how Barber's idea gradually secured support within the Department of Defense (DoD). Vine quotes Barber himself as writing that 'Our military criteria [for selection of an island] were location, airfield potential, anchorage potential', while the 'political criteria were minimal population, isolation, present [administrative] status, historical and ethnic factors'. Within the DoD, the idea was that the US would acquire sovereignty over such islands, but this was modified on the advice of the State Department to the proposal that Britain should detach them, retain sovereignty and make them available to the US. Diego Garcia was not the only island on Barber's list; so were Aldabra and Desroches, both part of Seychelles Colony.

Company gloom

Officials in London sought unsuccessfully to interest private companies involved in coconut oil production. They also considered whether the Colonial Development Corporation might invest, but noted that any approach would have to come from Mauritius itself, after weighing the Chagos requirement against other demands on its share of Commonwealth development funds. Many of the companies' directors were keen to sell up to anyone who might offer them the sum of Rs 4 million (by then much reduced in value by inflation) they had originally invested; but others persuaded the colonial government to examine the possibility of achieving a viable future for the islands. Eventually, in 1958, it was decided to send Mauritius' Director of Agriculture to examine the situation for himself. Mr Maurice Lucie-Smith was not able to make his tour of the Oil Islands until June 1959. To the Mauritian authorities' surprise, Lucie-Smith's report did not conclude that copra production could never become viable; but its enumeration of the fundamental changes required to every aspect of existing practices and of the need to replant most of the trees on Diego Garcia must have been profoundly depressing to the companies.[11]

The relationship between four formally distinct companies was by this time as follows: Diego Ltd. owned and operated the plantations on Diego Garcia, Peros Banhos and Salomon, as did Agalega Ltd. in the case of Agalega. These two companies shared (60%:40%) ownership of Diego-Agalega Shipping Ltd., a subsidiary which operated the mv *Sir Jules*; and they also owned (67%:33%) Innova Ltd., the company which processed copra from the islands to produce edible oil, soap and *poonac*. The financial situation of the two subsidiaries had become critical, with a joint indebtedness at the end of September 1958 of almost Rs 1.4 million. By the same date, the combined debit balance of the two principal companies had reached over Rs 1.2 million (rather more than half being accounted for by Agalega's losses).[12] However, since the four companies shared a common Chairman, Board of Directors, Managing Director, Secretary and Head Office, their difficulties were as hard to separate as were their pricing arrangements to discern. As the Governor of Seychelles commented, 'It apparently paid them to purchase their nuts as cheaply as possible, gaining on the roundabouts what they lost on the swings. This did not please those who had shares only in the copra producing companies'.[13]

Just how deep-seated were the problems of the Chagos plantations emerged very clearly from Lucie-Smith's report, which examined Diego Garcia in particular detail. There, trees were invariably planted too close, resulting in poorer crops, higher collection costs, increased infestation by weeds and pests; there was no selection of best seeds; no use of nursery plantations; such superior types as had been introduced from Ceylon were unsuitable (because their nuts did not fall naturally in the local conditions) and they had in any case become hybridised over the years with the natural *cocos bon Dié*; the method of planting was wrong in every respect – both labour-intensive and causing slow maturity, while the habit of placing two seeds in each hole ensured that neither sapling had a good start; the practice of under-planting of senescent palms with young ones made, at considerable extra cost, all the other problems worse; undergrowth clearance by slashing – *l'abattis* – was too infrequent on account of its cost in manpower, but the use of machinery was uneconomic in close and irregular plantations; and, in any case, the rotary hoes used did more harm than good, damaging the trees' roots. Similarly, the processing of gathered nuts was defective. De-husking and breaking the nuts as separate operations was inefficient, while the subsequent procedures for drying the copra were not only inefficient, but also reduced the quality of the product. The old sun driers, still used at Peros Banhos and Salomon, were unsuitable to so humid a climate as that of the Chagos, while the locally-made kilns were used at temperatures which gave the copra a crisp outer layer, thus preventing the internal moisture from escaping, and so encouraging both mould and attack by the copra beetle.

Lastly, the output of the Chagos labour force was very low. Lucie-Smith saw this as being primarily the consequence of the system, in operation since the very beginning, of setting each worker a single task, usually completed in under three hours. He considered that, with suitable incentives, which should be purely financial, the extra cost would be more than offset by greater productivity, given that the cost of the daily ration would be spread over two tasks rather than one. To underline the scope for improvement, Lucie-Smith made comparisons with the results of coconut plantations in Trinidad, where every procedure was more productive: even on the poorest soils, abandoned since the war as uneconomic, the output had been 0.29 tons of nuts per acre, whereas the average for the Oil Islands as a whole was a 'derisory' 0.14 tons and the yield of copra there from 'absurdly low'.

As George Wilson, the Mauritius Financial Secretary, then commented,

> For many years [the companies] have been insolvent … their total debts run to some Rs 1 million, they have closed down all operations except minimum care

and maintenance, they have repatriated almost all the Seychellois labour from the islands, and they have pressed us urgently to give them some form of financial assistance.[14]

The letter also explained the main reasons for this state of affairs: lack of interest in the company head offices, bad management and insufficient technical knowledge in the field, all leading to 'the most intractable current problem, the inefficiency of labour on the islands'. Lastly, he drew attention to the political impossibility of securing approval for any further subvention, even supposing the many practical problems could be overcome. The Labour Party, which had opposed the previous grant made under Scott's administration,[15] was now represented by Ministers in government and it was not worth the risk to the Administration's own political credit to try to get them to change their minds. Clearly, the balance of power was now shifting away from the Franco-Mauritian interests behind the Chagos enterprise. It was also shifting, as Wilson's colleague Robert Newton had pointed out earlier in the year, away from the Colonial Office and its local representatives and towards the elected representatives of the majority community: '… I am bound to advise you that from now on Mauritius will begin to emerge from its quiescent and passive role and join the ranks of the political blackmailers'.[16] From 10 July until 2 November, Newton, the Colonial Secretary, that is, the Governor's deputy, was (for the third time) the acting Governor in the interval between Scott's departure and his successor's arrival; it was in that capacity that his forceful warning was conveyed.

The islanders' view

As readers will have noticed, the views of the island workers were seldom articulated clearly. More often they were reflected in behaviour, occasionally in surviving songs, sometimes in the accounts of magistrates or other visitors, but also in the ease or difficulty of recruiting and retaining labour. And there was, throughout, a sort of tug o' war between Mauritius and the islands depending on perceptions of comparative satisfaction. During the 1950s, the working populations of Peros Banhos and Salomon appear to have remained virtually constant and undisturbed; in contrast, Diego Garcia never really recovered from the harm done during Henri D'Unienville's period as manager. With reduced Ilois interest in serving there and the introduction of another Seychellois (Lanier) to succeed him, it is no surprise that he should have introduced substantial numbers of Seychellois workers. The plethora of visitors during the decade between the 1952 and 1962 censuses provide an unusually clear picture of the patterns of change and continuity in the population of the Archipelago. Of

Fluctuations of population between 1952 and 1962 decennial censuses

The statistics shown here cannot be interpreted with complete accuracy. Some observers attempted to count everyone, distinguishing those who were actually employed [shown by square brackets]; others counted only the latter, while one provided only a rough estimate (round brackets). In 1955, Sir Robert Scott reported numbers only for the workers of non-Seychellois origin (*italics*). We believe however that, taken as a whole, they supply corroboration of the narrative which connects the different situations revealed by the 1952 and 1962 censuses.

Table 21.2   Population estimates available 1952–1962

	Diego Garcia	Peros Banhos	Salomon	Total
1952 census	619	327	212	1158
1953 *note 1*	583	319	204	1106
1953 *note 2*	[393]	[182]	[174?]	[749]
1954 *note 3*	656	305	181	1142
1955 (a) *note 4*	*511*	*328*	*189*	*1028*
1955(b) *note 4*	551 [437]	315 [187]	197 [125]	1063 [749]
1956 *note 5*	(600) [481]	(315) [181]	(200) [128]	(1115) [770]
1958 *note 6*	589 [394]	n/a [187]	n/a [119]	[700]
1960 *note 7*	428	?	?	?
1961 *note 8*	(300)	(250)	(150)	(700)
1962 census	200	342	205	747

Note 1. Report of Social Services director, Mary Darlow, who spent several weeks in the Chagos.
Note 2. Report of magistrate from Industrial Court, Mr Bouloux. The figure of 174 is dubious, given the size of the total Salomon population; also the same working population figures for Diego Garcia and Peros Banhos are elsewhere quoted together with a figure of 130 for Salomon, which looks much more plausible. We therefore consider a total <u>working</u> population of 705 to be more plausible.
Note 3. Figures provided by Visiting Magistrate J.Vallet in mid-1954 (file TNA CO 1036/138), Sir Robert Scott's Despatch No. 971 dated 10 December 1954.
Note 4. (a) Sir Robert Scott (TNA CO 1036/138 Despatch No. 3 dated 16 January 1956). Population in October 1955 excluding both management staff and Seychellois contract workers; (b) (file TNA CO 1036/421) Report of Mr Dubruel de Broglio, interim Chairman of Diego Ltd, November 1955.
Note 5. Details supplied by de Broglio by letter dated 15 January 1957 (folio 5, file TNA CO 1036/421).
Note 6. Figures for December 1958, quoted in report of M.N. Lucie-Smith, Director of Agriculture, mid-1959 (file TNA CO 1036/502).
Note 7. Newton Report (1964) paragraph 24 (file TNA CO 968/842). The sharp fall in Diego Garcia's working population during 1958–1959 evidently represents what was reported in Wilson's letter of 1 December 1959 (see pp. 450–451 above).
Note 8. Report of Marcelle Lagesse, Poor Law officer, who was concerned only with pension claimants. Her long familiarity with the islands gives her estimates some value. She too may have had in mind the working populations.

course, as always, it is impossible, in the absence of a full set of passenger lists, to know how far the same individuals and families were coming and returning, or new recruits replacing those who had departed for good. Table 21.2 (inset) shows roughly what happened.

The inset population figures suggest that the decline of the Chagos population during the 1952–1962 decade resulted wholly from the decline in Diego Garcia, and occurred only over its final four years. There seem to have been two forces at work. The first of these, as described in the preceding chapter, was the unpopularity of this island as a place of employment consequent upon the appalling management of D'Unienville. The immediate problem of recruitment was resolved by Capt. Lanier, who relied increasingly on labourers brought from Seychelles under short-term contracts. The first group of 111 appear to have arrived earlier, towards the end of 1950. De Broglio then reported that during 1954–55, 73 Seychellois departed, being replaced by a fresh contingent of 71.[17] It was anticipated that a similar changeover, involving 50–60 Seychellois workers, would take place at the end of 1955. To judge from the overall totals, there does not appear to have been any appreciable resumption of recruitment from Mauritius. Indeed, one visitor to Diego Garcia in 1958 referred to its population as being 'nearly all Seychellois'.[18] However, in 1958 Lanier retired and was replaced by the Mauritian Robert Talbot, who remained in charge of Diego Garcia until the sale of the Company in early 1962.

The second force at work was the need to reduce costs. This was the period during which the Board was vainly seeking outside investment and desperately making cost savings. Lucie-Smith, writing in June 1959, stated: 'Of the total population [in December 1958] in Diego Garcia of 589, which figure includes the families of the staff, 262 are Mauritian born and 327 Seychellois. Since then, 47 adults and 10 children have been repatriated to Seychelles and 9 adults and 3 children to Mauritius'.[19] Only months later, as just described, the Company had 'closed down all operations except minimum care and maintenance, and [had] repatriated almost all the Seychellois labour force'. Finally, when Talbot himself departed early in 1962, he took with him to Mauritius 'quite a number' (which he recalled in 2010 as having been around 30–40, presumably of Ilois workers).[20] No wonder then that the island's population in June 1962 amounted only to 200, its lowest figure since about 1820. The Mauritius domestic census figures for the number of residents born in the Chagos Archipelago tell a complementary story. In the 1944 census, only 57 were so recorded; in 1952, 245; and in 1962, 694 (in 1972, no equivalent record was kept). In 1955, Scott was told that 'until recently some 80% of the population were "natives", but that there is a growing tendency for islanders to visit Mauritius, where a number are settling'.[21] The statistics amply bear this out. Indeed, they show that the number of Chagos-born people in Mauritius by 1962 (694) was only 53 less than the total population of all origins then present in the Chagos (747).

An exit strategy devised

By 1961 the companies were in serious negotiations with both the hitherto unnamed Seychellois, Paul Moulinié (in relation to Agalega) and (in relation to the Chagos) with Rogers and Co., a Mauritian holding company having a wide range of interests. Moulinié (1914–1991) was an entrepreneur, who had transformed the decrepit coconut plantations of Farquhar Island by the introduction of mechanisation and modern techniques. The upshot of these discussions was a formal offer to Rogers & Co. of an option, in return for an initial lump sum of Rs 75,000, of a 55% controlling interest in Diego Ltd. at a price of Rs 742,000, the cost at par of the shares concerned. René 'Colo' Maingard, Managing Director of Rogers & Co, then visited all the Oil Islands, taking with him both Moulinié and a few trusted advisers, including Dr Wiehe, the agricultural expert who had already visited the Chagos in 1939 (see pages 358–359).[22] The party had available to them both Lucie-Smith's report and one from a visiting mission to Mauritius, headed by the distinguished economist, Professor Meade.[23]

Maingard and his companions found themselves facing very much the same situation as that reported by Lucie-Smith:

> the agricultural and productive aspects of the problem have not received from the central management in Mauritius all the attention they deserve. The standard of agricultural technique is very low indeed as a result of which the production of copra has also remained low. The managers do not receive any guidance but are left to get on with the job as best they can. Methods applied are either empirical or of a purely routine nature, while their equipment looks to be inadequate, unsuitable or uneconomical.

Noting that Diego Garcia, with its size, fertile soil and favourable rainfall, had by far the greatest potential, he also remarked that 'for some obscure reasons posting to Diego does not seem to be welcome among the personnel, all of whom seem to prefer their own islands'. Moulinié, for his part, was both appalled by the existing state of affairs, but also highly confident of his capacity to apply lessons learned from his experience of redeveloping Farquhar to the much more fertile conditions of Diego Garcia. He also took the view that capital expenditure to achieve profitability could and should be introduced more slowly than Lucie-Smith had envisaged.

Dr Wiehe's contribution was an interesting analysis of the historical performance of the Chagos plantations and a comparison of their output with that of competing plantations elsewhere. The first of these showed that production in 1960, though an improvement on recently preceding years, was virtually the same as that of 1939. There had therefore been no improvement in productivity in twenty years or more. Regarding the international comparison, the latest

The Dream of René Maingard

'We are on our way back to Mahé. I go to bed tonight trying to sleep, but dreams and reality keep me half awake. I dream that I have been visiting islands lost in the vast waste of oceans, where peace is undisturbed, time does not count, hurry is unknown and worry is an anachronism, the Tatamaka shade is bliss, the melody of coconut palms in the breeze is soft, fish abound and man is good and friendly. Then I wake up from the dream and whisper to myself 'I don't want to see another coconut in all my life or smell the rancid odour of copra ever again as long as I live'. The ship's engine purrs and the gentle roll to and fro helps to keep me half awake all night. My mind ticks and is busy in controversy with itself – To do or not to do business? If to do, how to do it? If not, why worry? I fight sleeplessness, but I'm afraid it wins the night.'

Next morning, after consulting his colleagues, Maingard sends a telegram to his board in Port Louis.

'SAME REMARKS APPLY TO CHAGOS ANCHORAGES QUITE SAFE STOP MOULINIE OF OPINION THAT REORGANISATION WOULD NOT COST EXCESSIVELY UNDER SUPERVISION EXPECT IMPROVEMENT FIVE YEARS TEN YEARS ESPECIALLY DIEGO WHOSE POTENTIALITIES ARE MUCH LARGER OCTAVE CONCURS STOP POLITICAL AND MARKET RISK TO BE CONSIDERED TO VALUE SHARES'

To which he received a reply, as follows:

'THANKS YOUR TELEGRAM OF 19TH STOP COPRA REPORT RECEIVED FROM LONDON VERY BAD FURTHER DECLINE LIKELY AS SUPPLIES EXCEED DEMAND AND RECORD PRODUCTION SOYA IN USA LIKELY TO REDUCE PRICE OF COCONUT OIL NO IMPROVEMENT IN THE MARKET ANTICIPATED FOR THE TIME BEING IF NOT FOR A LONG TIME STOP THIS HAS CONSIDERABLY REDUCED OUR ENTHUSIASM AND NOW FEEL WHETHER WOULD NOT BE ADVISABLE KEEP OUT OF THIS BUSINESS AND CONCENTRATE ON SHIPPING SIDE ONLY'

<u>Source</u>: Personal diary of R.H. Maingard, September 1961 (see Note 22).

figures showed a yield in Trinidad of up to 800 kilos of copra per acre, followed by Philippines (600), Ceylon (400), India and Seychelles (300), with Chagos trailing at an average of 156 kilos per acre. On the other hand, he judged that total production in the Chagos could be increased by around 60%.

Reporting back to his Board in September, Maingard stated that he could not recommend acceptance of the offer as it stood.[24] He believed however that a solution might be found by disposing of the Diego and Agalega companies' two subsidiaries, and transferring the Oil Islands to Seychelles, from where they would be run as a single entity, with the participation of both Moulinié and of Rogers' & Co. own subsidiary shipping company, which badly needed the business. He then made efforts to secure a promise of financial support from the Mauritius Governor, only to be told firmly that none would be forthcoming 'as the Colonial Office was dead against any new public money being thrown after bad'. Furthermore, Professor Meade had stated categorically that copra was not necessary for soap production, and that the islands were a liability and should be abandoned. For all that, Maingard was still inclined to purchase at least a one-third share in the islands, provided that Moulinié also participated. 'I feel,' he wrote, 'Diego particularly is bound to come into its own one day and *with the importance the Indian Ocean is taking* we should never abandon the old oil islands whose charms Père Roger Dussercle has sung so beautifully in his poems and books' [emphasis added].[25]

mv *Mauritius*. Image courtesy of Kirby Crawford.

Politics and strategy

In parallel with these commercial manoeuvres, the Governors of Mauritius and Seychelles were again exploring the idea of transferring administration of the Chagos to Seychelles, an idea which the Colonial Office declined to consider except in the event of a successful rejuvenation of the plantations under Seychellois management. Within months, however, Maingard's plan had come to partial fruition. Rogers & Co's subsidiary, the Colonial Steamship Company, took one third of the shares in a new company, Chagos-Agalega, with Moulinié as chairman and, together with various members of his family, owner of the remaining two thirds.[26] The price paid for all the islands was a mere Rs 1.5 million. The Mauritian company then sold off the *Sir Jules*. In consequence, direct links with Mauritius and the import of copra for the Innova factory became dependent on the mv *Mauritius*, the company's newer ship[27] with Rogers & Co.

obtaining a 50% subsidy from the Mauritius government for this purpose.

The Colonial Office then instructed the Governor to consult his Ministers about the transfer of the Chagos to Seychelles. In reply, Sir Colville Deverell said that he

> would like to know, before approaching Ministers, whether there is any near prospect of the US Government establishing a naval supply depot at Diego Garcia. If this were to take place and Mauritius lose opportunities of lucrative employment, they might not be well disposed to transferring the islands and in any case, they should be aware of the possibility, if it is a real one.

His request was brushed aside in the Colonial Office's reply:

> The Americans so far have expressed no more than a passing interest in siting a naval supply base there and we are unlikely to have any more definite news to give you in the near future.[28]

Evidently, the Governor had got wind of American military interest, as perhaps had Maingard, to judge from his allusion to the Indian Ocean's growing importance. Although nothing had appeared in public, the fact of a visit – if it was a fact – to Diego Garcia in 1957 of an American naval vessel with an Admiral aboard would surely have been reported by the local manager.

The first explicit approach to Britain had in fact been made on 31 October 1960 by the American Chief of Naval Operations, Admiral Burke, to his British counterpart, Admiral Sir Caspar John. Unfortunately, we have not been able to find any corresponding British record.[29] Possibly this was because the Top Secret document, about a meeting which also dealt with nuclear weapons issues, has yet to be released. Pressure within the Kennedy administration to increase the American presence in the Indian Ocean increased sharply after July 1961, when the British Defence Minister warned his counterpart, Robert McNamara, that financial pressures might force Britain to withdraw its forces east of Suez. It would appear, however, that knowledge of these developments – to judge from the paucity of material in the Colonial Office files – was restricted to a small circle of officials dealing with defence policy. For the time being, the Colonial Office continued to discuss the possibility of transfer of jurisdiction over the Chagos purely as a matter of colonial administration. We shall consider these developing complexities in the next chapter.

Implications for the islanders

The transfer of ownership to Moulinié's new company took effect in February 1962. As we shall see in the next chapter, its impact in the islands was cumulative. The transfer also released at a stroke the Diego and Agalega companies from all their responsibilities for the conditions of the islands' populations. This may therefore be an appropriate moment to take stock of what they had achieved in the Chagos during the 97 years of private ownership, obtained against an undertaking to invest in and modernise what had previously been held as supposedly insecure *jouissances*.

Under spasmodic and later more persistent pressure from the authorities in Port Louis, they had gradually improved the physical living conditions of their labourers. On the other hand, they had done nothing at all to alter the feudal methods of control they had inherited, nothing to develop alternative exports, nothing to hire or train their managers and staff to achieve greater competence, nothing to improve the labourers' lives, nothing to educate them let alone provide a relevant education, and virtually nothing to modernise methods of production. Whenever the Company was profitable, the benefits were retained by the directors and major shareholders; whenever times were hard, it was the island workers who felt the pinch. Greed and narrow-mindedness were evidently the owners' guiding principles. Even when this approach had resulted in the owners of Diego and Peros obtaining control of the whole Archipelago, they did not have the wit to rationalise their activities. So there was a certain justice in their own failings resulting in the collapse of their whole business. The pity of it was that their managerial subordinates found themselves out of work, while the islanders were simply stranded, having either to cope in the islands with whatever might result from the transfer of ownership to Seychelles or to take their chance of survival in Mauritius against competition from people having a better education and far more relevant skills. Over the generations, they had developed an approach to life and work that made the lack of wealth and amenities tolerable – but one that also reduced their own and the plantations' productivity. The English word 'exploitation' has both positive and negative connotations, while the French '*mise en valeur*' is purely positive. Sadly, the exploitation of the Chagos by Mauritian entrepreneurs had been largely of the negative kind.

Notes to Chapter 21

1 TNA CO 1036/421 (folio 12) M. Dubruel de Broglio *Report on Diego Ltd.*, January 1956.

2 The categorisation of the population as either Ilois or Seychellois suggests that management staff were excluded from these figures.

3 TNA CO 1036/138 (folio 13) Sir R. Scott, Despatch dated 24 April 1956.

4 Generally, quantities were calculated in metric tons (i.e., 'tonnes'). It is not possible to know whether significance should be attached to Scott's reference to imperial tons in this instance.

5 TNA CO 1036/421 (folio 5) M. Dubruel de Broglio, letter dated 15 January 1957 to P.V. Hunt.

6 The statistics forwarded showed an increase of 50 in the working population of Diego Garcia and also a near-halving of the estimated guano deposit. So Robert Talbot must have failed (or been forbidden) to recruit additional Ilois and the number of Seychellois recruited looks to have been fewer than the

80 hoped for.

7   TNA CO 1036/421 (folio 7) Sir Robert Scott, letter dated 27 June to H.P. Hall, Colonial Office.

8   TNA CO 1036/422 Sir Robert Scott, Secret letter dated 27 June to H.P. Hall, Colonial Office.

9   *Ibid.* Letter from T.C. Jerrom to Sir Robert Scott dated 6 August 1957.

10   Bandjunis, V.B., *Diego Garcia: creation of the Indian Ocean Base,* Writer's Showcase, Lincoln 2001. Bandjunis states (p.2) that Admiral Jerauld Wright was flown to Trincomalee, where he boarded a USN vessel to inspect Diego Garcia. David Vine, however, was unable to trace any documentary evidence earlier than July 1958 (*Island of Shame,* p. 221 (fn 22)).

11   TNA CO 1036/502 M.N.Lucie-Smith, *Report on the Coconut Industry of the Lesser Dependencies,* June 1959.

12   Detailed figures for the three most recent financial years showed losses in each year by Diego Garcia, especially in 1957–8, more than offset by profits of the other two plantations for the first two years, but worsened in 1957–8, when these plantations also made losses. Taking head office costs into account, Diego Ltd.'s overall loss in 1957–8 was just under Rs 300,000 on sales of Rs 1.04 million.

13   TNA CO 1036/421 Secret and Personal letter dated 18 February 1957 from Sir William Addis (Governor of Seychelles). In this letter, Addis also noted that 'a large percentage' of the labour in Diego Garcia and Agalega came from Seychelles.

14   TNA CO 141/1464 Secret and Personal letter dated 1 December 1959 from W.G. Wilson (Finance Department) to J.H. Robertson, Colonial Office.

15   We have been unable to discover a direct account of this action, which appears to have been taken in late 1955 or early 1956, apparently in the amount of Rs 2,000,000. It is evident that publicity must have been deliberately avoided.

16   TNA FCO 141/1464 Robert Newton, letter dated 28 August 1959 to H.P. Hall, Colonial Office.

17   These figures corroborate those of Sir Robert Scott, who had visited the islands a few weeks earlier.

18   TNA CO 1036/421 Report dated 17 July 1958.

19   TNA CO 1036/502 Report, paragraph 126.

20   NW-S. 'Population of the Chagos', in *Chagos News* No. 39 (January 2012).

21   TNA CO 1036/138 Despatch No. 3 dated 16 January 1956.

22   This set of records comprises eight papers, initially provided to us in confidence by the late Dr Donald Taylor in 2005; and independently offered in 2014 by Taylor's cousin Mr Tim Taylor, to whom we are deeply indebted, without restriction. They include not only Sir René Maingard's report to his fellow Directors of Rogers & Co., but also his personal diary of the voyage, and the individual observations of Paul Moulinié and Dr Wiehe. The latter's initials were P.O. and he was usually known as Octave. Here, he is occasionally referred to as 'Georges', evidently a nickname.

23   We have not seen Professor Meade's report, which is said to have concluded that the Chagos plantations were unviable and should be abandoned.

24   Maingard, R.H., 'Report on a visit to the Oil Islands', September 1961 (unpublished document in the possession of NW-S). Maingard was generally called by his nickname 'Colo' rather than his forename René.

25   *Ibid.*

26   TNA CO 2114/64 Full details of the formation of the Chagos-Agalega company and the financial background are contained in paragraphs 10–12 of Robert Newton's report, made as the British official participant in the Anglo-American Survey of 1964. Following his retirement in 1960, Newton had been elected to the Council of Exeter City, of which he soon became an Alderman.

27   The mv *Mauritius* entered service in 1955, her captain being Cyrille Nicolin.

28   TNA CO 1036/794 FCO letter dated 26 June 1962.

29   Vine, *op.cit.* p. 223 (fn 57). We are very grateful to David Vine for providing a copy of the document in question. As regards a corresponding British record, the still-closed TNA ADM 205/221 may be relevant.

PART THREE

Expulsion

22

1962–1965: Fateful Decisions

T HE final section of our story is titled Expulsion. This was not something sudden, but the end of a long accumulation of new pressures. These reflected the geopolitical changes that followed the Second World War. One such was the East–West so-called Cold War, in which the United States of America and the Soviet Union, together with their respective allies, confronted each other in a worldwide struggle. The second was the dismantling of the British and French empires as colonial demands for political independence increased. And, third, new economic and commercial forces emerged, putting a premium on education and adaptability. The events discussed in our preceding chapter reflected the early impacts of these underlying shifts of power; and, as ever, the Chagos islands and their inhabitants could not escape the consequences.

During July and August 1964, the survey vessel, HMS *Dampier* visited the Chagos and a number of other Indian Ocean island Dependencies of Mauritius and Seychelles. She bore a joint team of British and Americans to survey those identified as having potential to meet the two countries' future military requirements. The various linked developments leading up to and flowing from this important event form the subject of this chapter. Robert Newton, who, as Colonial Secretary in Port Louis, had dealt for many years with the political development of Mauritius and the problems of its Dependencies, was recalled temporarily from retirement by the Colonial Office to be its civilian representative on the team. His Report supplies much information on conditions in the islands at that time.[1]

New management and new workers

Paul Moulinié had moved promptly to take charge of his new domains. For transport, he had of course the services of the mv *Mauritius*, which maintained

Paul Moulinié. Photo
courtesy of Charles
Moulinié.

the connection between the Chagos and Mauritius. He also bought an elderly schooner with auxiliary engines, the *Isle of Farquhar*.[2] Soon too he appointed new Seychellois managers to all three plantations.[3] As the Governor of Seychelles reported, there had 'been a certain amount of friction with the managerial staff who had been taken over from the old company. Moulinié, a frugal man, was surprised to find on these remote and hitherto unprofitable islands considerable supplies of champagne and pâté de foie gras'.[4] Things were not easy for the new brooms. In Diego Garcia, the population had declined from around 600 to only 200. There had been a much smaller reduction on Peros Banhos. Only Salomon had maintained its numbers. In the case of Diego Garcia, Moulinié was convinced that the decline resulted from the deliberate action of the island's last Mauritian manager, Robert Talbot, who persuaded his workers that the new Seychellois management would prove hard taskmasters and that they would regret staying on. Talbot himself conceded only that 'quite a number, up to forty' had accompanied him back to Mauritius.[5] Equally, it seems clear that many islanders did find difficulties in getting on with the fresh influx of Seychellois workers and the new managers. Certainly, Harold Pouponneau, the manager appointed to Diego Garcia, later acquired a reputation for brutality on Agalega.[6]

In the case of Peros Banhos, Fernand Mandarin, whose experiences occupy Chapter 20, also recalled that it had been hard to socialise with the Seychellois and that their new managers 'lacked manners and became violent, giving hard tasks to elderly people or putting in prison those who had not completed their tasks'. There were other difficulties too, with different procedures and unfamiliar rations; Mandarin's uncle was the only one who, presented by Henri Gendron with the choice between accepting a new type of rice having tiny grains and leaving the island, took the latter course. Talbot thought Gendron's ploy was deliberately intended to get rid of Ilois. Mandarin has commented that there had anyway been a steady outflow beforehand of younger people and reckoned that anything up to 100 adults had left Peros Banhos by 1964; he recalled that their empty houses were subsequently destroyed, while children were called upon to undertake adult tasks. All the same, not many Seychellois had arrived to replace the Ilois who had left.[7]

Paul Moulinié made his third visit to the islands in March 1963. He concluded that, while they were very badly neglected and mismanaged, they were capable of high levels of production and profit, given investment and better organisation. Indeed, he spoke enthusiastically of the increases he expected to achieve from all of the islands, including the minuscule Three Brothers.[8] In fact, his ideas for exploiting the decrepit Chagos plantations were only part of a much wider scheme for developing a diversified economy for the islands of the western Indian Ocean, with linkages to Australasia and southern Africa, having Diego Garcia as its linchpin. Thus, for Moulinié, as for de Broglio and Lucie-Smith, Diego Garcia was the key priority, being both in a worse state and capable of greatest improvement. In February 1963 the Governor of Seychelles had reported information from Moulinié that 'about 350 Seychellois are employed at present. Another 100 are being taken next month and the total is expected to build up to 800 during the next 3 years'.[9] From the context, these figures clearly relate to Chagos and Agalega combined. The influx of new workers from Seychelles to Diego Garcia resulted in a rise of its population to 422 in 1963 and 483 in 1964, of which a substantial majority was now Seychellois (311:172),[10] including an even higher proportion of the male work force (156:48). It is thus unsurprising that, when the *Dampier* visited in August 1964, Newton should find 'little trace of the sense of a distinct Diego Garcian community described by Sir Robert Scott in his book *Limuria*'.[11] The visitors took less interest in Peros Banhos, and did not even visit Salomon, where there had been virtually no change in the size or composition of the island's population. In fact, the population figures in Newton's report were mostly obtained from Moulinié, whom he encountered at Farquhar later in the survey team's tour.[12]

Newton was able to give Moulinié credit for achieving a worthwhile increase in production of copra on Diego Garcia compared to 1962 (nearly 700 tons, as against 521). Nevertheless he remained sceptical about the realism of the entrepreneur's ideas in the absence of any sign of the new capital investment required, describing them as being 'more of a speculative prospectus than a properly costed business plan'. In one respect this judgment was unfair: with the results of the 1962 census being as yet unpublished, Newton compared the 1964 population (483) with that of 1958 (589), 1960 (428) and 1963 (422), seeing the result as a continuing tendency to decline. He had also been subjected to complaints from the local manager about the difficulty of recruiting labour to the island, whether from Mauritius or the Seychelles. Evidently, Newton thought, campaigns in Mauritius against the 'Seychellisation' of the Archipelago were having an effect, while Seychellois workers did not like the conditions obtaining at Diego Garcia. Also, 'Diego Garcia [was] undoubtedly suffering from rivalry between Mauritians and Seychellois, and bad management'. On the other hand, Moulinié had drawn to Newton's attention the French translation of an article in the *Economist* of 4 July 1964 about growing Anglo-American strategic interests in the Indian Ocean.[13] It was therefore certain that Moulinié would have considered what impact these interests might have on his own plans and wondered how he might profit from them. Talking up the value of his investment would in itself be useful; and Newton was also aware that Moulinié had discussed the wider situation with his business and political contacts in Port Louis.

American pressures

Following the initial American approaches (see page 459), the idea of securing an island base – and Diego Garcia specifically – reached increasingly senior levels in the Department of Defense and the State Department. Its progress has been chronicled in great detail by Professor David Vine.[14] In September 1962, the topic was included in talks between Robert McNamara, the US Defense Secretary and his British equivalent, Peter Thorneycroft, and in the following April the US proposed that the two countries discuss the matter formally. The British response was 'in principle [to] welcome the American initiative for exploratory discussions'.[15] What reached President Kennedy's desk first, in the summer of 1963, was a completely separate proposal to establish a communications facility, for which Diego Garcia would provide the ideal site. In August, under presidential orders to pursue this issue, the Administration sought the British government's permission to conduct an urgent and secret survey of the island. In November, while this request was still being considered,[16] McNamara ordered his officials to go ahead with plans to deploy an Indian Ocean Task Force, thus focussing immediate attention on its supply and communications requirements. This development, followed by the President's assassination later in the same month, brought to a head the need to consider together the various aspects of US policy in the Indian Ocean area. The resulting American proposals were then discussed with the British in London at the end of February 1964.[17] As the records show, additional to confirming their interest in establishing a communications facility on Diego Garcia, the Americans also had in mind the development of 'austere support facilities' there, as well as possibly (with less priority) in Cocos-Keeling, Aldabra and the remainder of the Seychelles area. The list of such facilities for the long term was formidable:

(a) Stockpile area for substantial portion of an Army division plus other pre-stockage facilities.
(b) Air base capable of supporting cargo, troop carrier and tanker aircraft. Facilities to support antisubmarine patrol operations and air logistic operations. Parking area for two to four squadrons.
(c) Naval anchorage and base area to support a carrier task force, amphibious and support ships.
(d) Communications station.
(e) Amphibious staging area.
(f) Space tracking and communications facilities.

(g) Fuel and ammunition storage.

(h) Secondary support anchorages and logistic air strips.

The United States delegation emphasised that they wished to avoid the political problems arising from the development of military facilities in populated areas and to have assured security of tenure for at least 25 years. The delegation also proposed that the United Kingdom should be responsible for making available the necessary land, at British expense, as well as for 'any resettlement of population and compensation'.

The only British reservation immediately recorded concerned the possible size of any space-tracking facilities the US might propose to put on Diego Garcia. In reporting the discussions to the Chiefs of Staff, the defence planners made clear their welcome for an American presence on Diego Garcia. The wider background to the two countries' coincidence of interest has been admirably described by Mauritian historian Jocelyn Chan Low.[18] However, the British still saw that island as being less important as an air staging post than Aldabra and entertained hopes that the US might contribute to the development of the latter.[19] Only if use of the existing runway on Gan (in Addu Atoll) were denied would Diego Garcia come into its own in that role. This consideration did not however affect the military planners' view that the Chagos should be detached from Mauritius as soon as possible and, rather than being incorporated into Seychelles (as the Colonial Office wished), should be directly administered by the UK. One factor not mentioned by Chan Low, but tending to focus British minds on maintaining air access to southern Africa, was the looming crisis in Southern Rhodesia, which was destined to come to a head at virtually the same moment in 1965 as the issue of the Chagos islands.

Issues arising for the Colonial Office

Whatever might have been the reasons leading the Colonial Office to act as if it were unaware of the American military interest in Diego Garcia, by early in 1963 it had no choice but to involve the two Governors concerned. The position of Seychelles was simple: as ever, the Governor was strongly in favour of transferring both Agalega and the Chagos to Seychelles. When the new Governor of Mauritius, Sir John Rennie, was invited to consult his Council of Ministers, he replied that, with elections looming, he could not advise that Mauritian Ministers should be approached in the existing pre-electoral period, if that could be avoided.[20] He maintained this position in September, following the American request to send a survey party in secrecy to Diego Garcia. This communication elicited from his Seychelles colleague a letter urging early transfer of the islands and from the Colonial Office the view that 'if Chagos and Agalega should be transferred to Seychelles on strategic grounds, economic and financial questions could probably be more easily resolved'.[21] That option was however discarded early in 1964, following the Mauritius elections held in October 1963 and the meeting with American officials described above. The Colonial Office now came round to the general Whitehall view that it would be preferable for all the islands of potential defence interest to be constituted as a separate entity and administered directly as such. In June, Rennie consulted Seewoosagur Ramgoolam, now Premier of a multiparty government, about the proposed survey of the Chagos and the islands' eventual excision from Mauritius. While Ramgoolam expressed important reservations on excision, he had no objection to the survey.[22] At the same time the Premier, who had that morning volunteered his interest in continuing defence relations with Britain, agreed that it was premature for his ministers to be consulted about the possible excision, although they should be informed of the survey. This action was duly taken in mid-July, shortly before the team's departure from Gan for Diego Garcia.

Eventual removal of Chagos islanders

While American sources make it clear that removal of the population of islands to be used for their installations was a fundamental element in their plans, and that the British would be responsible for undertaking this measure, British files suggest that officials were initially unclear of the wider implications of what they had agreed to do. However, immediately after the February meeting of officials, the two Governors primarily concerned were informed by telegram[23] and in mid-March a senior Colonial Office official, Trafford Smith, visited Mauritius and Seychelles to discuss matters with them. From Port Louis, he reported that

> it is not clear whether the intention is to remove the whole population from Diego Garcia. Presumably it is. Exactly what will be involved will depend on whether any of the people can be resettled elsewhere in the Chagos Archipelago (assuming the whole group does not have to be cleared) or whether some or all will have to be resettled in Mauritius or Seychelles. The former seems very unlikely, and indeed, assuming Diego Garcia only is to be cleared, will the copra economy of the rest of the Archipelago be able to carry on or not? If not, the problem is more serious still – but one can't say without closer investigation.[24]

Smith's letter then went on to outline the interlocking problems that would arise from detaching any or all of the dependencies of Mauritius, including the impact on negotiations for constitutional advance and the difficulty of establishing 'these coral island copra people' in Mauritius. It would be fair to categorise his analysis as a frustrated struggle with multiple uncertainties.

This is not at all surprising. The timing of American construction was unknown and even a decision to proceed conditional on the results of the survey visit; in the UK, elections were looming and – when they took place in October – led to a change of government; while in Mauritius too the political situation was highly volatile and, early in 1965, erupted into severe communal disturbances. Above all, there seems to have been an assumption that the removal of island populations would begin with that of Diego Garcia, with any further removals only being required in the event, in some distant future, that other specific islands would be used for defence installations. The Americans indeed confirmed the correctness of this assumption in February 1965, in response to a British request for clarification.[25] So it is equally unsurprising that Newton's report, made in September 1964, reflected the same assumption, which clearly underlay his oft-quoted remark that 'if it becomes necessary to transfer the whole population there will be no problem resembling, for instance, the Hebridean evictions'. Yet this perspective ignored both the fundamental importance of Diego Garcia to the viability of the Chagos economy – even perhaps of the oil islands generally – and the fact that the presence of a resident population in any part of the new colonial entity would entail consideration of its affairs by the United Nations under the terms of Article 73(e) of the Charter.

The first of these issues was considered in the Colonial Office in mid-1965, mainly stimulated by the colonial government in the Seychelles. In mid-June, partly as a result of unease being expressed by Moulinié, the acting Governor, Peter Lloyd, examined the commercial value of each of the islands that would comprise the planned British Indian Ocean Territory (BIOT) in order to calculate what compensation might have to be paid to the owners and to the inhabitants who could need to be transferred elsewhere.[26] The potential economic importance of the Chagos to Seychelles emerged clearly. In July, the Governors of both Mauritius and Seychelles were in Oxford for a conference and Smith took the chance to discuss with them the many administrative issues that would arise from the decision to create the new entity. These included such matters as the legal instrument required (an Order-in-Council), the staff required, the purchase of a vessel to service the detached islands and the need for collaboration with and compensation for Moulinié. In addition, the officials tried to envisage how to anticipate the removal of the 480 inhabitants of Diego Garcia and the possibility of the same process being applied later to other islands. In this, financial considerations loomed large: while Moulinié should be encouraged to use the Diego Garcia workforce elsewhere in his domains, the government should not promote substantial long-term development for which – if cut short – increased compensation would be required. Ideally, the displaced workers would be transferred to Agalega, which the participants hoped might be separately transferred to Seychelles jurisdiction.[27]

Britain and Mauritius

By far the best account available of this negotiation is that of Chan Low.[28] Relying on the British documentary records available before 2012, he traces the British Ministerial discussions in 1964 and, particularly, in 1965, together with the reports and activities of the British governors of Mauritius. He describes the differences of perspective between the Ministers primarily involved, in particular those between the Colonial Secretary, Anthony Greenwood and the Secretaries of State for Foreign Affairs, Defence and Commonwealth Affairs. Greenwood, deeply concerned about the communal tensions in Mauritius, was determined to avoid adding to them by inserting the potentially destabilising issue of the Chagos into the constitutional conference scheduled to be held in September. The other Ministers were acutely aware of American pressure to secure access to Diego Garcia on the terms already agreed. Although Chan Low does not make the point, the new Prime Minister, Harold Wilson, had to balance both these specific concerns and more general political differences between (in over-simplistic terms) the right and left wings of his administration – the latter, suspicious of America, being notably represented by Greenwood.[29] He also faced the highly divisive issue of Vietnam, on which President Johnson was seeking not just political support, but a British contribution of troops, however small. This being politically unacceptable, Wilson must have been casting about for some other way to demonstrate timely support for the USA.[30]

It is unnecessary to replicate Chan Low's impressively balanced and objective accounts of the progress of the constitutional talks and the increasingly frequent inter-ministerial discussions of their handling in relation to the Chagos issue.[31] As matters turned out, the Chagos issue did prove destabilising, to the extent that one of the four parties represented in the Mauritian government walked out of the conference. This was the Parti Mauricien Social Démocrate (PMSD), resolutely opposed to the country's independence, whose departure left the way clear for Ramgoolam to make his own judgment of what terms he might be able to achieve and hold to on his return home. The issue remained unresolved until, as Chan Low describes,

> On the morning of 23 September [1965] S. Ramgoolam met Harold Wilson at Downing Street. The British Prime Minister, after deploring that the Mauritians were raising the stakes too high, stated that 'there was a number of possibilities: the Premier (Ramgoolam) and his colleagues could return to Mauritius either

with independence or without it. On the Defence part, Diego Garcia could either be detached by Order in Council or with the agreement of the Premier and his colleagues. The best of all might be independence and detachment by agreement, although he could not of course commit the Colonial Secretary on this point.

As Chan Low comments, Ramgoolam understood perfectly what was at stake: 'Sir Seewoosagur Ramgoolam said that he was convinced that the question of Diego Garcia was a matter of detail. There was no difficulty in principle'.[32] When the conference resumed the same afternoon, the Mauritian delegation (the PMSD still being absent), given reassurances on various issues (including fishing rights), agreed to the excision of the Chagos in return for compensation of £3 million. This opened the way for Greenwood to close the conference the following morning with an announcement inviting the Mauritians to decide upon independence at their next general elections, that is, rejecting the PMSD's demand for a referendum on the subject.

Did this agreement entail, as Chan Low concludes, deceit and blackmail? Each of the two leaders had his own political objectives; each faced important political pressures, from the US in Wilson's case and, in Ramgoolam's, from strong domestic opposition to independence. As is in the nature of political bargains, each paid what he regarded as an acceptable price for reconciling their primary aims.[33]

Britain and the United States

Following the 1964 survey visit, as Bandjunis records,[34] enthusiasm for developing Diego Garcia grew sharply within the Department of Defense, and included, for the first time, expressions of interest from the US Air Force. Well-informed press reports also began to proliferate, inspiring expressions of concern at the United Nations. However, in the US there were also other political preoccupations. President Johnson, now standing for election in his own right, secured the passage through Congress of a resolution giving him greatly increased freedom of action in Vietnam and presaging a major escalation of hostilities there. The Chagos issue was lost to view. In December, the British urged the US to decide how exactly they wished to proceed. In January 1965, the Americans responded that they had definite military plans for Diego Garcia, but wished the rest of the Chagos Archipelago to be included, 'primarily in the interests of security and in order to have other sites available for future contingencies'. They also asked for Aldabra, Coëtivy, Agalega, Farquhar, Desroches and Cosmoledos to be included in the 'detachment package'.

In April, British ministers reacted favourably to the American requests, but decided to seek an American contribution to the costs of detachment. The Americans, after reminding the British of their previous acceptance of such costs (page 469 above), agreed to contribute up to half of the anticipated £10 million involved. At the prevailing rate of exchange (£1=$2.8), this share amounted to $14 million. However, in view of the likelihood that Congress would refuse to appropriate funds for this purpose, the payment would be made secretly by waiving part of the research and development costs of an ongoing missile programme.[35] Conveniently, the US Chiefs of Staff concluded that perpetual access was worth $15 million,[36] while the State Department official who presented the resulting draft agreements in September explained that the US Government wanted an 'Ascension-type' agreement with once-for-all compensation.[37] As in all their dealings concerning Diego Garcia, then and subsequently, the Americans sought to avoid any direct dealings with Mauritius concerning compensation. Their consistent policy was to deal only with Britain as the responsible sovereign power.

BIOT is born

With the political obstacles cleared, the way was now open to set up the new colonial entity and the British government lost no time in doing so. Instructions were sent to the Governors of Mauritius and Seychelles to seek formal agreement of the local representative bodies to the detachment of the various islands concerned. This was given by Seychelles on 1 November and Mauritius on 5 November.[38] On Monday 8 November 1965, by Order-in-Council, the British Indian Ocean Territory was formally promulgated (and soon became known by its acronym BIOT), with parliament informed two days later by Written Answer to an arranged parliamentary question. From the larger number of islands earlier proposed, only the Chagos, together with three Seychelles islands (Aldabra, Farquhar and Desroches) were included. The Order also provided for the Territory's administration by a Commissioner (the existing Governor of Seychelles) assisted by an Administrator. The Answer explained that 'the islands will be available for the construction of defence facilities by the British and US Governments, but no plans have yet been made by either Government. Appropriate compensation will be paid'. On 12 November, three PMSD Ministers of the Mauritius coalition government resigned, on the ground that Mauritius had been inadequately compensated. There followed a whole year before any further public moves were made.[39]

BIOT and the United Nations

Nevertheless, the announcement of the creation of BIOT occurred while the annual General Assembly of the UN was in session. As usual, Britain had many contentious issues to face, not least the decolonisation questions arising in the Fourth Committee. Here, the UK was accustomed to take a strong stand in defence of the right of the Falkland islanders to decide their own future. The potential embarrassment of having to defend the very different arrangements envisaged for BIOT was obvious and officials turned urgently to examine how oversight by the UN might legitimately be avoided. One option – to remove the populations of all the islands ahead of any defence construction, was quickly rejected as being indefensible, for economic reasons in Seychelles and political reasons in Mauritius. Officials concluded almost as quickly that the only basis for denying the existence of a permanent settled population in BIOT was to define their presence in terms solely of their employment and their links with either Mauritius or Seychelles. Vulnerability to criticism of this approach in UN fora was foreseen, but judged less damaging than the expected interference of UN bodies. Thought was then given to ways of presenting this choice so as to blunt criticism as far as possible. It could be pointed out that all those on the islands were contracted employees of the companies concerned (or dependants thereof) and all had established links with either Mauritius or Seychelles. No-one obtained a living from independent economic activity. On this last point, the views of Newton were sought. He replied that '… as a matter of personal interest, [he had been] anxious to try to find established communities on the islands, particularly people who had made their living by fishing or market gardening, etc. [He] failed to find any'.[40] However, as it turned out, the timetabling of the agenda that year made it unnecessary to deploy the proposed arguments.

Notes to Chapter 22

1 TNA CO 968/842 Robert Newton, CMG, *Report on the Anglo-American Survey in the Indian Ocean,* 1964, submitted to Secretary of State Duncan Sandys on 23 September 1964. Born in 1908, Newton had wide experience of colonial administration, having served in Nigeria, Palestine and Jamaica, before his appointment in 1953 as Colonial Secretary [deputy to the Governor] in Mauritius, from where he retired in 1961. He then obtained election to the Exeter City Council, later being chosen as one of its Aldermen.

2 This vessel had been built in the US in 1909, as the *Telma,* and later renamed *La Perle.* She was used regularly until 1971, her last voyage being that to remove the last islanders from Diego Garcia (article dated 10 May 2004 in the Seychelles *Nation*).

3 On Diego Garcia, Harold Pouponneau succeeded Robert Talbot; on Peros Banhos, Henri Gendron joined a M. Guillemin, later taking over; on Salomon, the new man was a M. Remy.

4 TNA CO 1036/796 Letter dated 27 September 1962.

5 Marcel Moulinié, Paul's nephew, sent to replace his uncle's initial appointee, Pouponneau, spoke forcefully in this sense to NW-S during his visit to Seychelles in 1995; Talbot's comment was made in answer to NW-S's question during a visit to Mauritius in 2010. Both conversations took place before the relevant census figures were known to the latter.

6 The Mauritian newspaper *L'Express* carried articles in its issues for 24 April and 7 July 1974 about the 'Eden and hell that was Agalega'. These reported a diatribe in the Mauritius parliament by the then PMSD deputy, Raymond d'Unienville, about the consequences of the Seychellisation of Agalega following its purchase by Paul Moulinié and the subsequent appointment of Pouponneau as manager. The population had halved from its previous figure of 400, and only 80 Ilois remained, who were, according to the article, treated much more harshly than the workers introduced from Seychelles.

7 Fernand Mandarin, as dictated to his collaborator, Robert Furlong (personal communication, July 2012). Official figures, however, show a decline of only about 60 between 1962 and 1964.

8 TNA CO 968/842 Report by Robert Newton.

9 TNA CO 1036/1582 Secret and Personal Telegram No. 49 of 22 February 1963.

10 All the Seychellois were employed on either two-year (heads of families) or eighteen-month (bachelors) contracts.

11 Newton *op. cit.*, paragraph 24. Critics of this view have suggested that Newton was deliberately seeking to minimise the extent and depth of Ilois links with the Chagos, in conformity with already-formed Whitehall views. However, the issues that later concerned the British government, in particular the status of the Ilois under the UN Charter, were not to surface for at least another year.

12 TNA FCO 141/1462 Governor Seychelles Telegram No. 159 dated 10 August 1964.

13 It was in that month that the US plans were described in American and British newspapers, immediately attracting international attention.

14 Vine, D., *Island of Shame*, Princeton University Press, 2009.

15 British Embassy, Washington Note to the State Department of 29 July 1963 (Vine, *op.cit* p. 71).

16 To the consternation of officials in Whitehall, the memorandum from the US Embassy in London envisaged an eventual requirement for 3,000 acres and accommodation for 350 operatives.

17 TNA CAB 21/5418 Chiefs of Staff paper 95/64; also TNA DEF 127/123/03 memorandum following the talks.

18 Chan Low, J., 'The Making of the Chagos Affair: myths and reality', in S. Evers and M. Kooy (eds.) *Eviction from the Chagos* Islands, Brill, Leiden 2011.

19 The British interest in Aldabra clearly reflected the government's deep anxieties about developments affecting Britain's very important economic and political engagement in central and southern Africa, as well as the possible need to intervene on behalf of the large numbers of British nationals in the area. Only a few months earlier, British forces had intervened to help put down mutinies in East Africa, while the situation in Rhodesia was becoming steadily more tense. When the possibility of developing Aldabra became public, the scientific community mounted sustained opposition to the project and its eventual abandonment gave rise to the belief, still held in some quarters, that the humans of the Chagos were sacrificed for the sake of the giant tortoises of Aldabra. The prosaic facts that the Americans declined to contribute and the British could not afford to undertake such development alone were as nothing compared to so powerful a myth.

20 TNA CO 1036/1582 Sir John Rennie, letter dated 6 June 1963.

21 TNA CO 1036/1582 Colonial Office Secret and Personal Telegram No. 39 to Port Louis, dated 16 December 1963.

22 TNA FCO 141/1464 Governor, Mauritius, Secret and Personal Telegram No. 83 dated 1 July 1964.

23 TNA FCO 141/1464 Colonial Office Secret and Personal Telegram No. 19 to Governor Mauritius (also to Governor Seychelles as No. 42) dated 6 March 1964.

24 TNA FCO 141/1464 Letter dated 23 March 1964 from Smith (in Port Louis) to J.G. Marnham.

25 TNA FCO 32/484 C.C.P. Heathcote-Smith, *BIOT: Chronological summary of events leading to its creation … and subsequent events relating to the establishment of UK/US defence facilities.* Item 7 quotes an American communication dated 10 February 1965 as follows: 'No reason to re-locate population prior

to Island coming into use to meet a requirement. This would apply to other islands of the Chagos Archipelago as long as our activity was confined to Diego Garcia'. [Heathcote-Smith, a Counsellor available between postings, had evidently been called in to summarise the material accumulated in a multitude of departmental files; the result remains an admirable aid to historians.]

26 TNA CO 1036/13 P. Lloyd, letter dated 22 June 1965.

27 TNA FO 371/184524, folio Z4/86 Letter dated 13 July 1965 from T. Smith (Colonial Office) to J.A. Patterson (HM Treasury).

28 Chan Low *op. cit.*

29 A Cabinet ally of Greenwood, Barbara Castle, referred in her published diaries to a meeting on 31 August 1965 to discuss the Chagos, remarking 'I approve the motive: to off-load on to the US some of our responsibilities East of Suez; but I don't like the method'. *The Castle Diaries 1964–70* Weidenfeld & Nicolson, 1984.

30 We do not think this suggestion is fanciful. It is, for example, put forward by Ashley Jackson (page 183 of his *War and Empire in Mauritius and the Indian Ocean*, Palgrave 2001). Also, NW-S consulted Sir Oliver Wright, the official responsible for recording what passed between Wilson and Ramgoolam. His reply, at the age of 89, was commendably Delphic, but cited another example where, in 'high politics', a favour was given, or returned, unrelated to the logic of immediate policy.

31 TNA CAB 48/18 is the main Whitehall source for this material'.

32 TNA CO 1036/253 The two quotations cited by Chan Low are from the record of conversation between Prime Minister and Premier of Mauritius at 10, Downing Street at 10 a.m. on Thursday 23 September 1965.

33 In 1982, following a general election in which Ramgoolam was defeated, he was summoned before a Select Committee on the Excision of the Chagos Archipelago, to whose questions he replied 'I thought that independence was much more primordial and more important than the excision of the island which is very far from here, and which we had never visited, which we never could visit … If I had to choose between independence and the ceding of Diego Garcia, I would have done again the same thing.' De l'Estrac, J.C., *Report of the Select Committee on the Excision of the Chagos Archipelago*, cited by L. Jeffery in *Chagos Islanders in the UK* (p.33) Manchester University Press 2011.

34 Bandjunis, V.B., *Diego Garcia: creation of the Indian Ocean base* (pp. 13–14) Writer's Showcase Lincoln 2001.

35 Bandjunis *op.cit.* (pp. 26–27) describes the arrangement in detail.

36 Vine *op. cit.* (p. 82).

37 TNA FCO 32/484 Heathcote-Smith *op. cit.* (item 43).

38 *Ibid.* (items 48 and 49) The two colonies' agreements came in response to Despatch No. 423 of 6 October 1965 to Port Louis and Telegram No. 338 to Seychelles, dated 20 October.

39 The procedure for announcing the government's decision was that traditionally used for reporting colonial legislation. It enabled the government to evade prior parliamentary debate and to hide both the financial arrangements (awkward for the US Administration) and questions about the treatment of the existing island inhabitants (highly embarrassing for the British). However, those (such as Vine *op. cit.* p. 83) who have claimed that the creation of BIOT was not announced publicly are mistaken.

40 TNA CO 1036/1344 Minuting by officials (T.C.D. Jerrom, H.P. Hall, K.W.S. Mackenzie) in November 1965.

23

1966–1971: The Price of Secrecy and Prevarication

A slower tempo

WHILE the 1965 session of the UN General Assembly ended without any detailed discussion of BIOT, a Resolution was passed in mid-December that included a paragraph calling upon the Administering Power to take no action to dismember the territory of Mauritius nor violate its territorial integrity.[1] This stark warning of future troubles was followed closely by a surprise development from the US: on 31 December, the Americans informed the British that they foresaw no use of Diego Garcia in 1966 such as might require removal of the islanders. In fact, the immediate problem of radio communications in the central Indian Ocean was on the way to being resolved by the developing capacity of satellites, while the wider case for major facilities stood little chance of Congressional approval while expenditure on the Vietnam war was being vastly increased.[2] It was therefore necessary for the British to plan for a period of uncertain length in which the plantations would be maintained and the status of the population need to be explained and defended. There were a series of interlocking aspects to their problems: how to prepare for the differing scenarios with which the Americans might confront them, not least the impact these might have on British defence policy east of Suez; what to do about the commercial activities of the Chagos islands; and how, on the diplomatic front, to deal with questions arising from Mauritius, India and above all in UN forums, without exposing the American Administration to premature scrutiny by a suspicious Congress. This complex situation was not to be resolved for a full five years. Necessarily, much of this chapter relates the twists and turns of the debates within and between the external participants.[3] As before, however, our story is more concerned with the impact of these forces upon the economy of the islands and the lives of the islanders.

Bilateral Agreement on the usage of BIOT

An American team present in London as the negotiations with Mauritius were concluded had left behind drafts of three agreements, covering the use of defence facilities in the Indian Ocean, the American financial contribution thereto and a satellite tracking station to be established in Seychelles. Notwithstanding the loss of immediate interest in setting up any installation, the US proposed that negotiations on the three agreements should go ahead. The British accepted, seeing in this a means to further their own interests. In July 1966, Harold Wilson visited Washington and invited the US to contribute to the costs of constructing an air staging post on Aldabra and to participate in surveying the island. The Americans agreed in principle, but asked the British to agree to a similar early survey of Diego Garcia.[4] As before, the British were seeking to retain a capacity to intervene in southern Africa, to reduce the level of their own commitments in the Indian Ocean and to encourage greater American involvement further east, while the latter were equally keen to keep British disengagement to a minimum.

Although problems with Congress prevented the allocation of funding for Diego Garcia, the US Navy was authorised to continue making plans. Under this authority, an American team returned to London in November 1966 to complete the bilateral agreements mentioned above. As far as Diego Garcia was concerned, the outcome was the signature of an Exchange of Diplomatic Notes on 30 December.[5] The documents, having for the British the force of a Treaty, consisted of the published Exchange, together with two unpublished exchanges, one concerning the limits to US financial commitment (see page 469) and the second setting out other 'understandings', most notably that it would be for the British to take any 'administrative measures' that might be required for 'modifying or terminating any economic activity then being pursued, resettling any inhabitants, and otherwise facilitating the availability of the islands for defence purposes'. These secret attachments did not see the light of day until 2005.

Policy towards the Ilois

In parallel to the discussions with the US, the British government spent much of 1966 in private debate about the administrative issues arising from the creation of the new Territory. Most of such information as has been released about this debate comes from documents disclosed in a succession of court cases which took place between 1999 and 2008. The gist of many such documents is available, but the texts only of those cited in full in court. Access to the latter (and to those mentioned in the preceding paragraph) has been greatly facilitated by their publication in a book by Dr Peter Sand, a well-known international jurist.[6] Inevitably, this material tends to be skewed towards issues of forensic interest.

One most important aspect of policy in relation to the newly-formed Territory had of course legal, but also practical implications: the status of its inhabitants. The initial ideas of officials (see page 475) were soon adopted by Ministers and in February 1966 directions were given to the BIOT Commissioner to work out ways by which, to avoid UN oversight, the inhabitants could be defined as either Mauritians or Seychellois temporarily resident on account of their employment.[7] Nevertheless, the problem and its detailed solution continued to occupy officials throughout the year, without an unequivocal decision being taken and with considerable uncertainty prevailing about the actual numbers living and working in the islands of BIOT or the closeness of their connections with the two colonies. The policy line was formulated more firmly on 4 January 1967, a few days after signature of the Agreement with the Americans. Officials meeting under the chairmanship of Sir Arthur Galsworthy, a Deputy Secretary of the Colonial Office, concluded that, in order to treat BIOT as other than subject to over-view by the UN, it was 'necessary to ensure that all inhabitants became "belongers" of either Seychelles or Mauritius and only in BIOT as temporary residents'.[8]

The Seychelles perspective

Long before Paul Moulinié had shown a commercial interest in the Chagos islands, indeed at the time of the separation of Seychelles from the colony of Mauritius in 1903, the idea of putting the Chagos under Seychelles jurisdiction had been mooted, but rejected on account of opposition by the Port Louis-based proprietors. The same had happened in 1931 for much the same reason (see page 351), despite the eagerness of the colonial government in Seychelles to increase the scale and economic potential of their own coconut industry. Immediately following the creation of BIOT, the Governor of Seychelles was appointed to the new post of Commissioner, with his deputy as the new territory's Administrator. At last the Chagos islands were – up to a point – in Seychelles' grasp. It was not surprising therefore to find official sympathy there for the plans Moulinié, already a member of the Governor's advisory Council, had made to modernise and expand the plantations he had acquired in 1962. Moulinié, however, being aware of the uncertainty surrounding the future of these acquisitions, had complained to the Governor about the problems military usage would entail for him.[9] Very recently, the opportunity arose to discuss with Charles Moulinié, one of Paul's sons and board members, his father's outlook on his Chagos-Agalega venture. It did not involve, in Charles's view, any strategic calculation of a possible capital gain from a governmental buy-out. Rather, as an enthusiastic planter, his success in revitalising Farquhar's output had convinced him that even greater success would attend investment of capital and skilled labour in the dilapidated islands of Chagos and Agalega, going for a song.[10] In fact, the British were already considering a plan to purchase the islands and lease them back and in February 1966 so informed Moulinié. The latter readily accepted this method of proceeding, although the process of establishing the basis of Moulinié's title proved time-consuming. Meanwhile, Moulinié carried on his efforts to increase copra production. This arrangement stood to benefit both parties. Moulinié might hope to make a profit from ongoing production in the plantations he had begun to rehabilitate. Britain could put the islanders' future 'on hold' under competent management, with probable benefit to the Seychelles economy; at the same time the government retained the flexibility to respond rapidly, should the US renew its interest in developing any part of BIOT for defence purposes.

So far as Seychelles was concerned, the approach adopted introduced a potential conflict of interest for the colony's Governor who was also Commissioner for BIOT: action to improve the Seychelles economy by resuscitating the Chagos plantations could very well complicate preparations to prepare for the eventual removal of the inhabitants of such islands as might be required by the US. Secondly, as had been foreseen (see page 471), the greater the investment made by Moulinié, the higher would be the compensation required if it had to be abandoned. Finally, of acute interest from a political and legal point of view, the local officials were required to institute a civil status system which conformed to the notion that the BIOT islands' workers and their families belonged either to Mauritius or Seychelles. As we shall relate, these problems were to make themselves felt most clearly[11] in the day-to-day dealings between Moulinié and John Todd, the BIOT Administrator.[12]

Todd had been transferred to Seychelles after four years' experience in the Anglo-French condominium of New Hebrides. For the next five years, he and

Moulinié were to work closely together, in a situation where political and commercial imperatives became increasingly hard to reconcile. That they succeeded in doing so in part reflected their own personalities, but also stemmed from a common wish to make the best of the situation in the islands now brought together in BIOT.[13] Todd did not make his first visit to the Chagos until May 1967, having visited the ex-Seychelles islands of Farquhar, Coëtivy and Aldabra in 1966. This order of priorities resulted from the temporary American loss of interest in Diego Garcia, while the British government remained actively

John Todd. Image courtesy of Mrs Todd.

engaged in its plan to develop Aldabra. However, during this period the British had also needed to secure the local powers required to turn the islands to military use. Although the Commissioner granted himself the possibility of acting by compulsory purchase, he was able to achieve his objective by negotiation. However, Moulinié's detailed negotiations with the War Office were only completed in April 1967.[14] The price paid to him for transfer of ownership was £660,000, while the basis of the lease-back was that he should receive 80% of the net income before taxation.

As Todd reported, the islands had been neglected during the preceding eighteen months, owing to the uncertainty as to their future; Diego Garcia required extensive clearing, while Peros Banhos and Salomon had similar though less severe problems.[15] By the end of 1966, the total population of the Chagos had fallen to 795, compared with 993 in 1964; much of the decline was accounted for by a reduction of Diego Garcia's numbers from 483 to 345.[16] Moulinié's plans were to increase the labour force, primarily with Seychellois; to manage Salomon from Peros Banhos; and to establish a subsidiary settlement in the latter, on Ile Diamant. Indeed, the mv *Mauritius*, aboard which Todd and Moulinié travelled, was making a round trip from Mauritius via Mahé on both outward and return passages, resulting in a net increase of 129 Seychellois adults, offset by a net decrease of 38 Ilois adults. There is no substantive evidence to suggest that Moulinié's key aims at this period – to focus on Diego Garcia and to substitute Seychellois for Ilois – were influenced, let alone decided, by the British.[17]

As required by his instructions, Todd's role was confined to counting the inhabitants and categorising them as Ilois, Seychellois or Mauritian. Taking account of the children arriving and departing, the population of the Chagos as a whole rose by 127 from 797[18] to 924; of the latter figure 487 were described by Todd as Ilois. A footnote to his report stated 'Ilois classified on basis of their own assessment and includes Mauritians who have worked on the islands for long periods and who wish to continue this employment'. By this time, under Moulinié's management, all those working for the company had contracts, leading the Commissioner to remark 'It is true to say that all those in Chagos are contract labour on contracts for one or two years and their dependents, but how often and over what period and over how many generations you have to renew contracts before becoming a belonger is not something about which argument would produce any great profit'.[19] As will be seen, however, lack of profit was to prove no barrier to indefinite debate on this topic. It also emerged, much later, that one individual born on Diego Garcia had never been subject to a contract.[20]

In March 1968, following his second visit, Todd identified the Ilois as 'persons born in Chagos or in Mauritius whose father or, in the case of illegitimate children, whose mother was born in Chagos', noting that those so classified were entitled to Mauritian citizenship under the country's 1968 independence constitution. Shortly afterwards, the new Commissioner, Sir Hugh Norman-Walker, examined the issue in a despatch.[21] In it, he concluded that there were at least 434 Ilois in the Chagos at that time, of whom 354 were at least third-generation Ilois and that an unknown number of people living in Mauritius were also of Ilois origin. Norman-Walker went on to point out that 'if we are to maintain that there are no permanent inhabitants … we shall have to find some other basis than birth to support our claim'. The solution, he suggested, was to rely on the facts that, from the start, the inhabitants of the islands had only been there because they were employed by the owners or lessees or were members of the family of persons so employed; that they did not own any land or houses; and that the owners/lessees had legal rights to remove and to refuse the return of all such people, subject only to respecting the terms of their individual contracts. In its essentials, this advice became the basis for the subsequent British stance on the status of the inhabitants of BIOT. It also introduced the question of Ilois in Mauritius affected by the reduction and eventual cessation of opportunities for employment or re-employment in the Chagos.

American constraints and delays

From the start, as demonstrated by the financial element of the 1966 Agreement, contortions were required to avoid Congressional scrutiny of the Pentagon's plans. These have been described in authoritative detail by one of the civilian staff involved, Vytautas Bandjunis.[22] The essentials of his account are, firstly, that there was great reluctance in Congress, especially in the Senate, to see the US committed to overseas entanglements additional to the Vietnamese quagmire. Consequently, there was a danger that inadvertent revelation of Pentagon thinking would result in outright rejection of the project. This danger was most acute in 1968 during the count-down to the Presidential election; indeed, officials of the State and Defense Departments became increasingly wary of expressing their views even to the British. Secondly, there were divisions between the US Navy and the higher civilian echelons of the DoD concerning the appropriate scale of any installations, with the Navy's concerns gradually gaining strength with successive indications of British withdrawal from the area. Perhaps the most pertinent of these was the announcement by Harold Wilson in late November 1967 that the projected staging post on Aldabra was to be abandoned as part of the government's deep cuts in defence expenditure.[23] The Americans had never been greatly interested in the Aldabra project, except as a lever to sustain a British presence, and they were not prepared to pay for it on their own.

Faced with the clearer prospect of a strategic vacuum in the Indian Ocean, the American Joint Chiefs of Staff put forward proposals, which were whittled down by those concerned with budgetary control and finally presented to Congress in November 1968 (shortly before the election of President Nixon) as 'an austere logistic support facility … for ship refuelling, limited aviation, and communications.'[24] Diego Garcia itself was not mentioned. The cost was put at about $10 million, as part of the budget for 1970. After much to-ing and fro-ing, the proposal was blocked in the Senate on 18 December 1969, but with the understanding that it could be presented again a year later. The project duly scraped through, but gained Congressional approval only as a communications facility. Finally, however, in December 1970 President Nixon named Diego Garcia as the site for the facility and spoke of it as a base which would provide support for American and British ships and planes in the Indian Ocean. The net result was that a detailed survey of Diego Garcia's lagoon in August 1967 had been followed by a hiatus of over three years in the Chagos. Throughout this period, it was essential to Britain's relations with the US that nothing be revealed about the Administration's intentions regarding Diego Garcia, thus precluding discussion with either Moulinié or the Mauritians.[25]

Continued functioning of the plantations

Meanwhile, Moulinié had been doing his best to make the islands profitable. Hence the introduction in May 1967, as soon as his lease had been signed, of the additional Seychellois workers. However, with the prospect of losing a substantial proportion of Diego Garcia's acreage to eventual military usage, Moulinié must quickly have despaired of obtaining the increased investment necessary to the fulfilment of his dreams; as early as July, he gave the required six months' notice of his intention to give up the lease. The year's results must have confirmed his judgment. By clearing neglected areas, he secured an increase of copra production for the year, to 1284 tonnes. However, this was still below the disappointing 1955–58 average of 1311 tonnes; and his balance sheet for 1967 showed that the BIOT government had made a small profit of Rs 60,000, while his company's profit amounted only to Rs 15,000.[26] He therefore terminated the lease at the end of that year, arranging instead to manage the plantations on behalf of the government in exchange for 8% of the gross sales. This at least guaranteed him a certain income while passing to the British the problem of securing commercial viability or making alternative arrangements for the future of the inhabitants. Not surprisingly, copra production for the next two years was substantially less (941 tonnes in 1968 and 982 tonnes in 1969). The condition of Peros Banhos was particularly poor.[27] For want of labour and boats, only the islands close to Ile du Coin were being worked, while the four easternmost islets were being worked from Salomon (Moulinié's plan to operate Salomon from Peros had clearly been abandoned). Todd's own concern was expressed in a letter of 16 July 1968, asking whether, by September, 'Diego Garcia has to be cleared and whether the other islands may continue to be run as coconut plantations'.[28]

The changed contractual arrangement with Moulinié was also reflected in the plantations' employment levels. When Todd visited the islands in March 1968, he found that, compared with 1967, the total population of Diego Garcia had fallen from 503 to 380, with Seychellois accounting for 97 of the reduction; on Peros Banhos, there had been small declines of both Ilois and Seychellois, resulting in a change in the total population from 253 to 244; on Salomon, the total had, in contrast, risen slightly, from 168 to 183, the change being accounted for by an increase in the number of Mauritians (up from 7 to 23). As mentioned briefly on page 484, the total of those identified as Ilois was 434 (128 + 168 +138). In addition, there were 68 Ilois on the Seychelles island of Desroches. These figures were reported by Todd to a meeting in London in early December.[29] The same figures were repeated in Todd's *Notes on the BIOT Islands*, which were mentioned in a letter from Norman-Walker in early January 1969 and forwarded to London later in the same month (see note 20). Norman-Walker reported a 'continuing decline in population. This is mainly due to the present difficulty of recruiting Seychellois to replace the Ilois who have left the islands ...'.[30] In November 1968, when Norman-Walker and Todd visited the Chagos together, they were also accompanied by a public health official. The latter's findings (it

mv *Nordvaer* at East Point, 1969. Image courtesy Kirby Crawford.[31]

seems) were only published in 1985.[32] He found that the total population (807 in March) had fallen to 666; of these 336 were on Diego Garcia, 162 on Peros Banhos and 168 on Salomon. Thus, as 1968 drew to its end, commercial uncertainty was added to the political.

Another important development in 1968 was that, immediately upon Mauritius' independence in March of that year, the new government removed the 50% subsidy it had provided to Rogers & Co. to maintain a regular link with the Chagos, while the Seychelles government (at a cost of £55,000) purchased its own vessel, the mv *Nordvaer*, to provide a direct service between Victoria and the BIOT islands.

This greatly complicated the movement of both individual Ilois employees[33] and the traditional patterns of recruitment. Unintentionally, the decision also added an unexpected problem for Moulinié: the imminent commencement of Seychelles' biggest ever building project, an international airport, made the recruitment of Seychellois labourers for Chagos nigh impossible. As recently released files show, British Ministers had agreed to allow Moulinié to recruit 100 workers, together with their families, from Mauritius and expected him to do so from the Ilois who had left the Chagos from 1967 and wanted to return. These were among 354 people who were the subject of Mauritian diplomatic representations on 17 September 1968.[34] They fell, according to a memorandum from the Prime Minister's Office, into two categories. The first concerned 55 male workers (and their 159 dependents), who '*on the expiry of the contract which they signed in Mauritius* [emphasis added] before the Magistrate of the Industrial Court … were returned to Mauritius on the 19th May, 1967, by the employing Company …'. The second group comprised '84 adults and 56 children who arrived in Mauritius from either Diego Garcia, Peros Banhos or Salomon Island, on the 30th March, 1968 and are stranded here'. 'Stranded' was an apt word: bereft of its subsidy, Moulinié's partner, Rogers & Co., was no longer prepared to offer a service to the Chagos. In November, however, the mv *Mauritius* did make a final visit to Diego Garcia, which Moulinié planned to use in order to recruit Ilois workers to make up the numbers he required. His scheme came to nought, because the vessel was, on safety grounds, refused permission to carry them.[35] It is worth mentioning, *en passant*, that Moulinié was facing similar problems in Agalega and invited Rogers & Co. to recruit 50 Ilois workers and their families. Only fourteen families volunteered, including nine of those named in the list attached to the Prime Minister's memorandum. No one at the time offered an explanation for this reluctance.[36]

Despite uncertainties in the arithmetical detail – not least because only a few of the movements of labour were counted, the purpose and outcome of Moulinié's actions were clear. He was trying to secure greater output and efficiency by employing Seychellois workers rather than Ilois. As owner (later lessee) of the

Chagos plantations, he had no special obligations to those employed by the previous Mauritian company.[37] The process of Seychellisation (such as he had already accomplished in Agalega) was, however, brought to a halt by the surge in demand for labour on Mahé for construction of the new airport and the infrastructure required for the development of tourism as the main component of the Seychelles economy. Hence the need to turn again to Ilois, whose direct route to the islands was, following the Mauritian government's decision to cancel its subsidy, no longer available. While the British government was keen to avoid any increase in the numbers of people whom it might later have to compensate or recognise as belongers of the new Colony, it had not by the end of 1968 taken any measures to run down the Chagos population. This was primarily a consequence of uncertainty over American intentions, combined with inability to discuss the issues openly with the Mauritians. The only moral scruple involved was a continuing wish to avoid exacerbating Mauritius' persistent problems of unemployment.

Policy dilemmas

From the Seychelles perspective, legal and diplomatic issues were by no means the only – or even preponderant – considerations facing those responsible for managing BIOT. As Todd commented in October 1968, humanitarian, economic and local political factors had also to be weighed:

> On humanitarian grounds one cannot but have sympathy with the displaced Ilois. In the past they have by their standards been among the most fortunate of labourers in that they have had an almost absolute guarantee of employment. Now, due to our defence requirements, they not only find that the guarantee has gone but that they are in Mauritius, a country with an acute unemployment problem and, as Mauritius has virtually no copra industry, with no opportunity to use the skills they possess …[38]

As regards the politics, Todd argued that it would be advantageous to re-employ Ilois from Mauritius ahead of any announcement of a defence project on Diego Garcia. These points were the prelude to his arguments in favour of increasing the labour force in order to develop the neglected plantations – a policy which, in his view, would carry risks only if the Americans required the whole of Chagos to be abandoned. Todd reckoned that the labour force on Peros Banhos and Salomon was only half that needed for care and maintenance break-even activity and about one third of that necessary for redevelopment and profitable operation. In November, the Governor also intervened, asking for the exploitation of Peros Banhos and Salomon to be maximised, with whatever extra recruitment might be required, expressing strong opposition to clearing the whole Archipelago ('the culpable waste of a fine asset'), and noting also that it was 'problematic how long [Moulinié] will be prepared to carry on his present uneconomic operations'.[39]

In early October 1968, FCO officials had begun to express their own dilemmas: 'It still remains possible that the Americans will urge us to clear the whole of Chagos – which despite difficulties would basically improve our long term position in the United Nations on the population question'.[40] Britain's growing frustration with American prevarication was reflected in a letter from a desk officer to the Washington embassy, which included the remarks that 'We are indeed on the point of having to take certain decisions in the local labour field which could have a direct effect on the Diego Garcia project. Our decisions may have political repercussions in Mauritius. If the Americans are really not prepared to discuss resettlement with us at this stage, there is considerable danger that the decisions we take will create difficulties for them and for us'.[41]

In fact, as soon as their election was over, the Americans stated that they had no objection to the continued use of Salomon and Peros Banhos or to the transfer there of islanders from Diego Garcia, but could not exclude future requirements for installations on other BIOT islands.[42] In short, they left the British to solve their dilemma by themselves. As the FCO explained to Norman-Walker, 'we have not ourselves taken a final decision that Peros Banhos and Salomon should be developed. There are possible long-term political dangers (particularly in the UN) about encouraging economic development anywhere in the BIOT, and thus allowing a population to become established and we shall be putting the matter to Ministers at the appropriate moment'.[43] These 'dangers' were spelled out in a letter from the head of the FCO's UN department to the UK Mission in New York. John Lambert, after describing the tactical and procedural issues involved, went on to write:

> I do not think we can either in the longer or the shorter term exclude the possibility that this semi-permanent population will find themselves in the international limelight. If interest in them became strong enough, the press for example may well discover that they exist in significant numbers. (You may recall the Press interest in the wild life of Aldabra). If attention were drawn to them we should find it difficult to assert that BIOT is not a 'non-self-governing territory' and that we had no obligations in respect of it under Chapter XI of the Charter. In particular we should find it extremely difficult to deny [sic] that we had sufficiently honoured or were now honouring our Charter obligation 'To ensure … their political, economic, social and educational advancement'. NO proper schools or hospitals exist in these islands and there are no representative political institutions. Already our political anxieties on this score coincide with the Treasury's anxiety to avoid an expanding financial commitment in these fields.

Policy decisions

The balance of argument soon swung decisively in favour of removing the whole Chagos population, when, in response to persistent requests, the Americans finally made clear (the very day after despatch of Lambert's letter) their refusal to agree to the grant of a twenty-year contract for Moulinié to develop the two northern atolls (see inset opposite).[44] Responding to a submission from the Foreign and Commonwealth Secretary to the Prime Minister, with input from other Ministers concerned during the month of April 1969, Harold Wilson agreed on 26 April that on balance it would be preferable to resettle those two as well, to Mauritius and Seychelles. The moves should be gradual and discussed with Mauritian ministers. Only if they could not reach a satisfactory deal with Mauritius would development of the two outer atolls be considered. The overriding consideration was 'the existence of the Ilois and their possible claim to belong to BIOT, [which] could cause us considerable problems, particularly in the United Nations'.[45] What could now be seen was that the initial commitment to the US had been made without adequate grasp of the character of the individual Chagos islands and the numbers of people inhabiting them, and without weighing sufficiently what was entailed by the inclusion in BIOT of islands other than Diego Garcia.[46]

At this stage, the British were under the impression that the moment was close when the Americans would disclose enough of their plans to enable the Mauritian government to be informed of them in confidence and for discussions on the related issues of resettlement and compensation to begin. Indeed on 2 June 1969 a preparatory telegram of the line to be taken in such an eventuality was despatched to the High Commissioner in Port Louis.[47] Shortly afterwards, the British sent the Americans a memorandum, explaining frankly their fears concerning the consequences of a detailed examination in UN forums (such as had not yet occurred) of the numbers and citizenship status of the Ilois inhabitants of the Chagos, especially those born after 1965.[48]

The implications for Seychelles and BIOT

For the Seychelles Governor and Todd, this decision would have been a major disappointment. It also presaged the end of Moulinié's hopes for expansion. These had been set down in a five-year budget plan, presented to the Commissioner in the very week of Stoddart's letter. Essentially, the plan envisaged substantially increasing output and profits, resulting from large, but later diminishing capital investment.[49] All that Moulinié might now hope for was to make the most of the government's reliance on him to keep operations going

Text of Secret letter dated 22 February 1969, with US Embassy letterhead

London, England
Richard A. Sykes, Esquire, C.M.G., M.C.
Defense Department
Foreign and Commonwealth Office
Whitehall, S.W. 1

Dear Richard:

We have now heard from Washington on the general subject of resettlement of workers to Peros Banhos and Salomon Islands, and on the specific question of reserving those two islands for economic exploitation for a twenty-year period which you discussed with us on February 5 and in paragraph 2 of your letter of February 6.

As we understand it, you propose that we undertake, for a period of twenty years, not to install any defense facility on Peros Banhos or Salomon which would require evacuation of migrant workers, or in the event that such facility should be installed, that we agree to compensate for any development which takes place during the interim period.

In our view, this proposal would seriously derogate from the principles underlying the 1966 BIOT agreements, which we interpret as (1) authorizing the transfer of local workers elsewhere, together with the curtailment or closure of copra plantations or other economic activity, and (2) placing the responsibility on the U.K. government for any relocation costs or compensation to private interests. For these reasons, we would not wish to enter a 20-year self-denying commitment regarding the use of the two islands, nor could we undertake to compensate for interim economic development costs in the event we should later find it desirable to use them.

Our acquiescence to the resettlement of Chagos copra workers to Peros Banhos and Salomon was with the caveat, as you will remember, that it should not prejudge the ultimate use of those islands for defense purposes, even to the exclusion of workers if that should some day be necessary. It remains our position that neither such use nor such exclusion is presently foreseen, but we do not wish to be tied to a commitment for any given number of years.

Finally, let me say that we fully recognize the desirability of solving resettlement problems within the BIOT in a manner so as not to contribute to labor problems on Mauritius and Mahe, if that is possible. We will bear this in mind as planning proceeds. We would prefer not to stimulate movement of workers from Diego Garcia to Peros Banhos and Salomon at the present moment, since we wish to meet both your desires and our 1966 commitment regarding the employment of local labor to the extent possible. We will have a clearer idea of how much employment may be feasible in March/April after Congressional review of the proposal. Accordingly, we believe that movement of workers at this time may be premature.

Yours truly,
Jonathon D. Stoddart
Chief, Politico-Military Affairs

pending closure. Todd's next visit to the islands took place during the second half of July, this being the sixth voyage in the *Nordvaer*'s first year of operation; he was accompanied by the company chairman's nephew, Marcel Moulinié, who had, since 1966, been installed as the local manager of Diego Garcia. On all three atolls, work was, once again, now being carried out on a care and mainte-nance basis.[50]

As usual, Todd's report included a population count. Numbers had declined since the previous November from 666 to 652, with Ilois predominating on Peros Banhos and Salomon, in sharp contrast to the position on Diego Garcia, which accounted for just under half the overall total. Although Todd did not refer to the point, it appears that the *Nordvaer* brought in some 90 Seychellois to replace a similar number leaving at the end of their contracts.[51] Simplifying Todd's more detailed table, the position was as follows:-

Table 23.1   Chagos population in July 1969

	Seychellois	*Mauritians*	*Ilois*	*Total*
Diego Garcia	225	1	93	319
Peros Banhos	26	4	121	151
Salomon	46	–	136	182
Total	297	5	350	652

The above totals include 11 Seychellois living *en ménage* with Iloises and 4 Ilois living *en ménage* with Seychelloises. The children of these partnerships have been assigned to the father's group of origin in the case of married couples and to the mother's in the case of natu-ral children.

Source: J.R. Todd Report of visit in July 1969.

These figures were well below London's understanding of the situation, as communicated to Washington in May 1969. 'The inhabitants of the three atolls number about 400 (D G), 250 (PB), and 200 (S) respectively. Of this total popu-lation of about 850 about 60 are Mauritians, 340 Seychellois and 450 Ilois. The latter are dual citizens of Mauritius and the UK and Colonies, some of whom have lived on the atolls for two or three generations. There are, in addition, [on Mauritian estimates] some 400 Ilois present in Mauritius.'[52] The telegram went on to explain that, as regards the Seychellois 'there should be no special problem ... as they are contract labourers recruited in Seychelles who would return to Mahé either at the end of their present contract or with appropriate contractual compensation'. As for the 'Ilois and mono-Mauritians', the government planned 'to enter into negotiations with the Mauritian government', which was pressing Britain to accept responsibility for resettling the Ilois already in the country. The telegram was issued in response to American indications that they were on the point of revealing their plans to develop Diego Garcia. This moment too passed.

The consequences of continued secrecy

More starkly than ever, the British government's ability to implement the policy it had finally settled upon was shown to be totally constrained by the US Administration's requirement to keep its intentions secret from Congress. With the approach of autumn came the next annual round of Congressional hearings and budgetary appropriations. By mid-November 1969 the Diego Garcia project had once more cleared the policy hurdles and the Administration had high hopes of obtaining, by late December, financial authority to proceed. The Administration then planned to act quickly, using a US Navy Mobile Construction Battalion ('Seabees') rather than employing civilian contract labour, which might offer openings for some Ilois. Moreover, the proposed work timetable would not allow Moulinié's employees to be given the requisite six months' notice. In communicating these developments to Todd, the FCO acknowledged the important implication that they would not allow time to negotiate compensation arrangements with Mauritius ahead of the depopulation of all three atolls.[53] Exasperated examination of ways to meet the American timetable was, however, cut short within a fortnight, by the decision of the Senate Appropriations Committee to reject funding for the Diego Garcia project in 1970.[54] There was of course no danger that the outstanding problems could be put to one side, but in mid-December Mauritius' newly-established Ministry of External affairs asked 'whether anything has yet been decided about the resettlement of the Ilois'.[55]

Production of Foodstuffs, July 1969

'So far as foodstuffs are concerned the [Diego Garcia] management at present runs a vegetable garden of about half an acre and herds of 50 pigs and 25 head of cattle. The labourers keep their own poultry and there is some citrus on the island. It would be possible to keep at least 300 head of cattle on the island and an equal number of pigs, to increase the area of gardens and build up a flock of poultry. I doubt however whether the produce would be of a standard acceptable to the Americans and we would probably find that they preferred to eat imported frozen and tinned food. This is certainly the pattern with the Americans at the Tracking Station to whom all eggs and most other items are only acceptable if they come in the super-large-giant-Emperor size.'[56]

In reporting on his visit that same month, Todd commented that the Diego Garcia vegetable garden was too small to provide vegetables for the whole population, while that on Salomon had fallen into disuse and that on Peros Banhos no longer existed; and that on none of the islands did the workers attempt to grow their own vegetables. However on Salomon, Rhode Island Red cockerels had been introduced to improve the chicken stock, while, on Diego Garcia, some promising litters had resulted from the introduction of Wessex Saddleback boars.[57]

By February 1970, the British government's thinking on resettlement had developed sufficiently to be communicated in outline to the Commissioner, ahead of a meeting in London with him and Todd, arranged for the following month.[58] The key element was that steps to depopulate the Chagos should, provided the Americans agreed, proceed without awaiting Congressional approval of the Diego Garcia project. At this point, FCO officials still entertained high hopes that many Ilois might be found employment on Moulinié's plantations in Agalega and that the Chagos could be cleared in a single operation, with the labourers moved as their contracts ended (and the Seychellois returned to Seychelles). In mid-March, following the meeting, this plan was put to the Americans.[59] It was explained that Moulinié would need to be informed that Britain could not justify spending the capital required to implement his plans for increased production in the Chagos, given the uncertainties over eventual American requirements; but the government would need to know his plans for developing Agalega, before they could initiate discussions with Mauritius. All this, London argued, would assist the Americans by reducing the possibility of delay, should they decide to go ahead in 1971.

Todd's 1970 visit

Todd visited the Chagos again in the second half of July 1970. The plantations remained as neglected as he had found them the previous year, although on Diego Garcia increased production had resulted from more intensive use of chosen areas, leaving others to become impenetrable. Overall, the amount of copra produced in the first six months of the year amounted to two-thirds of the total for 1969. Living conditions were adequate – the camps clean, food stores, hospitals and shops well supplied, but the housing was in increasingly poor condition. Only small numbers of children were attending the schools on Diego Garcia (30 out of 119) and Peros Banhos (24 out of 97), while on Salomon education had ceased in the absence of anyone competent to teach. As to population, there had been a slight increase over the year, mostly accounted for by increased numbers of Seychellois on Peros Banhos.

Table 23.2   Chagos population in July 1970

	Seychellois	Mauritians	Ilois	(inc. Children)	Total
Diego Garcia	215	1	108	(53)	324
Peros Banhos	88	3	111	(61)	202
Salomon	28	2	124	(78)	154
Total	331	6	343	(192)	680

Source: J.R. Todd, report of visit in July 1970.

Sudden acceleration

Meanwhile, the same Congressional procedures were being once more repeated. They included a secret briefing by the Administration, the record of which the British embassy inadvertently acquired. It included a brutally frank explanation of the purpose of having the British retain sovereignty over the Chagos: 'they [UK] act as a lightning rod to draw off international controversy and attention, leaving us relatively free to carry out the physical aspects of the project'. In London, officials decided that this remark would be better <u>not</u> drawn to the attention of their political masters.[60] As 1970 drew towards its end, the omens for success were much more positive. Plans were laid for consultations with interested governments and public announcements in mid-December. Suddenly, a week before the due date, the US also informed the British of the detailed programme they had in mind: in January 1971 a brief visit to Diego Garcia of a small reconnaissance party; on 10 March, arrival of a 20-strong advance party; on 20 March, the first contingent of 150 men; on 20 April, a second contingent of 200 men; and on 15 May, the third contingent of 265 men.[61] Their plan was to move all the inhabitants of the island's western limb to the eastern side in March and to have the whole population removed by July to Peros Banhos and Salomon. There followed a scramble to examine the feasibility of these plans and to ensure that Todd at least could visit Diego Garcia before the Americans arrived. As the Commissioner immediately explained, the American timetable would entail a prolonged stay on Peros Banhos and Salomon for the Ilois removed from Diego Garcia, since it would take at least a year to build the additional housing required on Agalega. Todd could however leave Seychelles on 9 January 1971 to visit and warn the islanders.[62]

At last, the end was in sight for the five years of American prevarication, British confusion, disappointment of Moulinié's commercial ambitions, damage to Britain's international relations, especially those with Mauritius, as that country emerged into independence, and, above all, the dispiriting neglect and deceit practised against the Chagos islanders. At last, the way was open to address the issue of resettlement costs, which lay behind much of the British scheming over patterns of employment in the islands and efforts to arrange for transfers of the Ilois to Agalega. The cost of the secrecy involved was very high and was to prove enduring.

Notes to Chapter 23

1 UNGA Resolution 2066 (XX) dated 16 December 1965.

2 TNA FO 371/184530 Letter dated 31 December 1965 from G.G. Arthur, Foreign Office, to H.P. Hall, Colonial Office.

3 A meticulously detailed account of this period is to be found in the Appendix to the High Court judgment of Mr Justice Ouseley in the case against the British Government on behalf of the Chagos Islanders on 9 October 2003 (HQ02X01287). This text is available at http://www.uniset.ca/naty/2003EWHC2222.htm.

4 TNA ZD 5/57 G Letter dated 12 August 1966 from J.R. Kitchen, US State Department to N.C.C. French, British Embassy, Washington. Amusingly, Vine's discussion of American thinking (*Island of Shame*, pp. 84–86) includes an account of a conversation in which, prior to a meeting with Harold Wilson, Robert McNamara explained to President Johnson how the word Aldabra was spelt.

5 UK Treaty Series (1967) No. 15 (Cmnd. 3231).

6 Sand, P.H., *United States and Britain in Diego Garcia* Palgrave Macmillan 2009. Texts of all the documents relating to the use of BIOT have very conveniently been included in this book.

7 *Ibid.* (pp. 16–17).

8 TNA FCO 32/128 Record of meeting held under chairmanship of Sir Arthur Galsworthy on 4 January 1967.

9 TNA FO 371/184530 Seychelles Telegram No. 355 dated 17 December 1965.

10 Email and telephone exchanges with NW-S in February 2016.

11 Sand, *op.cit.* (pp. 16–17).

12 J.R. Todd, born in 1929, became a Colonial Service cadet in Gambia in 1955, before being transferred to the New Hebrides in 1962. From 1966–1974 he combined the jobs of Deputy Governor of Seychelles with that of BIOT Administrator. After two years' secondment to the FCO, he spent the rest of his career in Hong Kong (1976–1988). An adaptable linguist, he became fluent in Mandinka, French, Kreol and Cantonese, as well as German (his wife was Austrian). He died in 2003.

13 Mrs Ingrid Todd, widow of John Todd, told NW-S in October 2015 of her husband's liking and respect for both Marcel and, especially, Paul Moulinié. Marcel's reciprocal liking for Todd was expressed in paragraph 10 of a draft Witness Statement prepared in 1977: 'I got on very well with John Todd, the Administrator'.

14 TNA WO 32/21295.

15 TNA FCO 32/128 (folio 11) J.R. Todd, Tour Report Chagos May 1967.

16 TNA FCO 141/1419 (folio 1) Report of Seychelles Director of Medical Services in November 1966. Its author categorised the inhabitants of Peros Banhos and Salomon, but for Diego Garcia merely remarked that its population 'is mainly Seychellois with a small number of Mauritians and Creoles des Iles'.

17 Vine (*op. cit.* p. 92) states that 'After May 1967, the BIOT Administration ordered Chagos-Agalega to prevent Chagossians … from returning to Chagos' [and, later] Moulinié & Co to 'prevent entry of anyone to BIOT without BIOT consent'. One of the files cited (FCO 31/13) does not concern Chagos at all, while the draft contract under which Moulinié operated informally, to which Vine refers without mentioning its file reference (WO 32/21295), merely provides for ceilings for the total numbers of male workers whom Moulinié could employ without reference to BIOT. Furthermore these ceilings, especially in the case of Diego Garcia, were set at levels well above the numbers actually employed at the time. As to the Ilois refused return passages by Rogers & Co in 1967, these are discussed later in this chapter (p. 487).

18 The minute difference between the figures for November 1966 and May 1967 presumably reflects a net increase resulting from births and deaths in the meanwhile.

19 TNA FCO 32/128 Sir Hugh Norman-Walker, letter of 2 October 1967.

20 Michel Vincatassin, the *chef commandeur*, who, on his forced departure from Diego Garcia in October 1971, chose to go to Mauritius, took legal action in 1975 against the British Government, resulting in an out-of-court settlement in 1982.

21 TNA FCO 32/128 Sir Hugh Norman-Walker, Despatch BIOT/SD/24 dated 4 June 1968.

22 Bandjunis, V.B., *Diego Garcia: creation of the Indian Ocean Base* Writer's Showcase, San José 2001.

23 There has been persistent speculation that the project was abandoned as a result of the vigorous opposition of British and American scientists of the Royal Society and Smithsonian Institute. Hence the myth that Aldabra's giant tortoises were judged more important than the human inhabitants of Chagos. The British government had however decided initially to disregard scientific views before later abandoning it for financial reasons, whilst for the Americans scientific opposition simply added weight to military considerations that were probably already determinant.

24 Bandjunis *op. cit.*, pp. 36–37.

25 Not surprisingly, the Mouliniés sensed and resented being kept in the dark. In a witness statement prepared for subsequent legal proceedings, Marcel Moulinié stated 'the administration of the islands and the evacuation was not carried out well. There was never any proper communication between us. My uncle's advice as to how the islands should be run and as to how the evacuation should be carried out was not taken. I felt we were not trusted.' The Mouliniés could not of course have been aware that until early in 1970 Todd and successive Commissioners had repeatedly sought authority to discuss matters in confidence with the Company, only to have their requests vetoed by London at American behest.

26 TNA WO 32/21295 (folio 185).

27 TNA FCO 141/1404 J.R. Todd *Notes on the Islands of BIOT* January 1969. 'The island shop is well stocked and supplies some simple luxury items in addition to the necessities of life. There is an increasing demand for wireless sets and guitars, which are ordered specially and only if the employee has enough savings to his credit for their purchase. The housing on the island is very poor and the general condition of the labour lines is unsatisfactory. The standard of personal and household hygiene on Peros Banhos is much lower than elsewhere in the group and can partly be attributed to the unsatisfactory living conditions.'

28 *Ibid.*

29 TNA FCO 31/401. Record of meeting held on 11 December 1968. In this report, the total of Ilois is shown as 404, manifestly a typographical error.

30 TNA FCO 141/1416 (folio 39) Letter dated 7 January 1969 from Norman-Walker to Jerrom. In the absence of fresh population statistics, Norman-Walker quoted figures supplied by Moulinié contrasting changes in the *working* populations of the three plantations between March and September 1968: Diego Garcia's was up from 221 to 232, Peros Banhos' down from 132 to 98 and Salomon's down from 100 to 91.

31 The cattle shown in this photograph are some of the 25 head introduced in September 1968. The photographer, Kirby Crawford, was leader of a small American team carrying out a geodetic survey, a project wholly unconnected with the military plans. We are far from being the only beneficiaries of Crawford's camera skills and his multi-faceted curiosity in the islanders' lives. One unique achievement is his recording of a *séga* in full swing, whose lyrics and drink-befuddled speech by the island manager have been transcribed and translated into English by our collaborator Chris Cuniah (available at www.chagos-info).

32 Grainger, C.J., 'A Retrospective Estimate of Some Vital Statistics for BIOT, 1965–1973', in *Journal of the Royal Society of Health*, October 1985 (pp. 178–183). The table reproduced in Dr. Grainger's article was compiled during a visit to BIOT by officials from the Seychelles Department of Health and contains no breakdown by origin or sex. It does however include calculations of the rates of infant mortality (98 per 1,000 live births) and death (averaging 11.6 per 1,000).

33 For example, Roger Velloo, aged 29 at the time, had left Salomon in 1969, accompanying his sick mother. He was taken in the *Nordvaer* to Seychelles and from there by the mv *Mauritius* to Port Louis. Then no direct return to the Chagos was possible. *L'Express* 1 September 1995 'Il y a 25 ans' (trans. NW-S).

34 TNA FCO 31/134 (folio 431) FCO Telegram No. BIOT 64 to Seychelles. The Mauritian document is also entered on TNA FCO 141/1416 (folio 14).

35 TNA FCO 141/1416 (folio 27) Seychelles Telegram No. BIOT 71 dated 5 November 1968. The *Mauritius* had been chartered by the American government to take supplies for the geodetic survey team. Because these included large quantities of fuel to power generators and the like, maritime regulations forbade the carrying of deck passengers. Instead, a large number of pigs were stowed on deck and deliv-

ered to Rodrigues.

36 TNA FCO 46/346 (folios 201 and 209).

37 TNA FCO 141/1416, FCO Telegram No. 423 to Port Louis dated 10 October 1968. The FCO strenu-ously (and fairly) denied that it was in any way responsible for those refused re-employment. However, when compensation eventually came to be distributed, no distinctions were made between the Ilois who had left the Chagos after 1965, whatever the circumstances.

38 TNA FCO 32/488 J.R. Todd, letter to Commonwealth Office dated 17 October 1968.

39 TNA FCO 141/1416 Seychelles Telegram No. BIOT 73 to FCO, dated 23 November 1968.

40 *Ibid.* FCO Telegram No. BIOT 63 to Seychelles dated 9 October 1968.

41 TNA FCO 46/342 (folio 3) Letter dated 18 October 1968 from Robin Johnstone to K.W. Wilford, British Embassy, Washington.

42 TNA FCO 32/488 Letter dated 22 November 1968 from Gerald Oplinger, US Embassy London, to Johnstone.

43 TNA FCO 141/1416 Letter dated 18 December 1968 from Jerrom, FCO, to Norman-Walker, Gover-nor Seychelles.

44 TNA FCO 46/343 (also on FCO 32/488) Letter dated 22 February 1969 from Jonathon D. Stoddart, US Embassy, London, to R.A. Sykes, FCO. Although some, for example Snoxell, D. R., in *Journal of Impe-rial and Commonwealth History*, 2009, have argued that the British government was principally and unnecessarily responsible for the decision to remove the populations of the northern atolls, the Ameri-cans were throughout, as the negotiating record demonstrates, consistent in making sure that the deci-sions reached, while formally Britain's, were consonant with their requirements; it would then be for the UK, not the US, to be accountable internationally for these actions.

45 TNA PREM 2565 (see also FCO 32/485).

46 TNA FCO 46/344 (folio 125) An internal FCO memorandum composed in early June 1969 con-firms this impression.

47 TNA FCO 46/344(folio 121) FCO Telegram No. 113 date 2 June 1969.

48 TNA FCO 46/346 (folio 125) Memorandum handed to US embassy, London on 13 June 1969.

49 TNA FCO 46/352 (folio 32) Seychelles Telegram No. BIOT 5 dated 21 February 1969.

50 TNA FCO 141/1416 (folio 70) Visit report by J.R. Todd dated 30 July 1969.

51 TNA FCO 46/344 Seychelles Telegram No. BIOT 19 dated 23 May 1969. No mention is made of arrivals or departures of Ilois, but Todd ascribed declining Ilois and Mauritian numbers to the absence of direct transport between Chagos and Mauritius (presumably, it was simpler for those leaving to be sure of onward transport from Mahé than for inhabitants of Port Louis to leave for Mahé without prior organised recruitment).

52 TNA FCO 46/344 (folio 109) FCO Telegram No. 1119 to Washington, dated 16 May 1969.

53 TNA FCO 46/346, letter from A.C.W. Lee dated 6 November 1969. In his reply, dated 21 November, Todd set out a scheme to provide for the removal of all the islanders during 1970, starting with the transfer of Diego Garcia's inhabitants; but, as Todd pointed out, the plan, involving transfer of many Ilois to Agalega, would be unworkable without explaining matters both to Moulinié and the Mauritians.

54 TNA FCO 46/346 Washington Telegram No. 3350 dated 3 December 1969.

55 TNA FCO 31/402 (folio 238) Port Louis letter dated 18 December 1969.

56 TNA FCO 141/1404 (folio 91) Letter dated 8 July 1969.

57 TNA FCO 141/1416 (folio 70).

58 TNA FCO 46/639 FCO Telegram No. BIOT 4 dated 18 February 1970.

59 *Ibid.* FCO Telegram No. 664 to Washington dated 20 March 1970.

60 TNA FCO 46/640 (folio 106).

61 TNA FCO 46/642 FCO Telegram No. BIOT 31 to Seychelles dated 11 December 1970.

62 TNA FCO 46/646 Seychelles Telegram No. BIOT 34 dated 14 December 1970.

24

1971–1973: The Axe Falls

FROM the start of 1971, we leave the world of policy for that of implementation. One aspect was the progressive arrival of US Naval Construction Forces, commonly known as the 'Seabees', their installation of facilities, including a substantial airfield, and their interaction with the islanders. Secondly, there was the management of the islanders' removal from Diego Garcia and, later, the other two atolls. Thirdly, the way was opened to resolve the long-suppressed problem of negotiating payment of resettlement costs for the islanders who had lost their livelihoods in the Chagos since November 1965.

The starting point

In January 1971, Todd had visited the islands once more.[1] This time the *Nordvaer*'s passengers included not only Paul Moulinié, but also the nine-strong reconnaissance party of Seabees. On 24 January, the day following their arrival at Diego Garcia, he warned the inhabitants there of the intention to close the island in July, sending as many people as possible to Peros Banhos and Salomon. A few of the Ilois asked if they might not instead return direct to Mauritius and receive some compensation for leaving their 'own country'. Todd avoided giving a direct answer by referring to transport difficulties. He and Moulinié then made brief visits to the other two atolls to consider how those removed from Diego Garcia might be accommodated, concluding that all the Ilois could be lodged without the need to cancel the contracts of any Seychellois already working there. For this purpose, his population count needed to look in detail at distribution by household. We have divided his single composite table to show population numbers for easy comparison with previous estimates and, separately, the number of families involved.

Table 24.1   Population in January 1971, distinguishing Men, Women and Children

	Diego Garcia			Peros Banhos			Salomon			Total
	M	W	C	M	W	C	M	W	C	
Seychellois	86	39	52	28	5	13	10	–	–	233
Ilois	36	27	64	27	25	75	30	22	81	387
Mauritians	3	–	–	1	2	1	1	1	–	9
Total (by island)	307			177			145			629

Source: TNA FCO 141/1417 (folio 50)

This table shows that the overall population had declined by 50 since July 1970, with a decrease of nearly 100 Seychellois being partly offset by an increase in the number of Ilois, perhaps mainly children.

Table 24.2   Number of family groups in January 1971

	Diego Garcia	Peros Banhos	Salomon	Total
Seychellois	92	28	10	130
Ilois	36	33	31	100
Mauritians	3	2	1	6

Source: as for Table 24.1

Of the Seychellois families, 42 were due to leave Diego Garcia before July on completion of their contracts, as were 4 from Peros Banhos and 5 of the single men on Salomon. In contrast, none of the 100 Ilois families were due to leave before that time (when all their contracts would have expired). Taking into account one Mauritian due to leave Diego Garcia, accommodation would need to be found for 37 families on the other two atolls, requiring some accommodation to be re-allocated, but no premature removal of any of the Seychellois working there (and providing badly-needed labour). On the other hand, it would not be economic to build additional houses on the other islands for the remainder of the Seychellois working on Diego Garcia. It would therefore be necessary to end the contracts of the 45 families concerned, at a cost of about £3,000.

Todd also considered other local costs of the manoeuvres involved, taking account of the desirability of covering as much as possible of them by continued production and drawing attention to the fact that any Ilois who wished to go to Mauritius could not be prevented from doing so. The details are unimportant, save that he envisaged payment of Rs 500 to each family transferred to the outer islands as compensation for the disturbance and loss of the possessions they were unable to take with them. This equated to twenty weeks basic pay. Finally, he sought in vain to discover from Moulinié how his plans for Agalega were developing; all that Moulinié volunteered was his willingness to provide jobs there for any Diego Garcians who expressed a wish to go there. Shortly after

Todd's visit to the islands, the BIOT Commissioner, Bruce Greatbatch, legislated for the islanders' removal by means of an Immigration Ordinance, which made it unlawful for any person (other than members of the armed forces or public servants) to enter or remain in BIOT without an official permit.[2]

Interaction of Ilois and Americans

In 2015, a full account was published of the Seabees' arrival and build-up in numbers and activities.[3] Its author, Commander Dan Urish, was the contingent's Commanding Officer and Island Commander. He sets the construction process in a wider historical and strategic context, and his illustrations of island life as experienced by both Americans and the Ilois they encountered are of particular interest. When the reconnaissance party arrived, they soon became acquainted with one of the island's oldest inhabitants: Elmour Jean-Pierre Cloridor, born there in 1903 and with memories of the visit of SMS *Emden*, for which he had gathered firewood. He was also well qualified to describe the geography and point out the traditional names for many locations, including information which we have not encountered from any other source (see map on page 503).

Elmour Cloridor with map of Diego Garcia. Image courtesy of Daniel Urish.

As mentioned in the preceding chapter (see page 495), the American plan was to begin by having all the Ilois living on the western limb of the island transferred to East Point. By 1971, there were, according to Marcel Moulinié, who carried out this operation well before the arrival of the first small Seabee contingent, only about 50 such individuals.[4]

In June, Marcel Moulinié informed Urish that some of the Ilois owners of sailing boats would be interested in selling their craft. As Urish explains,

> It was agreed that this would be a feasible purchase for qualified and responsible persons, as well as a substantial income benefit for the departing Ilois. In late June a fleet of sailing canoes arrived on our beach. The outriggers bought by various Seabees had the picturesque names of *Quincess, Onic, Flying Fish, Mondésir, Vidal, Genevieve, Melody, Malbar* and *Mares.* ... the prices ranged from $65 to $140 depending on condition ...[5]

Urish himself was one of the purchasers of the *Genevieve,* which 'handled beautifully as the wind filled its sail'. Moulinié acted as intermediary between sellers and buyers, ensuring that the prices paid were fair.

Ilois outrigger canoes on Seabee beach. Image courtesy of Larry Sellers.

Meanwhile the Seabees were busying themselves in the construction of living quarters and assembling the industrial equipment for production of fresh water, cement, coral rock and the other materials needed for the major project of building a runway 5,500 feet long (including over-runs). The latter received its first C-130 aircraft on 19 July. Shortly before, on 29 June, without warning, a flight of Sea Vixen fighter planes had roared low over the island, surprising the Americans and frightening the islanders. They were followed immediately by a helicopter, whose pilot handed Urish a bottle of Scotch whisky, accompanied by a

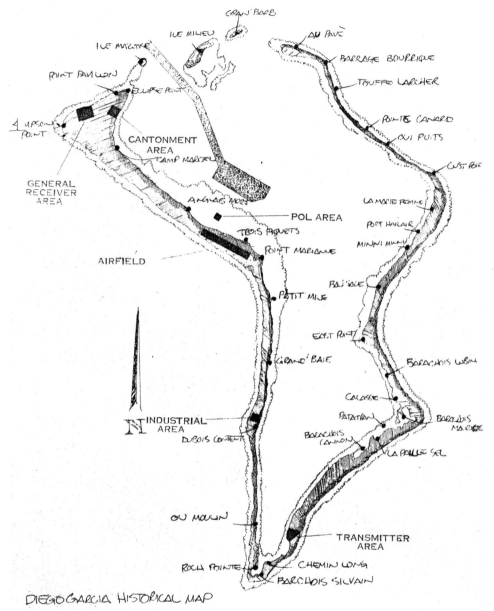

GRAN' BARB

ILE MILIEU

AU PAVÉ

BARRAGE BOURRIQUE

ILE MAGUERE

POINT PAVILLON

ECLIPSE POINT

TOUFFE LARCHER

POINTE CANARD

UPSEN POINT

OUI PUITS

CANTONMENT AREA

CAMP MAREE

CUST BOIS

GENERAL RECEIVER AREA

LA MORTE FEMME

ANGLAIS NOIR

POL AREA

POST HALLAIR

TROIS PAQUETS

MINNI MINNI

POINT MARIANNE

AIRFIELD

BOIS SECE

PETIT MILE

EAST POINT

GRAND' BAIE

BARACHOIS WBIN

CALASSE

N INDUSTRIAL AREA

PATATRAN

BARACHOIS MARICE

DUBOIS CONTENT

BARACHOIS CANNON

LA PAILLE SEL

OU MOULIN

TRANSMITTER AREA

ROCH POINTE

CHEMIN LONG

BARACHOIS SILVAIN

DIEGO GARCIA HISTORICAL MAP

RECORDED BY USIG GRANT IN INTERVIEW WITH MR ELMOUR JEAN PIERRE CLOPINOR, A MAN BORN ON DIEGO GARCIA ON 21 APRIL 1903

Traditional landmarks of Diego Garcia. Image courtesy of Daniel Urish.

From left, LCDR Rau, M. Moulinié, Lt. Col. McNamara, CDR Urish.
Image courtesy of Daniel Urish.

friendly note from the Admiral aboard the British aircraft carrier, HMS *Eagle*, on passage from the Cape to Singapore. The checks we have made confirm that these flights were of 'no operational importance'.[6]

As Urish recounts,[7] the Americans also became involved in providing various forms of practical assistance to the islanders. The need for this arose from what proved to be a three-month delay in closing down the plantations beyond the planned date of 15 July. This was caused by breakdowns of the *Nordvaer* and resulted in shortages of supplies. Expanding on the details given in his book, Urish adds, 'Much of this support fell by default to me. In addition to continuing medical and dental support, and the visit of a priest in August, we provided fresh water and a continuing supply of food. Following is a listing of these support items from my notes:

Milk. pint per 2 persons/day. More milk on Fridays.
Tea. 100 pounds.
Flour. 700 pounds per month.
Salve (medical) for horse.
Soda and ice for Prosper.
Prosper wants 2 dozen type D batteries.

[Willis] Prosper was Marcel's assistant manager with whom I coordinated when Marcel [Moulinié] was off island. I am sure there was more plantation support that I did not know of or record. In general, if Marcel or Prosper said they needed something, we tried to supply it. Certainly, we continued to provide whatever we could to sustain them as they awaited transportation off the island.'[8]

Urish goes on to describe the disposal of animals which the islanders were forced to leave behind, recording that Greatbatch had instructed Moulinié to ship as many as possible of the island's (eight) feral horses and to have the island's dogs destroyed. As Urish recalls the issue,

> The hundreds of dogs could not be taken to another location nor could they be allowed to remain to revert to a wild state, so had to be disposed of by the plantation manager by one means or another before the plantation was closed. Shooting was dangerous and imprecise with the possibility of only wounding; poisoning would be traumatic to those seeing the effect, as well as dangerous. Hence a 'sleeping death' by carbon monoxide appeared the most humane and practical way for all concerned. At the request of the plantation manager, Navy trucks were provided to pump their exhaust fumes into a confining copra drying shed enclosure for the purpose.[9]

Moulinié himself, in a signed witness statement made in 1999, largely confirmed this account, explaining that, as the population declined from 1968 onwards, it had become common for families to have four or five dogs each, with an increasing problem of stray animals. By the time the Seabees arrived the total number of dogs exceeded 800. Ordered by the Commissioner to destroy them, he

> first tried to shoot the dogs, using US sharpshooters armed with M 16s. If confronted with a hungry pack of dogs, it was often possible to shoot two or three of them, but the rest ran away into the jungle of overgrown plantation. I then experimented by poisoning dog meat with strychnine, but the animals which took this poison suffered so horribly I had to shoot them … I therefore had to find a method of large scale extermination, and hit upon the idea of gassing them in the *calorifère*. This is a small building in which copra is dried by burning husks on the shelf below.[10]

This slaughter took place, according to his testimony, shortly before the last group of Ilois departed, that is, in early October. Recently, Moulinié gave us some additional details.[11] It appears that he discussed his distasteful task with LCDR Don Cline, the US Navy communications officer attached to the Seabee contingent, who provided carpenters to block all the air intakes to the *calorifère*. The main door was left open and meat used to familiarise the animals with this new source of food. Finally, in batches, the dogs were locked in and killed. As Moulinié recalls, their corpses were not burnt, but buried in large pits. Moulinié thus suggests greater American involvement than Urish records. This difference of evidence is however, a great deal less significant than it may appear. Both parties were seeking the most humane way to accomplish an unpleasant, but

sv *Isle of Farquhar* at East Point jetty. Drawing by kind permission of Daniel Urish.

inescapable task. According to Moulinié, the import of dogs into Mauritius from the islands had never been permitted, on account of the potential spread of disease.

Expulsions

Delayed by technical problems, the plan to remove the Ilois from Diego Garcia was not put into effect until 1 August. Following the breakdown of the *Nordvaer* during her first visit to Peros Banhos, Paul Moulinié dispatched his own auxiliary schooner *Isle of Farquhar*, which in late August transferred most of the remaining Ilois inhabitants to the northern atolls. The *Nordvaer*, after being repaired at the Kenyan port of Mombasa, returned to Diego Garcia in mid-September to bring back many Seychellois, and to bring eight Ilois employees and their dependants to Seychelles; the latter, who had exercised their right to be returned to Mauritius, reached Victoria on 30 September and left for Port Louis on 8 October. This group consisted of seven men, six women and twelve children.[12] In addition, five members of Marcel Moulinié's management staff returned by this sailing; they do not appear to have been included in any list of potential claimants for resettlement expenses.[13] The *Isle of Farquhar* remained in the Archipelago. On 14 October she removed Marcel Moulinié and the 50 remaining Ilois from Diego Garcia, calling at the northern atolls before leaving the Archipelago for Seychelles on 31 October. The vessel then revisited Salomon and Peros Banhos, to deliver stores and return with copra. When this series of movements was completed, the combined population of Peros Banhos and Salomon (including those transferred from Diego Garcia) amounted to 332, comprising 65 men, 70 women and 197 children.[14]

Urish records that he took an official contingent of US Navy personnel to East Point for a ceremonial lowering of the Union Jack on the evening of 6 October, after which he dined with Moulinié. Next day, the flag was hoisted again, alongside the Stars and Stripes, at the emerging American establishment. For two months there were only US military personnel on Diego Garcia, until the arrival of Lt. Cdr. John Canter DSC on 12 December 1971. This officer was to be the symbol of British sovereignty and to provide local liaison between the Americans on Diego Garcia and the UK. Having no means of transport he had no role in respect of the other atolls or the Ilois.

Numbers affected, numbers expelled

Efforts to refine the calculation of the numbers of people in Mauritius having long-term connections with the Chagos, whether or not these were inter-generational, are unlikely to yield a precise result. However, in December 1971, the Mauritian Government presented a full list of the Ilois settled in Mauritius and known to have come from the Chagos since 1965.[15] Converted to tabular format (overleaf), the list provides valuable information about their years of arrival and islands of origin. By adding those discussed above, say 400, to the total given in Table 24.3, a round figure of 1550 would fairly describe the total of Ilois directly affected by the events from 1965 onwards which ended in closure. What proportion of the reduction should be ascribed directly to British governmental action

Table 24.3   Arrivals in Mauritius from Chagos 1965–1971

	1965	1966	1967	1968	1969	1970	1971	Other	Total
Diego Garcia									
Men	16	15	39	17	1	2	7	–	97
Women	16	12	38	24	–	1	6	–	97
Children	50	36	124	73	–	3	8	–	294
Sub-Total	82	63	201	114	1	6	21	–	488
Peros Banhos									
Men	16	13	51	16	1	–	–	–	97
Women	16	21	36	21	–	–	–	–	94
Children	47	64	98	56	3	–	–	–	268
Sub-Total	79	98	185	93	4	–	–	–	459
Salomon									
Men	3	6	8	14	2	–	1	–	34
Women	6	10	8	15	2	–	1	–	42
Children	30	29	25	46	10	–	7	–	147
Sub-Total	39	45	41	75	14	–	9	–	223
TOTAL	200	206	427	282	19	6	30	–	1170

Source: TNA FCO 31/915 folio 80.

Note. All the totals provided in the Mauritian government document (see also TNA FCO 141/1416, folio 14) have been accepted. However, in a few cases, notably one involving a couple with ten children, there was double counting. It also appears that most of the 25 individuals who exercised their right to be taken to Mauritius from Diego Garcia (see page 507) included the 21 shown above as having left the island in 1971.

is debatable. As discussed in preceding chapters, the post-war drift from the islands was accelerated by the rapid decline of Diego Ltd. in the later 1950s and the takeover by Chagos Agalega Ltd. in 1961–62. The determination of Paul Moulinié to improve productivity by replacing Ilois with Seychellois labour gave further impetus to this trend (the creation of BIOT in November 1965 could not, for example, have accounted for any of the continued reduction of the Ilois population of the Chagos during that year). The uncertainty and neglect of 1966, during which Moulinié let contracts expire as they reached their term, was followed, once his lease was signed in 1967, by his return to the active substitution of Seychellois for Ilois workers, for purely commercial reasons. In 1968, when the opportunity for renewed employment of Ilois arose, it was impeded, if unintentionally, by the action of the Mauritius Government in removing the shipping subsidy for voyages to the Chagos (see page 487). On the other hand, had there been no plans for militarisation, Moulinié might have needed both Ilois and increased Seychellois labour to implement his plans for a major increase in the production from Diego Garcia.

Only in 1969 did the British government accept that, in addition to Diego Garcia, the plantations of the two northern atolls would need to be closed. Strikingly, as Table 24.3 shows, there then followed almost three years of stability, before any deliberate removal of Ilois from the Chagos occurred, justifying the term 'expulsion'.[16] Indeed, as Peter Sand has pointed out, only in April 1971 were powers taken to permit such action.[17] It was, of course, British policy to minimise its exposure to eventual claims for compensation from both Moulinié and Mauritius (readers have been spared details of the relentless correspondence between the British Treasury and the spending departments concerned). However, any assumption that, in the absence of policy deriving from the militarisation of the Chagos, Ilois employment by a Seychelles-owned company would have returned to the levels obtaining prior to its Mauritian predecessor's financial collapse must remain speculative. Both in Agalega and in the outer Seychelles islands copra production and population levels were to decline rapidly. Last but not least, those declines were not simply local, but part of a worldwide trend towards substitution of coconut by other vegetable oils, especially (as vividly demonstrated by Table 24.4 below) palm oil.[18]

The Agalega 'option'

As soon as BIOT had been brought into existence in November 1965, officials had turned their minds to what appeared to be the immediate practical problems ('which should not be serious') requiring attention: staffing of the new entity and contingency planning for evacuation of Diego Garcia. Replying to the FCO's instruction to make such plans, Lord Oxford and Asquith, the High Commissioner to Seychelles, responded by pointing out that nothing practical could be done without Paul Moulinié's co-operation, for which progress in

Table 24.4 Comparison of world palm oil and coconut oil production, 1965–2004.

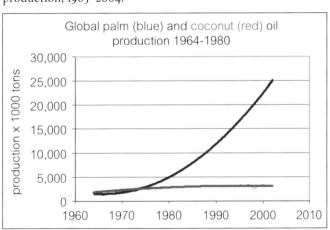

arranging his compensation would be a prior requirement. It was evident from this exchange that evacuation to Agalega was the solution all three parties had in mind.[19] Seen from Whitehall, its advantages were obvious. The island was owned by Moulinié, with transport arrangements in place, and other Ilois inhabitants already present, with similar lifestyles and working practices; moreover, the island was a Mauritian dependency, but not, as was Mauritius itself, suffering from severe unemployment. Moulinié, however, had more to consider than British convenience.

So long as resettlement of the Chagos Ilois remained a potential problem, there was no need for the British to press Moulinié to commit himself to accepting specific numbers; in any case constraints on discussion of the evacuation of Diego Garcia inhibited exploration of what might be possible on Agalega. In early 1970, however, when the British decided that they ought to talk to Moulinié without waiting for completion of procedures in Congress (see page 494), the Americans agreed that they might do so 'in the context of the declining viability of the Chagos copra plantations'.[20] One immediate complication was that Agalega had twice been struck by cyclones in the preceding weeks, causing the company to delay plans for expansion, until the island had been rehabilitated by the existing labour force.[21] No additional labour would be needed for 6–8 years. In further discussion with Moulinié's directors, it became clear that only half of the Chagos Ilois could be found work in Agalega and then only if they were to replace all of the Seychellois already there – a move that would be highly unwelcome to Moulinié and unacceptable to public opinion in Seychelles.[22] In some desperation, the FCO sought ways of encouraging Moulinié to accept those to be removed from the Chagos, by the provision of technical assistance and the offer of money to build additional accommodation, but to little avail. Moulinié himself sensed political opposition in Mauritius to his occupation of Agalega and feared that he might find himself landed with responsibility for the cost of eventual resettlement of the Chagos Ilois in Mauritius. All he would agree to was to continue to recruit labour from Mauritius, including Ilois being resettled there from the Chagos. In the end, as mentioned in our preceding chapter (see page 487) he tried to recruit 50 Ilois families for Agalega, but attracted only fourteen.[23]

With hindsight, it is easy to criticise the British officials involved for supposing that employment in Agalega could dispose of the problem of resettling the Ilois and avoiding the costs which that would entail. The fact was that Paul Moulinié was absent from Seychelles for months at a time, as he sought ways of building a profitable business from the plantations remaining in his possession after the excision of BIOT, with increased copra output not being the only option for Agalega (for example, he examined joint development of tourism with South African interests). His main concern, however, was with political obstruction from Mauritius. In November 1971, he told Greatbatch that he had changed his mind about a scheme to resettle Agalega jointly with the Mauritius Government.[24] Soon afterwards, Moulinié's business partner in Mauritius, René Maingard, informed the British High Commissioner in Port Louis that Moulinié was contemplating the sale of his Agalega freehold rather than developing the island in partnership with the Mauritius Government, 'which he distrusted'.[25] At the same time, as with his earlier manoeuvres in relation to his plans for the Chagos, he needed to present an optimistic front about the potential profitability of Agalega. Thus, when Mauritius, only a few years later (October 1975), bought him out (in response to strong domestic political pressure), Moulinié once again made, it seems, a handsome capital gain. However, he was not able to enjoy his prosperity in Seychelles, where, following his coup, President Albert René, confiscated many of his assets, leading Moulinié to leave for good and join his daughter and her family in the US, where he died in 1991.

Fulfilling the British commitment

From the start, that is, at the meeting between Greenwood and Ramgoolam in September 1965,[26] it had been agreed that the £3 million compensation for the excision of the Chagos from Mauritius would be 'over and above the direct compensation to landowners and the cost of resettling others affected in Chagos islands …', the last phrase being defined as 'persons necessarily removed from one or other of the islands because of defence facilities thereon'. Ramgoolam himself had repeated this commitment without the qualifying phrases. When, in 1969, Michael Stewart, then Foreign and Commonwealth Secretary, warned him in confidence of the possible development of Diego Garcia and a consequent need to displace Mauritians working in Chagos, Ramgoolam's 'only comment was that all this had been envisaged at the time of the 1966 Agreement. He agreed that we should talk about the workers when the time came'.[27]

It was not until March 1971 that the British High Commissioner to Mauritius was instructed to explain to Ramgoolam what his government had in mind. This was that Britain would now accept the full cost of resettling both those still in the Chagos and those Mauritians/Ilois (estimated at about 100 families) who had moved to Mauritius since December 1965; but that discussions would be needed to decide upon and cost a suitable resettlement plan. An expert could be made available to assist in this process. Britain also hoped that some of the Ilois might be found employment on Agalega.[28] At a meeting on 29 March, Ramgoolam did not dissent from the approach outlined, which he planned to discuss with British Ministers, when he visited London in the first week of May. The outcome was that a British agricultural expert was dispatched to examine ideas for developing Agalega and also to investigate Ramgoolam's proposal that a coconut industry be established in Mauritius. Prior to Ramgoolam's departure, British officials discussed Mauritian thinking with the Minister of Finance, Veerasamy Ringadoo, and others on 3 May. It emerged that the Economic Planning Unit had been investigating an idea to employ the Ilois to clear the small islands around the coast to prepare them for tourist ventures. The Minister however favoured 'a pig breeding and rearing project specifically for the Ilois', which could be established in Roche Bois where land was cheap, to be run 'on co-operative lines'.[29]

When Ramgoolam visited London, he held meetings with three British Ministers and only at his meeting with Lord Lothian, a junior FCO Minister, did the Chagos resettlement issue arise, on the latter's initiative. For Ramgoolam, other issues, notably Mauritian access to the European sugar market and security assistance, were much more important. No mention was made of Ringadoo's idea, but Ramgoolam agreed that opportunities for work on Agalega could continue to be explored for Ilois interested in taking them up. He himself thought that 'severance pay' would also be required under Mauritian law. Lothian conceded that this 'might be looked into'.[30] Ramgoolam visited London twice more in 1971. In mid-September, he discussed only the security risks arising from recent strikes and demonstrations, while on 1 December he made no mention of Chagos in a meeting with the Prime Minister, but discussed it inconclusively with Lord Lothian the following day: he claimed to believe that the British High Commissioner in Port Louis (Peter Carter) now agreed that there should be lump sum payments to the Ilois, which should incorporate severance payments; but he declined to commit himself to considering such payments as discharging Britain's obligation to bear the costs of resettlement. It was left that discussions would continue in Port Louis.[31]

These discussions had in fact been given a sharp impetus by the arrival in mid-October of the *Nordvaer*, carrying the 30 Ilois and Mauritians mentioned above (page 507). While the arrival of these passengers was not totally unexpected, its exploitation by Opposition politicians required Ramgoolam to make an early parliamentary statement to calm matters.[32] Behind the scenes, work continued both to establish how many claimants there might be and to consider specific proposals. The first sign of real progress was the provision in December of the detailed list of people (summarised on page 508 above) who had returned from the Chagos since the start of 1965. Early in January 1972, the High Commission reported the establishment of a Cabinet Sub-Committee to consider the alternatives.[33]

A month later, the High Commissioner reported the gist of the Sub-Committee's conclusions, ahead of a further visit to London by Ramgoolam. On the basis of consultations with Ilois family heads representing the great majority of the Ilois already in Mauritius it was proposed that two housing estates should be constructed. On each, a pig-breeding scheme should go ahead, supplemented by grants to heads of household to finance agricultural activity on the plots attached to each house. Higher cash payments would be made to families not willing to participate in the scheme. The overall cost, including reimbursement of social security payments already made, was calculated at Rs 8,558,000 (£642,000). This plan was endorsed by the Mauritian cabinet. When he met Lord Lothian on 23 February, Ramgoolam strongly urged its acceptance and Ringadoo handed over a copy of the Sub-committee's report containing it.[34] There followed three months of official deliberations in London in which quibbles about the technical soundness of the scheme and the problem of funding over-commitment of the £10 million originally authorised by the Treasury were set against the political arguments for agreeing at modest cost to discharge the commitment made to Mauritius in 1965 in the way favoured by the Mauritian Government itself. The latter finally won the day in time for Ramgoolam's next visit to London, where he met Lothian's successor, Lady Tweedsmuir, on 23 June and was given the news he sought. On 24 June a telegram was dispatched stating that the government would pay Mauritius £650,000 as being the estimated cost of its scheme for resettling those displaced from the Chagos since November 1965, provided that the Mauritius Government accepted the payment as full and final discharge of the undertaking given on 23 September 1965.[35] Ramgoolam replied personally on 4 September[36] and, as he requested, a cheque for the required amount was paid into the Mauritius Government's London account.

The last days

By mid-1972, while terms of compensation to be paid to Mauritius for resettlement of the displaced islanders were still under discussion, a further 53 islanders had returned to Mauritius,[37] with a much larger number following in early November (120 (*sic* – misprint for 128?), comprising 73 adults and 55 children).[38] By this time, all those remaining on Salomon had been transferred to Peros Banhos. In April 1973 the *Nordvaer* made a further voyage, taking 133 islanders (26 men, 27 women and 80 children) direct to Mauritius.[39] The ship's final voyage to the Chagos took place a month later. This time the *Nordvaer* travelled to Mauritius via Seychelles, with the last 46 islanders (8 men, 9 women and 29 children).[40] The number of Ilois evacuated from 1971 onwards thus totalled 377 (or perhaps 385), slightly fewer than the number present in January 1971.[41] Thus ended organised civil utilisation of the whole archipelago.[42]

Notes to Chapter 24

1   TNA FCO 141/1417 (folio 50), Letter from J.R. Todd dated 17 February 1971.

2   BIOT Immigration Ordinance, dated 16 April 1971.

3   Urish, Daniel W., *Coral, Copra and Concrete* 2015, Donning Co., Virginia Beach, VA .

4   Personal communication on 17 November 2015. Given the steadily reducing population of the island, the statement by Seewoo-Sankar Mandary (witness statement dated 21February 2005) that 'hundreds of people lived in these villages' is implausible.

5   Urish, D.W., *op. cit.* p. 68.

6   Fleet Air Arm Museum letter RRC2009/220 to NW-S, dated 7 July 2009.

7   Urish, D.W., *op. cit.*, p. 72 and associated Notes.

8   Personal Communication, Dan Urish , email dated 16 November 2015.

9   Urish, *op cit.*, p. 216.

10   Marcel Moulinié, draft witness statement (undated) 1977, as expanded in statement signed and dated 22 November 1999.

11   Telephone conversation NW-S/Marcel Moulinié 27 November 2015.

12   TNA FCO 31/915. Their stopover in Port Victoria occasioned highly-coloured press accounts of their having been cast into prison. They were in fact (Seychelles telegram No. BIOT 57 dated 21 October 1971, folio 41)'accommodated in an unused modern prison building completely separate from the main prison building and were supplied with cooked food whilst there'.

13   TNA FCO 31/915 (folio 41) Seychelles telegram BIOT 57 dated 21 October 1971.

14   TNA FCO 141/1417 Seychelles telegram BIOT 56 dated 21 October 1971. See also Court document (2003) 7–1203. Some of the material for this chapter has been obtained from the amended chronology supplied to the High Court for hearing of the Chagos Islanders Group Litigation (Claim No. HQ02X012870) before Justice Ouseley in October 2003. Access to the documents cited, except where they are to be found in the publicly available files at The National Archives, was not available; no document providing concordance between those files and the numbering system of the court documents is available, therefore, except where (as in this case) the material itself provides a firm connection, only the court reference – to bundles and the page number within them – is given.

15   TNA FCO 31/915 Letter from R.G. Giddens, Port Louis, dated 10 December 1971.

16   This question was debated in some detail in two papers published in 2012. In an article in *Chagos News* (No. 39), Wenban-Smith, N., discussed the 'Population of the Chagos Archipelago, 1820–1973'. In this article, he argued that 'some 500 [Ilois and Mauritians] might have lost their livelihoods and homes in the 1971–1973 expulsions', but that there could be 'confusion between the numbers of those expelled and the numbers who qualified for payments under terms subsequently negotiated between the parties concerned; however the latter figure, being based on links of birth and descent, not actual removal, [was] bound to have been a much larger one.' In response to this article, a paper by Gifford, R., and Dunne, R., 'A Dispossessed People: the Depopulation of the Chagos Archipelago 1965–1973' was published in the journal *Population, Space and Place*, Wiley Online Library, October 2012. This maintained that 'the British Government itself accepted in 1972 at the time of the deportations that at least 1,483 Ilois were affected'. The *Chagos News* article was wrong to claim that the agreement to pay resettlement costs was based on 'birth and descent' as opposed to the closure of the islands. As the present narrative describes, the British Government's commitment, which it honoured in 1972, was that made in 1965. A fresh calculation of the total numbers involved shows that up to 1150 were 'affected', with up to 400 more actually 'expelled'.

17   Sand, P.H., 'The Chagos Archipelago Cases: Nature Conservation Between Human Rights and Power Politics' *Global Community Yearbook of International Law and Jurisprudence* 2013, Oxford University Press.

18   Data from US Department of Agriculture. Since 2004, palm oil production has more than doubled further to 63.3 million tons, while coconut oil production remains at roughly previous levels (data also from USDA). Relevant internet references are:

http://chagos-trust.org/sites/default/files/images/Card_010_A4%20Coconuts%20and%20the%20
Oil%20Islands%2022%20%20Oct%2007.pdf

Current Palm oil production:
http://pecad.fas.usda.gov/highlights/2014/09/SEAsia/index.htm

Current coconut oil production:
http://www.ers.usda.gov/data-products/oil-crops-yearbook.aspx.

19 TNA CO 1036/1342 CO telegrams Nos. 373 and 398, dated 12 and 27 November 1965; Seychelles telegram No. 324 dated 19 November 1965.

20 TNA FCO 32/725 (folio 29), FCO telegram BIOT 5 to Seychelles dated 3 April 1970.

21 *Ibid.* Folio 25, letter from Todd to FCO dated 24 March 1970.

22 TNA FCO 46/640 (folio 87), letter dated 14 May 1970 to FCO. This letter also provides basic details of the numbers involved. The working population of Agalega was then about 200 men and women, half of them Seychellois and the other half Ilois.

23 The consideration of resettlement of Ilois in Agalega is here recorded in a rather summary fashion, since it proved to be a dead end. However, the idea generated a good number of documents, to be found mainly in the following files in TNA: FCO 31/915, FCO 31/1246, FCO 32/725, FCO 46/640, FCO 46/641 and FCO 141/1417. It is puzzling that so few Ilois took up the offer of employment in Agalega. One possibility is that they may have been reluctant to work for Harold Pouponneau, the unpopular manager of Diego Garcia, who had been transferred to Agalega in 1966.

24 TNA FCO 31/1246 (folio 201), Seychelles telegram BIOT 59, dated 12 November 1971.

25 TNA FCO 31/1222 Letter dated 23 February 1972 from P.A. Carter to FCO.

26 TNA FCO 141/1416 FCO telegram No. 423 to Port Loius dated 10 October 1968.

27 TNA FCO 31/402 (folio 183) FCO telegram No. 1519 to Washington dated 4 July 1969.

28 TNA FCO 31/915 (folio 2) Letter dated 12 March 1971 from Ian Watt to P.A. Carter.

29 TNA FCO 31/915 (folio 9) Internal minute from K.A. Woolverton dated 3 May 1971.

30 TNA FCO 31/920 Meeting record dated 13 May 1971 (folio 46. Other ministerial meetings recorded at folios 33 and 44).

31 TNA FCO 31/920 Meeting records (folios 59 and 69) and TNA FCO 31/915 Instructions to High Commissioner by FCO telegram No. 476 dated 2 December 1971 (folio 77).

32 TNA FCO 31/915 (folio 480) Port Louis telegram No. 431 dated 27 October 1971.

33 TNA FCO 31/1246 (folio 2) Port Louis telegram No. 11 dated 12 January 1972.

34 TNA FCO 31/1246 (folio 12).

35 TNA FCO 31/1247 (folios 57 and 58), FCO telegrams Nos. 318 and 319 dated 24 June 1972.

36 TNA FCO 31/1247 Letter dated 4 September 1972 from Sir S. Ramgoolam to British High Commissioner.

37 Court document (2003) 8–1334.

38 Court documents (2003) 8–1343 and 8–1516.

39 Court documents (2003) 8–1357 and 7–1178.

40 Court documents (2003) 8–1360 and 7–1180.

41 No account has been taken of the births and deaths that must have occurred during the period in question.

42 TNA FCO 141/1418 The names of the passengers taken by the *Nordvaer* on the voyages in 1972 and 1973 were later provided by Paul Moulinié, but much of this material was sent by facsimile, which is now barely decipherable.

Epilogue

THE history of the Chagos did not of course come to an end in 1973. On the contrary, the islands and their surrounding seas have been involved in much activity. They have also been the subject of increasingly animated and still unresolved debates. While we may attempt to provide a sketch of some of the themes of these debates, we consider it premature to attempt any general conspectus worthy of being called history. Apart from other considerations, many, perhaps most of the relevant official records have yet to be disclosed. On the other hand, the public interest which the Archipelago has attracted contrasts strongly with the neglect in which it languished in previous centuries; a mass of material is accumulating from which a complex historical account will surely emerge.

One principal theme has focused on the islands' dispossessed workers, their families and their descendants. It was not until the late 1960s that they began to be recognised as a distinct community and only in the late 1990s that they came to adopt the name 'Chagossian' to underscore their unique position as an exiled community among other disadvantaged groups. The Mauritian society into which many were thrust was in the throes of adaptation to its newly-achieved independence, with the Hindu-dominated leadership eager to assert its hegemony over the Franco-Creole groups who had, by and large, opposed independence. The latter had, however, retained a good deal of financial and commercial power and (of particular relevance to the islanders) were seen as the main beneficiaries of the exploitation of the Oil Islands.[1]

A second major theme has been the development of the US base on Diego Garcia. While this was readily foreseeable, the extent and variety of its operational use has probably exceeded all expectations, eclipsing anything experienced in the island's previous history.[2] However, no other BIOT island has been used for military purposes and indeed the islands detached from Seychelles were re-incorporated at the time of that colony's independence in 1976. BIOT now consists solely of the 55 islets of the Chagos Archipelago. All except Diego Garcia have been abandoned to Nature. Almost all the previous man-made structures have collapsed, while the plantation areas have been overtaken by a near-impenetrable jungle of palms and undergrowth.

Another theme has been the resumption since the mid-1970s of scientific interest in the Archipelago's ecology. From small beginnings, scientific under-standing of the ecological vulnerability of the atolls and their associated marine life has grown in parallel with the exponential loss of such habitats in all of the world's oceans. During the same period of time, the gradual warming of the Earth's climate – barely recognised in the 1960s – has begun to threaten the sustainability of human life on low-lying islands, most acutely in the Pacific, but discernibly too in the Indian Ocean. A measurable increase in the acidity of seawater presents a risk to all life forms having limestone skeletons, not least corals. Now, the Chagos reefs rank among the best preserved in the world, pro-viding a standard against which degradation elsewhere can be measured.[3]

These developments have been both linked to and further complicated by legal challenges to the establishment of BIOT and subsequent actions by the British authorities. The challenges range from the assertion of sovereignty over the Chagos by successive post-independence Mauritian administrations to a series of individual and group claims by Chagossians for additional compensa-tion for the loss of their livelihood. Other specific challenges question the right of the British Government to exclude former inhabitants of the Chagos from the islands and its authority to legislate unilaterally to prevent fishing in BIOT's ter-ritorial waters. To these diplomatic and legal challenges must be added domestic political challenge within the UK by the emergence of an active All-Party Parlia-mentary Group. This has increasingly concentrated its critique of the policies of successive administrations on the perceived inadequacy of investigation of the scope for resettlement of the Chagos.[4]

As this book goes to press, important decisions are awaited from the British Supreme Court and the British Government, while diplomatic negotiations are also in progress between the United States and United Kingdom concerning the possible adjustment of the terms of their 1966 Agreement. We do not seek to enter any aspect of these ongoing debates. We do, however, hope that the account we have sought to provide of the historical background to the bleak situation of today's Chagossian community will encourage the governments concerned to work together more amicably for their future well-being and development and inspire Chagossians to learn more about their own history.

Notes to the Epilogue

1 An excellent starting point for examination of the deep-seated communal differences in Mauritius would be a despatch written by the then-Colony's Governor, Sir Donald Mackenzie, in 1944. 'Hard-hitting' is a mild description of its contents. No segment of the population, including his own Administration, is spared scathing criticism. Mackenzie nevertheless strikes an optimistic note concerning the prospects for change, placing his hopes on 'one or two far-sighted Franco-Mauritians of sterling worth' and, in the Administration, 'a few outstanding British and Mauritian officers' (TNA CO 167/924/12). These underlying issues scarcely receive mention in modern writings about the Chagos. A partial exception is Jean Claude de l'Estrac's *Next Year in Diego Garcia*. As a former Foreign Minister, de l'Estrac naturally espouses the official Mauritian view of events, playing down Ramgoolam's role and ignoring his strategic viewpoint; but he writes with admirable clarity (de l'Estrac, J.C., *L'an prochain à Diego Garcia*, ELP Publications, Mauritius 2011; also available in English translation, by Touria Prayag, ISBN-978-99949-1-065-6). The structure and particular problems of the Creole population of Mauritius, including its Chagossian component, are the subject of an outstanding study by Rosabelle Boswell (Boswell, R., *Le Malaise Créole: ethnic identity in Mauritius*, Berghahn Books, 2006). Concerning the experiences of the Chagos islanders in Mauritius, the most useful discussion is to be found in Laura Jeffery's *Chagos Islanders in Mauritius and the UK* (Manchester University Press, 2011) and in a collection of essays of varying quality, edited by Sandra Evers and Marry Kooy (*Eviction from the Chagos Islands: displacement and the struggle for identity*, Brill, Leiden and Boston, 2011).

2 A brief –and perhaps only – account of the military development and usage of Diego Garcia is contained in Richard Edis's *Peak of Limuria* (2004 edition, published by Chagos Conservation Trust). However, online searches may enable those interested to acquire more detailed and more up-to-date information, as well as voluminous polemic.

3 As one of the outstanding global concerns, climatic change and its impact have attracted a vast literature. As regards scientific investigation of the Chagos, *Ecology of the Chagos Archipelago*, edited by Charles Sheppard and Mark Seaward (Linnean Society, 1999) is the essential starting point, now supplemented by an ever-expanding accumulation of reports in *Chagos News* (the online journal of the Chagos Conservation Trust, at www.chagos-trust.org).

4 There have been at least nine cases in the superior courts of Britain, Europe and the US, spawning huge volumes of evidential material and legal opinion. A very good point of access to this material, explaining the issues involved and the decisions reached, is to be found in a published essay by Ted Morris, Jr. (*A Brief History of the Ilois Experience*, Stalking Flamingo Productions, Galoot, New Mexico, 2013). The All-Party Parliamentary Group – Chagos Islands (BIOT) sponsors debates and stimulates parliamentary questioning of the government of the day, records of which are to be found in the official record (Hansard), which can be accessed online via the UK Parliament's website. The Group's pressure was largely responsible for the commissioning of a new study of the feasibility of resettling the Chagos islands. This was undertaken by the independent consulting group, KPMG, which reported in 2015. At the time of writing, the government's response is still awaited.

List of Tables

List of Acronyms and Abbreviations

Adm.	Admiral	Govt.	Government
ADM	Admiralty file series	ha	hectares
ADR	Archives Départmentales de la Réunion	HMAS	His/Her Majesty's Australian Ship
AFB	Advanced Forward Base	HMIS	His/Her Majesty's Indian Ship
AFC	Air Force Cross	HMS	His/Her Majesty's Ship
AN	Archives Nationales (French)	HMSO	His/Her Majesty's Stationery Office
ANOM	Archives Nationales d'Outre Mer (French colonial records)	Ibid.	Ibidem (to be found in the same work)
BIOT	British Indian Ocean Territory	IOR	India Office Records
C-in-C	Commander-in-Chief	kg	kilograms
Capt.	Captain	km	kilometres
CBE	Companion, Order of the British Empire	KWM	Kendall Whaling Museum
		Lat.	Latitude
Cdr.	Commander	lbs	pounds (weight)
cif	cost including freight	Lt.	Lieutenant
Col.	Colonel	M.	Monsieur
CSO	Central Statistical Office	MA	Mauritius National Archives
cwt.	Hundredweight (108 lbs)	Maj.	Major
d.	pence	Mass	Massachusetts
DOD	Department of Defense(US)	MC	Marina Carter
DOI	Department of Industry	Messrs	Messieurs
DSC	Distinguished Service Cross	Mgr.	Monsignor/Monseigneur
ed.	Editor/edited by	Mme	Madame
FCO	Foreign & Commonwealth Office	MSA	Maharashtra State Archives (India)
fnu	First/further name unknown	mv	motor vessel
fob	free on board	NAI	National Archives of India
Fr.	Father	NBWM	New Bedford Whaling Museum
Gen.	General		
GOC	General Officer Commanding	NCO	Non-commissioned Officer

NMM	(British) National Maritime Museum		RSM	Royal Society of Mauritius Archives
NW-S	Nigel Wenban-Smith		SA	Seychelles Archives
ODH	Old Dartmouth Historical		SHIM	Société d'Histoire de l'Ile Maurice
OIND	Océan Indien (sub-series of ANOM files)		ss	steam ship
op. cit.	opere citato (already cited work)		sv	sailing vessel
			TNA	The (British) National Archives
oz	ounces		TNA AIR	Royal Air Force/Air Ministry files
PD	Papiers Doyen			
p.m.	per month		TNA AVIA	Civil Aviation files
PMSD	Parti Mauricien Social Démocrate		TNA CO	Colonial Office files
			TNA FCO	Foreign & Commonwealth Office
Prof.	Professor			
q.v.	go to reference (from Latin *quod vide*)		TNA FO	Foreign Office
			TNA HCA	High Court of Admiralty
RAF	Royal Air Force		TNA WO	War Office/Army files
RCAF	Royal Canadian Air Force		UN	United Nations
RCP	Royal College of Physicians		UNGA	United Nations General Assembly
RHL	Rhodes House Library (Oxford)			
			US	United States
RN	Royal Navy		W/T	Wireless Telegraphy
Rs	Rupees		/-	British shillings

Brief Glossary of Sailing Vessel Types and Rigs
(a landlubber's guide)

The kit   Until the 19th century most vessels were made of wood, with wooden masts and poles used to support their sails. The poles, termed 'spars', had distinct names according to their function: from one or more 'yards', attached to the mast at their mid-point and set at right angles to the line of the hull, were suspended the sails of 'square rigged' vessels; while fore-and-aft rigged vessels would have a 'boom' along the sail's lower edge and sometimes also a 'gaff' at its top edge; and the gaff could either be set close to mast to increase its height, or at angle to allow a broader area of sail. The various arrangements of sails were known as 'rigs'. One long-enduring rig, both in the Mediterranean and eastern seas is the 'lateen', a triangular sail suspended from a very long spar hoisted to the top of a comparatively short mast, typically used for Arab dhows.

Boom   A spar attached to the bottom of sails, usually found only on fore-and–aft-rigged vessels (such as schooners) where the mainsail is attached directly to the mast and the sails pivot to the right and left of the centre line of the hull.

Sails   These may be triangular, rectangular or, roughly, trapezoid. They work by having the wind flow smoothly over them, such that there is high pressure on one side and low pressure on the other ; and in a 'billowing sail' more of the power comes from the convex than the concave side, i.e. the vessel is more 'pulled' than 'pushed'. This is why fore-and-aft rigged vessels, such as schooners, are much more efficient at sailing upwind than square-rigged ones, a difference that was discovered empirically over the centuries, long before the physics were understood.

Jibs and stay sails   Triangular sails attached by the longest side to a rope (stay) strung from the mast. Jibs are installed from the foremast, at the ship's bow end, often to a spar extending beyond the bow (the bowsprit), while staysails are installed from the main or rear (mizzen) mast. The free bottom corner is attached to ropes (sheets), which can be loosened or tightened to set the sail so that it pulls smoothly without flapping.

Vessel types

Brigantine   Two-masted vessel, having a fully square-rigged foremast and a main mast carrying at least two sails, a square-rigged topsail, plus a gaff-rigged mainsail.

Brig (Fr. *Brick*)   Larger than the brigantine, from which it was developed, having more sails, including a square mainsail, as well as a topsail and gaff sail attached to the main mast.

Being highly manoeuvrable and carrying more sails than other vessels of its size, it was much favoured by pirates and slavers.

Corvette   Somewhat larger than a sloop-of-war (*q.v.*), but smaller than a frigate (*q.v.*), this vessel was built for speed and manoeuvrability.

Cutter (Fr. *Cotre*)   Similar to a sloop (*q.v.*), but having two foresails. Large, full-rigged ships would usually carry a cutter, as well as smaller boats, for use in taking messages or exploring unknown coasts.

Frigate   A smallish fully-rigged warship, built for speed and manoeuvrability, generally having a single deck of carriage-mounted guns.

Grab (Arabic ghurab)   A shallow-draft vessel developed from ancient galleys; armed with cannons, including forward-pointing bow cannons. Much used by the East India Company to protect its merchant ships against pirates.

Ketch   Two-masted, but having the after mast (mizzen) shorter than the forward, main mast. The name is an old form of the word 'catch'; and, with the mainsail furled, the vessel could be held head to wind to facilitate the handling of fishing nets. Initially square rigged, these vessels came to be fore-and-aft-rigged, like schooners.

Lugger (Fr. *Lougre*)   Derived from the sails for square-rigged vessels, lugsails were fastened to a spar which was hauled up the mast by a rope attached near one end, such that the longer end was raised above the top of the mast. The rigging for the comparatively short mast was simple and the sail very easy to operate. Luggers were usually two-masted.

Nau   A Portuguese cargo ship of the 15th–18th centuries (see Chapter 1 Note 7 on p. 11).

Pinnace   While early pinnaces were smaller version of square-rigged ships, those mentioned in this book would have been shallow-draft sailing boats used as tenders to larger ships or employed for local use in and between the islands.

Pirogues   These ranged from dugout canoes made from local hardwood trees to the sailing skiffs, with or without outriggers, used to transport workers to and from their work

Schooner (Fr. *Goëlette*)   These vessels were fore-and-aft-rigged, that is having sails attached directly to the mast, with a boom along the bottom, with its front end also attached to the mast and its after end controlled by ropes (sheets) to limit its movement to left (port) or right (starboard). Generally two-masted, with the foremast shorter than the main mast.

Ship (full-rigged)   These had three or more masts, all of them square-rigged. Whether intended for trade or warfare, they were generally armed with carriage-mounted cannons.

Ships of the line   The largest fully rigged warships, three-masted and having two or even three decks of carriage mounted cannons.

Sloop (Fr. *Chaloupe*; Dutch. *Sloep*)   A sailing boat with a single fore-and-aft mainsail; and a single foresail. However the name was also used to describe 'sloops-of-war', used by the RN, having a single gun deck that carried up to 18 guns.

Snow (Dutch *snaw*, *lit.* 'beak')   Originally the name given to large two-masted vessels, snows came to be equipped with a small mizzen mast close to the mainmast from which a loose footed sail could be operated while the mainsail was furled; this made it easy to manoeuvre in confined spaces.

Bibliography

Allen, R.B., *A Traffic Repugnant to Humanity: Children and slave trading in the Southwestern Indian Ocean, 1770–1830 Conference on Slavery and Unfree Labour: Children and Slavery, Avignon, 19–21May 2004.*Anderson,

Camens, A., Clark, G. and Haberle, S. (In press) Investigating pre-modern colonisation of the Indian Ocean: the remote islands enigma. In *Connecting Continents: archaeology and history in the Indian Ocean* (ed. by K. Seetah & R. Allen). Ohio University Press, Athens (Ohio).

Aspley, W., *A True and Large Discourse of the Voyage …* William London, 1603 (reprinted in *East Indian Trade,* Gregg Press, London, 1968*)*.

Astley, T., *Voyages and Travels* (Vol 1), London 1745.

Baker, P. and Hookoomsingh, V.Y., *Diksyoner kreol morisyen/Dictionary of Mauritian Creole/ dictionnaire du Créole mauricien* Editions L'Harmattan, Paris 1987

Bandjunis, V.B., *Diego Garcia: creation of the Indian Ocean Base,* Writer's Showcase, Lincoln, USA 2001.

Banks, A., *Wings of the Dawning,* Images Publishing, Malvern 1996.

Bethencourt, F., and Curto, D.G. (eds.), *Portuguese Oceanic Expansion 1400–1800* Cambridge University Press 2007.

Boddam, R. H. *et al,* Bombay Castle to Court of Directors 18 March 1786 p 99–100.

Bolton, G.C., and Kennedy, B.E., 'William Eden and the Treaty of Mauritius, 1786–7' *The Historical Journal,* XV1, 4 (1973).

Boswell, R., *Le Malaise Créole* Berghahn Books 2006.

Bourne, G. C., 'On the Island of Diego Garcia of the Chagos Group', *Journal of the Royal Geographical Society* June 1886.

Boxer, C.R., *The Tragic History of the Sea*, Minnesota University Press 1961.

Boxer, C.R. (ed.), *The Tragic History of the Sea* Hakluyt Society 1959.

Brenton, E.P. *The Naval History of Great Britain*, Henry Colburn, London,1837.

Bruin, J.R. and others *Dutch Asiatic Shipping in the 17th and 18th centuries* (3 Vols.) Nijhoff, The Hague 1979–1987.

Burrows, E.H. *Captain Owen of the African Survey*, A.A. Balkema, Rotterdam, 1979.

Caron, F. *Le vicomte de Grenier, héritier de Bigot de Morogues ou fils spirituel de Suffren?* Institut de Stratégie Comparée, [www.stratisc.org].

Carter, M. *et al*, *The Last Slaves: Liberated Africans in 19th Century Mauritius,* CRIOS, Mauritius, 2003.

Castle, B., *The Castle Diaries 1964–70* Weidenfeld & Nicolson, 1984.

Castle, C., *Lucky Alex* Trafford Publishing, Victoria, Canada 2001.

Chaudhuri, K.N., *The English East India Company*, Frank Cass & Co., London, 1965.

Chelin, J-M., *Les Ziles La Haut*, privately printed J & S Printing, Mauritius 2012.

Chun, Carl *Aus den Tiefen des Weltmeeres,* Gustav Fischer, Jena, 1903.

Cortesão, A., 'A hitherto Unrecognized Map by Pedro Reinel in the British Museum' *The Geographical Journal*, Vol. 87, No. 6, June 1936 (pp. 518–524); see also his *History of Portuguese Cartography*, Junta de Investigações do Ultramar, Lisbon, 1969.

Dalrymple, A., *The Oriental Repertory.*

Davis. J., *Seaman's Secrets* London 1594.

Descroizilles, M., and Mülnier, A., *Bor' Endan Bor' Déhors* Editions de L'Océan Indien, Mauritius 1999.

Didier, M., *Pages Africaines de l'Ile Maurice*, Centre Culturel Africain, Mauritius 1987.

Documenta Indica, (Vol III, 1553–1557), Monumenta Historica Societatis Iesu, Jesuit Historical Institute, Rome.

Doeff, H., *Recollections of Japan*, translated and annotated by Annick M. Doeff, Trafford, Victoria, Canada, 2003.

Druett, J. & R., *Petticoat Whalers: whaling wives at sea, 1820–1920*, 2001.

Duffy, J., *Shipwreck and Empire* Harvard University Press 1955.

Dussercle, R., *Agalega: petite île* General Printing & Stationery, Port Louis 1949.

Dussercle, R., *Archipel de Chagos: en mission 10 Nov 1933– 11 Jan 1934* General Printing Company, Port Louis 1934.

Dussercle, R., *Archipel de Chagos: en mission Diégo-Six Iles-Péros, Sept – Nov 1934.*

Dussercle, R., *Dans les 'Ziles la-Haut* General Printing and Stationery, Port Louis 1937.

Dussercle, R., *Naufrage de la Barque Diégo à l'Ile d'Aigle aux Chagos* General Printing and Stationery, Port Louis 1936

Duyker, E. (ed.), *Mauritian Heritage: an anthology of the Lionnet, Commins and related families*, Australian Mauritian Research Group, Victoria, 1986.

Edis, R.S., *Peak of Limuria*, Bellew Publishing, London 1993.

Edis, R.S., *Peak of Limuria*, (revised edition), Chagos Conservation Trust 2004.

de l'Estrac, J.C., *L'an prochain à Diego Garcia* Editions Le Printemps, Mauritius 2011.

Evers, S.J., and Kooy, M., (eds.), *Eviction from the Chagos Islands* Brill, Leyden 2011.

Filliozat-Restif, M., unpublished doctoral thesis. *L'Océan Oriental: connaissances hydrographiques françaises aux XVIIe et XVIIIe siècles*, Paris, Ecole pratique des Hautes-Etudes, 2002.

da Fonseca, H. Q., *Os Portugueses no Mar*, Ministerio de Marinha, Lisbon, 1926.

van Fraassen, C.F., and Klapwijk, J.F. (eds), *Herinnering aan een reis naar Oost-Indië*, Linscho-ten-Vereeniging, 2008.

Fry, H.T., 'Early British Interest in the Chagos Archipelago and the Maldive Islands' *Mariners Mirror* vol. 53, no 4, 1967 pp. 343–356.

Furber, H., *Henry Dundas, First Viscount Melville, 1742–1811*, OUP London 1931.

Furlong, R. and Ramharai, V., (eds.), *La Production Créolophone* (volume 1) 2007.

Gomes de Brito, B. (compiler), *Historia Tragico-Maritima* Lisbon 1735.

Grenier, M., *Mémoires de la Campagne de Découvertes dans les Mers des Indes*, Brest 1770.

Hébert, J.C. 'Les Français sur la Côte Ouest de Madagascar au Temps de Ravahiny [1780–1812]'*Omaly Si Anio*, 1983–4 p. 235.

Herbert, W., *New Directory for the East Indies* London, 1774.

von Hohenhollern-Emden, F. J., *Emden – the last cruise of the chivalrous raider, 1914* Lyon Publishing International, Brighton, 1989.

Von Hohenzollern, F. J., *My Experiences in SMS Emden*, Herbert Jenkins, London, 1928.

Hough, R., *The Pursuit of Admiral von Spee* Allen & Unwin, London 1969.

Jackson, A., *War and Empire in Mauritius and the Indian Ocean*, Palgrave, Basingstoke 2001.

Jeffery, L., *Chagos Islanders in Mauritius and the UK* Manchester University Press 2011.

van Keulen, *De Nieuwe Lichtende Zee-Fakkel* 1753.

Lacroix, L., *Les Derniers Négriers*, Paris, 1977.

Lagesse, M., *Des Pas sur le Sable* Les Editions du Printemps, Mauritius 1975, re-published 2009.

Lagesse, M., *D'un Carnet* Editions Paul Mackay, Mauritius 1967.

Lassemillante, H., *L'esclavage aux Chagos Pendant les Dix-huitième et Dix-neuvième Siècles*, unpublished paper 1998.

Leitão, H., 'Identificão dos Baixos de Pero dos Banhos e das Chagas', in *Studia: Revista semestral do Centro de Estudos Ultramarinos*, 1 Lisbon, 1958.

Lepelley, R., *Croisières dans la Mer des Indes 1810–1811*, Keltia Graphic, France 1992. pp 142–144.

van Linschoten, H., *Voyages into the East and West Indies* London 1598.

Lohrli, A., *Household Words* Toronto University Press 1973.

Macmillan, A. (ed.), *Mauritius Illustrated*, W.H. & L. Collingridge, London 1914.

Malim, Michael, *Island of the Swan*, The Travel Book Club, London, 1953.

Martin, R.M., *History of the British Colonies*, London, James Cochrane, vol. 4, 1835.

Masselman, G., *The Cradle of Colonialism* Yale University Press, 1963.

Moitessier, Bernard, *Sailing to the Reefs*, Hollis & Carter, London 1971, translated and adapted from *Un Vagabond des Mers du Sud*, Flammarion, Paris 1960.

Moresby, R., and Elwon, T., article printed by the order of the Court of Directors, East India Company, London by Black & Co., 1841 and reprinted as 'Surveys of the Indian Navy' in *The Foreign Quarterly Review*, July 1845.

van Neck, J.C., and Warwijck, W., *De Tweede Schipvaart der Nederlanders naar Oost-Indië 1598–1600*, Der Linschoten Vereenigen, XLVIII, Nijhoff, The Hague, 1944.

North-Coombes, A., *La Découverte des Mascareignes par les Arabes et les Portugais: rétrospective et mise au point*, Service Bureau, Port Louis, 1979.

Ommaney, F.D., *The Shoals of Capricorn* Longmans, Green & Co, London, 1952.

Owen, W. F. W., *Journal of the Royal Geographical Society*, vol. 2, paper dated April 9 1832.

Parkinson, C.N. *Samuel Walters, Lieutenant R.N.* Liverpool University Press, 1949.

Peerthum, S., 'Origins & History of the Chagossians', *L'Express*, 11 Nov 2003.

Pereira, G. (ed.), *Roteiros Portuguezes da Viagem de Lisboa á India*, Sociedade Geographia de Lisboa, 1898.

Pereira, J.M. Malhão and Jin Guo Ping, *Navegações Chinesas no Século XV: realidade e ficção*, Academia de Marinha, Lisbon, 2006.

Pereira, J.M. Malhão, *O Cabo de Bõa Esperança e O Espólio Náutico Submerso*, Academia de Marinha, Lisbon, 2005.

Philips, C.H. & Misra, B.B., Fort William-India House *Correspondence, vol XV Foreign and Secret 1782–1786*, National Archives of India, Delhi, 1963.

Phillips, M., *Ships of the Old Navy* www.ageofnelson.org

Pollock, J. *Gordon: the man behind the legend* Constable, London 1993.

Prestage, E., *The Portuguese Pioneers* A & C Black, London 1933.

Pridham, C., *England's Colonial Empire: Mauritius and its Dependencies* Smith, Elder 1846.

Pridham, C., *An Historical, Political and Statistical Account of Mauritius and its Dependencies* 1849.

Purchas, S., *Purchas His Pilgrimes* William Stansby, London, 1625.

Quenette, R., *La franc-maçonnerie à l'Ile Maurice, 1778–1878* Port Louis 2006

Rouillard, G., and Guého, J. *Les plantes et leur histoire à l'Ile Maurice* (n.d.) [c. 1999].

Rangel, M., *Relação do naufragio da não Conceyção, História Trágico-Máritima, I, 169–217*

Rea, W.E., *Nil Desperandum*, privately printed 1936.

Régnaud, C., 'Quelques mots sur le véritable nom de l'île Diégo Garcia' *Transactions of the Royal Society of Mauritius, pp. 280–1, 1860.*

Richardson, W., *A Mariner of England: An Account of William Richardson from Cabin Boy in the Merchant Service to Warrant Officer in the Royal Navy [1780–1819] as told by himself*, London, John Murray 1908.

Rigby, B. *Ever Glorious, the Story of the 22nd [Cheshire] Regiment*, vol 1, Evans& Sons, Chester, 1982. See 'La Guerre aux Iles de France et Bourbon 1809–1810' by De Poyen *Nouvelle Revue Historique et Littéraire* April 1898, no 1.

Rochon, Abbé, *Voyage à Madagascar et aux Indes Orientales*, Paris, 1791.

Ryan, V.W., *Journals of an Eight Years' Residence in the Diocese of Mauritius, and of a Visit to Madagascar* Seeley, Jackson and Halliday, London 1864.

Samuels, A., *Palm Land* Lee and Shepard, Boston 1874.

Sand, P.H., *United States and Britain in Diego Garcia* Palgrave Macmillan 2009.

Sclater, P., 'The Mammals of Madagascar', *Quarterly Journal of Science* 1864.

Scott, R., *Limuria – the lesser dependencies of Mauritius*, Oxford University Press 1961.

Sheppard, C.S,. and Seward, M. (eds.), *The Ecology of the Chagos Archipelago* Linnean Society,

London, 1999.

da Silva Jayasuriya, S., *The Portuguese in the East* Tauris Academic Studies, London 2008.

Stevens, H. (ed.),*The Dawn of British Trade*, Henry Stevens & Son, London, 1886.

Taylor, P.G., *The Sky Beyond* Cassell Australia 1963.

Thompson, J.A., *Only the Sun Remembers* Andrew Dakers 1950.

Toussaint, A. *Histoire Des Iles Mascareignes*, Paris, 1972.

d'Unienville, R. *Histoire Politique de l'Ile de France*, Vol 2 1791–1794 Archives Publications no 13, 14, and 15, Mauritius 1975–1989.

d'Unienville, R. *Histoire Politique de l'Ile de France,* Vol. 3 1795–1803.

d'Unienville, R. *Malartic*, SHIM, Mauritius 2006.

Urish, D., *Coral, Copra and Concrete* Donning, Virginia Beach, VA 2015.

van der Vat, D., *Gentlemen at War* William and Morrow, New York, 1981.

Vine, D., *Island of Shame*, Princeton University Press 2009.

de Visdelou-Guimbeau, G., *La Découverte des Îles Mascareignes*, General Printing and Stationery, Port Louis, 1948.

Wade, G., 'The Zheng He Voyages: a reassessment', *Journal of the Malaysian Branch of the Royal Asiatic Society*, vol. 78, Part 1, No. 228, 2005.

Wanquet, C., 'Quelques remarques sur les relations des Mascareignes avec les Autres Pays de l'Océan Indien a l'Epoque de la Révolution Française' *Annuaire des Pays de l'Océan Indien* [APOI], vol. VII, 1980.

Whidden, J.D., *Ocean Life in the Old Sailing Ship Days: from forecastle to quarter-deck*, Little, Brown & Co, 1908.

Wray, P., & Martin, K., 'Historic Whaling Records from the Western Indian Ocean', *Report of the International Whaling Commission 5,* Cambridge, Mass. 1983.

Index of Names

Index of Ships

Subject Index

Extracted from Admiralty Chart No. 12805. Not to be used for navigation.

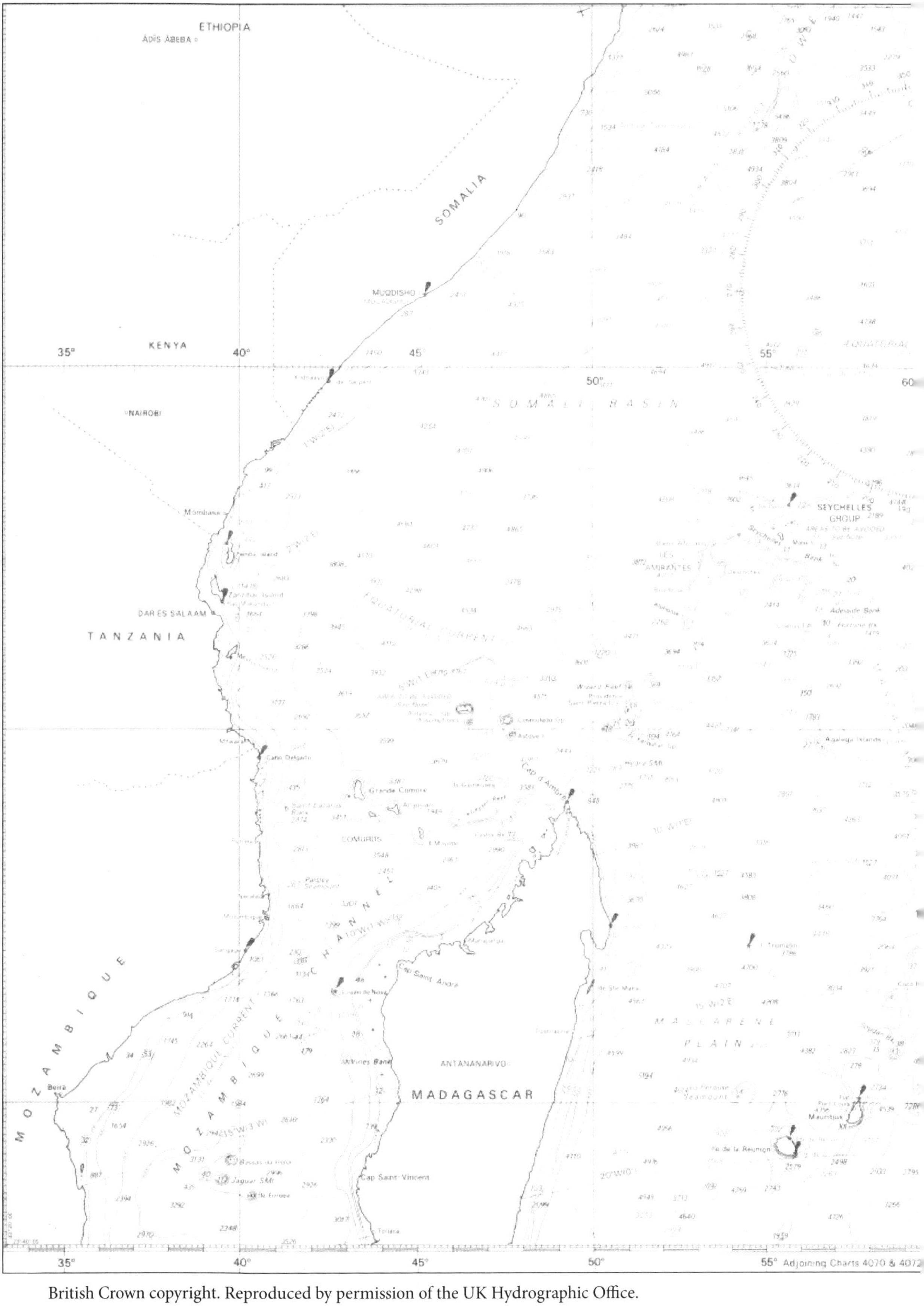